Word 97 Macro & VBA Handbook

Word 97 Macro & VBA Handbook

Guy Hart-Davis

SYBEX®

San Francisco • Paris • Düsseldorf • Soest

Associate Publisher: Amy Romanoff
Acquisitions Manager: Kristine Plachy
Acquisitions & Developmental Editor: Melanie Spiller
Editor: Julie Powell
Project Editor: Kim Wimpsett
Technical Editors: Renate Strub, Jim Bonelli
Book Designer: Catalin Dulfu
Graphic Illustrator: Patrick Dintino
Electronic Publishing Specialist: Alissa Feinberg
Production Coordinators: Nathan Johanson, Anton Reut
Proofreaders: Theresa Gonzalez, Jennifer Metzger
Indexer: Nancy Guenther
Cover Design: Design Site
Cover Photographer: David Bishop

Screen reproductions produced with Collage Complete.

Collage Complete is a trademark of Inner Media Inc.

SYBEX is a registered trademark of SYBEX Inc.

TRADEMARKS: SYBEX has attempted throughout this book to distinguish proprietary trademarks from descriptive terms by following the capitalization style used by the manufacturer.

Library of Congress Card Number: 96-72108
ISBN: 0-7821-1962-X

Manufactured in the United States of America

10 9 8 7

This book is dedicated to Jim.

ACKNOWLEDGMENTS

I'd like to thank the following people for their help on this book: Melanie Spiller for deciding the book was a good idea, asking me to write it, and prodding me when I was slow; Amy Romanoff for raising the page count and putting up with my joking about it; Julie Powell for excellent and tenacious editing from start to finish; Jim Bonelli for starting the technical edit, and Tanya Strub for finishing it; Kim Wimpsett for making the schedule work when I didn't, and preserving her equanimity throughout; Alissa Feinberg for typesetting the book; Nathan Johanson and Anton Reut for coordinating the production of the book; and Nancy Guenther for marshalling every important word into the index.

CONTENTS AT A GLANCE

TABLE OF CONTENTS

INTRODUCTION

Word 97 provides enough features to create just about any type of document—from a two-line memo in 12-point Courier to a fully typeset technical manual to an intranet or Web page packed with pictures, sounds, and hyperlinks. Using these features, people create millions of documents every day.

But almost nobody uses Word's best feature—one that can save the most time working with Word.

That feature is Word's powerful built-in macro language, Visual Basic for Applications (VBA for short). Yet upwards of 98 percent of the people who use Word never use VBA. And as a result, they waste huge amounts of time every day in their work.

What Can You Do with VBA?

With VBA, you can automate almost any action that you now do interactively (manually) with Word—creating a document, adding text or other items to it, formatting the document, saving it, and so on. VBA performs actions faster, more accurately, more reliably, and far more cheaply than any human. (The one thing VBA can't do is make a human decision, which is perhaps just as well for us.)

Better yet, Word's tight integration with the other Microsoft Office products—Excel, the spreadsheet; PowerPoint, the presentation package; Access, the relational database; and Outlook, the Desktop Information Manager—means that once you control Word, you can control the entire Microsoft Office environment. So by learning to automate Word procedures with VBA, you can also reduce complex multi-application maneuvers to the press of a key or the click of a button.

This book takes a practical approach to speeding up and automating your work in Word. Rather than focusing on theory and putting you to sleep within the first few pages, I'll focus on getting things done as quickly and as simply as possible. This means that some of the macros we look at in the earlier chapters of the book will not be particularly concise or pretty; they may in fact be crude and clumsy.

But they will get the job done. Later on in the book, we'll look at how you can bring concision or even elegance to your macros, how you can create reusable code, and how you can write macros that run at top speed.

What's in This Book?

This book contains all the information you need to learn to create powerful, time-saving VBA macros in Word 97.

The book is divided into three parts, as discussed in the following paragraphs.

Part I, "The Keys to Automating Word," discusses the features that Word provides to automate your work. In addition to VBA and macros, this part discusses such features as styles, fields, and templates, which you can use to automate many tasks in Word without using macros:

- Chapter 1 provides a quick introduction to what VBA is and why you should take advantage of it.

- Chapter 2 discusses how to use styles to apply formatting consistently across your documents. Even if you've worked with styles in the past, check out this chapter to make sure you understand their full potential.

- Chapter 3 covers how to use documents and templates effectively: what templates are for, how they work and how they affect documents, and what you can do with them.

- Chapter 4 discusses such features as AutoCorrect, AutoText, AutoFormat, fields, and bookmarks. It also shows you how to harness the power of complex Find-and-Replace operations, which you can use to swiftly change and reformat your documents either manually or in a macro.

Part II, "The Tools for Automating Word," begins the coverage of macros proper and comprises the heart of the book:

- Chapter 5 introduces you to the fundamentals of recording and editing macros. This chapter also introduces you to the Visual Basic Editor, the application in which you can both edit macros and create them from scratch.

- Chapter 6 shows you how to display status-bar messages, use message boxes to communicate with the users of your macros and let them make simple decisions about how the macros run, and use input boxes to allow them to supply information the macros need.

- Chapter 7 discusses how to create simple custom dialog boxes to allow the user to make decisions and direct the flow of your macros.

- Chapter 8 covers how you can use loops to repeat actions in your macros.

- Chapter 9 shows you how to use conditional statements (such as If statements) to make decisions in your macros.

- Chapter 10 shows you how to work with variables, strings, and constants, all of which provide you with the means to store information while you're running your macros.

- Chapter 11 explains the Word object model—the logical structure according to which VBA recognizes the components of Word.

- Chapter 12 takes you into working with text. You'll learn how to retrieve text from a document and how to insert it in a document; how to manipulate text; and how to get text from the user of a macro and make sure it's what you need.

- Chapter 13 discusses how to work with files and folders (a.k.a. documents and directories) within your macros. You'll learn how to create and save documents and folders as well as how to delete them when you no longer need them.

- Chapter 14 covers how to use fields and form fields in your macros.

- Chapter 15 shows you how to use bookmarks in your macros.

- Chapter 16 explains the principles of debugging your macros. If nothing has gone wrong in your macros by this point, feel free to skip this chapter.

- Chapter 17 illustrates the benefits of building reusable, modular code rather than monolithic macros, then shows you how to do so. This may not sound like much fun, but you'll love the time and effort it saves you.

- Chapter 18 discusses how to build well-behaved macros stable enough to withstand being run under the wrong circumstances and civilized enough to leave the user in the best possible state to continue their work.

- Chapter 19 picks up where Chapter 7 left off, and talks about how to create complex dialog boxes. These include both dynamic dialog boxes that update themselves when the user clicks a button and dialog boxes with hidden depths that the user can reveal to access infrequently used options.

- Chapter 20 discusses how you can use Word's built-in dialog boxes in your macros. You can choose to display a built-in dialog box, have the user interact with it, and then have it execute as usual, or you can commandeer the information the user enters in the dialog box for your own purposes.

Part III, "Automating Word Procedures and Documents," discusses how to apply the tools introduced in Part 2 to automate procedures that you perform and documents that you create in Word:

- Chapter 21 discusses how to use Word's five automatic macro names and how to use startup switches to control how Word launches. You'll also learn to use VBA to read information in the Windows registry—and write information to the registry.

- Chapter 22 takes a break from writing code to suggest how you should approach automating procedures that you and your colleagues perform regularly in Word.

- Chapter 23 explains how to use Word's VBA capabilities to communicate with other applications, from using high-tech methods to share information with other members of the Office 97 clan (for example, retrieving information from an Excel spreadsheet) to running applications that have never even heard of Microsoft.

- Chapter 24 discusses how you can build a special-purpose template in Word to enable the user to quickly create a particular type of document. The chapter presents a sample template (included on the CD) that illustrates many of the VBA commands discussed throughout the book.

Finally, there are two appendices: Appendix A discusses what's on the CD, and Appendix B provides a brief primer for converting WordBasic macros to VBA.

What Do You Need to Know Already?

In this book, I'll assume that you're reasonably familiar with your computer, with your operating system (Windows 95 or NT Workstation 4), and with the capabilities of Word 97. For example, I'll assume you know how to create and save documents, format them, and use regular Word features such as Print Preview, page numbers, and pictures. (If you don't, you might want to try a book such as *The ABCs of Word 97* or *Mastering Word 97*, also published by Sybex, to bring yourself up to speed.)

Listings and Analyses

Throughout this book, you'll find thousands of lines of code. Most of the lengthy sections of code appear as numbered listings (Listing 7.1, Listing 8.2, etc.) in which each line is identified by number:

Listing 7.1

```
1.    Private Sub cmdOK_Click()
2.        frmMoveParagraph.Hide
3.        Unload frmMoveParagraph
4.        If chkReturnToPreviousPosition = True Then
```

The line numbers are included only to identify the lines during the discussion in the Analysis section that follows each listing. The line numbers are not part of the code itself.

What's on the CD?

The CD-ROM included in the back of the book contains the following:

- All the numbered code listings from the book, presented in an automated document that lets you quickly access the code you need and transfer it to the Visual Basic Editor; from there you can run it, change it, or otherwise play with it.

- Video walk-throughs of key procedures from Chapters 5, 6, and 7, in which you'll explore the Visual Basic Editor and learn to use message boxes, input boxes, and dialog boxes in your macros. If you can't figure out what the written instructions are saying, fire up the relevant walk-through and watch VBA unfold in real time before your eyes.

- The sample template discussed in Chapter 24.

Appendix A contains details of where to find things on the CD, including a full list of the walk-throughs.

Conventions Used in This Book

This book uses a number of conventions to convey information:

- ➤ designates choosing a command from a menu. For example, "choose File ➤ Open" means that you should pull down the File menu and choose the Open command from it.

- + signs indicate key combinations. For example, "press Ctrl+Shift+F9" means that you should hold down the Ctrl and Shift keys, then press the F9 key. Some of these key combinations are confusing (for example, "Ctrl++" means that you hold down Ctrl and press the + key—i.e., hold down Ctrl and Shift together and press the = key), so you may need to read them carefully.

- Likewise, "Shift+click" means that you should hold down the Shift key as you click with the mouse, and "Ctrl+click" means you should hold down the Ctrl key as you click.

- ↑, ↓, ←, and → represent the arrow keys that should appear in some form on your keyboard. The important thing to note is that ← is *not* the Backspace key (which on many keyboards bears a similar arrow). The Backspace key is represented by "Backspace" or "the Backspace key."

- **Boldface** indicates items that you may want to type in letter for letter.

- `program font` indicates program items. Complete program lines will be offset in separate paragraphs like the example below, while shorter expressions will appear as part of the main text.

```
Sub Sample_Listing()
     Lines of program code will look like this.
End Sub
```

- *Italics* usually indicate either new terms being introduced or variable information (such as a drive letter that will vary from computer to computer and that you'll need to establish on your own).

- ➥ (a continuation arrow) indicates that a single line of code has been broken onto a second or subsequent line in the book. Enter these lines of code as a single line when you use them. For example, the three lines below represent a single line of code:

```
MsgBox System.PrivateProfileString("",
➥"HKEY_CURRENT_USER\Software\Microsoft\
➥Office\8.0\Common\AutoCorrect", "Path")
```

Feedback

VBA is a powerful and exciting new feature in Word 97. It's also very complex. I've been working with it for the best part of a year now, and I'm still learning new things about it every day—and even if I did already know everything about VBA and Word, I still could only have fit so much information into a book this size. If you've got an idea you'd like to share, a suggestion for information that I should have included in the book, or a question you'd like the next edition of the book to answer, drop me an e-mail at `wordvba@textbutcher.com`; likewise if you find something in the book that just doesn't seem right. I travel now and then, and even when I'm around, I'm usually behind on my e-mail (aren't we all?), so don't be offended if I don't get back to you immediately.

I'll be posting further information on VBA and Word on my Web site, `http://www.textbutcher.com/guy`, including answers to any entertaining questions that you send my way. So stop by and see what's happening.

Thank you for reading this book. I hope you find it useful in your day-to-day work with Word and VBA.

PART I

The Keys to
Automating Word

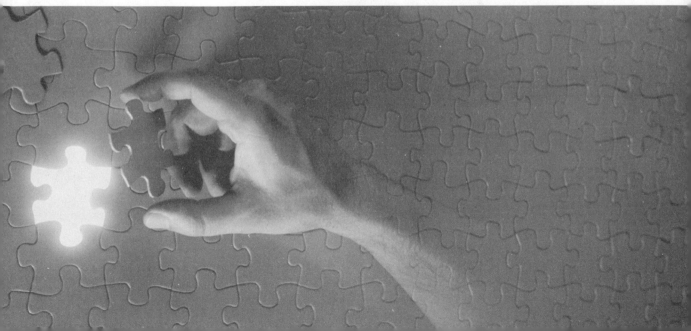

CHAPTER

ONE

1

What Is Visual Basic for Applications?

In this chapter, we'll set the scene for automating Word to do your bidding, laying out the different elements that we will examine and use in the course of this book. First, we'll look at Visual Basic and its subset, Visual Basic for Applications (VBA); VBA is the language in which you record and write macros and modules in Word. This will provide a conceptual introduction that will carry you through the rest of the book.

Then we'll look at the various features that Word provides for automating your work without using macros. This is a great place to start automating Word, because not only are these features powerful time-savers in their own right, but you can use them later in your macros.

Why Use Macros to Automate Word?

In the Introduction, we touched briefly on why you might want to use macros to automate procedures in Word. In this section, we'll look at a couple of concrete examples before we start to examine the tools you can use for such automation.

At the risk of stating the obvious, Word is designed for creating documents. These documents can be of various formats and types, from single-page items such as a recipe or tri-fold invitation all the way up to industrial-strength product manuals featuring photos, technical graphics, and cross-references. Complex documents may also be peppered with field codes that, for example, quickly create or update an index or provide links to relevant World Wide Web sites.

Whatever the type of document you're creating, Word offers various features to help you create it as quickly, easily, and efficiently as possible. You can use different shapes and sizes of paper; use any font (typeface) that your computer's operating system and your printer support; use styles to quickly apply complex formatting; use Find and Replace to make wholesale changes to your text; and so on. Once your masterpiece is almost complete, Word's table-of-contents and indexing tools remove from your sagging shoulders two of the most tedious and least-loved duties in the realm of publishing.

Because of the minimal skill required to start working in Word—namely the ability to navigate the Windows 95 graphical user interface (GUI) enough to start Word, plus rudimentary typing ability—it's possible to use Word at a wide variety of levels. To start with the ludicrous, you could easily use Word as you would a typewriter: type the text in, and then print out the resulting document. You could even skip the conventional stage of saving your documents to disk for the authentic typewriter experience of laboriously retyping each successive draft. With determination, you could even go so far as to start a page anew once you made a single mistake on it.

At the other end of the spectrum, you could customize your copy of Word so extensively that the amount of time you spent actually producing a document paled into insignificance alongside the time spent in preparation. At the end of the process, you could create a particular type of document with literally a single keystroke or a single click of the mouse, but you would have paid for the time saved many times over in the time spent producing such automation.

Most users settle for a modestly happy medium whereby they gradually identify the features of Word that are most useful to them in the creation of their documents. Once they've defined this set of Word tools, they stop exploring the other features that Word offers. If they're feeling ambitious, they customize the user interface of Word a bit to make their most-used commands easier to access. In this book, we'll start off by looking at such simple customization; after that, we'll move into the areas in which Word offers you remarkable powers of automation in exchange for a little study.

Two of the areas that most people leave unexplored are recording and writing macros, which are really two facets of the same topic. This is in large part because back when PCs were truly difficult to use, macros rapidly built up such a dreadful reputation that most people felt unwilling to risk contaminating their fair hands with them. These days, though, macros are easy to record and play back, and with a modicum of care one can avoid any actions that might lose data or damage one's computer system, which remains one of the great (and far from unfounded) fears of the typical macro-evader.

Word also offers significant automation through several features not directly related to macros, such as styles and templates, AutoCorrect and AutoText, and bookmarks. We'll look at all of these features briefly later in this chapter, and then in the succeeding chapters we'll discuss in detail how to use them most effectively. Don't feel cheated that this book is discussing other topics besides macros and VBA programming—there's no point in building a sledgehammer to crack a nut when Microsoft has provided decent (if underused) tools in Word. Not only that, you can use macros to manipulate all of these other automation features once you know how they work.

Visual Basic for Applications

First, a few words of explanation about the main tool we'll be using for automating operations in Word. Visual Basic for Applications (VBA) is a programming language built into the Office applications that you can use to automate operations. Word, Excel, PowerPoint, Outlook, Access (in Office Professional, not in Office Standard), and the Office Binder all use Visual Basic for Applications, so you can automate operations throughout the Office applications.

Visual Basic for Applications is based on Visual Basic, a programming language derived from BASIC, which (as you may remember from those joyous days of cassette-loaded programs and 16K of RAM) stands for Beginner's All-purpose Symbolic Instruction Code. BASIC is supposedly user-friendly in that it uses recognizable English words (or quasi-recognizable permutations of them) rather than completely incomprehensible programming terms. Visual Basic is visual in that it supports the Windows graphical user interface and provides tools for drag-and-drop programming and working with shared graphical elements.

The Difference between Visual Basic and Visual Basic for Applications

Visual Basic for Applications consists of Visual Basic variants that contain application-specific commands. The set of VBA commands available in Word is different from the set of VBA commands available in Excel because it supports functions contained in Word but not in Excel; however, the Visual Basic for Applications variants share a common core, so that you can quickly translate your knowledge of, say, Excel VBA to Word VBA. To give a concrete example, you would use the `Save` method to save a file in either Excel VBA or Word VBA. In Excel VBA, the command would be `ActiveWorkbook.Save`, whereas in Word VBA it would be `ActiveDocument.Save`. This difference probably seems small and unexciting, as indeed it is: in the former case, you're saving changes to the active workbook, and in the latter case, to the active document, so you'd expect them to be named differently. But as soon as you stray as far as the `SaveAs` method, you start getting into a sea of differences: Word has a number of options that Excel does not have, and vice versa. And when you get into formatting different parts of a document or spreadsheet, the differences are substantial, and potentially confusing.

Furthermore, the different applications contain different sets of the Visual Basic for Applications language to provide functionality for their different commands. For example, Word needs VBA commands for manipulating its bookmarks, whereas Excel doesn't—Excel doesn't have bookmarks. Likewise, Excel needs VBA commands for working with scenarios, which Word doesn't need.

A Brief History of VBA in the Office Applications

Excel has used its own variant of Visual Basic for Applications since version 5, and Access has used its own variant of VBA since version 2. (Both Excel and Access used leapfrog-numbering to get to version 7: Access went straight from 2 to 7, while Excel went from 5 to 7. So neither has had VBA for quite as long as it might seem.)

Word and PowerPoint are the newcomers to the VBA fold; both have VBA support for the first time in their current versions. Earlier versions of Word (up to Word 7 for Windows 95) used WordBasic instead, while PowerPoint didn't have a programming language.

Like VBA, WordBasic is a complete programming language, but it is limited to Word—it cannot command other Office applications in the way that VBA can. This meant that trying to build interapplication solutions with Word versions before Word 97 was frustrating. You could use Object Linking and Embedding (OLE) and Dynamic Data Exchange (DDE), two technologies for sharing information between applications written to certain standards, to shuttle information from, say, Excel or Access into Word; but you could not run a procedure in Word, switch to Excel and run a procedure there, do something else in Word that used the data resulting from the Excel procedure, and so on. Now that Word has VBA too, you can use Word to run procedures in the other VBA-enabled Office applications until the cows come home (or substantially later).

Also, in Office 97, the different VBA dialects (if you will) use different dynamic link libraries (DLLs) to implement the commands. This is a little clumsy, and Microsoft has announced that it intends to merge the DLLs in future releases of Office. (In practice, this doesn't make much difference to the user, except that you have multiple DLLs for VBA on your hard drive, taking up more space than one combined DLL for VBA would.)

Such trivial annoyances aside, Visual Basic for Applications is a complete programming language for use with the Office applications. You use VBA to create macros and modules. We'll discuss those in the next section.

Macros and Modules

First, let's clarify our terms. What's a macro and what's a module? Put simply, a *macro* is a set of instructions that tells a program to do things, and a *module* is a container for the VBA source code that makes up a macro.

A module can contain one macro or a whole bunch of macros. (It can also contain unfinished fragments of code that you may for some reason be proud of and want to keep, but we won't concern ourselves with those here.)

Word stores modules within templates or within documents (as we'll see in Chapter 3, Word 97 has blurred some of the distinctions between templates and documents). When you record a macro, you can choose to store it in a module within Normal.dot—the global template—or in a module within the template to which the current document is attached, or within the current document itself. (If you're working with a template rather than a document, you can choose to store the macro in a module within that template.) Any given template or document can contain no modules, one module, or multiple modules.

NOTE   Chapter 3 discusses templates in great detail. If the brief discussion of global templates and modules here doesn't make sense, hold your horses—we'll get there in just a little bit.

Automation

What kinds of automation can you achieve in Word with macros and Visual Basic for Applications? You can automate almost any Office operation from the extremely simple to the hideously complex, from a straightforward but tedious piece of formatting on a word or paragraph to building a mini-application that will run at a certain time each day, access information from a variety of sources, prepare a report from it, and even e-mail it to a number of worthy recipients. In this book, we'll discuss macros that run the gamut from the small to the extremely complex.

> **NOTE** Any macro that saves you time, effort, or keystrokes can more than justify the time it takes to create it. To improve your work, a macro doesn't have to contain 500 lines of code and use half the statements that VBA provides; for someone who composes or edits documents, small macros that simply move the current word forward or backward a word or two, or the current paragraph up or down a paragraph or two, can make work more efficient and less frustrating.

Before we get into Visual Basic for Applications and the wonders you can perform with it, we'll look at several other components that Word offers for automating day-to-day operations. These include:

- **styles**, which you can use to assign complex formatting quickly to paragraphs or characters. We'll look at styles in Chapter 2.

- **templates**, which are specialized documents that you use as skeletons for specific documents that you create regularly (such as a letter containing your company's name and address, or a form that always contains a number of fields). Templates can contain both styles and macros, which means you can create highly automated templates. We'll discuss templates in Chapter 3.

- **AutoCorrect**, which automatically corrects predefined typos into correctly spelled words on-the-fly. The great thing about AutoCorrect is that these typos don't have to be mistakes—it will also expand any predefined abbreviation into its full entry. You can even include graphics, tables, and other elements in AutoCorrect entries. We'll look at AutoCorrect in Chapter 4.

- **AutoText**, which changes predefined abbreviations into full-fledged entries at the push of a button or when you accept an AutoText pop-up suggestion. We'll look at AutoText in Chapter 4, too.

- **fields**, which are codes that Word uses to represent information that gets updated. For example, if you add a date or time field to a document, you can have Word update it automatically whenever you open the document or whenever you print it. Other commonly used fields include the page number of the current page and the number of pages in the document (for double-numbering—*page 1 of 111*, and so on). We'll cover fields in Chapter 4 as well.

- **bookmarks**, which provide a way of referring to a defined part of a document. By using bookmarks, you can set up documents so that you can quickly retrieve the contents of a given part of a document or insert information there. Again, turn to Chapter 4 for bookmarks.

- **Object Linking and Embedding (OLE)**, which provides a way of including in one Office application information created in another Office application. For example, you can use OLE to include part of an Excel spreadsheet or a PowerPoint presentation in a Word document. Because of the wonders of Cut and Paste (not to mention drag-and-drop), I'm assuming that you're familiar with OLE, so we won't go through it in the early chapters of the book, though we will examine later how to manipulate OLE with VBA.

CHAPTER
TWO

Using Styles Effectively

In this chapter, we'll look at how to use Word's styles to automate your Word documents. There are two reasons for doing this. First, Word's styles can save you a great deal of time and effort that you might otherwise be tempted to spend formatting your documents with macros (or, if you're a masochist, manually); and second, to use Word's styles effectively in your macros and thus save even more time, you need a thorough understanding of how styles work.

Before we get into the details of styles, we need to briefly discuss how character formatting and paragraph formatting work in Word, and we'll review how you select items in Word. If you think you already know all this, bear with me for a few minutes, or skim through the next couple of sections.

Understanding Formatting in Word

Straightforward formatting is very simple, and no doubt you're quite familiar with it: to double-space a paragraph, you make a choice in the Paragraph dialog box; to apply boldface to a selection, you click the Bold button on the Formatting toolbar. The first method is an example of paragraph-based formatting, the second an example of character-based formatting.

Formatting can be applied to characters in three ways:

- directly (as in the two examples above)
- through paragraph styles
- through character styles

We'll look first at direct formatting, then at paragraph styles and character styles.

Direct Formatting

The simplest form of character- and paragraph-formatting in Word is direct formatting—applied by the user to selected text, or to the current word (for character formatting) or the current paragraph (for paragraph formatting). As an example of direct character formatting, to apply italic to a word, you could place the insertion point within the word (by moving the mouse to it and clicking, or by using the arrow keys) and then either click the Italic button or press the Ctrl+I key combination. As an example of paragraph formatting, you could change the margins of a paragraph by placing the insertion point in the paragraph, and then adjusting the Left and Right settings in the Indentation group box on the Indents and Spacing tab of the Paragraph dialog box.

Applying Direct Character Formatting

With each new version, Word has made it a fraction easier to quickly apply formatting to characters. You can apply formatting by using the toolbars, keyboard combinations, or the Font dialog box.

- To apply formatting to a word, simply place the insertion point in the word and choose the formatting you want to apply.

- To apply formatting to a number of words, select them using the mouse, the keyboard, or both, and choose the formatting you want to apply.

If you select a number of words and apply formatting to them, the spaces between the words will also take on the formatting characteristics you apply. However, the space at the end of the selection will retain its previous formatting characteristics.

For complex character formatting, it's generally easier to use character styles instead. We'll look at how to create and apply character styles a little later in this chapter.

NOTE   Inline graphics—those in the text layer, not floating in the graphics layer—count as characters too. You can apply font formatting to them just as to any other character. For example, you can format a graphic with bold, or italic, or 20-point Tahoma. However, it won't do you much good, because the graphic won't display that formatting, even though Word will register it as having that property. (About the only good this *will* do you is if you ever need to find a graphic by its formatting rather than by using Edit ➤ Find and specifying the code for a graphic). More relevant for our purposes, because an inline graphic counts as one character, you can select it by moving the insertion point by one character in selection mode. Hold that thought for the moment.

Applying Direct Paragraph Formatting

The basis of all paragraph formatting in Word is the paragraph mark, in which Word stores information about the paragraph's style. The paragraph mark itself behaves as one character: you can select it like any other character (or inline graphic) and delete it. When you delete a paragraph mark (and thus join the paragraph it governed with the paragraph after it), the second paragraph takes on the style of the first paragraph. (A *style*, as we'll see in the next section, is a collection of formatting.) For example, if you delete the paragraph mark of a Heading 1 paragraph that's followed by a Body Text paragraph, the Body Text paragraph will be subsumed into the Heading 1 paragraph and will take on the Heading 1 style.

Paragraph formatting applies to the whole of any given paragraph and covers the following:

- line spacing (the distance between the lines of the paragraph) and paragraph spacing (the distance between one paragraph and the next, above and below)

- indents from the left and right margins

- alignment (left, right, centered, or justified)

- pagination—whether Word tries to suppress any widow (a line that appears by itself at the top of a page) or orphan (a line that appears by itself at the bottom of a page); whether Word keeps the lines of the paragraph together or breaks them onto the next page as necessary; whether Word keeps the paragraph with the paragraph after it or allows them to appear on separate pages as necessary; and whether Word automatically places a page break before the paragraph

- automatic bullets and numbering, including heading numbering

TIP

Suppressing typographical widows and orphans is good general practice for making your documents as readable as possible, whereas keeping all the lines of a paragraph together on the same page is seldom necessary and tends to create short pages if your paragraphs are more than a few lines long. Keeping a paragraph together with the paragraph after it is primarily useful for headings, because it prevents a heading from appearing at the bottom of one page unless the paragraph after it fits on that page too; and automatically placing a page break before a paragraph is mostly useful for part, chapter, and section headings that need to always start on a new page.

To apply paragraph formatting, place the insertion point anywhere in the paragraph (or select the whole of multiple paragraphs, or parts of multiple paragraphs). You can then apply formatting by using the buttons on the Formatting toolbar (such as the alignment buttons), by using keyboard combinations (such as Ctrl+1 for single-spacing, Ctrl+2 for double-spacing, and Ctrl+5 for 1.5-line spacing), or by choosing Format ➤ Paragraph and making choices on its tabs.

NOTE The final paragraph mark in a document contains document-formatting information, including page setup information (paper size and orientation, margins) and properties (the static information you see in the document's Properties dialog box).

What Are Styles?

While direct formatting works well for simple formatting, styles provide an efficient way of applying complex formatting to parts of your documents. Word supports two different kinds of styles: paragraph styles and character styles.

Paragraph styles bring together the various kinds of formatting that Word offers: character formatting, paragraph formatting (including alignment), tabs, language formatting, frames, bullets and numbering, and borders and shading. Each style contains complete formatting information that you can apply with one click of the mouse or one keystroke (or a tediously complex menu choice, if that's your preference). Every paragraph in Word uses a style; Word starts you off in the Normal style unless the template you're using dictates otherwise. Each paragraph can have only one style applied to it at a time.

Character styles are similar to paragraph styles but contain only character formatting—they have no alignment options, no line-spacing choices, no language or border formatting, and so on. Character styles are suitable for picking out elements in a paragraph already formatted with paragraph styles: you can apply multiple character styles to different parts of any paragraph, though any given

FIGURE 2.1

You can apply character styles on top of paragraph styles.

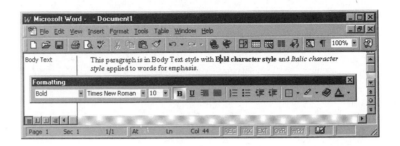

character can have only one character style applied to it at any time. For example, the paragraph shown in Figure 2.1 is in Body Text paragraph style with Italic character style and Bold character style applied to specific words. You couldn't apply both the Italic character style and the Bold character style to the same word at the same time, though you could create a Bold Italic style that contained both boldface and italic.

Using styles not only gives your documents a consistent look—every Heading 1 paragraph will appear in the same font and font size, with the same amount of space before and after it, etc.—but also saves you a great deal of time in formatting your documents.

You can either use Word's built-in styles—which are different in Word's various predefined templates—or create your own styles. If you so choose, Word will help you do the latter by automatically defining styles whenever it thinks you're trying to create one.

NOTE Most users start their adventures in Word by sticking with the Normal style and simply applying formatting to individual paragraphs as necessary. While this works fine for the short haul, for any document more than a page or so in length (or with anything beyond an absolute minimum of formatting), you'll usually save a significant amount of time by using styles.

Applying Styles

To apply a paragraph style, place the insertion point in the paragraph or select a number of paragraphs, and then click the Style drop-down list button (on the far left side of the Formatting toolbar) and choose the style you want from the list, as shown here. Paragraph styles are identified with a paragraph symbol (¶) and character styles with an underlined letter a. As you can see, the Style drop-down list shows formatting for the styles. This can make it tediously slow to display the first time you use it in each session if the current template has many styles—Word has to collate all the style-formatting information before it displays the list. Typically, the list displays quickly on subsequent use, because the information is already stored.

TIP

Some of the most popular styles have keyboard shortcuts: Ctrl+Shift+N for Normal style; Ctrl+Alt+1 for Heading 1, Ctrl+Alt+2 for Heading 2, Ctrl+Alt+3 for Heading 3; and Ctrl+Shift+L for List Bullet style. If you find keyboard shortcuts to be convenient for applying styles, you can define other keyboard shortcuts for other styles by customizing your templates. If you find them inconvenient, you can alter the keyboard shortcut for any style.

To apply a character style, click in the word to which you want to apply it, or select a number of words, and then choose the character style from the Style drop-down list.

You can also apply a paragraph or character style by choosing Format ➤ Style to display the Style dialog box (see Figure 2.2), choosing the style in the Styles list box, and clicking on the Apply button; however, this is much slower and less convenient than the drop-down list method.

You can always tell which style the current paragraph (or current text, for character styles) is in by looking at the name in the Style drop-down list box:

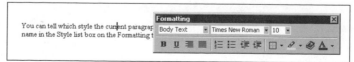

If multiple paragraphs with the same style are selected, the Style drop-down list box will display that style name. If multiple paragraphs with different styles are selected, the Style drop-down list box will be blank.

FIGURE 2.2

To apply a style, choose it in the Styles list box and click the Apply button.

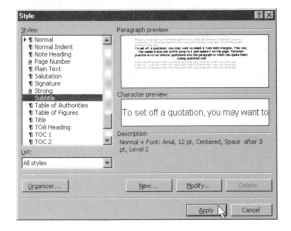

If you want to see which style all the displayed paragraphs are in, you can display the *style area*, a vertical bar at the left side of the Word window that displays the style name for each paragraph:

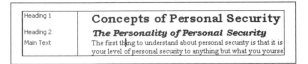

To display the style area, choose Tools ➤ Options to open the Options dialog box, and click on the View tab to bring it to the front. Enter a measurement (say, 1 inch, or 3 centimeters, or 6 picas, or 72 points) in the Style Area Width box in the Window area, and then click OK. Once you have the style area displayed, you can change its size by clicking on the line that separates it from the text area and dragging the line left (to decrease) or right (to increase). To get rid of the style area, either drag the line all the way over to the left side of the Word window or reduce the setting in the Style Area Width box to zero.

NOTE   You cannot display the style area in Page Layout view or Print Preview, because these show how the page will print, and the style area does not print.

TIP

If you use a relatively small number of styles with great frequency, you can make them easily accessible by creating a custom toolbar for them. Alternatively, you can create a Style menu (on the menu bar or on a toolbar) for your most-used styles, or you can define keyboard shortcuts for them. For a template that you'll distribute widely (e.g., throughout a department), you may want to cover your bases by making the styles quickly accessible in all three of these ways. We'll discuss how to customize a template in Chapter 3.

How Paragraph Styles, Character Styles, and Direct Formatting Are Related

One of the most important things to understand about formatting in Word is how paragraph styles, character styles, and character formatting relate to each other. Here are the main rules:

- **A character can have only one character style at a time.** When you apply a new style to a character, it loses the style it had before. (Also note that once you've applied a character style to some text, the text will retain that style until you replace it with another character style, or until you delete the text.)

TIP

If you use character styles to apply straightforward formatting, such as a Bold style to apply bold and an Italic style to apply italic, you'll probably want to create a Bold Italic style for the occasions when you want to apply both.

- **A paragraph can have only one paragraph style at a time.** When you apply a new style to a paragraph, it loses the style it had before.

- **Applying a paragraph style does not remove a character style** (and of course vice versa), but both paragraph styles and character styles will override direct formatting that contains attributes they share. For example, if you apply boldface directly to a word in a paragraph that is in Normal style (which I'm assuming does not contain boldface), then apply to the paragraph a style that contains bold formatting (e.g., a typical Heading 1), the word will lose its boldface.

- **You can apply direct formatting on top of paragraph styles and character styles**, but if you apply another paragraph style or character style to the text in question, you may lose the direct formatting.

This seems (and is) convoluted, but you'll need to understand these intricacies of character and paragraph formatting when working with macros.

Viewing Formatting

Unlike WordPerfect, Word has no Reveal Codes option, and it can be hard to see where character formatting starts and ends. For example, in most typefaces and at usable zoom levels, you can easily see when a word is boldfaced or italic, but it's impossible to see whether a space is boldfaced or italic—or indeed red or yellow, or formatted as all caps or small caps. Pretty much the only character formatting that a space will show is underline (single, double, or dotted—not word underline), and even that only when there is another character after it; an underlined space at the end of a paragraph will not show or print the underline.

When there is no selected text, Word displays formatting information in the boxes and buttons on the Formatting toolbar for the character to the left of the insertion point. This is the formatting you'll get if you continue typing from the position of the insertion point. For example, if the character to the left of the insertion point is bold or italic, the appropriate button will be highlighted, the font name will appear in the Font box, the font size will appear in the Font Size box, and so on.

When there is a selection, Word displays in the boxes and buttons on the Formatting toolbar any formatting information common to all the characters and paragraphs in the selection: the style name, font, font size, bold, italic, underline, alignment, etc. For example, if all the characters and paragraphs are in Times New Roman font, the Font box will display **Times New Roman**; if the characters have different fonts, the Font box will be empty. Likewise, the Bold and Italic buttons will be highlighted if all the characters are bold or italic (respectively); if the characters are not bold or italic, or not *all* bold or italic, the buttons will appear in their normal state.

> **WARNING**
>
> There is a tricky element to toggle formatting such as boldface or italic. When you toggle, say, boldface for a selection, Word checks the first character in the selection for its current formatting, and then toggles the formatting accordingly. So if the first character (or, more likely, the first word) in a selection is boldfaced but the rest of the selection is not, Word will toggle boldface off for the whole selection. This is seldom a problem when you're applying formatting manually, but it can provide odd effects when you record macros.

While you can use the information on the Formatting toolbar to quickly check the formatting of the character to the left of the insertion point (or of selected characters), this will usually not give you enough information to be useful, unless you simply need to know the font or font size, or you need to check whether a space is bold, italic, or underlined. For more detail, you can use either the Reveal Formats dialog box or the Font dialog box.

Using the Reveal Formats Dialog Box

For a quick snapshot of character and paragraph formatting applied to a particular piece of text, choose Help ➤ What's This? or click the Help button. Word will change the mouse pointer to an arrow with a large black question mark beside it; with this, click on the text in question to display the Reveal Formats dialog box (see Figure 2.3).

FIGURE 2.3

To check the formatting of a character or paragraph, click the Help button to display the Help mouse pointer, and then click on the character or paragraph in question to display the Reveal Formats dialog box.

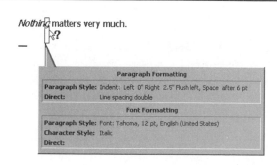

In the Reveal Formats dialog box, Word presents Paragraph Formatting information and Font Formatting information. The Paragraph Formatting section contains two categories of information:

- **Paragraph Style** displays paragraph-formatting information that you would find in the Paragraph dialog box, such as indents, space before and after, and line spacing. This paragraph-formatting information is contained within the style, so there will always be some information in this section of the Reveal Formats dialog box.

- **Direct** displays paragraph-formatting information added directly (manually) on top of the paragraph style. If you have added no paragraph formatting since applying the style (or since applying the most recent style), the Direct line will be blank. For example, if you apply Heading 3 style to a paragraph, and then apply double-spacing to it manually, the Paragraph Style line will show the indents, spacing, and line spacing for the style, and the Direct line will display Line Spacing Double to indicate that you have applied this formatting on top of the style. But if you then apply Heading 2 style to same paragraph and display the Reveal Formats dialog box again, the Direct line will be blank, because applying the style has reset the formatting.

The Font Formatting section of the Reveal Formats dialog box displays the following information:

- **Paragraph Style** displays font information for the current paragraph, as set in the paragraph style applied to the paragraph. There will always be some information in this section.

- **Character Style** displays font information for the character style that's applied to the current character or word. If you haven't applied any character style to the character or word, this line will be blank.

- **Direct** displays character-formatting information added manually on top of either the paragraph style or the character style.

After viewing the information in the Reveal Formats dialog box, you can then click on other characters or paragraphs to view their formatting information. To restore the regular mouse pointer, press the Esc key or choose Help ➤ What's This? again.

Using the Font Dialog Box

You can also use the Font dialog box to view formatting information. The advantage of using this over the Reveal Formats dialog box is that the Font dialog box is easier to use and allows you to change any of the settings more simply. For example, if you are unable to lowercase a word and suspect that it might be set in all caps, you can display the Font dialog box, see if the All Caps check box in the Effects group box is checked, and if it is, clear it.

Selecting Items

Selecting items in Word may seem peripheral to the business of styles, but in fact it ties in quite closely, as you'll see in just a moment. Beyond that, knowing how to easily and consistently select the items you intend to affect is a vital skill for creating robust macros that carry out your will rather than their own.

NOTE Selecting items ties in closely with understanding the Word Object Model, which we'll look at in Chapter 11.

Keyboard Selection

If you prefer to keep your hands on the keyboard as you work, you can select text quickly and easily by using the Shift key and the navigation keys. Table 2.1 provides a quick recap on what the navigation keys do.

NOTE If this all seems insufferably obvious, skip this section. Tedious as this is, though, we need these details for the macros.

TABLE 2.1   Selecting with the Navigation Keys

Key	Effect (with the Shift key held down)
←	Extends or reduces the selection by one character to the left.
→	Extends or reduces the selection by one character to the right.
↑	Extends or reduces the selection to the same insertion point position on the line above the current one (or to the end of the line above, if that line is shorter than the distance from the left margin to the current insertion point position).
↓	Extends or reduces the selection to the same insertion point position on the line below the current one (or to the end of the line below, if that line is shorter than the distance from the left margin to the current insertion point position).
Home	Selects from the insertion point to the beginning of the current line. If the insertion point is already at the beginning of a line, this has no effect.

WARNING   The beginning or end of the current line may fall in a different place depending on the view you're using (Normal view, Page Layout view, or Print Preview). In Normal view, it will also be affected by the Zoom setting, and by the Wrap to Window setting (located on the View tab of the Options dialog box).

Key	Effect (with the Shift key held down)
End	Selects from the insertion point to the end of the current line. If the insertion point is already at the end of the line, this has no effect.
Ctrl+←	Extends or reduces the selection by one word or word-equivalent (see the following section) to the left.
Ctrl+→	Extends or reduces the selection by one word or word-equivalent to the right.
Ctrl+↑	Selects from the insertion point to the beginning of the current paragraph. If the insertion point is currently at the beginning of a paragraph, selects the previous paragraph.
Ctrl+↓	Selects from the insertion point to the end of the current paragraph.

Key	Effect (with the Shift key held down)
PageUp	Selects what Word considers the previous screenful of material, starting at the insertion point. What you actually get can depend on the view you're using, the time of day, and whether a butterfly has recently flapped its wings over Shanghai.
PageDown	Selects what Word considers to be the next screenful of material, starting at the insertion point. What you actually get can vary; this is primarily useful as an active keyboard shortcut rather than as a key combination to use for selecting material in a macro.

WARNING   When using PageUp and PageDown, make sure that the Object Browser is set to browse by page rather than by anything else (such as Find). To set the Object Browser, click the Select Browse Object button at the foot of the vertical scroll bar.

Key	Effect (with the Shift key held down)
Ctrl+PageUp	Selects from the insertion point to the first character visible on the screen. (If the insertion point is currently at the first character on the screen, this does nothing at all.)
Ctrl+PageDown	Selects from the insertion point to the last character visible on the screen. (Again, if the insertion point is currently at the last character on the screen, this does nothing.)
Ctrl+Home	Selects from the insertion point to the start of the document.
Ctrl+End	Selects from the insertion point to the end of the document.

As noted in the table, some of these methods of selecting with the navigation keys are most useful when performing operations actively in Word—selecting text while watching what you're doing. But most of them also come in handy when you're recording macros, because you can control exactly the amount of text you're selecting. For example, to select a paragraph, you can use Ctrl+↑ to move to the start of it, then Shift+Ctrl+↓ to select to the end of it. (You'll need to make sure that the insertion point isn't already at the beginning of a paragraph— in which case the initial Ctrl+↑ would move the insertion point to the beginning of the previous paragraph rather than the start of the current one—but that's something that we'll consider in Chapter 12.)

What's a Word to Word?

Ctrl+← and Ctrl+→ (with the Shift key held down) extend or reduce the selection by one word or word-equivalent to the left or right, respectively. To use these key combinations successfully, you need to understand what Word considers a word. Here's a quick rundown:

- A word can be what you or I think of as a "regular" word: a number of letters preceded by a space, a punctuation mark, a hyphen, or a paragraph mark and followed by a space, a punctuation mark, a hyphen, or a paragraph mark. As a simple example, the phrase *this phrase contains five words* contains five words.

- When a word is followed by a space (or multiple spaces), Word includes that space (or spaces) in any selection or movement. For example, if you press Ctrl+→ with the insertion point before the word *phrase* as shown in the first line below, Word will move the insertion point one word to the right, to just before the word *contains:*

  ```
  this |phrase contains five words

  this phrase |contains five words
  ```

- When a word is followed by a punctuation mark, Word moves the insertion point to just before the punctuation mark:

  ```
  The sentence ends |here. This is the next sentence.

  The sentence ends here|. This is the next sentence.
  ```

- A punctuation mark counts as its own word, and again, Word will move the insertion point past any space or spaces following the punctuation mark:

  ```
  The sentence ends here|. This is the next sentence.

  The sentence ends here. |This is the next sentence.
  ```

- A symbol or inline graphic also counts as its own word; again, Word will move the insertion point past any space or spaces following it.

- Groups of punctuation marks that Word considers to belong together count as one word. For example, in the sentence below, the opening double quotes count as a word, but the exclamation point and the closing double quotes together count as only one word:

```
She said to the squirrel, "Get out of here!" and fired
the gun in the general direction of Texas.
```

If in doubt about what exactly Word is going to treat as a word in your macros, it's best to check before running them on any document you value.

Selecting with the F8 Key and Extend Mode

To select blocks of text, you can use Word's Extend mode. This is a potentially powerful feature, but with a couple of caveats. First, Extend mode is typically a clumsy and awkward way of selecting text; for most purposes, the mouse or keyboard (or a combination of the two) offers more speed and flexibility. Second, under some circumstances (which we'll look at in a moment), Extend mode can behave a little illogically and produce results drastically different from what you intended. That said, Extend mode can nevertheless be useful in macros, as we'll see later in this book (starting in Chapter 7), so don't disregard it completely.

Here's how Extend mode works with the F8 key:

- The first press of F8 toggles on Extend mode (and darkens the EXT indicator on the status bar to remind you that it's done so).

- The second press of F8 selects the current word or object. (If the insertion point is not in a word and has a space to its left and a word or object to its right, it selects the word or object to the right. If the insertion point is not in a word and has a space to its right, it selects the word or object to the left of the insertion point. If the insertion point is next to a blank paragraph, it will select the paragraph mark.)

- The third press of F8 selects the current sentence (but see the Warning below).

WARNING If the insertion point was next to a blank paragraph when you entered Extend mode, the third press of F8 will select the whole document. This won't bother you too much when you're working manually, but it can do horrible things with macros, so keep it in mind.

- The fourth press of F8 selects the current paragraph (but again, see the Warning above).

- The fifth press of F8 selects the whole document.

If none of the above choices appeals to you, at any point after entering Extend mode you can extend the selection from the insertion point toward the end of the document by pressing the character to which you want to extend the selection. For example, you can press the **e** key to extend the selection to the next letter *e* after the current position of the insertion point. To move to the letter *e* after that, press **e** again, and so on. So you can quickly select to the end of a sentence by pressing the period key, and to the end of a paragraph by pressing the Enter key. If you like, you can select the current word, sentence, or paragraph before pressing the character to which to extend the selection.

Once you've made your selection, you need to toggle Extend mode off before you do anything else. To toggle Extend mode off, press the Esc key or double-click the EXT indicator on the status bar. Alternatively, you can extend or decrease your selection by using the navigation keys, and then press Esc to toggle Extend mode off.

Mouse Selection

As with any Windows application, you can select any amount of text, even a single character, by clicking and dragging. This is unremarkable in itself and barely worth mentioning here, but Word offers a couple of features associated with it; see the next two sections.

Automatic Word Selection

Word's automatic word selection feature lets you quickly select the second and subsequent words as you click and drag. As soon as you drag the insertion point over part of the second word, Word selects the entire second word, along with any space after it and any unselected part of the first word. You don't need to click at the beginning of the first word in the selection—clicking anywhere in it will cause Word to select the whole word once the insertion point has moved into the second word. This means that you can quickly select a number of words with a relatively inaccurate swipe of your mouse—handy when you're using a dirty trackball or an uncooperative pointing stick.

WARNING Be careful when dragging down and to the left from one line to the line below it; if you drag over the word to the left of the insertion point on your way down to the next line, Word will select that word, too.

To temporarily override automatic word selection (for example, to select part of one word and part of the next), hold down the Alt key while you drag.

To switch automatic word selection off (or back on), choose Tools ➤ Options to display the Options dialog box and then clear (or select) the When Selecting, Automatically Select Entire Word check box on the Edit tab. (This check box is selected by default.)

Shift+Click Selection

Depending on the amount of text you're trying to select, and on the pointing device that you're using, you may find Shift+click selection easier than clicking and dragging. To use this method, place the insertion point at the beginning (or end) of what you want to select, and then move the mouse to the end (or beginning), hold down the Shift key, and click to select the block. (If you need to scroll up or down the document to reach the end of the selection, use the scroll bar; using the arrow keys or other navigation keys will move the insertion point from the beginning of the block.)

Creating a New Style

As you can see in the Style list box shown back in Figure 2.2, Word's templates come with a number of built-in styles. If these are not enough for you, you can create your own styles in any of three ways: by example, by definition, and by having Word do all the work for you.

Creating a New Style by Example

The easiest way to create a style is to set up a paragraph of text with the exact formatting you want for the style—character formatting, paragraph formatting, borders and shading, bullets or numbers, and so on. Then click in the Style box,  type the name for the new style into the box as shown here (replacing the current style name, which clicking in the Style box will have selected), and press Enter. Word will create the style, which you can immediately select from the Style drop-down list and apply to other paragraphs as necessary.

The disadvantage to creating a style by example is that you cannot choose the style on which it is based, the style for the following paragraph, or other more comprehensive settings. For these, you need to create a style by definition.

Creating a New Style by Definition

The more complex way of creating a style is by definition. This method gives you finer control over the style.

1. Choose Format ➤ Style to display the Style dialog box.

2. Click the New button. Word will display the New Style dialog box (see Figure 2.4).

FIGURE 2.4

Creating a new style in the New Style dialog box.

3. Set the information for your new style:

- In the Name box, enter a name for the style. Style names can be a decent length—Word will accept over 100 characters—but you'll do better to keep them short enough to fit in the Style box on the Formatting toolbar. If your style name is over 20 characters long, you should probably rethink your naming conventions.

- In the Based On drop-down list box, choose the existing style on which you want to base the new style. (We'll discuss how to make this decision in the sections "Create a Base Style" and "Use the Based On Setting Wisely" later in this chapter.) Bear in mind that if you change the Based On style later, the new style will change too. The Preview box will show what the Based On style looks like.

- In the Style Type box, choose whether you want to create a paragraph style or a character style.

- In the Style for Following Paragraph box (which is not available for character styles), choose the style that you want Word to apply to the paragraph immediately after this style. For example, after the Heading 1 style, you might want Body Text, or after Figure, you might want Caption. But for many styles you'll want to continue with the style itself.

4. To adjust the formatting of the style, click the Format button and choose Font, Paragraph, Tabs, Border, Language, Frame, or Numbering from the drop-down list. This will display the dialog box for that type of formatting. When you've finished, click the OK button to return to the New Style dialog box.

5. Repeat step 4 as necessary, selecting other formatting characteristics for the style.

6. Select the Add to Template check box to add the new style to the template.

7. Select the Automatically Update check box if you want Word to automatically update the style when you change it. (We'll look at this option more in a minute.)

8. To set up a shortcut key for the style, click the Shortcut Key button. Word will display the Customize Keyboard dialog box. With the insertion point in the Press New Shortcut Key box, press the shortcut key combination you'd like to set, click the Assign button, and then click the Close button.

WARNING Watch the Currently Assigned To area of the Customize Keyboard dialog box when selecting your shortcut key combination. If Word already has assigned that key combination to a command, macro, AutoText entry, style, or symbol, it will display its name there. If you choose to assign the key combination to the new style, the old assignment for that combination will be deactivated.

9. In the New Style dialog box, click the OK button to return to the Style dialog box.

10. To create another new style, repeat steps 2 through 9.

11. To close the Style dialog box, click the Apply button to apply the new style to the current paragraph or current selection, or click the Close button (into which the Cancel button will have changed when you created the style) to save the new style without applying it.

Having Word Create Styles Automatically

Microsoft must have noticed that only about one percent of Word users were using styles, so they decided to make creating styles easier in Word 97. Even if you do create your own styles, it can get tedious—so why not have Word create them for you? Not only that, when you change the formatting of a paragraph that has a certain style, you can have Word update the style for you, so that all other paragraphs that have the same style take on that formatting too.

By default, Word sets itself up to automatically create styles for you. If you're not sure whether it's creating styles for you, here's how to check:

1. Choose Tools ➤ AutoCorrect to display the AutoCorrect dialog box.

2. Click the AutoFormat as You Type tab to display it.

3. In the Automatically as You Type area at the bottom of the tab, make sure that the Define Styles Based on Your Formatting check box is selected. (If you want Word to cease and desist from creating styles on its own, clear this check box.)

4. Click the OK button to close the AutoCorrect dialog box.

Once you've set this option (or if it was set already), Word will attempt to identify styles you're creating and will supply names for them. For example, if you start a new document (with paragraphs in the Normal style, as usual) and bold and center the first paragraph, Word may define that bolding and centering as a Title style; if you simply increase the font size, Word may call that paragraph Heading 1 instead. This sounds creepy but works surprisingly well; and if it doesn't suit you, you can easily turn it off by clearing the Define Styles Based on Your Formatting check box.

Modifying a Style

Just as you can create a style by example, by definition, or by having Word create it automatically, you can modify a style with any of those three methods.

Modifying a Style by Example

To modify a style by example, you simply change the formatting of a paragraph that currently has that style assigned to it, and then choose the same style again from the Style drop-down list. Word will display the Modify Style dialog box (see Figure 2.5). Make sure that the Update the Style to Reflect Recent Changes option button is selected, and then click the OK button to update the style to include the changes you just made to it. If you want Word to automatically update the style without displaying this dialog box when you make future changes, select the Automatically Update the Style from Now On check box before clicking the OK button.

FIGURE 2.5

In the Modify Style dialog box, choose OK to update the style to reflect changes you just made to it. If you want Word to automatically update the style in the future, select the Automatically Update the Style from Now On check box.

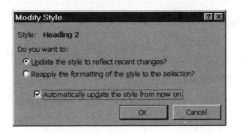

Modifying a Style by Definition

Modifying a Word style by definition is similar to creating a new style, except that you work in the Modify Style dialog box (a different one—not the one shown in Figure 2.5). This dialog box offers one less option than the New Style dialog box offers—you don't get to choose whether the style is a paragraph style or a character style because Word already knows which it is.

Open the Style dialog box by choosing Format ➤ Style, and then select the style you want to work on from the Styles list. (If you don't see the style you're looking for, make sure the List box in the lower-left corner of the Style dialog box is showing All Styles rather than Styles in Use or User-Defined Styles.)

Click the Modify button. Word will display the Modify Style dialog box. From there, follow steps 3 through 9 as outlined in the section "Creating a New Style by Definition" earlier in this chapter (except for selecting the style type), and then step 11 to exit the Style dialog box.

Removing a Style

Removing a style is much faster than creating one. Open the Style dialog box by choosing Format ➤ Style, select the style to delete in the Styles list, and click the Delete button. Word will display a message box confirming that you want to delete the style; click the Yes button.

You can then delete another style the same way, or click the Close button to leave the Style dialog box.

TIP
Two things to keep in mind here: First, you can't delete a Heading style once you've started using it. Second, when you delete a style that's in use (other than a Heading style), Word applies the Normal style to those paragraphs.

Copying Styles from One Template to Another

You can easily copy styles from one template to another by using the Organizer dialog box:

1. Choose Tools ➤ Templates and Add-ins to display the Templates and Add-ins dialog box; then click the Organizer button to display the Organizer dialog box, as shown in Figure 2.6. When this dialog box opens, it displays the styles in Normal (the global template) in one panel and the styles in the current document in the other panel.

TIP You can also get to the Organizer dialog box by choosing Tools ➤ Macro ➤ Macros to display the Macro dialog box, then clicking the Organizer button.

FIGURE 2.6

Use the Organizer dialog box to copy styles from one template to another.

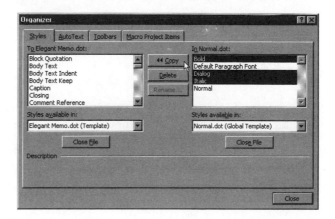

2. To work with the template for the current document, select it from the Styles Available In drop-down list in the panel listing the current document. Otherwise, open the templates or documents you want: click the Close File button on either side of the Organizer dialog box to close the file currently open on that side; then click the Open File button (into which the Close File

button will have metamorphosed) and choose the correct template or document from the Open dialog box that Word then displays.

3. If the Styles tab isn't foremost in the Organizer dialog box, click it to bring it to the front.

4. In the list box for the donor template or document, choose the styles you want to copy.

5. Click the Copy button to copy the styles from the donor template or document into the recipient template or document.

6. To copy more styles from other templates or documents, repeat steps 2 through 5. When you close a template or document to which you've made changes, Word will suggest you save it; do so.

TIP   If you need to create a new template that contains most but not all of the styles you have in an existing template, you'll probably find it quicker to copy the template and then remove the unnecessary styles than to create a new template and copy the styles into it.

Using the Style Gallery

Word provides the Style Gallery to give you a quick overview of its many templates and the myriad styles they contain. To open the Style Gallery, choose Format ➤ Style Gallery. Word will display the Style Gallery dialog box, shown in Figure 2.7.

To preview a template in the Preview Of panel, select it in the Template list box. Then choose the type of preview you want in the Preview box:

- *Document* shows you how your current document looks with the template's styles applied.

- *Example* shows you a sample document that uses the template's styles.

- *Style Samples* shows each of the styles in the document.

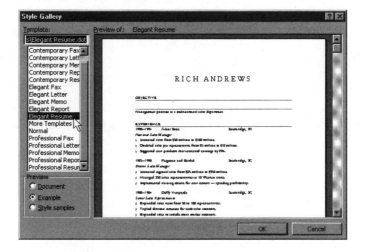

FIGURE 2.7

The Style Gallery dialog box gives you a preview of the styles available in Word's templates.

To apply to your document the template you've chosen, click on the OK button. Alternatively, click on the Cancel button to close the Style Gallery.

Attaching a Document to a Different Template

If you look behind the curtain, you'll notice that using the Style Gallery does not attach the document to the new template you chose—it just automatically copies styles from the template you chose to the template to which the document is currently attached.

If you want to attach the document to the other template, here's what to do:

1. Choose Tools ➤ Templates and Add-ins to display the Templates and Add-ins dialog box.

2. Click the Attach button to display the Attach Template dialog box, which you'll recognize as the Open dialog box in disguise.

3. Select the template to which you want to attach the document; then click the Open button to close the Attach Template dialog box and return to the Templates and Add-ins dialog box.

4. If you want the styles in the document to take on the formatting of their equivalents in the new template, make sure that the Automatically Update Document Styles check box is selected. (This is usually a good idea.)

5. Click the OK button to close the Templates and Add-ins dialog box and attach the document to the new template.

Including Your Own Templates in the Style Gallery

You can include your own templates in the Style Gallery. In fact, Word will automatically marshal into the Style Gallery any .dot files located in the folders specified for User Templates and Workgroup Templates on the File Locations tab of the Options dialog box (Tools ➤ Options).

The only drawback to including your own templates in the Style Gallery is that you cannot create example files for them. When the user chooses the Example or Style Samples option button, they will see a message that reads "There is no example for this template."

Styles That Word Applies Automatically

There are a number of styles that Word applies automatically to certain elements: annotations, headers and footers, macros, and more. For the moment, there's no need to memorize all of them—just be aware that Word will apply these styles to the corresponding elements without involving you, so your documents are likely to contain them.

Style	Automatically Applied To
Caption	Caption inserted using Insert ➤ Caption
Comment Reference	Character style for the initials of the person who inserted a comment
Comment Text	Comments inserted using Insert ➤ Comment
Endnote reference	Character style for the reference character for an endnote

Style	Automatically Applied To
Endnote Text	Text in endnotes
Footer	Text in footers
Footnote reference	Character style for the reference character for a footnote
Footnote Text	Text in footnotes
Header	Text in headers
Index 1–Index 9	Entries in an index created by Word
Line Number	Character style for automatic line numbers (e.g., for legal documents)
Page Number	Character style for automatic page numbers (Insert ➤ Page Numbers)
Table of Authorities	Entries in a table of authorities (for citing the sources referenced in a legal or scholarly work) created by Word
Table of Figures	Entries in a table of figures created by Word
TOC 1–TOC 9	Entries in a table of contents created by Word

Advice on Using Styles

Learning to use styles efficiently takes a bit of trial and error, and it's not really my intent to deprive you of that character-forming (and often enjoyable) experience. There's also a fair element of personal preference in the way you set up the styles in your templates. Still, I couldn't resist the temptation to dispense some advice, so this section contains a few suggestions you might want to consider following while finding your way with styles.

Plan Your Styles and Templates

At the risk of starting off with the most banal advice possible, plan carefully before investing any amount of time in a template. If you're the only person who will be using it, at least sketch out a rough list of the styles you think you'll be using and what you think you'll be using them for. This should help you identify any major gaps in your plan and work out the order in which to create the styles most efficiently. (We'll get into this in more detail in a section or two.)

If other people will be using the template as well as you, establish how that will affect your use of styles: Will you need to reduce the number of styles in a template to make it easy to use? Will you need to provide menus and toolbars of styles to help the others apply them most efficiently?

If possible, put together a small work party to decide what the template needs to do and to make sure you don't disregard the needs of one department or another. If this isn't possible, put together a prototype of the template for people to try, and solicit feedback.

Try to get answers to the following questions:

- Do you need to maintain backward compatibility with Windows 3.1 and Word 6? If so, you'll probably at least want to keep the template's name short (so that it doesn't show up in Word 6 with the dreaded ~1 extension); you may also want to restrict the length of document names in it.

- Do you need to maintain backward compatibility with the Word 6/95 format? If so, set up the template so that it will save files in that format by default rather than in the Word 97 format.

- Will everyone using the template have all the necessary typefaces, or will you need to distribute special typefaces? Can you reduce the set of typefaces to ones that everybody has without reducing the effect of the template?

- Will people be proofreading hard copy of documents created in the template? If so, make sure that all the styles are legible on paper (where the reader cannot zoom the view to help them deal with a small point size) and that the margins are a decent size.

NOTE   If you add a style to a template after creating a document that does not contain that style, you will need to reattach the document to the template in order to have that style available in the document.

Word's templates can contain several hundred styles, but usually you'll find it wiser to use only as many styles as you need for any project. Generally speaking, the Style drop-down list is manageable with up to thirty or so styles in use; if you're using more styles than that, you'll probably want to develop custom ways of applying them.

Use Consistent Style Names across Your Templates

This suggestion too may be stretching the bounds of your patience, but indulge me and consider it. By using consistent style names across a number of templates, you give yourself the ability to switch a document from one template to another swiftly and painlessly, changing its formatting either subtly or completely in the process.

Even if you don't need this ability, using consistent (or at least similar) style names in templates of the same kind makes it easier for you and your colleagues to work on them. For example, say your company produces several different newsletters, each of which has its own layout and look. If the templates for the newsletters all use the same style names, you can ask your contributors to use the appropriate styles for the elements of their pieces, no matter which newsletter they're destined for. Your contributors, most of whom probably wouldn't want to see the layout of the pieces as they were writing them, could use a common template that shared the style names with the other templates but could choose typefaces and font sizes suitable for writing and editing.

Use Logical Style Names

Again, this may seem obvious, but always try to create styles with logical style names. For example, if you have single-column lists and multi-column lists, create styles with parallel names such as List Single and List Multi-Column (which will appear close to one another in the Styles drop-down list) rather than Single List and Multi-Column List, which will appear far apart from each other.

Style names often matter less at the start of a project, when you're putting together a template, than later on, when you have to explain to a whole slew of people how to use it and why things don't work quite as logically as they might be expected to. For this reason, if for no other, they deserve your special consideration up front.

Set the Style for Following Paragraph Carefully

Always set the style for the following paragraph to the most appropriate style possible. This may be a tough choice: often, you'll need to create two or three paragraphs in a particular style before switching back to another style—for example, when you want to create three or four paragraphs of a bulleted list before switching back to a Body Text style for regular paragraphs. In such cases, it will usually be easiest to set the Style for Following Paragraph to the same style and then manually specify another style for the paragraphs that follow the end of that style.

TIP You may sometimes be able to use a line break (Shift+Enter) rather than a regular return (Enter) to continue a style from line to line that has a different style set for the following paragraph.

Create a Base Style

When you plan to have multiple styles of the same type, begin by creating a base style. For example, you might need several specialized types of lists. By creating one list style first and then specifying this style as the style on which the others are based, you can save yourself a lot of time setting up the details of the styles. See the next section for more on this.

Use the Based-On Setting Wisely

The Based-On setting can either save you a great deal of time and effort or cost you the same. For example, it's a great waste of time to base all the styles in a template on the Normal style.

Let's say that you want to use six levels of headings, each of which should bear a certain resemblance to the others. By using Heading 1 as the based-on style, you will be able to easily create a set of headings with common characteristics. Once you've created Heading 1 to your satisfaction, you can create Headings 2 through 6 based on Heading 1, varying each one enough to distinguish it—smaller point size, different indentation, more or less space above and below, etc.

There's another advantage to using the Based-On setting. To make changes such as altering the font in all the styles, you will only need to change the Heading 1 style; all the other styles will pick up the change automatically.

Combine Styles within Templates

To save time, you can combine styles within templates. As we saw earlier in this chapter, you can either copy styles from one template to another using the Organizer dialog box, or you can base a new template on an existing template so that the new template inherits all the other's styles.

Chapter 3 discusses templates and documents in detail.

Use Styles with Find and Replace

Find and Replace are features that you are probably already familiar with. Here I'll just mention a couple of the advantages of using styles consistently in your documents that relate to the Find and Replace features:

- You can search for single instances of a word or phrase that are in a particular style. This can save a great deal of time when you're working with large documents. Instead of trawling through an entire 200-page document looking at each instance of the word *import*, for example, you can search only for those in Discussion Note style.

- You can search for particular elements in your documents. For example, if you format all technical specifications in a manual with a style named Specifications, you can search for instances of that style so that you can check just those sections without trudging through the rest of the book.

- You can replace one style with another style. If the powers-that-be decide that the technical specifications would look better in the Maximum Impact style than the Specifications style, you can simply replace all instances of Specifications with Maximum Impact.

Use Styles with Macros

By using styles together with macros, you can create documents with macros and then quickly apply consistent formatting to them with styles. We'll delve deeper into this subject throughout the rest of the book.

CHAPTER

THREE

3

Using Documents and Templates Effectively

In this chapter, we'll dig into the powerful secrets housed in Word's templates and documents. That may sound a bit melodramatic, but understanding how templates and documents interact not only saves you a great deal of time and effort—such understanding is also vital for creating macros.

We'll start by examining what templates are and how they work, what you should use them for, and how you should use them. Then we'll go through customizing a template to present a suitable interface for the user. Last, we'll look at forms, specialized templates that you can use to quickly gather, manipulate, and disseminate information.

What Are Templates?

Word's templates are blueprints that you can use as skeletons for your documents. By creating the basic format of a certain type of document in a template, you can then use that template to create multiple documents of the same type.

For example, for your customer service needs, you could create a letter template that contained your company's name, address, phone number, URL, and logo, which all the customer service reps could use to create various letters. Better yet, each rep could use a different template that contained their name, title, signature, and contact information, so that they wouldn't have to enter this information multiple times (and risk introducing errors). Alternatively, you could add to the customer service template a macro that would customize the letter for whichever rep happened to be using it. The advantage of this would be that if you needed to change any of the basic information contained in the template (e.g., changing the URL, or adding an FTP site), you'd need to make changes in only one template rather than in a whole slew of them.

Templates also contain formatting information; in this case, all the customer-service letters going out from your company would use the same page setup (page size, margins, and indentation) and the same character and paragraph formatting (implemented through styles, as we saw in the previous chapter), ensuring that the letters had a uniform look and feel. Figure 3.1 shows how part of such a template might be laid out.

As you can see, template "skeletons" can be fully fleshed out: for example, by splitting your customer-service letters among several templates, you might create

FIGURE 3.1

A customer-service template, showing some of the possible features.

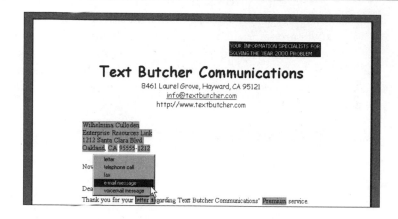

for each rep a letter template that required them to fill in only four or five fields for the document to be complete: customer name, customer address, product inquired about, and so on. Such a template would best be set up as a form, which we'll look at later in this chapter.

We're getting a little ahead of ourselves here; let's go back to basics for a moment.

How Do Templates Work?

Each Word document is based on a template; in Word's terminology, each document is *attached to* a template. If you choose to create a new default document by clicking the New button on the Standard toolbar, by pressing Ctrl+N, or by choosing Blank Document from the New dialog box, Word will start a document based on the Normal.dot global template. We'll look at Normal.dot in just a minute.

By default, Word's templates have a .dot extension (for *document template*) when you save them, but once you've saved them, you can rename them to anything you want. However, this can cause some problems, as we'll see later in the chapter. Depending on whether you have Windows 95 or NT 4 displaying file extensions, you may or may not see the .dot extension on file names. (This setting is controlled by the Hide MS-DOS File Extensions for File Types That Are Registered check box on the View tab of the Options dialog box [View ➤ Options] in the Windows Explorer or Windows NT Explorer.)

Templates can contain styles, macros, and AutoText entries, not to mention interface customizations including custom menus, custom toolbars, and custom keyboard shortcuts. You can start a document based on one template and then attach it to another, quickly switching the manifestation of its styles and making available to it all the styles, macros, AutoText items, and toolbars in the second template. We'll look at the implications of this in the following sections.

Word's Three-Layer Architecture

Word uses what Microsoft describes as a three-layer architecture. At the bottom of the structure, there's the Word application, which contains the Word menus, toolbars, commands, and so on, and which you see through Normal.dot. Sitting on top of that is the current template, which contains styles, AutoText entries, macro modules, and customized toolbars and settings for the template, along with any boilerplate text. On top of the current template is the current document, which contains the text and graphics in the document, the formatting, and the layout. Complicating things in Word 97 is that documents can also contain macro modules, custom toolbars, custom menus, and custom keyboard shortcuts.

Customized settings in the current template take precedence over those in Normal.dot, whose customized settings in turn take precedence over those in any other global templates or add-ins. So, for example, if you remove the Table menu from the menu bar in Normal.dot, documents attached to other templates will not show it either—unless you restore it in one of those templates, in which case that setting will take precedence over the setting in Normal.dot for documents based on that template.

The Normal.dot Global Template

Normal.dot is the mother of all global templates and is always loaded when Word is running, even when all currently open documents are attached to other templates. Word needs a Normal.dot to function correctly. If you delete your Normal.dot, move it to where Word cannot find it, or change the User Template directory (which we'll look at shortly) so that it no longer points to where Normal.dot is, Word will build itself a new Normal.dot the next time you start it.

Before you conclude that Normal.dot is indestructible and that you needn't worry what you do to it, bear in mind that if you delete Normal.dot, you'll lose any customization that you have saved in it—custom menus, toolbars, or keyboard shortcuts; macros; AutoText entries; or formatted AutoCorrect entries. With this in mind, you may want to make a backup of Normal.dot daily, or perhaps as often as you save changes to it.

TIP

You can use Word's automatic-backup feature to make sure that you always have a backup copy of Normal.dot: select the Always Create Backup Copy in the Save Options area of the Save tab of the Options dialog box to have Word automatically make a backup copy of each file you save, including Normal.dot. But if having Word help clutter your hard drive with backup copies of each file doesn't appeal to you, back up your Normal.dot manually at strategic moments. Just make sure that Word is closed before backing up Normal.dot—as I mentioned, Normal.dot is always loaded when Word is running, so if you try to back it up with Word running, you'll get an error.

In terms of Word's three-layer architecture, Normal.dot is the filter through which you see the application layer: by customizing Normal.dot, you change the appearance of the application layer. For example, you might add a couple of menus of frequently used commands to Normal.dot, and customize the Formatting toolbar by removing some buttons that you found useless. Thereafter, any documents you worked in would display those two extra menus and the customized toolbar.

Because macros contained in modules in Normal.dot are available to all documents, Normal.dot can be a great place to put the macros that you need to keep at your fingertips no matter which template the current document is based on. That said, try not to keep too much junk in Normal.dot, for a couple of reasons:

- First, customization in other templates builds on the current state of Normal.dot. As we saw a moment ago, templates other than Normal.dot sit on top of Normal.dot and the application layer, so changes you make to Normal.dot also show up in other templates unless you specifically remove them from the other templates. For example, if you add a menu named Peculiar Commands to Normal.dot, it will be added to your other templates as well. Likewise, if you've removed functionality from Normal.dot, it will be missing from your other templates until you specifically restore it in them.

- Second, if Normal.dot grows over a certain size—say, half a megabyte or so—it may start to slow down the running of Word (and other processes on your computer). If you create serious numbers of macros, consider storing less frequently used ones in a secondary template that you can load when necessary—or simply keeping them within the templates to which they belong. Alternatively, create your macros in a testing template and move them into Normal.dot only when they're ready for prime time.

Apart from macros, Normal.dot also contains a few other items:

- AutoCorrect entries that have formatting are stored in Normal.dot, which greatly increases your chances of swelling it to a significant size—especially if you create AutoCorrect entries for long sections of boilerplate text, which can save you a lot of time in creating documents. (As you'll see in the next chapter, AutoCorrect entries with formatting are supported only by Word, but AutoCorrect entries without formatting are shared among the Office applications.) Unfortunately, you can't park AutoCorrect entries in templates other than Normal.dot, so apart from avoiding defining AutoCorrect entries that have formatting (or avoiding defining AutoCorrect entries, period—which would be a mistake), you can't reduce the amount of space these take up in Normal.dot.

AutoText entries can also be stored within Normal.dot and can increase its size significantly; AutoText entries that contain complex graphics are especially guilty of this. But because Word stores AutoText entries in the template that's current when you create them, and because you can move AutoText entries from template to template (as you'll see in the next chapter), you can easily limit the space that AutoText entries take up in Normal.dot.

User Templates and Workgroup Templates

Word classifies templates into two groups: *user templates* and *workgroup templates*. User templates and workgroup templates are differentiated mostly by their location—there is actually no substantive difference between the two, but you can take advantage of their different locations to implement differences.

Put simply, user templates are *your* templates, the templates that you (the individual user) have on your workstation. Typically, these templates will be on your local hard drive and in the `\Program Files\Microsoft Office\Templates\` folder (or in one of its subfolders) that Word and Office create by default during installation; but if you want to, you can move them to pretty much any other location, either on your local hard drive or on a networked drive. (Generally speaking, you'll see better performance from templates on a local drive than on a networked drive.)

Workgroup templates are templates stored on a network, shared by anyone who has access to the folder the templates are in. You can implement workgroup templates in several ways, depending on whether or to what degree you need to protect them from unwelcome or ill-advised attentions from your coworkers. Essentially, you have a couple of options for protecting a template that you're sharing: First, you can mark the template itself as read-only, so that no one can save changes to it. Second, you can store the template in a read-only folder on the network so that only the network administrator (or administrator equivalent) can save changes to it. The second option is more elegant and restrictive than the first in that you can control more closely which templates are placed in the folder in question, but it can be more trouble to administer.

To set the locations for user templates and workgroup templates:

1. Choose Tools ➤ Options to display the Options dialog box.

2. Click the File Locations tab to display it if it's not already displayed (see Figure 3.2).

3. In the File Types list box, choose User Templates or Workgroup Templates as appropriate.

4. Click the Modify button to display the Modify Location dialog box (see Figure 3.3).

5. Navigate to the folder that you want to keep the templates in (create a new folder if necessary by clicking the New Folder button (the button showing a folder with a star behind its top-right corner) in the Modify Location dialog box), and then click the OK button.

6. Click the Close button to close the Options dialog box.

FIGURE 3.2

Changing the location of user templates on the File Locations tab of the Options dialog box.

FIGURE 3.3

In the Modify Location dialog box, choose the location for the templates.

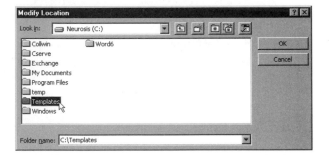

Global Templates

As mentioned earlier in the chapter, any template can contain AutoText entries, macros, custom toolbars, custom menus, and keyboard shortcuts. These will be available to the user for any document based on that template, but not for documents based on other templates. The exception to this is Normal.dot, the global template: any item stored in Normal.dot is available to any document, whether it's based on Normal.dot or based on another template.

If you want to make AutoText entries, macros, etc. from one template available to all other templates, you can load that template as a *global template*, in a similar way to how Word automatically loads Normal.dot. You can do this either manually, session by session, or automatically every time you start Word.

WARNING
Before you merrily designate ten different global templates to load automatically every time you start Word, bear in mind that each will take up a certain amount of system resources. Usually, you'll do better to concentrate your macros, AutoText entries, etc. in Normal.dot than in a number of other global templates—again, with the proviso that you don't make Normal.dot huge and unwieldy in the process.

Loading a Global Template Manually

1. Choose Tools ➤ Templates and Add-ins to display the Templates and Add-ins dialog box (see Figure 3.4).

FIGURE 3.4

Use the Templates and Add-ins dialog box to load global templates.

2. In the Global Templates and Add-ins area, click the Add button to display the Add Template dialog box (see Figure 3.5).

3. Choose the template to load as a global template, then click the OK button. Word will close the Add Template dialog box and display the name of the template in the Global Templates and Add-ins group box of the Templates and Add-ins dialog box.

FIGURE 3.5

FIGURE 3.5

In the Add Template dialog box, choose the template that you want to load as a global template, and click the OK button.

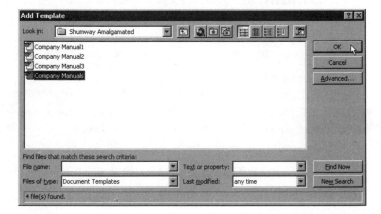

4. To load additional templates as global templates, repeat steps 2 and 3. (You cannot Shift+click or Ctrl+click in the Add Template dialog box to load multiple templates at once.)

5. Click the OK button to close the Templates and Add-ins dialog box.

Temporarily Deactivating a Global Template

You can deactivate a global template temporarily by displaying the Templates and Add-ins dialog box (Tools ➤ Templates and Add-ins) and clearing the check box next to the template in the Global Templates and Add-ins area. Reactivate it by selecting this check box again.

Unloading a Global Template Manually

1. Choose Tools ➤ Templates and Add-ins to display the Templates and Add-ins dialog box.

2. Select the template to remove in the Global Templates and Add-ins area.

3. Click the Remove button.

4. Repeat steps 2 and 3 to unload more global templates, or click the OK button to close the Templates and Add-ins dialog box.

Loading a Global Template Automatically When You Start Word

If you know you'll need to load a global template whenever you start Word, consider loading it automatically. To do so, you simply need to copy the template in question into the Startup file location specified on the File Locations tab of the Options dialog box (Tools ➤ Options). Usually, this is the Startup folder created by Office or Word in the `\Microsoft Office\Office\Startup\` folder, but you can specify any location from the File Locations tab. Word automatically loads all templates it finds in the specified startup folder.

> **TIP**
>
> At the risk of laboring the point, it's usually better to keep often-used items in Normal.dot than in a plethora of global templates. That said, at times you may find it useful to be able to load a global template from a shared network directory.

Temporarily Unloading a Global Template You've Loaded Automatically

You can temporarily unload a global template that you've loaded automatically by clearing its check box in the Global Templates and Add-ins group box of the Templates and Add-ins dialog box (Tools ➤ Templates and Add-ins).

To reload the global template, select its check box again.

Creating a Document Based on a Template

As you saw earlier, you can create a new default document based on Normal.dot by clicking the New button on the Standard toolbar, pressing Ctrl+N, or selecting File ➤ New and choosing Blank Document from the New dialog box.

To start a document based on a template other than Normal, choose File ➤ New rather than pressing Ctrl+N or clicking the New button on the Standard toolbar; when Word displays the New dialog box (see Figure 3.6), choose the tab

FIGURE 3.6

In the New dialog box, choose the template on which you want to base the new document, and then click the OK button.

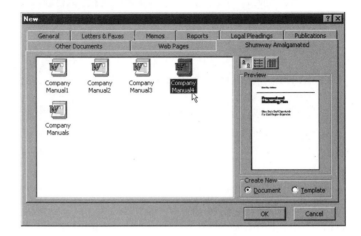

containing the type of document you want to create, and then choose the template from within the tab. Use the Preview box to verify that you've chosen the template you wanted, and then click the OK button to create the document.

TIP

Previews are available only for some templates. You can create previews of templates you've designed by selecting the Create Preview Picture check box on the Summary Info tab of the Properties dialog box. (The Properties dialog box is displayed when you first save a document or template if the Prompt for Document Properties check box on the Save tab of the Options dialog box is selected; otherwise, you can display the Properties dialog box at any time by choosing File ➤ Properties.)

Creating a New Template

Given that templates are just documents with special capabilities, it makes sense that you can base one template on another template. By doing so, you can quickly create several templates based on a single master template. If you were creating a number of templates for customer-service reps, to use our earlier example, you could proceed as follows: First, create one master template that contains the company's name, address, logo, and so forth, together with the page-layout and paragraph-formatting information. Next, create other, more specialized templates based on that first template—one for each rep, one for each type of customer-service letter, and so on.

To create a new template:

1. Follow the procedure described in the previous section for creating a new document: Choose File ➤ New to display the New dialog box, and choose the existing template on which you want to base the new template. In the Create New area of the dialog box, select the Template option button; then click the OK button. Word will display a new template based on the template you chose.

2. Enter text, tables, graphics, etc. in the template as usual and format it to suit your purpose. Insert any fields or bookmarks that the template will need for automation (I'll talk about fields and bookmarks in the next chapter).

3. Save your new template by choosing File ➤ Save to display the Save As dialog box. Word will automatically change directories to the Templates folder (or the folder designated for User Templates in the User Templates setting on the Save tab of the Options dialog box). Word will also suggest a name for your template, either a name based on the first line of any text you entered in the template or (if you entered no text) the name Dot1.dot; either way, you'll probably want to change it. If necessary, you can also change to a different folder: for example, you might want to create a new folder for your company's templates so that you can store them all together, or you might want to save the template to the directory for workgroup templates.

Attaching a Document to a Different Template

By attaching a document to a different template, you can instantly change its format. This can be very useful for a number of purposes. For example, say that you are writing a book or a company manual; you can write the book in a template that uses fonts and font sizes that are easy to work with on-screen, and then, when the writing is finished, attach the book to a typesetting template that looks good on paper.

NOTE
Remember that a document can be attached to only one template at a time; however, you can load other templates as global templates if you need to use macros, AutoText entries, etc. from them in a document that's attached to another template.

To attach the current document to a different template:

1. Choose Tools ➤ Templates and Add-ins to display the Templates and Add-ins dialog box (see Figure 3.7).

FIGURE 3.7

In the Templates and Add-ins dialog box, click the Attach button.

2. If you want the document to automatically take on the styles of the template to which you're attaching it, select the Automatically Update Document Styles check box.

3. Click the Attach button to display the Attach Template dialog box (see Figure 3.8).

4. Select the template to which you want to attach the document. (Navigate to a different folder if necessary.)

5. Click the Open button to attach the template. Word will close the Attach Template dialog box and return you to the Templates and Add-ins dialog box.

6. Click the OK button to close the Templates and Add-ins dialog box.

Should You Update the Document's Styles When You Change Templates?

It's almost always a good idea to select the Automatically Update Document Styles check box in the Templates and Add-ins dialog box when you attach a document to a different template. If you don't select this check box, you may find that the document appears not to have the styles from the new template available.

You can easily remedy this apparent problem by choosing to list All Styles rather than Styles In Use in the List drop-down list box in the Style dialog box, but it can be confusing to users and can occasion calls to your Help desk.

In my experience, there's seldom a good reason not to update a document's styles when you attach it to a new template—after all, if the new template turns out to be unsuitable, you can always reattach the document to its original template and give it back its original appearance.

FIGURE 3.8

In the Attach Template dialog box, choose the template to which you want to attach the current document.

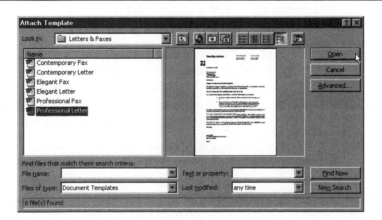

The document is now attached to the template you chose. If you selected the Automatically Update Document Styles check box in the Templates and Add-ins dialog box, the existing paragraphs in the document will take on the styles from the new template, as will paragraphs you subsequently create.

TIP

If you think you may need to frequently switch documents from template to template, use the same style names in each template. For example, if you have a style named Technical Listing in both your Company Manual 1.dot template and your Company Manual 2.dot template, you can attach a document created in Company Manual 1.dot to Company Manual 2.dot and have the paragraphs in the Technical Listing style change automatically to the style in the second template. If the second template does not have a style named Technical Listing, the style from the first template will remain even after you attach the document to the second template.

How Documents Differ from Templates

In versions of Word before Word 97, the main difference between documents and templates was that templates could contain macros, AutoText entries, styles, and customized toolbars, menu bars, and shortcut keys, whereas documents could not. Word 97 changes that, blurring the distinctions between the two and thereby eliminating a number of old problems while substituting some new ones.

One problem with the old distinction between a document and a template was that you could easily disguise a template as a document by renaming it from its .dot name to a .doc name. For example, you could rename Contract Template.dot to Contract for Joseph Takagi.doc, and it would show up in the Open dialog box as if it were a regular document. Unless you checked to see if the document had items that only a template could have, it was hard to tell the difference.

Such disguising proved helpful for distributing macros transparently. For example, you could create a template that contained a macro that ran automatically when the template was opened. You could use this macro, say, to pop up a dialog box offering to install other macros (or styles, or AutoText entries, or even other documents) to the user's computer. If the user chose OK or Yes, the macro would install the items, display a dialog box telling the user that the operation had been successful, and then close the document. If the user chose Cancel or No, the macro closed the document anyway. This was all very well and good, but you could also use automatic macros to make changes to a user's setup without their knowledge or approval. Such a macro could easily wreak havoc.

In Word 97, the differences between templates and documents in Word 97 are slight, and boil down to ease of use:

- You can base a new document on a template more easily than on another document. Word marshals templates onto the tabbed pages of the New dialog box so that you can quickly choose a template for each new document. (To base a document on an existing document, you would open the existing document, then use the File ➤ Save As command to save it under a different name.)

- You can quickly switch a document to a different template, as discussed in the previous section. Again, Word organizes the templates into folders in the Attach Template dialog box so that you can easily select the one you need. (To switch a document to the design you'd used on another document, you *could* create a new document based on the first document, as described in the previous bullet point, and then paste in the text from the first document—workable, but much clumsier and slower than using a template.)

Arranging Macros in Templates

I mentioned earlier in this chapter that macros contained in modules in Normal.dot are available to all open documents, no matter which template those documents are based on. As you'll see later in this book, this has advantages and disadvantages. The advantages include:

- All the macros are available whenever you need them.

- You'll have all your code at hand when you need to crib a line here and there for a macro you're working on.

The disadvantages include:

- All the macros are available whenever anyone needs them, whether you want them to be available or not. (You can write password protection into any macro, but it makes much more sense to store the macro where those who have no business using it will never encounter the temptation.)

- Normal.dot can become huge and can slow down Word on your computer.

Depending on your situation and how many macros you end up creating, you'll probably find it makes the most sense to do something like this:

- Keep everyday macros in Normal.dot so that they're always available when you need them.

- Keep suites of related macros in global templates that you can load and unload as necessary.

- Keep template-specific macros in the templates to which they belong.

- Keep a scratch global template for creating and testing macros until they work, at which point you can unleash them to suitable locations as described in the previous three bullet points.

Copying or Moving Macro Modules between Templates or Documents

As you may remember from Chapter 1, modules are containers for the code that makes up a macro. To copy or move macro modules from one template (or document) to another, open the Organizer dialog box by choosing Tools ➤ Macro ➤ Macros and clicking the Organizer button in the Macro dialog box. Word will display the Macro Project Items tab of the Organizer dialog box (see Figure 3.9), which shows the macro modules in Normal (the global template) in one panel and the macro modules in the current document in the other panel.

FIGURE 3.9

The Organizer box lets you quickly rename, copy, and move macro project items from one template or document to another.

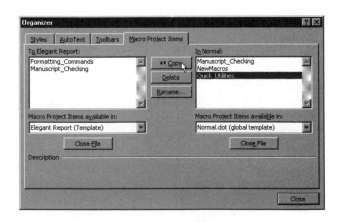

TIP Alternatively, choose Tools ➤ Templates and Add-ins, click the Organizer button in the Templates and Add-ins dialog box, and then click the Macro Project Items tab of the Organizer dialog box to display it.

To work with the template for the current document, select it from the Macro Project Items Available In drop-down list below the panel listing the current document. Otherwise, open the templates or documents you want: click the Close File button on either side of the dialog box to close the currently open file; then click the Open File button (into which the Close File button will have metamorphosed) and choose the correct template or document from the Open dialog box that Word then displays.

- To delete one or more macro modules from a template, choose the module 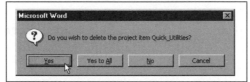 or modules from either panel of the Organizer dialog box, and click the Delete button. Choose Yes in the confirmation message box (shown here). Any copies of the macro module in other templates are unaffected.

- To rename a macro module, select it (from either the left-hand panel or the 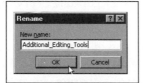 right-hand panel) and click the Rename button to open the Rename dialog box. Enter the new name for the module, and click the OK button. Again, copies of the module in other templates will be unaffected.

- To copy one or more macro modules from one template to another, open the templates in question in the Organizer dialog box. Select the module or  modules to copy in either panel of the dialog box (the arrows on the Copy button will change direction to point to the other panel). Then click the Copy button. If the recipient template contains a module of the same name as one you're copying, Word will display a warning message box telling you that the project item cannot be copied.

> **TIP**
> To move a macro from one template to another, copy it as described above, and then delete the macro from the source template.

Once you've deleted, renamed, copied, or moved macros as described above, click the Close button to close the Organizer dialog box. Word will invite you to save any changes to affected templates that are not open; click the Yes button unless you've made a mistake.

Word's Five Automatic Macros

Word provides names for five automatic macros that can be most helpful in customizing your Word environment. When you create a macro using one of these five names (or rename an existing macro with one of these names), the macro takes on the following automatic characteristics:

- **AutoExec** runs whenever you start Word. You can use an AutoExec macro to set screen preferences, to open the last couple of files you worked on, or to open, say, a log file that you need to update every morning at work.

- **AutoNew** runs whenever you open a new file based on the template containing an AutoNew macro (you can have more than one, in different templates). Adding an AutoNew macro to a template is a great way to create forms (which we'll look at later in the chapter) by automatically pulling the latest information from a database into the new document.

- **AutoOpen** runs whenever you reopen a file based on the template containing the AutoOpen macro. Again, AutoOpen is template-specific, so if you want to switch to a particular printer for a given type of document, this would be an easy way to do it.

- **AutoClose** runs whenever you close a file based on the template containing the AutoClose macro. You might want to pair AutoClose with AutoOpen to undo any environmental changes you make—for example, to switch back to the regular printer from the special one.

- **AutoExit** runs whenever you close down Word. This might be a great way to back up special files automatically every day—or to launch another application by using the Shell command.

WARNING You can either record an automatic macro using one of the above names or rename an existing macro. Either way, pay attention to which templates you put your AutoNew, AutoOpen, and AutoClose macros in, or you may find them running for the wrong documents and absent from the right ones.

Macro Viruses

The last year or so has seen a great deal of anxiety about macro viruses. The fun started with the Winword.Concept macro virus, also known as the Prank virus. This macro appeared to have been built as a demonstration of the capabilities of macro viruses. Rather than harboring code that would create havoc on computer systems it infected, it contained a macro named Payload that contained only the comment line "That's enough to prove my point."

Winword.Concept was relatively harmless. It installed a new FileSaveAs macro that supplanted the regular FileSaveAs command and caused you to save every document as a template in the templates directory designated in your Word settings. By saving every document as a template containing the macro virus, ready to install itself on any copy of Word that opened an infected template masquerading as a document, Winword.Concept was able to spread rapidly. At this writing, Winword.Concept is widespread throughout the world of Word users and accounts for up to 50 percent of all reported viruses.

Microsoft quickly created and distributed a fix for Winword.Concept called ScanProt.dot. (The fix is available from http://www.microsoft.com and from the online services, among other locations.) This consists of macros that remove the virus from your installation of Word; search for infected docu-templates, remove the virus, and save them as plain Word files; and replace the File ➤ Open command with a version that checks each document you open for automatic macros.

The Microsoft fix has a couple of minor disadvantages: First, you can open only one file at a time from the Open dialog box, rather than using Shift+click or Ctrl+click to open two or more files. Second, if you open a file without using the Open dialog box—for example, by double-clicking it in File Manager or Windows Explorer—the scanning macro fails to kick in.

A quick way around the WInword.Concept virus (before Word 97's built-in scanning) was not to install ScanProt.dot but to create a blank macro named Payload. When you opened a document infected with Winword.Concept, the virus macros checked for the Payload macro to see if it was already installed. If a macro named Payload was present, the Winword.Concept macros would not install themselves. This relatively elegant avoidance of the problem was limited to Winword.Concept, though, and did nothing to protect against other Word macros viruses, such as FormatC, which attempts to format your C: drive and has no interest in any macro named Payload.

Protection against macro viruses now takes several forms:

- First, Word 97 contains built-in scanning for documents that contain automatic macros. (You can turn this off by selecting or clearing the Macro Virus Protection check box on the General tab of the Options dialog box.)

- Second, McAfee, Norton, and the other anti-virus-product manufacturers have added macro virus–detection routines to their anti-virus programs. You can run these to actively scan documents you consider suspect. Alternatively, you can run them in the background, where they should detect any dangerous documents when you copy or move them to your computer. A quick word of warning here: some of these anti–macro virus routines have proven to be over-aggressive, at least in their early versions. Dr. Solomon's, in particular, has been known to flatline a computer while trying to refuse to copy a template containing a completely harmless automatic macro.

- Third, you can disable automatic macros to prevent them from running, as you'll see in the next section. This is an almost foolproof defense against macro viruses; unfortunately, it also prevents you from enjoying the benefits that automatic macros can offer. You can't have your checks unless you eat your balances too.

Disabling Automatic Macros

Now that you've seen some of the trouble that automatic macros can cause, you'll probably want to be able to disable them on occasion. You can disable them either temporarily or permanently.

Disabling Automatic Macros While Opening a Document

To temporarily disable automatic macros while you open a document, hold down the Shift key as you issue the Open command. For example, if you're using the Open dialog box, click to select the document, then hold down Shift as you click the OK button; if you're opening a document by double-clicking it on the Desktop or in an Explorer folder, hold down Shift as you double-click.

Permanently Disabling Automatic Macros

To permanently disable automatic macros, you can either start Word with a start-up switch, or you can create and run a macro to disable all automatic macros. We'll look at both these options in Chapter 21.

Customizing Templates

By including layouts, formatting, boilerplate text, and AutoText entries in your templates, you can greatly speed up the creation of documents. You can enhance usability even more by customizing the user interface—toolbars, menus, and the menu bar—to give instant access to the commands the user needs for a particular task.

Toolbars, the Menu Bar, and Command Bars

In Word 95 and earlier versions, there was a sharp difference between the menu bar and the toolbars. The menu bar stayed fixed at the top of the screen (unless you got rid of it by choosing View ➤ Full Screen), whereas the toolbars could be attached to any side of the Word window or float freely anywhere inside it or outside it on the Desktop. Right-clicking on a toolbar produced a context menu for quickly displaying and hiding toolbars.

Word 97 (and the other Office 97 applications) has melded toolbars and the menu bar into hybrid entities called *command bars*. To all intents and purposes, command bars behave like toolbars; because the menu bar is now a command bar, you can drag it about the Word window and the Desktop as you please, anchor it to any convenient side of the Word window, and so on (however, you can't hide the menu bar as you can a toolbar).

This change also means that what were previously toolbar items and menu items are now interchangeable: toolbars can have menus on them, and the menu bar can have buttons on it. I can see you're about to jump up and remind me that the Formatting toolbar has had the assorted menus (such as the Zoom Control menu and Font drop-down list box) on it for every version of Word in living memory, so let me reassure you that I haven't forgotten about those, but the command bars go far beyond that. As you'll see in a moment, once you've got the Customize dialog box open, you can drag and drop drop-interface elements from toolbar to menu bar to menu pretty much as you see fit.

Customizing Toolbars

You can create new toolbars, modify your own toolbars or Word's existing ones, and delete your own toolbars.

Creating a New Toolbar

To create a new toolbar:

1. Right-click on the menu bar or on any displayed toolbar to display the context menu of toolbars; then choose Customize to display the Customize dialog box.

2. On the Toolbars tab, click the New button to display the New Toolbar dialog box.

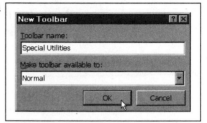

3. Enter a name for the new toolbar in the Toolbar Name text box.

4. If you want to make the toolbar available only to the current template, choose the template's name in the Make Toolbar Available To drop-down list. Otherwise, make sure Normal is selected in the Make Toolbar Available To drop-down list to make the template available to all documents.

5. Click the OK button to create the toolbar. Word will display the new toolbar (with space for just one button, and most of its name truncated) somewhere within easy commuting distance of the Customize dialog box.

6. Click the Commands tab to display it (see Figure 3.10), and then add the buttons you want to the new toolbar.

FIGURE 3.10

Drag buttons from the Customize dialog box to the new toolbar.

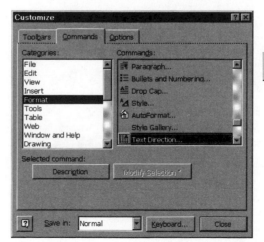

- From the Categories list, select the type of command you're looking for. The Categories list includes all the regular menus (from File through Help), together with Web, Drawing, AutoShapes, Borders, Mail Merge, Forms, Control Toolbox, All Commands, Macros, Fonts, AutoText, Styles, Built-in Menus, and New Menu.

- When you choose the category, the items available in that category appear in the Commands list box. Click the item you want and drag it to the toolbar. To see a description of the selected item (for example, to make sure you've gotten hold of the command you thought you had and not one of its close relatives), click the Description button to display a description of the command.

- If the item you dragged to the toolbar has a button associated with it, Word will add that button to the toolbar. (You'll see any button associated with an item beside its listing in the Commands list box.) If the item doesn't have a button associated with it, Word will create a text button containing a description of the button you dragged. For example, if you drag the Heading 1 style to the toolbar, Word will create a button named *Heading 1 Style*. You can now rename the button by right-clicking it and entering another name in the Name box, or you can choose an image for the button by right-clicking and choosing Change Button Image from the context menu.

- To rearrange the buttons on the new toolbar, drag and drop each button while the Customize dialog box is open. To remove a button from the toolbar, drag it off and drop it somewhere in the document or in the Customize dialog box.

7. When you've finished creating your toolbar, click the Close button in the Customize dialog box.

Modifying a Toolbar

To modify a toolbar:

1. Display the toolbar on-screen by right-clicking the menu bar or any displayed toolbar, then selecting that toolbar in the context menu of toolbars. Alternatively, choose View ➤ Toolbars and select the toolbar from the Toolbars submenu.

2. Add, move, copy, or remove buttons as appropriate:

- To add buttons to a toolbar, choose Tools ➤ Customize and add the buttons to the toolbar as described in step 6 of the previous instructions. Close the Customize dialog box when you've finished.

- To move a button from one toolbar to another, hold down the Alt key and drag the button from one toolbar to the other. You can also rearrange the buttons on a toolbar by holding down the Alt key and dragging the buttons.

- To copy a button from one toolbar to another, hold down Ctrl+Alt while dragging the button from one toolbar to the other.

- To remove a button from the toolbar, hold down the Alt key and drag the button off the toolbar and into an open space within a document. Drop the button there, and it'll disappear.

WARNING   If you remove a custom button (one that you've created) from a toolbar as described above, Word will delete the details of the button, so you'll have to re-create it from scratch if you want to use it again. To avoid this, you can create a storage toolbar and use it to safely store buttons for future use.

Deleting a Toolbar

To delete a toolbar you've created, right-click in the menu bar or any displayed toolbar and choose Customize from the context menu to display the Customize dialog box. On the Toolbars tab, select the toolbar you want to delete, and then

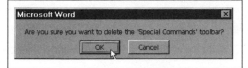

click the Delete button. Word will display a message box asking if you want to delete the toolbar; choose OK. Then click the Close button to exit the Customize dialog box.

NOTE   Word won't let you delete any of its own toolbars—only those you've created.

Renaming a Toolbar

To rename a toolbar you've created, right-click in either the menu bar or any displayed toolbar and choose Customize from the context menu to display the Customize dialog box. Highlight the toolbar to be renamed in the Toolbars list box on the Toolbars tab. Click the Rename button to display the Rename Toolbar dialog box, and specify the new name for the toolbar in the Toolbar Name text box. Click the OK button to rename the toolbar, and then click the Close button to close the Customize dialog box.

Customizing Menus

You can customize menus by adding items to them or by removing items that you don't use—or that you don't want other people to use. As if that weren't enough, you can remove entire menus and add menus of your own.

Adding Items to Menus

By strategically adding items to menus, you can have all the commands, styles, macros, and fonts that you need right on hand.

To add an item to a menu:

1. Open the Customize dialog box by right-clicking the menu bar or any displayed toolbar and then choosing Customize from the context menu, or by choosing Tools ➤ Customize.

2. Click the Commands tab to bring it to the front (see Figure 3.11).

NOTE   To make changes in a template other than Normal (the global template), open a document based on that template before starting these steps, and choose the template in the Save In drop-down list in the Customize dialog box.

3. In the Categories list box, select the category of item to add.

FIGURE 3.11

Adding items to menus
on the Commands tab of
the Customize
dialog box.

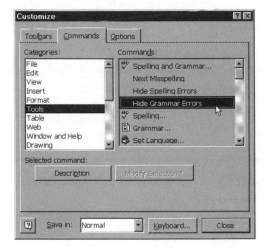

4. In the Commands list box, click the command and drag it to the name of the menu to which you want to add it. Keep holding the mouse button down as Word displays the menu, then drag the command down the menu (and across to any submenu if necessary) to where you want it to appear. Word will indicate with a horizontal black bar where the command will land. Drop it when it's in the right place. Alternatively, click the menu to display it before selecting and dragging the command to it.

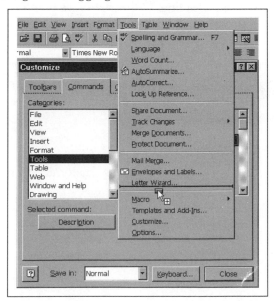

5. If the item you dragged to the menu has a button associated with it, Word will add that button along with the name of the command to the menu. (You'll see any button associated with an item beside the listing of the item in the Commands list box.) You can now rename the menu item by right-clicking it and entering another name in the Name box; or you can choose an image by right-clicking and choosing Change Button Image from the context menu (to add an existing button) or Edit Button Image (to create a new button in the Button Editor).

> **TIP**
>
> You can add an *access key* (also known as a "hotkey" or a "mnemonic") for the item by putting an ampersand (&) before the access key letter; just make sure the letter you choose isn't already an access key for another item on the menu.

6. Add more items to any of the menus, or click the Close button to close the Customize dialog box.

Modifying Menus and Removing Items

To remove one item quickly from a menu, press Ctrl+Alt+– (that's the hyphen key, but think of it as the minus key). The mouse pointer will change to a short, thick horizontal line. With this mouse pointer showing, pull down a menu and click the item you want to remove.

> **TIP**
>
> If you decide not to remove an item, press Esc to restore the mouse pointer to normal.

To remove a number of items from a menu, display the Customize dialog box by right-clicking and choosing Customize from the context menu or by choosing

Tools ➤ Customize. Then do one of the following:

- Reposition a menu item by clicking it and dragging it to a different position on that menu, on a different menu, or on a toolbar.

- Remove a menu item by dragging it and dropping it in blank space in the document (or anywhere in the Customize dialog box). As you drag the item, Word will display an "X" next to the mouse pointer to indicate that it will be removed.

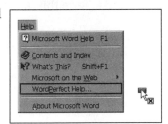

Restoring Word's Menus to Their Defaults

You can restore any of Word's predefined menus in a given template to its default state—and instantly wipe out any and all changes you've made to it—by opening the Customize dialog box, right-clicking the name of the menu you want to restore, and then choosing Reset from the context menu.

Customizing the Menu Bar

You can customize Word's menu bar by adding menus, removing menus, and renaming menus. To do so, first display the Customize dialog box by right-clicking either the menu bar or any displayed toolbar and choosing Customize from the context menu or by choosing Tools ➤ Customize. Then click the Commands tab to display it, and verify the setting in the Save Changes In drop-down list to make sure you're working in the right template.

Adding Menus

To add a menu to the menu bar or to a toolbar:

1. On the Commands tab of the Customize dialog box, select New Menu from the Categories list box.

2. Drag the New Menu item from the Commands list box and drop it where you want it to appear either on the menu bar or on a toolbar; Word will display a plus sign next to the mouse pointer to indicate that the item will be added where you drop it (see Figure 3.12). Word will name the new menu *New Menu*, which you'll probably want to change.

3. Right-click the menu name to display the context menu, then drag through the Name box to select its contents. Enter a suitable name for the new menu. Put an ampersand before the letter you want to use as an access key (make sure this access key letter isn't already assigned to another menu).

4. Repeat steps 2 and 3 if you need to add another menu. Otherwise, you can now add items to the menu as described in the section titled "Adding Items to Menus" earlier in the chapter.

5. When you're finished, click the Close button to close the Customize dialog box.

FIGURE 3.12

To add a new menu, drag the New Menu item to the menu bar or to a toolbar.

Removing Menus

You can remove a menu from the menu bar or from a toolbar in either of two ways:

- If you have the Customize dialog box open, click on the menu name, drag it off the menu bar or toolbar, and drop it either in open space in the Word window or in the Customize dialog box.

- If you do not have the Customize dialog box open, hold down the Alt key, click on the menu name, drag it off the menu bar or toolbar, and drop it in open space in the Word window.

Renaming Menus

To rename a menu, first display the Customize dialog box. Then right-click the menu name to display the context menu, edit the menu's name in the Name text box (putting an ampersand before the letter you want to use as an access key), and press Enter. Click the Close button to close the Customize dialog box.

Customizing Keyboard Shortcuts

While Word comes with an impressive array of preprogrammed keyboard short-cuts, you're likely to discover additional tasks that you'd like to have shortcuts for. When you do, you can speed and simplify your work by customizing the keyboard to suit your needs.

Assigning a Keyboard Shortcut

To set a keyboard shortcut:

1. Choose Tools ➤ Customize to display the Customize dialog box.

2. Click the Keyboard button to display the Customize Keyboard dialog box (see Figure 3.13).

3. If necessary, specify the template to change in the Save Changes In drop-down list. (Leave Normal selected if you want the changes to apply to all templates that don't have this keyboard combination set to another command.)

4. In the Categories list, select the category of item for the new keyboard shortcut.

FIGURE 3.13

Setting keyboard short-
cuts in the Customize
Keyboard dialog box.

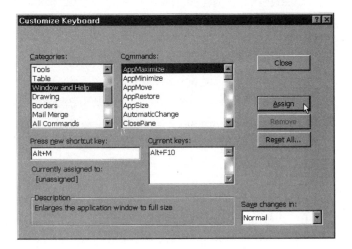

5. Choose the item to add in the Commands list box. (If you chose Macros, Fonts, AutoText, Styles, or Common Symbols in the Categories list, the list box will change its name to match your choice.)

6. Click in the Press New Shortcut Key box and press the key combination you want. A key combination can be any of the following:

    • Alt plus a regular key not used for a menu-access key

    • Alt plus a function key

    • Ctrl plus a regular key or function key

    • Ctrl+Alt plus a regular key or function key

    • Shift plus a function key

    • Ctrl+Shift plus a regular key or function key

    • Alt+Shift plus a regular key or function key

    • Ctrl+Alt+Shift plus a regular key or function key

    Because this last option involves severe contortions of the hands, it's not a great idea for frequent use.

TIP

You can set up shortcut keys that have two steps—for example, Ctrl+Alt+F, 1 and Ctrl+Alt+F, 2—by pressing the second key (in this case, the 1 or the 2) after pressing the key combination. However, these tend to be more trouble than they're worth unless you're assigning literally hundreds of extra shortcut keys.

7. Check the Currently Assigned To area under the Press New Shortcut Key box to see if that key combination is already assigned. (If it is and you don't want to overwrite it, press Backspace to clear the Press New Shortcut Key box, and then choose another combination.)

8. Click the Assign button to assign the shortcut.

9. Either assign more keyboard shortcuts, or click the Close button to close the Customize Keyboard dialog box.

Removing a Keyboard Shortcut

Usually you'll remove a keyboard shortcut by assigning that shortcut to another item—for example, if you assign Ctrl+P to a Photograph style you've created, Word will overwrite Ctrl+P as the shortcut for the Print command. But sometimes you may need to remove a shortcut without assigning it to another item—for example, if you want to prevent the user from performing certain actions.

To remove a keyboard shortcut:

1. Choose Tools ➤ Customize to display the Customize dialog box.

2. Click the Keyboard button to display the Customize Keyboard dialog box (refer back to Figure 3.13).

3. If necessary, specify the template you want to change in the Save Changes In drop-down list. (Leave Normal selected if you want the change to apply to all templates that don't have this keyboard combination set to another command.)

4. In the Categories list, select the category of the item that currently has the keyboard shortcut you want to remove.

5. Choose the item in the Commands list box. (If you choose Macros, Fonts, AutoText, Styles, or Common Symbols in the Categories list, the name of the list box will change to match your choice.)

6. In the Current Keys list box, select the key combination to remove (depending on the command, there may be several).

7. Click the Remove button.

8. Either remove more keyboard shortcuts, or click the Close button to close the Customize Keyboard dialog box.

Resetting All Keyboard Shortcuts

You can quickly reset all keyboard shortcuts for the template specified in the Save Changes In drop-down list by clicking the Reset All button in the Customize Keyboard dialog box. Word will display a confirmation message box to make sure you want to take this drastic step.

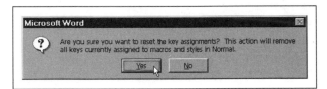

Choose Yes to reset the keyboard shortcuts, click the Close button to exit the Customize Keyboard dialog box, and then click the next Close button to close the Customize dialog box.

Putting Customization to Use

This section discusses how you might design and implement a special-purpose template that focuses a user—or yourself—precisely on their tasks. You could use such a template to improve productivity by putting all the commands (Word's own commands along with custom items you've created) needed for a particular task right where you need them.

Your steps toward creating such a template would include the following:

1. Work out exactly what the user needs to be able to do and which Word commands and features they'll need in order to fulfill their mission.

2. Rather than destroying your Normal.dot global template in the process, create a new template for this purpose. You could even use an AutoExec macro to start a new document based on your template whenever Word is run; this could help prevent a user from inadvertently starting their work in the wrong template.

3. Customize the menu bar and the toolbars to provide the most functionality with the least loss of screen real estate. For example, you could remove from the menu bar all the menus that aren't necessary and replace them with more useful menus or buttons. For some purposes, you may be able to reduce all the actions to one menu or one toolbar.

4. Write special-purpose macros for operations you know the user will need to perform for this type of document.

5. Customize keyboard shortcuts for the commands and macros needed most in this template, so that the user can work without removing their hands from the keyboard if they so choose.

This procedure will take some time and effort, but it yields very worthwhile results.

Forms

The benefits of templates extend to forms, which are a specialized type of template. Word's powerful features for creating business forms streamline the handling of repetitive information. You can create both printed forms that will be filled in by hand and online forms for gathering, storing, and distributing information. Online forms can be either Word documents or Web pages.

The usual procedure is to start a form as a new template, lay out the text and form fields, format the whole thing, and protect the form so the user can change only the form fields, not the text you've entered. Then the user can start a new copy of the form based on the template you've created, fill in the relevant fields, and save it as a document, leaving the template unaffected and ready for other users.

Creating a Form

First, start a new template for the form by choosing File ➤ New and clicking the Template option button in the Create New group box of the New dialog box. If Word offers a template suitable as a starting point for your new form, select it; otherwise, go with the Blank Document choice on the General tab. Click the OK button to close the dialog box and start the form.

Before you do anything else, save the form (as a template) in whichever of the folders in the Templates folder best suits your purpose, or in a workgroup template folder on the network. Then choose File ➤ Properties to display the Properties dialog box, and add a lucid description of the template in the Comments box on the Summary tab.

Next, display the Forms toolbar by right-clicking the menu bar or any displayed toolbar and choosing Forms from the context menu. The Forms toolbar contains nine buttons for working with forms, as shown in Figure 3.14.

Now enter the skeleton of your form as you would any regular Word document: type in text, insert graphics, and format the document. Figure 3.15 shows the beginning of an employment application form.

FIGURE 3.14

The Forms toolbar provides quick access to form fields.

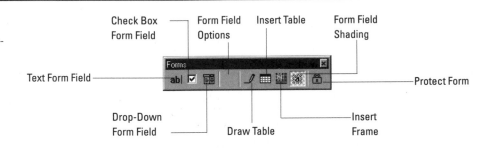

FIGURE 3.15

Putting together an online form with drop-down lists, text boxes, and check boxes.

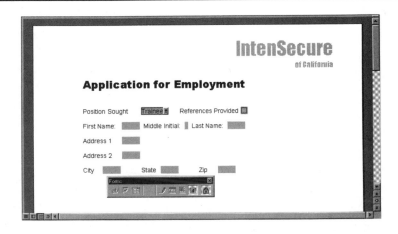

For many types of forms, you may also want to include tables, offset by the creative use of borders and shading. Draw tables by clicking the Draw Table button on the Forms toolbar and drawing with the mouse; insert tables as needed by clicking the Insert Table button.

Adding Form Fields

Once you've got the basic layout and text of your form in place, it's time to add form fields to it. Word provides the following basic form fields:

- check boxes, which can be selected (i.e., checked) or cleared (i.e., not checked)

- text boxes, in which the user can enter text of a type you choose

- drop-down lists, from which the user can choose one predefined option

NOTE   You can also use ActiveX controls in forms. See Chapter 19 for details.

Check Boxes   To insert a default-size check box in the form at the insertion point, click the Check Box Form Field button on the Forms toolbar.

To add customized settings, double-click the check box to open the Check Box Form Field Options dialog box (see Figure 3.16), and then choose the options you want:

- In the Check Box Size group box, choose Exactly and specify a point size for the check box if you don't like Word's automatic point size.

- If you want the check box to be selected by default, select Checked in the Default Value group box.

- If you want to run a macro when the user enters the check box or when they leave it, choose a macro name from the Entry or Exit drop-down list in the Run Macro On group box.

FIGURE 3.16

Set options for the check
box in the Check Box
Form Field Options
dialog box.

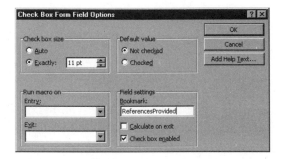

- In the Field Settings group box, enter an identifying name for the check box in the Bookmark text box, and then make sure the Check Box Enabled check box has been selected. (You may occasionally want to disable a check box so that the user can't access it at all.) If the check box will need to perform a calculation when the user moves the focus from the check box to another form field, select the Calculate on Exit check box.

Click the OK button when you've finished making your selections. Word will apply your choices to the check box you inserted.

Text Boxes To add a text box to the form at the insertion point, click the Text Form Field button on the Forms toolbar.

Double-click the text form field that Word inserts to open the Text Form Field Options dialog box (see Figure 3.17), and then choose the options you want:

- In the Type drop-down list, choose the type of text form field you want: Regular Text, Number, Date, Current Date, Current Time, or Calculation.

NOTE When you choose a type other than Regular Text, the Default Text and Text Format boxes change names accordingly—for example, Default Date and Date Format if you choose Date.

FIGURE 3.17

Set options for the text
form field in the Text
Form Field Options
dialog box.

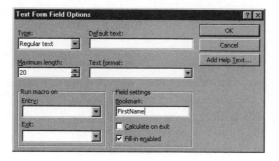

- In the Default Text box, enter a default or sample answer, if any, that you want the form to display. (If you choose Current Date, Current Time, or Calculation, this box isn't available.)

- In the Maximum Length box, you can choose to limit the text box entry to a specified number of characters. (For example, if you were adding text boxes for a phone number, you might use three boxes of three, three, and four characters, respectively. For a middle initial field, you'd probably set a one-character limit.)

- From the Text Format drop-down list, choose how you want the entry to look. The choices for text are Uppercase, Lowercase, First Capital (i.e., sentence case), and Title Case; for numbers, dates, times, and calculations, you get a more exciting range of choices.

- If you want to run a macro when the user moves to the text form field or when they leave it, choose a macro name from the Entry or Exit drop-down list in the Run Macro On group box.

- In the Field Settings group box, enter an identifying name for the text form field in the Bookmark text box, and then make sure the Fill-in Enabled check box has been selected. (If you choose Current Date or Current Time, this check box will be unavailable because Word will supply the information itself.) If the text box will need to perform a calculation when the user moves the focus from the text box to another form field, select the Calculate on Exit check box.

Click the OK button when you've finished making your selections. Word will apply your choices to the text form field.

Drop-Down Form Fields To add a drop-down form field to the form,
 position the insertion point at the appropriate place and click the Drop-Down Form Field button on the Forms toolbar.

Then double-click the drop-down form field to display the Drop-Down Form Field Options dialog box (see Figure 3.18), and choose options for the field:

- First, create the list by entering each item in the Drop-Down Item box and clicking the Add button to move it into the Items in Drop-Down List box. Repeat as often as needed, up to a maximum of 25 items. Use the Move buttons to move the selected item in the Items in Drop-Down List box up or down the list. Use the Remove button to remove a selected entry from the list.

- If you want to run a macro when the user moves to the drop-down form field or when they leave it, choose a macro name from the Entry or Exit drop-down list in the Run Macro On group box.

- In the Field Settings group box, enter an identifying name for the drop-down form field in the Bookmark text box, and then make sure the Drop-Down Enabled check box is selected.

FIGURE 3.18

Set options for the drop-down form field in the Drop-Down Form Field Options dialog box.

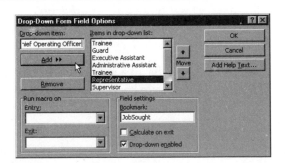

Click the OK button when you've finished making your selections. Word will apply your choices to the drop-down form field.

Adjusting Form Fields

Once you've inserted your form fields, you can drag and drop them (or cut and paste them) to move them to the most suitable place in your form.

You can format text form fields and drop-down lists by selecting them and applying formatting from the Font dialog box and Paragraph dialog box, just like any other character. You'll find this much easier to do if you keep form-field shading switched on (if it's off, click the Form Field Shading button on the Forms toolbar to turn it back on).

If you need to rename a form field, open its Form Field Options dialog box by either double-clicking the form field or right-clicking and choosing Form Field Options from the context menu. Enter the new name in the Bookmark text box and click the OK button to make the change.

Running Macros from Form Fields

As mentioned in the previous sections, you can set one macro to execute when the user enters a form field (using the mouse, the Tab key, or the Enter key) and another macro to execute when the user leaves that field. You can use this feature to automate your forms to a high degree. For example, you can make sure the user fills in a particular field by moving the insertion point to it when the user creates the copy of the form from the template (when they choose File ➤ New and specify the form's template) and running a macro when the user exits to make sure that *a)* the user has entered something in the field and *b)* the entry is suitable in format, length, and so on. If the user has failed on either count, you can make Word display a message box and then move the insertion point right back to that field time and time again until they get it right.

Less authoritarian, but equally helpful, might be a macro that runs on exit from a field and takes the user directly to the next relevant section of the form when they make a particular choice, so they don't have to tab their way through an entire subsection of fields that is meaningless to them.

TIP

You can also add AutoNew, AutoOpen, and AutoClose macros to form templates that automate your forms even further. We'll get into this later in the book.

Adding ActiveX Controls

In addition to the straightforward form fields discussed in the previous section, Word 97 provides ActiveX controls that you can use in forms and dialog boxes.

ActiveX controls include items such as toggle buttons (for toggling an option on and off), option buttons (for picking one choice out of two or more mutually exclusive choices), and spin buttons (for adjusting a number box), and they can store VBA code inside themselves.

To work with ActiveX controls, display the Control Toolbox toolbar (see Figure 3.19) by right-clicking the menu bar or any displayed toolbar and choosing Control Toolbox from the context menu of toolbars. I'll talk about actually using ActiveX components in Chapter 19, which covers creating complex dialog boxes.

FIGURE 3.19

Use the buttons on the Control Toolbox toolbar to insert ActiveX controls.

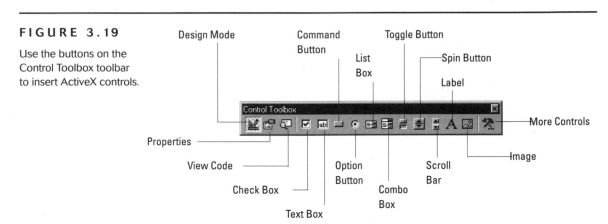

Testing Your Form

You can check to see how your form looks by protecting it with the Protect Form button on the Forms toolbar. This will allow you to see the drop-down form fields (and other form fields) in all their glory and to improve the layout of the form. You'll also be able to move through the text field-by-field by pressing Tab (or Shift+Tab to go backwards) or by clicking in fields with the mouse.

Adding Help Text to a Form Field

If you think users may need instructions to correctly fill out your form, you'll probably want to add help text to its form fields. To do so, display the Form Field Options dialog box by double-clicking the field you want to add help text to (or by right-clicking in it and choosing Form Field Options from the pop-up menu), and then click the Add Help Text button. Word will display the Form Field Help Text dialog box, as shown in Figure 3.20.

FIGURE 3.20

In the Form Field Help Text dialog box, add help text on either the Status Bar tab or the Help Key (F1) tab—or both.

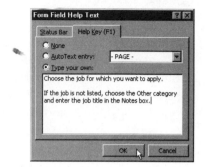

On the Status Bar tab of the Form Field Help Text dialog box, add any help text that you want to appear in the status bar when the user moves to the field in question. If you have a predefined AutoText entry suitable for help, select the AutoText Entry option button and specify the entry in the drop-down list; otherwise, click in the Type Your Own box (thereby selecting the Type Your Own option button) and enter the text. Status Bar help text can have a maximum of 138 characters; remember that some of these may not be visible if the user is running Windows at a low resolution (such as 640x480), because the later characters will run off the right edge of the screen.

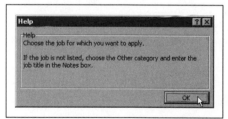

On the Help Key (F1) tab, add further help text as appropriate. Help Key help text can have up to 255 characters, and you can space the text over half a dozen lines, adding indents if need be. At left is an example of the Help box that the user will see when they press the F1 key.

TIP

For crucial fields, add both Status Bar help and Help Key help: use the status bar to provide a short explanation and invite the user to press F1 for more help; then provide a longer explanation (or a sample entry) in the Help Key help box.

When you are done adding help text in the Form Field Help Text dialog box, click the OK button to return to the Form Field Options dialog box. Choose OK to apply your changes to the form field and return to the form.

Protecting the Form

Once you've finished laying out the form, you need to protect it so that users will be able to fill in but not alter the form fields you've so carefully included. You can protect the form either with or without a password. If you protect it with a password, anyone will be able to fill in the form fields, but they'll need to enter the password to change the form itself; if you protect it without requiring a password, anyone can unprotect (and then alter) the form without any effort at all.

- To protect the form without a password, click the Protect Form button on the Forms toolbar. That's all there is to it.

- To protect the form with a password (which I strongly recommend), choose Tools ➤ Protect Document. Word will display the Protect Document dialog box (see Figure 3.21). Choose the Forms option button in the Protect Document For group box, enter a password (of up to 15 characters) in the Password text box, and click the OK button.

  To eliminate the chance of a typo, Word will ask you to confirm the password. Enter the password again in the Confirm Password dialog box, and click the OK button.

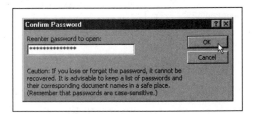

FIGURE 3.21

To protect your form against unauthorized changes, display the Protect Document dialog box, choose Forms in the Protect Document For group box, and enter a password in the Password box.

Filling in the Form

To fill in a form based on a template, simply open a document based on that

template and move from form field to form field, entering text in the text boxes, selecting and clearing check boxes, and making choices from drop-down lists.

Any macros set to run upon entering a form field will run when you move to that field (by using Tab or Shift+Tab, PageUp or PageDown, or by clicking in it); any macros set to run upon exiting a form field will run when you leave it.

When you've finished filling in the form, save it as you would any other document.

TIP A thoroughly automated form will offer to save itself. Consider offering the option to save the form as soon as the user starts filling in the form (either with an AutoNew macro or with a macro set to run on exit from, say, a Last Name text box, by which time the user should have filled in enough information for the form to start being useful); and to close it and save changes when the user completes the last required item.

Printing Out the Form

When you have filled in the form, you can print it in full by choosing File ➤ Print or by clicking the Print button on the Standard toolbar. But if you want to print only the data entered in the form without printing the standard text of the form, choose Tools ➤ Options to display the Options dialog box; click the Print tab; and select the Print Data Only for Forms check box in the Options for Current Document Only area. Then choose File ➤ Print, and Word will print just the data entered into the form.

TIP

This is a great way of filling in often-used preprinted forms on special paper: scan the form into your computer, and recreate it in Word with form fields. You can then fill in the form online and print out only the data onto the preprinted form sheets.

Saving Only the Data from a Form

Word also lets you save the data from a form without saving the form itself, which can help you quickly enter form data into a database. After all, your goal in life (or at least your work) is to get the data from the form in a usable format. For example, if you put together an online customer questionnaire for purchasers of your Deluxe Widgets, you'd probably want to transfer the data into a database so that you could sort the data by customer, by town, by quantity of Deluxe Widgets purchased, and so on.

To save the data without the form, display the Options dialog box by choosing Tools ➤ Options, click the Save tab, and select the Save Data Only for Forms check box on the Save Options tab. Then click the OK button to close the Options dialog box, and save the form as usual. The result will be a data file that you can transfer into, say, an Access database by using its Import Wizard or which you can manipulate with a Word macro.

TIP

If you automate your form using macros, you could design the save macro to automatically save data only for forms.

Retrieving Information from a Form

Having users fill in forms online so you can then print them out and get information from the hard copy is all well and good, but it makes much more sense to go for Double Jeopardy, where the stakes start to get interesting. If you're going to create a form online and have your victim fill it in online so you can then store it online, go the whole hog and use the information online, too. We'll look at how to do this in Chapter 19.

So much for templates in all their glory—at least for the time being. In the next chapter, we'll discuss how to use Word's automatic features to your best advantage—in essence, how to get things done *without* using macros. After that, in Chapter 5, we'll start on macros, and life will never be the same again.

CHAPTER

FOUR

4

Using Automatic Features Effectively

In this chapter, we'll look at the automatic features that Word provides for speeding up work in your documents. These features are useful as a way of avoiding using macros unless you have to, but several of them (for example, fields and bookmarks) are also critical components of successful macros.

Word's automatic features include the following:

- **fields,** which you use to place variable information in your documents and then update either automatically or manually at times of your choosing.

- **bookmarks,** which are electronic markers that you can use to identify parts of your documents. Once you've inserted bookmarks, you can get data from them, insert data into them, and otherwise manipulate your documents.

- **AutoCorrect,** a feature that checks what you type and automatically changes predefined typos and abbreviations on its list to their correct or full versions.

- **AutoText,** a feature that lets you keep a list of frequently used text or graphics (what old word-processing applications used to call *glossary entries*) that you can expand into their full form by typing an abbreviation and pressing F3 or accepting Word's prompt of the full entry.

- **AutoFormat,** a feature that applies automatic formatting to your choice of elements either as you type or when you choose to run AutoFormat on a whole document.

At the end of the chapter, we'll also discuss advanced uses of Word's Find and Replace features. It's hard to pretend that Find and Replace are truly automatic features, but they're so useful both inside and outside macros that I doubt you'll press the point.

Fields

In Word, fields are a subject that one can edge cautiously around but never avoid entirely. Most users of Word employ fields without realizing it: automatic page numbers in headers and footers, mail-merge instructions, automatic numbering and captioning, tables of contents and indexes, and master documents and sub-documents are all examples of Word using fields. In all of these instances, Word handles the fields more or less transparently, so that the user can benefit from the fields without having to worry about what they are and how to make them work.

Fields can be as confusing as they are powerful, but with a little patience, you can use them to help save time and effort.

What Is a Field?

Put simply, a field is a special code that tells Word to insert particular information in a document. For example, you can use fields to insert page numbers and dates in your documents and have them updated automatically.

Word lets you view either the field *codes* (the instructions that tell Word what information to put in your document) or the *results* of the field codes (the information the codes produce). Usually, you'll want to see the results, but when you're laying out a document that contains many fields, you may find it easier to display the codes. You may also want to display the codes when fields result in a blank—for example, if you cross-reference an empty bookmark, you will not see any result for the cross-reference field; or if you insert a field that may or may not contain information, such as the document properties Comment field. By displaying the field codes, you can check that each field code is where it should be and that it has not been deleted accidentally.

Fields get their information from a variety of sources, such as the following:

- Date and time information comes from your computer's clock. (If it's wrong, the fields will be wrong too.)

- User information comes from the information stored on the User Info tab of the Options dialog box and from the company information entered by whoever installed Word or Office on your computer.

- File information comes from the Properties dialog box. Some of it you can fill in when you save the document (Keywords, Comments, and so on), and some of it is generated automatically (details on who last saved the file and when, and so on).

What Should You Use Fields For?

Fields are good for inserting variable information in your documents and for automatically keeping that information up to date. For example, you can use index entry fields to mark the entries for your index, and then choose when to have Word generate the index instantly from the index entry fields. If you rearrange your document—either minor changes here and there, or a major reshuffling of the whole project—Word can update the index from the index entry fields in seconds.

Most people start off by using fields for inserting dates or page numbers in their documents—relatively simple information that is stunningly tedious to supply and update manually. You can also use fields to perform calculations, to reference bookmarks in your documents, and to provide hyperlinks to other documents or to Web pages.

Inserting Fields

For those users who want to enjoy the benefits of fields without having to mess with details, Word provides special ways to insert the most widely used fields—page numbers, dates and times (all from the Header and Footer toolbar), and so on. But you can also insert most any field code from the Field dialog box.

To insert a field code manually at the insertion point:

1.   Choose Insert ➤ Field to display the Field dialog box (see Figure 4.1).

FIGURE 4.1

Choose the field you want to insert in the Field dialog box.

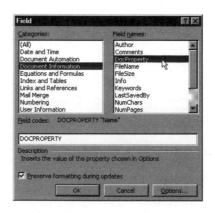

2. Choose the category of field from the Categories list. The first choice, (All), shows the fields in alphabetical order and is helpful if you know the name of the field but not which category Word lumps it into. Otherwise, choose a category, and Word will display all the fields for that category in the Field Names list box.

3. Choose the field you want from the Field Names list box.

4. To set options for the field, click the Options button to display the Field Options dialog box (see Figure 4.2):

   - The contents of the Field Options dialog box will vary depending on the field you've chosen: you may see just an Options tab, or it may contain tabs such as General Switches, Field Specific Switches, and Bookmarks. (A switch is an optional setting for a field.)

   - Choose formatting (e.g., uppercase or title case), formats (e.g., different date formats such as **28 November 1964** or **11/28/64**), properties (e.g., Author or Company, as shown in Figure 4.2), or switches for the field; then click the Add to Field button to add them to the field.

FIGURE 4.2

Make choices for the field in the Field Options dialog box.

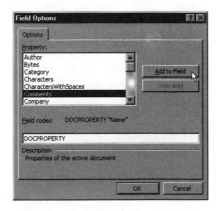

- Use the Undo Add button to correct any mistake you've just made, or click in the Field Codes box and edit out a part of the field that you've entered by mistake.

- When the field in the Field Codes box looks right with the formatting, formats, or switches you've added to it, click the OK button to return to the Field dialog box.

5. Click the OK button to close the Field dialog box and insert the field (and any formatting or switches) in the document at the insertion point.

WARNING You *can* type field codes straight into your document, provided you press Ctrl+F9 to insert the field-delimiter characters rather than trying to type them in from the keyboard—but it's a great waste of time and effort, and it's easy to make a small and stupid mistake that can take ages to find and fix. Using the Insert ➤ Field command and the Field dialog box is almost always faster and simpler unless you know fields inside and out.

Viewing Field Codes

By default, Word displays the results of field codes rather than the codes themselves, so if you insert a date code in your document, you'll see something like **January 16, 1997** rather than {**TIME \@"MMMM/d/yyyy"**} or a similar code.

To display a field code rather than the field result, right-click in any field and choose Toggle Field Codes from the shortcut menu. (To display the field result again, repeat the maneuver.) Alternatively, click in the field and press Shift+F9.

To toggle between field codes and field results for all fields in a document, simply press Alt+F9; alternatively, you can choose Tools ➤ Options to display the Options dialog box, bring the View tab to the front, and select the Field Codes check box in the Show area to display field codes; clear it to display field results. Click the OK button to close the Options dialog box.

TIP You may find it helpful to display field codes when arranging documents (e.g., forms) that contain many of them. You may find it even more helpful to split the window and view field codes in one half and field results in the other half: choose Window ➤ Split or double-click the split bar located at the top of the vertical scroll bar; then, to display the field codes in one pane, choose Tools ➤ Options to open the Options dialog box, select the Field Codes check box in the Show area on the View tab, and click OK. Alternatively, use the Alt+F9 shortcut to display all the codes in one pane. Don't use the Shift+F9 shortcut, which toggles the display of a single code in both panes at once.

To display index entry (XE), table of authorities (TA), table of contents (TC), and referenced document (RD) codes, you'll need to display hidden text rather than field codes—select the Hidden Text or the All box in the Nonprinting Characters area on the View tab of the Options dialog box (Tools ➤ Options).

Displaying Field Shading

To make things easier when working with documents that include fields, you can turn field shading on and off. Turning it on can not only help you see where all your fields are (with the exception of the XE, TA, TC, and RD fields), but also prevent you from deleting fields while under the impression that they're just text. At other times, though, field shading can be distracting, and you may want to turn it off so that you can treat the field results as regular text.

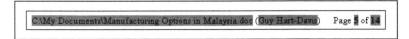

To turn field shading on and off, display the Options dialog box by choosing Tools ➤ Options. On the View tab, choose the appropriate option from the Field Shading drop-down list: Never, Always, or When Selected (the latter choice displays field shading when the insertion point is anywhere in the field, not just when the whole field is selected). Click the OK button to close the Options dialog box and implement your choice.

NOTE   Field shading is just a visual aid for working on-screen—it does not print under any circumstances.

Updating Fields

For your fields to be most useful, you'll need to update them so that the information is current. You can update fields one at a time manually, or all at once manually, or you can have Word update them all for you under certain circumstances, such as when you print a document.

TIP

If you have fields that you don't want to update, you can lock them or unlink them. See the section "Locking and Unlinking Fields" later in this chapter for details.

Updating Fields Manually

To manually update a single field, right-click anywhere in it and choose Update Field from the shortcut menu. Alternatively, click anywhere in the field and press the F9 key. Word will update the field with the latest information available for it.

To manually update several fields at once, select the text that contains them, then either right-click and choose Update Field from the shortcut menu or press the F9 key.

To update all the fields in a document at once, choose Edit ➤ Select All and press the F9 key.

Updating Fields Automatically When You Print

By updating fields whenever you print your documents, you can spare yourself the embarrassment of having your printouts contain out-of-date information.

To update fields when you print, display the Options dialog box by choosing Tools ➤ Options. On the Print tab, select the Update Fields check box in the Printing Options area and click the OK button. Now every time you print, Word will update all the fields first with the latest information. To stop updating fields when you print, clear the Update Fields check box on the Print tab of the Options dialog box once more.

TIP

You can also reach the Update Fields check box by choosing File ➤ Print and then clicking the Options button in the Print dialog box; this will display the Print tab of the Options dialog box in its own Print dialog box.

Updating Fields Automatically at Other Times

Word doesn't offer a built-in option for automatically updating fields other than when you print. But suppose you need to update all fields in your document automatically—for example, to see the latest sales figures and costs *right now* for the widgets your company has been manufacturing? This is one example of the usefulness of macros; you can create a macro to update fields at the touch of a button, or automatically when you open or close a document. We'll start looking at recording macros in the next chapter.

Locking and Unlinking Fields

Updating fields is all very well and good, but sooner or later you'll find yourself with a field that needs to stay the same while all the other fields in the document get updated. In this case, you can either *lock* the field for the time being to prevent updates (and unlock it later if need be) or *unlink* the field and prevent it from being updated from now until Armageddon.

To lock a field, click in it and press Ctrl+F11; to unlock it, click in the field and press Ctrl+Shift+F11.

TIP A locked field looks just the same as an unlocked field—for example, you'll still see field shading when the insertion point is in it (if field shading is turned on). One way to tell if it's locked is to try to update it—Word will beep if the field is locked.

To unlink a field, click in it and press Ctrl+Shift+F9. (If you do this by accident, you can choose Edit ➤ Undo to undo the action—but make sure you do so right away. If you don't catch the mistake in time to undo it, you can re-create the link from scratch.) Once you've unlinked a field, it will appear as regular text—no updating, shading, or other distinguishing characteristics.

Formatting Fields

Formatting fields could hardly be easier—simply format either the field code or the field result by selecting one or the other and using regular formatting techniques. Generally speaking, formatting the field results will give you a better idea of how your document will look.

TIP

You can also format fields by using special switches (such as * **CardText** * **Caps**); you'll find a horrendous number of them in the Word Help file (look under *Formatting Field Results*). If you get heavily into fields, you may want to investigate these switches. For all conventional documents, though, you can achieve the same effects by choosing options in the Field Options dialog box and then applying formatting by using the Font dialog box, thus having Word do all the work for you.

Moving from Field to Field

The easiest way to move from one field to another is by pressing the F11 key (going from the beginning of your document toward the end) and by pressing Shift+F11 to move to the previous field. This method takes you to the next or previous field without discriminating what kind of field it is.

If you need to move to a field of a particular type—for example, to move to each XE (index entry) field in turn—choose Edit ➤ Go To to display the Go To tab of the Find and Replace dialog box (see Figure 4.3). Choose Field in the Go to What list box (the list isn't alphabetical, so you'll need to scroll down), and then choose the type of field from the Enter Field Name drop-down list. You can then click the Next button to go to the next instance of that particular type of field (skipping all other intervening fields) or click the Previous button to go to the previous instance of that field. You can enter a + or − value after the field name to

FIGURE 4.3

Use the Go To tab of the Find and Replace dialog box to move quickly to a particular type of field.

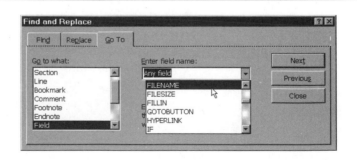

skip ahead (or back) a specified number of fields of the same type. For example, to skip ahead five index entry fields, enter **XE+5** and click the Next button.

You can also use the Object Browser to move from field to field. When you use the Go To tab of the Find and Replace dialog box to go to the next field as described in the previous paragraph, Word sets the Object Browser to browse by field and changes the Next Page and Previous Page buttons at the foot of the vertical scroll bar to Next Field and Previous Field buttons. You can then move from field to field by clicking these buttons. Like F11 and Shift+F11, the Object Browser doesn't discriminate among the various types of fields.

When you've finished moving through fields, reset the Object Browser to

browse by page (or whatever you prefer to browse by) by clicking the Select Browse Object button (located between the Previous and Next buttons below the vertical scroll bar) and choosing Browse by Page from the pop-up panel.

TIP
You can also set the Object Browser to browse by field by clicking the Select Browse Object button and then choosing Browse by Field from the pop-up panel.

Printing Out Field Codes

Normally you won't want your field codes to print—but should you ever need to,

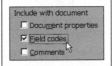

you can print them by opening the Options dialog box (Tools ➤ Options) and selecting the Field Codes box in the Include with Document area on the Print tab. Remember to clear it the next time you print, or Word will merrily keep printing the field codes rather than the results.

TIP
You can also access the Print tab of the Options dialog box by choosing File ➤ Print and then clicking the Options button in the Print dialog box.

Bookmarks

Word's electronic bookmarks provide a way of assigning names to parts of your documents so that you can access them quickly. A bookmark can mark a single point in the text, one or more characters, a graphic, etc.—pretty much any item in a document.

By using bookmarks in your macros, you can move instantly to a specified part of a document to write information to it, or you can retrieve information from a bookmark without moving to it. We'll look at the Visual Basic for Applications commands that Word provides for working with bookmarks in Chapter 15.

Adding a Bookmark

To add a bookmark to a document:

1. Position the insertion point where you want to insert the bookmark. If you want the bookmark to mark a particular section of text, a graphic, a frame, a table, or another element, select that item.

2. Choose Insert ➤ Bookmark to display the Bookmark dialog box, shown in Figure 4.4.

3. Enter the name for the bookmark in the Bookmark Name text box:

   • Bookmark names can be up to 40 characters long and can contain letters, numbers, and underscores, but no spaces or symbols. The names must start with a letter; after that, you can mix letters, numbers, and underscores to your heart's content. Each bookmark name must be unique for the document that contains it.

   • To reuse an existing bookmark name (effectively removing the old bookmark and creating another one with the same name), select it in the Bookmark Name list box.

4. Click the Add button to add the bookmark and close the Bookmark dialog box.

FIGURE 4.4

In the Bookmark dialog box, enter the name for the bookmark and then click the Add button.

Going to a Bookmark

Once you've added bookmarks to a document, you can quickly move to them by using either the Bookmark dialog box or the Go To tab of the Find and Replace dialog box.

To move to a bookmark using the Bookmark dialog box:

1. Choose Insert ➤ Bookmark to display the Bookmark dialog box.

2. In the Bookmark Name list box, select the bookmark to move to.

   To sort the bookmarks alphabetically by name, select the Name option button in the Sort By area (this is selected by default); to sort them by their location in the document (i.e., in the order in which they appear), select the Location option button.

3. Click the Go To button to move to the bookmark, and then click the Close button (into which the Cancel button will have changed) to close the Bookmark dialog box.

To move to a bookmark by using the Go To tab of the Find and Replace dialog box:

1. Choose Edit ➤ Go To to display the Go To tab of the Find and Replace dialog box (see Figure 4.5).

2. Choose Bookmark in the Go to What list box.

FIGURE 4.5

On the Go To tab of the
Find and Replace dialog
box, choose the book-
mark to move to, and
then click the Go To
button.

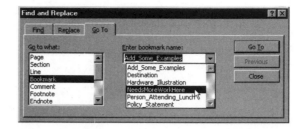

3. Select the bookmark from the Enter Bookmark Name drop-down list, and
    then click the Go To button.

4. Click the Close button to close the Go To dialog box.

Viewing Bookmarks

Word doesn't normally display bookmarks, which makes it easier to read your
documents. But when you do need to see where your bookmarks are, you can
display them as follows: choose Tools ➤ Options to display the Options dialog
box, select the Bookmarks check box in the Show area on the View tab, and click
the OK button.

Empty bookmarks appear as a heavy I-beam, disconcertingly similar to a
mouse pointer on steroids, while bookmarks that contain text or another item
appear as square brackets around the item. The illustration below shows both
types of bookmarks; the apparently missing word is marked by a bookmark so
that it can be filled in automatically.

Deleting a Bookmark

To delete a bookmark:

1. Choose Insert ➤ Bookmark to display the Bookmark dialog box.

2. In the Bookmark Name list box, select the bookmark you want to delete.

3. Click the Delete button to delete the bookmark. (This will delete just the bookmark—the bookmark's contents will not be affected.)

4. Repeat steps 2 and 3 as necessary, and then click the Close button to close the Bookmark dialog box.

TIP You can delete a bookmark *and* its contents by selecting it and pressing the Delete key.

AutoCorrect

Software mavens claim that any upgrade to an existing product has to have at least one killer feature for it to make any impression in the marketplace. In Word 6, the killer feature over Word 2 was AutoCorrect, which checks each word you type and automatically makes corrections from a predefined list of mistakes. Word 95 improved further on AutoCorrect, and now Word 97 integrates a number of other automatic features into AutoCorrect to capitalize on its popularity.

In Word 97, AutoCorrect includes AutoText and AutoFormat, which used to be separate features in previous versions of Word. We'll look at these in the next couple of sections; in this section, we'll examine AutoCorrect proper and how it can benefit you.

What Is AutoCorrect?

AutoCorrect offers five features that help you quickly enter your text in the right format. AutoCorrect works in a similar way to the on-the-fly Spelling feature that puts the squiggly red lines under words it doesn't recognize, but AutoCorrect has far greater potential for improving your working life. Every time you finish typing a word and press the spacebar, the Tab key, or the Enter key, or type any form of punctuation (such as a comma, a period, a semicolon, a colon, quotation marks, an exclamation point, a question mark, or even a % sign), Word checks it for a multitude of sins and, if it finds it guilty, takes action immediately.

To work with AutoCorrect, choose Tools ➤ AutoCorrect to open the AutoCorrect dialog box with the AutoCorrect tab displayed. The first four of AutoCorrect's features are straightforward; the fifth is a little more complex:

Correct TWo INitial CApitals stops you from typing an extra capital letter at the beginning of a word. If you need to type technical terms that need two initial capitals, clear the check box to turn this option off. (You can also use an Auto-Correct exception to get around this, as discussed in the section "Using AutoCorrect Exceptions" later in this chapter.)

Capitalize First Letter of Sentences does just that. If you and Word disagree about what constitutes a sentence, turn this option off by clearing the check box. For example, even if you start a new paragraph without ending the one before it with a period, Word will capitalize the first word of the new paragraph.

Capitalize Names of Days does just that.

Correct accidental usage of cAPS LOCK key is a neat feature that works most of the time. If Word thinks you've got the Caps Lock key down inadvertently, it will turn Caps Lock off and change the offending text from upper- to lowercase, and vice versa. Word usually decides that Caps Lock is stuck when you start a new sentence with a lowercase letter and continue with uppercase letters; however, the end of the previous sentence sometimes remains miscased. If you're deliberately using weird capitalization for your avant-garde poetry, this feature may bother you; clear the check box to turn it off.

Replace Text As You Type is the best of the AutoCorrect features. We'll look at it in detail in the next section.

Replace Text As You Type

The Replace Text As You Type feature of AutoCorrect keeps a list of AutoCorrect entries, starting with those included with the Office software and adding those that you create. Each time you finish typing a word, AutoCorrect scans this list for that word. If the word is on the list, Word substitutes the replacement text for the word.

Replace Text As You Type is a great way of fixing typos you make regularly, and in fact Word 97 ships with a decent list of AutoCorrect entries already configured—if you type *awya* instead of *away* or *disatisfied* instead of *dissatisfied*, Word will automatically fix the typo for you. But AutoCorrect is even more useful for setting up abbreviations for words or phrases that you use frequently in your day-to-day work, saving you not only time and keystrokes but also the effort of memorizing complex spellings or details. For example, while writing this book (in Word), I've been using any number of AutoCorrect entries, for everything from **db** for *dialog box* to **auc** for *AutoCorrect* to **uitodb** for *User Information tab of the Options dialog box*. This saves enough keystrokes to be worthwhile many times over—and if I occasionally forget an AutoCorrect entry for a particular piece of text and type the whole word or phrase, it's no big deal. The last phrase is a little too specialized—individual entries for *User Information tab* and *Options dialog box* are more useful—but there's no harm in having it lurking in the AutoCorrect list waiting for its set of keystrokes.

You can add AutoCorrect entries to Word's list in two ways—automatically while running a spelling check, or manually at any time.

Adding AutoCorrect Entries While Spell-Checking

It makes sense to begin building your list of AutoCorrect entries while spell-checking a document so that you can get Word to automatically fix your typos. When the Spelling checker finds a word it doesn't like, make sure the appropriate replacement word is highlighted in the Suggestions box; if the word isn't the right one, choose the appropriate word from the Suggestions box (or edit the word or type in the correct word). Then click the AutoCorrect button in the Spelling dialog box. Word will add the word from the Not in Dictionary box to the Replace list in AutoCorrect, and the word from the Suggestions box to the With list in AutoCorrect. In this way, you can build an AutoCorrect list tailored precisely to your typing idiosyncrasies.

Adding AutoCorrect Entries Manually

Adding AutoCorrect entries while spell-checking is great for building a list of your personal typos, but of little use for setting up AutoCorrect with abbreviations that will increase your typing speed dramatically. For that, you need to add AutoCorrect entries manually.

To add AutoCorrect entries manually:

1. If the replacement text for the AutoCorrect entry is in the current document, select it. Otherwise, proceed to step 2.

TIP

To create an AutoCorrect entry that contains formatting—bold, italic, paragraph marks, tabs, and so on—you need to select the formatted text in a document before opening the AutoCorrect dialog box.

2. Choose Tools ➤ AutoCorrect to display the AutoCorrect dialog box with the AutoCorrect tab at the front (see Figure 4.6).

FIGURE 4.6

The AutoCorrect tab of the AutoCorrect dialog box.

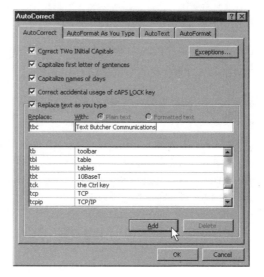

3. Make sure that the Replace Text As You Type check box is selected.

4. In the Replace box, enter the typo or abbreviation to be replaced.

TIP

When choosing the Replace text that will be an abbreviated AutoCorrect entry, avoid using a regular word that you might type in a document and not want to have replaced. Try reducing the word or phrase to an abbreviation that you'll remember—for example, omit all the vowels and include only the salient consonants.

5. Enter the replacement text in the With box.

   If you selected text before opening the AutoCorrect dialog box, that text will already appear in the With box. If the text needs to retain its formatting, make sure the Formatted Text option button is selected. (The Formatted Text option button also needs to be selected if your selection contains a paragraph mark or tab—that counts as formatting, too.)

6. Click the Add button or press Enter to add the AutoCorrect entry to the list.

   If Word already has an AutoCorrect entry stored for the text in the Replace text box, the Add button will have changed into a Replace button. When you press Enter or click this button, Word will display a confirmation dialog box to make sure that you want to replace the current AutoCorrect entry.

7. To add another AutoCorrect entry, repeat steps 4 through 6.

8. To close the AutoCorrect dialog box, click the Close button.

TIP You can include graphics, frames, borders, and so on in AutoCorrect entries. For example, you can easily include your company's logo with the company's address in an AutoCorrect entry to create instant letterhead. Be imaginative, and AutoCorrect can save you plenty of time.

Deleting AutoCorrect Entries

To delete an AutoCorrect entry, open the AutoCorrect dialog box (by choosing Tools ➤ AutoCorrect), click the AutoCorrect tab if it isn't displayed, and select the entry from the list box at the bottom of the dialog box. (You can also type the first few letters of an entry's Replace designation in the Replace box to scroll to it quickly.) Then click the Delete button.

   When you're finished deleting AutoCorrect entries, click the OK button to close the AutoCorrect dialog box.

TIP You can automatically add entries to the AutoCorrect list by writing a straightforward macro. We'll look at this in Chapter 23.

Advanced Use of AutoCorrect

Sometimes AutoCorrect can be too sharp for its own good—or rather, for yours. In this section, we'll look at a couple of "gotchas" that can diminish your enjoyment of the power of AutoCorrect—and (of course) ways to get around them.

Punctuation Keys and the Like

As mentioned earlier in this section, a number of keys in addition to the space bar, Enter key, and Tab key trigger the AutoCorrect checker; among these keys, the most-used are the punctuation keys (comma, period, semicolon, colon, exclamation point, question mark), the single-quotation mark and double-quotation mark key, the hyphen and dashes, and the slash key (/). The punctuation keys cause few problems because few of the abbreviations you define as Replace items for AutoCorrect will contain punctuation, but the other keys can be problematic. For example, if you define an AutoCorrect Replace entry that contains a single-quotation mark or apostrophe, by typing the single-quotation mark or apostrophe you will trigger an AutoCorrect check before the word is completed.

As an example of what might go wrong, consider that you might set up an AutoCorrect entry to change **os** into **operating system**. If you then try to type **OS/2**, the keystroke for the slash will cause AutoCorrect to change the first two letters into *operating system*, and you'll waste time having to fix it. This quirk turns **OS** into the equivalent of a word for AutoCorrect, making it better to use a different abbreviation for operating system, such as **ops**. (Of course, you could avoid ever typing **OS/** by setting up a different AutoCorrect entry for **OS/2**, but this type of cumulative AutoCorrect-building is guaranteed to confuse anyone else who has the misfortune to try to get any work done on your computer.)

NOTE AutoCorrect inherits its limited case-sensitivity from the Spelling checker: If you enter an AutoCorrect Replace item as lowercase, AutoCorrect will kick in whether you type it in lowercase, mixed case, or uppercase in the document. But if you enter a Replace item as uppercase, typing lowercase or mixed case will not trigger it.

Creating Multiple AutoCorrect Entries for One Result

Even if your installation of Word will be used by other persons, each with their own peculiar set of typos, AutoCorrect can still be useful. You simply need to adopt a multi-pronged approach. For example, to make sure that *10BaseT* never appears as *10BASET* or *10Base-T*, you could set up one Replace entry for 10BASET and another for 10Base-T, so that either of these mutations would be turned into the approved style.

So far, so good; but for enlightened users willing to learn a few abbreviations, you could also set up **10bt** and **tbt** entries to save them a few keystrokes (the latter is easier to type for those of us who never truly learned to touch-type the numbers).

Another example: To make sure that *TCP/IP* is easy to type, you could set up Replace entries for **tcp** and **tcp/ip** (and perhaps for **tpcip** and other typos of the acronym); if you also had discrete Replace entries that capitalized **tcp** and **ip** for use of these terms separately, the former would uppercase *tcp* as soon as the user pressed the slash key, but otherwise they would not interfere with the *tcp/ip* Replace entry.

An AutoCorrect entry that turned **tcp** into *Transmission Control Protocol* would be a different matter; if you then tried to type **tcp/ip**, as soon as you pressed the slash key AutoCorrect would assume you wanted Transmission Control Protocol. You might want to conclude from this that you shouldn't use AutoCorrect to expand an accepted abbreviation into the full phrase it maps to; instead, it is usually better to set up an AutoCorrect entry for something other than the accepted abbreviation. For example, you might set up an AutoCorrect entry that changed **tcp** into *TCP* and another entry that expanded **tcpp** to the full phrase.

Depending on the effort you've put into your typing lessons and the resulting dexterity (or otherwise) of your right pinkie, you may well find it easier to set up AutoCorrect entries that contain no apostrophes or quotation marks. For example, if you want to be able to type the word *OS/2's* quickly (e.g., for the perennial-favorite phrase *OS/2's imminent demise*), it would make much more sense to set up an AutoCorrect entry of **os2s** than one of **os2's** or **os/2's**. (In fact, if you want to type the phrase frequently, you might even set up an AutoCorrect entry for the whole of it—**os2id** or the like.)

Many of the frequently used words containing apostrophes are classic candidates for AutoCorrect entries, and indeed Word comes preconfigured with many of these: If you type **theyll** or **they;ll**, Word will automatically substitute *they'll*. But others you may well want to add yourself: if you add an AutoCorrect entry that substitutes **weren't** for **werent**, you're unlikely to cause problems for any users of your computer, and you can save them from the occasional underpress of the pinkie stroke.

TIP

For anyone who occasionally fumbles for the apostrophe key, it makes sense to set up AutoCorrect entries such as **werent** for *weren't*. The one thing to note here is the smart (curly) apostrophe: if you simply type **weren't** into the With text box in the AutoCorrect dialog box, you'll get a straight apostrophe instead of a smart one. There are two ways around this. One way is to type the word in a document, so that Word automatically enters the smart apostrophe for you; then select the word and create the AutoCorrect entry as usual. Alternatively, you can use the Alt-key combination to enter the smart apostrophe into the With box (**Alt+0146**). You can set up AutoCorrect entries for opening and closing quotation marks (**Alt+0147** and **Alt+0148**) in the same manner.

Using AutoCorrect Exceptions

If you've already managed to think up a couple more things that could cause problems with AutoCorrect, hold on a minute: AutoCorrect has an Exceptions feature that you can use to prevent specific items from triggering AutoCorrect corrections.

From the AutoCorrect tab of the AutoCorrect dialog box, click the Exceptions button to display the AutoCorrect Exceptions dialog box (see Figure 4.7).

FIGURE 4.7

In the AutoCorrect Exceptions dialog box, set exceptions to prevent specific terms you use from being corrected automatically.

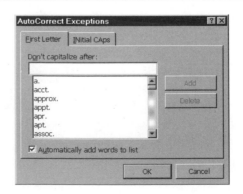

How Extensively Should You Use AutoCorrect?

Sensible uses of AutoCorrect depend very much on the person who's using the copy of Word that you're gimmicking. (The same is true of macros and the user interface, as you'll see later in this book.) Many of the most powerful uses of AutoCorrect depend on the user being prepared to type known abbreviations to achieve certain results, or to put up with the occasional glitch or awkwardness in the quest for everyday speed. For example, say you decide to use the letter *h* as the AutoCorrect entry for *the*, the letter *u* for *you*, and the letter *d* for *and*. As long as you're the only user of this installation of Word, all is well and good; but as soon as one of your colleagues comes along and starts typing a paper involving the chemical symbol for hydrogen (or pretty much any form of math), your AutoCorrect entries will change from a timesaver into a frustrating liability.

You may find these examples contrived and unconvincing; perhaps so. (For the record, I use those three AutoCorrect abbreviations.) But imagine the potential problems that can result from a "regular" user sitting down at a computer that has a highly gimmicked copy of Word. They'll spend half the time choosing Undo—or they'll wear out the Backspace key. (Off the record, AutoCorrect bombs would make a great way of frustrating self-important and ignorant users of Word...)

One option is to avoid using any single-letter AutoCorrect Replace items— sooner or later the user is going to want to type any given character on its own—as well as any Replace items that use real words the user might need to type. This means that you cannot save as many keystrokes on short common words as you might otherwise be able to, not to mention that your computer isn't as "personal" as it might be.

An alternative is to write an Auto_Exec macro that checks the user's name and turns the AutoCorrect Replace Text As You Type feature on and off accordingly. We'll look at this in the discussion of Auto_Exec macros in Chapter 21.

When Word doesn't recognize an abbreviation, it will think the period that denotes the abbreviation is the end of a sentence instead. To prevent this from happening, you can create exceptions to the Capitalize First Letter of Sentences feature: simply select the First Letter tab of the AutoCorrect dialog box, type the abbreviation into the Don't Capitalize After text box, and click the Add button. The abbreviation will be added to the list box below. To delete a first-letter exception, select it in the Don't Capitalize After list box and click the Delete button.

You can automate the First-Letter Exceptions feature by selecting the Automatically Add Words to List check box at the bottom of the First Letter tab; Word will automatically add first-letter exceptions to the list when you use Backspace to undo AutoCorrect's correction of them. For example, say you're writing about syntax and you need to use the abbreviation **prep.** for *preposition*. If you type **prep. used**, AutoCorrect will change **used** to **Used** because it thinks the period ends a sentence. But if you then use Backspace to delete **Used** and type in **used** to replace it, Word will create a first-letter exception for **prep.** and add it to the list.

On the cutely named INitial CAps tab, you can create exceptions for those rare terms that need two initial capitals (for example, IPng, the next-generation Internet Protocol). Enter the text in the Don't Correct text box, and then click the Add button. To delete an initial-cap exception, select it in the Don't Correct list box and click the Delete button.

When the Automatically Add Words to List check box at the bottom of the INitial CAps tab is selected, Word will automatically add two-initial-cap words to the list when you use Backspace to undo AutoCorrect's correction of them and retype them. For example, if you're writing about the next-generation Internet protocol and you type **IPng** and a space, AutoCorrect will change **IPng** to **Ipng**. But if you press Backspace four times (once for the space, once for the **g**, once for the **n**, and once for the **p**, leaving the **I** there) and then type **Png** and a space, Word will create a two-initial-cap exception for **IPng** and will cease and desist from lowercasing the second letter.

Using Multiple AutoCorrect Lists

As you may know, AutoCorrect entries come in two flavors:

- Entries with no formatting that are shared among the Office applications, so that you can use them in Excel and PowerPoint as well as Word

- Formatted entries that you can use only in Word

Windows 95 and Windows NT maintain a separate AutoCorrect list of shared entries for each user who logs in. Each user's file is stored in a file with the ACL extension in the Windows or WinNT folder. The Registry entries for these files are kept under `My Computer\HKEY_CURRENT_USER\Software\Office\8.0\ Common\AutoCorrect\Path`.

Using Multiple AutoCorrect Lists for the Same Login Name

If you must, you can use different AutoCorrect lists for the same login name in either of two ways. First, you can simply run a batch file (or a macro) to rename the current AutoCorrect file, then rename a second AutoCorrect file with the original name. We'll look at how to do this in Chapter 21, which deals with performing this kind of manipulation on unwary files. Second, you can achieve a similar effect by changing the Registry entry to a different file at the beginning of a Word session and then changing it back at the end of the session. We'll look at this in Chapter 21 too.

AutoText

Word's AutoText feature provides another way of inserting frequently used text and graphics in your documents. An AutoText entry is a piece of boilerplate text that you store ready for future use. This boilerplate could be anything from your name and address to a series of convoluted legal paragraphs. In Word 97, AutoText has grown much closer to AutoCorrect, which perhaps goes to show their relative popularity—AutoText, previously known as *glossaries* and a staple feature of Word from the early days, has been almost totally eclipsed by its late-coming and hyperactive cousin.

Nevertheless, AutoText remains an effective tool and an important weapon in your arsenal for making Word jump. It has several components that we'll look at in sequence in the following sections.

Creating an AutoText Entry

To create an AutoText entry:

1. Select the text (and/or graphics, etc.) from your document for the AutoText entry. Make sure that it contains all the formatting it needs.

2. Click the Create AutoText button (shown below) on the AutoText toolbar or press Alt+F3 to display the Create AutoText dialog box (see Figure 4.8).

FIGURE 4.8

In the Create AutoText dialog box, select a name for your AutoText entry and click the OK button.

---

3. In the Please Name Your AutoText Entry text box, enter the name you'll use to identify the AutoText entry.

    - If you chose text for the AutoText entry, Word will automatically display the first couple of words from your selection in the text box. Often you'll want to change this and use something catchy that you'll remember easily.

    - Unlike AutoCorrect entries, AutoText entries can have plain-English names that you'll type all the time, because AutoText does not automatically replace your typing.

    - If an AutoText entry with the same name already exists, when you click the OK button Word will ask if you want to redefine that entry. If you choose No, Word will let you choose another name for the new AutoText entry; if you choose Yes, Word will replace the existing Auto-Text entry with the new one.

4. Click the OK button to add the AutoText entry to Word's list and close the Create AutoText dialog box.

Inserting an AutoText Entry

You can insert an AutoText entry in several ways:

- by using the AutoText toolbar

- by typing and using the AutoComplete feature

- by typing and choosing the entry manually

- by using the Insert ➤ AutoText menu item

Inserting an AutoText Entry from the AutoText Toolbar

To insert an AutoText entry from the AutoText toolbar, you use the Insert AutoText

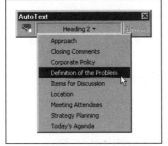

button. This button will bear the name of the style of the current paragraph, such as **Heading 1** or **Body Text**. Click the button to display a list of the AutoText entries associated with the current style.

To insert an entry associated with another style, or one of Word's predefined

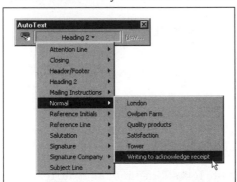

entries, hold down Shift as you click the Insert AutoText button. Word will display a menu of all the AutoText categories that it contains, including its predefined categories (Attention Line, Closing, Header/Footer, and so on) and all the styles that have AutoText entries defined. Select the category you want, and then choose the item from the submenu that appears.

Inserting an AutoText Entry by Using the AutoComplete Feature

To insert an AutoText entry quickly using the AutoComplete feature, start typing the name of the entry into your document. As soon as you've typed four letters of

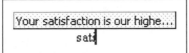

it (or enough of it to distinguish it from any other AutoText entry that starts with the same four letters), AutoComplete will pop up a suggestion box, as shown here. Press Enter, Tab, or

F3 to replace the name of the entry with the corresponding full text; keep typing to ignore the suggestion.

You can turn off the AutoComplete feature as follows:

1. Click the AutoText button or choose Insert ➤ AutoText ➤ AutoText to display the AutoText tab of the AutoCorrect dialog box.

2. Clear the Show AutoComplete Tip for AutoText and Dates check box.

3. Click the OK button to close the AutoCorrect dialog box.

Inserting an AutoText Entry Manually

When you've turned off AutoComplete, you can insert an AutoText entry by typing the first three letters of its name (or enough letters to distinguish it from any other AutoText entry) and then pressing F3 to insert the entry.

Inserting an AutoText Entry from the Insert Menu

You can also insert an AutoText entry from the Insert menu:

1. Display the appropriate AutoText submenu:

    - To display the AutoText submenu of AutoText entries associated with the current style, choose Insert ➤ AutoText.

    - To display the AutoText submenu of all AutoText categories, pull down the Insert menu, and hold down Shift as you select AutoText.

2. Choose the entry you want from the AutoText submenu or from a category on the AutoText submenu, as shown in Figure 4.9.

Changing an AutoText Entry

You can't edit an AutoText entry on the AutoText tab of the AutoCorrect dialog box. Instead, to change an AutoText entry, simply insert it in text (as described in the previous section), and then make edits to it by using regular Word editing techniques. Once you've got the material for the entry to your satisfaction, select

FIGURE 4.9

You can also insert
AutoText entries from
the Insert ➤ AutoText
submenu.

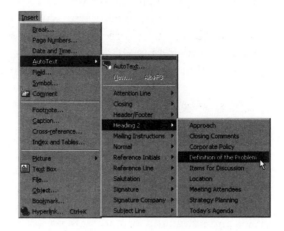

it, click the Create AutoText button to display the Create AutoText dialog box, re-enter the original name, click the OK button, and choose the Yes button in the message box that asks if you want to redefine the AutoText entry.

Deleting an AutoText Entry

To delete an AutoText entry:

1. Click the AutoText button or choose Insert ➤ AutoText ➤ AutoText to display the AutoText tab of the AutoCorrect dialog box.

2. Select the entry in the list box.

3. Click the Delete button to delete the entry.

4. Either delete more AutoText entries while you're at it, or click the Close button to close the AutoCorrect dialog box.

Using AutoText versus AutoCorrect

If you've read through the last few sections, you should be pretty clear on the differences between AutoCorrect and AutoText: AutoCorrect takes effect automatically whenever it can, whereas AutoText pops up suggestions and lets you choose whether or not to accept them. Any solid strategy for making life easier in Word will involve using both AutoCorrect and AutoText.

Whether to use AutoText or AutoCorrect for a particular purpose will depend to a large extent on the person who will be using that copy of Word. If having a large number of AutoCorrect entries replaced automatically is disconcerting—or if the user's typing is so bad that AutoCorrect abbreviations are inadvertently triggered all the time—then AutoText may prove a better option for that person.

AutoFormat

Word offers automatic formatting with its two AutoFormat features: AutoFormat regular, which applies styles and automatic formatting when you choose the Format ➤ AutoFormat command, and AutoFormat as You Type, which applies styles and automatic formatting to paragraphs as you finish them. In Word 97, AutoFormat is another feature that Microsoft has brought under the AutoCorrect umbrella, so you'll find the AutoFormat options in the AutoCorrect dialog box.

To set AutoFormat as You Type options:

1. Choose Tools ➤ AutoCorrect to display the AutoCorrect dialog box.

2. Click the AutoFormat as You Type tab to display it (see Figure 4.10).

3. In the Apply as You Type area, select the check boxes next to the auto-formatting options you want to use: Headings, Borders, Tables, Automatic Bulleted Lists, and Automatic Numbered Lists. These options apply the following formats:

Headings	Word applies Heading 1 style when you type a short paragraph starting with a capital letter and finish it by pressing Enter twice; it applies Heading 2 when that paragraph starts with a tab.
Automatic Numbered Lists	Word creates a numbered list when you type a number followed by a punctuation mark (such as a period, hyphen, etc.), and then a space or tab and some text.
Automatic Bulleted Lists	Word creates a bulleted list when you type a bullet-type character (e.g., a bullet, an asterisk, a hyphen, or a dash) and then a space or tab followed by text.

TIP You can stop the automatic numbered or bulleted list by pressing Enter twice.

FIGURE 4.10

On the AutoFormat as You Type tab of the AutoCorrect dialog box, set the autoformatting options you want.

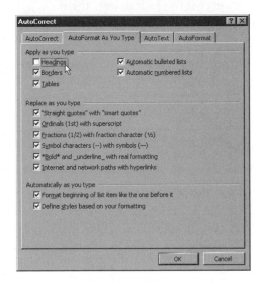

Borders	Word adds a border to a paragraph that follows a paragraph consisting only of three or more consecutive dashes, underscores, or equal signs: dashes produce a thin line, underscores produce a thick line, and equal signs produce a double line. (Word removes the paragraph consisting of dashes, underscores, or equal signs when it adds the border.)
Tables	Word creates a table when you type an arrangement of hyphens and plus signs (e.g., +--+--+--+). You need to type at least two plus signs (to indicate the vertical borders), one beginning the table and one ending it, and at least one hyphen or equal sign between them. This is one of the more bizarre and inconvenient ways of creating a table, but use it if it appeals to you.

4. Choose Replace as You Type options as necessary.

5. In the Automatically as You Type area, select the Format Beginning of List Item Like the One Before It check box if you want Word to try to mimic your formatting of lists automatically. Select the Define Styles Based on Your Formatting check box if you want Word to automatically create styles whenever it thinks it detects them.

6. Click the OK button to close the Options dialog box.

AutoFormat as You Type options will now spring into effect as you create your documents.

To set regular AutoFormat options:

1. Choose Tools ➤ AutoCorrect to display the AutoCorrect dialog box.

2. Click the AutoFormat tab to display it.

3. In the Apply area, select the check boxes next to the autoformatting options you want to use: Headings, Lists, Automatic Bulleted Lists, and Other Paragraphs. (For an explanation of the first three of these options, see the previous section. The fourth option, Other Paragraphs, applies styles to items other than headings, lists, borders, or tables, based on what Word judges your text to be.)

4. Choose Replace options as necessary.

5. In the Always AutoFormat area, select the Plain Text WordMail documents check box if you want Word to automatically format plain-text e-mail in WordMail.

6. Click the OK button to close the Options dialog box.

To use the regular AutoFormat feature, create your document and then choose Format ➤ AutoFormat. Word will display an AutoFormat dialog box (see Figure 4.11), which lets you access the Options dialog box to refine your predefined AutoFormat settings if necessary. Choose a type of document from the drop-down list, and then click the OK button to start the autoformatting.

FIGURE 4.11

In the AutoFormat dialog box, choose a type of document and indicate whether you want to review the changes Word proposes; then click the OK button.

Advanced Find and Replace

If you've done anything more than hack together a couple of memos in Word, you've undoubtedly already encountered Word's Find and Replace features, even if you've used them only to search for a particular *string* of text (a letter, several letters, a word, or a phrase) and replace either chosen instances or all instances of that string. As you'll see in this section, when you use their capabilities fully, Find and Replace are powerful tools for changing your documents rapidly—and of course you can also use Find independently of Replace to locate strategic parts of your document or to get to specific words in order to change the text around them.

With Find and Replace, you can search for special characters (such as tabs or paragraph marks), for special operators (such as a digit, a character, or a range of characters), for particular formatting (such as double underline, bold, or italic in Engravers Gothic font), or for a particular Word style (such as Heading 9 or Body Text). You can search for text in a particular language, for paragraphs with particular tab formatting, or for text that sounds like other text. You can even combine many of these elements to conduct searches of truly fiendish complexity that will confound your colleagues and impress your friends.

Finding Text

To find text:

1. Choose Edit ➤ Find to display Find tab of the Find and Replace dialog box (see Figure 4.12). If you see only the top half of the dialog box shown here, click the More button to display the rest of the dialog box.

FIGURE 4.12

The Find and Replace
dialog box gives you a
quick way to access any
combination of charac-
ters or formatting in your
document. If you're
seeing a smaller version
of the Find and Replace
dialog box, click the More
button to expand it.

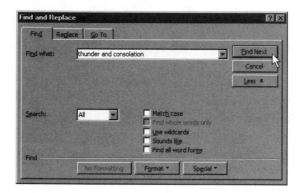

2. In the Find What box, enter the text you're looking for.

    • You can use *wildcard* characters to find a variety of characters. We'll get into this in the next section.

    • Word stores the Find operations from the current session in a drop-down list that you can access by clicking the arrow at the right-hand end of the Find What box.

3. Choose the direction to search from the Search drop-down list: Down, Up, or All.

    • If you choose Down or Up, Word will prompt you to continue when it reaches the end or beginning of the document (unless you started Find at the beginning or end of the document).

4. Choose the options you want from the column of check boxes. Each option you choose will be listed under the Find What box.

    • Match Case makes Word use the capitalization of the word in the Find What box as a search constraint. For example, with Match Case selected and **laziness** entered in the Find What box, Word will ignore instances of *Laziness* or *LAZINESS* in the document and find only *laziness*.

    • Find Whole Words Only makes Word look only for the exact word entered in the Find What box and not for the word when it is part of another word. For example, by selecting the Find Whole Words Only check box, you could find *and* without finding *land, random, mandible*, and so on. Find Whole Words Only is not available if you type a space in the Find What box.

- Use Wildcards provides special search options that we'll look at in the next section.

- Sounds Like finds words that, according to Word, sound like those in the Find What box. You may not always agree with Word's choices. For example, if you select the Sounds Like check box and enter **meddle** in the Find What box, Word will find both *middle* and *muddle*, but it won't find rhyming words, such as *peddle* and *pedal*.

- Find All Word Forms attempts to find all forms of the verb or noun in the Find What box. This is particularly useful with Replace operations: Word can change *break, broken, breaking,* and *breaks* to *fix, fixed, fixing,* and *fixes*. Enter the basic form of the words in the Find What and the Replace With boxes on the Replace tab of the Find and Replace dialog box—in this example, you'd use **break** and **fix**.

WARNING Find All Word Forms is an ambitious feature prone to random behavior if you use it unwisely. To give Microsoft credit, Word will warn you that choosing Replace All with the Find All Word Forms option selected may not be advisable—it's likely to find (and change) more than you bargained for. If you use it, use it carefully, and be especially careful with words such as *lead,* because the metal "lead" will likely be misinterpreted as the verb "to lead."

5. Make sure that no formatting information appears in the box under the Find What text box. If the No Formatting button at the bottom of the dialog box is active (not dimmed), that means Word will look for words only with the selected formatting; click the button to remove the formatting. If the No Formatting button is dimmed, you're OK.

6. Click the Find Next button to find the next instance of your chosen text. If Word finds the text, it will stop and select it in the document; otherwise, it will tell you that it was unable to find the text.

7. Click the Find Next button again to keep searching, or click the Cancel button to close the Find dialog box.

Once you perform a Find operation (or a Find and Replace operation), Word sets the Object Browser to browse by the item you last found. The Next Page and Previous Page buttons at the foot of the vertical scroll bar turn from black to blue and become Next Find/Go To and Previous Find/Go To, respectively. You can then click these buttons to move to the next or previous instance of the item you last found; you can also press Ctrl+PageDown or Ctrl+PageUp for the same effect.

To reset the Object Browser to browse by page, click the Select Browse Object button and choose the Browse by Page icon from the pop-up panel, as shown here. (To switch back to Browse by Find, you can click the Select Browse Object button again and choose the Browse by Find icon—the binoculars—from the pop-up panel.)

Finding Special Characters and Using Wildcards

Word's special characters and wildcards add great power and flexibility to Find and Replace operations. *Special characters* enable you to search for something more complex than plain text, such as an em dash, a paragraph mark, or any number. *Wildcards*—special search operators—let you search for words beginning with a specific character, or for words that contain a certain range of letters.

Special Characters

To find a special character, such as a paragraph mark, a tab character, or a graphic, click the Special button in the Find dialog box and choose the character from the drop-down list that appears, as shown in Figure 4.13.

You can combine special characters with regular text to make your Find operations more effective. For example, the special character for a paragraph mark is ^p; to find every instance where *Rhonda* appears at the beginning of a paragraph, you could search for **^pRhonda**.

FIGURE 4.13

You can find special characters, such as page breaks or endnote marks, by using the Special drop-down list.

When working in Word or when recording macros, it's usually easiest to enter special characters from the Special drop-down list; when writing or adapting macros in the Visual Basic Editor, you'll probably want to enter them manually. Here's the full list of characters and what they find:

Character	Finds
^?	Any one character
^p	A paragraph mark
^t	A tab
^a	A comment mark
^#	Any digit
^$	Any letter
^^	A caret (^)
^n	A column break
^+	An em dash (—)
^=	An en dash (–)

Character	Finds
^e	An endnote mark
^d	A field
^f	A footnote mark
^g	A graphic
^l	A manual line break
^m	A manual page break
^~	A nonbreaking hyphen
^s	A nonbreaking space
^-	An optional hyphen
^b	A section break
^w	A white space

Of these, you'll probably find yourself using ^? the most. For example, you could use **tr^?st** to find *trust* or *tryst*.

Using Wildcards

Word's wildcards go one stage beyond the special characters. You can search for one out of several specified characters, any character in a range, any character except the given one, and even a string of characters at the beginning or end of a word only. To enter these operators, select the Use Wildcards check box, and then click the Special button to display the drop-down list (see Figure 4.14).

Here is the list of wildcards and what they find:

Wildcard	Finds	Examples
*	A string of characters	**gr*d** finds *grid, groaned, "By great Scott!" thought Fitzgerald*, and any other combination of letters surrounded by *gr* and *d*.
[ ]	Any one of the given characters	**s[iou]n** finds *sin, son*, and *sun*.
[-]	Any one character in the range	**[g-x]ote** finds *note, mote, rote*, and *tote*. Enter the ranges in alphabetical order.

FIGURE 4.14

To search for wildcards, select the Use Wildcards check box and then choose the wildcards from the Special drop-down list.

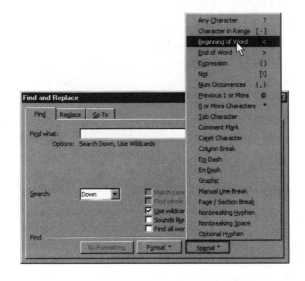

Wildcard	Finds	Examples
[!]	Any one character except the characters inside the brackets	[!f][!a]therhood finds *motherhood* and *brotherhood*, but not *fatherhood*.
[!x-z]	Any one character except characters in the range inside the brackets	a[!b-l]e finds *ape*, *are*, and *ate*, but not *ace*, *age*, or *ale*.
{x}	Exactly *x* number of occurrences of the previous character or expression	we{2}d finds *weed* but not *wed*, because *weed* has two *e*'s.
{x,}	At least *x* occurrences of the previous character or expression	we{1,}d finds *weed* and *wed*, because both words have at least one *e*.
{x,y}	From *x* to *y* occurrences of the previous character or expression	40{2,4} finds *400*, *4,000*, and *40,000*, because each has between two and four zeroes; it won't find *40*, because it has only one zero.
@	One or more occurrences of the previous character or expression	o@h! finds *oh!* and *ooh!*, which both contain one or more *o*s followed by an *h* and an exclamation point.

Wildcard	Finds	Examples
<	The following search string (in parentheses) at the beginning of a word	**<(work)** finds *working* and *workaholic,* but not *groundwork.*
>	The preceding search string (in parentheses) at the end of a word	**(sin)>** finds *basin* and *moccasin,* but not *sinful.*

As you can see from the Fitzgerald example, you need to be a little careful when using the * special character, particularly with only an identifying letter or two on either side of it. For a halfway realistic example of how you might actually use * in a search, see the section "An Example of Using Find and Replace" at the end of this chapter.

Finding and Replacing Text

To find and replace text:

1. Choose Edit ➤ Replace to display the Replace tab of the Find and Replace dialog box (see Figure 4.15). If you're already working on the Find tab of the Find and Replace dialog box, click the Replace tab.

2. In the Find What box, enter the text to find. To find text you've searched for before in the current Word session, click the arrow at the right-hand end of the Find What box and choose the text from the drop-down list.

FIGURE 4.15

The Replace tab of the Find and Replace dialog box.

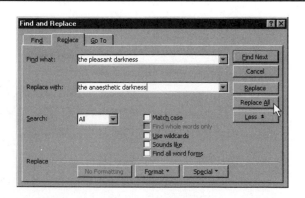

3. In the Replace With box, enter the text you want to replace the found text with. To reuse replacement text from the current session, click the arrow at the right-hand end of the Replace With box and choose the text from the drop-down list.

4. Choose a search direction from the Search drop-down list: All, Down, or Up.

5. Choose Replace options such as Match Case and Find Whole Words Only as appropriate (see the section "Finding Text" earlier in this chapter for an explanation of these options).

6. Start the Replace operation by clicking the Find Next button, the Replace button, or the Replace All button:

    *   Both the Find Next button and Replace button will find the next instance of the text in the Find What box. Once you've found it, either click the Find Next button to skip to the next occurrence of the text without replacing it with the contents of the Replace With box, or click the Replace button to replace the text with the contents of the Replace With box and have Word find the next instance of the Find What text.

    *   The Replace All button will replace all instances of the text in the Find What box with the text in the Replace With box. If you've chosen Up or Down in the Search drop-down list and started the search anywhere other than the end or the beginning of the document, Word will prompt you to continue when it reaches the beginning or end of the document.

7. When you've finished your Replace operation, click the Close button to close the Replace dialog box (this button will read Cancel if you haven't made any replacements).

WARNING When replacing simple text, make sure that Word is displaying no formatting information below the Find What box and Replace With boxes—otherwise Word will only find instances of the text that have the appropriate formatting information (bold, italic, Book Antiqua font, Heading 4 style, and so on), or it will replace the text in the Find What box with inappropriately formatted text from the Replace With box. To remove formatting information from the Find What box and Replace With box, click in the appropriate box and then click the No Formatting button.

Finding and Replacing Formatting

You don't always need to use text for Replace operations in Word—you can simply find one kind of formatting and replace it with another. For example, say you received an article for your newsletter in which the author had used boldface rather than italic for emphasizing words. To convert these words from bold to italic, you could replace all bold text with text with non-bold, italic text.

This use of the Replace function sounds suspiciously utopian, but it works well. Alternatively, you can replace particular strings of text that have one kind of formatting with the same strings of text that have different kinds of formatting (in which case you would enter text in the Find and Replace With boxes); or you can replace formatted strings of text with other formatted strings of text.

To replace one kind of formatting with another kind of formatting:

1. Choose Edit ➤ Replace to display the Find and Replace dialog box.

2. With the insertion point in the Find What box, click the Format button and choose Font, Paragraph, Tabs, or Language from the drop-down list. Word will display the Find Font, Find Paragraph, Find Tabs, or Find Language dialog box. These are versions of the Font, Paragraph, Tabs, and Language dialog boxes you're already familiar with.

3. Choose the formatting you want Word to find, then click the OK button to return to the Find and Replace dialog box. Word will display the formatting you chose in the Format box underneath the Find What box.

   > Find what: _____ ▾
   > Format: Font: Tahoma, 12 pt, Italic, Emboss

4. If necessary, add further formatting to the mix by repeating steps 2 and 3 with font, paragraph, tab, or language formatting.

5. With the insertion point in the Replace With box, click the Format button and choose Font, Paragraph, Tabs, or Language from the drop-down list. Word will display the Replace Font, Replace Paragraph, Replace Tabs, or Replace Language dialog box. Again, these are versions of the regular Font, Paragraph, Tabs, and Language dialog boxes.

6. Choose the replacement formatting, then click the OK button to return to the Find and Replace dialog box. Word will display this formatting in the Format box under the Replace With box.

7. Again, if necessary, add further font, paragraph, tab, or language formatting, this time by repeating steps 5 and 6.

8. Start the search by clicking the Find Next, Replace, or Replace All buttons.

TIP

If there's no text entered in the Find What box and Replace With box, Word will replace all instances of the formatting you chose. For example, you could replace all boldface with italic, non-boldface. You can also enter text in the Find What box and leave the Replace With box empty to have Word remove that text and put different formatting where it was. (This seems a bizarre concept until you find out how useful it is. We'll look at an example of this in the section "An Example of Using Find and Replace" at the end of this chapter.) Or you can enter replacement text in both the Find What box and in the Replace With box and replace both the text and the formatting at once. For example, you could replace all boldfaced instances of the word *break* with italicized, non-boldface instances of the word *fix*.

Finding and Replacing Styles

To replace one style with another:

1. Choose Edit ➤ Replace to display the Find and Replace dialog box.

2. Make sure that the Format boxes under the Find What box and the Replace With box don't contain any formatting information. To clear formatting information from the boxes, click in the appropriate box and then click the No Formatting button.

3. With the insertion point in the Find What box, click the Format button and choose Style from the drop-down list. Word will display the Find Style dialog box (see Figure 4.16).

4. Choose the style you want to find from the Find What Style list, then click the OK button to return to the Find and Replace dialog box. The area underneath the Find What box will display the style you chose.

5. Click in the Replace With box (or press Tab to move the insertion point there), then click the Format button and choose Style once more. Word will display the Replace Style dialog box, which is almost identical to the Find Style dialog box.

FIGURE 4.16

In the Find Style dialog box, choose the style you want Word to find.

6. Choose the replacement style from the Replace With Style list, and then click the OK button to return to the Find and Replace dialog box. The area underneath the Replace With box will display the style you chose.

7. If necessary, choose a search direction from the Search drop-down list.

8. Start the search by clicking the Find Next, Replace, or Replace All buttons. Word will search for the next instance or all instances of the style designated in the Find What dialog box.

TIP

To replace specific words or characters in one style with words or characters in another style, choose the styles as described above and then enter the appropriate text in the Find What box and the Replace With box.

An Example of Using Find and Replace

Once you've mastered them, Find and Replace can seem mundane and unexciting, and it's easy to forget how useful they can be. For example, by simply switching macro recording on and then performing a series of Find and Replace operations, you can completely reformat a document. Suppose you often need to reformat information that you receive in text format (e.g., .txt files or information people helpfully dump into e-mail messages instead of sending them as attachments); you may find the vigor of Word's AutoFormat feature (which was presented earlier in this chapter) distressing, and therefore prefer to develop a custom alternative.

Consider the following brief excerpt from a text file, in which the ellipses indicate more of the same:

```
Status Report from Pensacola Office¶
¶
¶
 Here are the highlights from this week:¶
¶
 o Sales increase of $4000¶
¶
 o New personnel manager hired¶
 ... ¶
¶
1. Sales Increase¶
==================================================¶
¶
 This week's surge in sales was driven by a¶
 breakthrough in accounts in the farming area. ¶
 ... ¶
¶
2. New Personnel Manager
==================================================¶
```

As you can see, this report contains several issues:

- You need to remove the extra paragraphs used for spacing.

- You need to remove the paragraphs that are, in fact, just line breaks.

- You need to replace the text-based formatting with Word formatting. For example, you need to replace the lines of equal signs used to denote the subheadings with Word styles to mark the headings themselves.

You could approach reformatting a report such as this as follows:

1. Select the whole document and apply Body Text style (or your favorite text style) to give yourself a base to build on.

2. Tag the subheadings by replacing ={2,} (two or more equal signs) with **Heading2** or another unique text string. Select the Use Wildcards check box in the Find and Replace dialog box to do this.

3. Tag the bulleted lists by replacing two spaces, an **o**, and another space with **BulletedList** or another unique text string. Clear the Use Wildcards check box for this replace.

4. Replace **^p^p** (two paragraph marks together; i.e., a real paragraph, as opposed to a line break) with **!realpara!** or some other phrase you can be sure won't appear in the rest of the text.

5. Replace **^p** (the remaining paragraph marks, which are really plain old line breaks) with a space.

6. Replace two spaces with one space (to get rid of any extra spaces inserted in the previous step).

7. Replace **!realpara!** with **^p** to restore all of the real paragraph breaks that the document should contain.

8. Replace the **BulletedList** text string with List Bullet style to create a bulleted list.

9. Replace the **BulletedList** text string with nothing to remove it from the document now that the style is safely applied.

10. Replace **Heading2** with the Heading 2 style to apply the style to the sub-headings and the text string paragraphs that were originally the lines of equal signs.

11. Replace the **Heading2** text string with nothing to remove it from the document now that the style is safely applied.

12. Apply Heading 1 style to the first paragraph.

A twelve-step program like this takes a while to slog through by hand, but for a long report it's substantially easier than manually formatting paragraph by paragraph—and when you create a macro to run the whole procedure for you, you can perform the whole operation at the touch of a button.

So—four chapters of relentless drilling on the basics of Word, much of it on features not immediately related to macros. I'll bet you're itching to start recording macros. So am I. Turn the page, and we'll get down to it.

PART II

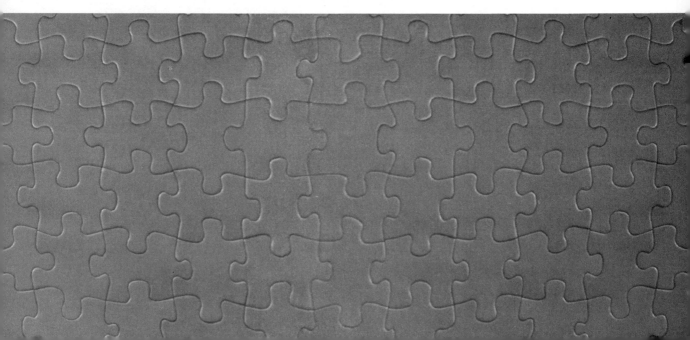

The Tools for
Automating Word

CHAPTER
FIVE

5

Recording and Editing Macros

In this chapter, we'll look at the easiest way of getting started with Word's macros and Visual Basic for Applications: recording simple macros using Word's built-in macro recorder. By recording macros, not only can you automate straightforward but tediously repetitive tasks and speed your regular work in Word, but you can also build the basis of a macro that you can then edit to give it more flexibility and power. After we look at recording a macro, we'll examine the tools that Word provides for editing recorded macros—and for writing macros from scratch.

What Are Macros?

A macro is a sequence of commands that you can repeat at will by using a single command or by setting the macro to run automatically. For example, you might create a macro to automate basic formatting tasks on a type of document you regularly receive in an inappropriate format.

In Word, you can create macros either by turning on Word's macro recorder and performing the sequence of actions you want the macro to contain, or by opening the Visual Basic Editor and typing in the commands yourself. You can also compromise by recording the basic sequence of actions, and then opening the macro and editing any inappropriate actions out of it so they're not repeated ad nauseam every time you run the macro. While editing the macro, you can add other actions one by one as needed; you can also add control structures, such as message boxes, input boxes, and dialog boxes, so that users of the macro can make decisions and choose options for how to run it.

Once you've created a macro, you can assign it to a menu item, a key combination, or a toolbar button and run it at any time. You can even create macros that run automatically when you start Word (for example, to customize your screen preferences or to present a menu of documents to work on); when you exit Word; or when you start a new document, open a document, or close a document.

Uses for Macros

There are any number of uses for macros, as you'll see throughout the rest of this book. You can create anything from a simple macro that applies intricate formatting to a word (bold, strikethrough, Abadi MT Condensed Light font, 14 points, magenta) without changing its style, all the way to an incredibly complex macro that draws information from three corporate databases every morning, adds in stock prices downloaded from the Dow Jones online service, formats all of this information attractively in your daily choice of five formats, and e-mails it to a distribution list of grateful recipients. As you can imagine, writing this second macro would be a much more complicated process than creating the first one—but far more rewarding.

Recording Macros

Recording a macro is by far the easiest way to create a macro. You simply switch on the macro recorder, assign a method for running the macro (a toolbar button, a menu item, or a key combination), perform the actions you want in the macro, and then switch the macro recorder off. As you perform the actions, Word records them as instructions—*code*—in the VBA programming language. Once you've finished recording the macro, you can view the code in the Visual Basic Editor, and change it if necessary; but if the code works perfectly as you recorded it, you never even have to look at it—you can simply run the macro at any time by choosing the toolbar button, menu item, or key combination you assigned to it.

Starting the Macro Recorder

To start the macro recorder, double-click the REC indicator on the status bar. Word will display the Record Macro dialog box, as shown in Figure 5.1.

FIGURE 5.1

In the Record Macro dialog box, enter a name for the macro you're about to record, and give it an illuminating write-up in the Description box.

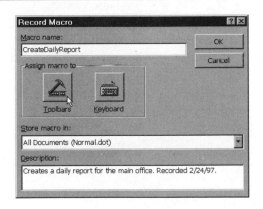

Naming the Macro

Enter a name for the new macro in the Macro Name text box. The macro name can be up to 80 characters long and can contain both letters and numbers, but it must start with a letter. It cannot contain spaces, punctuation, or special characters (such as ! or *), though underscores are allowed.

> **NOTE**   If you type a space or a forbidden character in the Record Macro Name text box, Word won't do anything to stop you—unlike previous versions of Word, in which this dialog box was smart enough to dim the OK button to keep you from proceeding if you tried to enter a macro name that wouldn't work. But as soon as you click the OK button to proceed, VBA will stop you with an Illegal Procedure Name error.

Enter a description for the macro in the Description box. This description is to help you (and anyone you share the macro with) identify the macro. If you want to restrict the macro to just the current template, choose that template from the Store Macro In drop-down list. If you want the macro to be available no matter which template you're working in, make sure the default setting, All Documents (Normal.dot), appears in the Store Macro In drop-down list box.

Assigning a Way to Run the Macro

Next, click the Toolbars button or the Keyboard button in the Assign Macro To group box.

- If you choose Toolbars, Word will display the Customize dialog box (see Figure 5.2) with the Commands tab displayed and Macros selected in the Categories list box. Click the macro's name in the Commands list box and drag it to any convenient toolbar or to the menu bar. Word will add a button or menu item for the macro, giving it the macro's full and unappealing name, such as **NORMAL.NEWMACROS.CREATEDAILYREPORT**. (This name consists of the template's name, the name of the module in which the macro is stored, and finally the macro's name.) You can now rename the button or menu item by right-clicking it and entering a more attractive and descriptive

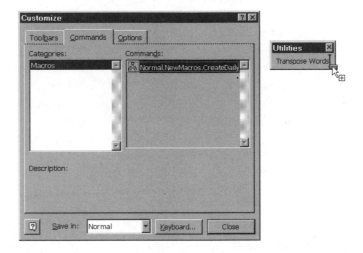

FIGURE 5.2

Choose a way to run the macro in the Customize dialog box.

(and probably shorter) name in the Name box that appears. To assign an access key to an item, put an ampersand (&) before the character that you want to use as the access key. Click the Close button to close the Customize dialog box.

NOTE

The access key does not have to be unique, but it's usually easiest if it is. If multiple menus or commands share the same access key, Word will select the first of them the first time you press the access key; you can then press the Enter key to display that menu or run that command, or you can press the access key again to access the next item associated with that key. For example, if you assign the access key T to the button for a Transpose_Word macro, Word will select the Tools menu (unless you have removed it) the first time you press Alt+T, and the Transpose _Word button the second time you press Alt+T.

TIP

Two points to keep in mind: First, the menu item name or button name for a macro doesn't have to bear any relation to the macro's name. Second, you can also create new toolbars and new menus as you need them. We'll look at this option briefly a little later in this chapter.

- If you choose Keyboard, Word will display the Customize Keyboard dialog box (see Figure 5.3). Place the insertion point in the Press New Shortcut Key box and then press the key combination you want. A key combination can be any one of the following: Alt plus either a regular key not used as a menu access key, or a function key; Ctrl plus a regular key or a function key; Shift plus a function key; Ctrl+Alt, Ctrl+Shift, Alt+Shift, or even Ctrl+Alt+Shift (for special occasions) plus a regular key or function key. Check the Current Keys list box to make sure the key combination you chose isn't already in use (if it is, press Backspace and press another combination), and then click the Assign button. Click the Close button to close the Customize Keyboard dialog box.

> **NOTE**
>
> While it's usually convenient to assign a toolbar button, menu item, or key combination to a macro when you start recording it, it isn't mandatory. You can avoid doing so by clicking the Close button in the Record Macro dialog box instead of the Toolbars button or the Keyboard button. You'll be able to run the macro from the Macros dialog box, as you'll see later in the chapter, or you can assign it a toolbar button, menu item, or key combination at any point after recording it.

FIGURE 5.3

Set a shortcut key combination for the macro in the Customize Keyboard dialog box.

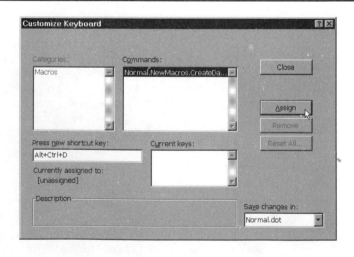

When you dismiss the Customize dialog box, the Customize Keyboard dialog box, or (if you chose to record a macro without assigning a custom way of running it) the Record Macro dialog box, Word will be ready to start recording the

 macro. You'll see Word display the Stop Recording toolbar (usually undocked in the upper-left corner of the screen, unless you or someone else has already dragged it to another location) and add a cassette-tape icon to the mouse pointer to remind you that you're recording. In case you miss these hints, the REC indicator in the status bar will be black.

Recording the Actions in the Macro

Now record the sequence of actions you want to immortalize. You can use the mouse to select items from menus and toolbars, and to make choices in dialog boxes, but not to select items within a document window—to select items in a document window, you must use the keyboard.

NOTE When you make choices in a dialog box—for example, the Paragraph dialog box—Word records the current settings for *all* the options on that tab of the dialog box when you click the OK button. So when you make a change to, say, the left indentation of a paragraph, Word will record all the other settings on the Indents and Spacing tab as well (Alignment, Before and After spacing, and so forth). You can, however, edit these out later if you don't want them.

To perform any actions that you don't want recorded, you can pause the macro recorder at any time by clicking the Pause Recording button on the Stop Recording toolbar. Click the Pause Recording button again to resume recording.

 To stop recording, click the Stop Recording button on the Stop Recording toolbar.

Word has now recorded your macro and assigned it to the control you chose.

Running a Macro

To run a macro, either click the toolbar button, choose the menu item, or press the key combination you assigned to it.

If you chose not to assign a button, menu item, or key combination (perhaps because you have too many macros, as I do), you can run a macro by choosing Tools ➤ Macro ➤ Macros to display the Macros dialog box, selecting the macro from the Macro Name list, and clicking the Run button. You can also run a macro from within the Visual Basic Editor, as you'll see shortly.

TIP   To stop a macro you've started running, press Ctrl+Break (Break is usually written on the front side of the Pause key). Visual Basic will display an annoyed dialog box telling you that "Code execution has been interrupted." Click the End button to dismiss this dialog box.

Recording a Sample Macro: Transpose_Word_Right

In this section, we'll quickly record a sample macro that we can work with throughout the rest of the chapter. This macro simply selects the current word, cuts it, moves the insertion point one word to the right, and pastes the word back in. This is a straightforward sequence of actions that we'll later view and edit in the Visual Basic Editor.

First, open up a new document in Word and enter a line or two of text. It doesn't have to say anything in particular, but it does need several words in a row (with spaces between them). Then place the insertion point in a word that has another word to the right of it, and follow these steps:

1. Start the process of recording the macro by double-clicking the REC indicator on the status bar or by choosing Tools ➤ Macro ➤ Record Macro. Either way, Word will display the Record Macro dialog box.

2. In the Macro Name text box, enter **Transpose_Word_Right**.

3. In the Store Macro In drop-down list, make sure All Documents (Normal .dot) is selected, unless you're sure you want to assign the macro to a different template. (In this example, I'll assume that the macro is in Normal.dot and that you'll take care of the consequences if you put it elsewhere.)

4. In the Description box, enter a description for the macro. The Description box will probably be showing something like "Macro recorded 4/1/97 by Joanna Bermudez," which is Word's best attempt to help you identify the macro later on when you've recorded four dozen macros with similar names. My advice is to be a little more explicit here and enter something like **Transposes the current word with the word to its right. Created 4/1/97 by Joanna Bermudez.**

TIP

> You can change the description for a macro later on, either in the Macros dialog box or in the Visual Basic Editor, but it's a good idea to start by entering an appropriate description when you're recording a macro. If you put off describing the macro until after you've finished creating it, you're apt to forget and eventually end up with dozens of macros bearing names that were clear as the light of noon when you created them but which now give little clue as to their function.

5. Now assign a method of running the macro as described in the previous section. Create a toolbar button or a menu item (or both), or assign a keyboard shortcut. (Which method you choose is strictly a matter of personal preference.)

6. When you've clicked the Close button to dismiss the Customize dialog box or the Customize Keyboard dialog box (or clicked the OK button to dismiss the Record Macro dialog box if you chose not to assign a way of running the macro), you're ready to record the macro. You should be seeing the Stop Recording toolbar on-screen (usually with its title truncated to "Stop R" because it only contains two buttons), and the mouse pointer should have a little icon of a cassette tape attached to it.

7. Now record the actions for the macro:

   a. With the insertion point in the word that you want to move, use the Extend Selection feature (discussed in Chapter 2) to select the word by pressing the F8 key twice. The EXT indicator on the status bar will be darkened to show that it's turned on.

   b. Press the Cancel key to cancel Extend mode. The EXT indicator on the status bar will go off.

   c. Press Shift+Delete or Ctrl+X to cut the selected word to the Clipboard. (You could also click the Cut button or choose Edit ➤ Cut if you preferred.)

   d. The insertion point will now be at the beginning of the word that was after the word you just cut. Press Ctrl+→ to move the insertion point right by one word.

   e. Press Shift+Insert or Ctrl+V to paste in the cut word from the Clipboard. (Again, you could click the Paste button instead, or you could choose Edit ➤ Paste.)

   f. Press Ctrl+← to move the insertion point one word back to the left. (This is an extra instruction that we're recording for later use when we edit the macro.)

8. Click the Stop Recording button on the Stop Recording toolbar to stop recording the macro.

That was pretty painless, but as you might imagine, the problem with straightforward recorded macros is that they are limited in what they can do—for example, you can't display a message box or dialog box. You can fix this by editing a macro—more accurately, editing the code that makes up a macro—in the Visual Basic Editor. But before we start exploring the Visual Basic Editor, let's take a quick detour through some of the terms you'll need to know.

The VBA Language

In this section, we'll blaze through a few elements of the Visual Basic for Applications programming language, so that you don't get lost in a welter of statements, keywords, expressions, operators, variables, and constants. Don't worry if these terms seem confusing at first. My goal in the next few chapters is to get you working with some of the more useful constructions in VBA without grinding through a couple hundred pages of theory. Here, though, I'm just going to present some definitions; rest assured that they'll make much more sense when we begin using them in context a little farther on.

Procedures

A *procedure* in VBA is a named unit of code, such as a function (which I'll discuss next) or a macro, that contains a sequence of statements to be executed as a group. For example, VBA contains a function named `Left`, which returns the left portion of a text string that you specify. The name simply gives you a way to refer to the procedure.

All executable code in VBA has to be contained in a procedure—if it isn't, VBA cannot execute it and throws an error. Procedures are contained within modules, which in turn are contained within documents or templates.

Functions

A *function* in VBA is a type of complete procedure designed to perform a specific task. For example, the `Left` function I just mentioned returns the left part of a text string, and its sibling the `Right` function returns the right part of a text string. Each function has a clear task that you use it for, and it doesn't do anything else. To take a ridiculous example, you can't use the `Left` function to print a document or make characters boldface—for those you need to use the appropriate functions.

Word comes with a plethora of built-in functions, but you can also create your own. When you do, you begin them with a `Function` statement and end them with an `End Function` statement.

Statements

A *statement* is a unit of code that describes an action, defines an item, or gives the value of a variable. VBA usually has one statement per line of code, though you can put more than one statement on a line by separating them with colons. You can also break a line of code onto a second line by using a line-continuation character—an underscore (_)—to make it easier to read. This is strictly for visual convenience; VBA still reads both lines as a single line of code.

Getting Help on Visual Basic for Applications

The Visual Basic Editor offers comprehensive help on the Visual Basic for Applications programming language. To view it, choose Help ➤ Microsoft Visual Basic Help, or choose Help ➤ Contents and Index. Most of the statements and functions have examples, which can be particularly helpful when creating and troubleshooting your macros.

If your computer doesn't offer you any help on VBA, whoever installed Word (or Office) on your computer might not have installed the relevant files (perhaps to save space). If that's the case, you'll need to dig out your CD of Word (or Office) and run the Setup program again to install them.

Keywords

A *keyword* is simply a word defined as part of the VBA language—for example, the name of a statement or of a function.

Expressions

An *expression* consists of keywords, operators, variables, and constants put together to produce a string, number, or object. For example, you could use an expression to run a calculation or to compare one variable against another.

Operators

An *operator* is an item used for comparing, combining, or otherwise working with values in an expression. VBA has *arithmetic operators* (such as + and -) for performing mathematical calculations, *comparison operators* (such as < and >, less than and greater than, respectively) for comparing values, *concatenation operators* (& and +, for joining two strings together), and *logical operators* (such as And, Not, and Or) for building logical structures.

Variables

A *variable* is a location in memory set aside for storing a piece of information that can be changed while a procedure is running. For example, if you needed the user to input their name via an input box or a dialog box, you would typically store the name in a variable so that you could work with it in the procedure.

You can declare variables either explicitly or implicitly. In the next few chapters, we'll use implicit variable declarations to keep things simple. Later on, we'll look at how to use explicit variable declarations to make your code faster and easier to read.

Strings

A *string* is a type of variable used for storing text characters (as opposed to, say, numbers). For example, if you had the user enter their name in an input box, you could store it in a string, because a name is a sequence of text characters.

Constants

A *constant* is a named item that keeps a constant value while a program is executing. For example, as you'll see in the next chapter, message boxes use constants for the buttons, and you use those constants to see which button was clicked in a message box.

Arguments

An *argument* is a constant, a variable, or an expression that you pass to a procedure. Some arguments are required; others are optional.

Objects

VBA thinks of Word as consisting of a series of *objects*. A document is an object, as is a paragraph or a table. Even a single character is an object. Most of the actions you can take in VBA involve manipulating objects. For example, you can close the active document by using the `Close` method on the `ActiveDocument` object:

```
ActiveDocument.Close
```

Collections

A *collection* is simply an object that contains several other objects. For example, the `Documents` collection contains all the open documents, each of which is itself an object. You could close all open documents by using the `Close` method on the `Documents` collection:

```
Documents.Close
```

Properties

Each object has a number of *properties*. For example, a document has properties such as its title, its subject, and its author, which you can set through the Properties dialog box that pops up by default the first time you save each document. Likewise, a single character has various properties, such as its font, font size, and various types of emphasis (bold, italic, strikethrough, etc.).

Methods

A *method* is an action that you can perform with an object. Different objects have different methods associated with them. For example, the `Document` object has the following methods associated with it:

- The `Activate` method activates the document (the equivalent of selecting the document's window with the keyboard or mouse).

- The `Close` method closes the document (the equivalent of choosing File ➤ Close).

- The `Save` method saves the document (the equivalent of choosing File ➤ Save).

- The `SaveAs` method saves the document under a specified name (the equivalent of choosing File ➤ Save As).

So that's a brief introduction to the VBA vocabulary. Now let's turn to the area in which you'll be working with all these mysterious pieces of code: the Visual Basic Editor.

The Visual Basic Editor

Once you've recorded a macro, you can run it as described earlier in the chapter. If the macro doesn't work as you expected it to, you can open it in the Visual Basic Editor and change it. As you'll see later in this chapter, you can also create macros directly in the Visual Basic Editor.

In this section, we'll look at how to open the Visual Basic Editor and navigate to the macro you just created. We'll then examine the various parts of the Visual Basic Editor and what they do. Once we've been through those, the next section will cover how to make some minor changes to the macro you recorded and how to create a second macro from it.

Opening the Visual Basic Editor

There are a couple of ways to open the Visual Basic Editor: directly, by choosing Tools ➤ Macro ➤ Visual Basic Editor and then navigating to the module containing the macro you want to work with; or indirectly, by choosing the macro to edit in the Macros dialog box, which opens the Visual Basic Editor with that macro displayed. (If the Visual Basic Editor is not already running, Word starts it and switches to it; if the Visual Basic Editor is running, Word simply switches to it.)

To open the Visual Basic Editor directly:

1. Choose Tools ➤ Macro ➤ Visual Basic Editor to start the Visual Basic Editor. As you'll see in a moment, the Visual Basic Editor contains a number of different windows and can have a variety of configurations. Figure 5.4 shows the type of configuration that you're likely to see when you open it up. (If you're seeing something different—for example, apparently lacking some of the windows shown here—stay with me; we'll get to that shortly.)

2. In the Project Explorer window in the top-left corner of the Visual Basic Editor, expand the object for the current template (e.g., Normal, if you're working in the Normal.dot global template) by clicking the + sign to the left of its name.

   This works just like a standard Windows 95 Explorer or Windows NT Explorer tree: the root objects are the Normal template, the template for the current document (if it's attached to a template other than Normal.dot), and the current document. Each of these contains a number of folders for Microsoft Word Objects, Forms, Modules, and References.

FIGURE 5.4

The Visual Basic Editor.

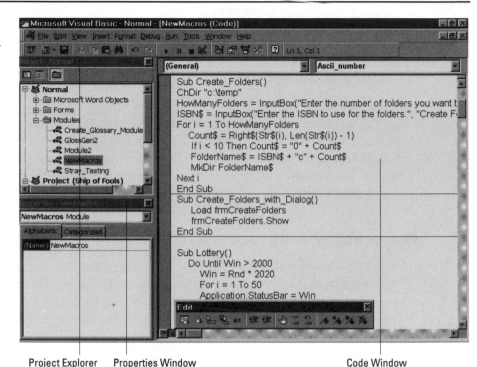

Project Explorer   Properties Window   Code Window

In the example below, Normal.dot is identified as **Normal** and the

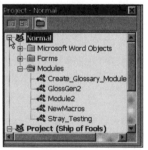

current document is identified as **Project (Ship of Fools)**. If the current document were attached to a template other than Normal.dot, the current template would be identified as **TemplateProject** (*templatename*).

3.   Expand the Modules object and double-click the module that contains the macro. By default, Word puts macros that you create into a module named NewMacros. Word will display the contents of the module in the code window on the right side of the Visual Basic Editor. In that window, select the macro you want to edit (in this case, **Transpose_Word_Right**) from the Procedure drop-down list (see Figure 5.5); or use the scroll bar to scroll to the macro you want to edit, which will be identified by the word "Sub",

the name you gave it, and a pair of parentheses—in this case, **Sub Transpose_Word_Right()**.

That's one way to open a macro in the Visual Basic Editor; now I'll show you an even easier way.

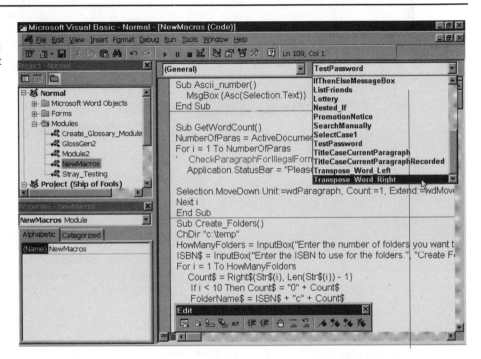

Procedure Drop-Down List

Opening the Visual Basic Editor with a Macro Selected

Instead of opening the Visual Basic Editor and then navigating to the module containing the macro you want to work with, you can also open the Visual Basic Editor with a specified macro you've already created (or someone else has already created) displayed and ready to work on:

1. Choose Tools ➤ Macro ➤ Macros to display the Macros dialog box.

2. Select the macro you want to edit (in this case, Transpose_Word_Right) and click the Edit button; this will open the Visual Basic Editor with the macro displayed and ready for editing (see Figure 5.6).

FIGURE 5.6

The Visual Basic Editor with the Transpose_ Word_Right macro open in the code window.

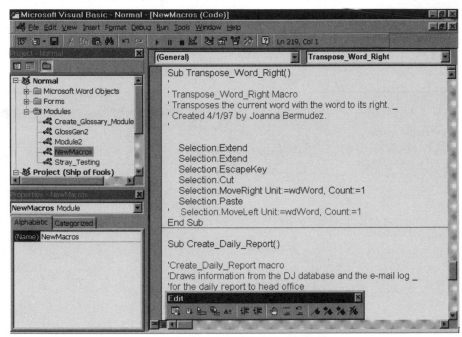

Now that you've got the `Transpose_Word_Right` macro open in the Visual Basic Editor, let's look at the component pieces of the Visual Basic Editor and what they do.

Components of the Visual Basic Editor

If you've spent any time working with macros in earlier versions of Word, you'll find a number of differences in the Visual Basic Editor that take some getting used to. Whereas Word versions through Word 95 used a macro-editing window within the Word window, the Visual Basic Editor runs as a separate application window. It has its own Taskbar button so that you can switch to it easily, and if it misbehaves, you can close it down from the Tasklist as you would any errant Windows application. (Be warned, though, that the Visual Basic Editor is sharing the same memory space as Word, so if you crash the Visual Basic Editor, it's wise to close and restart Word as well.)

Running the Visual Basic Editor as a separate application window removes a number of problems that the macro-editing window caused in previous versions of Word. For example, it was easy in previous versions of Word to accidentally change the active window from a Word document that the macro was operating on to the macro-editing window, so that the macro was trying to perform actions upon itself—usually with less than happy results. The new setup not only prevents this but also makes it easier to see both how the code is executing and how the macro will appear to the user (who will see the results of the macro in the Word window without seeing the Visual Basic Editor window). Another advantage of the Visual Basic Editor is that you can more easily switch from module to module to work with the code you need, rather than having to open a number of macro windows.

The price to pay for these new advantages of the Visual Basic Editor is that it is more complex than the macro-editing window in Word and has a steep learning curve. In this section, I'll go through the components of the Visual Basic Editor and discuss how they work. Again, some of this discussion may seem intimidating at first, but will make more sense as we begin actually working with code.

The Visual Basic Editor Toolbars

The Visual Basic Editor provides four toolbars, which you can display and hide by right-clicking anywhere in the menu bar or in any displayed toolbar and choosing the name of the toolbar from the context menu of toolbars; alternatively, you can choose View ➤ Toolbars and make your selection from the Toolbars submenu.

- The Standard toolbar (see Figure 5.7) provides commands for working with and running macros. We'll look at some of these commands in this chapter and others in coming chapters.

  The **View Microsoft Word** button displays Microsoft Word.

  The **Insert** *Item* button inserts the currently selected item—Userform, Module, Class Module, or Procedure. You can click the drop-down button and select a different item from the drop-down list.

  The **Save** *Project* button (in whose name *Project* will be the name of the current project) saves the current project and all code in it.

  The **Cut**, **Copy**, and **Paste** buttons work as usual.

  The **Find** button displays the Find dialog box for finding and replacing text.

FIGURE 5.7

Use the buttons on the Standard toolbar for working with macros.

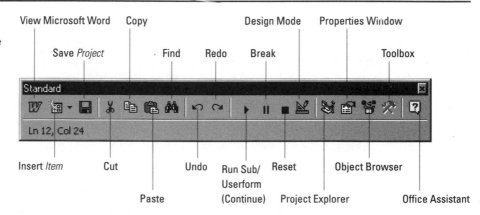

The **Undo** and **Redo** buttons work as usual.

The **Run Sub/Userform** button (which changes into the **Continue** button) starts (or restarts) the current procedure running. (If no procedure is current, clicking this button displays the Macros dialog box for you to choose the macro to run.)

The **Break** button pauses the currently executing procedure.

The **Reset** button stops the current procedure and clears all its variables.

The **Design Mode** button toggles Design mode on and off.

The **Project Explorer** button displays the Project Explorer window (if it is not displayed) and activates it.

The **Properties Window** button displays the Properties window (if it is not displayed) and activates it.

The **Object Browser** button displays the Object Browser (if it is not displayed) and activates it.

The **Toolbox** button displays or hides the Toolbox when it is available.

The **Office Assistant** button starts the Office Assistant.

- The Edit toolbar (see Figure 5.8) provides more commands for running and editing macros.

FIGURE 5.8

Use the buttons on the Edit toolbar for running and editing macros.

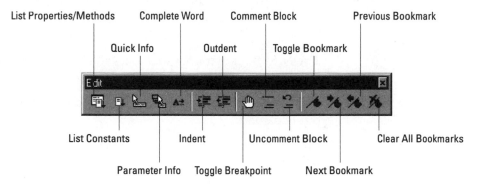

The **List Properties/Methods** button displays the pop-up List Properties/Methods list box when it is available.

The **List Constants** button displays the pop-up List Constants list box when it is available.

The **Quick Info** button displays information about the code at which the insertion point is currently located.

The **Parameter Info** button displays pop-up information about the parameter at which the insertion point is currently located.

The **Complete Word** button completes the word the insertion point is currently located in.

The **Indent** and **Outdent** buttons indent and un-indent the current line of code or the currently selected lines.

The **Toggle Breakpoint** button toggles on and off a breakpoint at the current line.

The **Comment Block** button "comments out" the current line or selected lines by putting an apostrophe at the beginning of the line. (The apostrophe tells VBA that this line is a comment, which means that VBA will not try to execute it. VBA displays comment lines in a different color so that you can readily identify them.)

The **Uncomment Block** button removes commenting from the current line or selected lines.

The **Toggle Bookmark** button adds a bookmark to the current line (if it doesn't already have one) or removes a bookmark if the line already has one.

The **Next Bookmark** button moves the insertion point to the next bookmark.

The **Previous Bookmark** button moves the insertion point to the previous bookmark.

The **Clear All Bookmarks** button removes all bookmarks from the current project.

- The Debug toolbar contains commands for running and debugging your macros. We'll take a closer look at this toolbar in Chapter 16.

- The Userform toolbar contains buttons for working with userforms (such as dialog boxes). We'll start working with this toolbar in Chapter 7.

The Project Explorer

The Project Explorer (shown in Figure 5.9) provides a way of navigating among the various components in the Visual Basic Editor. Each Word project can contain the following elements:

- userforms (forms that make up part of the Word user interface, such as a custom dialog box)

- modules containing macros

- references to other Word documents

Each open document and template is considered a project and is displayed as a root in the project tree.

You navigate the Project Explorer in the same way that you navigate the Windows Explorer or Windows NT Explorer tree: click the boxed plus sign to the left of a project item to expand the view and display the items contained within the project; click the resulting boxed minus sign to collapse the view and hide the items again. Double-click a module name to display the module's code in the code window; double-click a userform name to display the userform.

FIGURE 5.9

Use the Project Explorer
to navigate to the module
you want to work with.

You can display the Project Explorer by choosing View ➤ Project Explorer or by pressing Ctrl+R. To close the Project Explorer, click its close button. Because the Project Explorer provides fast and efficient navigation among the various elements of your VBA projects, it's usually easiest to keep it displayed unless you're desperately short of screen space.

The Object Browser

The Visual Basic Editor provides a full Object Browser for working with objects in VBA. We'll look at the Object Browser in detail when we examine the Word object model in Chapter 11, but in the meantime, take a quick look at Figure 5.10; the Document object is selected in the left-hand panel, and its list of properties is displayed in the right-hand panel. You'll find that a number of these properties

FIGURE 5.10

The Object Browser
provides a quick way to
look up objects and their
properties. Here, you
can see the properties
contained in the
Document object.

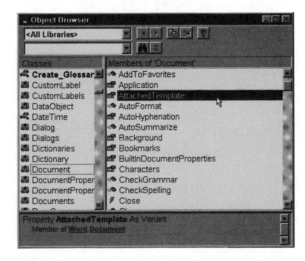

immediately make sense from your knowledge of Word documents. For example, the `AttachedTemplate` property tells you which template the document is currently attached to. Likewise, the `Bookmarks` property contains information on all the bookmarks in the document. The property information is displayed at the bottom of the Object Browser.

The Code Window

The Visual Basic Editor's code window is where you'll do most of the actual work of creating and editing your macros. The Visual Basic Editor provides a code window for each open project, for each document section within the project that can contain code, and for each code module and userform in the project. Each code window is identified by the project name, the name of the module within the project, and the word "Code" in parentheses. Figure 5.11 shows the Visual Basic Editor code window with the `Transpose_Word_Right` macro open in it.

FIGURE 5.11

The code window is where you create and edit your macros.

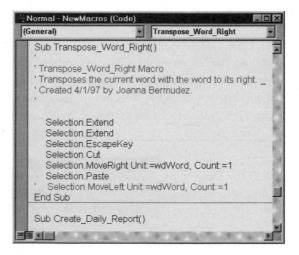

```
Normal - NewMacros (Code)
(General)                    Transpose_Word_Right
Sub Transpose_Word_Right()

' Transpose_Word_Right Macro
' Transposes the current word with the word to its right. _
' Created 4/1/97 by Joanna Bermudez.


    Selection.Extend
    Selection.Extend
    Selection.EscapeKey
    Selection.Cut
    Selection.MoveRight Unit:=wdWord, Count:=1
    Selection.Paste
'   Selection.MoveLeft Unit:=wdWord, Count:=1
End Sub

Sub Create_Daily_Report()
```

The Visual Basic Editor code window provides a half-dozen features for helping you create code efficiently and accurately:

- The **Complete Word** feature completes the word you're typing once you've typed enough letters to distinguish that word from any other. To activate Complete Word, press Ctrl+spacebar or click the Complete Word button on the Edit toolbar.

- The **Quick Info** feature on the Edit toolbar displays syntax information on

the current variable, function, method, statement, or procedure.

- The **List Properties/Methods** feature displays a pop-up list box containing properties and methods for the object you've just typed so that you can quickly complete the expression. List Properties/Methods is switched on by
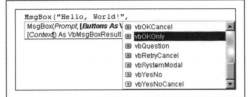
default and will automatically pop up the list box when you type a period within an expression. Select a property or method using either the mouse or the keyboard; enter the property or method into the code either by double-clicking it, by pressing Tab (if you want to continue working on the same line after entering the property or method), or by pressing Enter (if you want to start a new line after entering the property or method).

- The **List Constants** feature displays a pop-up list box containing constants for a property that you've typed so that you can quickly select the constant needed to complete the expression. Again, you can use either the mouse or

keyboard to select the constant, and you can enter the constant by double-clicking it or by pressing Tab (to continue working on the same line) or Enter (to start a new line).

- The **Data Tips** feature displays a screentip containing the value of a variable
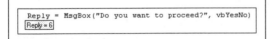
that the mouse pointer moves over when the Visual Basic Editor is in Break mode (a mode that you use for testing and debugging macros).

- The **Margin Indicators** feature lets you quickly set a breakpoint, the next statement, or a bookmark by clicking in the margin of the code window. We'll look at setting breakpoints, setting the next statement, and setting bookmarks later in this book.

Apart from these features, the Visual Basic Editor includes standard Office editing features such as copy and move; cut-and-paste; and drag-and-drop.

Drag-and-drop is particularly useful because you can drag code from one macro or module to another.

The Properties Window

The Visual Basic Editor provides a Properties window that you can use to view the properties of an object in VBA, such as a project (here, a template or a document), a userform (a form that becomes part of the user interface, such as a dialog box), or a control (such as a button or check box in a dialog box). The drop-down list at the top of the Properties window lets you pick the item whose properties you want to view; the Alphabetic tab presents an alphabetic list of the properties in the item, while the Categorized tab presents a list of the properties broken down into categories. Figure 5.12 shows the properties for a relatively straightforward Word document.

FIGURE 5.12

Use the Properties window to view the properties of a project, a userform, or a control.

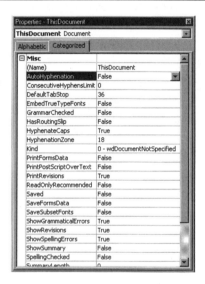

These are a little off-putting to behold at first, but a closer look at Figure 5.12 renders them more familiar. For example, the `Saved` property stores information on whether the document contains unsaved changes; if it does not, this property will be set to `True` (because all the information in the document is saved); if it does contain unsaved changes, this property will be set to `False`. Look through the other properties, and you'll see how their names map to options you'll be familiar with from your use of Word. The `AutoHyphenation` property records whether the Automatically Hyphenate Document check box in the Hyphenate dialog box (Tools ➤ Language ➤ Hyphenation) in Word has been selected (in this case, it hasn't, as indicated by the `False` setting); the `ConsecutiveHyphens-Limit` property records the setting in the Limit Consecutive Hyphens To text box in the same dialog box (here, 0 means that it is set to No Limit, not to zero hyphens in a row). The `HasRoutingSlip` property records whether the document has a routing slip attached to it (for routing the document around a network). And the `Kind` property records whether the document is a regular word document (0 - `wdDocumentNotSpecified`), a letter (1 - `wdDocumentLetter`), or an e-mail message (2 - `wdDocumentEmail`).

To display the Properties window, press F4 or choose View ➤ Properties Window. To change a property, click in the right-hand column and change the value. You'll be able to choose different values depending on the type of property: for a `True`/`False` property, you'll be limited to those two choices in the drop-down list; for a text property such as `Name`, you can enter any valid VBA name.

Choosing Options for the Visual Basic Editor

Like any good Windows application, the Visual Basic Editor lets you customize its look and its actions. To do so, choose Tools ➤ Options to open the Options dialog box and make choices on the four tabs. Figure 5.13 shows the Editor tab.

FIGURE 5.13

The Editor tab of the Options dialog box.

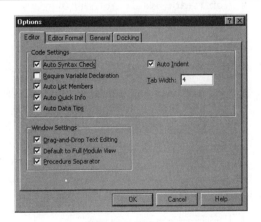

The Editor tab of the Options dialog box includes the following settings:

- **Auto Syntax Check** controls whether VBA automatically checks your syntax as you type expressions. This is usually helpful, because VBA can instantly point out errors that otherwise would have remained unseen until you tried to run or debug your code. But if your style is to flit from one unfinished line of code to another (and ultimately finish all the lines in your own good time), you may want to turn this feature off.

- **Require Variable Declaration** governs whether you declare variables explicitly or implicitly. (We'll look at this in Chapter 10.) For the moment, leave this check box cleared so that VBA does not require you to declare variables explicitly.

- **Auto List Members** controls whether the List Properties/Methods and List Constants features automatically suggest properties, methods, and constants as you work in the code window.

- **Auto Quick Info** controls whether the Quick Info feature automatically displays information as you work in the code window.

- **Auto Data Tips** controls whether the Visual Basic Editor displays screentips when you move the mouse pointer over a variable.

- **Auto Indent** controls whether the Visual Basic Editor automatically indents subsequent lines of code after you've indented a line.

- **Tab Width** sets the number of spaces in a tab. You can adjust this from 1 to 32 spaces.

- **Drag-and-Drop Text Editing** controls whether the Visual Basic Editor supports drag-and-drop. (This is usually a good idea.)

- **Default to Full Module View** controls whether the Visual Basic Editor displays all the macros in one module together in one list or displays them one at a time. If you're working with short macros, you may find the list view useful; for most other purposes, the individual view provides a less cluttered and more workable effect. To switch to individual view, clear this check box, close the Options dialog box, and then open the module you

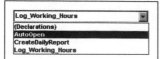

want to work with by choosing it from the Procedure drop-down list (shown here) at the top of the code window. (If you already have the macro displayed in the list view, you'll need to close this window to switch to the individual view.)

- **Procedure Separator** controls whether the Visual Basic Editor displays horizontal lines to separate the macros within a module shown in list view in

the code window. Usually these lines are helpful, providing a quick reference to where one macro ends and the next begins. (If you're using the individual view, this check box is not relevant.)

The Editor Format tab of the Options dialog box (see Figure 5.14) controls how text in the Visual Basic Editor appears.

FIGURE 5.14

The Editor Format tab of the Options dialog box.

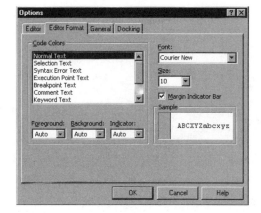

You can change the default colors for various types of text used in macros by choosing any of them (one at a time) in the Code Colors list box and selecting colors from the Foreground, Background, and Indicator drop-down lists. Here's what the choices mean:

- Choosing **Keyword Text** affects the color in which keywords (words recognized as part of the VBA language) are displayed, which accounts for a sizable portion of each macro.

- Choosing **Normal Text** takes care of much of the rest of the text in a typical macro. You'll probably want this to be a normal color (such as black).

- Choosing **Selection Text** affects the color of text that is simply selected (highlighted) text.

- **Syntax Error Text** affects the color VBA uses for offending lines. (By default, this is fire-engine red for ease of finding.)

- Choosing **Execution Point Text** affects the color VBA uses for the line currently being executed in Break mode. You'll usually want this to be highlighted so that you can immediately see the current line.

- Choosing **Breakpoint Text** affects the color in which VBA displays breakpoints (points where execution of the macro is to stop).

- Choosing **Comment Text** affects the color in which your comment lines appear. You may want to change this to emphasize your comments or to make them fade into the background.

- Choosing **Identifier Text** affects the color VBA uses for identifiers.

- Choosing **Bookmark Text** affects the color VBA uses for the bookmarks in your code.

- Choosing **Call Return Text** affects the color VBA uses for calls to other macros.

You can change the font and size of all the text in the code window by using the Font and Size drop-down lists on the Editor Format tab. You can also prevent the display of the margin indicator bar (in which items such as the Next Statement and Breakpoint icons appear) by clearing the Margin Indicator Bar check box. (Usually, these icons are helpful, but removing this bar can slightly increase your viewable-screen real estate.)

Figure 5.15 shows the General tab of the Options dialog box.

The General tab contains several different categories of settings:

- The **Form Grid Settings** control how the Visual Basic Editor handles userforms for items such as dialog boxes. We'll work with userforms to create dialog boxes in Chapter 7.

- The **Notify Before State Loss** check box controls whether the Visual Basic Editor warns you when you're running a module and you try to take an action that will require VBA to reset the values of all variables in the module. We'll look at resetting variables in Chapter 17.

- The **Error Trapping** group box controls how VBA handles errors that occur when you're running code. We'll look at these options in Chapter 17 as well.

FIGURE 5.15

The General tab of the
Options dialog box.

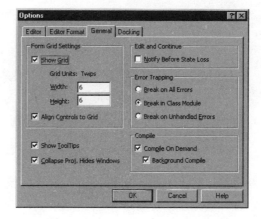

- The **Compile** group box controls when VBA compiles the code for a project. Select the Compile On Demand check box if you want the code to be compiled only as needed; if you do so, you can also select the Background Compile check box to have VBA use idle CPU time to compile the code while the project is not running. We'll thrash through the advantages of compiling code on demand in Chapter 17.

- The **Show ToolTips** check box controls whether the Visual Basic Editor displays ToolTips (a.k.a. screentips) for its toolbar buttons.

- The **Collapse Proj. Hides Windows** check box controls whether the Visual Basic Editor hides the code window and other project windows that you collapse in the Project Explorer.

The Docking tab of the Options dialog box (see Figure 5.16) controls whether the various windows in the Visual Basic Editor are dockable or not—that is, whether they attach automatically to a side of the window when you move them there. Keeping windows dockable usually makes for a more organized interface, but you may find it useful to make the windows undockable so that you can drag them off the edge of the screen as necessary and generally arrange them however makes the most sense to you.

FIGURE 5.16

The Docking tab of the
Options dialog box.

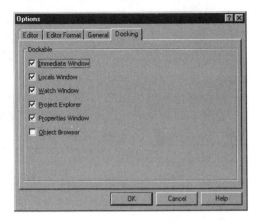

Editing Macros

Now that you've met the components of the Visual Basic Editor, let's take a look at how to apply them. There are three basic reasons for working with macros in the Visual Basic Editor:

- First, to fix any problems in the way a macro you recorded is executing. For example, if you made a misstep when recording the macro, the macro will keep faithfully performing that wrong instruction every time you run it, unless you remove or change the instruction.

- Second, to add further instructions to the macro to make it behave differently (as mentioned earlier). This is a great way to get started with VBA, because by making relatively simple changes to a recorded macro, you can greatly increase its power and flexibility.

- Third, to create new macros by writing them in the Visual Basic Editor instead of recording them. You can write a new macro from scratch or cull parts of an existing macro as appropriate.

The remainder of this book will largely be devoted to these topics. In this section, however, we'll examine some quick methods of detecting problems in your macros, and then we'll edit the `Transpose_Word_Right` macro you recorded earlier in the chapter.

Testing a Macro in the Visual Basic Editor

If a macro fails when you try to run it from the Word window, the quickest way to find out what's going wrong is to open the macro in the Visual Basic Editor and run it by clicking the Run Sub/Userform button on the Standard toolbar. If the macro encounters an error and crashes, Visual Basic for Applications will display an error box on-screen and will select the offending statement in the code window, where you can use the editing tools described in the previous sections to change the statement. (We'll look at full-scale debugging of macros in Chapter 16.)

WARNING Always test your macros on documents (or copies of them) that you don't care about.

Stepping Through a Macro

For subtler problems—say the macro is selecting almost, but not quite, the text you want, and you can't make out which command is superfluous (or plain wrong)— arrange the Visual Basic Editor and Word windows so that you can see them both (for example, by right-clicking in open space on the Windows Taskbar and choosing Tile Windows Horizontally from the context menu). Position the insertion point in a suitable place in the Word window, and click the Visual Basic Editor window to activate it. Then position the insertion point in the macro you want to run, and press F8 to step through the macro command by command (see Figure 5.17). The Visual Basic Editor will highlight each command as it's executed, and you can watch the effect in the Word window so that you can catch errors.

As I mentioned, we'll look at debugging macros in detail in Chapter 16, but in the meantime, you may want to try setting breakpoints and commenting out lines to quickly resolve problems in your macros.

FIGURE 5.17

FIGURE 5.17

To catch something that the macro is doing wrong, arrange the Word and Visual Basic Editor windows so that you can see them both, then step through the macro by pressing the F8 key.

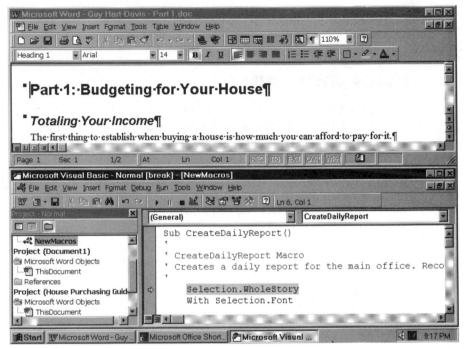

Setting Breakpoints

A breakpoint is a toggle switch you set on a line of code to tell VBA to stop executing the macro there. By using a breakpoint, you can run through fully functional parts of a macro at full speed, without having to go through them instruction by instruction, and then stop them where you want to watch the code execute line by line.

To toggle a breakpoint on or off, right-click in a line of executable code and choose Toggle ➤ Breakpoint from the context menu, or click in a line of executable code and click the Toggle Breakpoint button on the Edit toolbar. Breakpoints appear shaded in brown by default and are designated by a brown circle in the margin indicator bar.

> **NOTE**
> Breakpoints are a debugging tool that you don't want to leave in your code, so the Visual Basic Editor doesn't save them with your code; you have to place them for each editing session.

Commenting Out Lines

By commenting out a line of a macro, you tell VBA not to execute it. Commenting can be a useful technique for removing suspect lines of code from a macro so that you can see if their absence improves the macro.

To comment out the current line or selected lines, click the Comment Block button on the Edit toolbar. The Visual Basic Editor will place an apostrophe at the beginning of each line, which tells it to ignore that line. To uncomment the current line or selected lines, click the Uncomment Block button, and the Visual Basic Editor will remove the apostrophe from those lines.

> **NOTE**
> Two other points: First, you can also enter or delete comment apostrophes manually if you prefer. Second, you can use comment lines at any point in the macro to annotate or explain what the code is doing (or what it is supposed to be doing).

Editing the Transpose_Word_Right Macro

Now let's edit the `Transpose_Word_Right` macro and then use it to build another macro. To begin, open the macro in the Visual Basic Editor as described earlier in the chapter. In the code window, you should be seeing code something like this (without the numbers, which I've added to help easily identify the lines of the macro):

```
1.  Sub Transpose_Word_Right()
2.  '
3.  ' Transpose_Word_Right Macro
4.  ' Transposes the current word with the word to its right. _
```

```
 5.  ' Created 4/1/97 by Joanna Bermudez.
 6.  '
 7.       Selection.Extend
 8.       Selection.Extend
 9.       Selection.EscapeKey
10.       Selection.Cut
11.       Selection.MoveRight Unit:=wdWord, Count:=1
12.       Selection.Paste
13.       Selection.MoveLeft Unit:=wdWord, Count:=1
14.  End Sub
```

Here's what we've got:

- Line 1 starts the macro with the `Sub Transpose_Word_Right()` statement, and line 14 ends the macro with the `End Sub` statement. The `Sub` and `End Sub` lines mark the beginning and end of the macro procedure.

- Lines 2 and 6 are blank comment lines that the Visual Basic Editor puts in to make your macro easier to read. You can have any number of blank lines or blank comment lines in a macro to help separate statements into groups.

- Lines 3 through 5 are comment lines that contain the name of the macro and its description.

- Line 7 records the first keypress on the F8 key, which starts Extend mode.

- Line 8 records the second keypress on the F8 key, which continues Extend mode and selects the current word.

- Line 9 records the keypress on the Escape key, which cancels Extend mode.

- Line 10 records the Cut command, which cuts the selection (in this case, the selected word) to the Clipboard.

- Line 11 records the Ctrl+→ command, which moves the insertion point one word to the right.

- Line 12 records the Paste command, which pastes the selection into the document at the current position of the insertion point.

- Line 13 records the Ctrl+← command, which moves the insertion point one word to the right.

First, let's comment out line 13, which we recorded so that we could build a `Transpose_Word_Left` macro from this one. Just enter an apostrophe at the beginning of the line—anywhere before the start of the instruction is fine, but you may find it easiest to enter the apostrophe in the leftmost column so that it's clearly visible:

```
'    Selection.MoveLeft Unit:=wdWord, Count:=1
```

Alternatively, click anywhere in line 13 and then click the Comment Block button to have the Visual Basic Editor enter the apostrophe for you.

When you move the insertion point out of that line, VBA will check it, identify it as a comment line, and change its color to the color currently set for comment text. When you run the macro, VBA will now ignore this line.

Stepping through the Transpose_Word_Right Macro

Try stepping through this macro in Break mode using the F8 key. First, arrange your screen so that you can see both the Word window and the Visual Basic Editor window (for example, by right-clicking the Taskbar and choosing Horizontally or Vertically from the context menu). Then activate the Visual Basic Editor and click to place the insertion point in the `Transpose_Word_Right` macro in the code window. Press the F8 key to step through the code one active line at a time (i.e., skipping the blank lines and comment lines). VBA will high-light the current statement, and you'll see the actions taking place in the Word window.

The Visual Basic Editor will switch off Break mode when it reaches the end of the macro (in this case, when it executes the `End Sub` statement in line 14), but you can also exit Break mode at any time by clicking the Reset button on the Standard toolbar or the Debug toolbar.

Running the Transpose_Word_Right Macro

If stepping through the macro works fine, you may also want to run it from the Visual Basic Editor by clicking the Run Sub/Userform button on the Edit toolbar or the Debug toolbar. You can also click this button (which will then be identified as Continue) from Break mode to run a macro beginning from the instruction that you've reached by stepping through with the F8 key.

Creating a Transpose_Word_Left Macro

Now, create a `Transpose_Word_Left` macro by making minor adjustments to the `Transpose_Word_Right` macro:

1. In the code window, select all the code for the `Transpose_Word_Right` macro, from the `Sub Transpose_Word_Right()` line to the `End Sub` line. As in most any Windows application, you can select using the mouse, the keyboard, or a combination of the two.

2. Copy the code by issuing a Copy command (for example, by right-clicking and choosing Copy from the context menu, or by pressing Ctrl+C).

3. Move the insertion point to the line below the `End Sub` statement for the `Transpose_Word_Right` macro in the code window.

4. Paste the code in by issuing a Paste command (for example, by right-clicking and choosing Paste from the context menu, or by pressing Ctrl+V). The Visual Basic Editor will automatically enter a horizontal line between the `End Sub` statement for the `Transpose_Word_Right` macro and the new macro you've pasted in.

5. Change the name of the second `Transpose_Word_Right` macro to `Transpose_Word_Left` by editing the `Sub` line:

   ```
   Sub Transpose_Word_Left()
   ```

6. Edit the comment lines at the beginning of the macro accordingly:

   ```
   'Transpose_Word_Left Macro
   'Transposes the current word with the word to its left. _
   'Created 4/1/97 by Joanna Bermudez.
   ```

7. Now all you need to do is replace the `MoveRight` method with the `MoveLeft` method to move the insertion point one word to the left instead of one word to the right. While you could do that by typing in the correction or by using Cut and Paste to replace the `Selection.MoveRight` line with the commented-out `Selection.MoveLeft` line, try using the List Properties/Methods feature instead:

   a. Click to place the insertion point in the `MoveRight` method.

   b. Click the List Properties/Methods button on the Edit toolbar to pop up the list of properties and methods.

    c. Double-click the `MoveLeft` method to paste it in over the `MoveRight` method.

8. Now that we no longer need it even for reference, delete the commented `Selection.MoveLeft` line from the end of the macro.

You should end up with a macro that looks like this:

```
Sub Transpose_Word_Left()
'
' Transpose_Word_Left Macro
' Transposes the current word with the word to its left. _
' Created 4/1/97 by Joanna Bermudez.
'
    Selection.Extend
    Selection.Extend
    Selection.EscapeKey
    Selection.Cut
    Selection.MoveLeft Unit:=wdWord, Count:=1
    Selection.Paste
End Sub
```

Try stepping through this macro to make sure that it works. If it does, you're ready to save it—and perhaps to create a toolbar button, menu item, or keyboard shortcut for it in Word.

Saving Your Work and Closing the Visual Basic Editor

When you've finished working with this or any other macro, choose File ➤ Save *templatename* to save the template and the changes you've made to it. Then choose File ➤ Close and Return to Microsoft Word to close the Visual Basic Editor and return to Word.

Organizing Your Macros

If you use macros often, sooner or later you'll need to rename some of them, or you'll need to move or copy them from one template to another. To do so, open the Organizer dialog box by choosing Tools ➤ Macro ➤ Macros and clicking the

Organizer button in the Macro dialog box. Word will display the Macro Project Items tab of the Organizer dialog box (see Figure 5.18), with the macro modules in Normal (the global template) in one panel and the macro modules in the current document in the other panel.

FIGURE 5.18

The Organizer dialog box lets you quickly rename macro project items and copy or move them from one template to another.

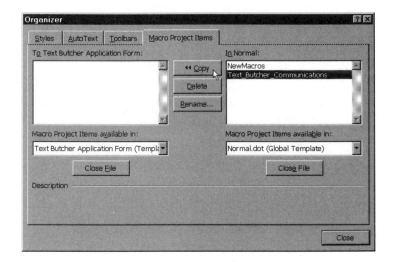

To work with the template for the current document, select it from the Macro Project Items Available In drop-down list in the panel listing the current document. Otherwise, open the templates you want: click the Close File button on either side of the Organizer dialog box's Macro tab to close the currently open file; then click the Open File button (into which the Close File button will have metamorphosed) and choose the correct template from the Open dialog box that Word then displays.

Once you've renamed, copied, or moved macros as described next, click the Close button to close the Organizer dialog box. Word will invite you to save any changes to affected templates that are not open; click the Yes button.

Renaming a Macro

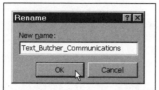

To rename a macro, select it in the Organizer dialog box (from either the left-hand panel or the right-hand panel) and click the Rename button. Enter the new name for the macro in the Rename dialog box and click the OK button. Copies of the macro in other templates will be unaffected.

Copying and Moving Macro Project Items between Documents or Templates

To copy one or more macros from one template or document to another, open the templates (or documents) in question in the Organizer dialog box. Select the macro project item or items to copy in either panel of the dialog box (the arrows on the Copy button will change direction to point to the other panel). Then click the Copy button.

If the recipient template contains a macro of the same name as one of the macros you're copying, Word will tell you that it cannot copy the project item.

TIP   To move a macro from one template to another, copy it as described here, and then delete the macro from the source template.

Deleting a Macro

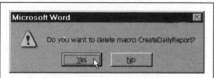

To delete a macro that you no longer need, the quickest way is to display the Macro dialog box by choosing Tools ➤ Macro. Choose the macro in the Macro Name list box, and click the Delete button. In the warning message box that appears, choose Yes.

TIP

Instead of deleting your macros, consider storing them in another template. (Create the template as usual by choosing File ➤ New and clicking the Template option button in the Create New group box in the New dialog box; then click the OK button.)

Deleting a Macro in the Organizer Dialog Box

To delete a macro or macros from a template, select the macros from either panel of the Organizer dialog box, and click the Delete button. Choose Yes in the confirmation message box:

Any copies of the macro in other templates are unaffected.

You should now be equipped to record macros using the macro recorder, open them up in the Visual Basic Editor, and make minor adjustments to the code you see there. That's excellent progress for one chapter. Take a quick bow and then turn the page. In Chapter 6, I'll discuss how you can add simple controls to a macro, starting with message boxes and input boxes.

Adding Simple Controls
to a Macro

In this chapter, we'll start looking at how you can modify a macro to increase its power and functionality. I'll discuss how you can communicate with the user of a macro, what controls you can add to the macro to enable the user to make decisions, how to decide which controls are appropriate to the needs of the macro, and how to implement the more straightforward of these controls. (We'll start looking at more complex controls for macros—dialog boxes—in the next chapter.)

Word offers four ways of communicating with the user of a macro:

- You can display messages on the status bar at the bottom of the Word screen. As you'll see in the next section, this can be an effective way of communicating with the user—with a couple of medium-sized caveats.

- You can display a message box (usually in the middle of the screen). Message boxes are useful both for communicating with the user and providing them with the means to make a single choice based on the information you give them. We'll spend the bulk of this chapter working with message boxes.

- You can display an input box (again, usually in the middle of the screen). Input boxes can be used to communicate with the user, but their primary purpose is to solicit one item of information. We'll look at input boxes in this chapter as well.

- You can display a dialog box (once again, usually in the middle of a screen). Dialog boxes can be used both to communicate with the user and to let them make a number of choices. As you'll know from your own experience with Windows and Windows applications, dialog boxes are best reserved for those times when other forms of communication will not suffice; in other words, there's no point in using a dialog box when a simple message box or input box will do. We'll look at creating simple custom dialog boxes in the next chapter.

Getting Started

Before we get into adding controls, we need to make sure you're all set for editing in the code window of the Visual Basic Editor.

First, get Word running if it isn't already. Then fire up the Visual Basic Editor by pressing Alt+F11, or by choosing Tools ➤ Macro ➤ Visual Basic Editor. Next, open a macro for editing in the code window: use the Project Explorer to navigate to the module that holds the macro, and then either scroll to the macro in the code window or choose it from the Procedure drop-down list in the code window. (As an alternative to the preceding steps, choose Tools ➤ Macro ➤ Macros to display the Macro dialog box, select a macro you've created in the Macro Name list box, and click the Edit button to display the Visual Basic Editor with the macro open in the code window.) Test the macro as described in Chapter 5 by using the F8 key to step through it in Break mode, or by clicking the Run Sub/Userform button to run it without highlighting each statement in turn.

If you want to work in a new macro rather than in an existing one—which is probably a good idea, since it'll help prevent you from doing any damage—you can create a new macro by entering Sub and the macro's name on a blank line in a module and pressing Enter; VBA will supply the parentheses and End Sub statement. For example, you could type the following:

```
Sub Experimentation_ Zone
```

VBA will add the parentheses and End Sub statement, together with a separator line to separate the macro from adjacent macros (if there are any):

```
Sub Experimentation_Zone()

End Sub
```

For working with the statements in this chapter, you'll want to start each statement on a new line. (As you'll see later in the book, you can include more than one VBA statement on one line by using a colon between statements, but this tends to be confusing.)

Now that you have a macro ready to work on, let's begin by looking at how to add a status-bar message to a macro, and the reasons for doing so.

Status-Bar Messages

Status-bar messages provide the best way to tell the user what's happening in a macro without halting execution of the macro. By including instructions to print information to (display information on) the status bar at strategic points in a macro, you can indicate to the user not only what the macro is doing but also that it is still running—sometimes a macro may appear to the user to have stopped, while in fact it is working furiously but displaying no changes on-screen.

> **TIP**
>
> Printing messages to the status bar is also a great help in debugging macros, especially when you've turned off screen updating to speed up execution of the macro. (We'll look at turning off screen updating in Chapter 18.)

The main disadvantage of displaying messages on the status bar is that the user may miss them if they're not paying attention or if they're not expecting to see messages there. Given Word's extensive use of the status bar for displaying information about ongoing processes, you wouldn't expect this to be a problem; but consider notifying your user in the greeting dialog box of a macro that screen updating will be turned off during execution of the macro and to watch the status bar for messages about what's going on.

As an alternative to displaying status-bar messages, you can disable input from the user for the duration of a macro, so that Word will ignore any flailing at the keyboard at inappropriate moments. This saves you from user input short of the Vulcan Nerve Pinch (a.k.a. the three-fingered salute of Ctrl+Alt+Delete) or hitting the power switch on their computer. We'll look at methods of constraining the user in Chapter 18.

Displaying a Status-Bar Message

To display information on the status bar, use the `Application.StatusBar` statement with the string you want to display:

```
Application.StatusBar = "The macro is searching for
unsuitable coding. Please wait...."
```

```
The macro is searching for unsuitable coding. Please wait....
```

This statement should go on its own line, but you can put it most anywhere in a macro (either one you've recorded, or one you're writing from scratch) between the starting `Sub... ()` and ending `End Sub` lines.

NOTE   In later chapters we'll look at how you can indicate the percentage of an action completed and display it in the status bar.

As you'll know from using it yourself, Word uses the status bar to display information about actions that it's performing, such as Find and Replace operations. If you run such an operation in a macro, Word will shoulder aside any message you've been displaying on the status bar so that it can display its own messages. Once Word has finished displaying messages on the status bar, you can resume control of it.

On the other hand, if your macro does not cause Word to perform actions about which it displays information on the status bar, the last message you have displayed on the status bar will remain there even after the macro has finished running. Usually, you'll want to either display another message saying that the macro has finished, or clear the status bar by displaying a blank string on it, as shown here:

```
Application.StatusBar = ""
```

Message Boxes

Your second tool for providing information to the user is the garden-variety message box, with which you'll be familiar from any number of Windows applications. As you'll see in this section, the humble message box can play an important role in almost any macro or module. Displaying your first "Hello, World!" message box tends to be exhilarating, but after a while you can grow blasé to the usefulness of the message box. This is a shame, because even a straightforward message box can significantly enhance the user-friendliness of the most complex macro.

Classic uses of message boxes include:

- Telling the user what a macro is about to do (and giving them the chance to cancel out of it if it isn't what they thought it was).

- Presenting the user with an explanation of what a macro will do next and asking them to make a simple decision (usually, to let it proceed or to send it on a different course).

- Warning the user of an error that the macro encountered and allowing them to take action on it.

- Informing the user that a macro ran successfully and that it has finished. This is particularly useful for macros that turn off screen updating, perhaps leaving the user unsure whether the macro is running or has finished. You can also use the message box to report what the macro has done—for example, that it changed particular items, or that it has discovered problems in the document that require attention.

In this chapter, I'll show you how to create a message box suitable for each of these tasks. In later chapters, we'll create specific message boxes to enhance various macros.

To any seasoned user of Windows, the advantages of using a message box are clear:

- The user cannot miss seeing the message box. (If you want, you can even display a message box that the user cannot escape by "coolswitching"— Alt+Tabbing—to another application. We'll look at this a little later in the chapter.)

- You can present the user with a simple choice among two or three options.

The limitations are also pretty clear:

- A message box can present only one, two, or three buttons, which means it can offer only a limited set of options to the user.

- The buttons in message boxes are predefined in sets—you can't put a custom button in a message box. (For that, you have to use a dialog box.)

- You can't use features such as text boxes, group boxes, or list boxes in message boxes.

Message Box Syntax

The basic syntax for message boxes is as follows:

```
MsgBox(prompt[,buttons] [,title][,helpfile, context])
```

Here's the brief translation of what this means:

MsgBox is the function that VBA uses to display a message box. You typically use it with a number of arguments enclosed in parentheses after it, as you'll see in a moment.

prompt is a required argument for the MsgBox function and controls the text displayed in the message box. prompt is a string argument, meaning you need to type in text of your choice, and can be up to 1,024 characters long, though it's usually a good idea to be more concise than this.

NOTE   As mentioned in Chapter 5, an argument is a piece of information that VBA uses with a function, method, or command.

buttons, title, and helpfile and context are optional arguments for the MsgBox function. You can tell they're optional because they're enclosed within brackets. You can include or omit the arguments displayed in the brackets. If any pair of brackets contains more than one argument, you have to use both of them together. For example, with the MsgBox function, you can specify a Help file by using the `helpfile` argument, but if you do, you have to specify the context as well by using the `context` argument.

`buttons` controls the type of message box that VBA displays by specifying which buttons it contains. For example, as you'll see in a couple of pages, you can display a message box with just an OK button, with OK and Cancel buttons, with Abort, Retry, and Ignore buttons, and so on. You can also add arguments to the `buttons` argument that control the icon in the message box and the modality of the message box. We'll also look at these options later in this chapter.

`title` controls the title bar of the message box. This too is a string argument.

`helpfile` controls which Help file VBA displays when the user presses F1 within the message box to get help. `context` controls which topic in the Help file VBA jumps to. If you specify the `helpfile` argument, you need to specify the `context` argument as well.

In the following sections, we'll look first at how you can build the simplest of message boxes, and then at how you can add the other arguments to it to make it more complex.

Displaying a Simple Message Box

You can display a straightforward message box by specifying only the `prompt` as a text string enclosed in double quotation marks:

```
MsgBox("This is a simple message box.")
```

This statement produces the simple message box shown here. With `prompt` as the only argument supplied, VBA produces a message box with just an OK button and with "Microsoft Word" in the title bar. This message box does nothing except display information.

You can enter this `MsgBox` statement on any blank line within a macro. After you type the **MsgBox** keyword, VBA's Auto List Members feature prompts you with the syntax of the function:

```
MsgBox
MsgBox(Prompt, [Buttons As VbMsgBoxStyle = vbOKOnly], [Title], [HelpFile], [Context])
As VbMsgBoxResult
```

Once you've entered the `MsgBox` statement with its required argument (`prompt`), you can display the message box by stepping through the code (by pressing the F8 key) or by running the macro (by clicking the Run Sub/Userform button).

Instead of entering a text string for the `prompt` argument, you can define a *string variable* (a variable containing a string) beforehand (using the $ character to identify the string) and then specify it for the `prompt` argument:

```
Prompt$ = "This is a simple message box."
MsgBox(Prompt$)
```

This method can be useful when you're working with long strings, or when you need to display a string that has been defined earlier in the macro.

Displaying a Multi-Line Message Box

By default, VBA displays short message strings as a single line in a message box and wraps longer strings onto two or more lines as necessary, up to the limit of 1,024 characters (1K of characters) in a string.

You can deliberately break a string over more than one line by including line-feed and carriage-return characters in the string as follows:

- `Chr(13)` represents a carriage return.

- `Chr(10)` represents a line-feed.

- `Chr(10) + Chr(13)` represents a line-feed–carriage return combination.

NOTE
"Line-feed" and "carriage return" seem like archaic terms better suited to the typewriter than to the computer. At least with the typewriter, you could distinguish between a line-feed (rolling the paper up by one line) and a carriage return (returning the carriage to the beginning of its run, usually by swinging a lever that drove a line-feed at the same time). But the different characters that originally represented these two actions are valuable in VBA as well: when you're not working in message boxes, `Chr(10)` and `Chr(13)` have different uses, as you'll see later in the book.

In message boxes, these three characters all have the same effect, so pick the one you find easiest to type and stick with it.

For example, to display the message box illustrated in Figure 6.1, you could use the code shown below. Note that each part of the text string is enclosed in double quotation marks (to tell VBA that they're part of the string). The Chr(149) characters are bullets, so the text after them starts with a couple of spaces to give the bullets some air.

```
Prompt$ = "Word has finished formatting the report you
⮞requested." + Chr(10) + Chr(10) + "You can now run the
⮞following macros:" + Chr(10) + Chr(10) + Chr(149) +
⮞" Distribute_Report will e-mail the report to the head
⮞office." + Chr(10) + Chr(149) + " Store_Report will copy
⮞the report to the holding directory." + Chr(10)
⮞+ Chr(149) + " Backup_Report will create a backup of
⮞the report on the file server."
MsgBox Prompt$
```

TIP

You'll notice that in this example, there's a space on either side of each of the plus signs and the equal sign. You can enter these spaces yourself, or you can have VBA enter them for you when you move the insertion point to another line, which causes VBA to check the line you've just been working on.

FIGURE 6.1

You can display a multi-line message box by using line-feed and carriage-return characters within the prompt string.

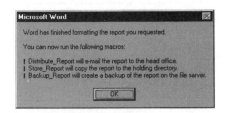

As you can see, this makes for an uncomfortably long string that is difficult to read or to edit in the Visual Basic Editor. One way to solve this problem is to break a line of code over two lines by using a single underscore between items (i.e., not within an expression):

```
Prompt$ = "Word has finished formatting the report you
➥requested." + Chr(10) _
+ Chr(10) + "You can now run the following macros:"
➥+ Chr(10) + Chr(10) + Chr(149)_
    + " Distribute_Report will e-mail the report
➥to the head office."
```

VBA treats these three lines of code as one line.

Choosing Buttons for a Message Box

As you saw a little earlier, the `buttons` argument controls which buttons a message box contains. VBA offers the following types of message boxes, controlled by the `buttons` argument:

Value	Constant	Buttons
0	vbOKOnly	OK
1	vbOKCancel	OK, Cancel
2	vbAbortRetryIgnore	Abort, Retry, Ignore
3	vbYesNoCancel	Yes, No, Cancel
4	vbYesNo	Yes, No
5	vbRetryCancel	Retry, Cancel

You can refer to these message box types by using either the value or the constant. For example, you can specify either **1** or **vbOKCancel** to produce a message box with OK and Cancel buttons. The value is easier to type; the constant is easier to read. Either of the following statements produce the message box shown at right:

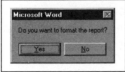

```
Response = MsgBox("Do you want to format the report?", vbYesNo)
Response = MsgBox("Do you want to format the report?", 4)
```

Whether you choose to use values or constants when creating message boxes for your macros is mostly a matter of personal choice—and a question of how easy you want to make life for other people who may have to thrash their way through your macros to debug them once you've distributed the macros or moved on from your current position.

> **TIP**
>
> As I mentioned in Chapter 5, you can use the Visual Basic Editor's many Help features to assist you in writing out commands quickly and accurately. By using the Help features when you are creating message boxes, you can avoid typos or missing arguments.

Choosing an Icon for a Message Box

You can also add an icon to a message box by including the appropriate value or constant argument. Here are your options:

Value	Constant	Displays
16	vbCritical	Stop icon
32	vbQuestion	Question mark icon
48	vbExclamation	Exclamation point icon
64	vbInformation	Information icon

Again, you can refer to these icons by using either the value or the constant: either **48** or **vbExclamation** will produce an exclamation point icon.

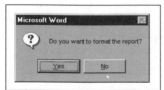

To link the value or constant for the message box with the value or constant for the icon, use a plus sign. For example, to produce a message box containing Yes and No buttons together with a question mark icon, you could enter **vbYesNo + vbQuestion** (or **4 + 32**, or **vbYesNo + 32**, or **4 + vbQuestion**).

```
Response = MsgBox("Do you want to format the report?",
➥vbYesNo + vbQuestion)
```

Setting a Default Button for a Message Box

You can set a default button for a message box by specifying it in the `MsgBox` statement. This is seldom necessary for every macro (unless you happen to write dangerous macros or you have colleagues prone to random behavior), but it can be a wise move when you distribute macros that take drastic action. For example, a useful macro that we'll look at later in the book is one for deleting the current document without having to close it and then switch to a file-management program (such as Explorer) or dredge around in one of the common dialog boxes (such as the Open dialog box or the Save dialog box). Because this macro can destroy someone's work if they run it inadvertently, you'd probably want to set a default button of No or Cancel in a confirmation message box so that the user has to actively choose to run the rest of the macro.

The arguments for default buttons are as follows:

Value	Constant	Effect
0	VbDefaultButton1	The first button is the default button.
256	VbDefaultButton2	The second button is the default button.
512	VbDefaultButton3	The third button is the default button.
768	VbDefaultButton4	The fourth button is the default button.

In VBA, unless you specify otherwise, the first button on each of the message boxes is automatically the default button: the OK button in a `vbOKCancel` message box, the Abort button in a `vbAbortRetryIgnore` message box, the Yes button in a `vbYesNoCancel` message box, the Yes button in a `vbYesNo` message box, and the Retry button in a `vbRetryCancel` message box. VBA counts the buttons in the order they're presented in the constant for the type of message box (which in turn is the left-to-right order in which they appear in the message box on-screen), so in a `vbYesNoCancel` message box, Yes is the first button, No is the second button, and Cancel is the third button.

To set a different default button, specify the value or constant as part of the `buttons` argument:

```
Response = MsgBox("Do you want to delete this document?",
➥vbYesNo + vbCritical + vbDefaultButton2)
```

This produces the message box shown here:

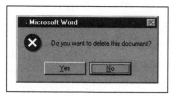

Controlling the Modality of a Message Box

Word (or, to be more precise, VBA) can display both *application-modal* message boxes and *system-modal* message boxes. The difference between the two is that application-modal message boxes stop you from doing anything in the current application until you dismiss them, while system-modal message boxes stop you from doing anything *on your computer* until you dismiss them. Most message boxes are application modal, allowing you to coolswitch (or switch via the Taskbar) to another application and work in that before you get rid of the message box. In contrast, some installation message boxes are system modal, and, in fact, General Protection Faults (GPFs) in Windows 3.*x* were so system modal it was painful.

You probably know from your own experience how frustrating system-modal message boxes can be, and when designing macros you'll use them only when absolutely necessary. In practice, this means almost never. For most conventional purposes, application-modal message boxes will do everything you need them to—and will not confuse or vex users of your macros.

You can control the modality of a message box by using these two `button` arguments:

Value	Constant	Result
0	`vbApplicationModal`	The message box is application modal.
4096	`vbSystemModal`	The message box is system modal.

By default, message boxes in Word are application modal, so you need to specify modality only on those rare occasions when you are producing a system-modal message box. When you do, add the **vbSystemModal** constant or **4096** value to the `buttons` argument:

```
Response = MsgBox("Do you want to delete this document?",
➥vbYesNo + vbCritical + vbDefaultButton2 + vbSystemModal)
```

System-modal message boxes do not look any different from application-modal message boxes.

Specifying a Title for a Message Box

The next component of the message box is its title bar, which is controlled by the `title` argument. As I mentioned earlier in this chapter, the title argument is optional; Word supplies the title "Microsoft Word" if you choose not to specify one yourself. This generic title bar is the perfect argument (that's *argument* in the conventional sense for once) for your specifying a title bar: just about anything you care to put in the title bar of a message box will be more informative than the default, so you might as well go ahead and do so.

`title` is a string expression and can be a full 1,024 characters in length, but in practice any title longer than about 75 characters gets truncated with an ellipsis; and if you want people to actually read the title bars of your message boxes, 25 characters or so is a reasonable maximum to aim for.

The title bar is usually the first part of a message box that the user notices, so make your title bars as helpful as possible. Conventional etiquette is to put the name of the macro or procedure in the title bar of a message box and then use the prompt to explain what choices the buttons in the message box will implement. In addition, if you expect to revise your macros, you may find it helpful to include their version number in the title so that users can easily check which version of the macro they're using (and update to a more current version as appropriate). For instance, in the next illustration, the Delete Document macro is identified as version 1.1.

Specify the `title` argument after the `buttons` argument like this:

```
Response = MsgBox("Do you want to delete this document?",
➥vbYesNo + vbCritical +vbDefaultButton2,
➥"Delete Document 1.1")
```

As with the `prompt` argument, you can use a string variable as the title argument, which can prove useful if you want to include in the title of the message box a string created or stored in the macro. For example, in a macro that offers to delete a document, you could retrieve the name of the document to be deleted and display it in the title bar of a message box or (perhaps better) in the prompt, so that the user couldn't misunderstand which document the macro was referring to. We'll look at how to work with strings in Chapter 10.

You *can* include line-feed and carriage-return characters in a `title` argument, but Word will display them as square boxes in the title bar rather than doing anything inventive like creating a two-line title bar, so there's little point.

Specifying a Help File for a Message Box

The final arguments you can use for a message box are the `helpfile` and `context` arguments. The `helpfile` argument is a string argument specifying the name and location of the Help file that Word will display when the user summons help from the message box. The `context` argument is a Help context number within the Help file. These arguments are primarily useful if you're writing your own Help files, because otherwise it's difficult to access the Help context numbers, which are buried in the Help files. If you are writing your own Help files, the syntax for specifying the `helpfile` and `context` is simple:

```
Response = MsgBox("Do you want to delete this document?",
➥vbYesNo + vbCritical +vbDefaultButton2,
➥"Delete Document 1.1", "//neuromancer/server_f\helpfiles\
➥word\macros.hlp", 1012)
```

In this case, the Help file is specified as `macros.hlp` in the `\helpfiles\ word\` folder on the `\server_f\` drive of the networked computer identified as `neuromancer`. VBA will go to the help topic numbered 1012.

Using Some Arguments without Others

As you've seen in this section, VBA lets you either specify or omit optional arguments. Until now, we've looked only at omitting optional arguments at the tail end of the syntax, but you can also omit earlier optional arguments and specify later ones.

If you want to specify later arguments for a function without specifying the ones before them, use a comma to indicate each unused optional argument. For example, if you wanted to display the message box we looked at in the previous example without specifying `buttons` and `title` arguments, you could use the following statement:

```
Response = MsgBox("Do you want to delete this document?",,,
➥"//neuromancer/server_f\helpfiles\word\macros.hlp", 1012)
```

Here, the triple comma indicates that the `buttons` and `title` arguments are omitted (which will cause VBA to display a `vbOKOnly` message box with a title bar of "Microsoft Word"), preventing VBA from confusing the `helpfile` argument with the `buttons` argument.

> **NOTE**
> Because the commands in VBA are laid out with the required arguments first, followed by the optional arguments in approximate order of popularity, you may not need to use commas to indicate omitted arguments very often.

Retrieving a Value from a Message Box

So far in this chapter, we've examined the different items you can specify for a message box:

- the prompt to the user (the only compulsory item)
- the buttons the message box contains, and the default button if necessary
- the icon for the message box
- the modality of the message box
- the title of the message box
- the Help file and its context

Apart from the `vbOKOnly` message box, the other message boxes have little usefulness until you retrieve a value from them that tells you which button the user clicked. Once you've established which button they clicked, you can point the macro in the appropriate direction.

To retrieve a value from a message box, you need to declare a variable for it. You can do so quite simply by telling VBA that the variable name is equal to the message box (so to speak):

```
Response = MsgBox("Do you want to create the daily report?",
➥vbYesNo + vbQuestion, "Create Daily Report")
```

When you run the code, VBA stores the user's choice of button as a value. You can then check the value and take action accordingly. Following is the full list of buttons; again, you can refer to them by either the constant or the value:

Value	Constant	Button Selected
1	vbOK	OK
2	vbCancel	Cancel
3	vbAbort	Abort
4	vbRetry	Retry
5	vbIgnore	Ignore
6	vbYes	Yes
7	vbNo	No

For example, to check a vbYesNo message box to see which button the user chose, you can use a straightforward If statement:

```
Response = MsgBox("Do you want to create the daily report?",
➥vbYesNo + vbQuestion, "Create Daily Report")
If Response = vbYes Then
    Goto CreateDailyReport
Else
    Goto Bye
EndIf
```

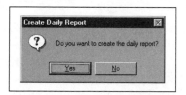

Here, if the user chooses the Yes button, Word goes to the CreateDailyReport label (a label is a way of naming a line of code) and continues running the macro from there; if not, it terminates the macro by going to the Bye label at the end. The If condition checks the Response generated by the choice the user made in the message box to see if it's a vbYes (generated by clicking the Yes button or pressing Enter with the Yes button selected); the Else statement runs if the Response was not vbYes—i.e., if the user chose the No button, there being only those two buttons in this message box.

We'll look at `If` conditions in detail in Chapter 9, but here's a quick example of how you can use an `If... ElseIf... Else` condition to handle a three-button dialog box:

```
ButtonChosen = MsgBox("Word was unable to find the file "
+ NextFile$ + "." + Chr(10) + Chr(10) + "Choose the Yes
button to search for the file; choose the No button to
skip this file and continue; choose the Cancel button to
terminate this procedure.", vbYesNoCancel + vbCritical,
"Concatenate Files v2.05")
If ButtonChosen = vbYes Then
    DisplaySearchDialog
ElseIf ButtonChosen = vbNo Then
    Goto SkipCurrentFile
Else
    Goto Bye
End If
```

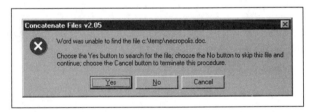

As you've probably guessed, the `If...ElseIf...Else` condition, works like this: if the `If` condition is met, the statements following it are executed; otherwise, the `ElseIf` condition is evaluated, and if it is met, the statements after it are executed; otherwise, the statements following the `Else` line are executed. So here, VBA compares the value of the `ButtonChosen` variable to `vbYes`; if the button chosen was `vbYes`, VBA executes the `DisplaySearchDialog` procedure, which we'll assume displays a dialog box for the user to find the missing file. If the button chosen was not `vbYes`, VBA compares `ButtonChosen` to `vbNo`; if the button was `vbNo`, VBA goes to the `SkipCurrentFile` label, which we're assuming is located elsewhere in the macro. Otherwise—if the Cancel button was chosen or the user clicked the close button on the input box—VBA executes the `Goto Bye` statement, going to the `Bye` label that we're assuming is located at the end of the macro.

Enough of message boxes for the time being. Let's take a look at Input boxes.

Input Boxes

For times when you want to retrieve one simple piece of information from the user, you can use an input box. You'll be familiar with input boxes by sight if not by name; they usually look something like this:

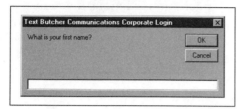

TIP

To retrieve two or more pieces of information from the user, you could use two or more input boxes in succession, but usually a custom dialog box is a better idea. We'll start looking at simple dialog boxes in Chapter 7.

Input Box Syntax

The syntax for displaying an input box is straightforward and similar to the syntax for a message box:

```
InputBox(prompt[, title] [, default] [, xpos] [, ypos]
➥[, helpfile, context])
```

Here's what the arguments mean:

- `prompt`, as with the `MsgBox` function, is a string that specifies the prompt that appears in the input box and is the only required argument. Again, as with `MsgBox`, `prompt` can be up to 1,024 characters long, and you can use line-feed and carriage-return characters to force separate lines.

- `title` is a string that specifies the text in the title bar of the input box. Again, if you don't specify a `title` argument, VBA enters "Microsoft Word" for you.

- `default` is a string that you can use to specify default text in the text box. Entering a `default` argument can be a good idea both for cases when the default text is likely to be suitable (for example, if you displayed an input box asking for the user's name, you could enter the name from the User Information tab of the Options dialog box as a suggestion) and when you need to display sample text so that the user can understand the type of response you're looking for.

- `xpos` and `ypos` are optional numeric values for specifying the on-screen position of the input box. `xpos` governs the horizontal position of the left edge of the input box from the left edge of the screen (not of the Word window), while `ypos` governs the vertical position of the top edge of the input box from the top of the screen. Each measurement is in *twips*, which are units of measurement not entirely unrelated to pixels. The short explanation is that you don't really want to know what twips are, but a computer screen at 800 x 600 resolution is around 10,000 twips across and 8,000 twips high. If you need to position your input boxes and dialog boxes precisely, experiment with twips at different screen resolutions until you achieve satisfactory results or until you give up in disgust. Otherwise, omit these two arguments, and VBA will display your input boxes at the default position of halfway across the screen and one-third of the way down it.

- `helpfile` and `context` are optional arguments for specifying the Help file and context in the Help file to jump to if the user summons help from the input box.

Again, you can omit any of the optional arguments, but if you want to use an optional argument later in the syntax sequence than one you've omitted, you need to indicate the omission with a comma.

Unlike message boxes, input boxes come with a predefined set of buttons—OK and Cancel, plus a Help button if you specify the `helpfile` and `context` parameters—so there's no argument for specifying the buttons for an input box:

```
NumFile = InputBox("How many files do you want to concatenate?", _
"Concatenate Files v0.99a", 10, , , "c:\temp\test.hlp", 11)
```

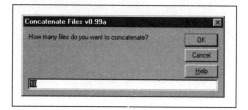

Retrieving Input from an Input Box

To retrieve input from an input box, you need to declare the numeric variable or string variable that will contain it. Here, the variable `TextEntered` will contain what the user enters in the input box:

```
TextEntered = InputBox("Please enter the file you want to
➡transfer.", "Transfer Files v1.0")
```

Once you've done that, and the user has entered a value or a string and chosen the OK button, you can use the value or string as usual in VBA. (We'll start working with strings in Chapter 10.) To make sure that the user has chosen the OK button, you can have VBA check to see that the input box has not returned a zero-length string (which it also returns if the user chooses the OK button with the text box empty) and take action accordingly:

```
TextEntered = InputBox("Please enter the file you want to
➡transfer.", "Transfer Files v1.0")
If TextEntered = "" Then Goto Bye
```

When Message Boxes and Input Boxes Won't Suffice

As you've seen in this chapter, a strategically positioned message box can greatly enhance a macro by enabling the user to make a choice at a turning point or by presenting the user with important information. But once you've used message boxes for a while, you're apt to start noticing their limitations. You can present only a certain amount of information, and you're limited in the way you can display it (to whatever layout you can conjure up with new paragraphs, line breaks, tabs, and spaces). You can use only seven sets of buttons, which limit the possibilities of message boxes. While you *can* get creative and enter complex messages in message boxes to make the most use of the buttons they present, you'll usually do better to use a custom dialog box instead; as you'll see in the next chapter, custom dialog boxes are relatively simple to create, and they give you far more power and flexibility than message boxes do. Figure 6.2 shows an instance where a dialog box would clearly be preferable to an overworked message box.

FIGURE 6.2

How to overuse a message box. If you're lucky, the user of the macro will take enough time to figure out what you're trying to do with the message box, but you'd do better to use a dialog box instead.

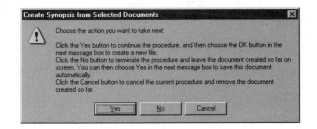

You'll generally want to avoid writing macros that present the user with a number of choices via a sequence of message boxes. Consider the sequence of message boxes and input boxes shown in Figure 6.3. This sequence would be better combined into one dialog box.

Similarly, input boxes are useful for retrieving a single piece of information from the user, but beyond that, their limitations quickly become apparent. If you find yourself planning to use two or more input boxes in immediate succession, that should raise a red flag that you should be using a dialog box instead.

FIGURE 6.3

This sequence of message boxes and input boxes could be combined into one dialog box.

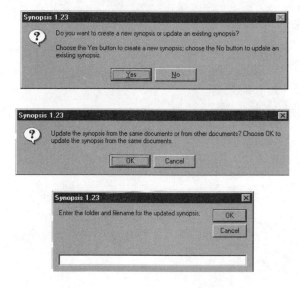

I'll show you how to create the simpler kinds of custom dialog boxes in the next chapter. The more complex kinds of custom dialog boxes can wait until Chapters 19 and 20, where we'll look at dynamic dialog boxes and discuss how you can use Word's built-in dialog boxes to avoid having to create custom dialog boxes in the first place unless absolutely necessary.

CHAPTER

SEVEN

7

Creating Simple Custom Dialog Boxes

In the previous chapter, we looked at how you could use VBA's built-in message boxes and input boxes to communicate with the users of your macros, allow them to make choices on how to run the macros, and provide necessary input for procedures. We finished up by looking at a couple of instances where message boxes and input boxes proved unsuitable for providing the user with the choices the macro needed—at least, for providing those choices in a logical and easy-to-use manner.

In this chapter, we'll start looking at the capabilities that Word and Visual Basic for Applications provide for creating custom dialog boxes that interact with the user. Dialog boxes are one of the most powerful and complex features of Word, and in this chapter we'll cover the more straightforward dialog box elements and how to manipulate them. These lessons will help us work with VBA in the coming chapters. Toward the end of the book, in Chapter 19, I'll show you how to create more complex dialog boxes, such as those that contain a number of tabbed pages and those that update themselves when the user clicks a control; and in Chapter 20 I'll show you how to shanghai Word's own dialog boxes and bend them to your will for quick results.

When Should You Use a Custom Dialog Box?

You'll often want to use a custom dialog box when simpler methods of interacting with the user fall short—for example, when you can't present the user with a reasonable choice using the limited selection of buttons provided in message boxes, or when you need to retrieve from the user information more involved than a straightforward input box can convey. You'll also need to use a custom dialog box when a macro requires that the user choose non-exclusive options by selecting or clearing check boxes, when you need to present mutually exclusive options via option buttons, or when you need to provide the user with a list box from which to make a selection.

Custom dialog boxes provide the full range of interface elements that the user will be familiar with from their experience with Word and with the other Office applications. With a little effort, you can create custom dialog boxes that look professional enough to fool inexpert users into thinking that they are built-in Word dialog boxes.

Typically, you'll use custom dialog boxes to drive your macros, so they usually will appear in response to an action taken by the user. For example, when the user starts a macro, you can have the macro display a dialog box presenting options that determine what the macro will do, such as choosing the files for the macro to manipulate. You can also create dialog boxes that trigger themselves in response to events in the computer system. For example, you could run an automatic macro that sets up Word to perform a specific action (such as displaying a dialog box) at a particular time. We'll look at how to work with Word's automatic macros in Chapter 21.

Because creating dialog boxes is relatively complex, it's wise to consider any practical alternatives to using them. As you'll see in Chapter 20, there are times when it's easier to use one of Word's built-in dialog boxes to return information for a macro. This has a couple of benefits: first, the user is likely to be familiar with the dialog box and what it does; and second, you can save time by using the built-in dialog boxes instead of laboriously constructing similar dialog boxes to achieve the same purpose.

Creating a Custom Dialog Box

Previous versions of Word used the Dialog Editor to build custom dialog boxes. The Dialog Editor was a separate application that provided a simple visual interface for creating custom dialog boxes and positioning their elements where you wanted them; once you'd gotten everything into place, you would select the dialog box, copy it to the Clipboard, and then paste it as a set of lines of WordBasic code into the appropriate macro in a macro-editing window within Word, where you would write further lines to display the dialog box and code it into the macro. Generally, the Dialog Editor worked well for straightforward dialog boxes, but it tended to lose track of information when you pasted complex information from the macro-editing window back into the Dialog Editor to adjust its layout.

Word 97 and VBA handle dialog boxes very differently. First, you work in the Visual Basic Editor instead of in the Dialog Editor. Second, VBA uses visual objects called *userforms* to implement dialog boxes. A userform (also sometimes referred to simply—and confusingly—as a *form*) is essentially a blank sheet on which you can place controls (such as check boxes, buttons, and so on) to create a dialog box. VBA stores the userform as a collection of code but displays it as a graphical object; likewise, each control on the userform has code attached to it that you can view and work with in the code window. Each userform becomes part of the application's user interface. In practical terms, this means that you can display a userform (i.e., dialog box) for the user to interact with, and you can then retrieve information from the userform and manipulate it with VBA.

> **NOTE**   You can also create userforms that are not dialog boxes.

Each userform is itself one *object* and contains a number of other objects that you can manipulate separately. (I'll discuss objects in greater detail in Chapter 11.) For example, you could create a simple dialog box with two option buttons, an OK button, and a Cancel button. Each option button would be an object; the OK button would be a third object; and the Cancel button would be a fourth object. You could set properties for each object—such as the action to take when the Cancel button was clicked, or the screentip to display when the user moved the mouse pointer over one of the option buttons—to make the dialog box as comprehensible, straightforward, and useful as possible.

Now we'll go through the process of creating a custom dialog box. This is mostly theory, but bear with me. Toward the end of the chapter, I'll give you a couple of examples that step through creating a macro and linking a dialog box to it.

Designing the Dialog Box

As you might imagine, there are several ways to design a custom dialog box:

- First, you can start from scratch and design the dialog box off-the-cuff. For straightforward dialog boxes, this works pretty well, but for dialog boxes that need a number of controls, you may find yourself wasting time and having to start over from scratch.

- Second, you can adopt a more methodical approach and plan what you need to include in the dialog box before you start creating it: State the intended function of the dialog box and list the elements it will need to include in order to perform this function. Then sketch a rough diagram of the dialog box to get an approximate idea of where you'll fit in each of the elements. Unless you can sustain an uncanny imitation of the various

Windows system fonts, the dialog box you end up creating will inevitably differ from your initial sketch, but by doing this you can make sure that you don't ruin an otherwise perfectly proportioned dialog box by having to add a couple of extra command buttons at the last minute.

- Third, you can draw the basic design for the custom dialog box from an existing dialog box. Study existing dialog boxes that perform a similar function to the dialog box you're intending to build. Would one of them be appropriate if you were able to remove a couple of elements from it or substitute, say, a list box for a combination box? (A combination box—also known as a *combo box*—contains both a list box and a text box.) If so, you may be able to create a custom dialog box similar in design to the existing dialog box. Bear in mind that Microsoft has conducted thousands upon thousands of hours of usability tests for its applications, and try to leverage this to your advantage. There's no point in reinventing the wheel, but if you find a particular Microsoft dialog box ill-constructed or hard to use, consider how you might be able to improve on the design, and implement those changes in dialog boxes that you create.

- Fourth, you can combine the previous three approaches into a method uniquely your own.

Inserting a Userform

Once you have a design in mind, the first step in creating a custom dialog box is to insert a userform in the appropriate template.

To insert a userform, select the document project or template project that you want to contain it by clicking in the Project Explorer window. (If the Project Explorer is not currently displayed, choose View ➤ Project Explorer or press Ctrl+R to display it.) If the current document is based on a template other than Normal, your choices of project will consist of that template, the Normal template, and the document itself. Then click the Insert button on the Standard toolbar in the Visual Basic Editor and choose Userform from the drop-down list. (If the button is already displaying the Insert Userform button, just click the button rather than bothering with the drop-down list.) Alternatively, choose Insert ➤ Userform. The Visual Basic Editor will open a new userform (see Figure 7.1), which it will identify as `UserFormn`—usually `UserForm1`, unless the project already contains a userform named `UserForm1`. At the same time, the Visual Basic Editor will display the Toolbox.

FIGURE 7.1

The first step in creating
a new dialog box is to
start a new userform.

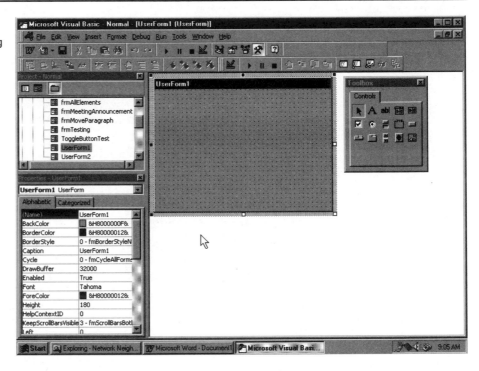

NOTE VBA will park the userform in the Forms object (the collection of
forms) for the project. If the project you chose did not already contain
a Forms object, VBA will add one to contain the new userform. You'll
see the Forms object displayed in the Project Explorer, as discussed in
Chapter 5.

Choosing Userform Grid Settings

As you can see in Figure 7.1, the Visual Basic Editor displays a grid in each user-
form to help you place controls relative to the dialog box and to align controls
relative to each other. To switch off the display of this grid or to switch off the
Visual Basic Editor's automatic alignment of controls to the grid, choose Tools ➤
Options to display the Options dialog box; select the General tab; and clear the
Show Grid check box or the Align Controls to Grid check box in the Form Grid

Settings group box. You can also adjust the units on the grid by specifying a different number of twips in the Width and Height text boxes. The Align Controls to Grid feature is usually a timesaver, so I'd suggest leaving it on.

Renaming the Userform

Once you've inserted the userform in a template, the next step is to change its default name of `UserFormn` to one that's more descriptive. (If you don't, it's surprisingly easy to get userforms confused when you start working with more than one of them at a time.) For advice on choosing names, refer to the following section, "Naming Conventions in Visual Basic for Applications," and then follow these steps:

1. If the Properties window isn't displayed, press F4 to display it. Figure 7.2 shows the two tabs of the Properties window, Alphabetic and Categorized. Alphabetic contains an alphabetic listing of the properties of the currently selected object; Categorized contains a listing broken down into categories, such as Appearance, Behavior, Font, Misc, Picture, and Position. (Some controls have more categories than those listed here.) You can expand a category by clicking the + sign beside it to display the properties it contains, and collapse it by clicking the resulting – sign. If the Alphabetic tab isn't selected, click it to select it.

FIGURE 7.2

You can work on either the Alphabetic tab or the Categorized tab of the Properties window.

NOTE You can enter the userform's name and caption on the Categorized tab of the Properties window if you want—you just have to look a little harder to find the right places. The `Caption` property is contained in the Appearance collection, and the `Name` is contained in the Misc collection.

2. Make sure the drop-down list is displaying the default name of the user-form. If it isn't, select the userform from the drop-down list.

3. Select the userform's default name in the cell to the right of the Name cell, and enter a new name for the userform. This name can be anything you want, with a few limitations:

    • The name must start with a letter.

    • The name can contain letters, numbers, and underscores, but no spaces or symbols.

    • The name can be up to 40 characters long.

WARNING Make sure you don't rename a userform or dialog box to a name that you've already used for a macro: "Well, this is the `Move_Current_ Paragraph` macro, so I'll name this dialog box `Move_Current_ Paragraph` so that I can remember what I called it." Because the names are not unique, VBA will object. Calling the dialog box `Move_Current_Paragraph_Dialog` does create a unique name and gets around the problem. For a more elegant solution, consult the naming guidelines on the next page.

4. Select the userform's default name in the cell next to the Caption cell and type the caption for the userform—this is the text label that appears in the title bar of the dialog box. This name has no restrictions beyond the con-straints imposed by the length of the title bar; you can enter a name longer than will fit in the title bar, but VBA will truncate it with an ellipsis at its maximum displayable length. As you type, you'll see the name appear in the userform title bar as well, so it's easy to see what's an appropriate length.

5. Press Enter or click elsewhere in the Properties window (or elsewhere in the Visual Basic Editor) to enter the userform's name.

TIP Naming other objects works the same way as just described.

Naming Conventions in Visual Basic for Applications

Names for objects in VBA can be up to 40 characters long, must begin with a letter, and after that can be any combination of letters, numbers, and underscores. You can't use spaces or symbols in the names, and each name must be unique in its context—for example, each userform or dialog box must have a unique name, but within any userform or dialog box, an object can have a name that is the same as an object in another dialog box.

Those are the rules; there are also conventions you can use to make the names of your VBA objects as consistent and easy to understand as possible. For example, by using the convention of starting a userform name with the letters `frm`, you can be sure that anyone else reading your code will immediately identify the name as belonging to a userform—and that you will do so yourself when you revisit old code you've written after a long interval. When you're writing code in a concentrated effort, you'll probably feel that the names you're using and the procedures you're putting together are crystal clear, and that everything is so self-explanatory that you don't want to slow yourself down by entering comment lines about what the code does. But when you revisit the code later, perhaps to troubleshoot it, you'll have a much harder time working through what things are and what they do if you haven't documented them at the time. So it's a good idea to quickly review the code at the end of a project and enter comment lines at strategic points, or to take a moment now and then as you're creating the code to enter a quick reminder of what's what.

The naming conventions for the most-used VBA objects are shown in the following list. We'll encounter the naming conventions for other VBA objects in due course later in the book.

Object	Prefix	Example
Check box	chk	chkReturnToPreviousPosition
Command button	cmd	cmdOK
Form (userform)	frm	frmMoveParagraph
Frame	fra	fraMovement
List box	lst	lstConferenceAttendees
Menu	mnu	mnuMacros
Option button	opt	optSpecialDelivery
Text box	txt	txtUserDescription

Note that the naming convention is to start the prefix for each object with lowercase letters and then start the rest of the object's name with a capital to make it a little easier to read.

Naming conventions tend to seem impossibly formal at first, and there's a strong temptation to use any name that suits you for the objects in your VBA userforms and dialog boxes. But if you plan to distribute your VBA modules or have others work with them, it's usually worth the time, effort, and formality to follow the naming conventions.

Adding Controls to the Userform

Now that you've renamed the userform, you're ready to add controls to it from the Toolbox (see Figure 7.3). VBA automatically displays the Toolbox when a userform is active, but you can also display the Toolbox when no userform is active by choosing View ➤ Toolbox.

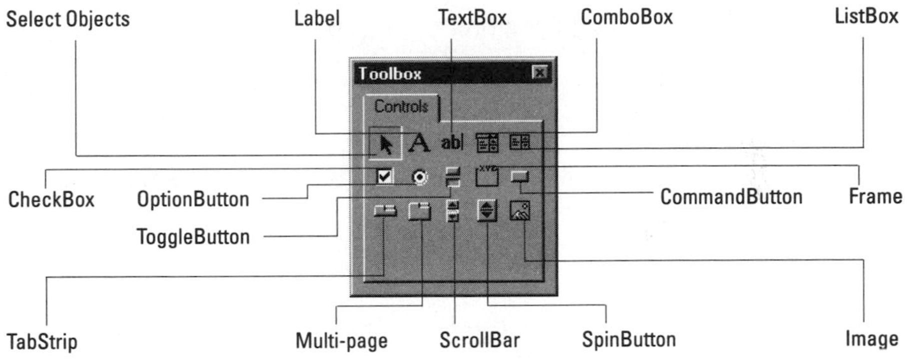

FIGURE 7.3

Use the Toolbox to add
controls to the userform.

Select Objects   Label   TextBox   ComboBox   ListBox

CheckBox   OptionButton   CommandButton   Frame

ToggleButton

TabStrip   Multi-page   ScrollBar   SpinButton   Image

Here's what the buttons on the Toolbox do:

Button	Action
Select Objects	Restores the mouse pointer to selection mode. The mouse pointer automatically returns to selection mode once you've placed an object, so usually you'll need to click the Select Objects button only when you've selected another button and then decided not to use it.
Label	Creates a label—text used to identify a part of the dialog box or to explain information the user needs to know in order to use the dialog box effectively.
TextBox	Creates a text box (also known as an *edit box*)—into which the user can type text.
ComboBox	Creates a combo box—a control that combines a text box with a list box. The user can either choose a value from the list box or enter a new value in the text box.
ListBox	Creates a list box—a control that lists a number of values. The user can pick one value from the list.
CheckBox	Creates a check box and an accompanying label. The user can select or clear the check box to turn the associated action on or off.
OptionButton	Creates an option button (also known as a radio button) and an accompanying label. The user can select only one option button out of any group of option buttons.

Button	Action
ToggleButton	Creates a toggle button—a button that shows whether or not an item is selected. A toggle button can be defined with any two settings, such as On/Off or Yes/No.
Frame	Creates a frame—an area of a userform or dialog box surrounded by a thin line—and an accompanying label. Use a frame (also known as a *group box*) to group related elements in your dialog boxes.
CommandButton	Creates a command button—a button used for taking action in a dialog box. Most dialog boxes contain command buttons such as OK, or Open, or Save, usually paired with a Cancel button or a Close button.
TabStrip	Creates a tab strip for displaying multi-page dialog boxes that have the same layout on each tab.
Multi-page	Creates a multi-page control for displaying multi-page dialog boxes that have different layouts on each of their tabs.
ScrollBar	Creates a stand-alone scroll bar. Stand-alone scroll bars are of relatively little use in dialog boxes. Combo boxes and list boxes have built-in scroll bars.
SpinButton	Creates a spin button control for attaching to another control. Spin buttons are useful for presenting sequential values with consistent intervals within an understood range, such as times or dates.
Image	Creates an image control for displaying a picture within the userform. For example, you might use an image control to place a corporate logo or a picture in a dialog box.

NOTE The Toolbox we're looking at in this chapter contains the basic set of tools provided by VBA. You can customize the Toolbox by adding other existing controls to it; creating additional pages for the controls; moving controls from page to page; and creating customized controls of your own making so that you can quickly place the elements you need most often. We'll examine these topics in Chapter 19.

Click in the userform to add a standard-size version of the selected control, as illustrated in Figure 7.4. VBA will place the top-left corner of the control where you click. As you place a control, it will snap to the grid on the userform (unless you've turned off the Align Controls to Grid feature as described in the earlier section "Choosing Userform Grid Settings").

FIGURE 7.4

When you click in the userform, VBA places a standard-size control of the type you chose. If the Align Controls to Grid feature is switched on (as it is by default), VBA will automatically align the control with the grid on the userform.

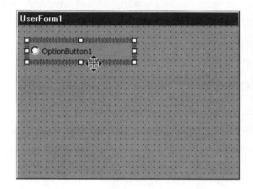

You can resize the standard-size control as necessary by selecting it, then clicking and dragging one of the selection handles (the white squares) that appear around it, as shown below. When you drag a corner handle, VBA resizes the control on both sides of the corner; when you drag the handle at the midpoint of one of the control's sides, VBA resizes the control only in that dimension. In either case, VBA displays a dotted outline indicating the size that the control will be when you release the mouse button.

You can also create a custom-size version of the control by clicking and dragging

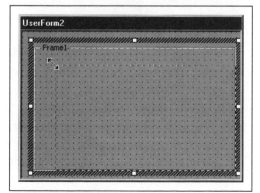

when you place the control in the userform (as opposed to clicking to place a standard-size control and then dragging it to the size you want). Usually, however, it's best to place a standard-size version of the control and resize it as necessary.

TIP To resize the userform itself, click its title bar to select it, then click and drag one of the selection handles that appear around it.

To delete a control, right-click it in the userform and choose Delete from the context menu, or select it by clicking it and then press the Delete key. To delete multiple controls at once, select them by holding down Shift as you select each control after the first, and then press Delete.

Renaming Controls

As with userforms, VBA gives each control that you add a default name consisting of the type of control and a sequential number for the type of control. For example, when you create the first text box in a userform, VBA will name it `TextBox1`; when you create another text box, VBA will name it `TextBox2`; and so on. Each control in a dialog box has to have a unique name so that you can refer to it in code.

Almost invariably, you'll want to change the controls' default names to names that describe their functions so that you can remember what they do. For example, if `TextBox2` is used for entering the user's organization name, you might want to rename it `txtOrganizationName`, `Organization_Name`, or something similar.

To rename a control:

1. Click the control in the userform to select it and display its properties in the Properties window.

    - When selecting a control, make sure the Select Objects button is selected in the Toolbox. (Unless you're performing another operation in the Toolbox, such as placing another control, the Select Objects button should be selected anyway.)

    - If you already have the Properties window displayed, you can select the control from the drop-down list instead of selecting it in the userform. VBA will then select the control in the userform, which helps you make sure that you've selected the control you want to affect.

- If you don't have the Properties window displayed, you can quickly display it with the properties for the appropriate control by right-clicking the control in the userform and choosing Properties from the context menu.

2. On either the Alphabetic tab or the Categorized tab, select the default name in the cell to the right of the `Name` property.

3. Enter the new name for the control. Remember that the name for a control (which is an object, as the userform is) must start with a letter, can contain letters, numbers, and underscores (but no spaces or symbols), and can be up to 40 characters long.

4. Press Enter to set the control name.

If you change your mind at some point and wish to change the name you assigned to a control, follow the above procedure again.

Moving a Control

To move a control that is not currently selected, click anywhere in it to select it, and then drag it to where you want it to appear, as shown here.

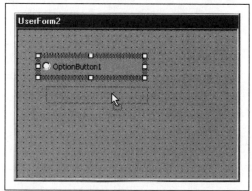

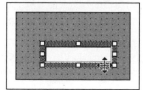 To move a selected control, move the mouse pointer over the selection border around it so that the mouse pointer turns into a four-headed arrow (as shown here), and then click and drag the control to where you want it to appear.

> **NOTE**
> You can use the Cut and Paste commands (either from the Standard toolbar, the Edit menu, or the keyboard) to move a control, but it's not a great way of proceeding: the Paste command places the control slap in the middle of the userform, so you have to drag it to its new position anyway.

Copying and Pasting Controls

You can use the Copy and Paste commands to copy and paste controls you've already added to a userform. You can paste them either to the same userform or to another userform. As mentioned above, the Paste command drops the copy of the control in the middle of the dialog box; from there you can you drag it to where you want it. The advantage of using Copy and Paste for creating new controls over using Cut and Paste to move existing controls is that the new controls take on the characteristics of their progenitors, so you can save time by creating a control, setting its properties, and then cloning it. All you then need to do is move each cloned copy to a suitable location, change its name from the default name VBA has given it to something descriptive and memorable, and set any properties this control needs to have different from its siblings. For copies you paste to another userform, you don't even need to change the names of the copies you paste—they just need to be named suitably for the code with which they work.

If you need to set all the properties separately for each control of the same type, you'll probably find it quicker to insert a new control by using the Toolbox buttons rather than Copy and Paste.

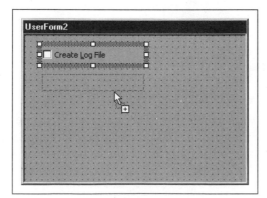

As an alternative to using the Copy and Paste commands, you can also copy a control by holding down the Ctrl key as you click and drag the control. VBA will display a + sign attached to the mouse pointer, as shown here, to indicate that you're copying the control rather than moving it. Drop the copy where you want it to appear on the userform.

Changing the Label on a Control

For a control with a displayed label, you can change the label by working in the userform as follows:

1. Click the control to select it.

2. 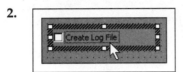 Click once in the label to select it. VBA will display a faint dotted border around the label, as shown here.

3. Click in the label to position the insertion point for editing it, or drag through the label to select the whole of it.

4. Edit the text of the label as desired.

5. Press Enter or click elsewhere in the userform to put the change to the label into effect.

TIP   You can also change the label by changing its `Caption` property in the Properties window.

Working with Groups of Controls

By grouping two or more controls, you can work with them as a single unit to size them, format them, or delete them.

Grouping Controls

To group controls, select them by Shift+clicking, then right-click and choose Group from the context menu. Alternatively, select the controls and then click the Group button on the Userform toolbar. VBA will create a new group containing the controls and will place a shaded border with handles around the whole group, as shown in Figure 7.5.

FIGURE 7.5

You can work with multiple controls at once by grouping them. VBA indicates a group of controls by placing a border around it.

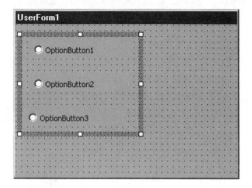

Ungrouping Controls

To ungroup controls, right-click any of the controls contained in the group and then choose Ungroup from the context menu. Alternatively, select the group of controls by clicking in any control in the group and then click the Ungroup button on the Userform toolbar. VBA will remove the shaded border with handles from around the group and will instead display a border and handles around each individual control that was formerly in the group.

Sizing Grouped Controls

You can quickly size all controls in a group by selecting the group and then

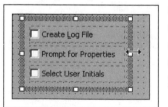

dragging the sizing handles on the surrounding border. For example, you could select the middle handle on the right side and drag it outward to lengthen the controls, as shown here. The controls will be resized proportionately to the change in the group outline.

Generally speaking, this procedure works best when you group a number of controls of the same type, as in the illustration. For example, sizing a group that consisted of several text boxes or several option buttons would work well, whereas sizing a group that consisted of a text box, a command button, and a combo box would seldom be a good idea.

Deleting Grouped Controls

You can quickly delete a whole group of controls by right-clicking in any of them and choosing Delete from the context menu, or by selecting the group and pressing the Delete key.

Working with One Control in a Group

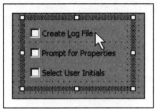

Even after you've grouped a number of controls, you can still work with them individually if necessary. To do so, click any control in the group to select the group, as shown here.

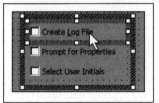

Now click the control you want to work with. As shown here, VBA will display a darker shaded border around the group (indicating that the group still exists) and display the lighter shaded border around the individual control, indicating that that control is selected.

You can then work with the individual control as if it were not grouped. When you've finished working with it, click another control in the group to work with that, or click elsewhere in the userform to deselect the individual control.

Aligning Controls

For all the wonders of the Snap to Grid feature, you'll often need to align controls manually. The easiest way to align selected controls is to right-click in any one of them and choose an option from the Align submenu: Lefts, Centers, Rights, Tops, Middles, Bottoms, or To Grid. Lefts aligns the left borders of the controls; Centers aligns the horizontal midpoints of the controls; Rights aligns the right borders of the controls; Tops aligns the tops of the controls; Middles aligns the vertical midpoints of the controls; Bottoms aligns the bottoms of the controls; and To Grid aligns the controls to the grid.

VBA aligns the borders or midpoints to the current position of that border or midpoint on the dominant control—the control that has white sizing handles around it rather than black sizing handles. After selecting the controls you want to align manually, make dominant the one that is already in the correct position by clicking it so that it takes on the white sizing handles. Then choose the alignment option you want.

WARNING   Make sure the alignment option you choose makes sense for the controls you've selected. VBA will happily align controls in an inappropriate way if you tell it to. For example, if you select a number of option buttons or text boxes and choose Tops from the Align submenu, VBA will obligingly stack all the option buttons or text boxes on top of each other, rendering them all but unusable.

Placing Controls

VBA offers a number of placement commands on the Format menu. Most of these are simple and intuitive to use:

- On the Format ➤ Make Same Size submenu, use the Width, Height, and Both commands to make two or more controls the same size in one or both dimensions.

- Use the Format ➤ Size to Fit command to have VBA decide on a suitable size for an element, based on the size of its name. This works well for, say, a toggle button with a medium-length name, but VBA will shrink an OK button to a meager size that your dialog boxes will be ashamed of.

- Use the Format ➤ Size to Grid command to size a control up or down to the nearest gridpoints.

- On the Format ➤ Horizontal Spacing and Format ➤ Vertical Spacing submenus, use the Make Equal, Increase, Decrease, and Remove commands to set the horizontal spacing and vertical spacing of two or more controls. The Remove option removes extra space from between controls, which works well for, say, a vertical series of option buttons (which look good close together) but is not a good idea for command buttons (which need a little air between them).

- On the Format ➤ Center in Form submenu, use the Horizontally and Vertically commands to center a control or a group of controls in the form. Centering controls vertically is seldom a good idea, but you'll often want to center a frame or a group of command buttons horizontally.

- On the Format ➤ Arrange Buttons submenu, use the Bottom and Right commands to quickly rearrange command buttons in a dialog box. (You may find, as I do, that VBA tends to put the buttons in the wrong order, such as putting the Cancel button to the left of the OK button in a Bottom arrangement instead of to the right, where it normally appears.)

Adjusting the Tab Order of the Dialog Box

The *tab order* of a dialog box (or other userform) is the order in which VBA selects controls in the element when you move through them by pressing the Tab key (to move forward) or the Shift+Tab key combination (to move backward). VBA makes it easy to adjust the tab order in userforms.

Your goal in setting the tab order for a dialog box should be to make the dialog box as easy as possible to use. The general rule of thumb is to arrange the tab order from left to right and from top to bottom of the dialog box or userform, but if you use group boxes (a.k.a. frames) in your dialog boxes, you will often want to set the tab order to cycle through the controls in a group box before moving on to the next control.

VBA assigns tab order to the controls in a dialog box on a first-come-first-served basis as you add them. Unless you have a supremely logical mind, this order will seldom produce the optimal tab order for a dialog box, so usually you'll want to adjust (or at least check) the tab order.

To change the tab order in a dialog box:

1. Right-click in open space in the userform and choose Tab Order from the context menu to display the Tab Order dialog box (see Figure 7.6).

2. Rearrange the controls into the order in which you want them to appear by selecting them in the Tab Order list box and clicking the Move Up button or Move Down button as appropriate. You can Shift+click to select a range of controls or Ctrl+click to select a number of noncontiguous controls.

3. Click the OK button to close the Tab Order dialog box.

FIGURE 7.6

Use the Tab Order dialog box to arrange the controls in your dialog box into a logical order for the user.

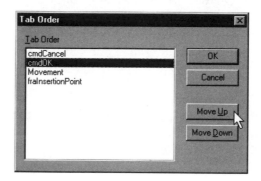

Linking a Dialog Box to a Macro

Designing a custom dialog box is only the first step in getting it to work in a macro. The interesting part is writing the code to display the dialog box and make it perform its functions.

Typically, the code you create for a dialog box will consist of the following:

- A macro that displays the dialog box by loading it and using the .Show method. Usually, this macro will be assigned to a menu item or a toolbar button so that the user can invoke it, but a macro can also run automatically in response to a system event (such as running at a specified time).

- The userform that contains the dialog box and its controls.

- The code attached to the userform. This code consists of macros for designated controls. For example, for a simple dialog box containing two option buttons and two command buttons (an OK button and a Cancel button), you would typically create one macro for the OK button and one for the Cancel button. The macro for the OK button, which would be triggered by a Click event on the OK button (i.e., either a click on the OK button or a press of the Enter key with the focus on the OK button) would ascertain which option button was selected and then take action accordingly; the macro for the Cancel button would cancel the procedure. (You could also assign a macro to the Click event for an option button, but usually it makes more sense to trap the command buttons in a static dialog box. In a dynamic dialog box, you may often want to trap the click on an option button and display further controls as appropriate.)

Once the code attached to a button has run, execution returns to the dialog box (if it's still displayed) or to the macro that called the dialog box.

NOTE   If you've used WordBasic to create dialog boxes in earlier versions of Word, you'll notice some significant differences in VBA. For example, whereas WordBasic includes the code for the dialog box and its controls in the macro, VBA separates the code into separate components: the macro that calls the dialog box, the code for the dialog box itself (which you see as a visual object—the dialog box—rather than as a series of instructions), and the code controlling how the controls in the dialog box respond to the user. While VBA's approach is ultimately much more flexible and powerful than WordBasic's, it tends to be initially confusing and takes a while to get used to. But with VBA, you can even assign a macro to be executed by a Click event on the dialog box itself—i.e., if the user clicks once with the mouse in open space in the dialog box, rather than on a command button.

Loading and Unloading a Dialog Box

You load a dialog box by using the `Load` statement and unload it by using the `Unload` statement. The `Load` statement loads the dialog box into memory so it is available to the program, but does not display the dialog box; for that you use the `.Show` method, which we'll look at in the next section. The `Unload` statement unloads the dialog box from memory and reclaims any memory associated with that object. If the dialog box is displayed when you run the `Unload` statement on it, VBA removes the dialog box from the screen.

The syntax for the `Load` and `Unload` statements is straightforward:

```
Load Dialog_Box
Unload Dialog_Box
```

For example, to load a dialog box named `frmOddDialog`, you could use the following statement:

```
Load frmOddDialog
```

Displaying and Hiding a Dialog Box

You can display a dialog box by using the `.Show` method and hide a dialog box by using the `.Hide` method. For example, if you want to display a dialog box named `frmMyDialog`, you could use the following statement:

```
frmMyDialog.Show
```

Run the macro with this line, and the `frmMyDialog` dialog box will obligingly pop up on-screen, where you can enter text in its text boxes, select or clear its check boxes, use its drop-down lists, and click its buttons as you wish. When you click one of its command buttons, the dialog box will disappear from the screen and the macro will continue to run, but until you retrieve settings from the dialog box and take action on them, the dialog box will have little effect beyond its graphical display.

You can display a dialog box by using the `.Show` method without explicitly loading the dialog box with a `Load` command first; VBA takes care of the implied `Load` command for you. There's no particular advantage to including the `Load` command, but it makes your code easier to read and to debug. For example, the two modules shown here have the same effect:

```
Sub Display_Dialog()
    Load frmOddDialog       'loads dialog box into memory
    frmOddDialog.Show       'displays dialog box
End Sub

Sub Display_Dialog()
    frmOddDialog.Show       'loads dialog box into memory and
                            'displays it
End Sub
```

NOTE   If you run a `.Hide` method without having loaded the dialog box into memory by using the `Load` statement or the `.Show` method, VBA will load the dialog box but not display it on-screen.

Once you've displayed the dialog box, take a moment to check its tab order by moving through it using the Tab key. When you open the dialog box, is the focus on the appropriate control? When you move forward from that control, is the appropriate next control selected? Adjust the tab order as necessary as described in "Adjusting the Tab Order of the Dialog Box" earlier in this chapter.

Setting a Default Button

To set a default button in a dialog box, set that button's `DefaultButton` property to `True`. The button will then be selected when the dialog box is displayed, so that if the user simply presses the Enter key to dismiss the dialog box, this button will receive the keypress.

As you'd expect, only one button can be the default button at any given time; if you set the `DefaultButton` property of any button to `True`, VBA automatically changes to `False` the `DefaultButton` property of any other button previously set to `True`.

Retrieving the User's Choices from a Dialog Box

Displaying a dialog box is all very well, but to actually do anything with a dialog box, you need to retrieve the user's choices from it. In this section, we'll look first at the VBA commands for retrieving information from a dialog box. After that, we'll go through an example of retrieving the user's choices from a relatively simple dialog box and then a more complex one. In each case, we'll record a straightforward macro and then create a dialog box to give it more power and flexibility.

Returning a String from a Text Box

To *return* (retrieve) a string from a text box, you simply check its `Value` property or `Text` property after the user has dismissed the dialog box. (For a text box, the `Value` property and the `Text` property return the same information; for other VBA objects, the `Value` property and the `Text` property return different information.) For example, if you have a text box named `MyText`, you could return its value and display it in a message box by using the following line:

```
MsgBox MyText.Value
```

VBA supports both one-line and multi-line text boxes. To create a multi-line text box, select the text box in the userform or in the drop-down list in the Properties window and set its `Multiline` property to `True`. The user will then be able to enter multiple lines in the text box and to start new lines by pressing Shift+Enter.

To add a horizontal or vertical scroll bar to a text box, set its ScrollBars property to `1- fmScrollBarsHorizontal` (for a horizontal scroll bar), `2 - fmScrollBarsVertical` (for a vertical scroll bar, which is usually more useful), or `3 - fmScrollBarsBoth` (for both).

Returning a Value from an Option Button

An option button can have only two values, `True` and `False`. A value of `True` indicates the button is selected, a value of `False` that it is unselected. You can check an option button's value with a simple `If...Then` condition. For example, if you have two option buttons named `optSearchForFile` and `optUseThis-File`, you can check their values and find out which was selected by using the following condition:

```
If optSearchForFile = True Then
    'optSearchForFile was selected; take action on this
Else 'optSearchForFile was not selected, so optUseThisFile was
    'take action for optUseThisFile
End If
```

With more than two option buttons, you'll need to use an `If...Then...ElseIf` condition or a `Select Case` statement. We'll look at the `If...Then...ElseIf` condition in the first example in the next section; the Select Case statement we'll investigate in Chapter 9.

Returning a Value from a Check Box

Like an option button, a check box can have only two values, True and False. Again, you can use an If...Then condition to check the value of a check box. For example, to check the value of a check box named DisplayProgress, you could use an If...Then condition such as this:

```
If DisplayProgress = True Then
    'Take actions for DisplayProgress
End If
```

You could also use an ElseIf condition to take effect if the check box was cleared rather than selected. The normal use of check boxes, though, is to present additional options rather than alternative ones, so often you'll want to take no action (as opposed to a different action) if a check box is cleared.

Returning a Value from a List Box

Returning a value from a list box is a little more complex than returning a value from a text box, an option button, or a check box. First, you need to tell VBA what choices you want to display in the list box.

To display items in a list box, you need to *initialize* (prepare) the userform and add the items to the list box before displaying it. To do this, right-click the name of the userform in the Project Explorer and choose View Code from the context menu to display in the code window the code for the controls assigned to the dialog box. Move the insertion point to the beginning of the code sheet (the sheet of code displayed in the code window) so that it isn't in any other macro, and then create a new macro named Private Sub UserForm_Initialize by entering that text and pressing Enter. VBA will automatically add the parentheses to the end of the macro's name, identifying it as a procedure, and the End Sub statement:

```
Private Sub UserForm_Initialize()
End Sub
```

Now, to add items to the list box, use the `AddItem` method for the list box object (here, `MyList`) with a text string in double quotation marks to specify each item in the list box:

```
MyList.AddItem "Receipt of complaint"
MyList.AddItem "Sorry, no free samples"
MyList.AddItem "Bovine Emulator Information"
MyList.AddItem "Leatherette Goblin Information"
```

> **TIP**
>
> By adding items when you initialize the form, you can add variable numbers of items as appropriate. For example, if you wanted the user to pick a document from a particular folder, you could create a list of the documents in that folder on-the-fly and then use them to fill the list box. We'll look at how to do this in Chapter 19.

You can display a list box as either a box containing a straightforward list or as a group of option buttons or check boxes. From a list of option buttons, the user can select only one item; from a list of check boxes, the user can select multiple check boxes.

Returning a Value from a Combo Box

Returning a value from a combo box (a combination list box and text box) is refreshingly similar to retrieving one from a list box: you add items to the combo box list in an `Initialize` procedure, and then check the value of the combo box after the user has dismissed the dialog box. For example, if your combo box is named `cmbMyCombo`, you could add items to it like this:

```
Private Sub UserForm_Initialize()
cmbMyCombo.AddItem "Red"
cmbMyCombo.AddItem "Blue"
cmbMyCombo.AddItem "Yellow"
End Sub
```

When you trap the Click event of the dialog box, you can retrieve the value of the combo box:

```
Result = cmbMyCombo.Value
```

The item retrieved from the combo box can be either one of the items assigned in the `Initialize` procedure or one that the user has typed into the text-box portion of the combo box.

Examples of Connecting Dialog Boxes to Macros

In this section, we'll go through two examples of how to record a macro and then build a dialog box into it to make it more useful and powerful.

Move-Paragraph Macro

The first macro moves the current paragraph up or down the document by one or two paragraphs.

Recording the Macro

We'll start by recording a macro to move the current paragraph. In the macro, we need to record the commands for selecting the current paragraph; for cutting the selection and then pasting it; for moving the insertion point up and down the document; and for inserting a bookmark, moving the insertion point to it, and then deleting the bookmark.

The finished macro will display a dialog box with option buttons for moving the current paragraph up one paragraph, up two paragraphs, down one paragraph, or down two paragraphs. There will also be a check box for returning the insertion point to its original position at the end of the macro. Because this is presumably desirable behavior for the macro, this check box will be selected by default; the user will be able to clear it if necessary.

First, create a scratch document and enter three or four paragraphs of text—just about anything will do, but it'll be easier to have recognizable text so that you can make sure that the macro is moving paragraphs as it should. Then place the insertion point in one of the paragraphs you've just entered and start recording a macro as discussed in Chapter 5: Double-click the REC indicator on the status bar, or choose Tools ➤ Macro ➤ Record New Macro to display the Record Macro dialog box. Enter the name for the macro in the Macro Name box, choose a template if necessary in the Store Macro In drop-down list, and enter a succinct description of the macro in the Description box. Then, if you want, use the Toolbars button or Keyboard button to create a toolbar button, menu option, or keyboard shortcut for the macro.

Record the following actions in the macro:

1. Insert a bookmark at the current position of the insertion point by using the Insert ➤ Bookmark command to display the Bookmarks dialog box, entering a name for the bookmark, and clicking the Add button. I'll call my bookmark `Move_Paragraph_Temp` to indicate that it's a temporary bookmark used for the `Move_Paragraph` macro.

2. Select the current paragraph by pressing F8 four times. As you'll remember from my denigration of Extend mode in Chapter 2, the first press of F8 activates Extend mode, the second selects the current word, the third selects the current sentence, and the fourth selects the current paragraph. Press the Escape button to turn off Extend mode once the paragraph is selected.

3. Cut the selected paragraph by using some form of the Cut command (e.g., by clicking the Cut button or pressing Ctrl+X or Shift+Delete).

4. Move the insertion point up one paragraph by pressing Ctrl+↑.

5. Paste the cut paragraph back in by using a Paste command (e.g., by clicking the Paste button or pressing Shift+Insert).

6. Move the insertion point down one paragraph by pressing Ctrl+↓.

7. Move the insertion point up two paragraphs by pressing Ctrl+↑ twice. (Moving the insertion point around for no immediately apparent purpose may feel weird, but do it to record the commands in VBA that we need for the macro.)

NOTE If you started with the insertion point at the beginning of the first paragraph in the document, you'll only be able to move the insertion point up one paragraph. This doesn't matter—press the keystroke anyway to record it.

8. Move the insertion point down two paragraphs by pressing Ctrl+↓ twice. (If in doing so you hit the end of the document after the first keypress, don't worry—perform the second keypress anyway to record it.)

9. Open the Bookmarks dialog box (Insert ➤ Bookmark), select the `Move_Paragraph_Temp` bookmark, and click the Go To button to go to it. Then click the Delete button to delete the `Move_Paragraph_Temp` bookmark. Click the Close button to close the Bookmarks dialog box.

10. Stop the macro recorder by clicking the Stop Recording button on the Stop Recording toolbar or by double-clicking the REC indicator on the status bar.

So far, so good: you've recorded the macro. Now open it in the Visual Basic Editor by choosing Tools ➤ Macro ➤ Macros, selecting the macro's name in the Macro dialog box, and clicking the Edit button.

You should see a macro that looks something like this:

```
1.    With ActiveDocument.Bookmarks
2.        .Add Range:=Selection.Range,
          ➥Name:="Move_Paragraph_Temp"
3.        .DefaultSorting = wdSortByName
4.        .ShowHidden = False
5.    End With
6.    Selection.Extend
7.    Selection.Extend
8.    Selection.Extend
9.    Selection.Extend
10.   Selection.EscapeKey
11.   Selection.Cut
12.   Selection.MoveUp Unit:=wdParagraph, Count:=1
13.   Selection.Paste
14.   Selection.MoveDown Unit:=wdParagraph, Count:=1
15.   Selection.MoveUp Unit:=wdParagraph, Count:=2
16.   Selection.MoveDown Unit:=wdParagraph, Count:=2
17.   Selection.GoTo What:=wdGoToBookmark,
          ➥Name:="Move_Paragraph_Temp"
18.   ActiveDocument.Bookmarks("Move_Paragraph_Temp").Delete
19.   With ActiveDocument.Bookmarks
20.       .DefaultSorting = wdSortByName
21.       .ShowHidden = False
22.   End With
```

So far, this is pretty straightforward: Lines 1 through 5 contain a `With` statement that adds the `Move_Paragraph_Temp` bookmark. Lines 3 and 4 are unnecessary here, but the macro recorder records all the settings in the Bookmark dialog box, including the setting for the Sort By option button and the Hidden Bookmarks check box. Lines 6 through 10 use the Extend Selection feature to select the current paragraph. Lines 12, 14, 15, and 16 record the syntax for moving the insertion point up and down, one paragraph and two paragraphs, respectively. Line 11 records the Cut command and Line 13 the Paste command. Finally, line 17 moves the insertion point to the `Move_Paragraph_Temp` bookmark, and line 18 removes the bookmark. Lines 19 through 22 again record the settings in the Bookmark dialog box, which we don't need here either.

We can quickly strip out the unnecessary lines (3 and 4, and 19 through 22) to give a more succinct version of the code:

```
1.   With ActiveDocument.Bookmarks
2.       .Add Range:=Selection.Range,
         ➥Name:="Move_Paragraph_Temp"
3.   End With
4.   Selection.Extend
5.   Selection.Extend
6.   Selection.Extend
7.   Selection.Extend
8.   Selection.EscapeKey
9.   Selection.Cut
10.  Selection.MoveUp Unit:=wdParagraph, Count:=1
11.  Selection.Paste
12.  Selection.MoveDown Unit:=wdParagraph, Count:=1
13.  Selection.MoveUp Unit:=wdParagraph, Count:=2
14.  Selection.MoveDown Unit:=wdParagraph, Count:=2
15.  Selection.GoTo What:=wdGoToBookmark,
     ➥Name:="Move_Paragraph_Temp"
16.  ActiveDocument.Bookmarks("Move_Paragraph_Temp").Delete
```

Creating the Dialog Box

Next, let's create the dialog box for the macro:

1. Start a userform by clicking the Insert button's drop-down list and choosing Userform from the drop-down list (or just click the Insert button if it's already showing the Userform icon) or by choosing Insert ➤ Userform.

2. Use the Properties window for the userform to set the `Name` and `Caption` properties for the userform. As before, click in the cell next to the `Name` cell and enter the `Name` property there, and then click in the cell next to the `Caption` cell and enter the `Caption` property there. I've named my userform `frmMoveCurrentParagraph` and given it the caption `Move Current Paragraph`, so that the name of the form is closely related to the text the user will see in the title bar of the dialog box but is different from the macro name (`Move_Current_Paragraph`).

3. Place two frames in the userform to act as group boxes in the dialog box:

   a. Click the Frame tool in the Toolbox, and then click and drag in the userform to place each frame.

   b. Align the frames by selecting them both and choosing Format ➤ Align ➤ Lefts.

   c. With the frames still selected, verify that the frames are the same width by choosing Format ➤ Make Same Size ➤ Width. (Don't choose Format ➤ Make Same Size ➤ Height or Format ➤ Make Same Size ➤ Both here—the top frame will need to be taller than the bottom frame.)

   d. Caption the top frame Movement and the bottom frame `Insertion Point` by selecting each in turn and then setting the `Caption` property in the Properties window. At the same time, name the top frame `fraMovement` and the bottom frame `fraOptions`.

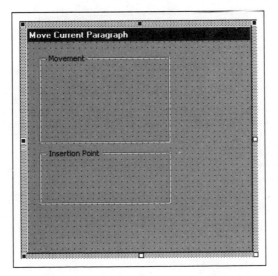

4. Place four option buttons in the Movement frame:

    a. Click the OptionButton tool in the Toolbox, and then click in the Movement frame to place each option button. This time, don't click and drag—just click to place a normal-width option button.

    b. When you've placed the four option buttons, select them and align them with each other by choosing Format ➤ Align ➤ Lefts. Then even out any disparities in spacing by choosing Format ➤ Vertical Spacing ➤ Make Equal. If necessary, use the other items on the Format ➤ Vertical Spacing submenu—Increase, Decrease, and Remove—to adjust the amount of space between the option buttons.

    c. Enter the captions for each option button by setting the `Caption` property in the Properties window. Caption them as follows: `Up one paragraph`, `Up two paragraphs`, `Down one paragraph`, and `Down two paragraphs`. These option buttons will control the number of paragraphs the macro moves the current paragraph.

    d. If you need to resize the option buttons, select them and group them by right-clicking and choosing Group from the context menu, by choosing Format ➤ Group, or by clicking the Group button on the Userform toolbar. Then select the group and drag one of the handles to resize all the option buttons evenly. For example, if you need to lengthen all the option buttons to accommodate the text you entered, drag the handle at the right midpoint of the group outward.

    e. Name the option buttons `optUpOne`, `optUpTwo`, `optDownOne`, and `optDownTwo`, respectively, by changing the Name property of each in turn in the Properties window.

TIP By default, all the option buttons on a userform are part of the same option group—i.e., only one of them can be selected at a time. If you want to provide multiple groups of option buttons on a userform, you need to specify the separate groups. The easiest way to do this is to position each group within a separate frame control, as we've done here (even though in this form we have only one group of option buttons).

f. Next, set the first option button's `Value` property to `True` by selecting

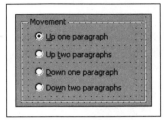

the default `False` value in the Properties window and entering `True` instead. This will select the option button in the user-form you're designing, and when the dialog box is displayed, that option button will be selected as the default choice for the option group, as shown here.

5. Place a check box in the Options frame, as shown in the illustration below:

   a. Click the CheckBox tool in the Toolbox and then click in the Options frame in the userform to place a check box of the default size.

   b. In the Properties window, set the name of the check box to `chkReturn-`

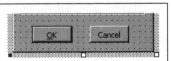

`ToPreviousPosition` (a long name but a descriptive one). Then set its `Caption` property to `Return to previous position`. Set its accelerator key to R by entering **R** as its `Accelerator` property. Finally, set the check box to be selected by default by entering `True` as its `Value` property.

6. Next, insert the command buttons for the form:

   a. Click the CommandButton tool on the Toolbox and click to place the first command button at the bottom of the userform. Repeat the process for the second command button.

   b. Size and place the command buttons by using the commands on the Format menu. (In the example, I grouped the buttons and then used

the Format ➤ Center in Form ➤ Horizontally to center the pair horizontally. Note that you need to group the buttons before doing this—if you simply select both of them, VBA will happily center one on top of the other so that only the uppermost button is visible.)

   c. Set properties for the command buttons as follows: For the left-hand button (which will become the OK button), set the Name property to `cmdOK`, the Caption property to `OK`, the Accelerator property to O (that's *O* as in OK, not a zero), and the Default property to `True`. For the right-hand button (which will become the Cancel button), set the `Name` property to `cmdCancel` and the `Caption` property to `Cancel`. Leave the `Default` property set to `False`.

7. Now we need to set the action for each command button.

First we'll set the Cancel button, because the code attached to it will be much shorter and simpler than that attached to the OK button. Double-click the Cancel button to display the code associated with it. You should see something like this:

```
Private Sub cmdCancel_Click()
End Sub
```

Add an End statement between the lines here:

```
Private Sub cmdCancel_Click()
    End
End Sub
```

This End statement removes the dialog box from the screen and ends the current procedure—in this case, the Move_Current_Paragraph macro. None of the code in the rest of the Move_Current_Paragraph macro will execute after the End statement.

Now we'll set the OK button, which is where things get interesting. When the user clicks the OK button, the macro needs to continue and do all of the following:

- Remove the dialog box from display by hiding it or by unloading it (or both). Again, the choice is yours, but using both commands is usually clearest.

- Check the Value property of the checkbox to see whether it was selected or cleared.

- Check the Value property of each option button in turn to see which of them was selected when the OK button was clicked.

Double-click the OK button to display the code attached to it. (If you're still working in the code attached to the Cancel button, scroll up or down from the Private Sub cmdCancel_Click() code to find the Private Sub cmdOK_Click() code.) Again, it should look something like this:

```
Private Sub cmdOK_Click()
End Sub
```

First, enter the following two lines between the `Private Sub` and `End Sub` lines:

```
frmMoveCurrentParagraph.Hide
Unload frmMoveCurrentParagraph
```

The `frmMoveParagraph.Hide` line activates the `.Hide` method for the `frmMoveParagraph` userform, hiding it from display on the screen. The `Unload frmMoveParagraph` line unloads the dialog box from memory.

NOTE It's not strictly necessary to hide or unload a dialog box to continue execution of a macro, but if you don't, you're likely to confuse your users. For example, if you click the OK button on a Print dialog box in a Windows application, you expect the dialog box to disappear and the command to be executed. If the dialog box didn't disappear (but started printing the job in the background), you'd probably think it hadn't registered the click, so you'd click again and again until it went away.

8. Next, the macro needs to check the `Value` property of the `chkReturnTo-PreviousPosition` check box to find out whether to insert a bookmark in the document to mark the current position of the insertion point. To do this, enter a straightforward `If...Then` statement:

```
If chkReturnToPreviousPosition = True Then
End If
```

If the `chkReturnToPreviousPosition` statement is set to `True`—that is, if the check box is selected—the code in the lines following the `Then` statement will run. The `Then` statement will consist of the lines for inserting a bookmark that we recorded earlier. Cut these lines from the macro and paste them into the `If...Then` statement like so:

```
If chkReturnToPreviousPosition = True Then
    With ActiveDocument.Bookmarks
        .Add Range:=Selection.Range,
        ➡Name:="Move_Paragraph_Temp"
    End With
End If
```

If the check box is selected, the macro will insert a bookmark; if the check box is cleared, the macro will pass over these lines.

9. Next, paste in the code for selecting the current paragraph and cutting it to the Clipboard. Remove the `Selection.EscapeKey` statement:

```
Selection.Extend
Selection.Extend
Selection.Extend
Selection.Extend
Selection.Cut
```

10. Now, we need to retrieve the `Value` properties from the option buttons to see which one was selected when the user chose the OK button in the dialog box. For this, we can again use an `If` condition—this time, an `If...Then ElseIf...Else` condition, with the relevant insertion-point-movement lines from the recorded macro pasted in:

```
If optUpOne = True Then
    Selection.MoveUp Unit:=wdParagraph, Count:=1
ElseIf optUpTwo = True Then
    Selection.MoveUp Unit:=wdParagraph, Count:=2
ElseIf optDownOne = True Then
    Selection.MoveDown Unit:=wdParagraph, Count:=1
Else
    Selection.MoveDown Unit:=wdParagraph, Count:=2
End If
Selection.Paste
```

Here, `optUpOne`, `optUpTwo`, `optDownOne`, and `optDownTwo` (which piggybacks on the `Else` statement here and is therefore not specified by name in the listing) are the four option buttons from the dialog box, representing the choice to move the current paragraph up one paragraph, up two paragraphs, down one paragraph, or down two paragraphs, respectively. The condition is relatively straightforward: If `optUpOne` is `True` (i.e., selected), the first `Then` condition kicks in, moving the insertion point up one paragraph from its current position (after cutting the current paragraph, the insertion point will be at the beginning of the paragraph that was after the current one). If `optUpOne` is `False`, the first `ElseIf` condition is evaluated; if it is `True`, the second `Then` condition runs; and if it is `False`, the next

ElseIf condition is evaluated. If that too is False, the Else code is run; in this case, the Else statement means that the optDownTwo option button was selected in the dialog box, so the Else code moves the insertion point down two paragraphs.

Wherever the insertion point ends up after the attentions of the option buttons, the next line of code (Selection.Paste) pastes in the cut paragraph from the Clipboard.

11. Finally, the macro needs to return the insertion point to where it was originally if the chkReturnToPreviousPosition check box is selected. Again, we can test for this with a simple If...Then condition that incorporates the go-to-bookmark and delete-bookmark lines from the recorded macro:

```
If chkReturnToPreviousPosition = True Then
    Selection.GoTo What:=wdGoToBookmark,
    ➥Name:="Move_Paragraph_Temp"
    ActiveDocument.Bookmarks("Move_Paragraph_Temp").Delete
End If
```

If the chkReturnToPreviousPosition check box is selected, VBA moves the insertion point to the temporary bookmark and then deletes that bookmark.

Listing 7.1 shows the completed code for the cmdOK button.

Listing 7.1

```
1.   Private Sub cmdOK_Click()
2.       frmMoveParagraph.Hide
3.       Unload frmMoveParagraph
4.   If chkReturnToPreviousPosition = True Then
5.       With ActiveDocument.Bookmarks
6.           .Add Range:=Selection.Range,
             ➥Name:="Move_Paragraph_Temp"
7.       End With
8.   End If
9.       Selection.Extend
10.      Selection.Extend
```

```
11.       Selection.Extend
12.       Selection.Extend
13.       Selection.Cut
14.   If optUpOne = True Then
15.       Selection.MoveUp Unit:=wdParagraph, Count:=1
16.   ElseIf optUpTwo = True Then
17.       Selection.MoveUp Unit:=wdParagraph, Count:=2
18.   ElseIf optDownOne = True Then
19.       Selection.MoveDown Unit:=wdParagraph, Count:=1
20.   Else
21.       Selection.MoveDown Unit:=wdParagraph, Count:=2
22.   End If
23.   Selection.Paste
24.   If chkReturnToPreviousPosition = True Then
25.       Selection.GoTo What:=wdGoToBookmark,
          ➥Name:="Move_Paragraph_Temp"
26.       ActiveDocument.Bookmarks("Move_Paragraph_Temp")
          ➥.Delete
27.   End If
28.   End Sub
```

Meeting-Announcement Macro

This macro displays a dialog box (see Figure 7.7) for quickly putting together a meeting announcement. Once the user has made their choices in the dialog box, the macro opens a new document and inserts the information.

FIGURE 7.7

The finished dialog box for the Meeting Announcement macro.

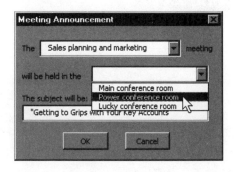

Recording the Macro

The recorded portion of this macro is short and sweet:

1. Start the macro recorder. Name the macro and enter a description, and then assign a toolbar button, menu item, or shortcut key as appropriate.

2. Create a new document based on the Normal.dot global template by clicking the New button on the Standard toolbar.

3. Type some text into the document (anything will do—we'll remove it from the macro when we add the dialog box) and press Enter.

4. Stop the macro recorder.

Now open the macro in the Visual Basic Editor. You should see code that looks something like this:

```
Sub Meeting_Announcement()
'
' Meeting_Announcement Macro
' Displays a dialog box for specifying the details of a meeting.
'
    Documents.Add
    Selection.TypeText Text:="Here is some bogus text."
    Selection.TypeParagraph
End Sub
```

This is all pretty clear. VBA automatically inserts the comment lines with the macro's name and description. The `Documents.Add` line creates the new document; the `Selection.TypeText Text:=` line enters the text you typed; and the `Selection.TypeParagraph` line is the Enter keypress.

Creating the Dialog Box

Now, let's create a dialog box to hook up to the macro:

1. In the Visual Basic Editor, start a new userform by choosing Insert ➤ Userform or by using the Insert button on the Standard toolbar.

2. Name the userform something appropriate by setting the `Name` property in the Properties window. I've named mine `frmMeetingAnnouncement`.

3. Add two combo boxes and one text box to the userform by using the ComboBox tool and the TextBox tool:

    a. Set the `Name` property for the first combo box to `cmbMeetingName`.

    b. Set the `Name` property for the second combo box to `cmbMeetingLocation`.

    c. Set the `Name` property for the text box to `txtMeetingSubject`.

4. Add two command buttons to the userform:

    a. Set the `Name` property for the first command button to `cmdOK` and set its `DefaultButton` property to `True`.

    b. Set the `Name` property for the second command button to `cmdCancel`.

5. Add four labels to the userform by using the Label tool. Set their `Caption` properties to `The`, `meeting`, `will be held in the`, and `The subject will be:`, respectively. For each, set the `AutoSize` property to `True` to have VBA shrink the control to just bigger than the size taken up by the text.

6. 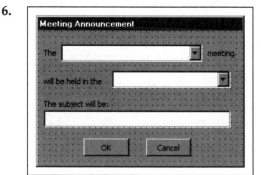 Arrange the controls on the userform approximately as shown here by using the commands on the Format menu. As in the previous example, select multiple items that you want to align, and group the command buttons before centering them horizontally.

7. Double-click the Cancel button to create the macro for its Click event on the code sheet for the userform, and then add an `End` statement between the `Private Sub` and `End Sub` lines:

```
Private Sub cmdCancel_Click()
     End
End Sub
```

8. In the userform, double-click the OK button to create the macro for its Click event on the code sheet. First, enter the `Unload` statement between the `Private Sub` and `End Sub` lines:

```
Private Sub cmdOK_Click()
    Unload frmMeetingAnnouncement
End Sub
```

9. Create a text string out of the Value properties of the `cmbMeetingName`, `cmbMeetingLocation`, and `txbMeetingSubject` controls, together with some boilerplate text to make a complete sentence, as shown below. The + signs concatenate (link together) the text strings, and the `Chr(13)` character is a carriage return. The $ tells VBA that this variable is a text string rather than any other kind of variable (we'll discuss strings in detail in Chapter 10).

```
MyText$ = "The " + cmbMeetingName.Value +
➥" meeting will be held in the "
➥+ cmbMeetingLocation.Value + "." + Chr(13)
➥+ "The subject will be "
➥+ txbMeetingSubject.Text + "."
```

10. Cut the recorded statements from the `Meeting_Announcement` macro and paste them into the OK button's macro after the `Unload` statement:

```
Private Sub cmdOK_Click()
    Unload frmMeetingAnnouncement
    Documents.Add
    Selection.TypeText Text:="Here is some bogus text."
    Selection.TypeParagraph
End Sub
```

11. Replace the text in double quotation marks with `MyText$` so that the macro inserts the string you just created:

```
Selection.TypeText Text:=MyText$
```

12. On the code sheet for the userform, create an `Initialize` procedure and use the `AddItem` method to add items to the `cmbMeetingLocation` and `cmbMeetingName` combo boxes:

```
Private Sub UserForm_Initialize()
    cmbMeetingLocation.AddItem "Main conference room"
    cmbMeetingLocation.AddItem "Power conference room"
    cmbMeetingLocation.AddItem "Lucky conference room"
    cmbMeetingName.AddItem "Strategy"
    cmbMeetingName.AddItem "Sales planning and marketing"
    cmbMeetingName.AddItem "Acquisitions and reductions"
    cmbMeetingName.AddItem "Review board considerations"
End Sub
```

13. Finally, in the `Meeting_Announcement` macro, enter the `Load` statement and `.Show` method to display the dialog box:

```
Load frmMeetingAnnouncement
frmMeetingAnnouncement.Show
```

Listing 7.2 shows the full listing for the `cmdOK` button.

Listing 7.2

```
Private Sub cmdOK_Click()
    Unload frmMeetingAnnouncement
    MyText$ = "The " + cmbMeetingName.Value + " meeting will
➥be held in the " + cmbMeetingLocation.Value + "."
➥+ Chr(13) + "The subject will be "
➥+ txtMeetingSubject.Text + "."
    Documents.Add
    Selection.TypeText Text:=MyText$
    Selection.TypeParagraph
End Sub
```

You should now be able to run the `Meeting_Announcement` macro (or whatever you named it), either in the Visual Basic Editor (by stepping through it with the F8 key or by clicking the Run Sub/Userform button) or in Word (by choosing it from the Macros dialog box and clicking the Run button).

NOTE If you get the error message "Compile error: Variable not defined" when you run this macro (or any other), you probably have the Visual Basic Editor set to require explicit declarations of variables. See page 323 for more information.

With message boxes and straightforward dialog boxes, you can transform a simple recorded macro into one that's ten times more versatile. In the coming chapters, we'll examine various occasions when you might want to add a dialog box to a macro to give the user the power of choice; and in Chapter 19, I'll show you how you can construct dynamic dialog boxes that change appropriately when the user chooses certain options in them. But in the meantime, a change of topic: in Chapter 8, we'll look at how to repeat actions in VBA by using loops. Combine message boxes and dialog boxes with loops, and you've really got something.

Using Loops to Repeat Actions

As in life, so in macros: at times, you may want to repeat an action to achieve a certain effect. Sometimes, you'll want to repeat an action a predetermined number of times: break six eggs to make an omelet, or create six new documents based on a certain template. More often, you'll want to repeat an action until a certain condition is met: buy two lottery tickets a week until you win more than $2,000 on the lottery, or repeat an action for every instance of a word that the Find feature identifies in a document. In this case, you don't know when you'll triumph against the wretched odds of the lottery, and you don't know how many instances of the relevant word there will be in any given document; you just carry on until the condition is met.

In VBA, you use *loops* to repeat actions. By using loops, you can transform a simple recorded macro into one that repeats itself as appropriate for the material it's working on. VBA provides a number of expressions for creating loops in your macros. In this chapter, we'll look at the different types of loops and typical uses for each.

When Should You Use a Loop?

To repeat an action or a series of actions in VBA, you can either record that repetition into a macro, or edit a macro containing the relevant commands and use copy and paste to repeat them. For example, you could record a macro containing the code for creating a new document based on the Normal global template (`Documents.Add`), open the macro in the Visual Basic Editor, and then simply copy that statement to five other lines to create a macro that created six new documents. But almost invariably, it's much better to use a loop structure to repeat the commands as necessary.

Loops have several straightforward advantages over simple repetition of code:

- Your macros will be shorter and will run faster.

- Your macros will be more flexible: instead of hard-coding the number of repetitions, you'll be able to control it as necessary. (Hard-coding means writing fixed code as opposed to variable code.)

- Your macros will be easier to test and debug, particularly for people other than you.

That said, if you simply need to repeat one or more actions two or three times in a macro, and that macro will always need to repeat the action the same number of times, there's nothing wrong with hard-coding the macro by repeating the code. It'll work fine, it's easy to do, and you won't have to spend time with the logic of loops. The code will likely be longer and will execute a little more slowly, but that's no big deal as long as it works.

> **NOTE** In Chapter 17, we'll start looking at how to break your code down into modules and how to strip it down to its essentials to make it run optimally. For the time being, we'll concentrate on just getting things done. I'm assuming your goal is to create effective macros with VBA to save yourself (and perhaps your colleagues) time and effort, and that you care less about the aesthetics of the code than about whether it works.

The Lowdown on Loops

In VBA, a loop is a structure that repeats a number of statements, looping back to the beginning of the structure once it has finished executing them. Each cycle of execution of a loop is called an *iteration*.

There are two basic categories of loops:

- *Fixed-iteration loops* are loops that repeat a set number of times.
- *Indefinite loops* are loops that repeat a flexible number of times.

The running of either type of loop is controlled by the *loop invariant*, also called the *loop determinant*. This can be either a numeric expression or a logical expression; fixed-iteration loops typically use numeric expressions (for example, to run through five iterations of a loop), whereas indefinite loops typically use logical expressions (for example, to continue taking an action until the end of the document is reached).

Visual Basic for Applications provides expressions for the following loops:

- Repeating an action or a sequence of actions a given number of times (For... Next)

- Repeating an action or a sequence of actions once for each object in a collection (For Each...Next)

- Performing an action or a sequence of actions if a condition is True and continuing to perform it until the condition becomes False (Do While... Loop); or vice versa, performing the action or sequence of actions while a condition is False until it becomes True (Do Until...Loop)

- Performing an action or a sequence of actions once, then repeating it if a condition is True until it becomes False (Do...Loop While); or vice versa, performing the action or sequence of actions once and repeating it while a condition is False until it becomes True (Do...Loop Until)

Let's look first at the For...loops, which deal with a fixed number of repetitions.

Using For...Loops for Fixed Repetitions

For...loops execute for a fixed number of times. For...Next loops repeat for a number of times of your choosing, while For Each...Next loops execute once for each element in the specified collection.

For...Next Loops

For...Next loops provide you with a straightforward way to repeat an action or a sequence of actions a given number of times, specified by a counter variable. The counter variable can be hard-coded into the macro, passed from an input box or dialog box, or even passed from a value generated by a different part of the macro (or a different module).

Syntax

The syntax for For...Next loops is as follows:

```
For counter = start To end [Step stepsize]
    [statements]
[Exit For]
    [statements]
Next [counter]
```

Here's what it all means:

counter	A numeric variable. By default, VBA increases the counter value by an increment of 1 with each iteration of the loop, but you can change this increment by using the optional Step keyword and stepsize argument. Note that counter is required in the For statement and is optional in the Next statement; however, it's a good idea to include counter in the Next statement to make your code clear, particularly when you're using multiple For...Next statements in the same macro.
start	A numeric variable or numeric expression giving the starting value for counter.
end	A numeric variable or numeric expression giving the ending value for counter.
stepsize	A numeric variable or numeric expression specifying how much to increase the value of counter. To use stepsize, use the Step keyword and specify the stepsize variable. As I just mentioned, stepsize is 1 by default, but you can use any positive or negative value (depending on whether you want the value to increase or decrease).
Exit For	A statement for exiting a For loop.
Next	The keyword indicating the end of the loop. Again, you can specify the optional counter here to make your code clear.

Here's what happens in a `For...Next` loop:

1. When VBA enters the loop at the `For` statement, it assigns the `start` value to `counter`. It then executes the statements in the loop; when it reaches the `Next` statement, it increments `counter` by 1 or by the specified `stepsize`, and loops back to the `For` statement.

2. VBA then checks the `counter` variable against the `end` variable. If `counter` is greater than `end`, it terminates the loop and continues execution of the macro with the statement immediately after the `Next` statement (which could be any action, or the end of the macro). If `counter` is less than or equal to `end`, VBA repeats the statements in the loop, increases `counter` by 1 or by `stepsize`, and loops back to the `For` statement again.

3. The `Exit For` statement exits the `For` loop early. We'll look at how to use the `Exit For` statement later in this chapter.

I'll show you the different uses of `For...Next` loops a little farther on in the chapter as well.

Straightforward For...Next Loops

In a straightforward `For...Next` loop, you first specify a counter variable and the starting and ending values for it:

```
For i = 1 to 200
```

Here, `i` is the counter variable, 1 is the starting value, and 200 is the ending value. As mentioned earlier, by default Word will increase the counter variable by an increment of 1 with each iteration of the loop. Here, it will be 1, 2, 3, and so on up to 200; a value of 201 (or greater—though in this example it cannot reach a greater value than 201 because the `stepsize` is 1) will terminate the loop. You can also use a `Step` keyword to specify a different increment, either positive or negative; more on this in the next section.

Next, you specify the actions to perform in the loop, followed by the `Next` keyword to end the loop:

```
Application.StatusBar = "Please wait while Word formats your
➥document: " + Str$(i) + "..."
Next i
```

This will produce a status bar readout indicating Word's progress in formatting your document:

```
Please wait while Word formats your document:  199...
```

So far, so good. But how about something a little more practical? Say you need to check every paragraph in documents you receive from contributors to make sure they don't contain any unsuitable formatting. You could retrieve the number of paragraphs in the document from its properties (I'll discuss this in Chapter 13), and then use this number (stored here in the variable NumberOfParas) to provide both an end point for the macro and a reference point for the user in the status bar display:

```
For i = 1 to NumberOfParas
    CheckParagraphForIllegalFormatting
    Application.StatusBar = "Please wait while Word checks the
    ➥formatting in this document: Paragraph" + Str$(i)
    ➥+ " out of " + Str$(NumberOfParas) + "..."
    Selection.MoveDown Unit:=wdParagraph, Count:=1,
    ➥Extend:=wdMove
Next i
```

This macro will start at the beginning of the document (probably by using a Selection.HomeKey Unit:=wdStory, Extend:=wdMove statement). It runs the CheckParagraphForIllegalFormatting macro on the current paragraph, displays a message in the status bar indicating which paragraph out of the total number it is working on, and then moves down a paragraph. When it reaches the Next statement, it increases the i counter by 1 (because no step-size variable is specified) and loops back to the For statement, where it compares the value of i to the value of NumberOfParas. The macro will continue to loop until i has reached the value of NumberOfParas, which will be the final iteration of the loop.

Likewise, you could use a simple For...Next loop to quickly build the structure of a document. For example, you could use the following loop to insert the hours for a timesheet or work log:

```
For i = 1 To 24
    Selection.TypeText Str$(i) + ":00" + Chr(13)
Next i
```

Here, the `Selection.TypeText` statement inserts the automatically increased string for the counter, `i`, together with a colon and two zeroes (to create a time format) and a `Chr(13)` to create a new paragraph after each. The loop runs from `i = 1` to `i = 24` and stops when the automatic increase takes `i` to 25.

For...Next Loops with Step Values

If increasing the counter variable by the default 1 doesn't suit your purpose, you can use the `Step` keyword to specify a different increment or decrement. For example, the following statement increases the counter variable by 20, so the sequence will be 0, 20, 40, 60, 80, 100.

```
For i = 0 to 100 Step 20
```

You can also use a decrement by specifying a negative Step value:

```
For i = 1000 to 0 Step -100
```

This statement produces the sequence 1,000, 900, 800, etc., down to 0.

Instead of the "x out of y" countdown example given in the previous section, you could produce a NASA-style countdown by decreasing the variable `NumberOfParas` to zero:

```
For i = NumberOfParas to 0 Step -1
    CheckParagraphForIllegalFormatting
    Application.StatusBar = "Please wait while Word checks the
    ➡formatting in this document: " + Str$(i)
    Selection.MoveDown Unit:=wdParagraph, Count:=1,
    ➡Extend:=wdMove
Next I
```

Using an Input Box to Drive a For...Next Loop

Sometimes you'll be able to hard-code the number of iterations into a For...Next loop, as in the previous examples; depending on the type of work you're involved in, this will probably be the exception rather than the rule. At other times, you'll take a number from another operation, such as the `NumberOfParas` variable in the example above. But often you'll need to use input from the user to drive the loop. The easiest way of doing this is to have the user enter the value into an input box.

NOTE   Chapter 6 discusses how to display input boxes and retrieve values from them.

For example, consider a `Create_Folders` macro designed to reduce the tedium of creating multiple folders with predictable names, such as for the chapters of a book. For the sake of argument, say that you're using a four-digit number to identify the book (perhaps part of the book's international standard book number, or ISBN), the letter *c* for *chapter*, and a two-digit number to identify the chapter. So you would end up with folders named 1234c01, 1234c02, 1234c03, and so on—simple enough to create manually, but very boring if you needed more than, say, a dozen.

To write the macro for naming the folders automatically, you might use code such as that shown in Listing 8.1.

Listing 8.1

```
1.   Sub Create_Folders()
2.       HowManyFolders = InputBox("Enter the number of folders
         ➥you want to create.", "Create Folders 1.0")
3.       ISBN$ = InputBox("Enter the ISBN to use for the
         ➥folders.", "Create Folders 1.0")
4.        For i = 1 To HowManyFolders
5.             Count$ = LTrim$(Str$(i))
6.             If i < 10 Then Count$ = "0" + Count$
7.             FolderName$ = ISBN$ + "c" + Count$
8.             MkDir FolderName$
9.         Next i
10.  End Sub
```

Analysis

This macro starts off by displaying two input boxes in immediate succession. The first input box, in line 2, prompts the user to supply the number of folders they want to create; it stores it in the variable `HowManyFolders`. The second input box, in line 3, prompts the user to enter the ISBN (the book number), which it stores in the string `ISBN$`.

Now that the macro has the necessary information, it goes into a `For...Next` loop to create the folders. Line 4 restricts the loop: it will run from `i = 1` to `i = HowManyFolders`, the variable supplied by the user in the first input box.

Line 5 creates a string named `Count$` that consists of the number from the counter, `i`; the `LTrim$` statement is necessary because of a quirk of VBA—when you convert a value to a string, it gains a leading space. We'll examine strings in detail in Chapter 10, so for now suffice to say that this statement takes all of the string but the unwanted leading space.

Line 6 modifies the `Count$` string so that the folder name will have a two-digit number rather than a one-digit number for the numbers 1 through 9: if the value of the counter `i` is less than 10, this line adds a zero to the `Count$` string. So if `i` is 1, `Count$` becomes 01; if `i` is 3, `Count$` becomes 03; and so on.

Line 7 builds a string for the name of the current folder to be created by concatenating the `ISBN$` string, the letter *c* (to stand for *chapter*), and the `Count$` string. It stores this name in the `FolderName$` string. Line 8 then uses the `MkDir` command with the `FolderName$` string to create a folder (i.e., make a directory—the old DOS command `mkdir` lives on in VBA).

Line 9 then loops back to the `For` statement, incrementing the `i` counter. VBA compares the `i` counter to the `HowManyFolders` variable and lathers, rinses, and repeats as necessary.

NOTE

Note that this macro creates the new folders in the current folder, without giving the user a choice of location. This is good enough for the example, but in practice it would be tasteless and antisocial. At a minimum, the macro should warn the user in an opening message box that it will create the new folders in the current folder and let them cancel the operation so that they can pick a more suitable folder before rerunning it. Better, the macro would display an input box that let the user type in the location they wanted for the folders; the macro would then make sure that the folder existed before attempting to proceed. Better still, the macro would display a dialog box that let the user pick the recipient folder from a standard Windows 95 tree. I'll show you how to add these capabilities to a macro later in the book: Chapter 13 covers working with files and folders, and Chapters 19 and 20 discuss how you can make dialog boxes supply this type of information.

Using a Dialog Box Control to Drive a For...Next Loop

For those occasions when an input box will not suffice, you can easily use a value from a dialog box to drive a For...Next loop. Instead of using the two input

boxes for the Create_Folders macro as described in the previous section, you could use a single dialog box. In its simplest form, this dialog box would provide a text box for the number of folders to be created (though you could also use a drop-down list for this, or even a spinner) and a text box for the ISBN of the book, and it might look like the example shown here:

As you learned in the previous chapter, you would display the dialog box by using the .Show method, probably with a Load statement first:

```
Load frmCreateFolders
frmCreateFolders.Show
```

As you can see, I've named my dialog box frmCreateFolders so that it's easily identifiable. The first text box, the one identified with the Number of Folders to Create label, is named HowManyFolders; the second text box is named ISBN. Using these names means that we can reuse most of the code from the version of the macro that had the two input boxes. So the OK button in the dialog box has the following code attached to its Click event:

```
Private Sub cmdOK_Click()
    frmCreateFolders.Hide
    Unload frmCreateFolders
    For i = 1 To HowManyFolders
        Count$ = LTrim$(Str$(i))
        If i < 10 Then Count$ = "0" + Count$
        FolderName$ = ISBN + "c" + Count$
        MkDir FolderName$
    Next i
End Sub
```

When the user clicks the OK button, VBA hides the dialog box and then unloads it from memory. Then the For loop runs from i = 1 to i = HowManyFolders, which is the value in the HowManyFolders text box. Just as before, the `FolderName$` string is constructed out of the ISBN (in this case, the contents of the `ISBN` text box), the letter *c*, and the `Count$` string derived from the counter `i`.

As in the example from the previous chapter, the Cancel button here has an `End` statement attached to its Click event, so that if the user clicks it, VBA ends the procedure:

```
Private Sub cmdCancel_Click()
        End
End Sub
```

For Each...Next Loops

The `For Each...Next` loop has the same basic premise as the `For...Next` loop—you're working with a known number of repetitions, in this case the number of objects in a collection. (I'll talk more about Word's collections of objects in Chapter 11.) For example, all of Word's bookmarks are stored in a collection, so you could choose to take an action that repeated itself for each bookmark in the collection—you wouldn't need to know how many bookmarks there were in the collection, provided there were at least one (if there were none, nothing would happen).

Syntax

The syntax for the `For Each...Next` statement is straightforward:

```
For Each object In collection
        [statements]
        [Exit For]
        [statements]
Next [object]
```

VBA starts by evaluating the number of objects in the specified collection. It then executes the statements in the loop for the first of those objects. When it reaches the `Next` keyword, it loops back to the `For Each` line, reevaluates the number of objects, and performs further iterations as appropriate.

Here's an example: The Windows collection contains the open windows in Word. So you could create a straightforward macro to close all the open windows by using a `For Each...Next` loop like this:

```
For Each Window in Windows
    ActiveDocument.Close
Next
```

For each open window, VBA closes the current document (by using the `Close` method in the second line above), which transfers focus to the next window. As long as there are open windows in the Windows collection, VBA repeats the loop, thus closing all open windows and then terminating the macro.

NOTE This example provides a straightforward illustration of how a `For Each...Next` loop works, but you probably wouldn't want to use the example in practice; instead, you would probably use the `Close` method with the `Documents` object (which contains all the open documents) to close all the open documents. (I'll discuss how to use the `Close` method in Chapter 13.) However, you might want to use a `For Each...Next` loop to check each open document for certain characteristics before closing it.

Using an Exit For Statement

As you saw earlier in the chapter when looking at the syntax for `For` statements, you can use one or more `Exit For` statements to exit a `For` loop if a certain condition or other is met. `Exit For` statements are optional and are seldom necessary; if you find yourself needing to use `Exit For` statements in all your macros, there's probably something wrong with the loops you're constructing. Still, if they work for you, that's fine by me.

On those occasions when you do need them to exit a loop early, you'll typically use `Exit For` statements with straightforward conditions. For example, if you wanted to close open windows until you reached a certain document that you knew to be open, you could use an `Exit For` statement like this:

```
For Each Window In Windows
    If ActiveWindow.Caption = "Document1" Then Exit For
    ActiveDocument.Close
Next Window
```

This `For Each...Next` statement checks the `Caption` property of the active window to see if it's Document1; if it is, the `Exit For` statement causes VBA to exit the loop. Otherwise, VBA closes the active document and returns to the start of the loop.

You can also use multiple `Exit For` statements if you need to. For example, you might need to check two or more conditions during the actions performed in the loop.

Using Do...Loops for Variable Numbers of Repetitions

`Do` loops give you more flexibility than `For` loops in that you can test for conditions in them and direct the flow of the macro accordingly. The various permutations of `Do` loops include the following:

- `Do While...Loop`
- `Do...Loop While`
- `Do Until...Loop`
- `Do...Loop Until`

These loops break down into two categories:

- Loops that test a condition before performing any action. `Do While...Loop` and `Do Until...Loop` loops fall into this category.

- Loops that perform an action before testing a condition. `Do...Loop While` and `Do...Loop Until` loops fall into this category.

The difference between the two types of loop in each category is that each `While` loop repeats itself *while* a condition is `True` (i.e., until it becomes `False`), whereas each `Until` loop repeats itself *until* a condition becomes `True` (i.e., while the condition is `False`). This means to some extent that you can get by using only the `While` loops or only the `Until` loops if you're feeling lazy—you'll just need to set up your conditions the other way around. For example, you could use a `Do While...Loop` loop with a condition of `x < 100` or a `Do Until...Loop` loop with a condition of `x = 100` to achieve the same effect.

In this discussion, I'll assume that you want to learn about all the different kinds of loops so that you can diligently use each when it is most appropriate. We'll start with the `Do While...Loop` loop, because I find it to be the most useful of the four types.

Do While...Loop Loops

In a `Do While...Loop` loop, you specify a condition that has to be `True` for the actions in the loop to be executed; if the condition is not `True`, the actions are not executed and the loop ends. For example, you might want to search a document for an instance of a particular word or phrase and take action once you find it. Figure 8.1 shows a `Do While...Loop` loop.

FIGURE 8.1

A `Do While...Loop` loop tests for a condition before performing the actions contained in the loop.

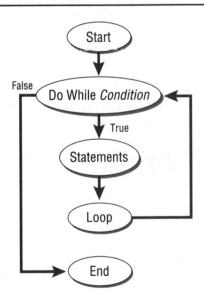

Syntax

The syntax for the `Do While...Loop` loop is straightforward:

```
Do While condition
    [statements]
    [Exit Do]
    [statements]
Loop
```

While the condition is met (`Do While`), the statements in the loop are executed. The `Loop` keyword returns execution to the `Do While` line, which is then re-evaluated; if the condition remains `True`, the loop continues; if the condition is `False`, execution continues with the statement on the line after the `Loop` keyword. You can use one or more `Exit Do` statements to break out of the loop as necessary.

Say you wanted to construct a glossary from a long document that used italics to explain main terms in the body text and list paragraphs, which both used Times New Roman font, without picking up italic variable names in code snippets. You could command Word to search for Times New Roman text with the italic attribute; if Word found instances of the text, it would take the appropriate actions, such as selecting the sentence containing the term, together with the next sentence (or the rest of the paragraph), and copying it to the end of another document. Then it would continue the search, performing the loop until it found no more instances of italic Times New Roman text.

Listing 8.2 shows an example of how such a macro might be constructed with a `Do While...Loop` loop. This listing includes a number of commands that we haven't examined yet and that I'll just mention briefly here as an illustration of how the loop works.

Listing 8.2

```
1.   Sub GenerateGlossary()
2.       Source = ActiveWindow.Caption
3.       Documents.Add
4.       GlossaryName$ = InputBox$("Enter the name for the
         ➥glossary document.", "Create Glossary 1.0")
5.       ActiveDocument.SaveAs FileName:=GlossaryName$,
         ➥FileFormat:=wdFormatDocument
```

```
 6.        Destination = ActiveWindow.Caption
 7.        Windows(Source).Activate
 8.        Selection.HomeKey Unit:=wdStory
 9.        Selection.Find.ClearFormatting
10.        Selection.Find.Font.Italic = True
11.        Selection.Find.Font.Name = "Times New Roman"
12.        Selection.Find.Text = ""
13.        Selection.Find.Execute
14.        Do While Selection.Find.Found
15.            Selection.Copy
16.            Selection.MoveRight Unit:=wdCharacter, Count:=1,
               ➥Extend:=wdMove
17.            Windows(Destination).Activate
18.            Selection.EndKey Unit:=wdStory
19.            Selection.Paste
20.            Windows(Source).Activate
21.            Selection.Find.Execute
22.        Loop
23.    End Sub
```

Analysis

This macro attempts to pull italic items in the Times New Roman font from the current document. It starts in line 2 by storing the `Caption` property of the current window in the `Source` variable, which it will use to activate this document as necessary throughout the procedure.

Line 3 creates a new document based on the Normal.dot global template. Line 4 displays an input box requesting the user to enter a name for the file that will contain the glossary entries pulled from the current document, and line 5 saves the document with this name. Line 6 stores the `Caption` property of this document in the `Destination` variable, again making it available to activate this document as necessary throughout the procedure. (We now have the source document identified by the `Source` variable and the destination document identified by the `Destination` variable.)

Line 7 uses the `Activate` method to activate the `Source` window. Line 8 moves the insertion point to the beginning of the document, which is where the macro needs to start working to catch all the italicized words in Times New

Roman. Lines 9, 10, 11, and 12 detail the Find operation the macro needs to perform: line 9 removes any formatting applied to the current Find item; line 10 sets the Find feature to find italic formatting; line 11 sets Find to find Times New Roman text; and line 12 specifies the search string, which is an empty string (" ") that causes Find to search only for the specified formatting. Line 13 then starts the Find operation by using the `Execute` method.

Lines 14 through 22 implement the `Do While...Loop` loop. Line 14 expresses the condition for the loop: `While Selection.Find.Found`, that is, while the Find operation is able to find an instance of the italic Times New Roman text specified in the previous lines. While this condition is met (is `True`), the commands contained in the loop will execute. Line 15 copies the selection (the item found with italic Times New Roman formatting). Line 16 moves the insertion point one character to the right, effectively deselecting the selection and getting the macro ready to search for the next instance in the document; you need to move the insertion point off the selection to the right so that the next Find operation does not find the same instance. (If the macro were searching up through the document instead of down through it, you would need to move the insertion point off the selection to the left instead.)

Line 17 activates the `Destination` window, putting Word's focus in it. Line 18 then moves the insertion point to the end of the document, and line 19 pastes the copied item in at the position of the insertion point. Moving to the end of the document is not strictly necessary here, provided that the Normal.dot global template does not contain any text—if Normal.dot is empty, the new document created in line 4 will be empty too, and the start and end of the document will be in the same position; and after each paste operation, Word positions the insertion point after the pasted item. However, if Normal.dot contains text, this step is necessary, so I've included it here.

Line 20 simply activates the `Source` document once more, and line 21 repeats the Find operation. The `Loop` statement in line 22 then loops execution of the macro back to line 14, where the `Do While Selection.Find.Found` condition evaluates whether this latest Find operation was successful (`True`). If it was successful, the loop continues; if it was not, execution of the macro continues at line 23 (which here happens to be the end of the macro but which could proceed in various ways, such as switching back to and then saving the document containing the glossary entries).

TIP To improve this macro, you could start it with a message box that asked the user to verify that they wanted to run the current procedure, and to run it on the current document, as this macro will do automatically.

Do...Loop While Loops

A Do...Loop While loop is similar to a Do While...Loop loop, except that in the former case, the actions in the loop are run at least once, whether the condition is True or False. If the condition is True, the loop continues to run until the condition becomes False. Figure 8.2 shows a Do...Loop While loop.

If Do While...Loop loops make immediate sense to you, Do...Loop While loops may well strike you as a little bizarre—you're going to take an action *before* checking a condition? The truth is, Do...Loop While loops can be very useful, but they lend themselves to different situations than Do While...Loop loops.

FIGURE 8.2

In a Do...Loop While loop, the actions in the loop run once before the condition is tested.

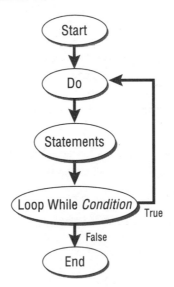

281

Consider the lottery example from the beginning of the chapter. In that situation, you execute the action before you check the condition that controls the loop: first, you buy a lottery ticket, then you check to see if you've won. If you haven't won, or have won only a paltry sum that doesn't meet your wealth cutoff point, you loop back and buy more tickets for the next lottery. (Actually, this is logically a Do...Loop Until loop rather than a Do...Loop While loop, because you continue the loop while the condition is False; when you win a suitably large amount, the condition becomes True.) Likewise, in a macro, you may want to take an action and then check whether you need to repeat it. For example, you might want to apply special formatting to a paragraph, then check to see if there were other paragraphs that needed the same treatment.

Syntax

The syntax for a Do...Loop While loop is as follows:

```
Do
    [statements]
    [Exit Do]
    [statements]
Loop While condition
```

VBA performs the statements included in the loop, after which the Loop While line evaluates the condition; if it is True, VBA returns execution to the Do line, and the loop continues to execute; if it is False, execution continues at the line after the Loop While line.

As an example of a Do...Loop While loop, consider this crude password checker that you could use to prevent someone from running a procedure without supplying the correct password:

```
Do
    Password = InputBox("Enter the password to start the
    ➥procedure:", "Check Password 1.0")
Loop While Password <> "CorrectPassword"
```

Here the Do...Loop While loop displays an input box for the user to enter the password. The Loop While line compares the value from the input box, stored in `Password`, against the correct password (here, `CorrectPassword`). If the two are not equal (`Password <> "CorrectPassword"`), the loop continues, displaying the input box again.

This loop is just an example—you wouldn't want to use it as is in real life. Here's why: choosing the Cancel button in the input box causes it to return a blank string, which also does not match the correct password, causing the loop to run again. The security is perfect; the problem is that the only way to end the loop is for the user to supply the correct password. If they are unable to do so, they will see the input box ad infinitum. If you wanted to build a password-checking procedure along these lines, you might specify a number of incorrect passwords that the user could enter (perhaps three) before the procedure terminated itself, or you could simply use an `End` statement to terminate the procedure if the user entered a blank string:

```
Do
    Password = InputBox("Enter the password to start the
    ➥procedure:", "Check Password 1.0")
    If Password = "" Then End
Loop While Password <> "CorrectPassword"
```

Do Until...Loop Loops

A `Do Until...Loop` loop is similar to a `Do While...Loop` loop, except that in a `Do Until...Loop` loop, the loop runs while the condition is `False` and stops running when it is `True`. Figure 8.3 shows a `Do Until...Loop` loop.

> **NOTE**
>
> `Do Until...Loop` loops are useful if you're not of a negative mindset and you need a condition to run when it is `False`. Otherwise, you can achieve the same effects using `Do While...Loops` and inverting the relative condition.

FIGURE 8.3

A Do Until...Loop loop runs while the condition is False and stops running when the condition becomes True.

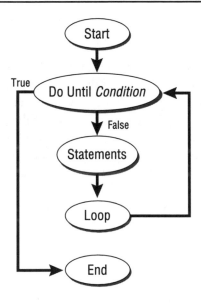

Syntax

The syntax for Do Until...Loop loops is as follows:

```
Do Until condition
    statements
    [Exit Do]
    [statements]
Loop
```

When VBA enters the loop, it checks the condition. If the condition is False, VBA executes the statements in the loop, encounters the Loop keyword, and loops back to the beginning of the loop, reevaluating the condition as it goes. If the condition is True, VBA terminates the loop and continues execution at the statement after the Loop line.

For example, consider our lottery experience redefined as a macro in Listing 8.3.

Listing 8.3

```
1.   Sub Lottery()
2.       Do Until Win > 2000
3.           Win = Rnd * 2100
4.           MsgBox Win,, "Lottery"
5.       Loop
6.   End Sub
```

Analysis

This macro is as straightforward as it is frivolous. Line 2 starts a Do Until loop with the condition that Win > 2000—the Win variable must be larger than 2,000 for the loop to end; until then, the loop will continue to run.

Line 3 defines the Win variable as being 2,100 times a random number produced by the Rnd function, which generates random numbers between 0 and 1. (In other words, the loop needs to receive a random number of a little more than .95 to end—a chance of a little less than one in 20, or considerably better than any lottery I've had the misfortune to be involved in so far.)

Line 4 displays a simple message box containing the current value of the Win variable so that you can see how lucky you are. Line 5 contains the Loop keyword that completes the loop.

Do...Loop Until Loops

A Do...Loop Until loop is similar to Do Until...Loop loop, except that in the former case, the actions in the loop are run at least once, whether the condition is True or False. If the condition is False, the loop continues to run until the condition becomes True. Figure 8.4 shows a Do...Loop Until loop.

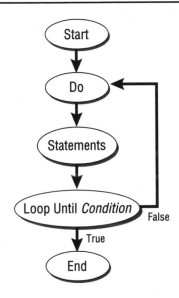

FIGURE 8.4

In a Do...Loop Until loop, the actions in the loop are run once before the condition is tested.

Syntax

The syntax for Do...Loop Until loops is as follows:

```
Do
    [statements]
    [Exit Do]
    [statements]
Loop Until condition
```

VBA enters the loop at the Do line and executes the statements in the loop. When it encounters the Loop Until line, it checks the condition: if it is False, VBA loops back to the Do line and again executes the statements; if it is True, VBA terminates the loop and continues execution at the line after the Loop Until line.

As an example, say you wanted to continue displaying an input box for putting together a list until the user chose the Cancel button or entered an empty string in the text box. You could use code such as that shown in Listing 8.4.

Listing 8.4

```
1.  Sub ListFriends()
2.  Do
3.      FriendName = InputBox("Enter the name of one of your
        ➥friends.", "List Friends 1.1")
4.      Selection.TypeText FriendName + Chr(13)
5.  Loop Until FriendName = ""
6.  End Sub
```

Analysis

This straightforward macro begins with a Do loop in line 2. Line 3 then displays an input box asking the user to enter the name of one of their friends. Line 4 enters what they typed into the current document, along with a carriage return to create a new paragraph. As long as the user enters anything except an empty string, or until they click the Cancel button (which also results in an empty string from the input box), the macro loops back to the Do line and displays the input box again; if they enter an empty string or click the Cancel button, the Loop Until FriendName = "" condition becomes True and terminates the loop. VBA then resumes execution at the line after the Loop Until line; in this case, the only command after that is End Sub, which ends the macro.

Except as an example, this macro is mostly worthless in its current state—the user might as well enter the names of their friends into a document directly and be done with it. But if you were to combine a simple Do...Loop Until like this with a dialog box or form that provided the user with an easy way to enter complex information, this macro could be most useful.

Using an Exit Do Statement

As with an Exit For statement in a For loop, you can use an Exit Do statement to exit a Do loop without executing the rest of the statements in it. Again, the Exit Do statement is optional, and you'll probably want to use Exit Do statements relatively seldom in your loops—at least, if they're properly designed.

When you do need an `Exit Do` statement, you'll usually use it with a condition. We could make our lottery example a little more interesting by adding an `If` condition with an `Exit Do` statement to take effect if the win is less than a certain amount—say, $500, as in Listing 8.5.

Listing 8.5

```
1.   Sub Lottery()
2.       Do Until Win > 2000
3.           Win = Rnd * 2100
4.           If Win < 500 Then
5.               MsgBox "Tough luck. You have been
                 ➥disqualified.", vbOKOnly + vbCritical,
                 ➥"Lottery"
6.               Exit Do
7.           End If
8.           MsgBox Win,, "Lottery"
9.       Loop
10.  End Sub
```

Analysis

This macro works in the same way as the one in Listing 8.3, except that line 4 introduces a new `If` condition. If the variable `Win` is less than 500, the statements in lines 5 and 6 run. Line 5 displays a message box announcing that the player has been disqualified from the lottery, and line 6 exits the `Do` loop.

Nesting Loops

You can nest one or more loops within another loop to create the pattern of repetition you need: you can nest one `For` loop inside another `For` loop, a `For` loop inside a `Do` loop, a `Do` loop inside a `For` loop, or a `Do` loop inside a `Do` loop.

For example, if you need to create a number of folders, each of which contains a number of subfolders, you could do so with a variation of the `Create_Folders` macro we looked at earlier in the chapter.

The dialog box for the macro will need another text box to contain the number of subfolders to create within each folder. In the example here, I've named the new dialog box `frmCreateFoldersAndSub-Folders` and the text box for the number of subfolders `HowManySubFolders`.

Listing 8.6 shows the code attached to the `Click` event on the `cmdOK` button of the form.

Listing 8.6

```
1.    Private Sub cmdOK_Click()
2.        frmCreateFoldersAndSubFolders.Hide
3.        Unload frmCreateFoldersAndSubFolders
4.        StartingFolder = CurDir
5.        For i = 1 To HowManyFolders
6.            Count$ = LTrim$(Str$(i))
7.            If i < 10 Then Count$ = "0" + Count$
8.            FolderName$ = ISBN + "c" + Count$
9.            MkDir FolderName$
10.           ChDir FolderName$
11.           For SubFolder = 1 to HowManySubFolders
12.               SubCount$ = Str$(SubFolder)
13.               SubFolderName$ = "Section" + SubCount$
14.               MkDir SubFolderName$
15.           Next SubFolder
16.           ChDir StartingFolder
17.       Next i
18.   End Sub
```

Analysis

Here's what the code does:

Line 2 hides the dialog box, and line 3 unloads it.

Line 4 stores the name of the current folder in the variable `StartingFolder`. We'll need this to make sure everything happens in the appropriate directory later in the macro.

Lines 5 through 9 and line 17 are the same as in the previous macro, building the folder name out of the contents of the ISBN box, the letter *c*, and a string derived from the i variable.

Line 10 uses a ChDir statement to change folders to the folder that has just been created, FolderName$.

In line 11, the nested For...Next loop starts. This loop is controlled by the loop invariant SubFolder and will run from SubFolder = 1 to SubFolder = HowManySubFolders, which is the value entered by the user in the Number of Subfolders to Create text box of the dialog box.

Line 12 defines the string SubCount$ as the string of the SubFolder loop invariant. SubCount$ in this loop works in the same way as the Count$ string in the first loop. The difference is that in this loop, we'll name the subfolders in such a way as to use the leading space that the string brings with it, so we don't need to use an LTrim$ statement to remove this space.

Line 13 builds the string SubFolderName$ out of the word *Section* and the string SubCount$. Note that, because of the leading space in the string, there's no need for a space between *Section* and the double quotation marks after it.

Line 14 creates the subfolder by using a MkDir statement with the SubFolderName$.

Line 15 then loops back to the beginning of the nested For...Next loop. VBA reevaluates the condition and repeats the loop as necessary.

Line 16 changes folders back to StartingFolder for the next iteration of the outside loop. (Otherwise, the next folder would be created within the current folder, FolderName$.)

Line 17 then loops back to the beginning of the outside loop.

TIP

When nesting For loops, make sure that you use the counter argument to identify the loop that is ending. Using this argument makes your macros much easier to read and may prevent VBA from springing any unpleasant surprises on you.

Avoiding Infinite Loops

If you create an infinite loop in a macro, it will happily run forever and a day, or until your computer crashes. For example, one type of loop we haven't examined yet is the Do...Loop loop. As you can see in the example in Listing 8.7, without a condition attached to it, this creates an infinite loop.

Listing 8.7

```
1.  Sub InfiniteLoop()
2.      x = 1
3.      Do
4.          Application.StatusBar = Str$(x)
5.          x = x + 1
6.      Loop
7.  End Sub
```

Analysis

Line 2 provides the starting value of the variable x, which is then displayed as a string in the status bar in line 4 and then increased by 1 in line 5. The effect of this loop is to display an ever-increasing number on the status bar until you press Ctrl+Break to stop the macro. This is all thoroughly pointless (except perhaps as a macro for burning in a new computer), and perhaps a good reason not to use the Do...Loop structure—at least, not without a condition attached to one end of it or the other.

No matter what type of loop you use, to avoid creating an infinite loop, you need to make sure that the condition that will terminate the loop will be met at some point. For example, for an editing or cleanup macro, you'll often want to perform an action until the end of the document is reached, and then stop. For a macro that works on and then closes all open documents, you could use the Windows collection or Documents collection to see if any windows or documents were still open before continuing the loop. In other cases, you may want to include some form of counting mechanism to make sure that a Do loop does not exceed a certain number of iterations.

In this chapter, we've looked at the formal types of loops that are available as VBA commands. These `For` loops and `Do` loops are a vital weapon in your VBA arsenal, and they are versatile enough to take care of almost all your looping needs. However, you can also implement loops in a number of other ways, such as by using `GoTo` statements (which have an unfortunate tendency to create infinite loops unless you use them with conditions) and by using `If` conditions, which we'll look at in detail (along with `Select Case` statements) in the next chapter.

CHAPTER

NINE

9

Using Conditional Statements to Make Decisions

In this chapter, we'll look at the conditional statements that VBA provides for directing the flow of your macros, branching to different sections of code depending on such things as the value of a variable or which button the user chooses in a dialog box.

VBA provides assorted flavors of If statements (some of which you've met without formal introduction in the previous chapters) suitable for taking simple or complex decisions, as well as the heavy-duty Select Case statement for simplifying the coding of truly involved decisions.

If Statements

As in most programming languages, If statements are among the most immediately useful and versatile statements in VBA. They're also surprisingly easy to use, at least in their simpler forms.

In this section, we'll look at the following types of If statements:

- If...Then
- If...Then...Else
- If...Then...ElseIf...Else

If...Then

If...Then statements tell VBA to make the simplest of decisions: if a condition is met, execute the following statement (or statements); if the condition is not met, skip to the line immediately following the conditional statement.

Syntax

If...Then statements can be laid out on either one line or multiple lines. A one-line If...Then statement looks like this:

```
If condition Then statement[s]
```

If the condition is met, VBA executes the statement or statements.

A multiple-line If...Then statement (more properly known as a *block* If statement) looks like this:

```
If condition Then
    statement
    [statements]
End If
```

> Note that the single-line If...Then condition has no End If to end it, whereas the block If requires one. VBA knows that a single-line If condition will end on the same line on which it starts, whereas a block If needs to have its end clearly specified.

Again, if the condition is met, VBA executes the statement or statements. Otherwise, VBA moves execution to the line after the End If statement.

Examples

In the past three chapters, we've already encountered a number of If statements—they're so necessary in VBA that it's hard to get anything done without them. In this section, we'll look at a couple more examples.

One-Line If Statements Here's an example of a one-line If statement in context:

```
Age = InputBox("Enter your age.", "Age")
If Age < 21 Then MsgBox "You may not purchase alcohol.",,
➥"Underage"
```

The first line prompts the user to enter their age in an input box, which stores it in the variable Age. The second line checks Age and displays an Underage message box if Age is less than 21.

Nothing to it. There's just one more thing to mention about one-line If statements: you can include multiple instructions on the same line as necessary by separating them with a colon. For example, if you wanted to end the procedure after displaying the Underage message box, you could include the End statement after a colon on the same line, as shown in the following example. (This is one line that I've had to break into two to fit onto the page of this book.)

```
If Age < 21 Then MsgBox "You may not purchase alcohol.",,
➥"Underage": End
```

VBA executes this as follows:

1. First, it evaluates the condition.

2. If the condition is met, it executes the first statement after Then—in this case, it displays the Underage message box.

3. Once the user has dismissed the Underage message box (by clicking the OK button, the only button it has), VBA executes the statement after the colon: End.

If desired, you could add several other statements on the same line, separated by colons. (End would have to be the last one, because it ends the procedure.) You could even add another If statement if you felt like it:

```
If Age < 21 Then If Age > 18 Then MsgBox
➥"You may vote but you may not drink.",, "Underage": End
```

Again, this would all be appearing on one line in the Visual Basic Editor.

As you'll see if you're looking at the Visual Basic Editor, there are a couple of problems with this:

- First, long lines of code go off the edge of the code window in the Visual Basic Editor, so that you have to scroll horizontally to read the ends of each line—you can't see the whole of each line at once. You *could* hide all windows but the code window, use a minute font size for your code, or buy a larger monitor, but you're probably still not going to have any fun working with long lines of code.

- Second, long lines of code that involve a number of statements tend to become visually confusing. Even if everything is blindingly obvious to you when you're entering the code, you may find the code hard to read when you have to debug it a few months later. Usually it's better to use block If statements rather than complex one-line If statements. Read on.

Block If Statements Block If statements work in the same way as one-line If statements, except that they are laid out on multiple lines, typically with one command to each line, and they require an End If statement at their end. For example, the one-line If statement from the previous section could also be constructed as a block If:

```
If Age < 21 Then
    MsgBox "You may not purchase alcohol.",, "Underage"
    End
End If
```

If the condition in the first line is True, VBA executes the statements within the block If, first displaying the message box and then executing the End statement.

As you can see from this example, block If statements are much easier to read (and thus to debug) than one-line If statements. This is especially true when you nest If statements within one another, which we'll do shortly.

To make block statements easier to read, the convention is to indent the lines of block If statements after the first line (VBA ignores the indentation). With short If statements, like the ones shown in this section, this doesn't make a great deal of difference; but with complex If statements, it can make all the difference between clarity and incomprehensibility, as you'll see in "Nesting If Statements" later in this chapter.

If...Then...Else

If...Then statements are all very well for taking a single action based on a condition, but often you'll need to decide between two courses of action. For this, you use the If...Then...Else statement. By using an If...Then...Else statement, you can take one course of action if a condition is True and another course of action if it is False. For example, as you saw in Chapter 7, If...Then...Else statements are a great way to deal with two-button message boxes.

NOTE Note that the If...Then...Else **statement is best used with clear-cut binary conditions—those that lend themselves to a** True/False **analysis. (A binary condition is like a two-position switch—if it's not switched on, it must be switched off.) For more complex conditions, such as those that can have three positions (for example, a switch that governs Off, Slow, or Fast on a kitchen appliance), you need to use a more complex logical structure, such as** If...Then...ElseIf...Else **or** Select Case.

Syntax

The syntax for the If...Then...Else statement is as follows:

```
If condition Then
    statements1
Else
    statements2
End If
```

If the condition is True, VBA executes *statements1*, the first group of statements. If the condition is False, VBA moves execution to the Else line and executes *statements2*, the second group of statements.

Again, you have the option of creating one-line If...Then...Else statements or block If...Then...Else statements. In almost all circumstances, it makes more sense to create block If...Then...Else statements, because they're much easier to read and debug, and because the If...Then...Else statement is inherently longer than the If...Then statement and thus more likely to produce an awkwardly long line.

Examples

As a straightforward example of an If...Then...Else statement, consider the one shown in Listing 9.1.

Listing 9.1

```
1.   If BookPages > 1000 Then
2.       MsgBox "The book is very long.", vbOKOnly
         ➥+ vbInformation, "The Electronic Book Critic"
3.   Else
4.       MsgBox "The book is not so long.", vbOKOnly
         ➥+ vbInformation, "The Electronic Book Critic"
5.   End If
```

Analysis

In this example, the macro compares the value of the variable BookPages (supplied through a macro or through user intervention, such as an input box) to the value 1,000 and displays an appropriate message box accordingly.

Line 1 compares BookPages to 1,000. If BookPages is greater than 1,000, VBA branches to line 2, which displays a message box sharing with the user the Electronic Book Critic's informed opinion that the book is very long. However, if BookPages is not greater than 1,000, VBA branches to the Else statement in line 3 and executes the statement following it—displaying a message box telling the user that the book is not so long.

The above example is clear enough but not particularly realistic. Let's look at an example that it might actually make sense to use in a macro, as shown in Listing 9.2.

Listing 9.2

```
1.      Response = MsgBox("Do you want to proceed?", vbYesNo
        ➥+ vbQuestion, "Create Glossary 1.0")
2.      If Response = vbYes Then
3.          CreateGlossary
4.      Else
5.          GoTo Bye
6.      EndIf
```

Analysis

Line 1 defines the variable Response as the result of the message box. Lines 2 through 6 implememnt an If...Then...Else statement that works with Response. Line 2 checks to see if Response was a vbYes; if it was, VBA branches to line 3 and runs the CreateGlossary macro. If Response was not a vbYes, VBA branches to the statements following the Else keyword—in this case, to line 5, where it executes the Goto Bye statement.

If...Then...ElseIf...Else

The last If statement we'll look at here is If...Then...ElseIf...Else, which you can use to help VBA decide between multiple courses of action. You can use any number of ElseIf lines, depending on how complex the condition is that you need to check.

Again, you can create either one-line If...Then...ElseIf...Else statements or block If...Then...ElseIf...Else statements. In almost all cases, block If...Then...ElseIf...Else statements are easier to construct, to read, and to debug. As with the other If statements, one-line If...Then...ElseIf...Else statements do not need an End If statement, but block If...Then...ElseIf...Else statements do need one.

Syntax

The syntax for If...Then...ElseIf...Else is as follows:

```
If condition1 Then
    statements1
ElseIf condition2 Then
    statements2
[ElseIf condition3 Then
    statements3]
[Else
    statements4]
End If
```

If the condition expressed in condition1 is True, VBA executes statements1, the first block of statements, and then resumes execution at the line after the End If clause. If condition1 is False, VBA branches to the first ElseIf clause and evaluates the condition expressed in condition2. If this is True, VBA executes statements2 and then moves to the line after the End If line; if it is False, VBA moves to the next ElseIf clause (if there is one) and evaluates its condition (here, condition3) in turn.

If all the conditions in the ElseIf statements prove False, VBA branches to the Else statement (if there is one) and executes the statements after it (here, statements4). The End If statement then terminates the conditional structure, and execution resumes with the line after the End If.

You can have any number of ElseIf clauses in a block If statement, each with its own condition, but if you find yourself using If statements with large numbers of ElseIf clauses (say, more than five or ten), you may want to try using the Select Case statement instead, which we'll look at toward the end of the chapter.

The Else clause is optional, though in many cases it's a good idea to include it to allow VBA to take a different course of action if none of the conditions specified in the If and ElseIf clauses turns out to be True.

Examples

In this section, we'll look at three examples of If...Then...ElseIf...Else statements:

- A simple If...Then...ElseIf...Else statement for taking action from a three-button message box

- An If...Then...ElseIf statement without an Else clause

- A complex If...Then...ElseIf...Else statement that uses a large number of ElseIf clauses to decide between multiple conditions

A Simple If...Then...ElseIf...Else Statement A simple If...Then... ElseIf...Else statement, as shown in Listing 9.3, is perfect for dealing with a three-button message box. As you can see, this listing is not a complete macro: it assumes that you've declared the variable FileToOpen and assigned it a string for which Word has searched without any success, that the module contains a SearchManually macro, and that the procedure contains a ResumeExecution label.

Listing 9.3

```
1.   Response = MsgBox("Word cannot find " + FileToOpen + "."
     ➥+ Chr(13)+ Chr(13) + "Do you want to search for the
     ➥file manually?", vbYesNoCancel + vbCritical,
     ➥"Concatenate Documents")
2.   If Response = vbYes Then
3.       SearchManually
4.   ElseIf Response = vbNo Then
5.       GoTo ResumeExecution
6.   Else
7.       End
8.   End If
```

Analysis

In this example, the macro is concatenating a number of files and has been unable to find one of them. Line 1 displays a message box offering the user a choice of actions controlled by the Yes, No, and Cancel buttons (vbYes, vbNo, and vbCancel, respectively); the user's choice in this message box is stored in the variable Response.

Line 2 compares the value of Response to vbYes. If Response = vbYes, VBA executes the SearchManually statement in line 3 (which runs the SearchManually macro, not shown in Listing 9.3). If Response is not vbYes, VBA evaluates the ElseIf clause in line 4, comparing Response to vbNo. If Response = vbNo, VBA executes the GoTo ResumeExecution statement in line 5, going to the ResumeExecution label elsewhere in the macro (also not shown in Listing 9.3) and resuming execution with the statements that follow it. If Response is not vbNo, VBA moves to the Else clause (line 6) and executes the statements that follow it—in this case, the End statement in line 7. The End If statement in line 8 ends the If statement.

An If...Then...ElseIf Statement without an Else Clause As I mentioned in the discussion on syntax, you can use an If...Then...ElseIf statement without an Else clause if need be. This is primarily useful when you do not need to take an action if none of the conditions in the If statement proves True. In the previous example, we looked at a situation that had three clearly defined outcomes: in the message box, the user could choose the Yes button, the No button, or the Cancel button. So we were able to use an If clause to test for the user's having chosen the Yes button, an ElseIf clause to test for the user's having chosen the No button, and an Else clause to take action if neither were chosen, meaning that the Cancel button was chosen. (Before you ask, clicking the close button on the title bar of this message box is the equivalent of choosing the Cancel button.) If the user were able to choose another option in the message box besides the Yes, No, or Cancel buttons, this Else clause would be unwise; but as it is, it works fine.

As an example of a situation where you do not need to take action if no condition is True, consider the If statement in Listing 9.4. This procedure checks to ensure that the password a user enters to protect an item is of a suitable length.

Listing 9.4

```
1.   BadPassword:
2.   Password = InputBox("Enter the password to protect
     ➥this item from changes:", "Enter Password")
3.   If Len(Password) = 0 Then
4.       End
5.   ElseIf Len(Password) < 6 Then
6.       MsgBox "The password you chose is too short."
         ➥+ Chr(13) + Chr(13) + "Please choose a
         ➥password between 6 and 15 characters in
         ➥length.", vbOKOnly + vbCritical,
         ➥"Unsuitable Password"
7.       GoTo BadPassword
8.   ElseIf Len(Password) > 15 Then
9.       MsgBox "The password you chose is too long." + Chr(13)
         ➥+ Chr(13) + "Please choose a password between 6 and
         ➥15 characters in length.", vbOKOnly + vbCritical,
         ➥"Unsuitable Password"
10.      GoTo BadPassword
11.  End If
```

Analysis

This procedure forces the user to enter a suitable password for the item they're supposed to protect.

Line 1 simply contains a label, BadPassword, to which VBA will loop if the password the user enters proves to be unsuitable. Line 2 displays an input box prompting the user to enter a password, which it stores in the variable Password.

Line 3 checks Password to see if its length is zero, which means it's a null string. This could mean either that the user clicked the Cancel button in the input box or clicked the OK button without entering any text in the text box of the input box; either of these actions causes VBA to branch to line 4, where it executes the End statement that ends the procedure.

If the length of Password is not zero (i.e., the user has entered text into the text box of the input box and clicked the OK button), the If clause in line 3 is False, and VBA moves to line 5, where it checks to see if the length of Password is less than 6 characters. If it is, VBA executes the code in lines 6 and 7. Line 6 displays a message box telling the user that the password is too short and specifying the length criteria for the password. This message box contains only an OK button, so when the user clicks it to continue, VBA continues with line 7, which returns execution to the `BadPassword` label on line 1, from which the procedure repeats itself, redisplaying the input box in line 2 so that the user can try again.

If the length of `Password` is not less than 6 characters, execution passes from line 5 to the second `ElseIf` clause in line 8, where VBA checks to see if the length of `Password` is more than 15 characters. If it is, VBA executes the code in lines 9 and 10: line 9 displays a message box (again, with only an OK button) telling the user that the password is too long, and line 10 returns execution to the `BadPassword` label on line 1, again restarting the procedure by displaying the input box again.

There is no need for an `ElseIf` statement in this case, because once the user has supplied a password that does not trigger the `If` clause or either of the `ElseIf` clauses, execution will continue at the line after the `End If` statement.

An If...Then...ElseIf...Else Statement Featuring Multiple ElseIf Clauses

So much for simple `If...Then...ElseIf...Else` statements. You can also create `If...Then...ElseIf...Else` statements with multiple `ElseIf` clauses to test for a variety of conditions and take action accordingly.

Toward the end of Chapter 7, we created a `Move_Paragraph` macro and hooked it up to a dialog box to allow the user to quickly move the current paragraph up or down the document by one or two paragraphs. To establish which of the four option buttons (`optUpOne`, `optUpTwo`, `optDownOne`, or `optDownTwo`) in the dialog box the user chose, we used a straightforward `If...Then...ElseIf...Else` statement:

```
If optUpOne = True Then
    Selection.MoveUp Unit:=wdParagraph, Count:=1
ElseIf optUpTwo = True Then
    Selection.MoveUp Unit:=wdParagraph, Count:=2
ElseIf optDownOne = True Then
    Selection.MoveDown Unit:=wdParagraph, Count:=1
Else
    Selection.MoveDown Unit:=wdParagraph, Count:=2
End If
```

To recap, VBA checks each of the first three option buttons in turn until it finds the one that is `True`, and then executes the statement after it, moving the insertion point up one or two paragraphs or down one paragraph as appropriate. If none of these options are `True`, VBA executes the `Else` statement, moving the insertion point down two paragraphs. (After moving the insertion point as specified by the option button, the macro goes on to paste in the paragraph it had previously cut, thus moving the paragraph.) You could easily expand the dialog box to contain, say, eight option buttons for moving the paragraph (four for up, named `optUpOne` to `optUpFour`, respectively; and four for down, named `optDownOne` to `optDownFour`, respectively) and expand the `If...Then...ElseIf...Else` statement accordingly:

```
If optUpOne = True Then
    Selection.MoveUp Unit:=wdParagraph, Count:=1
ElseIf optUpTwo = True Then
    Selection.MoveUp Unit:=wdParagraph, Count:=2
ElseIf optUpThree = True Then
    Selection.MoveUp Unit:=wdParagraph, Count:=3
ElseIf optUpFour = True Then
    Selection.MoveUp Unit:=wdParagraph, Count:=4
ElseIf optDownOne = True Then
    Selection.MoveDown Unit:=wdParagraph, Count:=1
ElseIf optDownTwo = True Then
    Selection.MoveDown Unit:=wdParagraph, Count:=2
ElseIf optDownThree = True Then
    Selection.MoveDown Unit:=wdParagraph, Count:=3
Else
    Selection.MoveDown Unit:=wdParagraph, Count:=4
End If
```

When this macro runs, VBA checks each condition in turn until it finds one that is `True`. Again, if neither the `If` clause nor any of the `ElseIf` clauses is true, the user must have chosen the `optDownFour` option button, so VBA runs the `Else` statement, which takes action accordingly.

Creating Loops with If and GoTo

In the previous chapter, we looked at the formal types of loop: the `For` loops for repeating loops a known number of times, and the `Do` loops for repeating loops while a condition is `True` or until it becomes `True`. If you wish, you can also create loops with `If` statements and the `GoTo` statement.

Syntax

The `GoTo` statement is very straightforward, and it's so useful that it's already come up a number of times in the examples we've looked at so far in this book:

```
GoTo line
```

Here, the `line` argument can be either a line number within the current procedure or a line label within the current procedure.

A line number is simply a number placed at the beginning of a line to identify it. For example, consider this demonstration of `GoTo`:

```
Sub Demo_of_GoTo()
1
    If MsgBox("Go to line 1?", vbYesNo) = vbYes Then
    ➥GoTo 1
    End If
End Sub
```

The first line contains only the line number 1, which identifies the line. The second line displays a message box offering the choice of going back to line 1; if the user chooses the Yes button, VBA executes the `GoTo 1` statement and returns to the line labeled 1, after which it displays the message box again. (If the user chooses the No button, the `If` statement ends.)

It's usually easier to use a line label than a line number. A line label, as you may have noticed in some of the earlier chapters, is simply a name for a line. A label starts with a letter and ends with a colon; apart from that, it can consist of any combination of characters. For example, earlier in this chapter we used the label `BadPassword:` to loop back to an earlier stage in a procedure when certain conditions were met. Perhaps the quintessential example of a label is the `Bye:` label traditionally placed at the end of a macro for use with this `GoTo` statement:

```
GoTo Bye
```

`GoTo` is usually used with a condition—if you use it without one to go back to a line earlier in the macro than the `GoTo` statement, you're apt to create an infinite loop; and if you were to use the `GoTo Bye` statement without a condition, you would guarantee that your macro would end at this statement (i.e., no statement after this line would ever be executed).

Example

As an example of a GoTo statement with a condition, you might use the GoTo Bye statement together with a message box that made sure that the user wanted to run a certain procedure:

```
Response = MsgBox("Do you want to create a daily report for the
➥head office from the current document?", vbYesNo
➥+ vbQuestion,  "Create Daily Report 2.3")
If Response = vbNo Then GoTo Bye
```

If the user chooses the No button in the message box that the first line here displays, VBA executes the GoTo Bye statement, branching to the Bye: label located at the end of the macro.

Nesting If Statements

You can nest If statements as necessary to produce the logical contortions you need in your macros. Each nested If statement needs to be complete in and of itself. For example, if you nest one block If statement within another block If statement and forget the End If line for the nested If, VBA will assume that the End If line for the outer If belongs to the nested If.

As I mentioned earlier, the convention is to use indentation with block If statements to make them easier to read. This is particularly important with nesting If statements, when you need to make it clear which If line is paired with each End If line. To see how this is done, check out the nested If statements below.

```
1.   If condition1 Then              'start of first If
2.       If condition2 Then          'start of second If
3.           If condition3 Then      'start of third If
4.               statements1
5.           ElseIf condition4 Then  'ElseIf for third If
6.               statements2
7.           Else                    'Else for third If
8.               statements3
9.           End If                  'End If for third If
10.      Else                        'Else for second If
11.          If condition5 Then      'start of fourth If
12.              statements4
13.          End If                  'End If for fourth If
```

```
14.       End If                    'End If for second If
15.   Else                          'Else for first If
16.        statements5
17.   End If                        'End If for first If
```

By following the layout, you can easily trace the flow of execution. For example, if *condition1* in line 1 is False, VBA branches to the Else statement in line 15 and continues execution from there. If *condition1* in line 1 is True, VBA evaluates *condition2* in line 2, and so on.

The indentation is for visual clarity only—it doesn't make one iota of difference to VBA —but it can be a great help to the human reader. I've annotated the above nested If structure to make it clear which Else, ElseIf, and End If line belongs with which If line, although with the nesting, this is unnecessary. On the other hand, check out the unindented version of this nested structure shown below. This version is murder for the human eye to follow, even when it's not buried in a morass of other code that might confuse things further.

```
1.    If condition1 Then            'start of first If
2.    If condition2 Then            'start of second If
3.    If condition3 Then            'start of third If
4.    statements1
5.    ElseIf condition4 Then        'ElseIf for third If
6.    statements2
7.    Else                          'Else for third If
8.    statements3
9.    End If                        'End If for third If
10.   Else                          'Else for second If
11.   If condition5 Then            'start of fourth If
12.   statements4
13.   End If                        'End If for fourth If
14.   End If                        'End If for second If
15.   Else                          'Else for first If
16.        statements5
17.   End If                        'End If for first If
```

There's seldom a pressing need to go to such ludicrous levels of nesting—often, you'll need only to nest a simple If...Then statement within an If...Then...Else statement or within an If...Then...ElseIf...Else statement. For example, you might create a macro that searched through a document for a specific style and, if it found it, offered to take an appropriate action (see Listing 9.5).

Listing 9.5

```
1.    Selection.HomeKey Unit:=wdStory
2.    Selection.Find.ClearFormatting
3.    Selection.Find.Style = ActiveDocument.Styles("Heading 5")
4.    Selection.Find.Text = ""
5.    Selection.Find.Execute
6.    If Selection.Find.Found Then
7.        Response = MsgBox("Make this into a special note?",
      ➥vbOKCancel, "Make Special Note")
8.            If Response = vbOK Then
9.                Selection.Style = "Special Note"
10.           End If
11.   End If
```

Analysis

This code searches through the active document for the Heading 5 style and, if it finds it, displays a message box offering to make it into a special note by applying the Special Note style.

Line 1 starts by returning the insertion point to the beginning of the document. Line 2 clears formatting from the Find command (to make sure that it's not searching for inappropriate formatting). Line 3 sets Heading 5 as the style for which the Find command is searching, and Line 4 sets the search string as an empty string (" "). Line 5 then runs the Find operation.

Lines 6 through 11 contain the outer If...Then loop. Line 6 checks to see if the Find operation in line 5 found a paragraph in Heading 5 style; if it did, VBA runs the code in lines 7 through 10. Line 7 displays a message box asking if the user wants to make the paragraph into a special note. Line 8 begins the nested If...Then statement and checks the user's response to the message box; if it is a vbOK—if they chose the OK button—VBA executes the statement in line 9, which applies the Special Note style (which I'll assume is included in the document or template) to the paragraph. Line 10 contains the End If statement for the nested If...Then statement, and line 11 contains the End If statement for the outer If...Then statement.

TIP

TIP — If you expected a document to contain more than one instance of the Heading 5 style, you would probably want to use a `Do While… Loop` loop to search for each instance.

Select Case Statements

The `Select Case` statement provides an effective alternative to multiple `ElseIf` statements, combining the same decision-making capability with tighter and more efficient code.

Syntax

The syntax for `Select Case` is as follows:

```
Select Case TestExpression
    Case Expression1
        Statements1
    [Case Expression2
        Statements2]
    [Case Else
        StatementsElse]
End Select
```

This looks complex at first, but stay with me: `Select Case` starts the statement, and `End Select` ends it. `TestExpression` is the expression that determines which of the `Case` statements runs, and `Expression1`, `Expession2`, and so on are the expressions against which VBA matches `TestExpression`. For example, you might test to see which of a number of buttons in a dialog box or userform the user chose. The `TestExpression` would be tied to a button having been chosen; if it was the first button, VBA would match that to `Expression1` and would run the statements in the lines following `CaseExpression1`; if it was the second button, VBA would match that to `Expression2` and would run the statements in the lines following `CaseExpression2`; and so on for the rest of the `Case` statements.

Case Else is similar to the Else clause in an If statement. Case Else is an optional clause that (if it is included) runs if none of the given expressions is matched.

Example

As a somewhat frivolous example of a Select Case statement, consider Listing 9.6, which prompts the user to enter their typing speed and then displays an appropriate response.

Listing 9.6

```
1.  TypingSpeed = InputBox("How many words can you type per
    ➥minute?", "Typing Speed")
2.  Select Case TypingSpeed
3.      Case ""
4.          End
5.      Case 0 To 50
6.          MsgBox "Please learn to type properly before
            ➥applying for a job.", vbOKOnly, "Typing Speed"
7.      Case 50 To 60
8.          MsgBox "Your typing could do with a little
            ➥brushing up.", vbOKOnly, "Typing Speed"
9.      Case 60 To 75
10.         MsgBox "We are satisfied with your typing speed.",
            ➥vbOKOnly, "Typing Speed"
11.     Case 75 To 99
12.         MsgBox "Your typing is more than adequate.",
            ➥vbOKOnly, "Typing Speed"
13.     Case Is > 99
14.         MsgBox "You wear out typewriters with your
            ➥blinding speed.", vbOKOnly, "Typing Speed"
15. End Select
```

Analysis

Line 1 displays an input box prompting the user to enter their typing speed. It stores this in the variable TypingSpeed. (In a more realistic procedure, the variable might be supplied from a person's resume or from a program that tests typing speed.)

Line 2 begins the `Select Case` statement, predicating it on the variable `TypingSpeed`.

Next, VBA evaluates each of the `Case` clauses in turn until it finds one that proves `True`. The first `Case` clause, in line 3, compares `TypingSpeed` to a blank string (`""`) to see if the user chose the Cancel button in the input box or clicked the OK button without entering a value in the text box. If `Case ""` is `True`, VBA executes the `End` statement in line 4, ending the procedure.

If `Case ""` is `False`, VBA moves execution to the next `Case` clause—line 5 in this example—where it compares `TypingSpeed` to the range 0–50 words per minute. If `TypingSpeed` is within this range, VBA displays the message box in line 6 and then continues execution at the line after the `End Select` statement. If `TypingSpeed` is not within this range, VBA moves to the next `Case` clause and evaluates it in turn. When it finds a `Case` clause that is `True`, it executes the statements following it and then continues execution at the line after the `End Select` statement.

NOTE If `Select Case` statements don't make much sense to you at the moment, feel free to stick with `ElseIf` statements instead. However, your code will probably be somewhat looser and might prove a little harder to read. It might even be a fraction less efficient, but you're unlikely to notice any substantial performance loss under normal circumstances, and everything will work just fine.

OK, enough conditions and decisions for the time being. It's time to get our hands dirty dealing with variables and constants, and to find out exactly how long a string is.

Working with Variables, Strings, and Constants

In this chapter, we'll cover the basics of working with variables, strings, and constants. *Variables* provide a way of storing and manipulating information derived from a procedure. *Strings*, which are a type of variable, are used for storing and manipulating text, and as such are the most useful type of variable for working in Word. *Constants* are named items that keep a constant value while a program is executing.

Variables and strings have been surfacing surreptitiously throughout the last five chapters, and we've also seen a few constants, such as those for the message boxes in Chapter 6. Now it's time to dig into the details, starting with variables.

Working with Variables

The good news is that VBA makes variables as easy to work with as possible. The bad news is that there is still a lot of information you'll probably want to know about variables, even if you don't need to learn all of it right away.

What Is a Variable?

Technically, a variable is a named area in memory that you use for storing data while a procedure is running. For example, as you've seen in previous chapters, you might use a variable to store a value from a counter that's augmenting itself in a loop, or to store a string that the user entered in an input box. The counter could terminate the loop when it reached a certain value; the string from the input box could be entered into a document, used as part of another string, or checked, manipulated, and changed as necessary.

Choosing Names for Variables

VBA imposes a number of constraints on variable names, but all in all, they're not too burdensome. Variable names must start with a letter and can be up to 255 characters in length. Usually, you'll want to keep them much shorter than this so that you can easily type them into your code and so that your lines of code don't rapidly reach absurd lengths. Variable names cannot contain characters such as periods, exclamation points, mathematical operators (+, -, /, *), or comparison operators (=, <>, >, >=, <, <=), or internally contain type-declaration characters

(@, &, $, #). (We'll look at the type-declaration characters later in this chapter.) Variable names cannot contain spaces but can contain underscores, which you can use to make variable names more readable. In other words, you're pretty safe if you stick with straightforward alphanumerics enlivened with the occasional underscore.

For example, all of the following variable names are fine and upstanding, though the last is awkwardly long to use:

```
i
John
MyVariable
MissionParameters
The_String_That_the_User_Entered_in_the_Input_Box
```

On the other hand, these variable names are not usable:

```
My Variable      My!Variable      Time@Tide
```

In the above example, the first variable name contains a space, the second contains an exclamation point, and the third contains a type-declaration character (@).

Each variable name must be unique within the scope it is operating in (to prevent VBA from confusing it with any other variable). Typically, the scope within which a variable is operating is a procedure, but if you declare the variable as public (which I'll discuss later in the chapter), its scope will be wider.

The other constraint on variable names is that it's not a good idea to assign to a variable a name that VBA already uses as the name of a function, a statement, or a method. Doing so is called *shadowing* a VBA keyword. It doesn't necessarily cause problems, but it may prevent you from using that function, statement, or method without specifically identifying it to VBA by prefacing its name with **VBA.** For example, instead of **Date**, you'd have to use **VBA.Date**—no big deal, but worth avoiding in the first place.

You're probably thinking that this isn't much of a restriction, and that anyone who hasn't taken leave of their senses should be able to easily avoid shadowing a VBA function, statement, or method with a variable name. But in fact, given the plethora of VBA commands, it's surprisingly easy to shadow a VBA keyword, especially when you suddenly lack inspiration for naming, say, a date or a time. Use Date or Time in this case, and you've shadowed a VBA function.

Declaring a Variable

VBA lets you declare variables either implicitly or explicitly. As I'll explain in a moment, each method has advantages and disadvantages.

Declaring a Variable Implicitly

Declaring a variable implicitly means you simply use it in your code without declaring it explicitly, which is what we've been doing with variables so far throughout this book. When you declare a variable implicitly, VBA checks to make sure that it isn't an already existing variable, and then automatically creates a variable and assigns it the Variant data type, which can contain any type of data except a fixed-length string.

For example, we've looked at a number of message boxes that used the following implicit declaration:

```
Response = MsgBox("Do you want to continue?", vbYesNo)
```

Here, `Response` is implicitly declared as a variable. VBA assigns it the Variant data type. In this case, the variable will be a number—as you'll recall, the `MsgBox` function returns a numerical value linked to a constant for the button chosen in the message box. VBA assigns the variable the value `Empty` when it creates it, but in this case the variable receives a value almost immediately—as soon as the user clicks one of the buttons in the message box.

The advantage of declaring a variable implicitly is that you don't have to code it ahead of time. If you want a variable, you can simply declare it on the spot. However, declaring a variable implicitly also has a couple of disadvantages:

- It's easier to make a mistake when re-entering the name of an implicitly declared variable later in the macro. For example, if you implicitly declare the variable `FilesToCreate` and then later type `FileToCreate` instead, VBA will not query the latter spelling with its missing *s*, but will create another variable with that name. When you're working with a number of variables, it can be difficult and time-consuming to catch little mistakes like these, which can throw a fairly large monkey wrench into your code.

- The Variant variable type takes up more memory than other types of variable, because it has to be able to store various types of data. This difference is negligible under normal circumstances, particularly if you're using only a few variables or writing only short macros; but if you're using large numbers of variables on a computer with limited memory, the extra memory that Variant variables take up might slow down a process or even run it out of memory. (We'll worry about this more in Chapter 17, where we'll consider how to optimize your code to make it run as fast and efficiently as possible.)

You can get around this second disadvantage in a couple of ways: by using a type-declaration character to specify the data type when you declare a variable implicitly, or by telling VBA to force you to declare variables explicitly.

A *type-declaration character* is a character that you add to the end of a variable's name in an implicit declaration to tell VBA which data type to use for the variable. For example, the type-declaration character for a string is $, and the type-declaration character for a currency variable is @. So you could implicitly declare the string variable UserName with the following statement:

```
UserName$ = InputBox("Please enter your name.")
```

And you could implicitly declare the currency variable Price by using this statement:

```
Price@ = Cost * Margin
```

Declaring a Variable Explicitly

Declaring a variable explicitly means telling VBA that the variable exists. VBA then allocates memory space to that variable and registers it as a known quantity. You can also declare the variable type at the same time.

You can declare a variable explicitly at any point in code before you use it, but custom and good sense recommend declaring all your variables at the beginning of the procedure that uses them. This makes them easy to find, which will help anyone reading through the code.

Declaring variables explicitly offers the following advantages:

- Your code will be easier to read and to debug. When you write complex code, this is an important consideration.

- It will be more difficult for you to unintentionally create new variables by mistyping the names of existing variables. As a corollary to this, it will also be more difficult for you to unintentionally wipe out an existing variable when trying to create a new variable.

- Your code will run a fraction faster because VBA will not need to determine while the code is running which type each variable is.

The main disadvantage of declaring variables explicitly is that doing so takes a little more time, effort, and thought. For most code, however, this is outweighed by the advantages.

To declare a variable explicitly, you use one of the following keywords: `Dim`, `Private`, `Public`, or `Static`. For example, you could use the following statement to declare the variable `MyValue`:

```
Dim MyValue
```

`Dim` is the regular keyword to use for declaring a variable, and you'll probably want to use it for most of your variable declarations. You use the other keywords to specify a different scope, lifetime, and data type for the variable in the declaration. (We'll examine these subjects in the next few pages, and we'll look at some examples of using the `Static` keyword in Chapter 17.) In the above example, the `MyValue` variable receives the default scope and lifetime and the Variant data type, which makes it suitable for general-purpose use.

TIP

As I mentioned earlier, it's usually a good idea to declare all variable names together at the beginning of a procedure. Doing so makes the names easy to find so that you can quickly refer back to make sure you've got the right name, instead of trudging through dozens of lines of code to find the relevant declaration; it also makes your code much simpler to read and debug.

You can also declare multiple variables on the same line by separating the variable statements with commas:

```
Dim Supervisor As Long, Controller As Long
```

Requiring Explicit Declarations for Variables

You can set VBA to require you to declare variables explicitly, either globally (for all modules you work with) or on a module-by-module basis. To require variable declarations globally, choose Tools ➤ Options in the Visual Basic Editor to display the Options dialog box; click the Editor tab to display it; select the Require Variable Declaration check box in the Code Settings area; and then click the OK button. (The Require Variable Declaration check box is cleared by default, enabling you to declare variables implicitly, which is usually the easiest way to start working with variables.) The Visual Basic Editor will then add an `Option Explicit` statement to new modules that you create. This statement requires explicit variable declarations for the module it is in.

When you select the Require Variable Declaration check box, VBA will not add the `Option Explicit` statement to your existing modules—you'll need to do that manually if you want to force explicit declarations in them too.

To require variable declarations only for specified modules, put an `Option Explicit` statement at the beginning of each module for which you want to require declarations. It needs to go before the `Sub` statement for the first macro in the module—if you put it inside a macro, or between macros, VBA will throw an error when you try to run any of the macros in the module.

If you've set Option Explicit either globally or for a module, VBA will test the procedure before it runs it—more precisely, VBA will complain when it tries to compile the macro and discovers that you haven't declared one or more of the variables—and will warn you if a variable is not explicitly declared, as shown here.

If you get this message box, you can solve the problem by either declaring the variable or by turning off the requirement of variable declarations for the module. To turn off the requirement, remove the `Option Explicit` statement from the module by selecting and deleting the line that contains it.

Choosing the Scope and Lifetime of a Variable

The *scope* of a variable is the area in VBA within which it can operate. Typically, you'll want to use a variable with its default scope—that is, within the procedure in which it is declared (implicitly or explicitly). For example, if you have a module named `Financial_Macros` that contains the macros `Breakeven_Table` and `Profit_Analysis_Table`, each of which contains a variable named `Gross_Revenue` and another named `Expenses`, the variables in each macro will be distinct from the variables in the other macro, and there will be no danger of VBA confusing the two. (For the human reader, though, using the same variable names in different macros rapidly becomes confusing when debugging. In general, it's a good idea to use unique variable names, even at the default procedure level.)

The *lifetime* of a variable is, not surprisingly, the period during which VBA remembers the value of the variable. You'll need different lifetimes for your variables for different purposes. A variable's lifetime is tied to its scope.

Sometimes you'll need to access a variable from outside the procedure in which it is declared. In these cases, you'll need to declare a different scope for the variable.

A variable can have three types of scope:

- procedure
- private
- public

We'll look at each of these in turn.

Procedure Scope

A variable with *procedure scope* (also known as *procedure-level scope* or *local scope*) is available only to the procedure that contains it. As a result, the lifetime of a local variable is limited to the duration of the procedure that declares it: as soon as the procedure stops running, VBA removes all local variables from memory and reclaims the memory that held them.

Procedure scope is all you'll need for variables that operate only in the procedure in which they are declared. For example, in previous chapters we've used a variable (declared either explicitly or implicitly) for retrieving the result of a message box, like this:

```
Response = MsgBox("Do you want to proceed?", vbYesNo
➥+ vbQuestion, "Delete File")
```

Here, the variable `Response` retrieves the value of the button clicked in the message box. Typically, you'll check the value and take action accordingly, directing the macro to a different branch of action depending on whether the Yes button or the No button was chosen. In this case, you'll seldom need to access the value of `Response` after you've checked what it was, and no other macro will need to access the variable.

NOTE **When you declare a variable implicitly, it is automatically assigned procedure scope. The variables we've used so far in this book have been declared implicitly and so have had procedure scope, which is suitable for general use.**

To explicitly declare a local variable, you use the `Dim` keyword or the `Static` keyword and place it inside the procedure like this:

```
Sub Create_Weekly_Report()
    Dim Supervisor As Long
    Dim Controller As Long
    Static ReportNumber As Integer
...
End Sub
```

Here, the second line declares the variable `Supervisor` as the Long data type, the third line declares the variable `Controller` as the Long data type, and the fourth line declares the variable `ReportNumber` as the Integer data type. (I'll go through the different data types in "Specifying the Data Type for a Variable" in a few pages' time.)

On the other hand, you might use a variable to store the result of an input box:

```
UserName = InputBox("Enter your name.", "Personal Information")
```

In this case, you might want to be able to pass the variable `UserName` to another macro that you call from this macro. For this purpose, procedure scope would not be sufficient—you would need to use either private scope or public scope.

Private Scope

A variable with private scope is available to all procedures in the module that contains it, but not to procedures in other modules. Using private variables enables you to pass the value of a variable from one procedure to another. Unlike local variables, which retain their value only as long as the procedure that contains them is running, private variables retain their value as long as the project that contains them is open.

To declare a variable with private scope, you can use either the `Dim` keyword or the `Private` keyword at the beginning of a module, placing it before the `Sub` statement for the first macro in the module:

```
Dim Supervisor As Long
Private Consultant As Long

Sub MyMacro()
```

You'll notice that the `Dim` statement here uses exactly the same syntax as the declaration for the local variable—the difference is that to declare a private variable, the statement is placed at the beginning of the module rather than within a procedure. But because the `Private` statement has the same effect as the `Dim` statement for declaring private variables and cannot be used within a procedure, it's clearer to use the `Private` statement rather than the `Dim` statement for declaring private variables. Your code will also be clearer if you stick with `Private` rather than mixing `Private` statements with `Dim` statements as I've done in the above example (although VBA will happily accept the mixture).

WARNING After you edit a macro in the Visual Basic Editor, private variables and public variables will be reset (their values will be erased) when the Visual Basic Editor recompiles the code. If you're testing a project that uses private or public variables, you will need to reinitialize (reassign values to) them after each edit you make.

Public Scope

A variable with public scope is available to all procedures in all modules in the project that contains it.

To declare a public variable, you use the `Public` keyword at the beginning of a module, before the `Sub` statement for the first macro in the module:

```
Public MyVar As Integer
```

This statement declares the variable `MyVar` as the Integer type.

Like private variables, public variables retain their value as long as the project that contains them is open. For example, if you wanted to track the user's name through a series of operations, you could create an `AutoExec` macro that prompted the user to enter their name when they started Word. By storing the result of their input in a public variable, you could then retrieve the value for use in macros later in the same Word session.

> **WARNING** Again, public variables are reset when the Visual Basic Editor recompiles code, so you will need to reinitialize them after editing your code.

We'll look at `AutoExec` macros and the other automatic Word macros in detail in Chapter 21, but for the moment you could quickly try the code shown in Listing 10.1.

Listing 10.1

```
1.  Public CurrentUser As String
2.  Sub AutoExec()
3.      CurrentUser = InputBox("Please enter your name.",
        ➥"Current User Identity")
4.  End Sub
5.
6.  Sub Identify_Current_User()
7.      MsgBox "The current user is " + CurrentUser,
        ➥vbOKOnly + vbInformation, "Current User"
8.  End Sub
```

Analysis

This code consists of three different parts:

- Line 1 declares the public variable `CurrentUser` as the String data type.

- Lines 2 through 4 contain the `AutoExec` macro. This will run each time the user starts Word. Line 3 displays an input box that prompts the user to enter their name and stores their response in the public variable `CurrentUser`.

- Lines 6 through 8 contain the `Identify_Current_User` macro, which simply displays a message box that gives the name of the user, along with prefatory text and an information icon and title bar for completeness.

You could step through the `AutoExec` and `Identify_Current_User` macros in the Visual Basic Editor by using the F8 key, but to see their effect, create the macros and then exit Word. When you restart Word, the `AutoExec` macro will display the input box for you to enter your name. At any point thereafter (until you exit Word), you can run the `Identify_Current_User` macro, and VBA will display a message box with the name you entered.

WARNING Because public variables retain their value when no procedure is running, they continue to take up space in memory. If you grossly abuse public variables, you might run short of memory or cause increased swap-file use on a computer with limited quantities of memory available.

Specifying the Data Type for a Variable

VBA supports the following *data types* for variables:

- Boolean
- Byte
- Currency
- Date
- Decimal
- Double
- Integer
- Long
- Object
- Single
- String
- Variant

Over the next few pages, we'll examine each of these data types in turn. First, though, I should mention that you don't have to specify data types if you don't want to. Almost always, you can use the default Variant data type (as we've been doing) and let VBA figure out how to handle the niceties.

The disadvantage to using the Variant data type is that it takes up more memory than some of the other data types. (In the next few sections, I'll mention how much memory each data type takes up; even if you don't care about this information now, you may want to refer back to it later on in your explorations of VBA.) Using the Variant data type also causes your code to run somewhat more slowly. With straightforward macros, such as those we've been working with so far in this book and those we'll be working with over the next few chapters, memory and speed are rarely an issue—in fact, you probably won't notice any speed difference unless you're dangerously hyper or you're running Word on a sorely underpowered computer (or both).

When we get to Chapter 17, in the context of optimizing your macros, I'll discuss the pros and cons of specifying data types for your variables. Right now, though, let's take a look at what the different data types mean.

Boolean

A Boolean variable is a two-position variable: it can only be set to True or False. You can use the keyword True or False to set the value of a Boolean variable, as in the second line below (the first declares the Boolean variable Product_Available):

```
Dim Product_Available As Boolean
Product_Available = True
```

You can then retrieve the result of the Boolean variable and take action accordingly:

```
If Product_Available = True Then
    MsgBox "The product is available."
Else             'Product_Available = False
    MsgBox "The product is not available."
End If
```

When you convert a Boolean variable to another data type, such as a numeric value, True returns –1 and False returns 0. When you convert a numeric value to a Boolean value, 0 returns `False` and all other numbers (whether positive or negative) return `True`.

Boolean variables are a good place to start declaring the data types of your variables, simply because they are so easy to use. Boolean variables take up 2 bytes each.

Byte

A Byte variable takes up the least memory of any of the data types (appropriately enough, just 1 byte) and can store a number from 0 to 255. Given this limitation, you probably won't want to use Byte variables very often.

Currency

The Currency data type, as you might guess, is designed for use with money. It allows for positive and negative numbers with up to fifteen digits to the left of the decimal point and four digits to the right of it.

To implicitly declare a currency variable, use the type-declaration character @. For example, you might indulge your curiosity by working out your weekly salary with a little simple math:

```
Sub Calculate_Weekly_Salary()
    Salary@ = InputBox("Enter your salary.",
    ➥"Calculate Weekly Salary")
    WeeklySalary@ = Salary@/ 52
    MsgBox WeeklySalary@
End Sub
```

Currency variables take up 8 bytes each.

Date

The Date data type is relatively complex. VBA works with dates and times as floating-point numbers (numbers in which the quantity is given by one number multiplied by a power of the number base), with the date displayed to the left of the decimal point and the time to the right. VBA can handle dates from 1 January 100 to 31 December 9999 and times from 0:00:00 to 23:59:59.

You can enter date variables as literal date values, such as **6/3/36** or **June 3, 1936**, by placing a # sign before and after the literal date value:

```
#June 3, 1936#
```

When you move the insertion point from the line in the code window in which you've entered a literal date value between # signs, VBA converts the data to a number and changes the display to the date format set in your computer. For example, if you enter **June 3, 1936**, VBA will probably display it as 6/3/36. Likewise, you can enter literal time values (for example, **#10:15PM#**) and VBA will convert them to a number and display them according to the current time format (for example, 10:15:00 PM).

Date variables take up 8 bytes each.

Decimal

The Decimal data type, which is only partly implemented in Word 97, stores unsigned integers scaled by powers of 10. (*Unsigned* here means that the integers carry no plus or minus designation, not that your check's going to be returned by the electric company.) In the Word 97 implementation of VBA, you cannot declare a Decimal variable—you can only use the Decimal data type within a Variant data type (which we'll examine in detail later in this section). In other words, you don't need to worry about the Decimal data type when working with VBA in Word.

Decimal variables take up 12 bytes each.

Double

The Double data type is for floating-point numbers and can handle negative values from $-1.79769313486232^{\wedge}308$ to $-4.94065645841247^{\wedge}-324$ and positive numbers from $4.94065645841247^{\wedge}-324$ to $1.79769313486232^{\wedge}308$.

> **NOTE** *Double* here stands for double-precision floating point, the way in which the number is handled by the computer. *Single* (which we'll look at later in the list) stands for single-precision floating point, which works with fewer decimal places and is consequently less accurate.

You can use the # type-declaration character to declare a Double variable implicitly. Double variables take up 8 bytes each.

Integer

The Integer data type is the most efficient way of handling numbers from –32,768 to 32,767, a range that makes it useful for macros. For example, if you wanted to repeat an action 300 times, you could use an Integer variable for the counter, as in the following lines:

```
Dim MyVar As Integer
For MyVar = 1 to 300
    'repeat actions
Next MyVar
```

Integer variables take up 2 bytes each.

Long

The Long data type is for integer numeric values larger or smaller than those the Integer data type can handle: Long variables can handle numbers from –2,147,483,648 to 2,147,483,647. (For numbers even larger or smaller than these, use the Double data type.) Long variables use the type-declaration character & and take up 4 bytes each.

Object

The Object data type is for storing addresses that reference objects (for example, objects in the Word object model, which we'll examine in the next chapter), providing an easy way to refer to an object. Object variables take up 4 bytes each.

Single

The Single data type, like the Double data type, is for working with floating-point numbers. Single can handle negative values from -3.402823^{38} to -1.401298^{-45} and positive values from 1.401298^{-45} to 3.402823^{38}; as noted earlier, these numbers use fewer decimal places than the Double data type provides.

Use the exclamation point type-declaration character to declare a Single variable implicitly. Single variables take up 4 bytes each.

String

The String data type is for handling text. We'll examine strings more closely in the next section of the chapter, but here's a quick preview:

- Variable-length strings can contain up to about two billion characters. They take up 10 bytes plus the storage required for the string.

- Fixed-length strings can contain from 1 to about 64,000 characters. They take up only the storage required for the string. If the data assigned to the string is shorter than the fixed length, VBA pads the data with trailing spaces to make up the full complement of characters. If the data assigned to the string is longer than the fixed length, VBA truncates the data after the relevant character. VBA counts the characters from the left end of the string: for example, if you assign the string **Output** to a fixed-length string that is four characters long, VBA will store **Outp**.

- Strings can contain letters, numbers, spaces, and punctuation.

- Use the $ type-declaration character to declare a string implicitly.

Variant

The Variant data type, as mentioned earlier in this chapter, is assigned by VBA to all variables whose data type is not declared. Variants can handle most of the different types of data, but there are a couple characteristics of Variants to keep in mind:

- First, Variants cannot contain fixed-length string data. If you need to use a fixed-length string, you need to specify a fixed-length string.

- Second, Variant variables can also contain four special values: `Empty` (which means the variable has not yet been initialized), `Error` (a special value used for tracking errors in a procedure), `Nothing` (a special value used for disassociating a variable from the object it was associated with), and `Null` (which you use to indicate that the variable deliberately contains no data).

Because of their extra capabilities, Variant variables take up more memory. Variant variables that contain numbers take up 16 bytes, and Variant variables that contain characters take up 22 bytes plus the storage required for the characters.

Deciding Among VariableTypes

If you found the details of the different types of variables confusing, relax. First, as already discussed, you can usually avoid the whole issue of choosing a variable type by declaring the variable either implicitly or explicitly and letting VBA assign the Variant data type. Second, if you do choose to specify data types for some of your variables, you can apply a few straightforward rules to direct your choices:

- If the variable will contain only the values `True` and `False`, declare it as the Boolean data type.

- If the variable will always contain an integer (i.e., will never contain a fraction), declare it as the Integer data type. (If the numbers may be too big for the Integer data type, declare it as the Long data type instead.)

- If the variable will be used for calculating money, use the Currency data type.

- If the variable may sometimes contain a fraction, declare it as the Single data type or the Double data type.

- If the variable will always contain a string (rather than a number), declare it as the String data type.

Working with Strings

String variables are among the most useful variables for working with Word in VBA. You can use them to store any quantity of text, from a character or two up to a large number of pages; you also use them to store file names and folder names. Once you've stored the data in a string, you can manipulate it and change it according to your needs.

In this section, we'll look at some of the most important commands in VBA for working with strings. These include removing spaces from a string, returning part of a string as another string, finding one string within another string, and joining strings together. First, though, let's recap briefly on how and when to declare a string.

Declaring a String

As you saw earlier in this chapter, you can declare a string either implicitly or explicitly:

- To declare a string implicitly, use the type-declaration character $:

```
UserName$ = InputBox("Enter your name.")
```

- To declare a string explicitly, use a straightforward statement like the one shown below. This statement explicitly declares the string variable UserName. This is a variable-length string that adjusts its length to match the data stored in it.

```
Dim UserName As String
```

- To declare a fixed-length string, use an explicit declaration with the * character and the length of the string. For example, the following statement declares the string Location and specifies that it is five characters long:

```
Dim Location As String * 5
```

When Should You Declare a String Explicitly?

While declaring strings implicitly using the $ type-declaration character is the easiest and quickest way to proceed in VBA, you'll often want to declare strings explicitly:

- When you need a string to have a scope wider than local scope, you'll have to declare it explicitly by using a Public statement or a Private statement at the beginning of the module:

```
Public MyString As String
Private ThisString As String
```

- When you need a fixed-length string, you have to declare it explicitly.
- When you want to make your code easy to read and debug, it is a good idea to declare all the variables you are using early in the code.

Assigning Data to a String

When you declare a string variable (either implicitly or explicitly), VBA assigns an empty string to it. An empty string (also known as a *blank string*) is a string that does not contain any characters and is represented by double quotation marks with nothing between them:

```
""
```

Once the string is declared, you can assign data to it by entering the text and the surrounding double quotation marks. You can enter any of the regular characters from the character set—that is, all the alphanumerics and all the symbols that you can type in by using the regular keys on the keyboard. (For characters such as a carriage return or a tab, refer to the section "Entering Special Characters in a String.")

Here's a simple example:

```
Dim UserName As String
UserName = "Gene Shumway"
```

The first line explicitly declares the variable `UserName` as a String variable. The second line assigns the data **Gene Shumway** to it.

Likewise, you can assign data to a string by using an input box:

```
Dim Company As String
Company = InputBox("Enter your company name:")
```

Here, the first line explicitly declares the variable `Company` as a string, and the second line assigns the data from the input box to it.

Concatenating Strings

By concatenating (linking together) strings, you can turn a variety of motley strings into coherent text or comprehensible messages. (You might experience a slight sense of déjà vu at this point, because we've been merrily concatenating strings for several chapters now in the name of producing halfway convincing message boxes and dialog boxes. Now, however, we get to examine them formally.)

To concatenate strings, use the + operator or the & operator. For example, to concatenate `string1` and `string2` into `string3`, you could use the following statement:

```
string3 = string1 + string2
```

Here, VBA joins the data in `string2` to the end of the data in `string1` and stores the result in `string3`. So if `string1` contained the data **Hello.** and `string2` contained the data **How are you today?**, `string3` would contain **Hello.How are you today?**

As you can see, VBA simply joins the two data items together: it doesn't bother with niceties like wondering if you'd want a space after the period. If you want a space there, you need to add one. You could do so either by adding a space to the end of `string1` or by adding a space between the two strings when you concatenate them.

To add a space to `string1`, you could use this line:

```
string1 = string1 + " "
```

Here, VBA adds the space entered between the double quotation marks to the end of `string1` and stores the result as `string1` again.

To add a space between the two strings when you concatenate them, you could use this line:

```
string3 = string1 + " " + string2
```

Entering Special Characters in a String

To add special characters (such as a carriage return or a tab) to a string, you need to specify them by their character codes using the `Chr` function. The syntax for the `Chr` function is straightforward:

```
Chr(charactercode)
```

Here, `charactercode` is a number that identifies the character to add.

Table 10.1 lists the most useful character codes.

TABLE 10.1 VBA Character Codes.

Code	Character
Chr(9)	Tab
Chr(10)	Line-feed
Chr(11)	Soft return (Shift+Enter)
Chr(12)	Page break
Chr(13)	Carriage return/line-feed
Chr(14)	Column break
Chr(34)	Double straight quotation marks (")
Chr(39)	Single straight quote mark/apostrophe (')
Chr(145)	Opening single smart quotation mark (')
Chr(146)	Closing single smart quotation mark/apostrophe (')
Chr(147)	Opening double smart quotation mark (")
Chr(148)	Closing double smart quotation mark (")
Chr(149)	Bullet
Chr(150)	en dash
Chr(151)	em dash

NOTE

The straight and smart quotes and apostrophes can sometimes be difficult to work with in Word because of Word's determination to help you make all your straight quotes smart. For example, during a Find and Replace operation, if you search for a single smart quote and replace it with another character, Word will assume that you want to affect the single straight quotes in your document as well. The solution is to specify the character number in the Find and Replace dialog box, or in a VBA Find and Replace operation, rather than using the character itself.

Let's say you wanted to build a string containing a person's name and address from individual strings that contained items of that information, and to have the individual items separated by tabs in the resulting string so that you could insert it into a document and then convert it into a table; to do this, you could use a statement like the one below. Here, VBA uses a For...Next loop to repeat the action until the counter i reaches the number stored in the variable NumberOfRecords.

```
For i = 1 to NumberOfRecords
    AllInfo = FirstName + Chr(9) + MiddleInitial + Chr(9)
    ➡+ LastName + Chr(9) + Address1 + Chr(9) + Address2
    ➡+ Chr(9) + City + Chr(9) + State  + Chr(9) + Zip
    ➡+ Chr(9) + BusinessPhone + Chr(9) + HomePhone + Chr(13)
    Selection.TypeText AllInfo
Next i
```

The second line (split here over four physical lines) assigns data to the string AllInfo by concatenating the strings FirstName, MiddleInitial, LastName, and so on with tabs—Chr(9) characters—between them. The final character added to the string is Chr(13), the line-feed/carriage-return character, which creates a new paragraph.

The third line enters the AllInfo string into the current document, thus building a tab-delimited list containing the names and addresses. This list can then be easily converted into a table whose columns each contain one item of information (the first column contains the FirstName string, the second column the MiddleInitial string, and so on).

Returning Part of a String

Frequently, you'll need to use only part of a string in your macros. For example, you might want to take only the first three characters of the name of a city to create the code for a location.

VBA provides several functions for returning from strings the characters you need:

- The Left function returns the specified number of characters from the left end of the string.

- The Right function returns the specified number of characters from the right end of the string.

- The Mid function returns the specified number of characters from the specified location inside a string.

Using the Left Function

The Left function, which returns a specified number of characters from the left end of a string, made a guest appearance earlier in the book. Now I'll show you how to use it.

Syntax   The syntax for the Left function is straightforward:

```
Left(string, length)
```

Here, the string argument is any string expression—that is, any expression that returns a sequence of contiguous characters. Left returns Null if string contains no data. The length argument is a numeric expression specifying the number of characters to return. Length can be a straightforward number (e.g., 4, or 7, or 11) or an expression that results in a number. For example, if you had the length of a word stored in the variable named LenWord, and you wanted to return two characters fewer than LenWord, you could specify LenWord - 2 as the length argument; to return three characters more than LenWord, you could specify LenWord + 3 as the length argument.

Example   You could use the Left function to separate the area code from a telephone number that was provided as an unseparated ten-digit chunk by your friendly local mainframe. Here, the telephone number is stored in the variable Phone, which we'll assume was created earlier in the procedure:

```
Area = Left(Phone, 3)
```

This statement creates the variable Area and fills it with the leftmost three characters of the variable Phone.

Using the Right Function

The Right function is the mirror image of the Left function and returns a specified number of characters from the right end of a string.

Syntax The syntax for the `Right` function is straightforward:

```
Right(string, length)
```

Again, the `string` argument is any string expression—that is, any expression that returns a sequence of contiguous characters—and `length` is a numeric expression specifying the number of characters to return. Again, `Right` returns `Null` if `string` contains no data, and `length` can be a straightforward number or an expression that results in a number.

Example To continue the previous example, you could use the `Right` function to separate the last seven digits of the phone number stored in the string `Phone` from the area code:

```
LocalNumber = Right(Phone, 7)
```

This statement creates the variable `LocalNumber` and fills it with the right-most seven characters from the variable `Phone`.

Using the Mid Function

The `Mid` function returns the specified number of characters from inside the given string. You specify a starting position in the string and the number of characters (to the right of the starting position) to return.

Syntax The syntax for the `Mid` function is as follows:

```
Mid(string, start[, length])
```

As in `Left` and `Right`, the `string` argument is any string expression. `Mid` returns `Null` if `string` contains no data.

`start` is a numeric value specifying the character position in `string` at which to start the `length` selection; if `start` is larger than the number of characters in `string`, VBA returns a zero-length string.

`length` is a numeric expression specifying the number of characters to return. If you omit `length` or use a `length` argument greater than the number of characters in `string`, VBA returns all characters from the `start` position to the end of `string`. Once more, `Length` can be a straightforward number or an expression that results in a number.

Example You could use `Mid` to return the local exchange code from a ten-digit phone number (e.g., 555 from 5105551212). Here, the telephone number is stored in the variable `Phone`, which we'll assume was created earlier in the procedure:

```
LocalExchange = Mid(Phone, 4, 3)
```

This statement creates the variable `LocalExchange` and fills it with the three characters of the variable `Phone` starting at the fourth character.

NOTE If the phone number were supplied in a different format, such as (510) 555-1212 or 510-555-1212, you would need to adjust the `start` value to allow for the extra characters. For example, if the area code is in parentheses and followed by a space, as in the first instance here, you would need a `start` value of 7; if the area code was divided from the rest of the phone number only by a hyphen, as in the second instance here, you would need a `start` value of 5.

Finding a String within Another String

The `InStr` function allows you to find one string within another string. For example, you could check a string derived from, say, the current paragraph to see if it contained a particular word. If it did, you could take action accordingly—for example, replacing that word with another word, or selecting the paragraph for inclusion in another document.

Syntax The syntax for `InStr` is as follows:

```
InStr([start, ]string1, string2[, compare])
```

`start` is an optional argument specifying the starting position in the first string, `string1`. If you omit `start`, VBA starts the search at the first character in `string1` (which is usually where you want to start). However, you do need to use `start` when you use the `compare` argument to specify the type of string comparison to perform.

`string1` is a required argument specifying the string expression in which to search for `string2`.

string2 is a required argument specifying the string expression for which to search in string1.

compare is an optional argument specifying the type of string comparison you want to perform: a *binary comparison*, which is case-sensitive, or a *textual comparison*, which is non-case-sensitive. The default is a binary comparison, which you can specify by using the constant vbBinaryCompare or the value 0 for compare; while this isn't necessary (because it's the default), you might want to use it to make your code ultra-clear. To specify a textual comparison, use the constant vbTextCompare or the value 1 for compare.

TIP

A textual comparison is a useful weapon when you're dealing with data that may arrive in a variety of cases. For example, if you wanted to search a selection for instances of a name, you would probably want to find instances of the name in uppercase and lowercase as well as in title case—otherwise you will find only title case (assuming you specified the name in title case).

Example You could use InStr to find the location of a certain string within another string so that you could then change that inner string. You might want to do this if you needed to move a file from its current position in a particular folder or subfolder to another folder that had a similar subfolder structure. For instance, suppose you work with documents stored in a variety of subfolders beneath a folder named "In" (e.g., f:\Documents\In\), and after you're done with them, you save them in corresponding subfolders beneath a folder named "Out" (e.g., f:\Documents\Out\). To write a macro that automatically saves the documents in the "Out" subfolders, you could use code like that shown in Listing 10.2.

Listing 10.2

```
1.  Sub Save_in_Out_Folder()
2.      OName = ActiveDocument.FullName
3.      ToChange = InStr(OName, "\In\")
4.      NName = Left(OName, ToChange - 1) + "\Out\"
        ➥+ Right(OName, Len(OName) - ToChange - 3)
5.      ActiveDocument.SaveAs NName
6.  End Sub
```

Analysis

Line 1 begins the macro, and line 6 ends it.

Line 2 implicitly declares the variable `OName` (as in *original name*) and assigns it the `FullName` property of the `ActiveDocument` object. We'll look at how to work with files in Chapter 13, but this property is easy to understand: it's the full name of the active document, including the path to the document (for example, `f:\Documents\In\Letters\My Letter.doc`).

Line 3 implicitly declares the variable `ToChange` and assigns it the value of the `InStr` function that finds the string `\In\` in the variable `OName`. If we use the example path from the previous paragraph, `ToChange` will be assigned the value 13, because the first character of the `\In\` string is the thirteenth character in the `OName` string.

Line 4 implicitly declares the variable `NName` (as in *new name*) and assigns to it the new file name created in the main part of the statement. This breaks down as follows:

- `Left(OName, ToChange - 1)` takes the left section of the `OName` string, returning the number of characters specified by `ToChange - 1`, the number stored in `ToChange` minus one.

- `+ "\Out\"` adds to the partial string specified in the previous bullet (to continue the previous example, `f:\Documents`) the characters `\Out\`, which effectively replace the `\In\` characters, thus changing the directory name (`f:\Documents\Out\`).

- `+ Right(OName, Len(OName) - ToChange - 3)` completes the partial string by adding the right section of the `OName` string, starting from after the `\In\` string (`Letters\My Letter.doc`), giving `f:\Documents\Out\ Letters\My Letter.doc`). The number of characters to take from the right section is determined by subtracting the value stored in `ToChange` from the length of `OName` and then subtracting 3 from the result. Here, the value 3 comes from the length of the string `\In\`; because the `ToChange` value stores the character number of the first backslash, we need count only the *I*, the *n*, and the second backslash to reach its end.

Line 5 saves the document using the name in the `NName` variable.

You'll notice that in this procedure, I've been lazy and used implicit declarations for all the variables. This means that VBA creates all the variables with the Variant data type and then determines what kind of information is stored in them: a string for OName and NName, and a value for ToChange. Were I more disciplined, I might have begun the procedure by declaring the variables with suitable types, as in the lines shown here:

```
Sub Save_in_Out_Folder()
    Dim OName As String, NName As String, ToChange As Integer
```

This would have saved a few bytes of memory and might have speeded up the macro by the blink of an eye—hardly worth the effort for a straightforward macro like this one.

Trimming Leading and Trailing Spaces from a String

Often you'll need to trim strings before concatenating them, to avoid ending up with extra spaces in inappropriate places such as in the middle of eight-character file names.

VBA provides three functions specifically for trimming leading spaces and trailing spaces from strings:

- LTrim removes leading spaces from the specified string.

- RTrim removes trailing spaces from the specified string.

- Trim removes both leading and trailing spaces from the specified string.

TIP   In many cases, you can simply use Trim instead of figuring out whether LTrim or RTrim is appropriate for what you expect a variable to contain. At other times, you'll need to remove either leading or trailing spaces while retaining their counterparts, in which case you'll need either LTrim or RTrim. RTrim is especially useful for working with fixed-length string variables, which will contain trailing spaces if the data assigned to them is shorter than their fixed length.

Syntax The syntax for the `LTrim`, `RTrim`, and `Trim` functions is straightforward:

```
LTrim(string)
Rtrim(string)
Trim(string)
```

In each case, `string` is any string expression.

Example You could use the `Trim` function to remove both leading and trailing spaces from a string derived from the current selection in the active document. The first line in the code below declares the variables `Untrimmed` and `Trimmed` as string variables. The second line assigns the data in the current selection to the `Untrimmed` string. The third line assigns the trimmed version of the `Untrimmed` string to the `Trimmed` string.

```
Dim Untrimmed As String, Trimmed As String
Untrimmed = Selection.Text
Trimmed = Trim(Untrimmed)
```

Checking the Length of a String

To check how long a string is, you use the `Len` function. Often, you'll need to check the length of a string to make sure that the string is not too long or too short, as we did with the password length–checking code in Listing 9.4. At other times, you'll need to determine the length of a string to determine how many characters to take from it, as you saw in Listing 10.2.

Syntax The syntax for the `Len` function is straightforward:

```
Len(string)
```

Here, `string` is any valid string expression. (If `string` is `Null`, `Len` also returns `Null`.)

Example You can use `Len` to make sure that a user's entry in an input box or in a text box of a dialog box is of a suitable length. For example, as shown in Listing 10.3, `Len` is used to make sure that the password the user entered was of a suitable length.

Listing 10.3

```
1.   BadPassword:
2.   Password = InputBox("Enter the password to protect this
     ➥item from changes:", "Enter Password")
3.   If Len(Password) = 0 Then
4.       End
5.   ElseIf Len(Password) < 6 Then
6.       MsgBox "The password you chose is too short." + Chr(13)
         ➥+ Chr(13) + "Please choose a password between 6 and
         ➥15 characters in length.", vbOKOnly + vbCritical,
         ➥"Unsuitable Password"
7.       GoTo BadPassword
8.   ElseIf Len(Password) > 15 Then
9.       MsgBox "The password you chose is too long." + Chr(13)
         ➥+ Chr(13) + "Please choose a password between 6 and
         ➥15 characters in length.", vbOKOnly + vbCritical,
         ➥"Unsuitable Password"
10.      GoTo BadPassword
11.  End If
```

Analysis

Here, the Len statement in line 3 checks to see if the length of the Password variable is 0 (which would mean that the user either clicked the Cancel button or the close button on the input box or clicked the OK button with no text entered in the input box); the Len statement in line 5 checks to see if the length of the Password variable is less than 6 (which would make for an unsuitably short password); and the Len statement in line 8 checks to see if the length of the Password variable is more than 15 (which would make for an unsuitably long password).

Changing the Case of a String

VBA provides a number of functions for changing the case of a string: StrConv (whose name comes from *string conversion*), LCase, and UCase. Of these, the easiest to use is StrConv, which can convert a string to a number of different formats varying from straightforward uppercase, lowercase, or propercase (as VBA refers to initial capitals) to the Japanese *hiragana* and *katakana* phonetic characters.

Using StrConv

The `StrConv` function has the following syntax:

```
StrConv(string, conversion)
```

Here, the `string` argument is any string expression, and the `conversion` argument is a constant or value specifying the type of conversion required. The most useful conversion constants and values are these:

Constant	Value	Effect
vbUpperCase	1	Converts the given string to uppercase characters
vbLowerCase	2	Converts the given string to lowercase characters
vbProperCase	3	Converts the given string to propercase (a.k.a. title case—the first letter of every word is capitalized)

For example, if you received a string `CustomerName` containing a person's name from a database program, you could use `StrConv` to make sure that it was in title case by using a statement such as this:

```
ProperCustomerName = StrConv(CustomerName, 3)
```

> **NOTE** `StrConv` doesn't care about the casing of the string you feed it—it simply returns the case you asked for. For example, you can feed `StrConv` uppercase and ask it to return uppercase, and it'll be perfectly happy.

Using LCase and UCase

If you don't feel like using `StrConv`, you can also use the `LCase` and `UCase` functions, which convert a string to lowercase and uppercase, respectively.

LCase and UCase have the following syntax:

```
LCase(string)
UCase(string)
```

Here, string is any string expression.

For example, you could lowercase the string MyString by using the following statement:

```
MyLowerString = LCase(MyString)
```

Converting a String to a Value

At times you'll need to create a value from a string, such as when you return a price from a document as a string and then need to perform math with it. VBA provides the functions Asc and Val for converting strings to values.

Using the Asc Function

The Asc (which stands for ASCII but in fact returns the ANSI—American National Standards Institute—number for a character) function returns the character code for the first character of a string. *Character codes* are the numbers by which computers refer to letters. For example, the character code for a capital *A* is 65 and for a capital *B* is 66; a lowercase *a* is 97, and a lowercase *b* is 98.

Syntax The syntax for the Asc function is straightforward:

```
Asc(string)
```

Here, string is any string expression.

Example You could use the Asc function to return the character code for the first character of the current selection in the active document and display that code in a message box by using these statements:

```
ThisCharacter = Asc(Selection.Text)
MsgBox ThisCharacter, vbOKOnly, "Character Code"
```

The first line declares the variable ThisCharacter and assigns to it the character code for the first character of the current selection. The second line displays a message box containing ThisCharacter.

Using the Val Function

The `Val` function converts the numbers contained in a string into a numeric value. `Val` is a bit weird:

- It reads only numbers in a string.

- It starts at the beginning of the string and reads only as far as the string contains characters that it recognizes as numbers.

- It ignores tabs, line-feeds, and blank spaces.

- It recognizes the period as a decimal separator, but not the comma.

This means that if you feed `Val` a string consisting of tabbed columns of numbers, such as the second line below, it will read them as a single number (in this case, 445634.994711).

```
Item#     Price    Available    On Order    Ordered
4456      34.99         4           7          11
```

If, however, you feed it something containing a mix of numbers and letters, `Val` will read only the numbers. For example, if fed the address shown below, it returns 8661, ignoring the other numbers in the string (because it stops at the *L* of *Laurel*, the first character that is not a number, a tab, a line-feed, or a space).

```
8661 Laurel Avenue Suite 3806, Oakland, CA 94610
```

NOTE You can also feed `Val` with octal (base 8) and hexadecimal (base 16) numbers, but I have this strange feeling you're probably not going to want to do that, so I won't go into that here.

Syntax The syntax for `Val` is straightforward:

```
Val(string)
```

Here, `string` is a required argument consisting of any string expression.

Example You could use the following statement to return the numeric variable `StreetNumber` from the string `Address1`:

```
StreetNumber = Val(Address1)
```

Converting a Value to a String

Just as you can convert a string to a value, you can also convert a value to a string. You'll need to do this when you want to concatenate the information contained in a value with a string—if you try to do this simply by using the + operator, VBA will attempt to perform a mathematical operation rather than concatenation. For example, if you have declared a string variable named `YourAge` and a value variable named `Age`, you cannot use a `YourAge + Age` statement to concatenate them, because they are different types; you need to first create a string from the `Age` value and then concatenate that string with the `YourAge` string.

To convert a value to a string, you use the `Str` function.

Syntax The syntax for the `Str` function is simply this:

```
Str(number)
```

Here, `number` is a variable containing a numeric expression (such as an Integer data type, a Long data type, or a Double data type).

Example As an example of converting a value to a string, consider the short macro in Listing 10.4.

Listing 10.4

```
1.  Sub Age
2.      Dim Age As Integer, YourAge As String
3.      Age = InputBox("Enter your age:", "Age")
4.      YourAge = "Your age is" + Str(Age) + "."
5.      MsgBox YourAge, vbOKOnly + vbInformation, "Age"
6.  End Sub
```

Analysis

Line 2 declares the variable `Age` as the Integer data type and the variable `YourAge` as the String data type. Line 3 then displays an input box prompting the user to enter their age; this is then stored in the `Age` variable. Line 4 assigns the data to the `YourAge` variable: a short text string, the string derived from the `Age` variable, and a period for grammar and completeness. Line 5 then displays a message box containing the `YourAge` string.

Comparing Strings Using the = Operator

Sometimes you'll want to compare one string with another string to see if you got the result you expected. The easiest way to do this is to use the = operator.

You can use a straightforward comparison with the = operator to compare two strings, as shown in the second line below:

```
Pet = InputBox("What is your pet?", "Pet")
If Pet = "Dog" Then MsgBox "We do not accept dogs."
```

The problem with this code as written is that the strings need to match exactly in capitalization for VBA to consider them equal: if `Pet` is `dog` or `DOG` rather than `Dog`, the condition is not met.

To get around this, you can use the `Or` operator to hedge your bets:

```
If Pet = "Dog" Or Pet = "dog" Or Pet = "DOG" Or Pet = "dogs"
➥Or Pet = "Dogs" or Pet = "DOGS" Then MsgBox "We do not
➥accept dogs."
```

As you can see, this rapidly becomes clumsy. One simple solution is to use one of the case-changing functions to make sure that you're at least comparing the same case. For example, you might use the `LCase` function to make sure that the string from the input box was lowercase before comparing it:

```
Pet = LCase(InputBox("What is your pet?", "Pet"))
If Pet = "dog" Or Pet = "dogs" Then
➥MsgBox "We do not accept dogs."
```

Now, the first line assigns to `Pet` the lowercased result of the input box, so that no matter what case the user chooses to type their response, the result is lowercase. The second line then compares `Pet` to the two lowercase strings, since there is no longer a need to compare it to the uppercase and title-case strings.

Working with Constants

As I mentioned way back at the beginning of this chapter, a constant is a named item that keeps a constant value during execution of a program.

We've looked at some constants already, such as the constants you can use for working with message boxes; `vbOK` is the constant for the value 1 returned when the user chooses the OK button in a `vbOKCancel` message box, which itself is a constant for the message box value 2.

VBA provides a number of constants, but you can also declare your own constants to help you work smoothly with information that stays constant through a procedure.

Declaring Your Own Constants

To declare your own constants, you use the `Const` statement. By declaring a constant, you can simplify your code when you need to reuse a set value a number of times in your macro.

Syntax   The syntax for the `Const` statement is as follows:

```
[Public/Private] Const constant [As type] = expression
```

Here, `Public` and `Private` are optional keywords used for declaring public or private scope for a constant. We'll examine how they work in a moment. `constant` is the name of the constant, which follows the normal rules for naming variables. `type` is an optional argument that specifies the data type of the constant. `expression` is a literal (a value written into your code), another constant, or a combination of the two.

As with variables, you can declare multiple constants in the same line by separating the statements with a comma:

```
Const conPerformer As String = "Rikki Nadir",
➥conTicketPrice As String = "$34.99"
```

Example As you can see from the syntax, declaring a constant in VBA works in a similar way to declaring a variable explicitly. The main difference is that you have to declare the value of the constant when you declare the constant (rather than at a later point of your choosing), and you cannot change its value afterwards (hence the name *constant*).

As an example, take a look at the statements below:

```
Const conVenue As String = "Davies Hall"
Const conDate As Date = #December 31, 1999#
MsgBox "The concert is at " + conVenue + " on "
➥+ Str(conDate) + "."
```

The first line declares the constant `conVenue` as a String data type and assigns it the data `Davies Hall`. The second line declares the constant `conDate` as a Date data type and assigns it the date `December 31, 1999`. (When you finish creating this line of code and move the insertion point to another line, VBA will change the date to the date format set in your computer's clock—`#12/31/99#`, for example.) The third line displays a message box containing a string concatenated from the three text items in double quotation marks, the `conVenue` string constant, and the string derived from the `conDate` date constant.

Choosing the Scope and Lifetime for Your Constants

The default scope for a constant declared in a procedure is local—that is, its scope is the procedure that declares it. Consequently, its lifetime is the time for which the procedure runs. However, you can set a different scope and lifetime for your constants in much the same way that you set a different scope for a variable: by using the `Public` or `Private` keywords when you declare the constants:

- To declare a private constant, place the declaration at the beginning of the module in which you want the constant to be available. A private constant's lifetime is not limited, but it is available only to procedures in the module in which it is declared.

```
Private Const conPerformer As String = "Rikki Nadir"
```

- To declare a public constant, place the declaration at the beginning of a module. A public constant's lifetime is not limited, and it is available to all procedures in all modules in the project in which it is declared.

```
Public conTicketPrice As String = "$34.99"
```

Enough of the minutiae of constants and variables, and quite enough of measuring the length of strings. It's time for a look at the big picture. In Chapter 11, we'll investigate the Word object model, the complex theoretical structure that explains how the different parts of Word relate to each other.

CHAPTER

ELEVEN

11

The Word Object Model

In this chapter, we'll look at the Word object model, which describes the theoretical architecture underlying Word. By understanding the Word object model, you can manipulate the objects from which Word is built and work quickly and effectively with VBA.

> **NOTE**
> I should warn you at the outset that the Word object model is too complex to be dissected thoroughly in this chapter. Instead, my goal is to help you understand the general structure of Word's plethora of objects, learn to navigate the object model to find the objects you need, and manipulate them efficiently once you've gotten ahold of them.

What Is the Word Object Model?

As I've already mentioned once or twice in this book, VBA works mostly with *objects*. Objects are the elements that VBA uses to manipulate Word ranging from the `Application` object that represents the whole of Word to `Document` objects that represent open documents and `Character` objects that represent individual characters within a document. When you need to perform a task in VBA, you usually end up working with a *property* of an object (for example, setting the `FullName` property of a document) or performing some action (a *method*) on an object. As a simple example of this, you've seen that to close the active document, you use the `Close` method on the `ActiveDocument` object:

```
ActiveDocument.Close
```

The *object model* is the structure that describes how the different objects in Word relate to each other. When you examine the object model, it begins to resemble a set of Chinese boxes: within each object is another object, which in turn contains other objects, inside each of which lurk still more objects. For example, a document object contains a number of word objects, which in turn contain a number of character objects. To use the object model, you open each box in turn until you reach the object you need, and then you start performing actions on it.

A VBA object that contains all the objects of a particular type is called a *collection*. The items in the collection are known as *members*; you refer to a particular member of a collection by using its name or its index number (more on index numbers in Chapter 19, when we look at arrays). You can also manipulate a collection as a single object. For example, the `Documents` collection contains all the documents that are currently open. By working with the `Documents` collection, you can manipulate all its members—all the open documents—at once. You could save and then close all the open documents by using the `Save` method and then the `Close` method on the `Documents` collection like this:

```
Documents.Save
Documents.Close
```

When you need to take action on all the open documents at the same time, working with the collection is much faster and much simpler than working with the individual documents. Likewise, you can work with collections of windows by using the `Windows` collection, with command bars by using the `CommandBars` collection, with words by using the `Words` collection, and so on.

The `Application` object is at the top level of the Word object model, which makes it a good place to start.

The Application Object

The `Application` object represents the Word application. Because you'll usually be working with Word in VBA, you seldom need to specify the `Application` object—in most cases it will be understood, although you can specify it if you want to. (You do need to specify the `Application` object when you're working with VBA in another application—Excel, for example—and you want to manipulate Word, or vice versa.)

Figure 11.1 shows the `Application` object and the objects it contains. The plural names with singular names in parentheses indicate collections and the individual objects they contain, respectively: for example, the `Addins` collection comprises all `Addin` objects in the `Application` object, and the `Documents` collection contains all the open `Document` objects in the `Application` object. The arrows to the right of the `AutoCorrect`, `Documents`, `Selection`, `Templates`, and `Windows` objects indicate that these objects contain further objects (beyond the objects in the collections)—for example, the `Documents` collection and the `Document` object, which we'll look at in the next section, contain a number of objects (and collections) from `Bookmarks` through `Words`. We'll start looking at some of these later in this chapter.

FIGURE 11.1

The `Application` object and the objects it contains. The shaded boxes denote objects and collections; the unshaded boxes denote objects only.

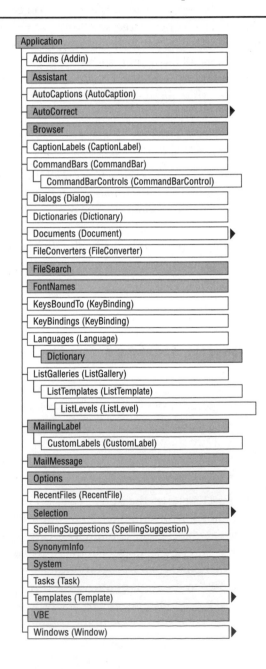

You can refer to the objects contained within the `Application` object by specifying their names. For example, if you want to refer to the name of the first of the command bars within the application, you can use the `Name` property of the first item in the `CommandBars` collection within the `Application` object:

```
Application.CommandBars(1).Name
```

Again, it's not necessary to use the `Application` object here, because it's understood—you can get the same effect by using `CommandBars(1).Name` instead.

The three most-used objects in the `Application` object are `Documents`, `Windows`, and `Selection`. By using these, you can manipulate the documents that are open, the windows that are open, and the current selection in the active document. Figure 11.2 shows some of the more important objects within each of these three objects.

FIGURE 11.2

Part of the `Word` object model, showing the `Documents` collection, the `Windows` collection, and the `Selection` object under the `Application` object.

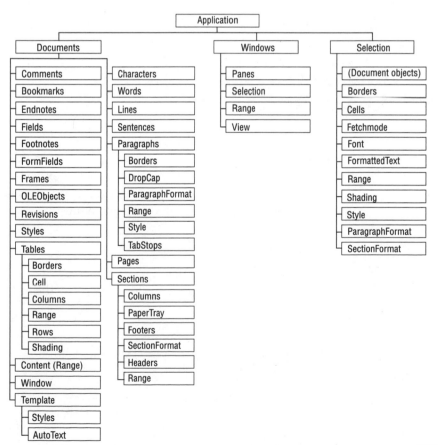

As you can see in the figure, the Documents collection contains collections for Characters, Words, Lines, Sentences, Paragraphs, Pages, and Sections, among others; the Paragraphs and Sections collections each contain objects of their own. So to access one of the paragraphs in a document, you would specify the Document object in the Documents collection and then the Paragraph object in the Paragraphs collection inside it:

```
Documents(1).Paragraphs(2)
```

This specifies the first object in the Documents collection (i.e., the first opened document) and the second object in the Paragraphs collection (i.e., the second paragraph in the document).

Once you've reached the object you want to refer to, you specify the property or method to apply to the object. In this case, you might specify the property Style = "Heading 1" to set the style of the paragraph to Heading 1:

```
Documents(1).Paragraphs(2).Style = "Heading 1"
```

The Documents Collection and the Document Object

The Documents collection contains a Document object for each of the open documents in Word. You refer to the Document objects in the Documents collection by using their index numbers or their names. For example, to refer to the second Document object in the Documents collection and display its full name in a message box, you could use the following statement:

```
MsgBox Documents(2).FullName
```

To refer to the Document object named Quarterly Analysis.doc and display a Print Preview window for it, you could use the following statement:

```
Documents("Quarterly Analysis.doc").PrintPreview
```

Figure 11.3 shows the collections and objects contained in the Documents collection and the Document object.

FIGURE 11.3

The collections and objects contained in the Documents collection and the Document object

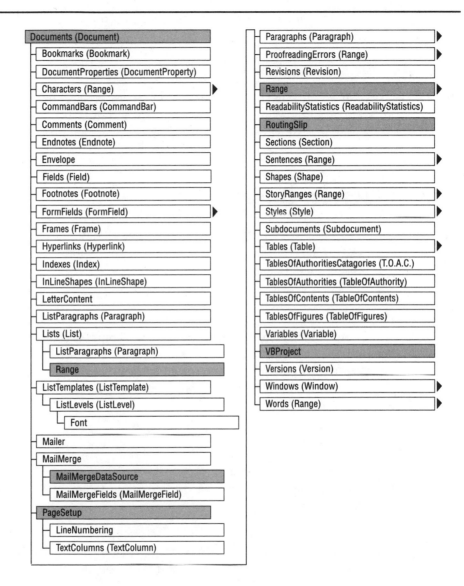

Of the collections that the Documents collection and the Document object contain, you'll often find yourself needing to work with the Characters collection, the Words collection, the Sentences collection, and the Paragraphs collection. You use these collections to reference the objects in the document that you want to work with. For example, if you wanted to apply Arial font to the first sentence in the document named `Promotion.doc`, you could use a statement like this:

```
Documents("Promotion.doc").Sentences(1).Font.Name = "Arial"
```

If you wanted to apply the font to several consecutive sentences, you could create a range containing the sentences and then apply formatting to the range. We'll look at working with ranges in the next chapter.

The Selection Object

The `Selection` object enables you to work with the current selection. (You can only have one selection at a time in a Word session, so `Selection` is an object rather than a collection.)

Figure 11.4 shows the collections and objects contained in the `Selection` object.

As you can see, the `Selection` object contains collections that include, among others, `Characters`, `Words`, `Sentences`, and `Paragraphs`, enabling you to work directly with the objects inside the selection. For example, if you wanted to display a message box containing the first word of the current selection, you could use this statement:

```
MsgBox Selection.Words(1)
```

If you wanted to change the font size of the first word of the current selection to 50-point type, you could use the following statement:

```
Selection.Words(1).Font.Size = "50"
```

This statement sets the `Size` property of the `Font` object of the first object in the `Words` collection in the `Selection` object to 50-point type.

FIGURE 11.4

The collections and objects contained in the Selection object.

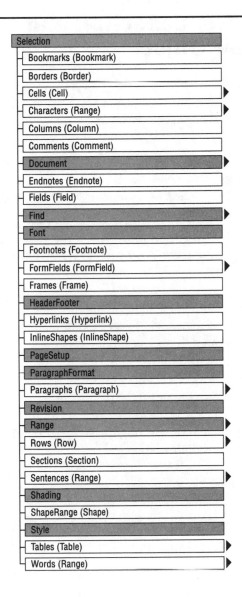

The Windows Collection and the Window Object

The `Windows` collection object gives you access to the `Window` objects for all the available windows in the application. Figure 11.5 shows the collections and objects contained in the `Windows` collection object.

> **NOTE**
> There are two `Windows` collections—one for the application, and one for the windows displaying the document with which you are working. The `Windows` collection for the `Document` object can be useful if you have multiple windows open for the same document (as you can do with the Window ➤ New Window command), but usually you'll want to use the `Windows` collection for the `Application` object.

If you want to manipulate the view of the windows currently displayed, you can use a `For Each...Next` statement with the `Windows` collection. Below, the statement in the second line sets the `ShowAll` property of the `View` object to `False`, the equivalent of clearing the All check box in the Nonprinting Characters area of the View tab of the Options dialog box, or of clicking the Show/Hide ¶ button to toggle off the display of nonprinting characters. The statement in the third line sets the `WrapToWindow` property of the `View` object to `True`, the equivalent of selecting the Wrap to Window check box in the Window area of the Options dialog box.

```
For Each Win In Windows
    Win.View.ShowAll = False
    Win.View.WrapToWindow = True
Next Win
```

FIGURE 11.5

The collections and objects contained in the `Windows` object.

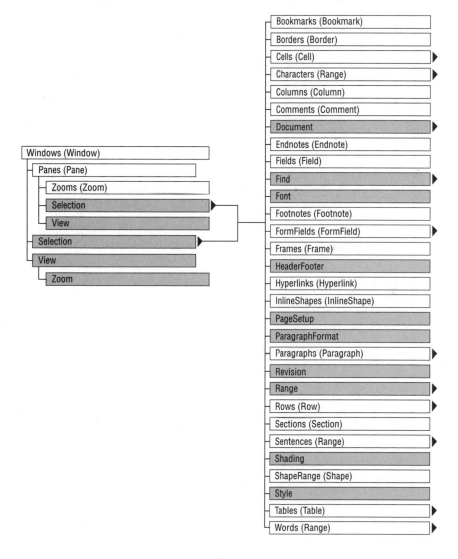

Navigating the Word Object Model

The Visual Basic Editor provides a number of tools for navigating the Word object model:

- the macro recorder, which we started working with in Chapter 5
- the Object Browser, which I mentioned in Chapter 5 but which we've been avoiding until now
- the online Help system, which has detailed pictures of the hierarchy of the Word object model
- the List Properties/Methods feature, which we looked at briefly in Chapter 5

Using the Macro Recorder to Record the Objects You Need

One of the best tools with which to start your exploration of the Word object model is the macro recorder. As you've seen in the preceding chapters, by recording the actions you perform, the macro recorder creates code that you can then work with in the code window of the Visual Basic Editor.

However, there are a couple of problems with using the macro recorder to navigate your way through the object model:

- First, you can't record all the actions that you might want. Say you want to create a statement that performed an action on a specified document in the `Documents` collection rather than on the active document; but with the macro recorder, you can only record actions performed on the active document. (This is because the macro recorder can record only those actions you can perform interactively in Word, and you can't work interactively with any document other than the active one.)
- Second, the macro recorder is apt to record statements that you don't strictly need, particularly when you're trying to record a setting in a dialog box.

As an example of the second point, try recording a quick macro to create an AutoCorrect entry: start the macro recorder, choose Tools ➤ AutoCorrect, enter the text to be replaced in the Replace box and the replacement text in the With box, click the OK button to close the AutoCorrect dialog box, and stop the macro recorder. Then open the resulting macro in the Visual Basic Editor. You'll probably see code something like this:

```
Sub Add_Item_to_AutoCorrect()
'
' Add_Item_to_AutoCorrect Macro
' Macro recorded 4/4/97 by Rikki Nadir
'
    AutoCorrect.Entries.Add Name:="reffs",Value:="references"
    With AutoCorrect
        .CorrectInitialCaps = True
        .CorrectSentenceCaps = True
        .CorrectDays = True
        .CorrectCapsLock = True
        .ReplaceText = True
    End With
End Sub
```

Here, you get eleven lines of padding around the one line you need:

```
AutoCorrect.Entries.Add Name:="reffs", Value:="references"
```

This line shows you that the object you need to work with to add an AutoCorrect entry is the `Entries` collection object in the `AutoCorrect` object. You use the `Add` method on the `Entries` collection to add an AutoCorrect entry to the list.

By removing the seven lines containing the `With...End With` statement from this recorded macro, you can reduce it to just the line it needs to contain (together with the comment lines, which you could also remove if you wanted):

```
Sub Add_Item_to_AutoCorrect()
'
' Add_Item_to_AutoCorrect Macro
' Macro recorded 4/4/97 by Rikki Nadir
'
    AutoCorrect.Entries.Add Name:="reffs",Value:="references"
End Sub
```

In spite of its limitations, the macro recorder does provide quick access to the objects you need to work with, and you can always adjust the resulting code in the Visual Basic Editor.

Using the Object Browser

The macro recorder is a good tool for recording the object you want to get a grip on, but the primary tool for navigating the Word object model is the Object Browser, which you met briefly in Chapter 5. In this section, you'll get to know the Object Browser better and will learn to use it to find the information you need on objects.

Components of the Object Browser

The Object Browser provides the following information on both built-in objects and custom objects you create:

- Classes (formal definitions of objects)
- Properties (the attributes of objects or aspects of their behavior)
- Methods (actions you can perform on objects)
- Events (for example, the opening or closing of a document)
- Constants (named items that keep a constant value while a program is executing)

Figure 11.6 shows the different components of the Object Browser. Here's what they do:

- The **Project/Library drop-down list** provides a list of object libraries available to the current project. (An *object library* is a reference file containing information on a collection of objects available to programs.) Use the drop-down list to choose the object libraries you want to view. For example, you might choose to view only objects in Word by choosing Word from the Project/Library drop-down list. Alternatively, you could stay with the default choice of <All Libraries>.

- In the **Search Text box**, enter the string you want to search for: either type it in, or choose a previous string in the current project session from the drop-down list. Then either press Enter or click the Search button to find members containing the search string.

FIGURE 11.6

The Object Browser provides information on built-in objects and custom objects.

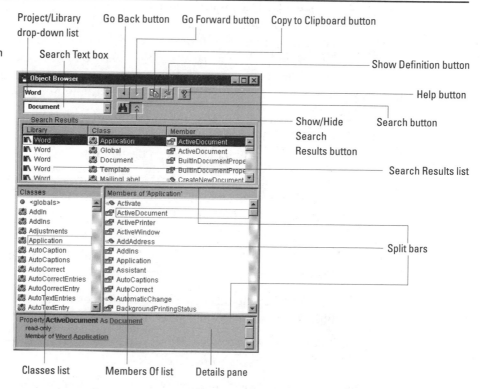

Project/Library drop-down list

Go Back button

Go Forward button

Copy to Clipboard button

Search Text box

Show Definition button

Help button

Search button

Show/Hide Search Results button

Search Results list

Split bars

Classes list

Members Of list

Details pane

TIP

To make your searches more specific, you can use wildcards such as **?** (representing any one character) and ***** (representing any group of characters). You can also choose to search for a whole word only (rather than matching your search string with part of another word) by right-clicking anywhere in the Object Browser (except in the Project/Library drop-down list or in the Search Text box) and choosing Find Whole Word Only from the context menu. The Find Whole Word Only choice will have a check mark next to it in the context menu when it is active; to deactivate it, choose Find Whole Word Only again on the context menu.

- Click the **Go Back button** to go back one by one through your previous selections in the Classes list and the Members Of list. Click the **Go Forward button** to go forward through your previous selections one by one. The Go Back button will become available when you go to a class or member in the Object Browser; the Go Forward button will become available only when you use the Go Back button to go back to a previous selection.

- Click the **Copy to Clipboard button** to copy the selected item from the Search Results box, the Classes list, the Members Of list, or the Details pane to the Clipboard so that you can paste it into your code.

- Click the **Show Definition button** to display a code window containing the code for the object selected in the Classes list or the Members Of list. The Show Definition button will be available (undimmed) only for objects that contain code, such as macros and userforms that you've created.

- Click the **Help button** to display any available Help for the currently selected item.

- Click the **Search button** to search for the term entered in the Search Text box. If the Search Results pane is not open, VBA will open it at this point.

- Click the **Show/Hide Search Results button** to toggle the display of the Search Results pane on and off.

- The **Search Results list** in the Search Results pane contains the results of the latest search you've conducted for a term entered in the Search Text box. If you've performed a search, the Object Browser will update the Search Results list when you switch to a different library by using the Project/Library drop-down list.

- The **Classes list** shows the available classes in the library or project specified in the Project/Library drop-down list.

- The **Members Of list** displays the available elements of the class selected in the Classes list. A method, constant, event, property, or procedure that has code written for it appears in boldface. For example, in the Members Of list shown in Figure 11.7, the procedures `Add_Item_to_AutoCorrect` and `Area_Code_from_Phone_Number` contain code and so appear in boldface. The Members Of list can display the members either grouped into their different categories (methods, properties, events, etc.) or ungrouped as an alphabetical list of all the members available. To toggle between grouped and ungrouped, right-click in the Members Of list and choose Group

Members from the context menu; click to place a check mark (to group the members) or to remove the check mark (to ungroup the members).

- The **Details pane** displays the definition of the member selected in the Classes list or in the Members Of list. For example, if you select a macro in the Members Of list, the Details pane will display its name, the name of the module and template or document in which it is stored, and any comment lines you inserted at the beginning of the macro. The module name and template name will contain hyperlinks (jumps) so that you can quickly move to them.

- Drag the three **split bars** to resize the panes of the Object Browser to suit you. (You can also resize the Object Browser window.)

FIGURE 11.7

Procedures that contain code are displayed in boldface in the Members Of list.

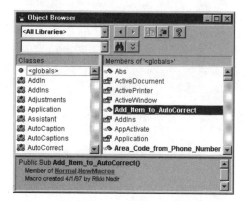

Adding and Removing Object Libraries

You can add and remove object libraries by using the References dialog box. By adding object libraries, you can make available additional objects to work with; by removing object libraries that you do not need to view or use, you can reduce the number of object references that VBA needs to resolve when it compiles the code in a project, thus allowing it to run faster.

You can also adjust the priority of different references by adjusting the order in which the references appear in the References dialog box. The priority of references matters when you use in your code an object whose name appears in more than one reference: VBA checks the order in the References list of the references that contain that object name and uses the first of them.

TIP

You probably won't want to mess with object libraries until you find that parts of your code are not working as you expect them to. For the moment, though, take a look at the references that appear in the References dialog box to make sure you're not loading a large number of object libraries that you don't need. My recommendation is to load the following object libraries in this order: Visual Basic for Applications; Microsoft Word 8.0 Object Library; OLE Automation; Microsoft Forms 2.0 Object Library; and Microsoft Office 8.0 Object Library. This forms a core group that will provide functionality for most operations in Word; if you're not using any of the Office functions, you might want to try unloading the Microsoft Office 8.0 Object Library, and if you think you're not using OLE Automation, you could remove that as well. But given the prevalence of OLE in Microsoft's applications, the OLE Automation object library is a good bet for most circumstances. If later on you wanted to work with objects from, say, Outlook, you could add the Microsoft Outlook 8.0 Object Model library. You can also add global templates to make their contents available to all open projects; and you can add references to open templates and documents so that you can use macros in them (I'll discuss this in Chapter 17).

To add or remove object libraries:

1. In the Object Browser window, right-click in the Project/Library drop-down list (or in the Classes window or the Members window) and choose References from the context menu; alternatively, choose Tools ➤ References in the Visual Basic Editor; either action will display the References dialog box, shown in Figure 11.8.

FIGURE 11.8

You can add and remove object libraries from the References dialog box.

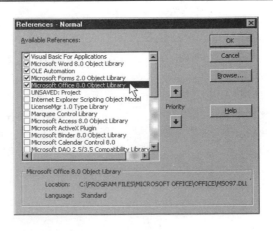

2. In the Available References list box, select the check boxes for the references you want to have available, and clear the check boxes for the references you want to remove.

3. Adjust the priority of the references if necessary by selecting a reference and using the up- and down-arrow Priority buttons to move it up or down the list. Usually, you'll want to keep Visual Basic for Applications and the Microsoft Word 8.0 Object Library at the top of your list if you're working with VBA and Word.

> **TIP**
>
> You can add further reference libraries by clicking the Browse button to display the Add Reference dialog box, selecting the library file, and clicking the Open button.

4. Choose the OK button to close the References dialog box and return to the Object Browser.

Navigating with the Object Browser

Now that you've seen the components of the Object Browser, let's look at how to use them to browse the objects available to a project:

1. First, activate a code module by double-clicking it in the Project Explorer.

2. Display the Object Browser by choosing View ➤ Object Browser, by pressing the F2 button, or by clicking the Object Browser button on the the Standard toolbar. (If the Object Browser is already displayed, make it active by clicking in it or by selecting it from the list at the bottom of the Window menu.)

3. In the Project/Library drop-down list, select the name of the project or the library that you want to view. The Object Browser will display the available classes in the Classes list.

4. In the Classes list, select the class you want to work with. For example, if you chose a template in step 3, select the module you want to work with in the Classes list.

5.   If you want to work with a particular member of the class or project, select it in the Members Of list. For example, if you're working with a template project, you might want to choose a specific macro or userform to work with.

Once you've selected the class, member, or project, you can take the following actions on it:

- View information about it in the Details pane at the bottom of the Object Browser window.

- View the definition of an object by clicking the Show Definition button. Alternatively, right-click the object in the Members Of list and choose View Definition from the context menu. (Remember that the definition of a macro is the code that it contains; the definition of a module is all the code in all the macros that it contains; the definition of a userform is the code in all the macros attached to it.) As I mentioned before, the Show Definition button will be available (undimmed) only for objects that contain code, such as macros and userforms that you've created.

- Copy the text for the selected class, project, or member to the Clipboard by clicking the Copy to Clipboard button or by issuing a standard Copy command (e.g., Ctrl+C, Ctrl+Insert).

Using Help to Find the Object You Need

VBA's Help system provides another easy way to access the details of the objects you want to work with. The Help files provide you with a hyperlinked reference to all the objects, methods, and properties in VBA, including graphics that show how the objects are related to each other.

The quickest way to access VBA Help is to activate the Visual Basic Editor and then press the F1 key. VBA will respond by displaying the Visual Basic Reference window (see Figure 11.9). If you've disabled the Office Assistant (as most people do after a while of suffering its merry pranks), you can also choose Help ➤ Microsoft Visual Basic Help; if you haven't disabled the Office Assistant, choosing Help ➤ Microsoft Visual Basic Help will display the Office Assistant.

TIP   To get help on a specific object, keyword, etc. referenced in your code, place the insertion point in the appropriate word before pressing the F1 key. VBA will display the Help for that topic.

FIGURE 11.9

The Visual Basic Reference window. From here, click the Help Topics button to display the Help Topics dialog box.

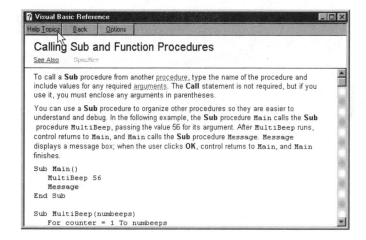

Click the Help Topics button at the top-left corner of the Visual Basic Reference window to display the Help Topics dialog box, shown in Figure 11.10. Click the Index tab to display it if it isn't already displayed. In the top text box, start typing the name of the object about which you want to get information, and then select the appropriate entry in the list box and click the Display button to display the entry.

For example, if you display help on the Document object, you'll see a Help window like the one shown in Figure 11.11.

FIGURE 11.10

Use the Index tab of the Help Topics dialog box to find the object about which you want to get information.

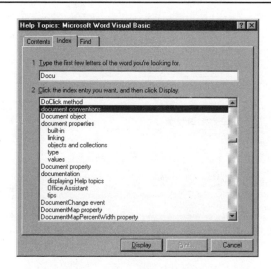

FIGURE 11.11

Here's what you'll get if you search for help on the `Document` object.

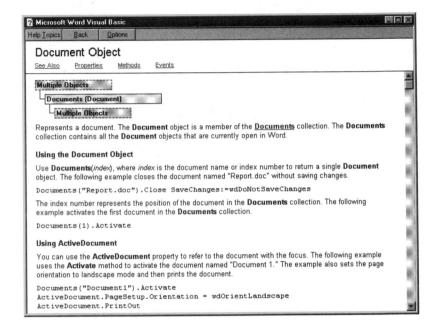

Apart from the regular Help information you'll find in the Help window, there are a few items that deserve comment here:

- The graphic at the top of the Help listing shows the relationship of the current object (in this case, `Document`) to the object (or objects) that contain it and to the objects it contains. You can click on either of these objects to display a list of the relevant objects, as shown in Figure 11.12.

FIGURE 11.12

Click on one of the objects in the graphic to see a list of the objects it contains. Here, you can see that the `Document` object contains a plethora of other objects from `Bookmarks` and `Characters` to `Windows` and `Words`.

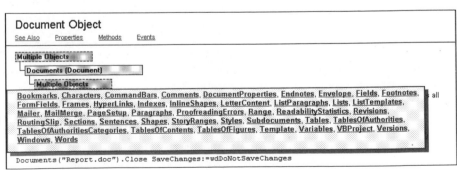

- If there is a See Also hyperlink at the top of the window, you can click it to display a Topics Found dialog box showing associated topics. For example, as you'd discover if you clicked on the hyperlink, one of the See Also topics from the Document Object Help screen is Help on the Template object.

- Click the Properties hyperlink at the top of the window to display a Topics Found dialog box listing the help available on the properties of the object. You can then display one of the topics by selecting it in the list box and clicking the Display button (or by double-clicking it in the list box).

- Click the Methods hyperlink at the top of the window to display a Topics Found dialog box listing the help available on the methods available for use on the object. Again, you can display one of these topics by selecting it in the list box and clicking the Display button or by double-clicking it in the list box.

- Some objects also have one or more events associated with them. If the object has any events associated with it (as the Document object does here), you can access them by clicking the Events hyperlink at the top of the window to display a Topics Found dialog box.

Using the List Properties/Methods Feature

We looked briefly at the List Properties/Methods feature in Chapter 5. To recap, when you're entering a statement in the Visual Basic Editor and type the period at the end of the current object, the List Properties/Methods feature displays a list of properties and methods appropriate to the statement you've entered so far.

The List Properties/Methods feature provides a quick way of entering statements, but you need to know the object from which to start. Sometimes using this feature is a bit like finding your way through a maze and being given paradoxical directions that mostly consist of "You can't get there from here."

Once you know the object from which to start, though, it's clear sailing. For example, to put together the statement Application.Documents(1).Close to close the first document in the Documents collection, you could work as follows:

1. Place the insertion point on a fresh line in an empty macro (between the Sub and End Sub statements).

2. Type the word **Application**, or type **Appl** and press Ctrl+spacebar to have the Complete Word feature complete the word for you.

3. Type the period after **Application**. The List Properties/Methods feature will display the list of properties and methods available to the `Application` object.

4. Choose the `Documents` item in the List Properties/Methods list. You can

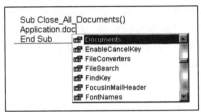

```
Sub Close_All_Documents()
Application.doc
End Sub
```

either scroll to it using the mouse and then double-click it to enter it in the code window, scroll to it by using the ↑ and ↓ keys and enter it by pressing Tab, or scroll to it by typing the first few letters of its name (as shown here) and then enter it by pressing Tab.

5. Type the **(1).** after **Documents**. When you type the period, the List Properties/Methods feature will display the list of properties and methods available to the `Documents` collection.

6. Choose the `Close` method in the List Properties/Methods list by scrolling to it with the mouse or with the ↑ and ↓ keys. Because this is the end of the statement, press the Enter key to enter the method and start a new line rather than pressing the Tab key (which would enter the method and continue the same line).

Using For Each...Next Loops with Collections

Earlier in this chapter, I touched briefly on how you can save time by working with the collections in the Word object model rather than working with the individual objects they contain. You can use a method on a collection to affect all the objects contained in it, such as closing all `Document` objects in the `Documents` collection, maximizing all `Window` objects in the `Windows` collection, and so on.

However, you don't need to take such sweeping actions: you could also use a `For Each...Next` loop with the `Documents` collection to work on each member of the collection in turn. For instance, you might want to search the contents of each document for a particular word or phrase and close each document that did not contain it. To do so, you could use code like that shown in Listing 11.1. One of the advantages of using the collection and the `For Each...Next` loop is that you do not need to know how many objects there are in the collection—you just tell VBA to repeat the loop for each object in the collection, and VBA handles the rest. (If there are no objects in the collection, VBA terminates the loop on the first iteration.)

Listing 11.1

```
1.   Sub Close_Documents_without_Specified_Text()
2.       Dim SearchText As String
3.       SearchText = InputBox("Enter the text to search for:",
         ➥"Close Documents without Specified Text")
4.       For Each Doc in Documents
5.           Selection.Find.Text = SearchText
6.           Selection.Find.Execute
7.           If Selection.Find.Found = False Then
             ➥Documents(Doc).Close
8.       Next Doc
9.   End Sub
```

Analysis

Here, line 2 declares the string variable `SearchText`. Line 3 then prompts the user for the text for which to search and stores the result of the input box in `SearchText`.

Line 4 begins a `For Each...Next` loop that runs for each member of the `Documents` collection. Here, the counter variable for the `Documents` collection is named `Doc`; you could use any valid name for it. Line 5 sets Word to find `SearchText`, and line 6 executes the search. Line 7 uses an `If...Then` condition to verify whether the search was successful; if it was not—as specified by `Selection.Find.Found = False`—VBA closes the current document in the `Documents` collection. Line 8 completes the loop, and line 9 ends the macro.

Using With...End With Statements with Objects or Collections

VBA's `With` statements let you simplify complex code that deals with the same object or collection. Instead of referring repeatedly to the same object, you can identify the object and then use a `With...End With` statement to perform a series of actions on it. The result is code that is easier to read and that runs faster.

The syntax for a `With` statement is as follows:

```
With object
    statements
End With
```

Here, `object` can be any object, including a collection.

As an example, consider the formatting you might want to apply to a paragraph to spice up its current style without applying a different style. Let's say you decided to apply a different font, a larger font size, and no underline, but still have the paragraph identified as a Heading 1 style. You could apply this formatting to it with the following three statements:

```
Selection.Font.Name = "Arial Black"
Selection.Font.Size = 24
Selection.Font.Underline = wdUnderlineNone
```

Alternatively, you could use a `With` statement to simplify the code:

```
With Selection.Font
    .Name = "Arial Black"
    .Size = 24
    .Underline = wdUnderlineNone
End With
```

Here, all the statements between the `With` statement and the `End With` statement apply to the object defined in the `With` statement, `Selection.Font`.

Likewise, you could use a `With` statement to apply paragraph formatting to the current selection. The statements below set the space before the paragraph to 0 points and the space after the paragraph to 12 points.

```
With Selection.ParagraphFormat
    .SpaceBefore = 0
    .SpaceAfter = 12
End With
```

Here, all the statements between the `With` statement and the `End With` statement apply to the `Selection.ParagraphFormat` object.

You could also combine these two `With` statements by using the object `Selection`, which is common to them both, as follows:

```
With Selection
    .Font.Name = "Arial Black"
    .Font.Size = 24
    .Font.Underline = wdUnderlineNone
    .ParagraphFormat.SpaceBefore = 0
    .ParagraphFormat.SpaceAfter = 12
End With
```

You can also nest `With` statements, as in the following example. In this case, the nesting is not strictly necessary (though it works fine), but in other cases, you may find it necessary:

```
With Selection
    With .Font
        .Name = "Arial Black"
        .Size = 24
        .Underline = wdUnderlineNone
    End With
    With .ParagraphFormat
        .SpaceBefore = 0
        .SpaceAfter = 12
    End With
End With
```

TIP The easiest way to create a `With` statement when you're learning to use VBA is by using the macro recorder to record the method of accessing the objects you want to work with and the actions you want to perform on them. Once you've done that, edit the code in the Visual Basic Editor and create a `With` statement that uses a stripped-down version of the recorded code to perform the actions.

If you've reached this point in the chapter without skipping ahead, you're probably ready for a break. Take a walk, or some refreshment, or even get a good night's sleep. When you come back, we'll start putting the theory we examined in this chapter into practice by working with text.

CHAPTER

TWELVE

12

Working with Text

In this chapter, we'll go through the primary methods of working with text in VBA, a vital set of skills for creating and manipulating documents automatically.

We'll start with methods of inserting text in either the current document or in a specified document. Then we'll examine how you can select text to work with in a macro. After that, I'll discuss how you can work with text without selecting it, by using the objects in the Word object model (which we looked at in the previous chapter). Finally, we'll look at how you can apply style formatting and direct formatting to text.

Working with the Active Document versus Working with the Word Object Model

Before we start working with text, I'd like to go back for a second to the Word object model. As you'll recall, VBA and the Word object model give you much greater flexibility than you have when working interactively in Word or when working with the WordBasic macro language in previous versions of Word. In macros written with WordBasic, your only choice was to work with the active window, as you would if you were working interactively in Word. For example, if you wanted to underline the first paragraph of a document manually, you would make sure the document was active, then move the insertion point to the beginning of the document (perhaps by pressing Ctrl+Home), select the paragraph (perhaps by pressing Ctrl+Shift+↓), and then apply underline; and in a WordBasic macro, you would use statements that performed the equivalent actions.

For many operations in Word 97, this is still the best way to proceed: in many instances, you will want to identify particular text located at an undetermined place in your documents and manipulate it. But VBA also enables you to format text that is not selected, provided that you can identify it by other means. For example, if you want to underline the first paragraph in the document, or the last paragraph, or the fifth paragraph, you can easily do so by identifying the paragraph to VBA without actually selecting it. The document that you want to work with does not even have to be active at the time (though it does have to be open).

Because of the possibilities that VBA and the Word object model offer, the material in this chapter is more complex than it might otherwise have been. Instead of discussing only how to work in the active document, this chapter discusses how to work both in the active document and in documents that are not active. When you're creating and working with macros in VBA, you'll find you need to choose between various ways of performing the same (or equivalent) actions.

The other thing you need to be aware of when reading this chapter are the differences in VBA code between recorded macros and written macros. These differences are much greater than the differences you'd see in WordBasic. In both languages, the macro recorder is at a disadvantage, because it is recording the actions you take without any overall understanding of their purpose. The result is code that, while faithfully mimicking the actions you took, by its nature cannot be optimized to its task. Because VBA offers depth that WordBasic does not (as discussed in the preceding paragraphs), its disparity between recorded code and written code is greater than with WordBasic.

To take a simple example, consider a single press of the → key. The effect of this is to move the insertion point one character to the right—or off the current selection, if there is one. If you recorded this keypress in WordBasic, the macro recorder would record this action as `CharRight`—the same command you'd use if you were writing the macro in a macro-editing window. In VBA, however, the macro recorder would record the following statement:

```
Selection.MoveRight Unit:=wdCharacter, Count:=1
```

You could create this statement in the Visual Basic Editor, but you would probably want to create a statement that gave you more flexibility. This statement works only with the current selection. If you want to work with a document that is not active, or with a part of the active document other than the current selection, you need to use a statement that you cannot record—one that you have to write in the Visual Basic Editor.

This distinction between recorded macros and written macros in VBA is not a big problem in itself, but it can prove a hurdle to surmount when you're learning VBA. As discussed earlier in the book, the best way to start getting acquainted with VBA is to record some macros, then open them in the Visual Basic Editor and examine the statements that correspond to the actions you took. The problem with this is that, because you can only record macros that deal with the active document, you'll inevitably miss many of the complexities of the Word object model, which may offer a faster and better way to work.

At some point in your investigation of macros, you'll need to wean yourself away from recorded macros and start using the Word object model to direct your macros. In the meantime, use written statements to augment and improve your recorded macros as you come to grips with the Word object model. As I've mentioned, VBA gives you a variety of choices for performing the same action, and if your code works, there's little point in wasting time worrying whether there's a more elegant way of achieving the same effect.

Inserting Text

One of the more straightforward things you'll want to do with text in your macros is insert it at the appropriate point in the right document. We'll start off here by examining how you can insert text; later in the chapter, we'll look at the best ways of making sure the text ends up where you want it to be.

You can either insert text at the current position of the insertion point, or you can specify exactly where you want to insert text by using a reference to the Word object model. The advantage to inserting text at the insertion point is that you do not need to identify the document with which you want to work. For a macro that performs a simple editing action, such as transposing two words or deleting everything from the insertion point to the end of the paragraph, you'll almost always want to have it work in the active document. For a macro that creates a new document and enters text into it from a document that's already on-screen, you'll probably want to work in the new document without needing to move the insertion point to it.

Inserting Text at the Insertion Point

When working in the active document, you'll often want to insert text at the position of the insertion point. To do so, use the TypeText method of the Selection object like this:

```
Selection.TypeText string
```

Here, `string` is a required string expression containing the text you want to insert in double quotation marks. For example, to insert the string **The meeting will be held at 10:00AM.**, you could use the following statement:

```
Selection.TypeText "The meeting will be held at 10:00AM."
```

To insert the text contained in the string variable `MyString`, you could use the following statement:

```
Selection.TypeText MyString
```

Before inserting text at the insertion point, you'll probably want to make sure that you do not have any text selected (unless you intend to overwrite it). We'll look at how to do this later in the chapter.

Inserting Text Before or After the Current Selection

You can also insert text before or after the current selection by using the `InsertBefore` and `InsertAfter` methods on the `Selection` object. These methods take the following syntax:

```
Selection.InsertBefore string
Selection.InsertAfter string
```

Here again, `string` is a required string expression containing the text you want to insert. For example, to insert the text **Dr.** before the current selection and insert a carriage return and the text contained in the string `Address` after the current selection, you could use the following statements:

```
Selection.InsertBefore "Dr. "
Selection.InsertAfter vbCr + Address
```

When you use the `InsertAfter` method or the `InsertBefore` method, VBA extends the selection to include the text you inserted, so in this case the selection will expand to include **Dr.** and the text contained in the `Address` string.

NOTE Remember that when you have a whole paragraph selected, the selection includes the paragraph mark at the end of the paragaph, so that any text you add to the end of the selection will in fact appear at the beginning of the next paragaph.

Inserting Text in a Specified Document

To insert text in a specified document, you first need to identify the document by using the appropriate Document object. You can work in either the active document or in a document that you specify by name. If you're working in the active document, you can either position the insertion point where you want the text to appear, or use the Word object model to identify the place in the document where you want to insert the text. If you're working in a Document object other than the active document, you need to use the Word object model to identify the location.

For example, to insert the text contained in the string Title at the beginning of the active document, you could use the following statement, which uses the InsertBefore method to insert Title before the first character in the document:

```
ActiveDocument.Characters(1).InsertBefore Title
```

To insert Title at the beginning of the document named Weekly Report.doc, you could use the following statement:

```
Documents("Weekly Report.doc").Characters(1).InsertBefore
➡Title
```

As you'll see in the later chapters of this book, there are a couple of advantages to inserting text by using the Word object model to identify the document:

- You do not need to activate the document in which you want to insert the text—you just need to identify it.

- You can hide background processing from the user. For example, if the user invokes a macro that accesses other documents than the currently active document, you can make it appear that only the active document is working, saving the user from seeing potentially ugly manipulations of text in the background documents.

Inserting a Paragraph

To lay out text suitably, you'll often need to insert a paragraph. There are several ways of doing so:

- You can insert a paragraph at the current position of the insertion point by using the `InsertParagraph` method:

```
Selection.InsertParagraph
```

- When you're working with a selection or range, you can use the `InsertParagraphAfter` or `InsertParagraphBefore` method to insert a paragraph either after or before the selection or range. For example, to insert a paragraph before the selection, you could use the following statement:

```
Selection.InsertParagraphBefore
```

- When you're working with the active document, you can insert a paragraph by inserting the carriage-return character (`Chr(13)`) or the `vbCr` constant at the position of the insertion point. The following statements each insert a paragraph:

```
Selection.TypeText Chr(13)
Selection.TypeText vbCr
```

Once you've inserted a paragraph, you'll often want to apply a style to it. I'll discuss how to do this in "Applying Paragraph Styles" later in this chapter.

Selecting Text

For some operations in your macros, you'll need to select text and then manipulate it directly. This is usually the case when you need to work with words, phrases, or other elements that might be located anywhere in the document or might not be there at all (as opposed to, say, applying specific formatting to the first paragraph of the document).

Working with the Current Selection

To work with the current selection, use the `Selection` object. For example, to copy the current selection to the Clipboard, you could use the following statement:

```
Selection.Copy
```

To work with part of the current selection, specify it by using the appropriate object. For example, the statement below sets the font size of the second word in the selection to 48 points:

```
Selection.Words(2).Font.Size = 48
```

> **NOTE** As you saw in the previous chapter, only one selection can be active at a time in a single session of Word. (If you have two sessions of Word running at the same time, each will have an active selection.)

To work with the current paragraph (the paragraph in which the insertion point resides, or the paragraph that is selected or partially selected), use the `Paragraphs` object to specify it:

```
Selection.Paragraphs(1)
```

This identifies the current paragraph, or the first paragraph in the selection if more than one paragraph is selected.

Extending a Selection

To extend a selection, you can use the `EndOf` method for a `Range` or `Selection` object. The syntax for the `EndOf` method is as follows:

```
expression.EndOf(Unit, Extend)
```

Here, `expression` is a required expression that returns a `Range` or `Selection` object, such as an object in the `Characters`, `Words`, `Sentences`, or `Paragraphs` collection. `Unit` is an optional variant specifying the unit of movement:

Unit	Meaning
wdCharacter	A character
wdWord	A word. (This is the default setting if you omit the argument.)
wdSentence	A sentence
wdLine	A line. (This can be used only with `Selection` objects, not with ranges.)
wdParagraph	A paragraph
wdSection	A section of a document
wdStory	The current story (I'll discuss Word's concept of stories in "Using Range Properties" later in this chapter.)
wdCell	A cell in a table
wdColumn	A column in a table
wdRow	A row in a table
wdTable	A whole table

`Extend` is an optional variant specifying whether to move or extend the selection or range. `wdMove` moves the selection or range and is the default setting; `wdExtend` extends the selection or range.

For example, to extend the current selection to the end of the paragraph, you could use the following statement:

```
Selection.EndOf Unit:=wdParagraph, Extend:=wdExtend
```

To move the selection (i.e., the insertion point) to the end of the paragraph, you could use the following statement:

```
Selection.EndOf Unit:=wdParagraph, Extend:=wdMove
```

To select from the current insertion point to the end of the current Word story, you could use the following statement:

```
Selection.EndOf Unit:=wdStory, Extend:=wdExtend
```

To select the whole of the active document, use `ActiveDocument.Content.Select`. This has the same effect as choosing Edit ➤ Select All when working interactively.

Canceling a Selection

When you've finished working with a selection, you'll probably want to cancel it (deselect it). There are several ways to cancel a selection:

- You can collapse the selection to the start of the selection by using a `Selection.Collapse wdCollapseStart` or `Selection.Collapse 1` statement. (Here the 1 is the value for the `wdCollapseStart` constant.)

- You can reduce the selection to just one point (an insertion point) by setting the end of the selection to be equal to the start of the selection with the statement shown below. This has a similar effect to pressing ← (the left-arrow key) when you have text selected in Word: VBA collapses the selection to a point at the start of what was selected.

  ```
  Selection.End = Selection.Start
  ```

- Alternatively, you can reduce the selection to one point by setting the start of the selection to be equal to the end of the selection with the statement shown below. This has a similar effect to pressing → when you have text selected in Word and is useful in a macro running a process that loops as it runs through the document. For example, you might use Find to locate a word (thus selecting it), perform some operations on the selection, and then cancel the selection like this so that you can move on to the next instance of the word:

  ```
  Selection.Start = Selection.End
  ```

- You can move the insertion point to the end of the selection by using the statement shown below, which collapses the selection and moves the insertion point to its end:

  ```
  Selection.Collapse wdEnd
  ```

Checking the Type of Selection

When you're working in the active document, you'll often need to check what type of selection is active, so that you know whether you're dealing with a block of selected text, no selection, or a special type of selection such as a table or a graphic. Depending on the current selection, you may not be able to take certain actions in a macro, and you may not want to take others.

Word differentiates the following types of selections:

wdSelectionType constant	Value	Meaning
wdNoSelection	0	There is no selection.
wdSelectionIP	1	The selection is a plain insertion point—nothing is selected.
wdSelectionNormal	2	A "normal" selection, such as a selected word or sentence.
wdSelectionFrame	3	A frame is selected.
wdSelectionColumn	4	A column or part of a column (two or more cells in a column, or one cell in each of two or more columns) is selected.
wdSelectionRow	5	A full row in a table is selected.
wdSelectionBlock	6	A block is selected (a vertical part of one or more paragraphs, selected by holding down the Alt key and dragging with the mouse).
wdSelectionInlineShape	7	An inline shape or graphic is selected (i.e., a shape or graphic that is in the text layer rather than floating over it).
wdSelectionShape	8	A shape object is selected. (A text box counts as a shape object.)

To find out what type of selection you currently have, you return the Type property of the Selection object. For example, you could use the following statements to check that the current selection is an insertion point before inserting a text string `MyString`:

```
If Selection.Type = wdSelectionIP Then
    Selection.TypeText MyString
End If
```

Getting Other Information about the Current Selection

VBA can provide an impressive amount of information about the current selection, from its font and size to its borders to when it last cleaned its teeth. You access this information by checking the property of the relevant object—for example, to find out the name of the font, you check the `Name` property of the `Font` object:

```
Selection.Font.Name
```

The `Information` property provides a mass of information about where the selection is and what's happening in the Word environment. After finding out what type of selection you have, in many cases you'll want to determine where the selection is by checking the position of the insertion point before you take any action; this will enable you to make sure that the action has the effect you intend. For example, as you saw in Chapter 2, if you press Ctrl+↑ when the insertion point is within a paragraph, Word will move the insertion point to the beginning of the paragraph; but if the insertion point is already at the beginning of a paragraph, pressing Ctrl+↑ will move it to the beginning of the previous paragraph. Delicate differences such as this can ruin sensitive operations in your macros, so you'll often need to make sure that the insertion point is where the macro expects it to be—and if it is not, either move it to somewhere suitable or perform a different action instead. In this case, you would check to see that the insertion point was *not* at the beginning of a paragraph before proceeding on the assumption that it was.

You can use the `Information` property to return information about a selection or range. Table 12.1 lists the available information.

TABLE 12.1 Information Available in the Information Property.

wdInformation Constant	Returns This Information

Environment Information

wdCapsLock	True if Caps Lock is on.
wdNumLock	True if Num Lock is on.
wdOverType	True if Overtype mode is on. (You can turn Overtype mode on and off by changing the Overtype property.)
wdRevisionMarking	True if change-tracking is on.
wdSelectionMode	A value that specifies the current selection mode: 0 indicates a normal selection; 1 indicates an extended selection (i.e., that Extend mode is on); and 2 indicates a column selection.
wdZoomPercentage	The current zoom percentage.

Selection and Insertion Point Information

wdActiveEndAdjusted-PageNumber	The number of the page containing the active end of the selection or range. This number reflects any change you make to the starting page number; wdActiveEndPage-Number does not.
wdActiveEndPageNumber	The number of the page containing the active end of the selection or range.
wdActiveEndSectionNumber	The number of the section containing the active end of the selection or range.
wdFirstCharacterColumn-Number	The character position of the first character in the selection or range. If the selection or range is collapsed to an insertion point, this returns the character number immediately to the right of the insertion point. (Note that this "column" is relative to the currently active left margin and does not have to be inside a table. This is the number that appears in the Col readout in the status bar.)
wdFirstCharacterLine-Number	In Page Layout view and Print Preview, this returns the line number of the first character in the selection. In non-layout views (e.g., Normal view), this returns −1.

TABLE 12.1 Information Available in the `Information` Property. (continued)

Selection and Insertion Point Information

`wdFrameIsSelected`	`True` if the selection or range is a whole frame or text box.
`wdHeaderFooterType`	A value that specifies the type of header or footer containing the selection or range: −1 indicates that the selection or range is not in a header or footer; 0 indicates an even page header; 1 indicates an odd page header in a document that has odd and even headers, and the only header in a document that does not have odd and even headers; 2 indicates an even page footer; 3 indicates an odd page footer in a document that has odd and even footers, and the only footer in a document that does not have odd and even headers; 4 indicates a first-page header; and 5 indicates a first-page footer.
`wdHorizontalPosition-RelativeToPage`	The horizontal position of the selection or range—the distance from the left edge of the selection or range to the left edge of the page, measured in twips (20 twips = 1 point; 72 points = 1 inch).
`wdHorizontalPosition-RelativeToTextBoundary`	The horizontal position of the selection or range—the distance from the left edge of the selection or range to the text boundary enclosing it, measured in twips.
`wdInCommentPane`	`True` if the selection or range is in a comment pane.
`wdInEndnote`	`True` if the selection or range is an endnote (this is defined as appearing in the endnote pane in Normal view or in the endnote area in Page Layout view).
`wdInFootnote`	`True` if the selection or range is in a footnote (this is defined as appearing in the footnote pane in Normal view or in the footnote area in Page Layout view).
`wdInFootnoteEndnotePane`	`True` if the selection or range is in a footnote or endnote.
`wdInHeaderFooter`	`True` if the selection or range is in a header or footer (defined as appearing in the header or footer pane in Normal view or in the header or footer area in Page Layout view).
`wdInMasterDocument`	`True` if the selection or range is in a master document (a document containing at least one subdocument).
`wdInWordMail`	A value that specifies the WordMail location of the selection or range: 0 indicates that the selection or range is not in a WordMail message; 1 indicates that it is in a WordMail send note; and 2 indicates that it is in a WordMail read note.

TABLE 12.1 Information Available in the `Information` Property. (continued)

Selection and Insertion Point Information

`wdNumberOfPagesInDocument`	The number of pages in the document in which the selection or range appears.
`wdReferenceOfType`	A value that specifies where the selection is in relation to a footnote, endnote, or comment reference. (We won't look at these here.)
`wdVerticalPosition-RelativeToPage`	The vertical position of the selection or range—the distance from the top edge of the selection to the top edge of the page, measured in twips.
`wdVerticalPosition-RelativeToTextBoundary`	The vertical position of the selection or range—the distance from the top edge of the selection to the text boundary enclosing it, measured in twips.

Table Information

`wdWithInTable`	`True` if the selection is in a table.
`wdStartOfRangeColumn-Number`	The number of the table column containing the beginning of the selection or range.
`wdEndOfRangeColumnNumber`	The number of the table column containing the end of the selection or range.
`wdStartOfRangeRowNumber`	The number of the table row containing the beginning of the selection or range.
`wdEndOfRangeRowNumber`	The number of the table row number containing the end of the selection or range.
`wdAtEndOfRowMarker`	`True` if the selection or range is at the end-of-row marker in a table (not the end-of-cell marker).
`wdMaximumNumberOfColumns`	The largest number of table columns in any row in the selection or range.
`wdMaximumNumberOfRows`	The largest number of table rows in the table in the selection or range.

An Example of Working with Selected Text: the Transpose_Three_Words Macro

As an example of working with selected text, consider the macros shown in Listing 12.1. The base macro here is `Transpose_Three_Words`, which (as its name implies) transposes the selected three words to an order of the user's choosing. This macro appears in a macro module; the other three macros—`Userform_Initialize`, `cmdOK_Click`, and `cmdCancel_Click`—appear on the code sheet for the `frmTranspose_Three_Words` userform.

Listing 12.1

```
1.   Sub Transpose_Three_Words()
2.       If Selection.Words.Count <> 3 Then
3.           MsgBox "Please select three words before
             ➥running this macro.", vbOKOnly + vbCritical,
             ➥"Transpose Three Words 1.0"
4.           End
5.       End If
6.       frmTranspose_Three_Words.Show
7.   End Sub
8.
9.
10.  Private Sub UserForm_Initialize()
11.
12.      Dim First As String, Second As String, Third As
         ➥String, FirstMix As String, SecondMix As String,
         ➥ThirdMix As String, FourthMix As String,
         ➥FifthMix As String
13.      First = Selection.Words(1)
14.      Second = Selection.Words(2)
15.      Third = Selection.Words(3)
16.
17.      If Right(First, 1) <> " " Then First = First + " "
18.      If Right(Second, 1) <> " " Then Second = Second + " "
19.      If Right(Third, 1) <> " " Then Third = Third + " "
20.
```

```
21.        FirstMix = First + Third + Second
22.        SecondMix = Second + Third + First
23.        ThirdMix = Second + First + Third
24.        FourthMix = Third + Second + First
25.        FifthMix = Third + First + Second
26.
27.        OptionButton1.Caption = FirstMix
28.        OptionButton2.Caption = SecondMix
29.        OptionButton3.Caption = ThirdMix
30.        OptionButton4.Caption = FourthMix
31.        OptionButton5.Caption = FifthMix
32.        OptionButton1 = True
33.        Label1.Caption = Selection.Text
34.
35.    End Sub
36.
37.
38.    Private Sub cmdOK_Click()
39.        Unload frmTranspose_Three_Words
40.        If OptionButton1 = True Then
41.            Selection.TypeText OptionButton1.Caption
42.        ElseIf OptionButton2 = True Then
43.            Selection.TypeText OptionButton2.Caption
44.        ElseIf OptionButton3 = True Then
45.            Selection.TypeText OptionButton3.Caption
46.        ElseIf OptionButton4 = True Then
47.            Selection.TypeText OptionButton4.Caption
48.        Else
49.            Selection.TypeText OptionButton5.Caption
50.        End If
51.    End Sub
52.
53.
54.    Private Sub cmdCancel_Click()
55.        End
56.    End Sub
```

Analysis

There are four macros here that work together:

1. The first macro, `Transpose_Three_Words`, listed in lines 1 through 7, makes sure there is an appropriate selection. Line 2 checks to see if the number of words in the selection (`Selection.Words.Count`—the `Count` property of the `Words` object in the `Selection` object) is different than 3. If it is, the macro displays a message box (line 3) prompting the user to select three words before running the macro and then ends execution (line 4). If the condition in line 2 is not met—meaning the selection is three words long—the statement in line 6 starts the display of the `frmTranspose_Three _Words` dialog box, in effect starting the second macro.

2. The second macro, `Private Sub UserForm_Initialize`, initializes the userform that makes up the dialog box:

   - Line 12 declares eight string variables. The first three are `First`, `Second`, and `Third`: line 13 assigns to `First` the first word in the `Selection` object; line 14 assigns to `Second` the second word; and line 15 assigns to `Third` the third word. The last five strings, `FirstMix` through `FifthMix`, will be created from combinations of `First`, `Second`, and `Third` later in the macro.

   - Lines 17 through 19 check to make sure that each of the strings `First`, `Second`, and `Third` end in a space—that the rightmost character of each string is a space. If any of them does not, the `Then` statement adds the space to the string. (Each string needs a space at the end to make sure there is a space between them when they are concatenated in the next step of the macro.)

   - Lines 21 through 25 assign data to the strings `FirstMix` through `FifthMix` by concatenating combinations of the `First`, `Second`, and `Third` strings: the `FirstMix` string is `First + Third + Second`, the `SecondMix` string is `Second + Third + First`, and so on for the other three possible combinations (aside from `First + Second + Third`, which is the starting combination and so does not need to be represented in the dialog box).

- Lines 27 through 31 assign `FirstMix` through `FifthMix` to the `Caption` property of `OptionButton1` through `OptionButton5`, respectively, the five option buttons in the dialog box.

- Line 32 sets the first option button, `OptionButton1`, to `True`, so that it will appear selected when the dialog box is displayed.

- Line 33 sets the `Caption` property of the label `Label1` to the current selection (`Selection.Text`). This completes the initialization of the dialog box, and it appears on-screen as shown below.

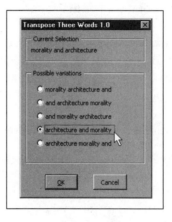

3. The third macro, `Private Sub cmdOK_Click`, runs if the OK button in the dialog box is clicked. Here's what happens:

- Line 39 unloads the form `frmTranspose_Three_Words` (to remove its display from the screen and prevent the user from clicking frenziedly at it).

- Lines 40 through 50 contain an `If...Then...ElseIf...Else` statement to check which of the option buttons in the dialog box was selected when the dialog box was dismissed. If the condition in line 40 is `True`—meaning `OptionButton1` was selected—the statement in line 41 inserts in the document the `Caption` property of the option button, which is the combination of the words defined in the `Initialize` procedure. If the condition in line 40 is `False`, the `ElseIf` condition in line 42 is checked; likewise for the `ElseIf` conditions in lines 44 and 46; and if none of the conditions is `True`, the `Else` statement in line 48 inserts the `Caption` property from the fifth option button, `OptionButton5`.

4. The fourth macro, `Private Sub cmdCancel_Click`, runs if the Cancel button in the dialog box is clicked. This macro simply terminates execution of the macro with its `End` statement.

Creating and Using Ranges

In Word, a *range* is a contiguous area of a document with a defined starting point and ending point (rather like ranges used to be in Excel until Excel learned to deal with ranges that consisted of noncontiguous cells as well as contiguous ones). For example, in Word you can define a range that consists of the first paragraph in a specified document. The starting point of the range will be the beginning of the paragraph, and the ending point of the range will be the end of the paragraph (after the paragraph mark). Likewise, you can define a range that consists of the 100th to 200th characters in a document, or a range that consists of a specified number of consecutive words in a certain paragraph.

You can use ranges with VBA in a similar way to how you use bookmarks when working interactively with Word: to mark a location in a document that you want to be able to access quickly or manipulate easily. Like a bookmark, a range can contain any amount of text in a document, from a single character to all the contents of the document; a range can even have the same starting point and ending point, which gives it no contents and makes it in effect an invisible mark in the document that you can use to insert text. Once you've created a range, you can refer to it, access its contents or insert new contents in it, or format it, all by using the properties of the range and the methods that apply to it.

The main difference between a range and a bookmark is that the lifetime of a range is limited to the VBA procedure that defines it, whereas a bookmark is saved with the document or template that contains it and can be accessed at any point (whether or not a procedure is running).

Using range objects gives you far more flexibility than working with the current selection. Whereas there can be only one active selection in a given Word session, you can define multiple ranges in each of the documents you have open. Moreover, by using the Word object model, you can define and manipulate ranges in documents other than the active document, and you can work with ranges without affecting the current selection.

Defining a Named Range

The terminology for working with ranges is a little confusing at first: to create a `Range` object, you use a `Set` statement and either the `Range` method on a `Document` object or the `Range` property for an object that supports it. The syntax for using the `Range` method looks like this:

```
Set RangeName = Document.Range(Start, End)
```

Here, `RangeName` is the name you are assigning to the range, and `Start` and `End` are optional arguments specifying the starting and ending points of the range.

The syntax for using the `Range` property on an object looks like this:

```
Set RangeName = Object.Range
```

For example, to define a range named `FirstPara` that consists of the first paragraph of the active document, you could use the following statement, which uses the `Range` property of the `Paragraphs` collection. Note that this statement does not use `Start` and `End` arguments because the starting point and ending point of the paragraph are clearly defined.

```
Set FirstPara = ActiveDocument.Paragraphs(1).Range
```

As another example, to uppercase the first three words at the start of a document (as you might do with, say, an article or a book chapter), you could use the following statements:

```
Set FirstThree = ActiveDocument.Range(Start:=ActiveDocument.
➡Words(1).Start, End:=ActiveDocument.Words(3).End)
FirstThree.Case = wdUpperCase
```

The first statement defines the range `FirstThree` as a range in the active document, from the beginning of the first word to the end of the third word. The second statement changes the case of the `FirstThree` `Range` object to uppercase.

Because `FirstThree` is now defined as a `Range` object for the duration of the procedure that declares it, you can return to `FirstThree` and manipulate it later in the procedure if you want to.

Working with Unnamed Ranges

You don't have to assign a name to a range to work with it—you can also use the `Range` object without assigning a name. For example, if you didn't want to revisit the `FirstThree` range that we defined in the previous example, you could skip the step of naming the range and instead apply the `Case` method to the `Range` object, as in the following statement:

```
ActiveDocument.Range(Start:=ActiveDocument.Words(1).Start,
➡End:=ActiveDocument.Words(3).End).Case = wdUpperCase
```

Redefining a Range

Once you've defined a `Range` object, you may need to redefine it to make it refer to different parts of a document. You can redefine a range by using the `SetRange` method, whose syntax is as follows:

```
expression.SetRange(Start, End)
```

Here, `expression` is a required expression that returns a `Range` or `Selection` object, and `Start` and `End` are (once again) optional arguments specifying the starting and ending points of the range.

For example, if you wanted to redefine the range `FirstThree` (which was defined as the first three words of the active document) to refer to the first character of the document (so that you could apply formatting to that character), you could use the following statement:

```
FirstThree.SetRange Start:=0, End:=1
```

You can also redefine a range by using the `Set` method again, in essence re-creating the range from scratch. For instance, if you'd assembled an alphabetical list of terms for inclusion in a glossary, you might need to make sure that no term appeared twice (or more times). To do so, you could create a macro that repeatedly redefined a pair of ranges and compared them to each other, as does the `RemoveRepeatedParagraphs` macro shown in Listing 12.2.

Listing 12.2

```
1.   Sub RemoveRepeatedParagraphs()
2.       NumParas = ActiveDocument.Paragraphs.Count
3.       For i = 1 To NumParas
4.           Set FirstRange = ActiveDocument.
             ➥Paragraphs(i).Range
5.           If i = NumParas Then Exit For
6.           Set SecondRange = ActiveDocument.
             ➥Paragraphs(i + 1).Range
7.           If SecondRange.Text = FirstRange.Text Then
8.               FirstRange.Delete
9.               i = i - 1
10.              NumParas = NumParas - 1
11.          End If
12.      Next i
13.  End Sub
```

Analysis

Line 2 implicitly declares the variable NumParas and assigns to it the Count property of the Paragraphs collection of the active document (the number of paragraphs in the document).

Line 3 begins a For...Next loop that ends in line 12. This loop runs from i = 1 to 1 = NumParas.

Line 4 defines the Range object FirstRange as the paragraph in the active document identified by the i counter—the first paragraph on the first iteration, the second paragraph on the second iteration, and so on. Line 6 defines the Range object SecondRange as the paragraph in the active document with the number one greater than i—that is, ActiveDocument.Paragraphs(i + 1). Before this, line 5 uses an If...Then condition to compare the value of i to the variable NumParas; if i is equal to NumParas, the macro has reached the end of the document, so the Exit For statement terminates the For loop.

Line 7 compares the Text property of SecondRange to the Text property of FirstRange, checking to see if the paragraphs are the same. If the paragraphs are the same, the statements in lines 8 through 10 run; if not, the loop continues, with the Next statement on line 12 returning execution to line 3.

Line 8 uses the `Delete` method to delete the `FirstRange` object, the paragraph that has been found to be the same as the paragraph after it. Line 9 subtracts 1 from the value of the counter `i` to make Word check the second paragraph of the previous pair (`SecondRange`) again, because deleting the paragraph has reduced the number of paragraphs in the document by one, thus moving the `SecondRange` paragraph to a number one higher than it was before. Line 10 subtracts 1 from the value of `NumParas` to keep the count of the paragraphs in the document accurate.

NOTE As I mentioned, this macro assumes that the terms are arranged in an alphabetical list; if they are not, the macro will miss repeated terms that do not appear consecutively. In the real world, you might want to sort the whole document anyway at the start of the macro to make sure that the list was in alphabetical order. You might also want to check for different capitalization of the same text—as the macro stands, it matches only identical text.

Using Range Properties

In addition to the `Text` property used in the previous macro, the `Range` object has a large number of other properties associated with it, from contents properties such as a `Words` property and a `Characters` property (as well as a `Cells` property, `Columns` property, and `Rows` property for ranges that contain tables) to formatting properties such as a `Font` property, a `Bold` property, and an `Italic` property. For manipulating a range, though, the most important properties to understand are the `Start` property, the `End` property, and the `StoryType` property.

As you've already seen, you use the `Start` property to set or return the starting character position of the `Range` object in question, and the `End` property to set or return the ending character position of the `Range` object in question. The `StoryType` property returns the type of *story* associated with the `Range` object. Word uses eleven different types of story to identify the different items of text within a document: the main text, the comments, footnotes and endnotes, text in frames, and the various types of header and footer. The following list shows the `wdStoryType` constants and the items of text that they correspond to.

wdStoryType Constant	Value	Meaning
wdMainTextStory	1	Main text of the document
wdCommentsStory	4	Comments section
wdEndnotesStory	3	Endnotes section
wdFootnotesStory	2	Footnotes section
wdTextFrameStory	5	Text in frames
wdPrimaryFooterStory	9	Main footer
wdEvenPagesFooterStory	8	Even-page footer
wdFirstPageFooterStory	11	First-page footer
wdPrimaryHeaderStory	7	Main header
wdEvenPagesHeaderStory	6	Even-page header
wdFirstPageHeaderStory	10	First-page header

For example, to make sure that the CurrentRange you were working with was in the main text of a document, you could use the following statements:

```
If CurrentRange.StoryType <> wdMainTextStory Then
    MsgBox "This range is not in the main text."
End If
```

To find out if the CurrentRange was in boldface, and apply boldface if it was not, you could use the following statement:

```
If CurrentRange.Bold = False Then CurrentRange.Bold = True
```

Working with a Range

Once you've defined a range, you can specify it by name to work with its contents. You've already seen an example of this in Listing 12.2, which used the Delete method to delete the range containing a repeated paragraph.

Likewise, you could define a range named WorkRange that referenced the first sentence in the document and then work with it by using statements such as the following:

```
Set WorkRange = ActiveDocument.Sentences(1)
WorkRange.Font.Name = "Arial"
```

```
WorkRange.Font.Size = "48"
WorkRange.Font.Underline = wdUnderlineSingle
```

The first line defines `WorkRange`. The second line specifies the Arial font for the `WorkRange` range, the third line specifies 48 as the point size for the range, and the fourth line specifies single underline. The named range provides a simpler way to work with the sentence, but you could also work directly with it by using statements such as these:

```
ActiveDocument.Sentences(1).Font.Name = "Arial"
ActiveDocument.Sentences(1).Font.Size = "48"
ActiveDocument.Sentences(1).Font.Underline = wdUnderlineSingle
```

You could also use a `With` statement to work more simply with the range:

```
With WorkRange
    .Font.Name = "Arial"
    .Font.Size = "48"
    .Font.Underline = wdUnderlineSingle
End With
```

Or you can use a `With` statement without naming the range:

```
With ActiveDocument.Sentences(1)
    .Font.Name = "Arial"
    .Font.Size = "48"
    .Font.Underline = wdUnderlineSingle
End With
```

An Example of Working with a Range of Text

Ranges prove useful, for example, in a macro designed to remedy the defects of the Title Case option in Word's Change Case command (Format ➤ Change Case). As you'll probably have noticed, Word implements Title Case by capitalizing the first letter of each word; this causes editors to froth at the mouth in distress and noted grammarians to gyrate in their graves, because title case should technically mean an initial capital on all words except articles (*the, a, an*), conjunctions (*but, and*, etc.), and prepositions (*in, on, under*, etc.), although even these words should receive an initial capital if they're first or last in the title. Listing 12.3 shows a macro that implements title case correctly within these constraints. (We'll ignore one of the more complex issues that presumably have deterred the Word team from implementing title case properly: if prepositions are part of a verbal phrase, they often need to be initial-capped as well. For example, in title case, the phrase *putting on your clothes* should appear as *Putting On Your Clothes* rather than *Putting on Your Clothes*—at least, if it is to carry its conventional meaning of dressing oneself rather than implying a bizarre form of sartorial golf.)

Listing 12.3

```
1.    Sub RealTitleCase()
2.        Dim HeadingSoFar As String, Q As String,
          ➥NumWords As Integer
3.        HeadingSoFar = ""
4.        If Selection.Type <> wdSelectionIP Then
          ➥Selection.Collapse
5.        Selection.Paragraphs(1).Range.Select
6.        NumWords = Selection.Words.Count
7.        For i = 1 To NumWords
8.            Q = Selection.Words(i)
9.            If Q = "a " Or Q = "above " Or Q = "after "
              ➥Or Q = "an " Or Q = "and " Or Q = "as "
              ➥Or Q = "at " Or Q = "beside " Or Q = "but "
              ➥Or Q = "by " Or Q = "down " Or Q = "for "
              ➥Or Q = "from " Or Q = "in " Or Q = "into "
              ➥Or Q = "of " Or Q = "off " Or Q = "on "
              ➥Or Q = "onto " Or Q = "or " Or Q = "out "
              ➥Or Q = "the " Or Q = "to " Or Q = "under "
              ➥Or Q = "up " Or Q = "with " Or Q = "within "
              ➥Or Q = "without " Then
10.               If i <> 1 And i <> NumWords Then
                  ➥Selection.Words(i).Case = wdLowerCase
```

```
11.          ElseIf Q = "DOS " Or Q = "dos " Or Q = "FTP " or
        ➥Q = "ftp " Or Q = "HTML " or Q = "html " Or
        ➥Q = "HTTP " Or Q = "http " Or Q = "IP " Or
        ➥Q = "ip " Or Q = "TCP " or Q = "tcp " Then
12.              Selection.Words(i).Case = wdUpperCase
13.          Else
14.              Selection.Words(i).Case = wdTitleWord
15.          End If
16.          HeadingSoFar = HeadingSoFar + Selection.Words(i)
17.          Application.StatusBar = HeadingSoFar
18.      Next i
19.      Selection.Collapse wdEnd
20.      Application.StatusBar = ""
21.  End Sub
```

Analysis

The `RealTitleCase` macro applies "real" title casing to the current paragraph, which I'm assuming is a heading within the document.

Line 2 declares the string variable `HeadingSoFar`, which the macro uses to display on the status bar the words in the heading that the macro has processed so far (more on this in a moment); it also declares the string variable `Q` and the integer variable `NumWords`. Line 3 then assigns a blank string to the `HeadingSoFar` variable.

Line 4 checks the current selection type. If the selection type is not an insertion point (`wdSelectionIP`—a plain insertion point, meaning that nothing is selected), the `Then` statement collapses the selection with the `Selection.Collapse` command, reducing it to the plain insertion point at the beginning of what was the selection. (At this point, you could also have the macro make sure that the selection was not in a table, in a header, and so on as necessary.)

Line 5 selects the current paragraph. Line 6 then checks the number of words in the selection (the paragraph selected in line 5) by returning the `Count` property of the `Selection.Words` object.

Lines 7 through 18 contain a `For...Next` loop that checks each of the words in turn to see what type of capitalization they require:

- Line 8 assigns to the string variable `Q` the word specified by the loop counter `i` in the selection—the first word, the second word, the third word, and so on. (The reason for using the string Q instead of repeating Selection. Words(i) here is to keep the lengthy Or conditions in lines 9 and 11 a little shorter than they would otherwise have been.)

- Line 9 contains a long If condition that compares the contents of the string Q to prepositions and articles that will need to be lowercased in a title-case line. If a match is made in line 9, VBA executes line 10; if not, VBA branches to the ElseIf statement in line 11.

- Line 10 uses an If condition to make sure that the word currently being evaluated for casing is not the first word or last word in the paragraph by comparing the counter i to the value 1 and to the integer variable NumWords, which stores the number of words in the paragraph. If the word is not the first or the last in the paragraph, the Then statement runs, applying lowercase to the word.

TIP

The articles and prepositions in the If...Then statement in line 9 are arranged in alphabetical order for ease of reference, but to speed up the code, you could place the most frequently used articles and prepositions (*the*, *a*, *an*, *in*, *on*, etc.) at the start of the list, and relegate *within* and *beside* to the end of the list. Because VBA proceeds to the next line as soon as it makes a match in the condition, putting the most frequently used words first in the statement should make the code run a little faster.

- Line 11 contains an ElseIf condition that checks to see if the current word should appear in uppercase. Here, the ElseIf statement compares the current word to *DOS*, *dos*, *FTP*, *ftp*, *HTML*, *html*, *HTTP*, *http*, *IP*, *ip*, *TCP* and *tcp*, but you could use any words that always needed to be uppercased. The lowercase repetition of each word is necessary so that the user can enter the words either in uppercase (as they should end up) or in lowercase.

- Line 12 contains the statement that runs if the ElseIf condition in line 11 is met. This statement uppercases the current word.

- Line 13 contains the Else keyword for the statement in line 14 that runs if the If condition and the ElseIf condition are not met. The current word does not need to be lowercase or uppercase, so this statement applies title case to it. Line 15 then ends the If statement.

- Line 16 assigns to the `HeadingSoFar` string the data already contained in the string plus the current word. The result of this is to add each word that is evaluated to the string, which is then displayed on the status bar by the statement in line 17. Neither of these lines is necessary, but including them provides a visual signal that the macro is running properly. This can be especially useful when you're testing a macro.

- Line 18 contains the `Next` statement for the `For...Next` loop.

Line 19 collapses the selection (the current paragraph) by moving the insertion point to the end of it. Line 20 then clears the status bar by printing an empty string to it.

Using Find and Replace in Macros

Word's Find feature is as effective a tool in macros as it is when working interactively with Word: you can locate a word (or part of a word, or a phrase, or even a graphic object or text) that has particular formatting attributes, and, once you've located it, manipulate it to within an inch of its life.

Likewise, Word's Replace feature is a terrific weapon to have on your side in a macro. As discussed in Chapter 4, you can automatically replace text, formatting, or other elements. An automated Replace operation is a great first step in hammering out any unevennesses in layout or formatting contained in documents that you receive from a variety of contributors.

You can run Find and Replace operations on either the active document (by using the `ActiveDocument` object) or in a document you specify using the `Documents` collection. We'll look at how to do both in just a few pages' time. But in either case, to find and replace text or formatting, you use the `Find` and `Replacement` objects.

The Find Object

The `Find` object, which applies to the `Range` and `Selection` objects, has properties and methods that match the options in the Find and Replace dialog box.

The easiest way to use the Find object is with the Execute property, as you'll see in just a moment. When you do this, you specify the parameters for the Find operation as arguments in the Execute statement, but you can also set them beforehand using properties.

The following list describes the properties you'll find most useful for common search operations. You'll see a lot of overlap between these and the arguments for the Execute statement, which we'll look at in a moment; essentially, they cover the same ground, but with different syntax.

Find Property	Meaning
Font	Font formatting you're searching for (on either specified text or an empty string).
Forward	A Boolean argument specifying whether to search forward (True) or backward (False) through the document.
Found	A Boolean property that is True if the search finds a match and False if it does not.
Highlight	A Long argument controlling whether highlighting is included in the formatting for the replacement text (True) or not (False).
MatchAllWordForms	A Boolean property—True or False—corresponding to the Find All Word Forms check box.
MatchCase	A Boolean property corresponding to the Match Case check box.
MatchSoundsLike	A Boolean property corresponding to the Sounds Like check box.
MatchWholeWord	A Boolean property corresponding to the Find Whole Words Only check box.
MatchWildcards	A Boolean property corresponding to the Use Wildcards check box.
ParagraphFormat	Paragraph formatting you're searching for (on either specified text or an empty string).
Replacement	Returns a Replacement object containing the criteria for a replace operation.

Find Property	Meaning
`Style`	The style for the search text. Usually, you'll want to use the name of a style in the current template, but you can also use one of the built-in Word constant style names, such as `wdStyleHeading1` (which applies Heading 1 style).
`Text`	The text you're searching for—what you would enter in the Find What box in the Find and Replace dialog box. This can be an empty string (`" "`) if you want to search only for formatting.
`Wrap`	A Long property that governs whether a search that starts anywhere other than the beginning of a document (for a forward search) or the end of a document (for a backward search), or a search that takes place in a range, *wraps* (continues) when it reaches the end or beginning of the document or the end or beginning of the selection.

The Replacement Object

You use the `Replacement` object, as you'd expect, to specify the replace criteria in a replacement operation.

The `Replacement` object has the following properties, which correspond to the properties of the `Find` object (but pertain to the replacement operation instead): `Font`, `Highlight`, `ParagraphFormat`, `Style`, and `Text`.

Using the Execute Method

The easiest way to execute a Find operation is to use the `Execute` method with the `Find` object. The syntax for the `Execute` method is as follows:

```
expression.Execute(FindText, MatchCase, MatchWholeWord,
➡MatchWildcards, MatchSoundsLike, MatchAllWordForms,
➡Forward, Wrap, Format, ReplaceWith, Replace)
```

The parts of this statement are as follows:

- `expression` is a required expression that returns a `Find` object. In practice, you'll almost always want to use the `Find` object itself.

- `FindText` is an optional variant specifying the text for which to search. Though this argument is optional, you'll almost always want to specify it, even if you specify only an empty string (`" "`) to allow you to search for formatting. (If you do not specify `FindText`, you run the risk of searching inadvertently for the previous item searched for.) You can search for special characters by using the codes discussed in "Special Characters" in Chapter 4 (e.g., **^p** for a paragraph mark or **^a** for an annotation), and for wildcards by using the codes discussed in "Using Wildcards" in Chapter 4. For wildcards to work, you need to set `MatchWildcards` to `True`. You can search for a symbol by entering a caret and a zero followed by its character code. For example, to search for a smart double closing quote, you would specify **^0148**, because its character code is 148.

- `MatchCase` is an optional variant that you can set to `True` to make the search case-sensitive.

- `MatchWholeWord` is an optional variant that you can set to `True` to restrict the search to finding whole words rather than words contained in other words.

- `MatchWildcards` is an optional variant that you can set to `True` to use wildcards in the search.

- `MatchSoundsLike` is an optional variant that you can set to `True` to have Word find words that it thinks sound similar to the Find item specified.

- `MatchAllWordForms` is an optional variant that you can set to `True` to have Word find all forms of the Find item specified (for example, different forms of the same verb or noun).

- `Forward` is an optional variant that you can set to `True` to have Word search forward (from the beginning of the document toward the end) or `False` to have Word search backward.

- `Wrap` is an optional variant that governs whether a search that begins anywhere other than the beginning of a document (for a forward search) or at the end of a document (for a backward search), or a search that takes place in a range, *wraps* (continues) when it reaches the end or beginning of the document. Word offers the following options for `Wrap`:

WdFindWrap Constant	Value	Meaning
wdFindAsk	2	Word searches the selection or range, or from the insertion point to the end or beginning of the document, and then displays a message box prompting the user to decide whether to search the rest of the document.
wdFindContinue	1	Word continues to search after reaching the end or beginning of the search range, or the end or beginning of the document.
wdFindStop	0	Word stops the Find operation upon reaching the end or beginning of the search range, or the end or beginning of the document.

- `Format` is an optional variant that you can set to `True` to have the search operation find formatting as well as (or instead of) any Find text you've specified.

- `ReplaceWith` is an optional variant specifying the replacement text. You can use an empty string for `ReplaceWith` to simply remove the `FindText` text; you can also use special characters for `ReplaceWith` as you can for the `FindText` argument. To use a graphic object, copy it to the Clipboard and then specify ^c (the contents of the Clipboard).

> **NOTE** To use a graphic object as described in the previous paragraph, it needs to be in the text layer (not floating over text). If the graphic was floating over text, ^c will paste in the previous text contents of the Clipboard.

- `Replace` is an optional variant that controls how many replacements the Find operation makes: one (`wdReplaceOne`), all (`wdReplaceAll`), or none (`wdReplaceNone`).

Using the ClearFormatting Method

The other method you need to know is the `ClearFormatting` method, which you use to clear any formatting specified under the Find What box or the Replace With box. Using the `ClearFormatting` method has the same effect as clicking the No Formatting button with the focus on the Find What box or the Replace With box. The following statements clear formatting from the `Find` and `Replacement` objects, respectively:

```
.Find.ClearFormatting
.Replacement.ClearFormatting
```

You could clear formatting on both the `Find` and `Replacement` objects by using a `With` statement like this:

```
With ActiveDocument.Content.Find
     .ClearFormatting
     .Replacement.ClearFormatting
End With
```

Find and Replace in Action

The simplest way to use Find and Replace is to specify as many parameters as you need in an `Execute` statement, leaving out any optional parameters that you don't need to specify. For example, to replace all extra paragraph marks in the active document, you could search for **^p^p** and replace it with **^p** with the following statement:

```
ActiveDocument.Content.Find.Execute FindText:="^p^p",
➥ReplaceWith:="^p",Replace:=wdReplaceAll
```

You can also use a `With` statement to specify the properties for a Find and Replace operation, as in the following statements:

```
With ActiveDocument.Content.Find
     .Text = "^p^p"
     .Replacement.Text = "^p"
     .Forward = True
     .Wrap = wdFindContinue
     .Execute Replace:=wdReplaceAll
End With
```

As another example, to change all bold formatting in the open document named `Submission.doc` to italic formatting, you could use the statements shown in Listing 12.4.

Listing 12.4

```
 1.   With Documents("Submission.doc").Content.Find
 2.       .ClearFormatting
 3.       .Font.Bold = True
 4.       With .Replacement
 5.           .ClearFormatting
 6.           .Font.Bold = False
 7.           .Font.Italic = True
 8.       End With
 9.       .Execute FindText:="", ReplaceWith:="",
          ➥Format:=True, Replace:=wdReplaceAll
10.   End With
```

Analysis

Here, line 1 identifies the `Document` object (`Submission.doc` in the `Documents` collection) with which to work and begins a `With` statement with its `Find` object. Line 2 uses the `ClearFormatting` method to clear any formatting from the `Find` object, and line 3 then sets the `Bold` property of its `Font` object to `True`.

Lines 4 through 8 contain a nested `With` statement for the `Replacement` object. Line 5 uses the `ClearFormatting` method to clear formatting from the `Replacement` object; line 6 sets its `Bold` property to `False`; and line 7 sets its `Italic` property to `True`.

Line 9 then uses the `Execute` method to execute the replacement operation. Both `FindText` and `ReplaceWith` here are specified as empty strings to cause Word to work with formatting only; `Format` is set to `True` to activate the formatting set in the `Find` and `Replacement` objects; and `Replace` is set to `wdReplaceAll` to replace all instances of the bold formatting with the italic formatting.

Line 10 ends the outer `With` statement.

Finding Text by Comparing Strings

Powerful though it is, at times the Find feature does not offer enough capability to help you find the items you need. For example, the Style option on the Find feature can be a great help when you need to find text that is assigned a certain style. But if you need to find text that has more than one paragraph style assigned to it, you're out of luck.

To illustrate, say you want to find a word in a certain style at the beginning of a paragraph; you could search for instances of that word with a paragraph mark (^p or ^13) before it. But if that paragraph mark is in a different style from the style of the word you're searching for, Find will not find the search string. In this case, your best bet is to search for the word in the style you need to find, and, when you find each instance, check the character before it to see if it is a paragraph mark, which will mean that the word you searched for is at the beginning of its paragraph. Alternatively, you could search for the paragraph mark and the word, move the insertion point to the right off the instance you found, and then check the paragraph style of that paragraph using the Style property.

Here's another example: Say you need to make sure that each Heading 2 paragraph is preceded by a Heading 2 Rule paragraph. To do this, you need to search for each Heading 2 paragraph in turn and, when each is found, check the style name of the paragraph before it. If the style name of the paragraph before the Heading 2 paragraph is not Heading 2 Rule, you can insert a new paragraph, apply the Heading 2 Rule style to it, and then continue searching for other Heading 2 paragraphs. Listing 12.5 shows one way of doing this.

Listing 12.5

```
1.    Sub ApplyHeading2Rule()
2.        With Selection
3.            .HomeKey Unit:=wdStory
4.    RuleLoop:
5.            With .Find
6.                .ClearFormatting
7.                .Style = ActiveDocument.Styles("Heading 2")
8.                .Text = ""
9.                .Forward = True
```

```
10.                      .Wrap = wdFindStop
11.                      .Format = True
12.                  End With
13.                  .Find.Execute
14.                  If .Find.Found = True Then
15.                      .MoveLeft Unit:=wdCharacter, Count:=1
16.                      .MoveUp Unit:=wdParagraph, Count:=1
17.                      If .Style <> "Heading 2 Rule" Then
18.                          .MoveDown Unit:=wdParagraph, Count:=1
19.                          .InsertParagraph
20.                          .Style = "Heading 2 Rule"
21.                      End If
22.                      .MoveDown Unit:=wdParagraph, Count:=2
23.                  Else
24.                      Exit Sub
25.                  End If
26.                  If .Type = wdSelectionIP And Selection.End =
                     ➥ActiveDocument.Content.End - 1 Then
27.                      Exit Sub
28.                  Else
29.                      GoTo RuleLoop
30.                  End If
31.          End With
32.  End Sub
```

Analysis

Here's how this macro works:

All the statements in the macro execute within a giant `With Selection` statement that begins in line 2 and ends in line 31. This allows simpler code (and impressive levels of indentation).

Line 3 moves the selection (i.e., the insertion point) to the beginning of the document. (This is a recorded statement—the equivalent of pressing the Ctrl+Home key combination.)

Line 4 contains the label `RuleLoop` to which the macro will loop back to repeat the search for Heading 2 paragraphs.

Lines 5 through 12 contain a nested `With` statement that sets up the Find operation: line 6 clears any current formatting; line 7 sets the style to search for as Heading 2; line 8 sets an empty string as the search text; line 9 specifies the direction of the search (forward); line 10 specifies the `Wrap` argument as `wdFindStop`, to stop the Find operation when Word reaches the end of the document; and line 11 sets the `Format` property to `True` to make Word search for the Heading 2 style as specified in line 7.

Line 13 uses the `Execute` method to execute the Find operation. Line 14 begins an `If` condition that checks whether the Find operation found its target; if it did, the statements in lines 15 through 22 run. Line 15 moves the selection left one character so that the insertion point is at the beginning of the Heading 2 paragraph (again, this is a recorded statement; you could also use a `.Collapse wdCollapseStart` statement here). Line 16 moves the selection up one paragraph, so that the insertion point is at the beginning of the paragraph before the Heading 2 paragraph.

Line 17 uses a nested `If` condition to check the style of the current selection, the paragraph before the Heading 2 paragraph. (Here at last is the string comparison hidden in the code.) If the style name does not match "Heading 2 Rule," line 18 moves the selection down by one paragraph to the beginning of the Heading 2 paragraph, line 19 inserts a paragraph, and line 20 applies the style Heading 2 Rule to the new paragraph. Line 21 then ends the nested `If` condition.

Line 22 moves the selection down two paragraphs from its position at the start of the Heading 2 Rule paragraph (either a previously existing Heading 2 Rule paragraph or a paragraph the macro has just inserted and applied the style to) to the beginning of the paragraph after the Heading 2 paragraph, so that the selection is in a suitable position for searching for the next Heading 2 paragraph.

Line 23 contains an `Else` statement that runs if the `.Find.Found` statement in line 14 is not `True`. This means that there are no more Heading 2 paragraphs in the document after this point, so line 24 contains an `Exit Sub` statement to exit the procedure and end execution of the macro. Line 25 ends the first `If` condition.

Line 26, to which execution moves once line 22 has run, checks to see if the macro has reached the end of the document. It first checks that the selection type is `wdSelectionIP`—an insertion point, a selection with no contents. It then (indicated by `And`) checks that the end of the selection is at the position just before the end of the content in the document (`ActiveDocument.Content.End - 1`). If these criteria are met, the macro has reached the end of the document, so the `Exit Sub` statement in line 27 exits the procedure. If not, the `Else` statement in line 28 causes execution to move to line 29, where the `GoToRuleLoop` statement moves execution back to line 4, from which the Find operation continues. Line 30 ends the `If` condition, line 31 the outer `With` statement, and line 32 the macro.

Formatting Text

In your macros, you'll often need to apply formatting to the documents you're working with, either to the current selection or to characters, words, paragraphs, or ranges you identify by using the Word object model.

In this section, we'll look first at how to apply a paragraph style, then at how to apply a character style, and finally at how to apply direct formatting. I'll assume that you remember the various types of formatting; if you don't, refer back to Chapter 2, which discusses them.

Applying Paragraph Styles

To apply a paragraph style, use the `Style` property of either the `Paragraphs` collection, a `Range` object, or the `Selection` object. For example, you could apply the Heading 1 style to the current selection by using the following statement:

```
Selection.Style = "Heading 1"
```

You can apply a style to all the paragraphs in the document by specifying the `Paragraphs` collection without a restricting argument. For example, you could use the following statement to apply the Body Text style to all the paragraphs in the active document:

```
ActiveDocument.Paragraphs.Style = "Body Text"
```

To return the name of the style applied to a paragraph, you can again use the `Style` property, as in the following statement, which uses a simple message box:

```
MsgBox "This paragraph uses the style " + Selection.Style
```

Applying Character Styles

To apply a character style, identify the target text and use the `Style` property of a suitable object, such as the `Characters` collection or the `Words` collection. For example, to apply the character style Bold Italic to the first word of the second paragraph of the active document, you could use the following statement:

```
ActiveDocument.Paragraphs(2).Range.Words(1)
➥.Style = "Bold Italic"
```

To apply a character style to selected text, use the `Style` property of the `Selection` object. For example, to apply the character style Dialog Text to the current selection, you could use the following statement:

```
Selection.Style = "Dialog Text"
```

> **NOTE**
> You cannot apply a character style to a `Paragraph` object directly—you need to specify a range, some characters, or some words.

Likewise, you can return the character style for a specified word or range by using the `Style` property for the object. The following statement displays the name of the character style of the third word of the active document in an unadorned message box:

```
MsgBox ActiveDocument.Words(3).Style
```

Applying Direct Formatting

As you saw in Chapter 2, you can apply direct formatting as well as (or instead of) paragraph styles and character styles. While direct formatting has a number of disadvantages (such as that carelessly applying other styles to text that has direct formatting can remove formatting attributes from it), you may want to use direct formatting from time to time in your macros.

Applying Font Formatting

To apply font formatting, manipulate the `Font` property of the object in question. For example, to italicize the first paragraph in the document named `Arizona Sales.doc`, you could use the following statement:

```
Documents("Arizona Sales.doc").Paragraphs(1).Range.Font.Italic
➥= True
```

To apply boldface to the current selection in a document, you could use the following statement:

```
Selection.Font.Bold = True
```

Applying Paragraph Formatting

To apply paragraph formatting to a paragraph, use the `ParagraphFormat` object. For example, to apply Left alignment to the current selection, you could use the following statement:

```
Selection.ParagraphFormat.Alignment = wdAlignParagraphLeft
```

There's a lot to learn about working with text effectively in your macros, but I hope that this chapter has given you enough information to get started, because it's time for us to consider greater things than text. Sooner or later in your macros, you'll need to create documents in which to store your text, as well as folders in which to store your documents. In the next chapter, I'll discuss how to do both—and how to kill off documents and folders when you no longer need them.

CHAPTER
THIRTEEN

13

Working with
Files and Folders

Oftentimes in a macro, you'll need to create files or folders; at other times, you'll need to delete files or folders (or both), or you'll need to gather information about the current file. In this chapter, we'll look at how you can manipulate files and folders in your macros.

We'll start by examining how you can check to see if a file actually exists before trying to do anything to it. This is an important technique that can help you both avoid overwriting existing files when automatically creating new ones and avert the errors that result from trying to open or manipulate a file that doesn't exist.

Checking to See If a File Exists

Before performing many file operations, you'll want to check whether a particular file exists. If you're about to save a new file automatically with a macro, you might want to make sure that the save operation won't overwrite an existing file; and if you're going to open a file automatically, you may want to check that it exists in its supposed location before you issue an Open method—otherwise, VBA will throw an error.

> **NOTE**
> The alternative to checking whether a file exists is to "trap" any error that results from the Open method. Logic suggests this to be an ugly way to proceed, but it's quite effective. We'll look at how to do this in Chapter 16.

To test whether a file exists, you can use a straightforward macro such as the one shown in Listing 13.1.

Listing 13.1

```
1. Sub Does_File_Exist()
2.     Dim TestFile As String, NameToTest As String
3.     NameToTest = InputBox("Enter the file name and path:")
4.     TestFile = Dir(NameToTest)
```

```
5.     If Len(TestFile) = 0 Then
6.         MsgBox "The file " + NameToTest +
       ➥" does not exist."
7.     Else
8.         MsgBox "The file " + NameToTest + " exists."
9.     End If
10.  End Sub
```

Analysis

This macro uses the `Dir` function to check whether a file exists and displays a message box indicating whether it does or doesn't. This message box is for demonstration purposes only—in most cases, you'll want to use the result of the test to direct the flow of the macro according to whether or not the file exists. We'll do this later in the chapter.

Line 2 declares the string variables `TestFile` and `NameToTest`. Line 3 then displays an input box prompting the user to enter a file name and path; VBA assigns the result of the input box to `NameToTest`.

Line 4 assigns to `TestFile` the result of running the `Dir` function on the `NameToTest` string. If `Dir` finds a match for `NameToTest`, `TestFile` will contain the name of the matching file; otherwise, it will contain an empty string.

Line 5 begins an `If...Then` statement by testing the length of the `TestFile` string. If the length is 0, the statement in line 6 runs, displaying a message box saying that the file does not exist; otherwise, VBA branches to the `Else` statement in line 7 and runs the statement in line 8, displaying a message box saying that the file does exist. Line 9 ends the `If` statement, and line 10 ends the macro.

Getting Document Information

As you probably know from working with the Properties dialog box, Word retains an impressive amount of information about each document, from the number of characters it contains to the dates it was created, last modified, last accessed, and last printed. Here, I'll discuss how to access and manipulate the most useful items of information.

To find a document's path (and have the information displayed in a message box), use the `Path` property:

```
MsgBox ActiveDocument.Path
```

Use the `Application.PathSeparator` property to add to the path the backslash used to separate folders and drive letters:

```
MsgBox ActiveDocument.Path + Application.PathSeparator
```

The `Name` property returns the file name without the path:

```
MsgBox ActiveDocument.Name
```

You could retrieve a document's full path and name by combining the previous two statements:

```
MsgBox ActiveDocument.Path + Application.PathSeparator
➥+ ActiveDocument.Name
```

However, it's usually easier to use the `FullName` property (which returns the file name together with the path):

```
MsgBox ActiveDocument.FullName
```

To get a count of the characters, words, sentences, or paragraphs in the document, use the `Count` property of the `Characters`, `Words`, `Sentences`, or `Paragraphs` collection object, as shown here:

```
Sub Document_Information()
    Dim C As String, W As String, S As String, P As String
    C = Str(ActiveDocument.Characters.Count) + " characters"
    W = Str(ActiveDocument.Words.Count) + " words"
    S = Str(ActiveDocument.Sentences.Count) + " sentences"
    P = Str(ActiveDocument.Paragraphs.Count) + " paragraphs"
    MsgBox "This document contains: " + Chr(13) + C
    ➥+ Chr(13) + W + Chr(13) + S + Chr(13) + P,
    ➥vbOKOnly + vbInformation, "Document Information"
End Sub
```

Retrieving Built-in Document Properties

You can also retrieve built-in document properties by using the `BuiltIn-DocumentProperties` property for a document. Word provides the following built-in document properties:

Property	Meaning
wdPropertyBytes	The number of bytes the file occupies.
wdPropertyCharacters	The number of characters in the document. This gives a different value from the `Characters.Count` method because it does not include spaces, paragraph marks, and other "non-character" characters (which `Characters.Count` includes).
wdPropertyComments	The contents of the Comments field in the Properties dialog box.
wdPropertyKeywords	The contents of the Keywords field in the Properties dialog box.
wdPropertyLastAuthor	The name of the last user to work on the document.
wdPropertyLines	The number of lines in the document.
wdPropertyPages	The number of pages in the document.
wdPropertyParas	The number of paragraphs in the document. This is the number of paragraphs in the document that have contents; it does not include blank paragraphs (which the `Count` property of the `Paragraphs` object does).
wdPropertyRevision	The number of times the document has been saved.
wdPropertySubject	The contents of the Subject field in the Properties dialog box.
wdPropertyTemplate	The template to which the document is attached.

Property	Meaning
`wdPropertyTimeCreated`	The date and time at which the document was first created.
`wdPropertyTimeLast-Printed`	The date and time at which the document was last printed. This property returns an error if the document has never been printed.
`wdPropertyTimeLast-Saved`	The date and time at which the document was last saved. This property returns an error if the document has never been saved.
`wdPropertyTitle`	The contents of the Title field in the Properties dialog box.
`wdPropertyVBA-TotalEdit`	The editing time spent on the document.
`wdPropertyWords`	The number of words in the document. This is the number of what humans consider "words" in the document (the `Count` property of the `Words` collection counts "word units"—punctuation, paragraph marks, etc.—as well as words).

To use one of these built-in document properties, specify it like this:

```
ActiveDocument.BuiltInDocumentProperties(wdPropertyWords)
```

Returning the Current Path

You can return (get) the current path (the path to which Word is currently set) on either the current drive or on a specified drive by using the `CurDir` function. Often, you'll need to change the current path to make sure the user is saving files in or opening files from the right location.

To return the current path, use `CurDir` without an argument:

```
CurDir
```

To return the current path for a specified drive, enter the drive letter as an argument. For example, to return the current path on drive D, use this statement:

```
CurDir("D")
```

We'll use `CurDir` in macros later in this chapter.

Changing the Drive and Path

You can change the drive and path by using the `ChDrive` and `ChDir` statements, respectively.

`ChDrive` changes the current drive and requires one argument of an existing drive:

```
ChDrive drive
```

For example, to change to drive D, you could use the following statement:

```
ChDrive "D"
```

`ChDir` changes the current folder (or directory, hence the name) on the specified drive and takes one named argument of a path. If this path contains a drive letter at the beginning, `ChDir` works on that drive; otherwise it works on the current drive. For example, to change folders on drive C to `C:\My Documents`, you could use the following statement:

```
ChDir "C:\My Documents"
```

NOTE `ChDir` does not change drives *to* the drive letter specified in the path; it simply changes the folder *on* the specified drive. To change drives, you need to use `ChDrive` rather than `ChDir`.

To change folders to a folder on a different drive, you need to use a ChDrive statement before the ChDir statement. For example, to change folders to the \Temp folder on drive D, you could use the following statements:

```
ChDrive "D"
ChDir "\Temp"
```

ChDrive is (refreshingly) intelligent enough to use only the first letter of any drive string that you feed it. This means that you can supply the same path string to both ChDrive and ChDir, and both will work properly: you don't need to create another string that contains only the leftmost character from the path by using a TargetDrive$ = Left$(TargetPath$, 1) statement—you can simply use ChDrive TargetPath$.

By using CurDir to return the path, you could write a macro that quickly switched from the current folder on one drive to the current folder on another drive and then back again, displaying the Save As dialog box along the way. This could be useful for making sure that you save a particular type of document in, say, a shared folder on a network drive while being able to save other types of documents to whichever folder on a local drive suited you, without either drilling down through the tree in the Save As dialog box or designating both of the folders as Favorite folders.

The macro might look like this:

```
Sub Switch_between_Drives()
    Dim CurrentFolder As String, TargetFolder As String
    CurrentFolder = CurDir()
    TargetFolder = "f:\users\mary\home"
    ChDrive TargetFolder
    ChDir TargetFolder
    Application.Dialogs(wdDialogFileSaveAs).Show
    ChDrive CurrentFolder
    ChDir CurrentFolder
End Sub
```

Alternatively, you could write a more sophisticated macro that checked the current path on the local drive using CurDir and then changed folders to the corresponding folder on a network drive:

```
Sub Smart_Switch_between_Drives()
    CurrentFolder = CurDir()
```

```
        TargetFolder = "f:\users\mary\" + Right(CurrentFolder,
        ➥Len(CurrentFolder) - 3)
        ChDrive TargetFolder
        ChDir TargetFolder
        Application.Dialogs(wdDialogFileSaveAs).Show
        ChDrive CurrentFolder
        ChDir CurrentFolder
    End Sub
```

Here, the macro checks the current folder and stores it in the `CurrentFolder` string, then builds the target folder name in the `TargetFolder` string by adding to `f:\users\mary\` the `CurrentFolder` string minus its leftmost three characters (the drive letter, its colon, and its backslash). It then changes to the target drive and target folder, displays the Save As dialog box for the user to save the document there under a different path, and then switches back to the current drive and folder.

Note that the `ChDrive` statement here may well be superfluous in many cases (because the drive will often be the same), but it's hardly worth running an `If` statement to check the current drive and then change it only if necessary; it's quicker to simply specify the required drive.

Changing the Folder in the Open Dialog Box

When working with the Open dialog box in macros, there's one complicating factor for changing drives and folders: for reasons best known to Microsoft, VBA uses a special method for setting the folder to display in the Open dialog box. This method is named `ChangeFileOpenDirectory`; it applies to the `Application` object (and the `Global` object, which returns `Application` objects) and changes the folder that is shown when you display the Open dialog box. You can use `ChDrive` and `ChDir` to change the current drive and folder until you're blue in the face, but the Open dialog box won't pay a blind bit of notice—you need to use `ChangeFileOpenDirectory` instead.

Syntax

The syntax for `ChangeFileOpenDirectory` is straightforward:

```
expression.ChangeFileOpenDirectory(path)
```

Here, `expression` is an optional expression that returns an `Application` object. If you're working strictly with Word, you won't need to specify it; if you want to specify it anyway, use `Application.ChangeFileOpenDirectory`. `path` is a required string that indicates the path to the appropriate folder.

Example

To change the folder shown when you display the Open dialog box to `c:\My Documents\Corporate\In\`, you could use the following statement:

```
ChangeFileOpenDirectory("c:\My Documents\Corporate\In\")
```

That's a pretty bland statement, but here's an example of how you put `ChangeFileOpenDirectory` to good use: you can save a surprising number of mouse-clicks (not to mention an engaging amount of frustration) with a macro that changes the current folder to that of the currently active document. If you work with documents that reside in a number of different folders, you probably find yourself drilling up and back down your directory tree to get to the documents you need. By creating a macro that grabs the path of the current document and switches the current path to it, you can quickly open further documents in the same folder:

```
Sub Change_Folder_to_Folder_of_Current_Document()
    ChangeTo = ActiveDocument.Path
    ChangeFileOpenDirectory(ChangeTo)
    Application.Dialogs(wdDialogFileOpen).Show
End Sub
```

There are two other things you need to remember about the File-Open-Directory setting, which you are probably already aware of: first, this is set to a default folder when you start Word, and second, it changes when the user manually changes folders in the Open dialog box. The latter point means that you'll almost always need to set the File-Open-Directory setting when you want to present the user with the Open dialog box pointed at the right folder; and the former point means that you may want to change the default file path if you want the user to start off in a particular folder. By fortunate coincidence, the next section is about setting default file paths. Read on.

Changing the Default File Paths

Apart from changing drives and folders on-the-fly, you may also need to make permanent or semi-permanent changes to the default file paths that Word uses to keep files and templates in appropriate places. For example, every time you go to open a file in a new session of Word, Word goes to the default file path until you tell it to go look somewhere else.

Table 13.1 displays many of Word's default file paths. You'll recognize some of these as the ones shown on the File Locations tab of the Options dialog box, which we visited in Chapter 3; others are not so exposed in the Word interface, and you need to use VBA to get at them. You can return and set the default file paths by entering the constants shown in the table. (These variables are read/write strings and are stored in the registry.)

TABLE 13.1 Default File Paths.

Constant	Specifies the Path To
wdAutoRecoverPath	AutoRecover files (the files that Word saves automatically so that it can restore some of your work after a crash).
wdBorderArtPath	Border art (usually the `Microsoft Office\Office\Borders\` folder).
wdCurrentFolderPath	The current folder.
wdDocumentsPath	The default location for documents.
wdGraphicsFiltersPath	The location of graphics filters (usually the `Common Files\Microsoft Shared\Grphflt\` folder).
wdPicturesPath	The default location in which to look for picture files (usually the `Microsoft Office\Clipart\` folder).
wdProgramPath	The location of the Word .EXE files (usually the `Microsoft Office\Office\` folder).
wdProofingToolsPath	The location of the spelling and grammar tools (usually the `Common Files\Microsoft Shared\ Textconv\` folder).

TABLE 13.1   Default File Paths (continued)

Constant	Specifies the Path To
wdStartupPath	The Startup folder.
wdStyleGalleryPath	The style gallery (usually the `Microsoft Office\Templates\` folder).
wdTempFilePath	The folder where Word stores temporary files.
wdTextConvertersPath	The folder containing the text converters (usually `Common Files\Microsoft Shared\TextConv\`).
wdToolsPath	The folder containing Word tools (usually the `Microsoft Office\Office\` folder).
wdTutorialPath	The folder containing the Word or Office tutorial files (if they were installed).
wdUserOptionsPath	The folder in which user options are stored.
wdUserTemplatesPath	The folder containing user (local) templates (usually the `Program Files\Templates\` folder).
wdWorkgroupTemplatesPath	The folder containing workgroup (shared) templates.

Syntax

The syntax for setting a default file path is as follows:

```
expression.DefaultFilePath(Path)
```

Here, `expression` is a required argument that returns an `Options` object, which usually means the `Application` object. (Typically, you'll use `Options.DefaultFilePath` to return these options—you don't need to specify `Application`, which is understood, though you can include it if you want.) `Path` is a required Long argument specifying the folder to set; for this argument, use one of the wdDefaultFilePath constants shown in Table 13.1.

Examples

You can return a default file path setting by assigning it to a variable. For example, the two lines below assign the AutoRecover path to the `AutoRec` variable and display the variable in a message box:

```
AutoRec = Options.DefaultFilePath(wdAutoRecoverPath)
MsgBox AutoRec, vbOKOnly + vbInformation, "AutoRecover Path"
```

As another example, you could set the workgroup templates folder to f:\users\common\templates by using this statement:

```
Options.DefaultFilePath(wdWorkgroupTemplatesPath)
➥= "f:\users\common\templates"
```

This second example might be useful for setting up a user in a networked environment. What's convenient is that when you set one of the default file paths, the setting takes effect immediately—you don't need to restart Word (let alone Windows). If you later need to remove a setting from the registry (for example, if you needed to remove our mythical user here from the network and stop their copy of Word from looking for workgroup templates), simply use an empty string (""):

```
Options.DefaultFilePath(wdWorkgroupTemplatesPath) = ""
```

Opening a File

You can open a file in a macro by using the Open method. But before you try to open a file, you may want to check that it exists, as described at the beginning of this chapter. If you try to open a file that doesn't exist, Word will respond with a run-time error 5174, to tell you that it cannot find the file. (Although you can trap this error, as you'll see in Chapter 16, for the moment we'll concentrate on avoiding the error in the first place.) If you issue an Open method for a file that's already open, Word is sensible enough not to try to open it again; in fact, Word doesn't even throw an error when you do this. You'll see why in just a moment.

Syntax

The syntax for the Open method is as follows:

```
expression.Open(FileName, ConfirmConversions, ReadOnly,
➥AddToRecentFiles, PasswordDocument, PasswordTemplate,
➥Revert, WritePasswordDocument, WritePasswordTemplate,
➥Format)
```

Here, `expression` is a required expression that returns a `Documents` collection object. Usually, you'll want to use the `Documents` collection itself.

`FileName` is a required variant argument specifying the name (and path, if necessary) of the document to open.

`ConfirmConversions` is an optional variant argument that you can set to `True` to have Word display the Convert File dialog box if the file is a format other than Word.

`ReadOnly` is an optional variant argument that you can set to `True` to open the document as read-only.

`AddToRecentFiles` is an optional variant argument that you can set to `True` to have Word add the file name to the list of recently used files at the foot of the File menu.

`PasswordDocument` is an optional variant that you can use to set a password for opening the document.

`PasswordTemplate` is an optional variant that you can use to set a password for opening the template.

`Revert` is an optional variant that specifies what Word should do if the `FileName` supplied matches a file already open. By default (i.e., if you do not include the `Revert` argument), `Revert` is set to `False`, which means that Word activates the open instance of the document and does not open the saved instance; you can set `Revert` to `True` to have Word open the saved instance of the document and discard any changes to the open instance.

`WritePasswordDocument` is an optional variant that indicates the password for saving changes to the document.

`WritePasswordTemplate` is an optional variant that indicates the password for saving changes to the template.

`Format` is an optional variant that you can use to specify the file converter with which to open the document. You can use a `wdOpenFormat` constant to specify the file converter:

Constant	Effect
`wdOpenFormatAuto`	Word chooses a converter automatically. This is the default setting.
`wdOpenFormatDocument`	Word opens the document as a Word document.

Constant	Effect
`wdOpenFormatRTF`	Word opens the document as a Rich Text Format file.
`wdOpenFormatTemplate`	Word opens the document as a template.
`wdOpenFormatText`	Word opens the document as a text file.
`wdOpenFormatUnicodeText`	Word opens the document as a unicode text file.

To specify an external file format (one not included in the above list), you need to specify the appropriate `FileConverter` object and use the the `OpenFormat` property. For example, you could open the Write file `Test.wri` by using the following statement:

```
Documents.Open FileName:="Test.wri", Format:=FileConverters
➥("MSWinWrite").OpenFormat
```

The easiest way to find out the names of the `FileConverter` objects you need is as follows:

1. In Word, choose Help ➤ About Microsoft Word to display the About Microsoft Word dialog box; or, in the Visual Basic Editor, choose Help ➤ About Microsoft Visual Basic to display the About Microsoft Visual Basic dialog box.

2. Click the System Info button to run the Microsoft System Information application in its own window.

3. In the tree in the left panel, expand the Text Converters object (if it's collapsed) by clicking the boxed plus sign to its left.

4. Select the Registry Settings item under Text Converters. Microsoft System Information will display a list of installed text converters in the right-hand panel. The Key column shows the name you need to specify. For example, the import filter for Word 6 is named `MSWord6` and the import filter for WordPerfect 6.x is `WordPerfect6x`. Specify this name for the `FileConverter` object.

5. To close Microsoft System Information, click its close button or choose File ➤ Exit.

Examples

You could open the document Good Times.doc in the C:\My Documents\ folder by using the following statement:

```
Documents.Open "C:\My Documents\Good Times.doc"
```

You could open the file Statistics.doc in the D:\Temp\ folder as read-only and add it to the list of most recently used files by using this statement:

```
Documents.Open "D:\Temp\Statistics.doc", ReadOnly:=True,
➥AddToRecentFiles:=True
```

Closing a File

To achieve balance in your life and maintain your VBA karma, you'll need to close as many files as you open. To close a file, you use the Close method.

Syntax

The syntax for the Close method is as follows:

```
expression.Close(SaveChanges, OriginalFormat, RouteDocument)
```

Here, expression is a required expression that returns a Document object or a Documents object. Usually, you'll want to use the ActiveDocument object (for working with the active document), a Document object (for working with the active document by name, or with a document that is not active), or the Documents collection itself (to work with all open documents).

SaveChanges is an optional variant you can use to specify how to handle unsaved changes. Use wdDoNotSaveChanges to discard changes, wdPromptToSaveChanges to have Word prompt the user to save changes, or wdSaveChanges to save changes without prompting.

OriginalFormat is an optional variant you can use to specify the save format for the document. Use wdOriginalDocumentFormat to have Word use the original document format, wdPromptUser to have Word prompt the user to choose a format, or wdWordDocument to use the Word document format.

`RouteDocument` is an optional variant that you can set to `True` to route a document that has a routing slip attached.

Examples

You could close the active document by using the following statement:

```
ActiveDocument.Close
```

You could close all open documents and save changes automatically by using this statement:

```
Documents.Close SaveChanges:=wdSaveChanges
```

Creating a File

You can create a file in a macro by using any of the following techniques:

- Create a new file, and then save it under a name of your choosing or the user's choosing. I'll discuss creating a new file in this section, and saving it later in this chapter.

- Open an existing file (as described earlier), and then save it under a different filename by using the `SaveAs` method.

- Copy the contents of an existing file, paste it into another document, and then save the resulting file with a new filename.

- Copy a file that is not open to a different filename.

To create a new file, you use the `Add` method for the `Documents` collection.

Syntax

The syntax for using the `Add` method is as follows:

```
expression.Add(Template, NewTemplate)
```

Here, `expression` is a required expression that returns a `Documents` object. Usually, you'll want to specify the `Documents` collection as the object.

`Template` is an optional variant specifying the template on which to base the new document. If you omit `Template`, Word uses the Normal template (as if you'd clicked the New button on the Standard toolbar); so you need specify a `Template` argument only when you need to base the new document on a template other than Normal.

`NewTemplate` is an optional variant that you can set to `True` to create a template rather than a document. `NewTemplate` is set to `False` by default, so you can safely omit this argument unless you're creating a template.

Examples

You could create a new document based on the Normal.dot global template by using this statement:

```
Documents.Add
```

To create a new document based on the Professional Report template, you could use the following statement:

```
Documents.Add Template:= "C:\Program Files\Microsoft Office\
➥Templates\Reports\Professional Report.dot"
```

To create a new template based on the template named `Overhead.dot` stored in the default template folder, you could use the following statement:

```
Documents.Add Template:="Overhead.dot", NewTemplate:=True
```

Note that in this last example, the path to the template is not specified because the template is in the default template folder.

Saving a File

To save a document or template in a macro, you use the `Save` method or `SaveAs` method, depending on whether you're saving a previously saved file, saving a file for the first time, or saving a previously saved file under a new name.

Saving a Previously Saved File

To save a previously saved file, use the `Save` method. For example, you could save the active document by using the following statement:

```
ActiveDocument.Save
```

You could save the open document named `Strife in Georgia.doc` by using the following statement, which identifies it by name in the `Documents` collection:

```
Documents("Strife in Georgia.doc"). .Save
```

And you could save all open documents by using the following statement, which saves all the documents in the `Documents` collection:

```
Documents.Save
```

> **NOTE** If you use the `Save` method the first time you save a file, Word will display the Save As dialog box (just as if you'd chosen File ➤ Save) so that you can enter a name and choose a location for the document.

Saving a File for the First Time

To save a file for the first time, when you need to specify a name and path for it, you use the `SaveAs` method.

Syntax

The syntax for the `SaveAs` method looks unfriendly but is actually fairly straightforward:

```
expression.SaveAs(FileName, FileFormat, LockComments,
➡Password, AddToRecentFiles, WritePassword,
➡ReadOnlyRecommended, EmbedTrueTypeFonts,
➡SaveNativePictureFormat, SaveFormsData,
➡SaveAsAOCELetter)
```

Here, `expression` is an expression that returns a `Document` object. For example, you could use the `ActiveDocument` object or specify a member of the `Documents` collection (e.g., `Documents(1).Save`).

`FileName` is an optional variant that specifies the name for the document. While this variable is technically optional, you'll almost always want to specify one, because otherwise VBA will use the current folder and the default file name of `Docn.doc` for a document and `Dotn.dot` for a template, where *n* is the next available number (e.g., `Doc5.doc` for a document or `Dot2.dot` for a template). You may also want to check if a document with this name and location already exists—if it does, VBA will overwrite it without warning, which could cause data loss.

`FileFormat` is an optional variant that specifies the format in which to save the document. Word provides eight `wdSaveFormat` constants for quick reference:

Constant	Saves Document As
wdFormatDocument	A Word 97 document
wdFormatDOSText	A DOS text file
wdFormatDOSTextLineBreaks	A DOS text file with layout
wdFormatRTF	A Rich Text Format file
wdFormatTemplate	A Word template
wdFormatText	A text file (plain ASCII)
wdFormatTextLineBreaks	A text file with line breaks
wdFormatUnicodeText	A text file with Unicode characters

For example, you could save the active document as a text file under the name `Investigation.txt` by using the following statement:

```
ActiveDocument.SaveAs FileName:="Investigation.txt",
➥FileFormat:=wdFormatText
```

Apart from these constants, you can save documents in other formats for which you have file converters installed by specifying the appropriate value for the `SaveFormat` property of the `FileConverter` object. For example, the value for the Word 5.1 for the Macintosh converter is 15, so you could specify saving the active document in Word 5.1 for the Macintosh format by using the following statement:

```
ActiveDocument.SaveAs FileFormat:=FileConverters(15).SaveFormat
```

`AddToRecentFiles` is an optional variant that you can set to `True` to have Word add the document to the list of recently used files on the File menu. (Often, when working with documents in macros, you'll want to avoid listing them on the most-recently-used list, leaving the user's previous list of recent files undisturbed.)

To protect the document as you save it, there are four different protection features you can use:

- `LockComments` is an optional variant that you can set to `True` to lock the document so that reviewers can only enter comments but cannot change the text of the document.

- `Password` is an optional variant that you can use to set a password for opening the document.

- `WritePassword` is an optional variant that you can use to set a password for saving changes to the document.

- `ReadOnlyRecommended` is an optional variant that you can set to `True` to have Word recommend that the user open the document as read-only.

Finally, there are four optional variables you'll want to use infrequently:

- `EmbedTrueTypeFonts` is an optional variant that you can set to `True` to save TrueType fonts with the document. (This is a good idea only if you're distributing the document to someone who you know does not have the TrueType fonts to view the document correctly.)

- `SaveNativePictureFormat` is an optional variant that you can set to `True` to have graphics imported from another platform saved as Windows graphics.

- `SaveFormsData` is an optional variant that you can set to `True` to save the data entered in a form as a data record (as opposed to saving the whole form, including its static text).

- `SaveAsAOCELetter` is an optional variant that you can set to `True` to save the document as an AOCE letter (a mailing format for routing documents).

Examples

Usually, when saving a file for the first time, you'll only need to specify its name and path; if you want to save it in a format other than Word 97 document, you'll need to specify that, too. So to save the active document under the name `Controlled Experiment.doc` in the folder `D:\My Documents\Corporate\`, you could use the following statement:

```
ActiveDocument.SaveAs "D:\My Documents\Corporate\
➥Controlled Experiment.doc"
```

As you can see in this example, you can specify the `FileName` argument without naming it. Beyond this one, though, you need to specify the arguments by name:

```
ActiveDocument.SaveAs "D:\My Documents\Corporate\
➥Controlled Experiment.doc", LockComments:=True
```

If you're using other arguments in addition to `FileName`, you may find it easiest to specify the `FileName` argument as well to keep your code clear:

```
ActiveDocument.SaveAs FileName:="D:\My Documents\
➥Corporate\Controlled Experiment.doc", LockComments:=True
```

Specifying the arguments by name means that you do not get tangled in a lengthy series of commas when you're using arguments a long way down the statement. For example, if you wanted to set `SaveFormsData` to `True`, you could simply use `SaveFormsData:=True` after the `FileName` argument:

```
ActiveDocument.SaveAs FileName:="D:\My Documents\
➥Corporate\Controlled Experiment.doc", SaveFormsData:=True
```

This is much easier than including a comma for each argument in between that you were not using:

```
ActiveDocument.SaveAs "D:\My Documents\Corporate\
➥Controlled Experiment.doc",,,,,,,,, True
```

Saving a File Under a Different Name

To save a previously saved file under a different name, you need to use the `SaveAs` method rather than the `Save` method. This has the same effect as choosing File ➤ Save As instead of File ➤ Save when working with a previously saved file. (If the file was not saved before, the `SaveAs` method has the same effect as the `Save` method.)

For example, you could save the current file under a different name by using this statement:

```
ActiveDocument.SaveAs "c:\temp\Newname.doc"
```

Checking Whether a File Contains Unsaved Changes

When manipulating documents within macros, you'll often need to find out whether or not a file contains unsaved changes. If a file contains no unsaved changes, you can close it without bothering to save it.

To find out whether a file contains unsaved changes (or, in technical terms, if it is *dirty*) or not (*clean*), you check the `Saved` property of the document object in question. This a Boolean property, meaning that it can be set to either `True` (the file contains no unsaved changes) or `False` (the file contains unsaved changes). For example, you could check whether the active document contained unsaved changes, and save it if it did, by using the following statement:

```
If ActiveDocument.Saved = False Then ActiveDocument.Save
```

> **NOTE**
>
> The question of whether a file is clean or dirty is a little more complex than it might appear, because a newly created document is considered clean until you make changes to it, even if it contains a vast amount of text from the template on which it is based. So a document that has never been saved to disk can be clean or dirty, and you won't be able to tell from its contents (or lack of them). As soon as the user enters even a space in the document, though, it's dirty.

Deleting Files

You can delete files from within your macros by using the `Kill` statement. As its name implies, this statement can be lethal to your hard work, but it's a good tool when used with care.

> **WARNING**   `Kill` deletes files irrevocably—it does not send them to the Recycle Bin.

Syntax

The syntax for the `Kill` statement is straightforward:

```
Kill pathname
```

Here, `pathname` is a required string argument indicating the name of the file or files to delete, including the drive and folder as necessary. If you do not specify a full path, Word assumes you're working in the current folder. Usually, you'll want to either specify a full path (to make sure you don't inadvertently delete the wrong file) or explicitly change folders to the appropriate folder first.

> **WARNING**   `Kill` will not work if the file in question is open—instead, you'll get a run-time error 75 in Windows 95 ("Path/File access error") and a run-time error 70 in NT ("Permission Denied"). To kill an open file, you need to do a little preliminary maneuvering. See the section "Deleting the Current File" below for details.

Deleting a Single File

To delete a single file, identify it in the `Kill` statement. For example, if you wanted to delete the `Elegant Memo.dot` template (perhaps for its gross abuse of the Garamond typeface) in the `Templates` subfolder of your `Microsoft Office` folder, you could use a statement like this:

```
Kill "c:\Program Files\Microsoft Office\Templates\Memos\
➥Elegant Memo.dot"
```

Deleting the Current File

From time to time, you'll want to delete the current document without having to close it and switch to a file-management application. As I mentioned, Kill will not work on an open file. So to delete the current file, first retrieve its path and name, then close the file and include its details as a variable in the Kill statement:

```
Sub Delete_the_Current_File()
    Dim FileToKill As String
    FileToKill = ActiveDocument.FullName
    ActiveDocument.Close
    Kill FileToKill
End Sub
```

Here, the name of the file to be deleted is contained in FileToKill, which is assigned the FullName property of the active document.

If you distribute a macro like this, you'll probably want to include a message box confirming the action before deleting the current file (for when users trigger the macro by accident). The confirmation for the deletion is straightforward. All you need is a two-button message box and a simple If...Then statement, like this:

```
Response = MsgBox("Do you want to delete " + FileToKill
➥+ "?", vbYesNo + vbCritical + vbDefaultButton2,
➥"Delete the Current File")
If Response = vbYes Then
    ActiveDocument.Close
    Kill FileToKill
End If
```

You'll also need to find out whether the file has ever been saved to disk. If the file has never been saved to disk, you won't be able to use Kill on it; instead, you'll need to get rid of it by closing it and not saving changes.

Listing 13.2 shows how you might construct a macro to delete the current file.

Listing 13.2

```
1.  Sub Delete_the_Current_File()
2.      Dim FileToKill As String, TestFile As String
3.      FileToKill = ActiveDocument.FullName
```

```
4.        Response = MsgBox("Do you want to delete "
          ➥+ FileToKill + "?", vbYesNo + vbCritical
          ➥+ vbDefaultButton2, "Delete the Current File")
5.        If Response = vbYes Then
6.            TestFile = Dir(FileToKill)
7.            ActiveDocument.Close SaveChanges:
              ➥=wdDoNotSaveChanges
8.            If Len(TestFile) <> 0 Then
9.                Kill FileToKill
10.           End If
11.       End If
12.   End Sub
```

Analysis

When this macro runs, the user will see the message box shown below. If the user chooses Yes, Word will close the file and then delete it if it has ever been saved to

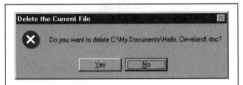

disk; if the document has never been saved to disk, closing it without saving changes gets rid of it. If the user chooses No, the macro terminates without either closing or killing the file.

Line 2 declares two string variables, FileToKill and TestFile. Line 3 then assigns to FileToKill the FullName property of the active document.

Line 4 displays a message box asking the user to confirm that they want to delete the file. The default button is No (set by vbDefaultButton2 in the statement defining the message box), so that if the user blindly presses the Enter key without reading the message, that button is chosen and the macro terminates.

Line 5 begins an If...Then condition which runs if the user chooses the Yes button in the message box.

Line 6 uses the Dir statement to establish whether the document exists on disk. Line 7 closes the document without saving changes. Lines 8 through 10 contain a nested If...Then condition: if the length of the TestFile string is not zero—meaning the document exists on disk—the Kill statement in line 9 is executed, deleting the document from disk. Line 10 ends the nested If...Then condition, and line 11 ends the outer If...Then condition. Line 12 ends the macro.

Using Wildcards to Delete Multiple Files

You can delete multiple files at the same time by using the wildcards * (for multiple characters) and ? (for single characters). For example, if you'd been working with a number of scratch files named `scratch1.doc`, `scratch2.doc`, etc., in the `c:\windows\temp\` folder, you could wipe them off the face of your hard disk by using the following command:

```
Kill "c:\windows\temp\scratch*.doc"
```

Deleting All Currently Open Files

You could even delete all currently open files by using a `For Each...Next` loop with the `Documents` collection to delete each file in turn:

```
Sub Delete_All_Open_Documents()
    For Each d In Documents
        KillMe = ActiveDocument.FullName
        TestFile = Dir(KillMe)
        ActiveDocument.Close SaveChanges:=wdDoNotSaveChanges
        If Len(TestFile) <> 0 Then
            Kill KillMe
        End If
    Next d
End Sub
```

Copying a File

In your work with Visual Basic for Applications, you'll frequently need your macros to copy files or the contents of files from one place to another. Generally, there are three kinds of copy operations that you'll find useful:

- Copying an open file to a different folder or a different file name
- Copying the contents of an open file to another file
- Copying a file that's not open to a different folder or a different file name

Copying an Open File

Perhaps the most common copy operation you'll find yourself using with VBA is copying an open file to a different folder or a different file name (or both). For example, you might want to create a copy of the currently open document so that you could manipulate its contents into a new document without changing the original. To do so, you would use the `SaveAs` method on the `ActiveDocument` object, as discussed earlier in this chapter.

Copying the Contents of an Open File

At other times, you may need to copy the contents of an open file to a new document or another existing document. If you copy the contents to a new document, you can either use the new document to manipulate the information in the existing document, then return it to the original document or to another document, or you can save the information under a new filename, again by using the `SaveAs` method as discussed earlier in the chapter.

To copy the contents of an open file to another existing document, open the document (if it isn't already open). Then use the `Copy` method to copy the contents of the source document (its `Content` object) to the Clipboard and the `Paste` method with a suitable range to paste the contents of the Clipboard into the destination document. For example, to copy the contents of the open document `CEO's Speech---First Draft.doc` to the document `CEO's Speech---Second Draft.doc` (which I'll assume is not currently open), you could use the following statements:

```
Documents("c:\Speeches\CEO's Speech---Second Draft.doc").Open
Documents("CEO's Speech---First Draft.doc").Content.Copy
Documents("CEO's Speech---Second Draft.doc").Range.Paste
```

Copying a File That's Not Open

The third method of copying a file involves files that are not open, though you can close an open file if you want to copy it by using this method. The statement to use for copying a file that's not currently open is `FileCopy`.

Syntax

The syntax for `FileCopy` is straightforward:

```
FileCopy source, destination
```

Here, `source` is a required string expression containing the name of the file to be copied, including the full path if necessary. `destination` is a required string expression containing the filename (and path as necessary) for the destination of the copy.

Copying a file that's not open is a great way of making backups of critical files before you carry out entertaining or dangerous experiments on them. That way, if things go wrong, you can easily restore the files to their original pristine condition, and no permanent damage will have been done.

Example

Listing 13.3 displays a macro that closes an open file, copies that file, and then reopens both the original file and its new copy and makes the original file the active document.

Listing 13.3

```
1.   Sub Copy_an_Open_File()
2.       Dim Source As String, SourcePath As String,
         ➥Destination As String
3.       Source = ActiveDocument.FullName
4.       SourcePath = ActiveDocument.Path
         ➥+ Application.PathSeparator
5.       Destination = InputBox("Enter the destination for "
         ➥+ Source, "Copy Open File 1.1", SourcePath)
6.       If Destination <> "" Then
7.           ActiveDocument.Close
8.           FileCopy Source, Destination
9.           Documents.Open FileName:=Source
10.          Documents.Open FileName:=Destination
11.          Documents(Source).Activate
12.      End If
13.  End Sub
```

Analysis

Line 2 declares three strings: `Source`, `SourcePath`, and `Destination`. Line 3 assigns to `Source` the `FullName` property of the active document. Line 4 assigns to `SourcePath` the `Path` property of the active document (i.e., the `FullName` property minus the document's name), together with the `PathSeparator` object (a backslash).

Line 5 displays an input box prompting the user to enter the destination for the open file, supplying `SourcePath` as the default contents of the text box in the input box so that the user can quickly give the copy of the file a different name in the same folder. VBA stores the result of the input box in the `Destination` string.

Line 6 begins an `If`...`Then` condition that verifies that the input box did not return a blank string (because the user either chose the Cancel button or chose the OK button with no text in the text box). If the input box did return a blank string, the macro ends. Otherwise, line 7 closes the active document; line 8 copies the file identified by `Source` to the `Destination` location; line 9 opens the `Source` document and line 10 the `Destination` document; and line 11 activates the `Source` document. Line 12 ends the `If` condition, and line 13 ends the macro.

Moving a File

Now and then, you'll need a macro to move a file from one location to another. Usually, it's easier to move a file that's not open than a file that's currently open, so we'll look at that first. At times, though, you'll want to move an open file as part of a macro—technically an impossible maneuver, but easy enough to counterfeit. We'll look at this too, later in this section.

Moving a File That's Not Open

You can easily move a file that isn't open to another location on the same drive by using the `Name` statement.

Syntax

The syntax for the `Name` statement is as follows:

```
Name oldpath As newpath
```

`oldpath` and `newpath` are string expressions that indicate filenames. Both `oldpath` and `newpath` can include the full path, including a drive letter if necessary.

`Name` will return an error (run-time error 58: "File already exists") if the file name specified in `newpath` already exists. This prevents you from overwriting an existing file by carelessly renaming or moving a file.

Example

The `Name` statement is most useful in parts of macros that do not require user participation, such as moving a file to a different location once the user has finished working with it or when a certain time has elapsed. You could accomplish this by using variables based on the current file name. For example, to move the file `Berlin Speech.doc` from `C:\Speeches` to `F:\Chairman\Private\Speeches\`, you could use the following statement:

```
Name "C:\Speeches\Berlin Speech.doc" As
➥"F:\Chairman\Private\Speeches\Berlin Speech.doc"
```

Moving an Open File

You can't really move an open file, but you can fake it. To move an open file, as you might guess, you first close it (saving any changes) and then move it to the desired location. To the user, the file appears to have simply moved to the new location, and they can continue working with it (as soon as the macro has finished running) as if nothing has happened. Listing 13.4 shows the code for a macro that does this.

> **TIP**
> Instead of moving an open file, you can save it under a new name and then delete the original version of the file. This method has the virtue of simplicity to recommend it, particularly because you can execute the procedure without actually closing the open file, which makes it a little quicker than the procedure for moving an open file. The disadvantage is that by doing so, you create a new file that has different properties than the previous file; this may cause problems if you need to search for the file by property (such as by its creation date).

Listing 13.4

```
1.  Sub Move_Open_File()
2.      Dim MoveMe As String, MoveFile As String,
        ➥MoveTo As String, CurPath As String
3.      MoveFile = ActiveDocument.FullName
4.      MoveMe = ActiveDocument.Name
5.      CurPath = ActiveDocument.Path
6.      MoveTo = InputBox("Enter the destination folder
        ➥for " + MoveMe + vbCr + vbCr + "Current folder: "
        ➥+ CurPath, "Move Document")
7.      If MoveTo <> "" Then
8.          MoveTo = MoveTo + Application.PathSeparator
            ➥+ MoveMe
9.          Documents(MoveFile).Close
10.         Name MoveFile As MoveTo
11.         Documents.Open MoveTo
12.         Application.GoBack
13.     End If
14. End Sub
```

Analysis

Line 2 starts the macro by declaring four string variables: `MoveMe`, `MoveFile`, `MoveTo`, and `CurPath`. Line 3 assigns to `MoveFile` the `FullName` property of the active document; line 4 assigns to `MoveMe` the `Name` property; line 5 assigns to `CurPath` the `Path` property; and

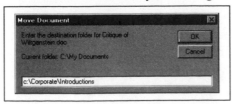

line 6 assigns to `MoveTo` the result of an input box that prompts the user to specify the destination folder for the document. In line 6, `vbCr` is a constant for `Chr(13)`, the carriage-return character used to create a new paragraph, so the prompt in the input box consists of two paragraphs.

Line 7 starts an `If...Then` condition by making sure that the user did not click the Cancel button in the input box (or didn't click the OK button with no entry in the text box). If all is well, line 8 builds the full name for the destination by concatenating `MoveTo`, the path separator (a backslash), and `MoveMe`, and assigns the result to the `MoveTo` string again. Line 9 uses the `Close` method to close the file to be moved; line 10 moves the file to its new destination using the `Name` statement; line 11 opens the file from its new location; and line 12 uses a `GoBack` statement to restore the insertion point to its previous position in the document, allowing the user to pick up work where they left it when they started the macro.

Creating a Folder

You'll often need to create folders in your macros, either for temporary storage or for permanent storage. To create a folder, use the `MkDir` (make directory) statement.

Syntax

The syntax for `MkDir` is encouragingly simple:

```
MkDir path
```

`path` is a required string expression indicating the folder (and path, including drive, as necessary) to be created.

TIP If you do not specify a drive in the `path` argument, `MkDir` works on the current drive.

Example

You could create a folder named `Testing` in the folder `C:\Temp\` by using the following statement:

```
MkDir "C:\Temp\Testing"
```

For an example of how to use `MkDir` to create a number of folders, refer back to Listing 8.1.

Deleting a Folder

You can write a macro that deletes a folder by using the `RmDir` (remove directory) statement.

Syntax

`RmDir` takes the following syntax:

```
RmDir path
```

Before you use `RmDir`, you have to remove all the contents of your target folder *and* make sure the target folder is not the current folder. (If it is, Word throws an error.) To avoid a macro that attempts to remove the current folder, either run a `CurDir` statement on it (and explicitly change the folder to something else if necessary) or else change to a different folder first by using `ChDir`.

If you do not specify a drive, `RmDir` works on the current drive. In most cases, you'll do better to explicitly specify the drive on which you want `RmDir` to operate. Alternatively, you can check the current drive by using `CurDir` and compare it to the drive on which you want `RmDir` to work, but this offers no advantages over simply specifying the drive.

Example

You could delete the empty folder named `Testing` in the folder `C:\Temp\` by using the following statement:

```
RmDir "C:\Temp\Testing"
```

To delete any files in `C:\Temp\Testing\` and then remove the directory, you could use `RmDir` preceded by a `Kill` statement:

```
Kill "C:\Temp\Testing\*.*"
RmDir "C:\Temp\Testing"
```

Using DELTREE to Delete Folders That Have Contents

If you're in a real hurry, you can use a `Shell` statement and the DELTREE command (which should be familiar from your DOS days) to remove a folder that contains files or subfolders. DELTREE is a powerful and dangerous command that you shouldn't use lightly. If you run DELTREE with the `/Y` parameter, Windows won't even prompt you to make sure that you want to delete the folder and any subfolders or files it contains: it will simply delete the lot.

To use DELTREE from Word, specify the path in the `Shell` statement, and add the `/Y` parameter as necessary. For example, to delete the folder `Scratch Documents to Remove` and all its contents, you could use the following syntax:

```
Shell "DELTREE /Y c:\Scratch Documents to Remove"
```

Windows will open a DOS box in which to execute the DELTREE command. Windows NT will close the DOS box after it is done, whereas Windows 95 will leave it running with a Finished title bar. (If you don't use the `/Y` parameter, you'll need to switch to the DOS box and press Y or N and then Enter to complete or cancel the operation.)

In this chapter, you've seen how to build macros that create and delete documents and templates, copy and move them, and create and delete the folders that hold them. In the next chapter, we move on to fields, which you can use to automate your documents and templates and keep the information in them up to date.

CHAPTER

FOURTEEN

14

Working with Fields and Form Fields

In this chapter, I'll discuss how to work with fields to keep the information in your documents up to date. In Chapter 4, we looked briefly at the reasons for using fields in your documents; here, we'll examine how you can manipulate fields in your macros.

First I'll show you how to use Word's regular fields—the ones you can insert interactively with the Insert ➤ Field command. Then I'll discuss how you can work with form fields, which we last visited in our discussion of forms in Chapter 3.

Working with Fields

VBA treats fields as `Field` objects and groups them into the `Fields` collection, which contains all the `Field` objects in a specified selection, range, or document. So if you have, say, a paragraph selected, you can use the `Fields` collection for its range to work with the fields contained in that paragraph.

You can refer to the fields in the `Fields` collection by number (the number indicates their position among the fields in the document). For example, to select the second field in the document, you could use the following statement:

```
ActiveDocument.Fields(2).Select
```

Counting the Fields in a Document or Range

To get a count of the number of fields in a document, use the `Count` property for the `Fields` collection object in the appropriate document. To get a count of the number of fields in a selection or range, use the `Count` property for the appropriate `Range` object. For example, you could use the following statements to display a message box that indicated the number of fields in the current selection:

```
Set CurRange = Selection.Range
FCount = CurRange.Fields.Count
If FCount = 0 Then
    Msg = "The current selection contains no fields."
```

```
ElseIf FCount = 1 Then
    Msg = "The current selection contains 1 field."
Else
    Msg = "The current selection contains" + Str(FCount)
    ➥+ " fields."
End If
MsgBox Msg, vbOKOnly + vbInformation, "Field Count"
```

Returning the Result of a Field

To get, or *return*, the result of a field, use the `Result` property of either the `Field` object or the specified object in the `Fields` collection. For example, to return the result of the second field in the active document, you could use this statement:

```
ActiveDocument.Fields(2).Result
```

Returning the Code of a Field

To return the code of a field, use the `Text` property of the `Code` object for the appropriate `Field` object in the `Fields` collection. For example, to display a message box containing the code for the first field in the document `Field Work`, you could use the following statement:

```
MsgBox Documents("Field Work").Fields(1).Code.Text
```

Inserting Fields

To insert a field, you add it to the `Fields` collection by using the `Add` method.

Syntax

The syntax for the `Add` method is as follows:

```
expression.Add(Range, Type, Text, PreserveFormatting)
```

Here, `expression` is a required expression that returns a `Fields` object. Typically, you'll use the `Fields` collection object of a `Document` object (e.g., `ActiveDocument.Fields`).

`Range` is a required argument specifying the `Range` object where you want to insert the field. The field replaces the range unless you collapse the range to a single point. When working in the active document, you'll often want to use the current selection—`Selection.Range`—for the `Range` argument.

`Type` is an optional variant specifying the type of field to insert. There are approximately 90 `wdFieldType` constants, of which I've listed below only the ones that are most immediately useful. (You can view the full list in the Visual Basic Editor by starting a `Fields.Add` statement in the code window, clicking the List Properties/Methods button on the Edit toolbar (or right-clicking and choosing List Properties/Methods from the shortcut menu) when you've entered `Type:=`, and typing or scrolling down to the entries starting with `wdField`.)

wdFieldType constant	Field Description
`wdFieldAuthor`	The Author property for the current document.
`wdFieldComments`	The Comments property for the current document.
`wdFieldCreateDate`	The date and time when the current document was created.
`wdFieldEditTime`	The time (in minutes) spent editing the current document.
`wdFieldEmpty`	An empty field (the braces—{}—in which you can enter field information manually). This is the default value if you don't specify `Type`, but it's not of much use in macros, so you'll usually want to specify `Type`.
`wdFieldFileName`	The name of the current document (without its path).
`wdFieldFileSize`	The file size (in bytes) of the current document.
`wdFieldKeyWord`	The Keywords property of the current document.
`wdFieldLastSavedBy`	The name of the user who last saved the document.
`wdFieldNumChars`	The number of characters in the document.
`wdFieldNumPages`	The number of pages in the document.

`wdFieldNumWords`	The number of words in the document.
`wdFieldPage`	The current page number.
`wdFieldPrintDate`	The date and time when the current document was last printed.
`wdFieldRevisionNum`	The revision number of the current document (i.e., how many times it has been saved).
`wdFieldSaveDate`	The date and time when the current document was last saved.
`wdFieldSection`	The number of the current section in the current document.
`wdFieldSectionPages`	The number of pages in the current section of the current document.
`wdFieldSubject`	The Subject property of the current document.
`wdFieldTemplate`	The template to which the current document is attached.
`wdFieldTime`	The current time.
`wdFieldTitle`	The Title property of the current document.
`wdFieldUserAddress`	The address entered on the User Information tab of the Options dialog box.
`wdFieldUserInitials`	The initials entered on the User Information tab of the Options dialog box.
`wdFieldUserName`	The name entered on the User Information tab of the Options dialog box.

`Text` is an optional variant specifying any additional text for the field (such as switches).

`PreserveFormatting` is an optional variant that you can set to `True` to have Word preserve any formatting applied to the field when Word updates the field.

Examples

You can insert a `wdFieldSubject` field at the current selection (thus replacing the current selection) in the active document by using the following statement:

```
ActiveDocument.Fields.Add Range:=Selection.Range,
➥Type:=wdFieldSubject
```

If you want to insert a field without replacing the current selection, you'll need to collapse it first:

- To insert the field before the current selection, collapse the selection to its beginning either by using a `Selection.Collapse wdCollapseStart` or `Selection.Collapse 1` statement, or by setting the end of the selection to be the same as its start (`Selection.End = Selection.Start`).

- To insert the field after the current selection, collapse the selection to its end either by using a `Selection.Collapse wdCollapseEnd` statement or by setting the start of the selection to be the same as its end (`Selection.Start = Selection.End`).

For example, to insert the file name of the current document before the current selection, you could use the following statements:

```
With ActiveDocument
    Selection.Collapse wdCollapseStart
    .Fields.Add Range:=Selection.Range, Type:= wdFieldFileName
End With
```

When you need to manipulate a field in a macro, you'll often find it convenient to set a name for the field when you insert it. You can do so by using a `Set` statement, as in the following example, which assigns the variable name `Author` to the `wdFieldAuthor` field it inserts:

```
Set Author = ActiveDocument.Fields.Add(Range:=
➥Selection.Range, Type:=wdFieldAuthor)
```

You can then refer to the field by name instead of needing to specify it in the `Fields` collection:

```
Author.Update
```

Going to a Field

To go to a specific field, use the `Select` method with the `Field` object. For example, to go to the first field in the active document, you could use the following statement:

```
ActiveDocument.Fields(1).Select
```

Updating Fields

As you saw in Chapter 4, you can have Word automatically update fields when you open a document and/or when you print a document. To update all the fields in a document at any other time, you need to record or write a macro. The differences between the two methods provide an interesting demonstration of the advantages of using the Word object model with VBA.

While you can quickly and easily record a simple macro to automatically update all fields in the current document (start the macro recorder, then choose Edit ➤ Select All, press F9, press ← to deselect the selection, and then stop the macro recorder), you can write a macro to update all fields in the current document even more simply:

```
Sub Update_All_Fields
    ActiveDocument.Fields.Update
End Sub
```

This macro uses the Update method to update all the fields in the Fields collection in the ActiveDocument object. You can also update a single field by specifying its object in the Fields collection and using the Update method; for instance, the following statement updates the third field in the document named Personnel Policy.doc:

```
Documents("Personnel Policy.doc").Fields(3).Update
```

> **NOTE**
>
> The Update_All_Fields macro shown here is in fact a little simplistic, because you may want to check that the document has no locked fields before you try to update all its fields. In the next section, I'll discuss how to lock a field, how to unlock a field, and how to tell whether or not one or more fields is locked.

Locking Fields

As you saw in Chapter 3, locking a field prevents anyone from updating its result and is a good way to prevent a field from being inadvertently updated when it shouldn't be. (Because an ill-intentioned user can unlock a locked field, field locking doesn't provide any security against malevolence.)

Syntax

To lock a field, you set its Locked property to `True`. `Locked` is a variant property and can be set to `True`, `False`, or `wdUndefined`. `True` indicates that the field or fields in question are locked; `False` indicates that the field or fields in question are unlocked; and `wdUndefined` indicates that some of the fields in question are locked and others are unlocked. (For obvious reasons, a single field cannot have `wdUndefined` status for its `Locked` property.) To lock all the fields in the current document, you could use the following statement:

```
ActiveDocument.Fields.Locked = True
```

Likewise, to lock all the fields in the current selection, you could use the following statement:

```
Selection.Fields.Locked = True
```

Examples

By using the following statements, you could insert at the current position of the insertion point a field containing the name of the user who created the document and the date when they created it, and then lock the field:

```
Selection.TypeText "This document was created by "
Set UserField = ActiveDocument.Fields.Add
➥(Range:=Selection.Range, Type:=wdFieldUserName)
UserField.Locked = True
Selection.TypeText " on "
Set DateField = ActiveDocument.Fields.Add(Selection.Range,
➥Type:=wdFieldCreateDate)
DateField.Locked = True
Selection.TypeText "." + vbCr
```

This produces a sentence such as "This document was created by Rikki Nadir on 6/21/97 12:04 AM." The three `Selection.TypeText` statements in the listing supply the static text, and the two fields supply the variable information.

If you write an `Update_All_Fields` macro, as I suggested in the previous section, you'll probably want to make it check the `Locked` status of all the fields in a document before it tries to update the fields. Then, once you've identified any locked fields, you can have the macro unlock them first if you need to update them.

Consider the `Update_All_Fields` macro shown in Listing 14.1, which prompts the user with one message box if all the fields in the document are locked and another message box if only some of the fields are locked.

Listing 14.1

```
1.  Sub Update_All_Fields()
2.      Dim MTitle As String, AllLockMsg As String,
    ➥LockMsg As String
3.      MTitle = "Update All Fields 1.2"
4.      If ActiveDocument.Fields.Locked = True Then
5.          AllLockMsg = "All the fields in this document are
        ➥locked, and you will not be able to update
        ➥them. Do you want to unlock the locked fields?."
6.          If MsgBox(AllLockMsg, vbYesNo, MTitle) = vbYes Then
7.              ActiveDocument.Fields.Locked = False
8.              ActiveDocument.Fields.Update
9.          Else
10.             End
11.         End If
12.     ElseIf ActiveDocument.Fields.Locked = wdUndefined Then
13.         LockMsg = "Some of the fields in this document are
        ➥locked, and you will not be able to update
        ➥them. Do you want to unlock the locked fields
        ➥before updating the other fields?"
14.         Choice = MsgBox(LockMsg, vbYesNoCancel
        ➥+ vbQuestion, MTitle)
15.         If Choice = vbYes Then
16.             ActiveDocument.Fields.Locked = False
17.             ActiveDocument.Fields.Update
18.         ElseIf Choice = vbNo Then
19.             ActiveDocument.Fields.Update
20.         Else    'Choice = vbCancel
21.             End
22.         End If
23.     Else
24.         ActiveDocument.Fields.Update
25.     End If
26. End Sub
```

Analysis

Line 2 declares the strings `MTitle`, which will contain the title-bar string for the two message boxes, `AllLockMsg`, which will contain a message if all the fields are locked, and `LockMsg`, which will contain a message if some of the fields are locked. Line 3 then assigns a suitable string for the title bar.

Line 4 begins the outer `If` condition by checking whether all the fields in the active document are locked. If so, the statements in lines 5 through 11 run as follows:

- Line 5 assigns the string for the message box to `AllLockMsg`.

- Line 6 starts a nested `If` condition that displays a message box containing the text in the `AllLockMsg` string, Yes and No buttons, and the title bar string `MTitle`.

- If the user chooses the Yes button, line 7 unlocks all the fields in the `Fields` collection, and line 8 updates the fields; if the user chooses the No button, the `Else` statement in line 9 runs the `End` statement in line 10, ending the macro.

- Line 11 ends the first nested `If` statement.

If the `If` condition in line 4 is not met, execution continues at line 12, where VBA evaluates the `ElseIf` condition, which checks if some of the fields in the `Fields` collection are locked (`ActiveDocument.Fields.Locked = wdUndefined`). If this condition is `True`, the statements in lines 13 through 22 run as follows:

- Line 13 assigns the string for the second message box to `LockMsg`.

- Line 14 displays a message box containing the text in the `LockMsg` string; Yes, No, and Cancel buttons; and the title bar string `MTitle`. The result of this message box is stored in the variable `Choice` (for once a change from `Response`, the variable name I've mostly been using in these examples).

- Line 15 starts a second nested `If` condition that evaluates the user's choice in the message box by checking the value of `Choice`. If `Choice` is `vbYes`, the statement in line 16 unlocks all the fields in the `Fields` collection, and line 17 updates the fields.

- If `Choice` is not `vbYes`, execution moves from line 15 to line 18, where VBA checks to see whether `Choice` is `vbNo`. If it is, the statement in line 19 runs, updating all fields that are not locked.

- If `Choice` is not `vbNo`, execution moves from line 18 to line 20, where an `Else` statement captures the third possibility from the message box: the user clicked the Cancel button. The `End` statement in line 21 then ends execution of the macro.

- Line 22 ends the second nested `If` condition.

If the `ElseIf` condition in line 12 is not met, execution continues at line 23, where an `Else` statement takes care of the third possible state of the fields: none of them are locked. In this case, there is no need to display a message box prompting the user to take action, so line 24 simply updates all the fields in the document. Line 25 then ends the outer `If` condition, and line 26 ends the macro.

Unlinking a Field

As you saw in Chapter 4, you can unlink a field by breaking its link so that the field can never again be updated. This is useful for information that you know you will never need to change again after a certain point. For example, if you were creating an annual report, you might want to use fields for the income, expense, and profit (or loss) figures while you were creating the report. Then, when the final draft had been approved, you could unlink the fields to finalize the information and prevent any of the figures from being updated by accident.

To break the link to a field, you use the `Unlink` method with the appropriate `Field` object in the `Fields` collection of the document object. For example, to unlink all fields in the active document, you could use the following statement:

```
ActiveDocument.Fields.Unlink
```

Working with Form Fields

As discussed in Chapter 3, form fields are fields that you use in forms (documents containing items of information that are to be filled in by users). Form fields in Word merge some of the features of fields with the features of bookmarks, which I'll discuss in the next chapter. Unlike fields, each form field is identified by a bookmark name, which gives you a way to quickly access specific form fields in your macros. VBA handles form fields as `FormField` objects that fit into a `FormFields` collection. This collection represents all the form fields in a document, a selection, or a range.

Many of the features of form fields work in a similar way to the features of fields, and I'll go through them quickly in the next few sections. At the end of the chapter, I'll show you how you can extract information from the form fields in a form. Given that it's much easier to design forms interactively in Word than to build them using macros, most of the time you spend working with form fields in VBA will probably be devoted to retrieving the contents of the form fields and taking appropriate action with them rather than inserting them automatically.

Inserting a Form Field

When you do need to insert a form field, you use the `Add` method with the `FormFields` collection. The syntax is the same as for adding a field:

```
expression.Add(Range, Type)
```

Here, `expression` is a required expression that returns a `FormFields` object, such as `ActiveDocument.FormFields`.

`Range` is a required argument specifying the range in which to insert the form field.

`Type` is a required Long argument specifying the type of form field to insert:

`wdFieldFormCheckBox`	Check box form field
`wdFieldFormDropDown`	Drop-down form field
`wdFieldFormTextInput`	Text box

For example, to add a text box to the range named `FormRange` in the active document, you could use the following statement:

```
Selection.Collapse Direction:=wdCollapseEnd
ActiveDocument.FormFields.Add Range:=FormRange,
➥Type: = wdFieldFormTextInput
```

Naming a Form Field

In most cases, you'll want to name your form fields so that you can quickly access them. To do so, use a `Set` statement when you insert the field, as in the following example, which inserts the same text box as in the previous example but this time assigns the name `TBox` to it:

```
Set TBox = ActiveDocument.FormFields.Add(Range:=FormRange,
➥Type: = wdFieldFormTextInput)
```

Assigning a Bookmark Name to a Form Field

Once you've set the name for a form field, you can easily assign a bookmark name to it. This is the equivalent of assigning the bookmark name in the form field's Options dialog box. For example, you could assign the bookmark name `UserCompany` to the text box named `TBox` by using the following statement:

```
TBox.Name = "UserCompany"
```

Assigning Other Properties to a Form Field

You can assign other information to a form field by setting its properties. These are the most useful of the form field properties:

Property	Description
Name	The name of the bookmark.
EntryMacro	The name of the macro that runs when the user moves the insertion point to the form field.
ExitMacro	The name of the macro that runs when the user moves the insertion point out of the form field.
Enabled	A Boolean setting determining whether the form field is available to the user. Leave this set to True unless you need to disable the form field so that the user cannot use it.

Property	Description
OwnHelp	A Boolean argument governing whether the form field has Help-key help associated with it.
HelpText	A string specifying the Help-key help.
OwnStatus	A Boolean argument governing whether the form field has status-bar help text associated with it.
StatusText	A string specifying the status-bar help.
Value	Applicable to check box fields only; indicates whether the check box is selected or cleared.
TextInput	Applicable to text box fields only. Returns the TextInput object, which has the following properties:
Type	Can be wdRegularText (regular text), wdCalculation-Text (calculation), wdCurrentDateText (the current date), wdCurrentTimeText (the current time), wdDate-Text (a date, not necessarily the current date), or wd-NumberText (a number).
Default	An optional variant that specifies the default text for the text box.
Format	An optional variant specifying the type of formatting for the text, number, or date. You can choose a variety of formats depending on the Type argument. For example, for wdRegularText, you can choose Title Case, Uppercase, Lowercase, or Initial Capital.
Width	The number of characters for the width of the text box. This number must be equal to or larger than the width of the Default text string (if there is one).

To illustrate, the following statements add a check box named MyCheck to the active document at the insertion point; assign to it the bookmark name Registered and the entry macro Display_Registration_Information; and then select the check box:

```
Set MyCheck = ActiveDocument.FormFields.Add(Range:=
➡Selection.Range, Type:=wdFieldFormCheckBox
```

```
With MyCheck
    .Name = "Registered"
    .EntryMacro = "Display_Registration_Information"
    .CheckBox.Value = True
End With
```

Assigning Items to a Drop-Down List Box

To assign items to a drop-down list box, you use the Add method with the ListEntries object for the DropDown object of the form field. For example, to add two entries named 100 and 200, you could use the following statements:

```
With ActiveDocument.FormFields("MyDropDown").DropDown.
➥ListEntries
    .Add Name: = "100"
    .Add Name: = "200"
End With
```

Deleting a Form Field

To delete a form field, use the Delete method with its object. For example, to delete the form field named MyDropDown in the active document, you might use the following statement:

```
ActiveDocument.FormFields("MyDropDown").Delete
```

Going to a Form Field

To go to a form field, use the Select method with its object. For example, to go to the form field named Address1 in the document Registration Form.doc, you could use the following statement:

```
Documents("Registration Form.doc").FormFields("Address1).Select
```

Setting the Result of a Form Field

To set the result (i.e., the contents) of a form field, you set its Result property. For example, to assign the string FirstName to the form field named FirstName in the active document, you could use the following statement:

```
ActiveDocument.FormFields("FirstName").Result = FirstName
```

Retrieving the Result of a Form Field

To retrieve the result of a form field, you check its `Result` property. For example, to retrieve the result of the form field named `LastName` in the active document and display it in a message box, you could use the following statement:

```
MsgBox ActiveDocument.FormFields("LastName").Result
```

As I mentioned earlier in the chapter, each form field is identified by a bookmark name, and so is also included in the `Bookmarks` collection. But there are a lot of other uses for bookmarks, as you'll see in the next chapter.

Working with Bookmarks

In Chapter 4, I discussed how you can use Word's bookmarks—electronic markers—for identifying and referring to parts of documents quickly and easily. In this chapter, I'll talk about how you can use bookmarks in your macros to automate the flow and transfer of information from document to document.

As you saw in Chapter 12, VBA's ranges provide another way of working with a specified part of a document. The advantage of a bookmark over a range is that you can save a bookmark in a document, whereas a range lasts only while the procedure that defines it is running.

In the first part of this chapter, I'll discuss how you can set and use bookmarks of your own. In the second part, we'll investigate how you can use Word's hidden, built-in bookmarks to make life easier in your macros.

The Basics of Bookmarks

As you might guess, VBA handles bookmarks as `Bookmark` objects, and all the `Bookmark` objects in a document or template are members of the `Bookmarks` collection. For most purposes, you access the `Bookmark` objects through the `Bookmarks` collection.

Word privately sets a number of bookmarks for each document. These bookmarks contain a variety of information about the document, including the starting and ending positions of the current selection, the contents of the current line or paragraph, and the contents of the entire document. You can use these built-in bookmarks for your own purposes in macros, as you'll see later in this chapter.

Working with User-Defined Bookmarks

In this section, I'll discuss how VBA handles user-defined bookmarks—the ones that you add to a document either manually or by using macros.

Inserting a Bookmark

To insert a bookmark, you use the Add method (this adds the Bookmark object to the Bookmarks collection). The syntax for the Add method is as follows:

```
expression.Add(Name, Range)
```

Here, expression is a required expression that returns a Bookmarks collection object. Usually, you'll want to use the Bookmarks collection in the active document or in a specified document for expression.

Name is a required string argument containing the name of the bookmark. As you saw in Chapter 4, bookmark names can contain underscores but not spaces, alphanumerics but not symbols, and can be up to 40 characters long.

Range is an optional variant specifying the range for the bookmark to mark. The range can contain text or graphical elements or can be collapsed to a single point.

Here's an example: to add a bookmark named Meeting_Location to the active document at the current position of the insertion point or the current selection, you could use the following statement:

```
ActiveDocument.Bookmarks.Add Name:="Meeting_Location"
```

You could also explicitly specify the range for the bookmark. The following statement specifies the range as the Range property of the Selection object:

```
ActiveDocument.Bookmarks.Add Name:="Meeting_Location",
➥Range:= Selection.Range
```

Likewise, you can set a bookmark in a document other than the active document. The following statement adds a bookmark named Request_Number to the first word of the open document named Personnel Request.doc:

```
Documents("Personnel Request.doc").Bookmarks.Add
➥Name:="Request_Number",Range:=Documents("Personnel
➥Request.doc").Words(1)
```

Finding Out Whether a Bookmark Exists

To find out whether a bookmark exists, you use the `Exists` property for the `Bookmark` object in the `Bookmarks` collection. This is a Boolean property, so it can be set only to `True` or `False`. For instance, you could use the following statements to tell you whether the bookmark `Request_Number` exists in the document `Personnel Request.doc`:

```
If Documents("Personnel Request.doc").Bookmarks.Exists
➥("Request_Number") = True Then
    MsgBox "The bookmark exists."
Else
    MsgBox "The bookmark does not exist."
End If
```

If the bookmark does not already exist, you might want to add it, as shown in the following lines of code. I've used a `Set` statement to set the variable `CurDoc` (for "current document") to represent `Personnel Request.doc`; this makes the code easier to handle—instead of specifying `Documents("Personnel Request.doc")` in each line, you can specify `CurDoc` instead.

```
Set CurDoc = Documents("Personnel Request.doc")
If CurDoc.Bookmarks.Exists("Request_Number") = False Then
➥CurDoc.Bookmarks.Add Name:="Request_Number",
➥Range:=Selection.Range
```

> **NOTE** In this example, `Personnel Request.doc` **needs to be the active document because the range is specified as** `Selection.Range`, **and the selection can only be in the active document.**

Going to a Bookmark

To move the insertion point to a bookmark, you use the `Select` method for the `Bookmark` object in the `Bookmarks` collection. For example, to move the insertion point to the bookmark named `MyTemp` in the active document, you would use the following statement:

```
ActiveDocument.Bookmarks("MyTemp").Select
```

If the bookmark consists of a single point in text, this statement will position the insertion point there, ready to insert text (which you could then do with the TypeText method). If the bookmark contains text or a graphic object, this statement will select that text or that object; so if you want to insert text without removing the current contents of the bookmark, you will need to move the insertion point off the contents first or use a method such as InsertBefore or InsertAfter rather than TypeText.

After selecting a bookmark, you can use the Selection object to work with its contents if you want to. This can be useful for adding to the contents of the bookmark. However, if you want to work with the contents of the bookmark and then apply them elsewhere in that document or in another document, you'll usually find it more efficient to first retrieve the contents of the bookmark and then manipulate it as a string. I'll show you how to do this in in just a moment.

Finding Out Where a Bookmark Is Located

To find out where a bookmark is located, you use the Start and End properties of its Range object, which return the character position of the start and end, respectively, of the bookmark's range. For instance, you could display a message box listing the start and end positions of the bookmark by using the statements shown below. Here, BookStart and BookEnd are variables in which the statements store the start and end positions of the bookmark.

```
Set CurDoc = Documents("Personnel Request.doc")
BookStart = CurDoc.Bookmarks("Request_Number").Range.Start
BookEnd = CurDoc.Bookmarks("Request_Number").Range.End
MsgBox "Start position:" + Str(BookStart) + vbCr +
➡"End position:" + Str(BookEnd), vbOKOnly
➡+ vbInformation, "Bookmark Information"
```

NOTE   If the start and end of the bookmark's range are in the same place— i.e., if the bookmark marks a collapsed selection—the start and end positions will be the same.

As another example, you could check to see whether the start of the bookmark MyTemp was at the beginning (character position 1) of the active document, and delete it if it was, by using the following statements:

```
With ActiveDocument.Bookmarks("MyTemp")
    If .Range.Start = 1 Then .Delete
End With
```

Retrieving the Contents of a Bookmark

To retrieve the contents of a bookmark, you use the Text property of the Range object of the Bookmark object in the Bookmarks collection. For example, you could retrieve the contents of the bookmark named Request_Number in Personnel Request.doc and display it in a message box by using the following statement:

```
MsgBox Documents("Personnel Request.doc").Bookmarks
➥("Request_Number").Range.Text
```

Finding Out Whether a Bookmark Is Empty

To find out whether a bookmark is empty, check to see if its Empty property is True. For example, to find out if the bookmark Employee_Name in Personnel Request.doc is empty and, if so, display the finding in a message box, you could use the following statements:

```
If Documents("Personnel Request.doc").Bookmarks
➥("Employee_Name").Empty = True Then
    MsgBox "The bookmark is empty."
End If
```

Changing the Contents of a Bookmark

Often, you'll want to change the contents of a bookmark in a macro. You can do this in two ways: by replacing the contents of the bookmark, or by adding to it.

To replace the contents of a bookmark, first select it by using the Select method. Then using the MoveLeft method move left one character to deselect the final character, so as not to overwrite the end of the bookmark (assuming the Typing Replaces Selection check box on the Edit tab of the Options dialog box is selected, as it is by default). Then use a method such as the TypeText method to insert the text to replace it, as in the following statements, which replace the contents of the bookmark `User_Name` in the active document with the user's input from an input box. (The `If` condition here checks to make sure that the result of the input box was not a blank string. The example assumes that the bookmark has contents—even a space—rather than being a point in text.)

```
Dim Employee_Name As String
Employee_Name = InputBox("Enter your name:", "Request Form")
If Employee_Name <> "" Then
    With ActiveDocument.Bookmarks("Employee_Name")
        .Select
        Selection.MoveLeft Unit:=wdCharacter, Count:=1,
        ➡Extend:=wdExtend
        Selection.TypeText Employee_Name
    End With
End If
```

Displaying Bookmark Markers

You can have a macro display bookmark markers by simply switching the `ShowBookmarks` property of the `View` object of the active window to `True`, and hide them again by setting the `ShowBookmarks` property to `False`. To display bookmark markers in the active document, you could use the following statement:

```
ActiveDocument.ActiveWindow.View.ShowBookmarks = True
```

To hide bookmark markers again, you could use this statement:

```
ActiveDocument.ActiveWindow.View.ShowBookmarks = False
```

Deleting a Bookmark

To delete a bookmark, use the `Delete` method with a `Bookmark` object. For example, to delete the bookmark named `MyTemp` in the active document, you could use the following statement:

```
ActiveDocument.Bookmarks("MyTemp").Delete
```

To delete the bookmark named `Employee_Idea` in the document `New Ideas.doc,` you could use this statement:

```
Documents("New Ideas.doc").Bookmarks("Employee_Idea").Delete
```

To delete all the bookmarks in a document, you could use a `For Each…Next` statement with the `Bookmarks` collection. The following macro deletes all bookmarks in the active document:

```
Sub Delete_All_Bookmarks()
    With ActiveDocument
        For Each Mark In .Bookmarks
            .Bookmarks(Mark).Delete
        Next Mark
    End With
End Sub
```

Using Word's Built-in Bookmarks

Word provides a number of built-in bookmarks that it uses in the background to perform standard operations. You can use these bookmarks for your own purposes:

Bookmark	Returns
\Sel	The current selection if there is one; otherwise, the location of the insertion point.
\PrevSel1	The location of the most recent edit. This is the position to which Word will return if you use the `GoBack` method once in VBA or press Shift+F5 once when working interactively.
\PrevSel2	The location of the second most recent edit. This is the position to which Word will return if you use the `GoBack` method twice in VBA or press Shift+F5 twice when working interactively.

TIP

Before using the PrevSel1 or PrevSel2 bookmark, check that it exists by using a statement such as `If ActiveDocument.Bookmarks .Exists("\PrevSel2") = True Then ActiveDocument .Bookmarks("\PrevSel2").Select`

Bookmark	Returns
\StartOfSel	The start of the current selection if there is one; otherwise, the location of the insertion point.
\EndOfSel	The end of the current selection if there is one; otherwise, the location of the insertion point.
\Line	The first line of the current selection if there is one; otherwise, the line on which the insertion point resides. If the insertion point is positioned at the end of any line other than the last line in the paragraph, this bookmark includes the whole of the next line. Note that if there's a space after the insertion point at the end of the line, you'll get the current line instead of the next line.
\Char	The first character of the current selection if there is one; otherwise, the character to the right of the insertion point.
\Para	The current paragraph (the paragraph containing the insertion point), or the first paragraph if part or all of two or more paragraphs are selected. This bookmark includes the paragraph mark unless the paragraph in question is the last paragraph in the document.
\Section	The current section (the section containing the insertion point), or the first section if there is a selection that contains part or all of two or more sections.
\Doc	All the contents of the active document except for the last paragraph mark.
\Page	The current page (the page containing the insertion point), or the first page if there is a selection that spans two or more pages. If the page in question is the last page in the document, this bookmark does not include the last paragraph mark.
\StartOfDoc	The beginning of the document.
\EndOfDoc	The end of the document.
\Cell	The current cell in a table (the cell containing the insertion point), or the first cell if there is a selection that spans two or more cells.

Bookmark	Returns
\Table	The current table (the table containing the insertion point or the current selection), or the first table if there is a selection that spans part or all of two or more tables.
\HeadingLevel	The current heading (the heading containing the insertion point) and any subordinate headings or text. If the current selection is not a heading, VBA selects the heading that precedes the selection, together with any subordinate headings or text.

As an example of how you might use these built-in bookmarks, consider Listing 15.1, which contains a macro for deleting the current paragraph.

Listing 15.1

```
1.  Sub Delete_Current_Paragraph()
2.  Msg = "Do you want to delete the current paragraph:"
    ➥+ vbCr + vbCr
3.  Msg = Msg + ActiveDocument.Bookmarks("\Para").Range.Text
4.  If MsgBox(Msg, vbYesNo + vbQuestion,
    ➥"Delete Current Paragraph") Then
5.      ActiveDocument.Bookmarks("\Para").Select
6.      Selection.Delete
7.  End If
8.  End Sub
```

Analysis

Line 2 implicitly declares the variable Msg and assigns to it a string of text and two carriage-return characters that will separate the string from the paragraph text. Line 3 then adds to Msg the Text property of the Range object of the \Para bookmark in the active document—that is, it adds to the string, after the two carriage-return characters, the contents of the paragraph in which the insertion point is currently residing.

Line 4 contains an `If` condition to display a message box containing the `Msg` variable, which asks the user if they want to delete the paragraph. If they choose the Yes button, the statements in lines 5 and 6 run: line 5 uses the `Select` method to select the `\Para` bookmark, and line 6 uses the `Delete` method on the `Selection` object to delete the selection. (If the user chooses the No button, the macro ends.)

As you've seen already in this book, and as you'll see in the coming chapters, bookmarks provide a great way of accessing and manipulating most any part of a document, from a single point or a single word to a whole section or a form field. Now, though, it's time for a change of topic to something I've been promising you for a number of chapters: rooting the bugs out of your macros. Turn the page.

CHAPTER

SIXTEEN

16

Debugging a Macro

In this chapter, we'll look at some of the things that can go wrong in macros and what you can do about them. We'll examine the types of errors that can occur, from simple typos to infinite loops to errors that happen only when the moon is blue *and* it's a leap year (or the turn of the millennium).

We'll start by going quickly through the principles of debugging. Then we'll work with the tools that Visual Basic for Applications offers for debugging macros and use them to get the bugs out of a few statements. Finally, I'll discuss the various ways of handling errors and when to use each one.

Principles of Debugging

A bug, as I'm sure you know, is an error in hardware or software that causes a program to execute incorrectly. (There are various explanations of the etymology of the word *bug* in this context, ranging from apocryphal stories of moths being pulled out from the circuit boards of malfunctioning computers to musings that the word came from the mythological *bugbear*, an unwelcome beast; but in fact, this usage of *bug* seems to come from the early days of the telegraph rather than originating in the computer age.) *Debugging* means removing the bugs from hardware or (in this case) software.

Your goals in debugging should be straightforward: you need to remove all detectable bugs from your code as quickly and efficiently as possible. Your order of business will probably go something like this:

- First, test your macro to see if it works as it should. If you're confident that the code will work, you'll probably want to test it by simply running the macro once or twice on suitable documents (or on suitable data). Even if that seems successful, continue testing for a reasonable period on sample documents (or sample data) before unleashing the macro on the world.

- If your code does not work as you expected it to, you'll need to debug it. That means following the procedures in this chapter to locate the bugs and then remove them. Once you've removed all the bugs that you can identify, test the code as described in the first step.

- When testing your code, try to anticipate the unorthodox applications that users will devise for your macro. For example, you might write a macro on the (perfectly reasonable) assumption that it will work on the document text in Normal view. You can test it on the document text until you're blue in the face, and it'll work fine every time. But if a user tries to run the code in Page Layout view, or Outline view, or in a header or footer or footnote area, things are apt to go wrong.

- When you are ready to distribute your macro, you may want to write instructions for its use. In these instructions, you may also need to document any bugs that you cannot squash or circumstances under which the macro should not be run.

Debugging a macro tends to be idiosyncratic work. There's no magic wand that you can wave over your code to banish bugs (although, as I'll discuss in a moment, the Visual Basic Editor does its best to help you eliminate certain types of errors from your code as you create it); moreover, such simple things as forgetting to initialize a variable can wreak havoc on your code. You'll probably develop your own approach to debugging your macros, partly because they will inevitably be written in your own style. But when debugging, it helps to focus on understanding what the code is supposed to do. You then correlate this with your observations of what the code actually does. When you reconcile the two, you'll probably have worked out how to debug the macro.

TIP   The more complex your code, the higher the probability that you will get bugs in it. Keep your code as simple as possible by breaking it up into separate procedures and modules. I'll discuss how to do this in the next chapter.

The Different Types of Errors

You'll encounter four basic kinds of errors in your macros:

- Language errors
- Compile errors
- Run-time errors
- Program logic errors

We'll look at these in turn and discuss how to prevent them. After that, we'll examine the tools VBA provides for fixing them.

Language Errors

The first type of error is a *language error* (also known as a *syntax error*). When you mistype a word in the code window, omit a vital piece of punctuation, scramble a statement, or leave out the end of a construction, that's a language error. If you've gotten this far in the book, you've probably already made dozens of language errors as part of the learning process and through simple typos.

VBA helps you eliminate many language errors as you create them, as you'll see in the next section. Those language errors that the Visual Basic Editor doesn't catch as you create them usually show up as compile errors, so we'll look at examples of both language errors and compile errors in the next section.

Compile Errors

Compile errors are errors that occur when VBA cannot compile a statement correctly —that is, when it cannot turn a statement that you've entered into viable code. For example, if you tell VBA to use a property for an object that doesn't have that property, you'll cause a compile error.

The good news about language errors and compile errors is that, as you'll have noticed, the Visual Basic Editor detects many language errors and some compile errors when you move the insertion point from the offending line. For example, try typing the following statement in the code window and pressing Enter to create a new line (or ↑ or ↓ to move to another line):

```
If X > Y
```

The Visual Basic Editor will display a "Compile Error: Expected: Then or GoTo" message box to tell you that the statement is missing a vital element: it should be `If X > Y Then` or `If X > Y GoTo`. This vigilance on the part of the Visual Basic Editor prevents you from running into this type of error deep in the execution of your code.

On the other hand, you will also make language errors that the Visual Basic Editor does *not* identify when you move the insertion point from the line in which you've inserted them. Instead, VBA will identify these errors as compile errors when it compiles the code. For example, if you enter the following statement in the code window, the Visual Basic Editor will not detect anything wrong. But when you run the macro, VBA will compile the code and will then discover and object to the error before running any of the statements in the macro.

```
ActiveDocument.SaveAs FileMame:="My File.doc"
```

This error is a straightforward typo—`FileMame` instead of `FileName`—but VBA cannot identify it until it runs the code.

The Visual Basic Editor does help you pick up some errors of this type. Say you're trying to enter a `Documents.Close` statement and mistype `Documents` as `Docments`. In this case, the Visual Basic Editor will not display the Properties/Methods list because you haven't entered a valid object. Not seeing the list should alert you that something is wrong. If you continue anyway and enter the `Docments.Close` statement (which is easy enough to do if you're typing at speed without watching the screen), the Visual Basic Editor will not spot the mistake, and it will show up as a "Run-time error 424: Object required" when you try to run the macro.

In a similar vein, if you specify a property or method for an object to which that property or method does not apply, VBA will generate a compile error. For example, say you forget the `Add` method and enter `Documents.Create` instead. VBA will highlight the offending word and will generate the compile error "Method or data member not found," which tells you there's no `Create` method for the `Documents` collection.

Run-Time Errors

The third type of error you'll see is the *run-time error*, which occurs while code is executing; you create a run-time error when you write a statement that causes VBA to try to perform an impossible operation, such as opening a document that doesn't exist, closing a document when no document is open, or performing something mathematically impossible such as dividing by zero.

As an example of an impossible operation, consider the archetypal division by zero. The following statement gives a "run-time error 11: Division by zero":

```
DZ = 1 / 0
```

I know—you're unlikely to enter anything as witless as this demonstration line in your code; this line will inevitably produce a division-by-zero error because

the divisor is zero. But it's easy to enter a valid equation, such as `MonthlyPay =
Salary/Months,` and forget to assign a value to `Months` (if a variable is empty,
it counts as a zero value), or to produce a zero value for `Months` by addition or
subtraction.

To avoid run-time errors, track the values of your variables by using the Watch
window, which I'll discuss a little later in the chapter.

Program Logic Errors

The fourth type of error is the *program logic error*, which is an error that produces
incorrect results. With program logic errors, there is no syntactical problem with
the code, so VBA is able to compile and run it without generating any errors, but
the result you get is not the result you were expecting. Program logic errors range
in scope from the relatively obvious (such as creating an inventory from the
wrong document by forgetting to activate the right document) to the subtle (such
as extending a range to the wrong character). In the first example, the inventory
macro is likely to run perfectly, but the resulting document will bear little resemblance to the inventory you were trying to produce; in the second example, you
might get a result that was almost correct—or the error might cause you to get
perfect results sometimes and slightly wrong results at other times.

Program logic errors tend to be the hardest errors to catch. To nail them down,
you need to trace the execution of your code and pinpoint where things start to go
wrong. For this, you need the tools that I'm going to introduce in the next section.

Uncatchable Bugs

The more complex your code, the more likely you are to create bugs that are
truly difficult to catch. Usually, with determination and ingenuity, you can track
down the bugs in a macro, but bugs that depend on several unforeseen and
improbable circumstances occurring simultaneously can be the devil's own
job to isolate. For example, an error that occurs in a macro when the user
makes a certain choice in a dialog box is relatively easy to catch; but if the
error occurs only when the user has made two particular choices in the dialog
box, it's much harder; and if the error is contingent on three specific choices
the user has made in the dialog box, or on an element in the document on
which the macro is being run, you'll have a much tougher time pinpointing it.

Hacker folklore defines various kinds of bizarre bugs by assigning them names derived from such disciplines as philosophy and quantum physics. For instance, a *heisenbug* is defined as "a bug that disappears or alters its behavior when one attempts to probe or isolate it." Heisenbugs are frustrating, as are Bohr bugs and mandelbugs, which we won't get into here. But the worst kind of bug is the *schroedingbug*, which is a design or implementation bug that remains quiescent until someone reads the code and notices that it shouldn't work, whereupon it stops working until the code is made logically consistent.

These bugs are of course ridiculous—until you start to discover them yourself...

VBA's Debugging Tools

VBA provides a solid assortment of debugging tools to help you remove the bugs from your macros. The main tools for debugging are the Locals Window, the Watch Window, and the Immediate Window, which I'll discuss in this section. As you'll see, you can access these tools in various ways, one of which is by using the Debug toolbar (see Figure 16.1). Three of the buttons—Run Sub/Userform (Continue); Break; and Reset—are shared with the Standard toolbar; the others I'll introduce later in this chapter as appropriate, except for the Design Mode/Exit Design Mode button, which I'll save for Chapter 19.

FIGURE 16.1

The Debug toolbar provides thirteen commands for debugging your macros.

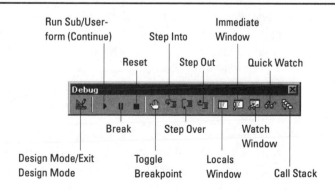

But before we dig into the debugging tools, let's go through a quick refresher on Break mode, which we visited briefly in Chapter 5. There, you saw how you can step through a macro one statement at a time, and how you can check the value of a variable with the Data Tips feature by moving the mouse pointer over the name of the variable in the code. Here, we'll build on that knowledge to get results faster.

Break Mode

Break mode is a vital tool for debugging your macros because it lets you watch your code execute step-by-step in the code window. For example, if you have an `If...Then...ElseIf...Else` statement that appears to be executing incorrectly, you can step through it in Break mode and watch exactly which statements are executing to produce the result.

In Chapter 5, I showed you the two easiest ways of entering Break mode:

- Placing the insertion point in the macro you want to run in the code window and pressing the F8 key (or clicking the Step Into button on the Debug toolbar) to start stepping through it.

- Setting one or more breakpoints in the macro to cause VBA to enter Break mode when it reaches one of the marked lines. As I mentioned briefly in Chapter 5, a breakpoint allows you to stop execution of code at a particular point in a macro; the easiest way to set a breakpoint is to click in the Margin Indicator Bar to the left of the code window beside the line you want to affect (you can also right-click in the line and choose Toggle ➤ Breakpoint from the context menu). You can set any number of breakpoints. They are especially useful when you need to track down a bug in a macro, because they allow you to run the parts of a macro that have no problems at full speed, then stop the macro where you think there might be problems; from there, you can step through the statements that might be problematic and watch how they execute.

You can also enter Break mode in a couple of other ways:

- Interrupting your code by pressing Ctrl+Break and then clicking the Debug button in the resulting dialog box (see Figure 16.2). This is not a particularly useful way of entering Break mode unless your code gets stuck in an endless loop; VBA will highlight the statement that was executing when you pressed Ctrl+Break, but (depending on your timing) this is unlikely to be the statement that is causing the problem in your code.

- Choosing the Debug button in a run-time error dialog box such as the one shown in Figure 16.3. In the code window, VBA will highlight the statement that caused the error. (You can also choose the Help button in the run-time error dialog box to get an explanation about the error before choosing the Debug button.)

FIGURE 16.2

You can enter Break mode by pressing Ctrl+Break and then clicking the Debug button in this dialog box.

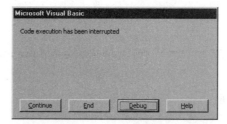

FIGURE 16.3

Entering Break mode from a run-time error dialog box like this one takes you straight to the offending statement in your code.

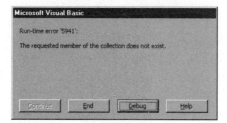

The Step Over and Step Out Commands

In Chapter 5, I showed you how to step through a macro by using the F8 key. More formally, this is known as the Step Into command; you can also issue the command by clicking the Step Into button on the Debug toolbar or choosing Debug ➤ Step Into. But there are two more features of Break mode that you should know about: the Step Over command and the Step Out command, both of which you use in Break mode to speed up stepping through your code.

NOTE   The Step Over and Step Out commands are not available until you enter Break mode (for example, by using the Step Into command).

The Step Over command, which you can issue by clicking the Step Over button on the Debug toolbar, by pressing Shift+F8, or by choosing Debug ➤ Step Over, executes the whole of a procedure or function called from the current procedure, instead of stepping statement-by-statement through the called procedure, as the Step Into command would do. (It "steps over" that procedure or function.) Use the Step Over command when you're debugging a procedure that calls another procedure or function that you know to be error-free and that you do not need to test step-by-step.

The Step Out command, which you can issue by clicking the Step Out button on the Debug toolbar, by pressing Ctrl+Shift+F8, or by choosing Debug ➤ Step Out, runs the rest of the current procedure at full speed. Use the Step Out command to quickly execute the rest of the macro once you've gotten through the part that you needed to watch step-by-step.

The Locals Window

The Locals window provides a quick readout of the value and type of all expressions in the active procedure via a collapsible tree view (see Figure 16.4). The Expression column displays the name of each expression, listed under the name of the macro in which it appears; the Value column displays the current value of the expression (including `Empty` if the expression is empty, or `Null` or `Nothing` as appropriate); and the Type column displays the data type of the expression, with variants listed as "Variant" along with their assigned data type (for example, "Variant/String" for a variant assigned the String data type).

To display the Locals window, click the Locals Window button on the Debug toolbar or choose View ➤ Locals Window; to remove the Locals window, click its close button.

From the Locals window, you can also click the button marked with an ellipsis (...) to display the Call Stack dialog box, which I'll discuss in "The Call Stack Dialog Box" section later in the chapter.

FIGURE 16.4

Use the Locals window to see at a glance all the expressions in the active procedure.

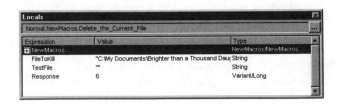

The Watch Window

The Watch window (the window identified as Watches at the bottom of Figure 16.5) is a separate window that you use for tracking the values of variables and expressions as your code executes. To display the Watch window, click the Watch Window button on the Debug toolbar or choose View ➤ Watch Window in the Visual Basic Editor. To hide the Watch window again, click its close button (clicking the Watch Window button or choosing View ➤ Watch Window again does not hide it).

FIGURE 16.5

Use the Watch window to track the values of variables and expressions in your code.

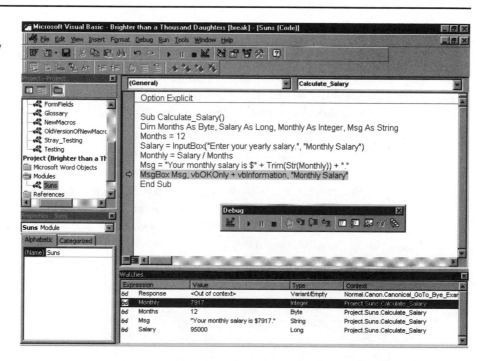

The Watch window displays *watch expressions*, which are expressions you set ahead of time to give you a running display of the value of a variable or an expression. This allows you to pinpoint where an unexpected value for a variable or an expression occurs as your code executes. Look at the Watch window for the `Calculate_Salary` macro in Figure 16.5: execution has reached the `MsgBox` line, so all the variables in the macro have been initialized and assigned values. The Watch window lists the names of the watched expressions or variables in the Expression column, their values in the Value column, their type (Integer, Byte, String, Long, etc.) in the Type column, and their context (the module and macro in which they are operating) in the Context column. So to track the value of, say, the Monthly variable, you need only look at the Watch window at any given point during Break mode.

NOTE If a variable or expression listed in the Watch window has not been initialized, the Watch window will display "<Out of Context>" in the Value column and "Empty" (for a variable other than a Variant) or "Variant/Empty" (for a Variant) in the Type column.

The Visual Basic Editor updates all watch expressions in the Watch window whenever you enter Break mode and whenever you execute a statement in the Immediate window (more on this window in the next section). So if you step through a macro in the code window by using the F8 key, which keeps you in Break mode, you can watch the value of a variable or an expression as each statement executes. This is a great way to pinpoint where an error or an unexpected value occurs, and much easier than having to move the mouse over each variable or expression in question to check its value by using the Auto Data Tips feature.

Before you can display a variable in the Watch window, you need to declare it (otherwise the Visual Basic Editor will respond with a "Variable not created in this context" error). This is another good reason for declaring variables explicitly at the beginning of a macro rather than declaring them implicitly in mid-macro.

Because watch expressions slow down execution of your code, the Visual Basic Editor does not save them with the code—you need to place them separately for each editing session. The Visual Basic Editor stores watch expressions during the current editing session, so you can move from procedure to procedure without losing your watch expressions.

Setting Watch Expressions

To set a watch expression, you add it to the list in the Watch window:

1. Select the variable or expression in your code, or just position the insertion point in it. (This is an optional step, but recommended.)

2. Right-click in the code window or in the Watch window and choose Add Watch from the context menu, or choose Debug ➤ Add Watch, to display the Add Watch dialog box (see Figure 16.6). If you selected a variable or an expression in step 1, it will appear in the Expression text box.

FIGURE 16.6

In the Add Watch dialog box, specify the watch expression you want to add.

3. If necessary, change the variable or expression in the Expression text box, or enter a variable or an expression if you didn't select one in step 1.

4. If necessary, adjust the settings in the Context group box. The Procedure drop-down list will be set to the current macro, and the Module drop-down list will be set to the current module.

5. In the Watch Type group box, adjust the option button setting if necessary:

    • The default setting, Watch Expression, adds the variable or expression in the Expression text box to the list in the Watch window.

    • Break When Value Is True causes VBA to enter Break mode whenever the value of the variable or expression changes to True.

    • Break When Value Changes causes VBA to enter Break mode whenever the value of the watch expression changes. Use this setting either when dealing with a watch expression whose value you do not expect to change but which appears to be changing, or with a watch expression whose every change you need to observe.

TIP

The Break When Value Is True option button allows you to run your code without stepping through each statement that does not change the value of the watch expression to True. The Break When Value Changes option button allows you to run your code and stop with each change of the value.

6. Click the OK button to add the watch expression to the Watch window.

> **TIP**
>
> You can also drag a variable or an expression from the code window to the Watch window. In that case, you set a default watch expression in the current context; to set Break When Value Is True or Break When Value Changes, you need to edit the watch expression after dragging it to the Watch window.

Editing Watch Expressions

To edit a watch expression, right-click the watch expression in the Watch window and choose Edit Watch from the context menu, or select the expression in the Watch window and choose Debug ➤ Edit Watch; either action will display the Edit Watch dialog box with the watch expression selected in the Expression box, as shown in Figure 16.7. Change the context or watch type for the watch expression by using the settings in the Context group box and the Watch Type group box, and then click the OK button to apply your changes.

FIGURE 16.7

You can edit your watch expressions in the Edit Watch dialog box.

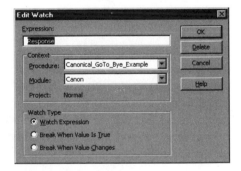

Deleting Watch Expressions

To delete a watch expression, right-click it in the Watch window and choose Delete Watch from the context menu. You can also delete the current watch expression by clicking the Delete button in the Edit Watch dialog box.

Using the Quick Watch Feature

For times when you don't want to create a watch expression for an expression or a variable, you can use the Quick Watch feature, which displays the Quick Watch dialog box (see Figure 16.8) containing the context and value of the selected expression. To use Quick Watch, select the expression or variable in the code window and then either click the Quick Watch button on the Debug toolbar, choose Debug ➤ Quick Watch, or press Shift+F9. (If you're already working in the Quick Watch dialog box, you can click the Add button to add the expression to the Watch window.)

FIGURE 16.8

Use the Quick Watch dialog box to get quick information on a variable or expression for which you don't want to set a watch expression in the Watch window.

The Immediate Window

The Visual Basic Editor provides an Immediate window (see Figure 16.9) that you can use as a virtual scratchpad to enter lines of code that you want to test without entering them in the macro itself, or to display information to help you check the values of variables while a macro is executing. In the first case, you enter code in the Immediate window; in the second, you use statements entered in the code window to display information in the Immediate window, where you can easily view it.

FIGURE 16.9

Use the Immediate window for on-the-fly work and information when you're running a macro in Break mode.

To display the Immediate window, click the Immediate Window button on the Debug toolbar, choose View ➤ Immediate Window, or press Ctrl+G. To hide the Immediate window again, click its close button. (Clicking the Immediate Window button, choosing View ➤ Immediate Window, or pressing Ctrl+G when the Immediate window is displayed does not hide the Immediate window.)

When Can You Use the Immediate Window?

You can execute code in the Immediate window *only* when your code is running—for example, when you're stepping through a macro in the code window by using the F8 key. If you try to execute code in the Immediate window when you don't have any code running, the Visual Basic Editor will display a "Can't execute immediate statements in design mode" error. (*Design mode* or *design time* is any time other than *run time*, when code is running.)

There are a number of restrictions on the code you can use in the Immediate window:

- You cannot use declarative statements (such as `Dim`, `Private`, `Public`, `Option Explicit`, `Static`, or `Type`) or control-flow statements (such as `GoTo`, `Sub`, or `Function`). These will cause VBA to throw an "Invalid in Immediate Pane" error.

- You cannot use multi-line statements (such as block `If` statements or block `For...Next` statements) because there is no logical connection between statements on different lines in the Immediate window: each line is treated in isolation. You can get around this limitation by entering block `If` statements on a single line, separating the statements with colons (which you'll remember I recommended against for general use in Chapter 9 because code crammed together like this is hard to read), and using the line-continuation character (the underscore) to break the resulting long lines onto two physical lines (while keeping them as one logical line). For example, the following statement works in the Immediate window as a single line, though it would not work as a block `If`:

```
If X < Y Then:MsgBox "X is smaller than Y.":Goto
➥End:Else:MsgBox "X is greater than Y.":End If
```

- You cannot place breakpoints in the Immediate window.

Entering Code in the Immediate Window

The Immediate window supports a number of standard Windows key combinations, such as Ctrl+X (Cut); Ctrl+C (Copy); Ctrl+V (Paste); Ctrl+Home (move the insertion point to the start of the window); Ctrl+End (move the insertion point to the end of the window); Delete (delete the current selection); and Shift+F10 (display the context menu).

The Immediate window also supports the following Visual Basic Editor keystrokes and key combinations:

- F5 continues running a macro.
- Alt+F5 runs the error-handler code for the current procedure.
- F8 single-steps through code (executing one statement at a time).
- Shift+F8 procedure-steps through code (executing one procedure at a time).
- Alt+F8 steps into the error handler for the current procedure.
- F2 displays the Object Browser.

Finally, the Immediate window has a couple of peculiar commands that you need to know:

- Pressing Enter runs the current line of code.
- Pressing Ctrl+Enter inserts a carriage return.

Printing Information to the Immediate Window

As well as entering statements in the Immediate window for quick testing, you can include in your macros statements to print information to the Immediate window by using the `Print` method on the `Debug` object. This provides you with a way of viewing information as a macro runs without having to be in Break mode or having to display a message box or dialog box that stops execution of the macro.

The syntax for the `Print` method is as follows:

```
Debug.Print [outputlist]
```

`outputlist` is an optional argument specifying the expression or expressions to print. You'll almost always want to include `outputlist`, because if you don't, the `Print` method prints a blank line, which is of little use to human or beast. Construct your `outputlist` using the following syntax:

```
[Spc(n) | Tab(n)] expression
```

Here, `Spc(n)` inserts space characters and `Tab(n)` inserts tab characters, with *n* being the number of spaces or tabs to insert. Both are optional arguments, and for simple output, you'll seldom need to use them.

`expression` is an optional argument specifying the numeric expression or string expression to print:

- To specify multiple expressions, separate them with either a space or a semicolon.

- A Boolean value will print as either `True` or `False` (as appropriate).

- If `outputlist` is `Empty`, `Print` will not print anything. If `outputlist` is `Null`, `Print` will print `Null`.

- If `outputlist` is an error, `Print` prints it as `Error` *errorcode*, where `errorcode` is the code specifying the error.

As an example, you could log the contents of the string expressions `CustName`, `Address1`, `Address2`, `City`, `State`, and `Zip` to the Immediate window in an address format by using the following statements:

```
Debug.Print CustName
Debug.Print Address1 + ", " + Address2
Debug.Print City + ", " + State + "  " + Zip
```

As another example, you could print the names and paths of all open files to the Immediate window by using the following statements in a macro:

```
For Each doc in Documents
    Debug.Print doc.FullName
Next
```

The Call Stack Dialog Box

When working in Break mode, you can summon the Call Stack dialog box (see Figure 16.10) to display a list of the active *procedure calls*, which are the procedures that are being called by the current procedure. When you start running a macro, that macro is added to the call stack list in the Call Stack dialog box; if that macro then calls another procedure (for instance, another macro), the name of that procedure is added to that list for as long as the procedure takes to execute; it is then removed from the list. By using the Call Stack dialog box, you can find out which procedures are being called by a macro, which can help you establish which parts of your code you need to check for errors.

FIGURE 16.10

Use the Call Stack dialog box to see a list of the procedures that are being called by the current procedure.

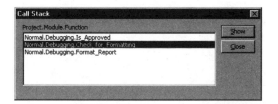

To display the Call Stack dialog box, click the Call Stack button on the Debug toolbar or select View ➤ Call Stack. To display one of the procedures listed in the Call Stack dialog box, select it in the Project.Module.Function list box and click the Show button. To close the Call Stack dialog box, click its Close button.

Dealing with Infinite Loops

You shouldn't find it hard to tell when a macro gets stuck in an infinite loop: you'll notice that the macro simply doesn't stop executing. To interrupt an infinite loop, press Ctrl+Break; this will display a "Code execution has been interrupted" dialog box.

There are several ways to guarantee that you'll get stuck in infinite loops, such as using GoTo statements without If conditions or Do loops without While or Until constraints. These are easy enough to avoid, but even if you do, it's still possible to have infinite loops occur in your code because of conditions you haven't been able to anticipate.

The best way to approach detecting and eliminating an infinite loop is to use breakpoints or a watch expression to pinpoint where the macro enters the infinite loop. Once you've reached it, you can use the Step Into command to step into the procedure and then use the Watch window or the Locals window to observe the variable and expressions in the loop, which should give you an indication of when something is going wrong and causing the loop to be endless.

If your code contains a loop that should execute for only a set number of times but which you suspect is running endlessly, you can use a counter in the loop with an `Exit For` statement or an `Exit Do` statement (whichever is appropriate) to exit from the loop if it runs more than a certain number of times.

Choosing Debugging Options

The General tab of the Options dialog box in the Visual Basic Editor (Tools ➤ Options) offers a number of options for debugging your macros. We looked at some of these in Chapter 5, and now we'll examine the remaining options in more detail.

Choosing How to Trap Errors

Your first choice is how to handle error trapping—how to direct execution of the macro when it encounters an error. The Error Trapping group box on the General tab of the Options dialog box offers three option buttons for error trapping: Break on All Errors, Break in Class Module, and Break on Unhandled Errors. We'll look at these in turn.

Break on All Errors

When you select Break on All Errors in the Error Trapping group box, you set VBA to enter Break mode when it encounters any error, no matter whether an error handler (code designed to handle errors) is active or whether the code is in a class module. Break on All Errors is useful for pinpointing where errors occur, which helps you track them down and remove them.

If you have an error-handling mechanism (which I'll discuss in "Dealing with Run-Time Errors" later in the chapter) in place, you probably won't want to use this option.

Break in Class Module

Break in Class Module is the default setting for the Error Trapping group box, and it's the most useful option for general use. When VBA encounters an unhandled error in a class module (a private module), VBA enters Break mode at the offending line of code in the module.

Break on Unhandled Errors

The third option in the Error Trapping group box is Break on Unhandled Errors. This option is useful when you have constructed an error handler to handle predictable errors in the current module. If there is an error handler, VBA allows the handler to trap the error, and does not enter Break mode; but if there is no error handler for the error generated, VBA enters Break mode on the offending line of code. An unhandled error in a class module, however, causes the project to enter Break mode on the line of code that invoked the offending procedure of the class, thus enabling you to identify (and alter) the line that caused the problem.

Choosing When to Compile Your Code

As you saw in Chapter 5, another choice you get to make on the General tab of the Options dialog box is when to compile the code in the current module. As you'll recall, VBA needs to compile the statements you write into executable code before it can execute them.

Compiling on Demand

When the Compile on Demand check box is selected, VBA compiles the code in the module that contains the macro when the code in the module is needed. VBA compiles the code in the macro you're running before starting to execute that macro, but it does not compile code in other macros in the same module unless the macro you're running calls them. This means that execution of the macro you run first in a module can start as soon as VBA finishes compiling the code for that macro; if the macro then calls another macro in the module, VBA compiles the code for the second macro when the first macro calls it, not when you start running the first macro.

Compile on Demand is usually a good option. It is especially useful when you are building a number of macros in a module. In contrast, if you clear the Compile on Demand check box, VBA will compile all the code in all the macros in the module before starting to execute the macro you want to run. This means that not only will the procedure start a little later (more code takes more time to compile), but any language error or compile error in any of the macros in the module will prevent you from running the macro you want to run, even if the code in that macro contains no errors.

Say you have a module named Compilation that contains two macros, GoodCode and BadCode, which look like this:

```
Sub GoodCode()
    MsgBox "This code is working."
End Sub

Sub BadCode()
    Application.Destroy
End Sub
```

GoodCode simply displays a message box to indicate that it is working; BadCode contains an invalid statement (there is, fortunately, no Destroy method for the Application object).

If you try to run GoodCode with Compile on Demand switched on, the macro will run fine: VBA will compile the code in GoodCode, will find no errors, and will run it. But if you try to run GoodCode with Compile on Demand switched off, VBA will compile the code in BadCode as well before starting to run GoodCode, and it will stop with a compile error at the bogus Application.Destroy statement. This thorough checking before running any code is good for finished modules that contain code that works together, but it's the kiss of death for experimenting with code in a module.

On the other hand, you can see the advantage of compiling all the code in the module when GoodCode calls BadCode, as in the third line of the version of the macro below.

```
Sub GoodCode()
    MsgBox "This code is working."
    BadCode
End Sub
```

Here, compiling the code in BadCode before starting to run GoodCode is a good idea, because it prevents GoodCode from running if BadCode has an error in it. If you run this version of GoodCode with Compile on Demand switched on, VBA will compile GoodCode and start to run it, displaying the message box in the second line. The BadCode call in the third line will then cause VBA to compile BadCode, at which point it will stop with the compile error. As you can imagine, you don't want this to happen in the middle of a complex macro; in such a case, you'd want Compile on Demand switched off.

Background Compiling

The Background Compile check box, which is available when the Compile on Demand check box is selected, controls whether the Visual Basic Editor uses idle CPU time to compile code. This can save a little time when it comes to executing the code.

You'll probably want to keep Background Compile switched on if your computer is tolerably fast with it active. If your computer is sluggish, you may find you get a little better response by switching Background Compile off and preventing the Visual Basic Editor from grabbing all your idle CPU time.

Dealing with Run-Time Errors

Despite the help that VBA provides in eliminating language errors and compile errors, run-time errors remain an unpleasant fact of life. Sooner or later, you're inevitably going to get errors in your code, but you don't have to take them lying down. VBA enables you to write *error handlers*, which are pieces of code that trap errors, analyze them, and take action if they match given error codes.

When Should You Write an Error Handler?

Consider writing an error handler in the following circumstances:

- When a run-time error can cause your code to fail disastrously. For a macro that applies minor formatting to a couple of words, you're unlikely to need an error handler; for a macro that creates, deletes, or moves files, you'll probably want an error handler.

- When you can identify particular errors that are likely to occur and that can be trapped. For example, when the user tries to open a file, certain errors can occur, such as if the file does not exist or is currently in use by another computer.

TIP In some instances, you may find it simpler to trap a resulting error from a procedure than to anticipate and try to forestall the various conditions that might lead to the generation of the error. For example, in Chapter 13, we looked at how you could check to make sure a file or folder existed before you tried to open it or manipulate it; instead of doing this, however, you can simply trap any error that results if the file or folder does not exist.

Trapping an Error

As you might guess, *trapping* an error means catching it so that you can do something about it; usually, you'll want to prevent an error from stopping your VBA code, but you can also anticipate particular errors and use them to determine a suitable course of action to follow from the point at which they occur.

To trap an error, you use the On Error statement. The usual syntax for On Error is as follows (we'll look at the other syntax variations in a minute):

```
On Error GoTo line
```

Here, line is a label specifying the line to which execution is to branch when a run-time error occurs. For example, to branch to the label named ErrorHandler, you could use a structure like this:

```
Sub ErrorDemo()
    On Error GoTo ErrorHandler
    'statements here
ErrorHandler:
    'error-handler statements here
End Sub
```

Usually, you'll want to place the error trap early in a procedure so that it is active and ready to trap errors for the rest of the procedure. If necessary, you can place several different error traps in a document by entering multiple On Error statements where they are needed, but only one can be enabled at a time. (*Enabled* means that an error trap has been switched on by an On Error statement. When an error occurs and execution branches to the error handler, that error handler is *active*.) Having multiple error handlers in a procedure can be useful when you're dealing with statements that require different types of action to be trapped. In the following structure, the first On Error statement directs execution to ErrorHandler1, and the second On Error statement directs execution to ErrorHandler2:

```
Sub ErrorDemo2()
    On Error GoTo ErrorHandler1
    'statements here
    On Error GoTo ErrorHandler2
    'statements here
ErrorHandler1:
    'statements for first errorhandler here
ErrorHandler2:
    'statements for second error handler here
End Sub
```

Each error handler is limited to the procedure in which it appears, so you can create different error handlers for different procedures and have each enabled in turn as the procedures run.

Because the error handler appears as code in the procedure, you need to make sure that it does not run when no error has occurred. You can do this by using either an Exit Sub statement before the error handler statement (to end execution of the macro) or a GoTo statement that directs execution to a label beyond the error-handling code. The Exit Sub statement is better if you choose to place your error handler at the end of its procedure, which is standard practice and usually makes sense; the GoTo statement may prove easier to use if you choose to place your error handler elsewhere in the procedure.

NOTE   For a function, use an Exit Function statement; for a property, use an Exit Property statement.

The following structure uses an `Exit Sub` statement to cause execution to end before the error handler if no error occurs:

```
Sub ErrorDemo3()
    On Error GoTo ErrorHandler
    'statements
    Exit Sub
ErrorHandler:
    'statements for error handler
End Sub
```

This next structure uses a `GoTo` statement to skip the error handler, which is placed within the code of the procedure, unless an error occurs. When execution reaches the `GoTo SkipErrorHandler` statement, it branches to the `SkipErrorHandler` label, thus bypassing the code in the error handler:

```
Sub ErrorDemo4()
    On Error GoTo ErrorHandler
    'statements
    GoTo SkipErrorHandler
ErrorHandler:
    'statements for error handler
SkipErrorHandler:
    'statements
End Sub
```

Disabling an Error Trap

As I mentioned, an error trap works only for the procedure in which it appears, and VBA disables it when it has finished executing the code in the procedure. You can also disable an error trap before the end of a procedure in which it appears by using the following statement:

```
On Error GoTo 0
```

You might want to disable an error trap while testing a macro to enable yourself to pinpoint errors that occurred after a certain point while retaining error-trapping for the first part of the macro.

Resuming after an Error

You use the `Resume` statement to resume execution of a macro after trapping an error or handling an error with an error-handling routine. The `Resume` statement takes three forms: `Resume`, `Resume Next`, and `Resume` *line*.

Using a Resume Statement

`Resume` itself causes execution of the procedure to resume with the line that caused the error. Use `Resume` with an error-handling routine that detects and fixes the problem that caused the offending statement to fail. For example, look at the error handler in Listing 16.1, which runs when VBA is unable to apply a specified style.

Listing 16.1

```
1.   Sub StyleError()
2.       On Error GoTo Handler
3.       Selection.Style = "Executive Summary"
4.       GoTo SkipHandler
5.   Handler:
6.       If Err = 5834 Then
7.           ActiveDocument.Styles.Add Name:="Executive
             ➥Summary", Type:=wdStyleTypeParagraph
8.           Resume
9.       End If
10.  SkipHandler:
11.       'execution of macro continues here
12.  End Sub
```

Analysis

Line 2 uses an `On Error` statement to enable the error handler `Handler`, which is identified by the `Handler` label in line 5. Line 3 applies the style named Executive Summary to the current selection. If all is well, the `GoTo SkipHandler` statement in line 4 directs execution to the `SkipHandler` label in line 10, and execution continues at line 11 (in which I've put only a comment, but which could be the first of a number of lines containing further statements). Line 12 then ends the macro.

If the `Selection.Style` statement in line 3 causes an error, execution branches to the `Handler` label in line 5, and the error handler is activated. Line 6 compares the error value to 5834, the code for the specified style not existing. If it matches, line 7 then adds the missing style to the document, and the `Resume` statement in line 8 causes execution to resume where the error occurred, with line 3. Because the specified style is now available, the `Selection.Style` statement will now run without an error, and the `GoTo SkipHandler` statement in line 4 will bypass the error-handler code.

Using a Resume Next Statement

`Resume Next` causes execution to resume with the next statement after the statement that caused the error. You can use `Resume Next` in either of the following circumstances:

- with an error-handling routine that ignores the error and allows execution to continue without executing the offending statement

- as a straightforward `On Error Resume Next` statement that causes execution to continue at the next statement after the statement that caused an error, without using an error handler to fix the error

As an example of the first circumstance, if the style specified in the previous example was not available, you could use a `Resume Next` statement to skip applying it:

```
Sub StyleError()
    On Error GoTo Handler
    Selection.Style = "Executive Summary"
    GoTo SkipHandler
Handler:
    Resume Next
SkipHandler:
End Sub
```

> **NOTE** The descriptions of `Resume` and `Resume Next` apply if the error occurred in the procedure that contains the error handler. But if the error occurred in a different procedure from the procedure that contains the error-handler, `Resume` causes execution to resume with the last statement to call out of the procedure that contains the error handler; `Resume Next` causes execution to resume with the statement *after* the last statement to call out of the procedure that contains the error handler.

How to Find Out Error Numbers

The VBA Help file provides a modest list of error numbers and descriptions under the Trappable Errors topic (choose "error messages, working with" from the Index tab of the Help Topics dialog box, then choose Trappable Errors in the Topics Found dialog box). Alternatively, you can generate a less-comprehensive list of your own by using a simple macro like this:

```
Sub Generate_List_of_Errors()
    For i = 1 to 1000
        If Error(Err) <> "Application-defined or object-
        ➥defined error" Then Selection.TypeText
        ➥Str(i) & Chr(9) & Error(Err) & vbCr
    Next i
End Sub
```

Here, the line inside the `For...Next` statement compares the error generated for the value of the counter `i` to *Application-defined or object-defined error*, which is VBA's generic description for any error VBA itself doesn't have a description of. If the error is other than the generic message, the `Selection.TypeText` statement enters the error in the active document, together with the value of `i`. You'll end up with a list that includes gems such as these:

- "96 Unable to sink events of object because the object is already firing events to the maximum number of event receivers that it supports"

- "97 Can not call friend function on object which is not an instance of defining class"

Beyond these lists of errors, the best way of finding out the number for a particular error is to cause the error yourself and note the number and description in the resulting dialog box.

Using a Resume Line Statement

`Resume line` causes execution to resume at the specified line. Use a label to indicate the line, which must be in the same procedure as the error handler.

For example, for a macro that tried open a particular file, you could create a simple error handler that used a `Resume line` statement, as shown in Listing 16.2.

Listing 16.2

```
1.  Sub Handle_Error_Opening_File()
2.  StartHere:
3.      On Error GoTo ErrorHandler
4.      FName = InputBox("Enter the name of the file to open.",
        ➡"Open File")
5.       If FName = "" Then End
6.      Documents.Open FName
7.      Exit Sub
8.  ErrorHandler:
9.      If Err = 5174 Then MsgBox "The file " + FName + "
        ➡does not exist." + vbCr + "Please enter the name
        ➡again.", vbOKOnly + vbCritical, "File Error"
10.      Resume StartHere
11.  End Sub
```

Analysis

Line 2 contains the `StartHere` label, to which execution will return from the `Resume` statement in line 10. Line 3 uses an `On Error` statement to enable the error handler `ErrorHandler`. Line 4 displays an input box prompting the user for the name of the file they want to open and stores the name in the variable `FName`, which line 6 then tries to open. Line 5 checks `FName` against a blank string and ends execution if it matches.

If the file exists and can be opened, execution passes to line 7, where an `Exit Sub` statement exits the macro, ending its execution. Otherwise, an error is generated, and execution branches to the `ErrorHandler` label in line 8, where the error handler becomes active. Line 9 then compares the value of the error to 5174, the code for VBA being unable to find the file. If the code matches, line 9 displays a message box advising the user of the error and prompting them to enter the correct file name. The `Resume` statement in line 10 then returns execution to the `StartHere` label in line 2. Line 11 ends the macro.

> **WARNING** You cannot use a `Resume` statement anywhere other than in an error-handling routine. (If you do, VBA produces an error.)

Handling User-Interrupts

Errors may seem quite enough of a problem, but you also need to decide what will happen if a user tries to interrupt your code by pressing Ctrl+Break while it is executing. You have three options here:

- You can allow a user-interrupt to stop your code dead in the water. This is the easy way to proceed (and, as the default condition, needs no effort on your part), but in complex macros, it may cause problems.

- You can prevent user-interrupts by disabling user input while the macro is running. This is simple to do, but you run the risk of creating unstoppable code if a procedure enters an endless loop.

- As a compromise between the above two options, you can allow user-interrupts during certain parts of a macro and prevent user-interrupts during more critical parts of a macro.

Disabling User Input While a Macro Is Running

To disable user input while a macro is executing, you disable the Ctrl+Break key combination by setting the `EnableCancelKey` property of the `Application` object to `wdCancelDisabled`:

```
Application.EnableCancelKey = wdCancelDisabled
```

VBA will automatically enable user input again when the macro stops executing. You can also enable user input again during a macro by setting the `EnableCancelKey` property to `wdCancelInterrupt`:

```
Application.EnableCancelKey = wdCancelInterrupt
```

Disabling User Input While Part of a Macro Is Running

You might want to temporarily disable user input while a macro was executing a procedure that didn't bear interruption and then re-enable user input when it was safe for the user to stop the macro again. For example, in a macro whose actions included moving a number of files from one folder to another, you could prevent the code that executed the move operations from being interrupted so that there was no risk of the user stopping the macro with some files still in the source folder and some in the destination folder:

```
'interruptible actions up to this point
Application.EnableCancelKey = wdCancelDisabled
For i = 1 to LastFile
    SourceFile = Source + "\Section" + Trim(i)
    DestFile = Destination + "\Section" + Trim(i)
    Name SourceFile As DestFile
Next i
Application.EnableCancelKey = wdCancelInterrupt
'interruptible actions after this point
```

WARNING   Never disable user input for any code that may get stuck in an endless loop. If you do, you'll have to close down the program from the Close Program dialog box in Windows 95 (reached by pressing Ctrl+Alt+ Delete) or the NT Task Manager in NT. This will cause you to lose any unsaved work in Word and might cause other applications to crash in Windows 95 (in NT, other applications should be protected by the operating system).

Documenting Your Code

You can greatly simplify debugging your macros by documenting your code; you do this by adding comments to it, either as you create the code or when you've finished creating it.

I recommend documenting your code as you create it in any macro in which you're exploring your way and trying different methods to reach your goal. Add comments to explain what action each group of statements is trying to achieve. Once you've gotten the macro to work, you can plow through the code and rip out abortive efforts wholesale, using the comments to identify which sections are now useless and which still worthwhile, and leaving only the comments that are relevant to how the remaining code functions. (You might also want to leave comment lines on any methods of achieving the same goal that you decided not to use. For example, if you think that you might be able to rewrite a macro to run a little faster when you have a few hours and some brain cells to spare, you could make a note of that. You could also note other possible applications for parts of the code in this macro to help you locate it if you need to reuse it in another macro.)

Likewise, add comments when you're changing an existing macro so that you don't lose track of your changes. Once you've got the macro working to your liking, remove any unnecessary comments.

On the other hand, documenting your code when you've finished writing it allows you to enter only the comment lines that you want to be there permanently. This is the way to go when writing code the direction of which you're fairly sure of when you start writing the macro, and which needs only a few pointers to make its code clear once it's complete.

To document your code, use comments prefaced by either the apostrophe character (') or the Rem keyword (short for *remark*). You can comment out either a whole line or part of a line: anything to the right of the apostrophe or the Rem keyword is commented out. For partial lines, the apostrophe is usually the better character to use; if you choose to use the Rem keyword, you need to add a colon before it to make it work consistently (some statements will accept a Rem without a colon at their end; others will generate a compile error):

```
Rem This is a comment line.
Documents.Add: Rem create a document based on Normal.dot
```

Generally, apostrophe-commented remarks separated by a few spaces from any statement the line contains, as in the second line below, are easier to read than comments using Rem:

```
'This is a comment line
Documents.Add          'create a document based on Normal.dot
```

If that was an eyebrow or a finger I saw you raising when I mentioned documenting your code, let me guess what you're thinking: you don't need to document your code because you'll be able to remember what it does. Trust me: you won't, not when you've written a good number of macros. Coming back to a macro six months after writing it, you'll find it as unfamiliar as if someone else had written it. And if you've advanced in your usage of VBA, you may even find it hard to think down to the clumsy methods you were using at that time.

Most programmers have a distinct aversion to documenting their code; in some, it's almost pathological. You can see why: when you're writing the code, documenting what it does slows you down and distracts you from your purpose; and when the code works, documenting it is tedious work. Besides, anyone worth their salt should be able to read the code and see what it does... shouldn't they?

Maybe so, but consider this: First, it's likely that you will not always be the person working on your code—at times, others will work on it too, and they'll appreciate all the help they can get in understanding your code. Second, the code on which you work will not always be your own—you may at times have to debug code that others have written, and in this case *you'll* be the one in need of comments.

I mentioned earlier in the chapter that you should split your code up into separate modules to simplify debugging it. Turn the page, and you'll find me discussing what modular code is and how you can create it.

CHAPTER

SEVENTEEN

17

Building Modular Code

So far in this book, we've concentrated on getting things done in Word by using Word's automation features and Visual Basic for Applications. The Visual Basic for Applications code we've constructed and examined up to now has been effective, but not particularly concise or elegant.

> **NOTE** *Elegant* in the context of computer code means not only that the code is bug-free and impeccably put together, and that the interface is well designed, but that the code contains nothing extra—it has been stripped down to the minimum required to achieve the desired effect.

In this chapter, we'll start looking at how to be more concise (and perhaps even more elegant) in your macros. We'll also start examining how you can create reusable code that you can apply to other macros, and how you can create your own non-macro procedures and functions. Fortunately, all these endeavors go together. The secret is to write modular code.

First, though, a quick word on the differences between macros, procedures, and functions.

Macros, Procedures, and Functions

I've been using the word *macro* in this book to denote a series of instructions starting with a `Sub` statement and ending with an `End Sub` statement. This is pretty accurate most of the time. As you'll see later in this chapter, though, `Sub` procedures break down into two basic types: those that do not take arguments and those that do. Technically, macros are `Sub` procedures that do not take arguments. So all macros are `Sub` procedures, but not all `Sub` procedures are macros. Some of the `Sub` procedures we'll be looking at in this chapter are macros; others take arguments and so are not macros. I mention the technical distinction in case you wanted to know; if you don't want to worry about this distinction, I'm right with you. The only practical difference between a macro and a `Sub` procedure is that you can run a macro on its own, but you cannot run a `Sub` procedure that is not a macro on its own. Instead, you have to call a non-macro `Sub` procedure from within a macro (or from another non-macro `Sub` procedure that you have called from a macro).

Functions are also procedures. Functions are easy to distinguish from macros and other `Sub` procedures because they start with a `Function` statement and end with an `End Function` statement. As you've seen, functions take arguments, and you call functions from within a macro (or from a `Sub` procedure run from a macro).

What Is Modular Code?

As you know from your work in the Visual Basic Editor, a module is a section or chunk of code in a Word document or template. Each document or template can contain no modules, one module, or multiple modules, and each module can contain any number of procedures, macros, and functions (or none of any). Within a module, you can run the individual macros separately, and you can call the individual functions and procedures separately from within the macro.

The terminology is a little confusing, because *modular code* is not so much code divided up into modules as I've just described, but code composed of different procedures that you can use in combination. For example, you could take a monolithic approach and create a single macro that created a document based on the user's choice of template, performed certain operations on it (e.g., inserting text and formatting it), saved the document in a particular folder under a name of the user's choice, printed the document to a specific printer, and then closed the document. Alternatively, you could take a modular approach and create a number of separate procedures—one for creating a document based on the user's choice of template, another for performing the text and formatting operations, another for saving the document, another for printing the document to the correct printer, and another for closing the document. You could then create a macro that ran these procedures to achieve the same effect as the monolithic macro; you could also create other macros that used the individual procedures in different combinations with other procedures to achieve different effects.

Advantages of Using Modular Code

Modular code has a number of advantages over code that lumps everything together in one long listing. For one thing, it is easier to write modular code, because you create a number of short procedures, each of which performs a specific task. You can usually debug these procedures relatively easily too, because their shorter length makes it simpler to identify, locate, and eliminate bugs. The procedures will also be more readable because they are less complex, and you can more easily follow what they do.

In addition, modular code provides a more efficient approach to programming, for four reasons:

- First, by breaking down your code into procedures, you can repeat actions at different points in a sequence of procedures without needing to repeat the lines of code, which makes for less code to compile and thus greater speed.

- Second, by reusing parts of your code (whole procedures), you can greatly reduce the amount of code you have to write.

- Third, if you need to change an item in the code, you can make a single change in the appropriate procedure instead of having to make changes at a number of locations in a long macro (and perhaps missing some of them). This change will then carry through to all macros that call the procedure.

- Fourth, you will be able to call individual procedures from other procedures without having to assimilate them into another macro.

How much you worry about creating modular code will vary from project to project, and from macro (or Sub procedure) to macro. For example, if you record a quick macro on-the-fly to perform a one-time task on a number of documents, there's no need to worry about stripping it down into its components and formalizing them as procedures. On the other hand, when you sit down to plan a macro that's going to revolutionize life as people know it in your workplace, you can benefit greatly from planning the code as a set of procedures—even if you decide to start the project by recording the macro.

You can go about creating modular code in two main ways:

- Record or write a macro as usual, then examine it and break it up into modules as necessary. This is a great way to start creating modular code, but it's usually less efficient: you'll end up spending a lot of time retrofitting your macros as you break them into procedures.

- Plan the different actions that a macro will take, and create each action (or set of actions) as a separate procedure. This method requires more forethought, but usually proves more efficient in the long run.

Arranging Your Code in Modules

Once you've created a set of procedures, you can move them to a different module within the same template, or even to a different template. By grouping your procedures in modules, you can easily distribute the procedures to your colleagues without including procedures they don't need. And by grouping your modules in templates, you not only give yourself an even easier way of distributing the modules and procedures, but you can remove from your immediate working environment (Normal.dot, or any other global templates you're loading) modules of code that you don't need, thus avoiding slowing down your computer.

> **TIP** Give your modules descriptive names so that you can instantly identify them in the Organizer dialog box.

Calling a Macro or Procedure

When a macro needs to use another macro or a procedure, it *calls* it. To call a macro in the same project, you simply enter the name of the macro to be called as a statement in the calling macro. For example, to call the macro `FormatDocument` from the macro `CreateReceiptLetter`, you could use the following statements:

```
Sub CreateReceiptLetter()
    'other actions here
    FormatDocument
    'other actions here
End Sub
```

As well as calling a macro or procedure in the same project, you can call a macro or procedure in another open project. To call a macro or procedure in another project, you need to add a reference to that project in the References dialog box (Tools ➤ References). For example, if you need to call the `Save_on_F_ Drive` macro in Normal.dot from the `CreateReceiptLetter` macro in the Receipt Letter.dot template (a different project), you would add a reference to Normal.dot in the References dialog box.

> **WARNING** You can't add a reference to a project that already contains a reference to the project to which you want to add the reference. For example, if Receipt Letter.dot already contains a reference to Normal.dot, you cannot add to Normal.dot a reference to Receipt Letter.dot: when you add the reference and close the References dialog box, the Visual Basic Editor will display a message box with the warning "Cyclic reference of projects not allowed" and will not place the reference.

Using Static Variables

In Chapter 10 I mentioned the `Static` keyword, which you can use for declaring variables whose values you want to preserve between calls to the procedure in which they are declared. This means that static variables are similar to public variables in that their lifetime is not limited to the duration of the procedure that declares them; the difference is that static variables, once declared, are available only to the procedure that declares them, whereas public variables are available to all procedures once they've been declared.

Static variables are useful for maintaining information on a process that you need to run a number of times during a Word session, either to maintain a running total (for example, a count of the times you performed a procedure) or to keep at hand a piece of information that may prove useful when you run a procedure a second or subsequent time.

> **NOTE** Like public variables, static variables take up memory once you've created them, so don't use them unnecessarily.

Listing 17.1 provides a straightforward example of how static variables work.

Listing 17.1

```
1.   Sub MakeStatic()
2.       Static LastTime As Date, TimesUsed As Integer
3.       If TimesUsed > 0 Then
4.           MsgBox "You have used this macro " & TimesUsed &
             ➥" times." & vbCr & vbCr & "You last used this
             ➥macro at " & LastTime & ".", vbOKOnly
             ➥+ vbInformation, "Demonstration of Static"
5.       End If
6.       LastTime = Time
7.       TimesUsed = TimesUsed + 1
8.   End Sub
```

Analysis

The MakeStatic macro uses one static variable to track the last time the macro was used and another to track how many times the macro has been used.

Line 2 declares the static variable LastTime as the Date data type and the static variable TimesUsed as the Integer data type. If this is the first time the macro has been run in the current Word session, VBA will create the variables and assign memory space to them; if the macro has already been run, the variables will retain their current memory space and their values. Line 3 then uses an If statement to check the value of TimesUsed; if it is greater than 0, line 4 displays a message box informing the user how many times they have run the macro and the time of the last use. Line 5 ends the If statement.

Line 6 sets `LastTime` to the current system time (returned by the `Time` function), and line 7 increases the value of `TimesUsed` by 1, making it reflect the number of times the macro has been run.

So the first time the macro is run, VBA creates the `LastTime` and `TimesUsed` static variables and assigns values to them. The second time and subsequent times the macro is run, VBA displays the message box, updates the `LastTime` variable, and increases the value of the `TimesUsed` variable.

Improving Your Code

So from now on you'll be writing modular code—but what else can you do to refine your code and make it run faster? Well, there are at least two other types of improvements you can make: logical improvements and visual improvements. We'll look at logical improvements first.

Logical Improvements

Breaking a macro into procedures can improve the logic of your code by forcing you to consider each set of actions the macro takes as modular, separate from other sets of actions (or even from other individual actions). But you can also improve the logic of your code by using explicit variable declarations, by simplifying any code you record, and by using `With` statements to reduce the number of object references.

Using Explicit Variable Declarations

As you saw in Chapter 10, you can declare variables either implicitly or explicitly. If you declare variables explicitly, you can specify which type each variable is, which allows VBA to allocate only as much memory as that variable type needs. (You can also specify a data type for an implicitly declared variable, by using its type-declaration character.)

Here again are the details on the amounts of memory that the different types of variables require:

Variable	Memory Needed (Bytes)
Boolean	2
Byte	1
Currency	8
Date	8
Decimal	12 (as I mentioned, only partly supported in Word 97)
Double	8
Integer	2
Long	4
Object	4
Single	4
String	Variable-length strings: 10 bytes plus the storage required for the string, which can be up to about 2 billion characters Fixed-length strings: the number of bytes required to store the string, which can be from 1 to about 64,000 characters long
Variant	Variants that contain numbers: 16 bytes Variants that contain characters: 22 bytes plus the storage required for the characters

How much memory can you reasonably expect to save by specifying data types, and how much difference will carefully choosing variable types make to your macros? Typically, the answer is not a lot. But in extreme circumstances—such as when using huge numbers of variables on a computer with limited memory—specifying the appropriate data types for your variables *might* save enough memory to enable your macro to run where it otherwise would not have been able to. The other bird you'll kill with this stone is to ensure optimal speed in your macros, which is always a noble aim, even if the users of your macros don't notice the efforts you've been making on their behalf.

The other reason for declaring your variables explicitly rather than implicitly is to make your code easier to read and to debug. In this case, you yourself will be the beneficiary of your good practice (or of whoever created the code and declared the variables explicitly).

The bottom line is that using explicit variable declarations is a good programming technique that can save you confusion and make your code easier to read. If you don't have time for this right now, keep it in mind for when you will have time.

Simplifying Recorded Code

As I've mentioned before, the macro recorder often provides a great way to kick-start your writing of a macro by letting you quickly identify the objects the macro will need to work with and the methods and properties you'll need to use with them. But as you've seen, the drawback of the macro recorder is that it tends to record a ton of code that you don't actually need in your macros, because it's faithfully detailing everything you *might* be trying to record. For example, when you record a macro that changes one setting in a dialog box such as the Font dialog box, the macro recorder records all the other settings on not only that tab of the dialog box but all other tabs as well—in case you wanted them, too.

Once you've finished recording the macro, you'll often want to open it to make minor adjustments, add loops or control structures (message boxes, input boxes, dialog boxes, etc.), or even crib parts of the macro wholesale for use in other macros or procedures. At the same time, you'll do well to study the code the macro recorder has recorded and, where possible, strip it down to leave only the pieces that you need.

For example, compare the `Recorded_Macro_Applying_Arial_Font` below with the `Stripped_Down_Macro_Applying_Arial_Font` that comes after it.

```
Sub Recorded_Macro_Applying_Arial_Font()
'
' Recorded_Macro_Applying_Arial_Font
' Macro recorded 7/11/97 by Rikki Nadir
'
    With Selection.Font
        .Name = "Arial"
        .Size = 10
        .Bold = False
        .Italic = False
```

```
            .Underline = wdUnderlineNone
            .StrikeThrough = False
            .DoubleStrikeThrough = False
            .Outline = False
            .Emboss = False
            .Shadow = False
            .Hidden = False
            .SmallCaps = False
            .AllCaps = False
            .ColorIndex = wdAuto
            .Engrave = False
            .Superscript = False
            .Subscript = False
            .Spacing = 0
            .Scaling = 100
            .Position = 0
            .Kerning = 0
            .Animation = wdAnimationNone
        End With
    End Sub

    Sub Stripped_Down_Macro_Applying_Arial_Font()
        With Selection.Font
            .Name = "Arial"
        End With
    End Sub
```

As you can see, the `Stripped_Down_Macro_Applying_Arial_Font` has the same effect as the recorded macro, but it contains five lines to the recorded macro's thirty. But because the `With` statement contains only one statement, you could make the macro even more economical by eliminating the `With` statement:

```
    Sub Apply_Arial()
        Selection.Font.Name = "Arial"
    End Sub
```

Using With Statements to Simplify Your Code

You just saw how you can tighten code by eliminating a `With` statement, but this tends to be the exception rather than the rule. When you're performing multiple actions with an object, you can often use `With` statements to reduce the number of object references involved, and thus simplify and speed up the code. When you need to work with multiple objects in a single object, you can either use separate With statements or pick the lowest common denominator of the objects you want to work with and use a common With statement along with nested With statements.

For example, the following statements contain multiple references to the Paragraphs(1) object in the ActiveDocument object:

```
ActiveDocument.Paragraphs(1).Range.Font.Bold = True
ActiveDocument.Paragraphs(1).Range.Font.Name = "Times New Roman"
ActiveDocument.Paragraphs(1).LineSpacingRule = wdLineSpaceSingle
ActiveDocument.Paragraphs(1).Borders(1).LineStyle =
➥wdLineStyleDouble
ActiveDocument.Paragraphs(1).Borders(1).ColorIndex = wdBlue
```

Instead, however, you could use a With statement that referenced the Paragraphs(1) object in the ActiveDocument object to simplify the number of references involved:

```
With ActiveDocument.Paragraphs(1)
    .Range.Font.Bold = True
    .Range.Font.Name = "Times New Roman"
    .LineSpacingRule = wdLineSpaceSingle
    .Borders(1).LineStyle = wdLineStyleDouble
    .Borders(1).ColorIndex = wdBlue
End With
```

You can further reduce the number of object references here by using nested With statements for the Font object in the Range object and for the Borders(1) object:

```
With ActiveDocument.Paragraphs(1)
    With .Range.Font
        .Bold = True
        .Name = "Times New Roman"
    End With
    .LineSpacingRule = wdLineSpaceSingle
    With .Borders(1)
        .LineStyle = wdLineStyleDouble
        .ColorIndex = wdBlue
    End With
End With
```

Visual Improvements

The second category of improvements you can make to your code consists of visual improvements—not aesthetics, but making your code as easy to read (and modify, if necessary) as possible.

Indenting the Different Levels of Code

As you've seen in the examples so far in this book, you can make your code much easier to follow by indenting the lines of code with tabs or spaces to show their logical relation to each other. You can click the Indent and Outdent buttons on the Edit toolbar, or press Tab and Shift+Tab, to quickly indent or unindent a selected block of code, with the relative indentation of the lines within the block remaining the same.

> **NOTE**
> You can't indent labels; if you try to indent a label, the Visual Basic Editor will remove all spaces to the left of the label as soon as you move the insertion point off the line containing the label. This can make for an unfortunate look to your otherwise neatly indented code, but it does make labels easy to spot.

Using Line-Continuation Characters to Break Long Lines

Use the line-continuation character (an underscore after a space) to break long lines of code into a number of shorter lines. This not only has the advantage of making long lines of code fit within the code window on an average-size monitor at a readable point size, but also enables you to break the code into more logical segments. For example, the statement below is uncomfortably long to read on-screen:

```
Application.Documents("Document with Long Name.doc")
➡.Paragraphs(1).Range.Words(1).Font.Size = 12
```

Instead, you could break the statement with a line-continuation character to make it easier to read:

```
Application.Documents("Document with Long Name.doc") _
.Paragraphs(1).Range.Words(1).Font.Size = 12
```

Because of the physical constraints of the line length in this book, I haven't been using line-continuation characters as much as I normally do. If I did, you'd be seeing lines with ➡ continuation arrows that led almost immediately to an underscore line-continuation character, which would be visually confusing.

Using the Concatenation Character to Break Long Strings

Because you can't use the line-continuation character to break a long string, you have to be a bit more creative and divide the string, then use the concatenation character (&) to sew the parts back together again; you can then separate the parts of the string with the line-continuation character. For example, consider a long string such as this:

```
BogusText = "Now is the time for all good men to come to the
➡aid of the party."
```

Instead, you could divide the string into two and then rejoin it like this:

```
BogusText = "Now is the time for all good men to come " & _
"to the aid of the party."
```

You can also use the addition character (+) for concatenating one string with another, but not for concatenating a string and a numeric variable—VBA will try to add them instead of concatenating them.

Using Blank Lines to Break Up Your Code

To make your code more readable, use blank lines to separate statements into logical groups. For example, you might segregate all the variable declarations in a macro as shown in the example below so that they stand out more clearly:

```
Sub Create_Rejection_Letter()

    Dim ApplicantFirst As String, ApplicantInitial As String,
    ➡ApplicantLast As String, ApplicantTitle As String
```

```
Dim JobTitle As String
Dim DateApplied As Date, DateInterviewed As Date
Dim Experience As Boolean

'next statements in the macro
```

> **NOTE** You'll notice that in the listings in this book, I've been using blank lines only to separate individual macros from one another; to save space in the book, I haven't been using blank lines to separate statements within macros, as I normally do.

Using Variables to Simplify Complex Syntax

You can use variables to simplify and shorten complex syntax. For example, you could display a message box by using an awkwardly long statement such as this one:

```
If MsgBox("The document contains no text." + vbCr + vbCr
➥+ "Click the Yes button to continue formatting the
➥document. Click the No button to cancel the procedure.",
➥vbYesNo + vbQuestion,
➥"Error Selecting Document: Cancel Procedure?") Then...
```

Alternatively, you could use one string for building the message, another for the title, and even another for the message box type:

```
Dim Msg As String
Dim TBar As String
Dim OKQ As Long
Msg = "The document contains no text." + vbCr + vbCr
Msg = Msg + "Click the Yes button to continue formatting the
➥document. "
Msg = Msg + "Click the No button to cancel the procedure."
TBar = "Error Selecting Document: Cancel Procedure?"
OKQ = vbYesNo + vbQuestion
If MsgBox(Msg, OKQ, TBar) Then...
```

At first sight, this looks more complex than the straightforward message box statement, mostly because of the explicit variable declarations that increase the length of the code segment. But in the long run, this type of arrangement is much easier to read, and much easier to modify. (For the record, though, I don't recommend replacing the `vbOKCancel + vbQuestion` part of the `MsgBox` statement with the variable—I just wanted to show that it's possible. Usually, you'll find it easier to read the `MsgBox` statement if you state the buttons in the conventional format than if you replace them with a custom designation. It's also usually easier to read the VBA constants than the values—the `vbOKCancel` constant rather than the value 1, the `vbQuestion` constant rather than the value 32, and so on—even though the values are much shorter to enter in code.)

Passing Information from One Procedure to Another

Often when you call another macro, you'll need to pass information to it from the calling macro, and, when the macro has run, either pass back other information or a modified version of the same information. You can pass information either by using arguments or by using private or public variables.

Passing Information with Arguments

Using arguments is the more formal way to pass information from one procedure to another: you have to declare the arguments you're passing in the declaration line of the `Sub` procedure in the parentheses after the procedure's name. You can pass either a single argument, or multiple arguments separated by commas:

```
Sub PassOneArgument(MyArg)
Sub PassTwoArguments(FirstArg, SecondArg)
```

You can pass an argument either *by reference* or *by value*. When a procedure passes an argument to another procedure by reference, the recipient procedure gets access to where the original variable is stored in memory and can change the original variable. By contrast, when a procedure passes an argument to another procedure by value, the recipient procedure gets only a copy of the information in the variable, and cannot change the information in the original variable. Passing an argument by reference is useful when you want to manipulate the variable in the recipient procedure and then return the variable to the procedure from which it originated. Passing an argument by value is useful when you want to use the information stored in the variable in the recipient procedure and at the same time make sure that the original information in the variable does not change.

By reference is the default way to pass an argument, but you can also use the `ByRef` keyword to state explicitly that you want to pass an argument by reference. Both the following statements pass the argument `MyArg` by reference:

```
Sub PassByReference(MyArg)
Sub PassByReference(ByRef MyArg)
```

To pass an argument by value, you must use the `ByVal` keyword. The following statement passes the `ValArg` argument by value:

```
Sub PassByValue(ByVal ValArg)
```

If necessary, you can pass some arguments for a procedure by reference and others by value. The following statement passes the `MyArg` argument by reference and the `ValArg` argument by value:

```
Sub PassBoth(ByRef MyArg, ByVal ValArg)
```

You can explicitly declare the data type of arguments you pass in order to take up less memory and ensure that your procedures are passing the type of information you intend them to. But when passing an argument by reference, you need to make sure that the data type of the argument you're passing matches the data type expected in the procedure. For example, if you declare a string and try to pass it as an argument when the receiving procedure is expecting a variant, VBA will throw an error.

To declare the data type of an argument, include a data-type declaration in the argument list. The following statement declares `MyArg` as a string to be passed by reference and `ValArg` as a variant to be passed by value:

```
Sub PassBoth(ByRef MyArg As String, ByVal ValArg As Variant)
```

You can specify an optional argument by using the `Optional` keyword. Place the `Optional` keyword before the `ByRef` or `ByVal` keyword if you need to use `ByRef` or `ByVal`:

```
Sub PassBoth(ByRef MyArg As String, ByVal ValArg As Variant,
➥Optional ByVal MyOptArg As Variant)
```

Listing 17.2 shows a stripped-down segment of a procedure that uses arguments to pass information from one procedure to another.

Listing 17.2

```
1.   Sub GetCustomerInfo()
2.       Dim CustName As String, CustCity As String,
         ➥CustPhone As Variant
3.       'Get CustName, CustCity, CustPhone from sources
4.       CreateCustomer CustName, CustCity, CustPhone
5.   End Sub
6.
7.   Sub CreateCustomer(ByRef CName As String, ByRef CCity
         ➥As String, ByVal CPhone As Variant)
8.       Dim Customer As String
9.       Customer = CName & " " + CCity + " " + CPhone
10.      'take action with Customer string here
11.  End Sub
```

Analysis

This listing contains two minimalist procedures, `GetCustomerInfo` and `CreateCustomer`, intended to show how to use arguments to pass information between procedures rather than do anything that's actually useful.

The first procedure, `GetCustomerInfo`, explicitly declares three variables in line 2: the string variables `CustName` and `CustCity`, and the variant variable `CustPhone`. Line 3 contains a comment indicating where the procedure would get the information for the variables. Line 4 calls the `CreateCustomer` procedure and passes to it the variables `CustName`, `CustCity`, and `CustPhone`.

Execution then switches to line 7, which starts the `CreateCustomer` procedure by declaring the arguments it uses:

- `CName` is declared as a string, to be passed by reference.
- `CCity` is declared as a string, to be passed by reference.
- `CPhone` is declared as a variant, to be passed by value.

Line 8 declares the string variable `Customer`. Line 9 then assigns to `Customer` the information in `CName`, a space, the information in `CCity`, another space, and the information in `CPhone`. Line 10 contains a comment indicating where the procedure would take action with the `Customer` string, and line 11 ends the procedure.

Passing Information with Private or Public Variables

Using private or public variables is the less formal way to pass information from one procedure to another, but it's quick and effective. You can use private variables if the procedures that need to share information are located in the same module; if the procedures are located in different modules, you'll need to use public variables to pass the information.

The disadvantage to using private variables or public variables to pass information among procedures is that doing so takes up more memory than passing information with arguments. But unless you grossly abuse private or public variables, you're unlikely to notice any problems from the extra memory overhead: a few private or public variables here and there aren't going to make much difference to the performance of most computers macho enough to run Office 97 at a decent clip.

Listing 17.3 contains an oversimplified example of how you can pass information by using private variables.

Listing 17.3

```
1.    Private PassMe As String
2.
3.    Sub PassingInfo()
4.        PassMe = "Hello."
```

```
5.       PassingInfoBack
6.       MsgBox PassMe
7.   End Sub
8.
9.   Sub PassingInfoBack()
10.       PassMe = PassMe + " How are you?"
11.   End Sub
```

Analysis

Listing 17.3 begins by declaring the private string variable `PassMe` at the beginning of the code sheet for the module. `PassMe` is then available to all the procedures in the module.

The `PassingInfo` macro (lines 3 to 7) simply assigns the text `Hello.` (with the period) to `PassMe` in line 4 and then calls the `PassingInfoBack` procedure in line 5. Execution then shifts to line 9, which starts the `PassingInfoBack` procedure. Line 10 adds `How are you?` with a leading space to the `PassMe` string variable. Line 11 ends the `PassingInfoBack` procedure, whereupon execution returns to the `PassingInfo` macro at line 6; line 6 displays a message box containing the `PassMe` string, which is now *Hello. How are you?* Line 7 ends the macro.

Using Functions

So far in this book we've mostly been talking about creating your own macros, but as I mentioned way back in Chapter 5 you can also create your own functions in VBA. As you may recall, a *function* is a procedure that returns a value to the procedure that called it. For example, we've used the built-in `Left` function to return the left part of a string.

As you just saw, you can create `Sub` procedures that take arguments so that they can receive information from a macro or another procedure. Likewise, the built-in Word functions we've looked at in earlier chapters use arguments to get information. For example, when you use the `Left` function, you indicate a `string` argument and a `length` argument:

```
Left(string, length)
```

Here, the `string` argument is a string expression specifying the string from which to take the leftmost number of characters specified by the `length` argument, which is a numeric expression. You pass the arguments to the `Left` function by substituting for `string` in the above syntax the string expression you want to use and for `length` the numeric expression you want to use. For example, to return the leftmost three characters from the string expression `Industrialization`, you could use the following statement:

```
X = Left("Industrialization", 3)
```

You can also use variables instead of the expressions. For example, you can return the number of characters denoted by the variable `MyValue` from the variable `MyString` by using the following statement:

```
X = Left(MyString, MyValue)
```

Functions that you create start with a `Function` statement and end with an `End Function` statement:

```
Function NeedsSmogCheck(CarYear As Integer)
    'contents of function
End Function
```

There are a couple of good reasons why I've saved functions until this point in the book. For one thing, functions are a little more complex to work with than macros. For another, creating and using functions means using modular code, because functions are stand-alone units that you can't run by themselves (you have to call them from a macro or procedure). Thirdly, because Word ships with a wide array of built-in functions (including the ones we've been looking at in the earlier chapters), under normal circumstances you won't need to create that many functions for working with VBA in Word. With Excel, on the other hand, because of the nature of the task you're likely to be performing, you're much more likely to want to create functions; they tend to be much better for crunching numbers than for manipulating text.

That said, let's take a look at how you can create your own functions when you need them.

Creating Your Own Functions

You create a function just like a macro, by working in the code window for the module in which you want to store the function. (You can't record a function; you have to write it.) Functions follow the same naming rules as other VBA items: alphanumerics and underscores are fine, but no spaces, symbols, or punctuation. To start creating a function, you type **Function**, the name of the function, and the necessary arguments in parentheses (we'll get to the arguments in a moment), and then press Enter; VBA will enter a blank line and an `End Function` statement for you:

```
Function MyFunction(MaxTemp, MinTemp)

End Function
```

The `Function` statement assigns to the given function name (here, `MyFunction`) the value that the function returns. In parentheses, separated by a comma, are the arguments that will be passed to the `Function` statement: here, the function will work with an argument named `MaxTemp` and an argument named `MinTemp` to return its result. If you want, you can define the data type of the arguments by including an `As` statement with the data type after the argument's name. For example, you could use the following statement to set the `MaxTemp` argument and `MinTemp` argument to the Double data type:

```
Function MyFunction(MaxTemp As Double, MinTemp As Double)
```

Like a macro, a function can have private or public scope; private scope makes the function available only to procedures in the module that contains it, and public scope makes the function available to all open modules. If you do not specify whether a function is private or public, VBA makes it public by default, so you don't need to specify the scope of a function unless you need it to have private scope. That said, if you do use explicit `Public` declarations on those functions you intend to be public, your code will be somewhat easier to read than if you don't:

```
Private Function MyFunction(MaxTemp, MinTemp)
Public Function AnotherFunction(Industry, Average)
```

Let's look at an example of how a function works. First, you declare it and its arguments. The following statement declares a function named `NetProfit`:

```
Function NetProfit(Gross, Expenses)
```

`NetProfit` uses two arguments, `Gross` and `Expenses`. Armed with this knowledge, you call `NetProfit` as you would a built-in Word function, by using its name and supplying the two arguments it needs:

```
MyProfit = NetProfit(44000, 34000)
```

Here, the variable `MyProfit` is assigned the value of the `NetProfit` function run with a `Gross` argument of `44000` and an `Expenses` argument of `34000`.

Once you've created a function, the Visual Basic Editor will display its argument list when you type the name of the function in a procedure in the code window, as shown here:

```
NetProfit(
    NetProfit(Gross, Expenses)
```

As you've seen earlier in this book, you call a function from within a macro (or within another function, if necessary). Listing 17.4 contains an example of calling a function: the `ShowProfit` macro calls the `NetProfit` function and displays the result in a message box.

Listing 17.4

```
1.    Sub ShowProfit()
2.        MsgBox (NetProfit(44000, 34000)),, "Net Profit"
3.    End Sub
4.
5.    Function NetProfit(Gross, Expenses)
6.        NetProfit = (Gross - Expenses) * 0.9
7.    End Function
```

Analysis

Lines 1 to 3 contain the `ShowProfit` macro, which simply calls the `NetProfit` function in line 2, passes it the arguments `44000` for `Gross` and `34000` for `Expenses`, and displays the result in a message box titled `Net Profit`.

Lines 5 to 7 contain the `NetProfit` function. Line 5 declares the function as working with two arguments, `Gross` and `Expenses`, telling VBA what to do with the two arguments that line 2 has passed to the function. Line 6 sets `NetProfit` to be 90 percent (`0.9`) of the value of `Gross` minus `Expenses`. Line 7 ends the function, at which point the value of `NetProfit` is passed back to line 2, which displays the message box containing the result.

Listing 17.5 contains a function that returns a string argument.

Listing 17.5

```
1.   Sub TestForSmog()
2.       Dim CYear As Integer, ThisCar As String
3.   BadValueLoop:
4.       On Error GoTo Bye
5.       CYear = InputBox("Enter the year of your car.",
     ➥"Do I Need a Smog Check?")
6.       ThisCar = NeedsSmog(CYear)
7.       If ThisCar = "Yes" Then
8.           MsgBox "Your car needs a smog check.", vbOKOnly
                 ➥+ vbInformation, "Smog Check"
9.       ElseIf ThisCar = "BadValue" Then
10.          MsgBox "The year you entered is in the future.",
             ➥vbOKOnly + vbExclamation, "Smog Check"
11.          GoTo BadValueLoop
12.      Else
13.          MsgBox "Your car does not need a smog check.",
             ➥vbOKOnly + vbInformation, "Smog Check"
14.      End If
15.  Bye:
16.  End Sub
17.
18.  Function NeedsSmog(CarYear As Integer)
19.      If CarYear > Year(Now) Then
```

```
20.           NeedsSmog = "BadValue"
21.       ElseIf CarYear <= Year(Now) - 3 Then
22.           NeedsSmog = "Yes"
23.       Else
24.           NeedsSmog = "No"
25.       End If
26. End Function
```

Analysis

This listing contains the macro TestForSmog (lines 1 to 16) and the NeedsSmog function (lines 18 to 26). The TestForSmog macro calls the NeedsSmog function, which returns a value indicating whether the user's car needs a smog check. TestForSmog uses this value to display a message box informing the user whether or not their car needs a smog check.

TestForSmog starts by declaring the integer variable CYear and the string variable ThisCar in line 2. Line 3 contains the BadValueLoop label, to which execution returns from line 11 if the user has entered an unsuitable value for the year of their car.

Line 4 contains an On Error statement to direct execution to the Bye label in line 15 if an error occurs. An error will occur if the user cancels the upcoming input box (or chooses its OK button with no value entered in its text box).

Line 5 displays an input box prompting the user to enter the year of their car. This line assigns to the CYear variable the value the user enters in the input box.

Line 6 then sets the value of the string ThisCar to the result of the NeedsSmog function running on the CYear integer variable. Execution now shifts to the NeedsSmog function (line 18), which evaluates CYear and returns the value for ThisCar.

Line 18 declares the function, assigning its value to NeedsSmog. The function takes one argument, CarYear, which is declared as an integer data type. Line 19 checks to see whether CarYear is greater than the value of the current year (Year(Now)). If so, line 20 sets the value of NeedsSmog to BadValue, which will be used to indicate that the user has entered a date in the future. If not, the ElseIf statement in line 21 runs, checking if the value of CarYear is less than or equal to Year(Now) - 3, the current year minus three. If so, line 22 sets the value of NeedsSmog to Yes; if not, the Else statement in line 23 runs, and line 24 sets the value of NeedsSmog to No. Line 25 ends the If statement, and line 26 ends the function. Execution then returns to the calling line (line 6) in the `TestForSmog` macro, to which the `NeedsSmog` function returns the value it has assigned to the `ThisCar` variable.

The rest of the `TestForSmog` macro then works with the `ThisCar` variable. Line 7 compares `ThisCar` to `Yes`; if it matches, line 8 displays a message box stating that the car needs a smog check. If `ThisCar` does not match `Yes`, line 9 compares `ThisCar` to `BadValue`. If it matches, line 10 displays an alert message box, and line 11 returns execution to the `BadValueLoop` label in line 3. If `ThisCar` does not match `BadValue`, the `Else` statement in line 12 runs, and line 13 displays a message box stating that the car does not need a smog check. Line 14 ends the `If` statement; line 15 contains the `Bye` label; and line 16 ends the macro.

You don't have to use a function as simply as the examples I've been showing here: you can also include a function as part of a larger expression. For example, you could add the results of the functions `NetProfit` and `CurrentBalance` (which takes a single argument) by using a statement such as this:

```
CurrentEstimate = NetProfit(44000, 33000) +
➥CurrentBalance(MainAccount)
```

In summary, to improve your macros, you'll probably want to graduate from monolithic code to modular code. The good news is that you don't have to make any great leaps to do so: you can build a macro, then strip it down into separate procedures as suits you; or you can plan your macros as a series of discrete procedures and create them that way from scratch.

Another aspect of improving your macros is learning how to build well-behaved ones—that is, macros that behave as you intended. We'll look at that next.

CHAPTER

EIGHTEEN

18

Building Well-Behaved Macros

Once you've built a macro that works consistently, you'll probably want to distribute it to as many of your coworkers as might possibly be able to use it, or at least to those who might be impressed by your imagination or industry. Before you distribute it, though, you should make sure that the macro is as civilized as possible in its interaction with the user and with the settings the user may have chosen on their computer. It's all too easy to distribute an apparently successful macro that runs roughshod over the user's preferences in Word or one that fails unexpectedly under certain circumstances. In this chapter, we'll look at how to avoid such problems and how to construct your macros so that the user will have no problem putting them into action.

What Is a Well-Behaved Macro?

Briefly put, a well-behaved macro is one that leaves no trace of its actions beyond those that the user expected it to perform. This means:

- making no detectable changes to the user environment, or restoring the previous settings if the macro needs to make changes.

- presenting the user with relevant choices for the macro and relevant information once the macro has finished running.

- showing or telling the user what is happening while the macro is running.

- making sure (if possible) that the macro is running on the appropriate item.

- anticipating or trapping errors wherever possible so that the macro does not crash; or if it does crash under exceptional circumstances, doing so as gracefully as possible and minimizing damage to the user's work.

- leaving the user in the optimal position to continue their work after the macro finishes executing.

- cleaning up any bookmarks, scratch documents, or folders that the macro creates in order to perform its duties.

Retaining or Restoring the User Environment

To ensure that your macros run properly, you'll frequently need to make changes to the user environment. For example, if the Track Changes feature is turned on, you'll need to turn it off if you want to perform any edits without having Word mark them with revision marks. Likewise, in certain views of Word, there are some actions you cannot perform, while other actions may produce results different from those you intended. For instance, selecting paragraphs in Outline view is a risky business because the outline can be collapsed to various degrees, each of which will cause a regular selection operation to select a different amount of text.

In these cases, you'll need to change the user environment at the beginning of the macro and then, at the end of the macro, restore the user environment to its original state. This means that at the beginning of a macro, you will need to store any settings that the macro will change. As I'll explain below, public or private variables usually provide the best means of storage for such information while a macro is running. Once the macro has finished its work, you retrieve the information from the variables and restore the settings.

Storing Environment Information

You'll often want to retrieve information about various Word settings at the beginning of a procedure, store that information during execution of the procedure, and then at the end of the procedure use that information to restore the user's working environment.

You can use local variables to store this type of information. This works well for any macro that does not need to call other macros, but it is no good for complex macros that call other macros in the same module or in other modules; for this, you need to use variables with greater scope.

Private and public variables provide the most convenient means of storing environment information while a macro is executing. As you'll recall from Chapter 10, private variables retain their value as long as the project that contains them is open, and can be accessed by any macro in the module that declares them. This makes them suitable for storing information that needs to be accessed by different macros in the same module that call each other.

If you need to make information available to procedures in other modules, you'll need to use public variables. Once you've declared a public variable, it will be available to all procedures in all modules during the current session of Word. For example, if you need to know the user's name and company for various macros, you might use an `AutoExec` macro to confirm these when the user started Word. You could then store these in public variables so that you could access them from any macro in any module.

> **NOTE** As I mentioned before, using public variables takes up memory, so don't use vast numbers of them unnecessarily, especially on any computer that is short of RAM.

Checking and Restoring the Browse Object in the Object Browser

As you saw in Chapter 11, the Object Browser provides an easy way to move quickly from object to object in the documents you work with, and so you may want to use it via VBA in your macros as well.

As you'll have noticed from working interactively in Word, settings in the Object Browser remain as they were last set (to use the technical term, the settings are *sticky*, so they *stick*). For example, when you use Find and Replace to search for some text or an object, the Object Browser changes to Find, so that after closing the Find and Replace dialog box you can continue the Find operation by clicking the Previous Find/Go To and Next Find/Go To buttons, into which the Previous Page and Next Page buttons at the foot of the vertical scroll bar will have transformed themselves. Therefore, when you use the Object Browser in a macro, you'll usually need to restore the previous Browse object at the end of a procedure to enable the user to continue using the Object Browser as they were before.

NOTE   A couple things to keep in mlnd: First, when you're working with the Object Browser in VBA, running a `GoTo` operation does not set the Browse object, but any other Browse object does stick. For example, if you set the Browse object to Find in a macro and then set it to GoTo, neither will be set as the Browse object after the macro ends (the Browse object will still be whatever it was before the Find and the GoTo operations); but if you simply set the Browse object to Find, the Browse object will remain set to Find when the macro ends. Second, if you use the Find feature from VBA without invoking the Object Browser, Find will not set the Browse object in the Object Browser. For example, if you run a `Selection.Find` statement or an `ActiveDocument.Content .Find` statement, the Object Browser will retain its previous setting.

To return or set the Browse object, you use one of the `Target` properties of the `Browser` object. These are the available `wdBrowse` objects:

Constant	Value	Meaning
wdBrowsePage	1	Page (the default setting)
wdBrowseSection	2	Section
wdBrowseComment	3	Comment
wdBrowseFootnote	4	Footnote
wdBrowseEndnote	5	Endnote
wdBrowseField	6	Field
wdBrowseTable	7	Table
wdBrowseGraphic	8	Graphic
wdBrowseHeading	9	Heading
wdBrowseEdit	10	Edit
wdBrowseFind	11	Find
wdBrowseGoTo	12	GoTo

To illustrate, you could set the Browse object to Table with the following statement:

```
Application.Browser.Target = wdBrowseTable
```

Once you've set the Browse object, you use the `Previous` and `Next` methods to move from instance to instance of the object. For example, to set the Object Browser's Browse object to Graphic and then move to the previous graphic in the document, you could use the following statements:

```
With Application.Browser
    .Target = wdBrowseGraphic
    .Previous
End With
```

Checking and Restoring the Current View

Before performing any intricate maneuvers, it's a good idea to check which view Word is in. If Word is in the "wrong" view for what you're trying to do, certain commands may fail. As you undoubtedly know from your everyday work in Word, some commands are not available in Print Preview; some are not available in Page Layout view; others are not available in Outline view or Master Document view; and a few are not available in Normal view. So you need to check the view Word is currently in, change it if it may prove problematic for your macro, and then restore the view afterward so that the user can proceed with their work.

To check the view, you return the `Type` property of the `View` object for either the `ActiveWindow` object itself or the `ActivePane` object in the `ActiveWindow` object. These are the available `WdViewType` constants:

Constant	Value	Meaning
wdNormalView	1	Normal view
wdOutlineView	2	Outline view
wdPageView	3	Page Layout view
wdPrintPreview	4	Print Preview
wdMasterView	5	Master view
wdOnlineView	6	Online Layout view

For example, to display the value representing the current view of the active window in a message box, you could use the following statement:

```
MsgBox ActiveWindow.View.Type
```

To change the view, you set the `Type` property. For instance, to change the view in the active window to Page Layout view, you could use the following statement:

```
ActiveWindow.View.Type = wdPageView
```

If you wanted to make sure that a procedure ran in Normal view and then restored the view to whatever the user was using before they ran the macro, you could use code like this:

```
UserView = ActiveWindow.View.Type
If UserView <> wdNormalView Then
    ActiveWindow.View.Type = wdNormalView
End If
'statements here
If UserView <> wdNormalView Then
    ActiveWindow.View.Type = UserView
End If
```

Here, the first line stores the current `Type` setting in the variable `UserView`. The second line then compares `UserView` to `wdNormalView`; if `UserView` is different than `wdNormalView`, the third line changes the view to `wdNormalView`. The fifth line is a comment line indicating where the other statements in the macro would appear. The sixth line again compares `UserView` to `wdNormalView`; this time, if `UserView` is different than `wdNormalView`, the seventh line switches the view back to `UserView`.

Checking and Restoring the Track-Changes Settings

Apart from being in the wrong view, one of the easiest ways to spoil the effect of a macro is to run it when Track Changes (known as *revision marking* in earlier versions of Word) is switched on when you didn't expect it to be. All the harmless little changes that you could otherwise make unnoticed—for example, replacing two paragraphs with one, removing stray spaces, adding an appropriate header and footer, and so on—will instead be revealed as brutal hacking at the text. Worse, if you've written any type of loop to remove unnecessary repeated items (such as spaces or paragraphs) until there are none left, the fact that Track Changes leaves the item marked as deleted but still present will cause the macro to go into an infinite loop.

To avoid either of these undesirable outcomes, check that Track Changes is not switched on before you make any changes to a document. If Track Changes is on, turn it off for the duration of the macro.

To find out the current state of Track Changes, you simply check the `Track-Revisions` property of the `Document` object; to change the state of Track Changes, you change the setting of this property. This is a Boolean property, which means it can only be `True` or `False`. So you could check to see if Track Changes was on, and turn it off if it was, by using the following statement:

```
If ActiveDocument.TrackRevisions = True Then
➡ActiveDocument.TrackRevisions = False
```

If you're building or maintaining a reputation of being considerate toward users of your macros, you'll probably want to store the setting for Track Changes in a variable. That way, you can turn Track Changes back on at the end of the macro, and the user will be none the wiser. Here's one example of how you might do so:

```
TrackChanges On = ActiveDocument.TrackRevisions
If TrackChanges On= True Then
    ActiveDocument.TrackRevisions = False
End If
'statements here
If TrackChanges On = True Then
    ActiveDocument.TrackRevisions = True
End If
```

At other times, you may need to turn Track Changes on, such as when you want to make sure that the user can review changes that a document makes to a macro. Say you wanted to create a macro that edited a sentence or a paragraph and then displayed it on-screen with revision marks and a dialog box allowing the user to accept or reject the changes. In such cases, you will need to check not only whether Track Changes is on, but whether the changes are being displayed on-screen.

The `ShowRevisions` property of the `Document` object controls the display of revisions on-screen. Like `TrackRevisions`, `ShowRevisions` is a Boolean property, so it's easy to work with. You could use the following statements to check whether revisions were being displayed and display them if they weren't:

```
If ActiveDocument.ShowRevisions = False Then
➥ActiveDocument.ShowRevisions = True
```

Tracking All the Properties You Need to Know About

When you're writing a macro, checking to see what esoteric settings the user has chosen is likely to be one of the last things on your mind. However, you can save a lot of time by putting together a short check of the user's environment before you run any macro that contains a command contingent on some settings being in a certain state: the view, the pane or story, the position of the insertion point, and so on.

To track the relevant properties, you could write a procedure that returned and stored the user's settings and run it as a matter of course at the beginning of every procedure for which you needed to retrieve some information. While running extra information that you do not strictly need will take a little time during execution of a macro that calls it, having the stored environment information on hand may save you time in the construction of your macros and so prove worthwhile.

Leaving the User in the Best Position to Continue Work

In order to leave the user of your macros in the best position to continue their work—in other words, without needing to reposition the insertion point in the current document, or switch to another document, or reopen a file—you need to plan carefully which document a macro will leave active and where in the document the current selection will be:

- For a straightforward text-manipulation macro, you'll usually want to restore the selection to where it was when the user started the macro. This enables the user to proceed from where they left off without repositioning the insertion point manually or finding their place. You saw one example of this in the `Move_Current_Paragraph` macro back in Chapter 5, when we added a bookmark to identify the starting selection at the beginning of the macro, and then moved the selection back to the bookmark and deleted the bookmark at the end of the macro.

- For a macro that adds text to the active document, you'll typically want to end the macro with the insertion point either immediately after the added text or at the beginning of a new paragraph, depending on what kind of text the macro inserts and what the user is likely to want to do afterwards.

- For a macro that performs formatting tasks on the active document, you'll usually have the user start the macro while the range that they want to affect is selected. After such a macro, you'll probably want to move the selection to the end of the selected range so that the user can continue their work from that point.

- If a macro needs to temporarily make active a document other than the document the user was working in, you'll usually need to make the original document active again at the end of the macro. On the other hand, if a macro creates a new document that the user will need to work in right away, you'll need to make that document active rather than the document the user was working in. To make a document active, use the `Activate` method for the appropriate document.

- Likewise, if the macro creates a new document containing fields that the user will need to fill in, you'll probably want to move the insertion point to the first of those fields.

Keeping the User Informed during the Macro

A key component of a successful macro is keeping the user adequately informed throughout the process. In a simple macro, adequate information may entail nothing beyond a lucid description in the macro's Description field to assure the user they're choosing the right macro. In a more complex macro, adequate information will also be much more complex; you may need to display a starting message box or dialog box, show information on the status bar during the macro, display an ending message box, and/or create a log file of information so that the user has a record of what took place during execution of the macro.

The first consideration, though, is whether to disable user input during the macro. As you saw in Chapter 16, you can disable user input to protect sensitive sections of your macros by setting the `EnableCancelKey` property of the `Application` object to `wdCancelDisabled`. When you do so, you may want to indicate to the user at the beginning of the macro that input will be disabled, and explain why.

To keep the user informed about other aspects of the macro, you have several options, which I'll discuss in the following sections. But first, let's look at how you can *hide* information from the user (and the reasons for doing so) by disabling screen updating.

Disabling Screen Updating

For many macros, you'll want to disable screen updating—that is, stop the redrawing of the information in the document area of the Word window. (The other parts of the Word window—the title bar, command bars, status bar, scroll bars, and so on—continue to update, but these items are usually relatively static while you're working with Word and so do not take much updating. Still, if you change the size of the application window or the document window, you'll see that change even with screen updating disabled.)

There are two advantages to disabling screen updating:

- First, you can speed up the running of your macros quite significantly, particularly on computers that have slow graphics cards. This applies especially to macros that cause a lot of changes to what is displayed on-screen. For example, in a macro that strips a certain type of information out of the current document, pastes it into a new document, creates a table out of it, and applies functional formatting to the table, your computer will spend a fair amount of effort updating what is appearing on the monitor. This is wasted effort if the user isn't hanging on every operation, so you might as well turn screen updating off.

- Second, you can hide from the user any parts of the macro that you don't want them to see. This sounds totalitarian, but it's usually more like a cross between benevolent dictatorship and public television: there are certain things you shouldn't see because they might upset you, and there's a lot that you don't *really* need to know about. So with macros: if the user doesn't know about the operations that a macro will routinely perform to achieve certain effects, they may be surprised or dismayed by what they see on-screen. For example, in a macro that moves an open file (the procedure shown in Listing 13.4), you might want to hide from the user the fact that the macro closes the open file, moves it, and then reopens the file from its new location. By disabling screen updating, you can achieve this effect.

The major disadvantage to disabling screen updating is that, as you might imagine, doing so prevents the user from seeing information that might be useful to them. In the worst case, the user might assume from the lack of activity on-screen that the macro has entered an endless loop or the computer has hung, and so they might try to stop the macro by pressing Ctrl+Break or shake up Windows by pressing Ctrl+Alt+Delete until they get a reaction.

To forestall the user from disrupting a macro or an application with a two- or three-finger salute, it's a good idea to warn them in advance that a macro will disable screen updating. For instance, you might mention the fact in a message box at the beginning of the macro, or you might display a dialog box that allowed the user to choose whether to disable screen updating and have the macro run faster or to leave screen updating on and have the macro run at its normal speed.

If you don't display a message box or dialog box at the beginning of a macro, you may want to display information on the status bar to tell the reader what's going during the macro. (As I mentioned, Word updates the status bar and the title bar of the application even if screen updating is turned off—at least, if the status bar and the title bar are visible.) To display information on the status bar, use the `StatusBar` property of the `Application` object as discussed in Chapter 6.

Alternatively, you can disable screen updating for parts of a macro and turn it back on for other parts. Consider a macro that creates and formats a number of documents from an existing document. If you turn screen updating off at the beginning of the macro, restore it briefly once each document has been created and formatted and then turn it off again until the next document is finished, the user will see each document in turn (which conveys the progress the macro is making) without seeing the ugly details of the formatting. What's more, the macro will run significantly faster than if the screen were showing all of the formatting taking place.

Displaying Information at the Beginning of a Macro

At the beginning of many macros or procedures, you'll probably want to display a message box or a dialog box. A message box for this purpose will typically be a Yes/No or OK/Cancel message box that tells the user what the macro will do and gives them the chance to cancel the macro without running it any further. A dialog box will typically present options for the macro (for example, mutually exclusive options via option buttons or non-exclusive options via check boxes), allowing the user to enter information (via input boxes, list boxes, or combo boxes) and of course allowing them to cancel the macro if they've cued it by accident.

TIP As I mentioned earlier, you can also use a message box or dialog box to warn the user that the macro is going to turn off screen updating. Likewise, if the macro will disable user-interrupts for part or all of its duration, warn the user about that, too.

Displaying Information in a Message Box or Dialog Box at the End of a Macro

With some macros, you'll find it useful to collect information on what the macro is doing so that you can display that information to the user in a message box or dialog box when the macro stops running. As you saw in Chapters 6 and 7, message boxes are easier to use but are severely limited in their capabilities for laying out text (you're limited to the effects you can achieve with spaces and carriage returns), whereas with dialog boxes you can lay out text however you need to (by using labels or text boxes).

The easiest way to collect information while running a macro is to build one or more strings containing the information you want to display. To illustrate, let's go back to the `Create_Folders` macro we looked at in Chapter 8 and collect some simple information from it (see Listing 18.1).

Listing 18.1

```
1.   Private Sub cmdOK_Click()
2.       frmCreateFolders.Hide
3.       Unload frmCreateFolders
4.       ChDir "c:\work"
5.       Msg$ = "The Create_Folders macro has created the
             following folders:" + vbCr + vbCr
6.       For i = 1 To HowManyFolders
7.           Count$ = Trim$(Str$(i))
8.           If i < 10 Then Count$ = "0" + Count$
9.           FolderName$ = ISBN + "c" + Count$
10.          Msg$ = Msg$ + "     " + FolderName$ + vbCr
11.          MkDir FolderName$
12.      Next i
13.      MsgBox Msg$, vbOKOnly + vbInformation, "Create Folders"
14.  End Sub
```

Analysis

This code is attached to the OK button in the Create Folders dialog box and runs on the `Click` event for that dialog box. As before, line 2 removes the `frmCreate-Folders` dialog box from the display, and line 3 unloads it from memory. Line 4 changes folders to the `c:\work` folder.

Line 5 implicitly declares a string called Msg$ and assigns to it the first line for the message box and two carriage returns to end its paragraph and create a blank paragraph after it. Lines 6 through 12 then contain the loop that builds the folder names and creates them using the MkDir statement in line 11. Line 10 adds to the Msg$ string four spaces (to produce an indent), the current contents of FolderName$ (the name of the folder about to be created), and a carriage return to end the paragraph.

At the end of the loop, line 13 displays a message box containing the Msg$ string, informing the user which folders were created.

Creating a Log File

If you need to collect a lot of information during the course of running a macro and present it to the user once the macro has finished, you may want to use a log file rather than a message box or dialog box. Log files are useful for lengthy procedures involving critical data: by writing information periodically to a log file (and by saving it frequently), you can keep a record of what the macro achieved before any crash it suffered.

For example, if you wrote a macro that collected information from a variety of sources each day and wrote it into a report, you might want to keep a log file that tracked whether information from each source was successfully transferred, and at what time. You could do so by using code such as that shown in Listing 18.2. At the end of the macro, you could leave the log file open so that the user could check whether the macro was successful in creating the report, or leave the summary file open so that the user could read the report itself.

Listing 18.2

```
1.   Sub Log_File_Example()
2.       Dim CurDate As String, CurPath As String,
         ➡Chicago As String, Toronto As String,
         ➡NewYork As String, LogText As String,
         ➡LogName As String, Summary As String,
         ➡TestFile As String
3.       On Error GoTo Crash
4.       CurDate = Month(Date) & "-" & Day(Date) & "-"
         ➡& Right(Year(Date), 2)
5.       CurPath = "u:\Daily Data\"
```

```
6.      Chicago = CurPath + "Chicago " + CurDate + ".doc"
7.      Toronto = CurPath + "Toronto " + CurDate + ".doc"
8.      NewYork = CurPath + "New York " + CurDate + ".doc"
9.      LogName = CurPath + "Reports\Log for " + CurDate
➥+ ".doc"
10.     Summary = CurPath + "Reports\Summary for " + CurDate
➥+ ".doc"
11.     Documents.Add
12.     ActiveDocument.SaveAs Summary
13.     TestFile = Dir(Chicago)
14.     If TestFile <> "" Then
15.         Documents.Open Chicago
16.         Documents(Chicago).Paragraphs(1).Range.Copy
17.         Documents(Chicago).Close
18.         With Documents(Summary)
19.             Selection.EndKey Unit:=wdStory
20.             Selection.Paste
21.             .Save
22.         End With
23.         LogText = LogText + "Chicago: OK" + vbCr
24.     Else
25.         LogText = LogText + "Chicago: No file" + vbCr
26.     End If
27.     TestFile = Dir(NewYork)
28.     If TestFile <> "" Then
29.         Documents.Open NewYork
30.         Documents(NewYork).Paragraphs(1).Range.Copy
31.         Documents(NewYork).Close
32.         With Documents(Summary)
33.             Selection.EndKey Unit:=wdStory
34.             Selection.Paste
35.             .Save
36.         End With
37.         LogText = LogText + "New York: OK" + vbCr
38.     Else
39.         LogText = LogText + "New York: No file" + vbCr
40.     End If
41.     TestFile = Dir(Toronto)
42.     If TestFile <> "" Then
43.         Documents.Open Toronto
44.         Documents(Toronto).Paragraphs(1).Range.Copy
45.         Documents(Toronto).Close
```

```
46.            With Documents(Summary)
47.                 Selection.EndKey Unit:=wdStory
48.                 Selection.Paste
49.                 .Save
50.            End With
51.            LogText = LogText + "Toronto: OK" + vbCr
52.        Else
53.            LogText = LogText + "Toronto: No file" + vbCr
54.        End If
55.  Crash:
56.        Documents.Add
57.        Selection.TypeText LogText
58.        ActiveDocument.SaveAs LogName
59.        Documents(LogName).Close
60.        Documents(Summary).Close
61.  End Sub
```

Analysis

This macro creates a new document to contain a summary, opens a number of files in turn, copies the first paragraph out of each and pastes it into the summary document, and then closes the file. As it does this, it maintains a string of log information from which it creates a log file at the end of the macro or if it runs into an error during the macro.

Line 2 explicitly declares nine string variables that the macro will use: `CurDate` (for the current date), `CurPath` (for the current path), `Chicago` (the name of the file from the Chicago office), `Toronto` (the name of the file from the Toronto office), `NewYork` (the name of the file from the New York office), `LogText` (the log information), `LogName` (the name for the log file), `Summary` (the name for the summary file), and `TestFile` (the result of a `Dir` search for a specified file).

Line 3 uses an `On Error` statement to set up error handling for the macro, directing execution to the `Crash` label in line 55 if an error occurs.

Line 4 assigns to `CurDate` a date string created by concatenating the month, the day, and the rightmost two characters of the year for the current date (with a hyphen between each) by using the `Month`, `Day`, and `Year` functions, respectively. For example, April 11, 1997 will produce a date string of `4-11-97`. (The reason for creating a string like this is because Windows cannot handle slashes in file names—slashes are reserved for indicating folders.)

Line 5 sets CurPath to the u:\Daily Data\ folder. Line 6 then builds a file name for the day's report from the Chicago office by concatenating CurPath, the word Chicago (with a space after it), CurDate, and .doc at the end (for example, u:\Daily Data\Chicago 4-11-97.doc). Line 7 similarly creates a file name for the Toronto office and line 8 a file name for the New York office. Line 9 creates a file name for the log file in the \Reports\ subfolder, and line 10 creates a file name for the summary file, also in the \Reports\ subfolder.

Line 11 creates a new document based on Normal.dot, and line 12 saves this under the name stored in the Summary variable.

Line 13 then assigns to TestFile the result of searching for the file with the name stored in the variable Chicago. Line 14 checks to see if TestFile is an empty string, which would indicate that no file of that name was found; if it is not an empty string, the statements for the If condition run: line 15 opens the file, line 16 copies the first paragraph from it, and line 17 closes the file. Lines 18 to 22 then use a With statement to work with the Summary document: line 19 moves the selection to the end of the document, line 20 pastes in the paragraph copied from the Chicago document, and line 21 saves the document. Line 23 adds to the string LogText the information that Chicago was OK.

If TestFile is an empty string, and the file is not available, execution shifts to the Else statement in line 24. Line 25 then executes, adding to the string LogText the information that no file was found for Chicago. Line 26 ends the first If clause.

Lines 27 through 40 then repeat lines 13 to 26 for the filename stored in the NewYork variable, and lines 41 to 54 repeat them again for the Toronto variable.

Line 55 contains the label Crash to which execution moves if VBA encounters an error in the macro; if VBA encounters no error, the macro reaches the label after executing the End If statement in line 54 and passes over the label to the next line. Line 56 creates a new document based on Normal.dot; line 57 enters the LogText string into the document; line 58 saves the document under the name stored in LogName; and line 59 closes the document. (Alternatively, you could leave the document open so that the user could view it.)

Line 60 closes the Summary document (which has remained open since it was created; again, you might want to leave this open so that the user could view it), and line 61 ends the macro.

Making Sure the Macro Is Running under Suitable Conditions

Another important element of creating a well-behaved macro is to check that it is running under suitable conditions. This is nearly impossible to achieve under all circumstances, but you should take some basic steps, such as the following:

- making sure that a document is open in a macro that needs a document to be open

- checking that the macro is running on an appropriate item, if it has definable requirements

- making sure the macro is working with the appropriate story

- making sure the document contains the element required by the macro

We'll look at each of these points in turn in the following sections.

Making Sure That a Document Is Open

First and simplest, for many macros you'll want to make sure that a document is open before you run them. For example, any macro that performs straightforward text manipulation or formatting on a document needs a document to be open; if none is, VBA will return an error.

To check that a document is open, use the `Count` property of the `Documents` collection object. For example, the first of the following statements makes sure that the `Documents` collection contains at least one open document before applying the Heading 1 style to the first paragraph of the active document:

```
If Documents.Count > 0 Then
    ActiveDocument.Paragraphs(1).Range.Style = "Heading 1"
End If
```

Checking That the Macro Is Running on an Appropriate Item

Second, where possible, check that the macro is running on an appropriate item. For example, the `Transpose_Three_Words` macro in Chapter 12 checked to make sure that three words were selected before it took any action. If the current selection was not three words, the macro didn't run, because it would probably not be able to accomplish what it was supposed to do; instead, it displayed a message box explaining the problem to the user and prompting them to select three words and run the macro again.

Making Sure You're Working with the Appropriate Story

The next thing to check is that the macro is starting off in the appropriate story in Word—that is, in the appropriate part of the document. As you'll remember from Chapter 12, Word identifies eleven different story types, from the `wdMainTextStory` that represents the main text of the document to the `wdFirstPageFooterStory` that represents the contents of the first-page footer (if the document has one).

To make sure that a macro does not run on any part of a document other than the main text, you could use the following statement early in a macro:

```
If Selection.StoryType <> wdMainTextStory Then End
```

This will spare your macro the embarrassment of producing a beautifully formatted table from, say, the text in the Comments pane rather than the contents of the document.

Making Sure the Document Contains the Required Object

Before performing an action on an object in a document, check that the document actually contains the object in question. If the document does not contain the object you've specified, VBA will return an error.

For example, to select the last table in a document and apply the Table Body style to it, you could use the following statements. The `If` condition in the second line checks to make sure that the `Tables` collection object in the active document contains a table before running the `Select` and `Style` statements:

```
With ActiveDocument
    If .Tables.Count > 0 Then
        .Tables(.Tables.Count).Select
        Selection.Style = "Table Body"
    End If
End With
```

In some cases, you won't need to formally check whether an object exists. For example, if you wanted to take action on all the tables in a document one after another, you could use a `For... Next` loop like the one in the following statements, without checking whether the document contains a table; if it contains no table, the loop will not run (because `ActiveDocument.Tables.Count` is 0):

```
For i = 1 to ActiveDocument.Tables.Count
    Selection.Style = "Table Body"
Next i
```

> **TIP**
>
> Another alternative to checking for an object's existence is to trap the error resulting from the object not being found; but for something as simple as checking whether a document contains a table or a bookmark, it's usually more complicated to figure out which errors might occur than to prevent them from occurring in the first place.

Cleaning Up after a Macro

It goes without saying that your macros should clean up after themselves. This involves the following:

- undoing any changes that the macro had to make to enable itself to run
- removing any bookmarks that the macro added to perform its duties
- closing any documents that no longer need to be open

- removing any scratch files or folders that the macro has created to achieve its effects

Undoing Changes the Macro Has Made

In some (usually rare) cases, you'll need to make changes to a document in order to carry out certain formatting operations. For example, if you need to manipulate half of a table, you may find it easier to split the table into two tables so that you can select columns in the relevant part and format or change them without affecting the columns in the other half of the original table. If you perform a procedure like this, you'll want to join the table together again afterward by removing the break you've inserted between its two halves. The easiest way to do this is to bookmark the break that you insert; you can then go back to the bookmark and delete it and the break at the same time. Alternatively, you could use a `Set` statement to define a range for the break, and then return to the range and remove the break.

Removing Bookmarks the Macro Has Added

If you add bookmarks to a document to help, say, identify a location in text or reposition the insertion point at the end of a macro exactly where it was at the start of the macro, be sure to remove the bookmarks afterward; see Chapter 15 for instructions on deleting a bookmark.

Removing Scratch Files and Folders

During a complex macro, you may need to create scratch files in which to temporarily store or manipulate information, or scratch folders in which to store files. For example, if you need to perform complex formatting on a few paragraphs of a long document, you may find it easier to copy and paste those paragraphs into a new blank document, and manipulate them there rather than continue working in the same document and risk unintentionally affecting other paragraphs as well.

Creating scratch files, while often necessary for the safe and successful operation of a macro, is antisocial toward the user of the computer: you're cluttering up their drive with information that's probably of no use to them. Creating scratch folders in which to save the scratch files is even worse. Always go the extra distance to clean up any mess that you've made on the drive, and remove both scratch files and scratch folders that you've created.

If your macro is going to remove any scratch files it creates, you may be tempted to conceal from the user their creation and subsequent deletion. This usually isn't a good idea; in most cases, the best thing is to warn the user that the macro will create scratch files. You might even let the user specify or create a suitable folder for the scratch files. This will allow the user to safely remove any scratch files left on their computer if a macro goes wrong or is interrupted during execution.

Building a Scratch Folder

You can use the `MkDir` statement to create a folder, as described in Chapter 13. For example, you could create a folder named `Scratch Folder` on the C: drive by using the following statement:

```
MkDir "c:\Scratch Folder"
```

Before creating a folder, check to see that the name isn't already in use; if a folder with that name already exists, Word will throw an error. To check if a folder exists, use the `Dir` statement as discussed in Chapter 13.

> **TIP**
>
> For temporary storage, you may want to build a folder name based on the date and time to lessen the chance that a folder with that name already exists.

Deleting the Scratch Folder

You can use the `RmDir` statement (also discussed in Chapter 13) to remove an empty folder. For example, to remove the scratch folder named `Scratch Folder` on the C drive, you could use the following statement (after making sure that the folder was empty):

```
RmDir "c:\Scratch Folder"
```

Enough on good behavior for macros for the moment. It's time for me to practice a little good behavior of my own. For the rest of the book, I'll try to put these principles into effect in the macros I show you.

CHAPTER
NINETEEN

19

Building Complex Dialog Boxes and ActiveX Forms

In this chapter, we'll pick up the discussion of dialog boxes that we left way back in Chapter 7, where I showed you how to create straightforward dialog boxes that used straightforward controls such as command buttons, check boxes, option buttons, and list boxes. These dialog boxes were static—the information in them remained the same as the user worked in them. Here, we'll start by investigating how to create *dynamic* dialog boxes—ones that change and update themselves when the user clicks a control within them. Dynamic dialog boxes cost you a little more work than static dialog boxes, but they're a great way both to present information and choices and to impress your colleagues.

In the middle of the chapter, I'll digress a little from building complex dialog boxes to cover a couple of topics that will at first seem only tangentially related to dialog boxes. The first topic is arrays, which are variables that can store multiple pieces of information. First, I'll explain how arrays work; then I'll show you how to use an array to get a directory listing into a list box of a dialog box. The second topic is the Toolbox, which we used earlier in the book when constructing simple dialog boxes. Here, I'll discuss how you can customize the Toolbox so that you have all the tools you need right at hand.

Toward the end of the chapter, we'll also look briefly at creating forms with ActiveX components, which work in a similar way to the components of custom dialog boxes.

What Is a Complex Dialog Box?

In a nutshell, complex dialog boxes are more complicated versions of the simpler dialog boxes we looked at in Chapter 7. Even those dialog boxes varied in complexity, but all used a single page to contain all the controls they included. Not only that, but the dialog boxes we looked at earlier were static, in that the information in them remained the same until the user dismissed them (beyond necessary changes such as reflecting the check boxes, option buttons, or list items selected, or the text entered in a text box).

In contrast to static dialog boxes, many complex dialog boxes are dynamic in that they change when the user clicks certain elements in them. Such changes can include the following:

- The application (for instance, Word) changes the information in the dialog box to reflect choices the user made. For example, if they select a particular check box, the application may make another check box unavailable because the option controlled by the second check box is not available or applicable when they use the option controlled by the first check box.

- The dialog box displays a hidden section of secondary options when the user clicks a button in the primary area of the dialog box.

- The application uses the dialog box to keep track of a procedure and to guide the user to the next step by displaying appropriate instructions and by activating the relevant control.

Other complex dialog boxes include multi-tab and multi-page dialog boxes, which provide you with the means to pack a lot of information into a single dialog box. I'll discuss these various types of complex dialog boxes in the following sections.

Creating and Working with Complex Dialog Boxes

Before we get further into complex dialog boxes, I'll risk making an obvious point: never go to the trouble to construct a complex dialog box where a simple one would do the trick. By keeping dialog boxes as simple as possible, you will make life easier for the users of your macros—for whom you're presumably creating the dialog boxes. That said, let's start by looking at how to create complex dialog boxes.

Updating a Dialog Box to Reflect the User's Choices

You'll find it relatively easy to update a dialog box to reflect the options the user chooses in it. Your primary tool for doing this is the `Click` event to which most of the controls in a dialog box react, and to which you can add a macro on the code sheet attached to the dialog box. (Some controls have different events than `Click`, such as `Change`.)

We'll look at an example of such updating in Listing 19.1 in the next section, because it ties in neatly with revealing an extra part of a dialog box.

Revealing an Extra Part of a Dialog Box

Hiding part of a complex dialog box is a great way to simplify the user's initial interaction with the dialog box. Consider the Find and Replace dialog box: when you first display it by choosing Edit ➤ Replace, you see only the part of the dialog box shown in the top picture of Figure 19.1. (If you choose Edit ➤ Find, you see an even smaller part of the dialog box.) If you need to use the more complex options that the Find and Replace dialog box offers, you can click the More button to display the bottom part of the dialog box, as shown in the lower picture of Figure 19.1.

FIGURE 19.1

The Find and Replace dialog box initially hides some of its options (above) until you click the More button to display its lower half (below).

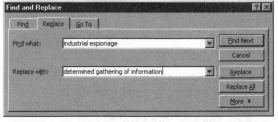

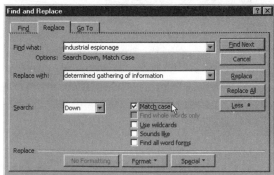

You may want to follow a similar strategy with complex dialog boxes that contain a subset of actions with which most users will be content most of the time. To do so, you can use two methods, either separately or in tandem:

- Set the `Visible` property to `False` to hide a control that appears in a displayed part of the dialog box. Set the `Visible` property to `True` when you want to display the control.

- Increase the height or width (or both) of the dialog box to reveal an area containing further controls.

TIP

With either of the above methods, you'll typically want to set the `Enabled` property for hidden controls to `False` until you reveal them so that the user cannot move to a control that they cannot see.

As a simple example of the latter technique, consider the dialog box shown in Figure 19.2. When you display the dialog box, only the top part is visible; when you click the More button, the bottom half is displayed. Listing 19.1 contains the code behind the dialog box; you'll find it's surprisingly simple.

FIGURE 19.2

The top part of the Inventories dialog box (above) offers the usual options. Clicking the More button reveals the rest of the dialog box (below), which contains less-used controls.

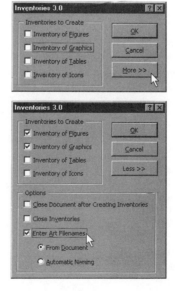

Listing 19.1

```
1.   Private Sub Userform_Initialize()
2.       frmInventories.Height = 120
3.   End Sub
4.
5.   Private Sub cmdMore_Click()
6.       If cmdMore.Caption = "More >>" Then
7.           cmdMore.Caption = "Less >>"
8.           cmdMore.Accelerator = "L"
9.           frmInventories.Height = 240
10.          fraOptions.Enabled = True
11.      Else
12.          frmInventories.Height = 120
13.          cmdMore.Caption = "More >>"
14.          cmdMore.Accelerator = "M"
15.      End If
16.  End Sub
17.
18.  Private Sub chkArtNames_Click()
19.      If chkArtNames = True Then
20.          optFromDocument.Enabled = True
21.          optFromDocument = True
22.          optAutoNames.Enabled = True
23.      Else
24.          optFromDocument.Enabled = False
25.          optFromDocument = False
26.          optAutoNames.Enabled = False
27.          optAutoNames = False
28.      End If
29.  End Sub
30.
31.  Private Sub cmdOK_Click()
32.      frmInventories.Hide
33.      Unload frmInventories
34.      'create inventories here
35.  End Sub
36.
37.  Private Sub cmdCancel_Click()
38.      End
39.  End Sub
```

Analysis

This listing contains five short macros that control the behavior of the dialog box:

- `Userform_Initialize`, which initializes the dialog box before it is displayed

- `cmdMore_Click`, which runs when the More button is chosen

- `chkArtNames_Click`, which runs when the Enter Art Filenames check box is chosen

- `cmdOK_Click`, which runs when the OK button is chosen

- `cmdCancel_Click`, which runs when the Cancel button is chosen

Here's what happens:

The `Userform_Initialize` macro simply sets the `Height` property of the `frmInventories` userform to `120`, which is enough to display only the top part of the dialog box. (To find the appropriate height for your dialog box, drag it to the depth that looks right and note the `Height` property in the Properties window.)

The `cmdMore_Click` macro starts by checking in line 6 if the `Caption` property of the `cmdMore` command button is `More >>`; if so, that means that only the top half of the dialog box is displayed. Line 7 then sets the `Caption` property of the `cmdMore` command button to `Less >>`, because it will be used to hide the bottom part of the dialog box again if necessary, and line 8 sets the `Accelerator` property of the `cmdMore` command button to `L` (to make the `L` in *Less* the accelerator key for the button). Line 9 sets the `Height` property of `frmInventories` to `240`, which is the depth required to show all the contents of the dialog box. Line 10 enables the `fraOptions` frame (identified as Options in the dialog box, and disabled in the userform, as are the `optFromDocument` option button and the `optAutoNames` option button), making it and the controls it contains available to the user.

If the condition in line 6 is `False`, execution shifts from line 6 to the `Else` statement in line 11. This must mean that the `Caption` property of the `cmdMore` button is already set to `Less >>`, so the dialog box is already at its expanded size; the `Less >>` button is being clicked to shrink the dialog box again. Line 12 sets the `Height` property of the userform back to `120`, thus hiding the lower part of the dialog box; line 13 restores the `Caption` property of the `cmdMore` command button to `More >>`; and line 14 sets the `Accelerator` property of the `cmdMore` command button back to `M`. Line 16 ends the `cmdMore_Click` macro.

The `chkArtNames_Click` macro (lines 18 to 29) runs when the Enter Art Filenames check box is clicked and enables and disables the option buttons below it as appropriate. Line 19 checks to see if the `chkArtNames` check box is selected. If it is, the statements in lines 20 through 22 run. Line 20 sets the `Enabled` property of the `optFromDocument` option button (identified as From Document in the dialog box) to `True`, thus making it available, and line 21 selects this option button as the default choice. Line 22 enables `optAutoNames`, the option button identified as Automatic Naming in the dialog box.

If the `chkArtNames` check box is not selected, execution shifts to the `Else` statement in line 23, which directs execution to line 24; this line sets the `Enabled` property of the `optFromDocument` option button to `False`, disabling it. Line 25 then deselects this option button (whether it is selected or not). Line 26 disables the `optAutoNames` option button, and line 27 deselects it (again, whether it is selected or not). The `End If` statement in line 28 ends this `If` statement, and line 29 ends this macro.

The `cmdOK_Click` macro in lines 31 to 35 shows the beginning of the macro that would run once the OK button was clicked. Line 32 hides the Inventories dialog box, and line 33 unloads it from memory. Line 34 contains a comment indicating that the instructions for creating the inventories would appear here.

The `cmdCancel_Click` macro contains only an `End` statement to end execution of the procedure if the user chooses the Cancel button.

Tracking a Procedure in a Dialog Box

The next stage of complexity in a dialog box is using it to track the different stages of a procedure and guide the user as to how to continue. As an example of this, consider the Mail Merge Helper dialog box, which provides instructions that walk you through the many steps of the various mail-merge operations (merging to a letter, mailing labels, a form, or a catalog; using different merge sources, such as a Word document, an Excel worksheet, or your Outlook address book; and merging the results to a printer or to e-mail).

Figure 19.3 shows the Mail Merge Helper dialog box nearing the end of a merge. The frame at the top of the dialog box contains information on the current state of the procedure and instructs the user to choose the Merge button to complete the merge; the Merge button is already selected so that the user can continue by simply pressing Enter. Underneath the "1" and "2" that denote the previous main steps of the mail merge, the Mail Merge Helper records the details of the choices the user has made: the merge type, the name of the main document, and the name of the data source. Underneath the Merge button, the Mail Merge Helper lists the options in effect for the merge. Even if Murphy himself were around to use this dialog box, he'd be hard-pressed to find something to do wrong with it.

FIGURE 19.3

The Mail Merge Helper dialog box keeps updating its information to give the user guidance during a mail-merge operation.

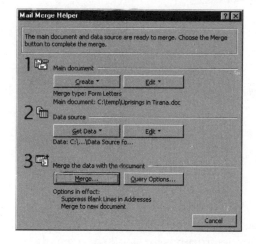

In your more complex macros, you may want to produce a dialog box that walks the user through a procedure like this; depending on the complexity of the procedure and the amount of time you have to cosset its users, your dialog box will probably be much less complex than this one.

Take a look at the Create Information Package dialog box shown in Figure 19.4. This dialog box guides the user through a three-stage procedure to create an information package consisting of a report (a Word document, we'll assume, rather than an Access report) and a spreadsheet (probably an Excel workbook). The first step is selecting the appropriate report, the second step is selecting the appropriate spreadsheet, and the third step is saving the information package under a suitable name.

> **NOTE**
>
> The more effort you put into making your macros instantly understandable to their users, the better your life will be—and I don't mean karma; rather, that you'll suffer fewer demands on your time to explain for the umpteenth time what you thought was a straightforward procedure. Along with following the guidelines for creating well-behaved macros covered in Chapter 18, providing clear information and relevant instructions in a dialog box can save you substantial amounts of grief.

FIGURE 19.4

The Create Information Package dialog box provides the user with instructions that it updates as they work their way through the procedure.

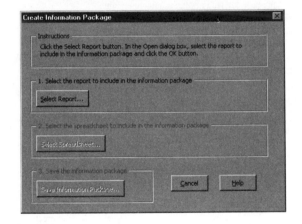

When the user first displays the Create Information Package dialog box, they will see the version of the dialog box shown in Figure 19.4, with steps 2 and 3 disabled and instructions for step 1 shown in the Instructions box at the top. When the user follows the instructions and clicks the Select Report button, the cmdSelect-Report_Click macro shown in Listing 19.2 runs, displaying the Open dialog box so that the user can choose a file and then updating and redisplaying the Create Information Package dialog box when the user has dismissed the Open dialog box. Figure 19.5 shows the updated version of the Create Information Package dialog box. You'll notice that the following changes have occurred:

- The text of the label in the Instructions box at the top of the dialog box now contains information for step 2 of the procedure.

- The name of the report document that the user chose is listed alongside the Select Report button.

- The frame for step 2 is enabled, as is the Select Spreadsheet button.

FIGURE 19.5

The second stage of the
Create Information
Package dialog box.
Notice the changes from
the first stage.

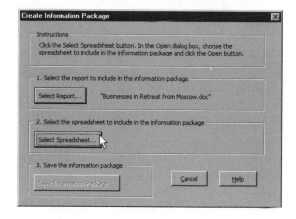

Listing 19.2

```
1.   Private Sub cmdSelectReport_Click()
2.       frmInformationPackage.Hide
3.       Set OpenDialog = Dialogs(wdDialogFileOpen)
4.       OpenDialog.Display
5.       lblReport.Caption = OpenDialog.Name
6.       fraStep2.Enabled = True
7.       lblSpreadsheet.Enabled = True
8.       cmdSelectSpreadsheet.Enabled = True
9.       cmdSelectSpreadsheet.SetFocus
10.      lblInstructions.Caption = "Click the Select
       ➡Spreadsheet button. In the Open dialog box,
       ➡choose the spreadsheet to include in the
       ➡information package and click the Open button."
11.      frmInformationPackage.Show
12.  End Sub
```

Analysis

This macro is pleasingly terse for the effects it achieves.

Line 2 hides the `frmInformationPackage` userform, removing the dialog box from the screen. Note that there is no `Unload` command, because we will summon the dialog box back up in just a moment.

Line 3 creates an object named `OpenDialog` refers to Word's built-in Open dialog box. (We'll look at how to work with built-in dialog boxes in the next chapter. This guest appearance is just to whet your appetite.) Line 4 then uses the `Display` method to display the dialog box. At this point the user chooses a file in the Open dialog box as if they were going to open it, but when they select the Open button, execution returns to the macro.

Line 5 sets the `Caption` property of the `lblReport` label (which is located to the right of the Select Report button but has so far contained an empty string and thus remained invisible) to the `Name` argument from the `OpenDialog` object. This assigns to the label the name of the file the user chose in the Open dialog box.

Line 6 enables the `fraStep2` control, the frame for the second step. Line 7 enables `lblSpreadsheet`, the label to the right of the Select Spreadsheet button. (This label will hold the name of the spreadsheet the user selects in the next step, which will parallel the first step.) Line 8 enables the Select Spreadsheet button (`cmdSelectSpreadsheet`), and line 9 uses the `SetFocus` method to select it.

Line 10 changes the `Caption` property for the `lblInstructions` label, thus changing the instructions that appear in the Instructions frame at the top of the dialog box.

Finally, line 11 uses the `Show` method to redisplay the Create Information Package dialog box with its updates.

Using Multi-Page and Multi-Tab Dialog Boxes

In addition to the controls we've looked at so far in this book, VBA provides controls that give you the capability to create multi-page dialog boxes and multi-tab dialog boxes. You'll be familiar with multi-page dialog boxes from your work in Word (and, in fact, pretty much any Windows application). For example, the Options dialog box contains ten pages, which you can access by clicking the tab at the top of the page. Each page contains a different set of controls and has a different layout appropriate to the controls. Likewise, the Font dialog box has three pages, the Paragraph dialog box has two pages, and so on. To confuse things, most everyone refers to the pages as "tabs"; for example, in the Word

Help file, you'll read instructions such as "On the Tools menu, click Options, and then click the View tab."

Multi-page dialog boxes are great for packing a lot of information into a single dialog box without having it take up the whole screen and become visually bewildering. You'll need to divide the information up into discrete sets of related information to fit it onto the pages, as in the three dialog boxes mentioned above.

A multi-tab dialog box differs from a multi-page dialog box in that it contains multiple tabs but not multiple pages: the rest of the dialog box apart from the tab strip stays the same no matter which tab is selected. This means that the dialog box has only one layout, so the controls do not change, although because you reference the controls through the tab, the controls can have different settings for each tab; for instance, the value of a text box might show one customer's name on the first tab of a dialog box and another customer's name on the second tab. Multi-tab dialog boxes are good for sets of information that need the same layout, such as the records you might maintain on your company's customers: each customer has an account number, a name (or several), an address, phone numbers, e-mail addresses, URLs, etc., so you can assign each customer a tab in a multi-tab dialog box and use the same set of fields for the customer information.

NOTE The Visual Basic Editor allows you to create dialog boxes with dozens of tabs or dozens of pages; if you run out of horizontal space to display the tabs, the Visual Basic Editor adds a scroll bar to enable you to scroll through the tabs. For most purposes, though, any dialog box with more than ten or a dozen pages or tabs is likely to prove awkwardly complex to use. If you need more than a dozen pages to organize the information in a dialog box, you're probably trying to present the user with too much information at once; and if you need more than a dozen or so tabs, you should probably consider an alternative way of displaying the information.

You won't find any examples of multi-tab dialog boxes in Word: they're more suited to custom applications. Generally speaking, multi-page dialog boxes provide more flexibility than multi-tab dialog boxes, so in the discussion in this section, I'll concentrate on multi-page dialog boxes. In case your primary interest is in multi-tab dialog boxes, I'll give an example of a multi-tab dialog box at the end of the discussion.

Multi-Page Dialog Boxes

To create a multi-page dialog box, you begin by placing a `MultiPage` control: click the `MultiPage` button in the Toolbox and then click in the userform where you want the control to appear. The Visual Basic Editor will place a `MultiPage` control with two pages, whose tabs will carry the labels `Page 1` and `Page 2`. You can then move and size the control as usual. For most purposes, you'll want to create a `MultiPage` control that is only a little smaller than the userform it inhabits (as in most of the multi-page dialog boxes you'll see in Windows applications).

Once you've created a `MultiPage` control, you work with a page on it by selecting the page's label and then right-clicking and using the context menu it produces. To select the label, click it so that a dotted outline appears around it. Right-clicking the label then produces a context menu for the page (whereas right-clicking the page without selecting the label produces a context menu for the userform).

Once you've selected the page (by selecting its label), you can do the following

- To add a page, right-click the label and choose New Page from the context menu. VBA will add a new page of the default size and will name it `Pagen`, where *n* is the next number after the current number of pages (even if the other pages have names other than `Page1`, `Page2`, and so on).

- To rename a page in a `MultiPage` control, right-click the label and choose Rename from the context menu. VBA will display the Rename dialog box (see Figure 19.6). Enter the caption (the label text) for the page strip in the Caption text box, the accelerator key in the Accelerator Key text box, and any control tip text (the tip the user will see when they move the mouse pointer over the tab for the page) in the Control Tip Text text box. Click the OK button to close the Rename dialog box.

FIGURE 19.6

Use the Rename dialog box to set the caption, accelerator key, and control tip text for a page.

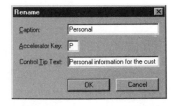

- To delete a page from a `MultiPage` control, right-click the label and choose Delete Page from the context menu.

- To move a page to a different place in the `MultiPage` control, right-click the label and choose Move from the context menu to display the Page Order dialog box (see Figure 19.7). In the Page Order list box, select the page or pages that you want to move (Shift+click to select multiple contiguous pages, Ctrl+click to select multiple pages individually) and then use the Move Up and Move Down buttons to rearrange the page or pages as desired. When you've finished, select the OK button to close the Page Order dialog box.

FIGURE 19.7

Use the Move Up and Move Down buttons in the Page Order dialog box to change the order of pages in a `MultiPage` control.

To specify which page of a multi-page dialog box to display by default, you use the `Value` property of the `MultiPage` control. For example, you could use an initialization macro such as the one shown here to display the third page (identified by the value 2, because the page numbering starts at 0) of a dialog box with a `MultiPage` control called `MyMulti`:

```
Sub Userform_Initialize()
    MyMulti.Value = 2
End Sub
```

Once you've created a multi-page dialog box, you can populate its pages with controls the same way you would with any dialog box, as described in Chapter 7. Each control has to have a unique name within the dialog box (not just within the page on which it appears). When designing a multi-page dialog box, keep the following issues in mind:

- What is the best way to divide up the information or options in the dialog box? What belongs on which page? Which information or options will the user expect to find grouped together?

- Which controls should appear on each page? In most dialog boxes, you'll want to have at least a pair of command buttons such as OK and Cancel or OK and Close on each page to allow the user to dismiss the dialog box from whichever page they happen to end up on. In rare instances, you may want to force the user to return to a particular page in order to close a dialog box. In these cases, make sure that each page that does not contain a command button to dismiss the dialog box gives the user an indication of where they will find such a command button.

- For settings, do you need to have an Apply button as well as an OK button to apply the changes on a particular page without closing the dialog box?

Because each control in a multi-page dialog box has a unique name, when returning information from a multi-page dialog box you need specify only the relevant object—you do not need to specify which page it is on.

Figure 19.8 shows an example of a multi-page dialog box. The first page contains the customer's personal contact information, the second the customer's professional information, the third the associations the customer belongs to, and the fourth the certifications the customer holds.

FIGURE 19.8

By using multiple pages in a dialog box, you can present a clean and uncluttered look that the user will be able to navigate easily.

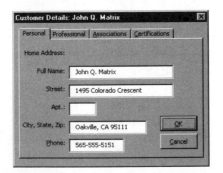

Multi-Tab Dialog Boxes

Here's a quick example of a multi-tab dialog box to round out the section. As I mentioned earlier, the main difference between a multi-tab dialog box and a multi-page dialog box is that the different tabs of a multi-tab dialog box share a common area: any control that appears in that area will appear on each tab of the dialog box. Figure 19.9 shows the first two tabs in a multi-tab dialog box used for entering and updating customer information. Each tab contains the same arrangement of controls, but these can be populated with different sets of information. (In this example, the customer and her spouse share the same address.)

FIGURE 19.9

The tabs of a multi-tab dialog box share a common area, but their controls can be populated with different sets of information.

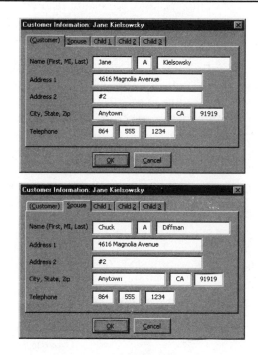

To create a multi-tab dialog box, you use the TabStrip control, a horizontal strip that can contain one or more tabs; obviously, you'll want to use at least two tabs to justify a tab strip, and, by no coincidence, each tab strip you place comes with two tabs. You can then add further tabs to the tab strip as necessary. (You can also remove one of the two tabs on the default tab strip, but there's no point in having only one tab in a dialog box.)

To create a tab strip, click the TabStrip button in the Toolbox, then click in the userform where you want the tab strip to appear. You can then size and move the tab strip as necessary, and add, rename, move, and delete tabs in the same way as pages in a MultiPage control.

Using a Picture in a Dialog Box

You can add a picture to a dialog box by using an Image control. Applied appropriately, a picture can provide a real boost to a dialog box by showing the user, for example, the effect that a setting in the dialog box will achieve or the type of document that a certain macro will produce. Of course, you can also use a picture to show a company logo. For example, if you're creating a set of macros for a company, they might want you to include the company's logo in the dialog boxes to emphasize that the code is proprietary.

If adding a picture is so straightforward, why didn't I show you how to use the Image control in Chapter 7? Simply because the Image control carries with it the temptation to overuse pictures in your dialog boxes, and I couldn't bear the thought of your needlessly decorating your fledgling dialog boxes with pictures of your family, your boss, or even (I shudder) yourself. But now that you've slogged through some serious chapters of VBA, my editors have persuaded me that you've shown enough self-restraint to be able to handle the temptation of Image controls with aplomb.

To place an Image control in a dialog box, click the Image button in the Toolbox and then click in the userform where you want the picture to appear. Once you've placed the Image control, you can size and move the picture just like any other control.

To choose the picture that will appear in the Image control, select the Picture property in the Properties window and click the ellipsis button that appears to the right of the entry, as shown here. The Visual Basic Editor will display the Load Picture dialog box. Select the picture file and choose the Open button. The Picture property in the Properties window will register the type of picture you selected (e.g., (Bitmap)) but not its file name, and the picture will appear in the Image control so that you can see if it is an appropriate size.

I'll let you experiment with pictures on your own after I point out one obvious thing to do with them: use a picture's `Click` event to trigger an action. For example, if you present the user with a choice of two formats for a document, you could have them click the appropriate picture to make their choice instead of having them select the picture and then click a command button. Figure 19.10 shows an example of such a dialog box.

When Should You Add a Picture to a Dialog Box?

Used appropriately, a picture enhances a dialog box; used inappropriately, it can severely detract from both the aesthetics and the effectiveness of the dialog box. The basic rule of thumb goes like this: don't add a picture to a dialog box unless the picture improves the dialog box's comprehensibility or is necessary for other reasons (such as the company logo).

One disadvantage of a picture is that it slows down the display time for the dialog box, which can look unprofessional. Test the display time for pictures in VBA dialog boxes on a slow computer to make sure the delay is not unreasonable.

Worse, if the computer displaying the dialog box does not have the graphics filter for the picture type installed, the user may see an error message box. When the dialog box then displays, there will be an empty space where the picture was supposed to be. If you do need to display a picture in a dialog box, make sure that the picture and the appropriate graphics filter are both available to the users of the dialog box. If the picture is not available or the computer does not have the appropriate graphics filter to display it, you could display a different version of the dialog box (or the same dialog box with its dimensions shrunk) to hide the missing picture, but having a picture in a dialog box is seldom worth this amount of effort.

FIGURE 19.10

You can use a picture
instead of a command
button to take action
from a dialog box.

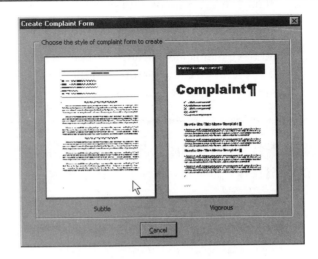

Adding Screentips and Help to a Dialog Box

As I've said before, the more straightforward you can make your dialog boxes, the less difficulty users of your macros will have with them; and the more helpful information you can put in your dialog boxes (without cluttering them and making them confusing, of course), the easier they will be to understand. When you have information that will be of value only to some users, or the volume of information that a user might need is such that it would clutter up the dialog box, you may want to add Help to the dialog box instead.

VBA offers several ways to add Help to a dialog box. The easiest way is to add screentips to the individual controls in the dialog box so that the user can get extra information about them by simply moving the mouse pointer over them. I'll show you how to do so in this section. Other possibilities, which go beyond the scope of this book, include adding to the dialog box a What's This button (the question-mark button that appears to the left of the close button in the title bar of some dialog boxes) linked to specific topics in a Help file. The user can click the What's This button and then click the control in the dialog box about which they need more information, and VBA will display the appropriate topic in the Help file. For this purpose, you'll probably want to create a custom Help file. The other alternative if you create a Help file for the macro is to link it to a Help button in the dialog box. When the user clicks the Help button, VBA will display the Help file, which they can consult as they attack the options in the dialog box. For users not familiar with the What's This button, this option provides a more friendly interface.

To add a screentip to a control in a dialog box, enter the text for the screentip in the `ControlTipText` property for the control. When the dialog box is displayed, moving the mouse pointer over the control displays the screentip, as shown in Figure 19.11. VBA restricts screentips to a single line—it won't wrap a screentip—but will happily display a screentip that goes off the right edge of the screen if it's long enough (or, if it's really long, off both edges of the screen); so plan your screentips to be fully visible at the lowest screen resolution your users will be working with (this usually means 640 x 480 pixels).

FIGURE 19.11

The easiest way to add Help to a dialog box is to use screentips.

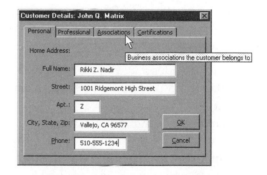

Creating a Help File

Various programs are available for creating Help files from Word documents; two programs worth mentioning are Doc-to-Help and RoboHelp, which you can find at your friendly neighborhood computer superstore or from a catalog computer company. If you're looking for something cheaper, you'll also find various freeware and shareware utilities lurking in FTP archives in dark recesses of the Net. Needless to say, the commercial programs are more powerful and much easier to use, and you pay accordingly for these benefits.

TIP

If your resources don't extend to creating a Help file, you could instead set up a Help button in a dialog box to display a separate dialog box that contained nothing but instructions for working with the current dialog box. This is clumsier than using a screentip but allows you to present more information.

Using Arrays

Here's the first of the diversions I promised you in the introduction to this chapter: arrays. The reason we're dealing with them here is that they're especially useful for putting lists of files into a list box or combo box in a dialog box. I'll show you how to do that after I've explained what arrays are and how they work.

An *array* provides a way of working with a number of values that have the same data type. VBA treats an array as a single variable that can store multiple values. You can refer to the array itself to work with all the values it contains, or you can refer to the individual values stored within the array by using their *index numbers*, which indicate their position within the array. If you're having difficulty visualizing what this means, try picturing an array as a list. Each item in the list is located in its own row and is identified by an index number, so you can access the value of the item by specifying the index number.

That's a simple array, one that has only one dimension. You can also declare multidimensional arrays, which I'll get to in a couple of minutes.

An array is delimited by a lower bound and an upper bound. By default, the lower bound is zero, so the first item in an array is indexed as zero. This can be confusing, because you're always working with an index number that's one lower than the item's position in the array. However, you can change the default index number of the first item in an array by using an Option Base statement at the beginning of the module that contains the array. If you do so, you'll typically want to set the default index to 1 so that the index number for each item in the array is the same as the item's position in the array:

```
Option Base 1
```

Declaring an Array

An array is a kind of variable, so you can declare an array by using the regular keywords discussed in Chapter 10: `Dim`, `Private`, `Public`, or `Static`. The difference is that when declaring an array, you need to declare the number of items in it. For example, you could declare an array named `MonthProfit` as the Currency data type containing twelve items by using the following statement:

```
Dim MonthProfit(11) As Currency
```

As I mentioned, index numbering for the array begins at 0, so 1 is the second item, 2 the third, and 11 the twelfth. If you used an `Option Base` statement at the beginning of the module, you would declare the array like this:

```
Option Base 1      'at the beginning of the code sheet

Dim MonthProfit(12) As Currency
```

In this example, the array is assigned the Currency data type, but you can omit the data type and have VBA automatically use the Variant data type. The price for this is slightly increased memory usage, which could, under extreme circumstances, slow down the performance of the computer; because an array needs storage for each item it contains, a large array can consume a significant amount of memory. This is particularly true with multidimensional arrays, which I'll discuss in the next section.

> **NOTE** Because working with arrays is much easier if you use an `Option Base 1` statement, I'll assume you're using an `Option Base 1` statement through the rest of this discussion.

Multidimensional Arrays

The `MonthProfit` example in the previous section is a one-dimensional array, which is the easiest kind of array to use. But VBA supports arrays with up to 60 dimensions—enough to tax the visualization skills of anyone without a Ph.D. in multidimensional modeling. You probably won't want to get this complicated with arrays—two, three, or four dimensions are enough for most purposes.

To declare a multidimensional array, you separate the dimensions with commas. For example, to declare a two-dimensional array named `MyArray` with ten items in each dimension, you could use the following statement:

```
Dim MyArray(10, 10)
```

Multidimensional arrays sound forbidding, but a two-dimensional array is quite straightforward if you think of it basically as a table with rows and columns. Here, the first series of ten elements would appear in the first column of the (imaginary) table, and the second series of ten elements would appear in the second column. The information in each series doesn't need to be related to information in the other series. For example, you could assign ten folder names to the first dimension of the array, and ten file names (or the names of your ten cats) to the second dimension of the array. You can then access the information in the array by specifying the position of the item you want to access (such as the second item in the first column of the imaginary table). We'll look at how to do this in just a minute.

Declaring a Dynamic Array

You can declare both *fixed-size* arrays and *dynamic* arrays. The examples we've looked at so far were fixed-size arrays; for instance, the size of the `MonthProfit` array was specified as 12 items.

Dynamic arrays are useful when you need to store a variable number of items. For example, for a macro that arranges two windows side by side, you might create an array to contain the name of each open document. Because you won't know how many documents will be open when you run the macro, you may want to use a dynamic array to contain the information. (The alternative is to use the `Count` property of the `Documents` collection to determine the upper bound of the array.)

To declare a dynamic array, you use a declaration statement without specifying the number of items, by including the parentheses but leaving them empty. For example, the following statement declares the dynamic array `TestArray` and has VBA assign it the Variant data type:

```
Dim TestArray()
```

Redimensioning an Array

You can reinitialize, or *redimension*, a dynamic array by using the ReDim statement. For example, to redimension the dynamic array TestArray declared in the previous example and assign it a size of five items, you could use the following statement:

```
ReDim TestArray(5)
```

When you use ReDim to redimension an array like this, you will lose the values currently in the array. If so far you've only declared the array as a dynamic array, and it contains nothing yet, this won't bother you; but at other times, you'll want to increase the size of an array without trashing its current contents. To preserve the existing values in an array when you raise its upper bound (if you lower the array's upper bound, you will lose information), use a ReDim Preserve statement instead of a straight ReDim statement:

```
ReDim Preserve TestArray(5)
```

Assigning Values to an Array

To assign a value to an item in an array, you use the index number to identify the item. For example, to assign the values London, Hong Kong, and Taipei to the three items in the array Locations, you could use the following statements:

```
Dim Locations(3) As String
Locations(1) = "London"
Locations(2) = "Hong Kong"
Locations(3) = "Taipei"
```

Typically, you'll want to assign information to an array shortly after you create it. For example, if you wanted to declare an array named Years with ten items and assign the years **1997** to **2006** to those items, you could use the following statements:

```
Dim Years(10) As Integer
For i = 1 to 10
    Years(i) = 1996 + i
Next i
```

Here, the third line assigns to the item i in the Years array the value of 1996 + i: for the first iteration of the For...Next loop, 1997; for the second, 1998, and so on.

Returning Information from an Array

To return information from an array, you use the index number to specify the position of the information you want to return. For example, to return the fourth item in the array named MyArray and display it in a message box, you could use the following statement:

```
MsgBox MyArray(4)
```

To return the fifth item in the second dimension of a two-dimensional array named My2DArray and display it in a message box, you could use the following statement:

```
MsgBox My2DArray(2,5)
```

> **NOTE**   To return multiple items from an array, specify each item individually.

Erasing an Array

To erase the contents of an array, use the Erase statement with the name of the array. This statement reinitializes the items in a fixed-size array, and frees up the memory taken by items in dynamic arrays (i.e., completely erasing the array). For example, to erase the contents of the fixed-size array named MyArray, you could use the following statement:

```
Erase MyArray
```

Finding Out Whether a Variable Is an Array

Because an array is a type of variable, you may occasionally need to check whether a particular variable name denotes an array or a *scalar variable* (a variable that isn't an array). To find out whether a variable is an array, use the `IsArray` function with the variable's name, as in the following statements, which check the variable `MyVariable` and display the results in a message box:

```
If IsArray(MyVariable) = True Then
    Msg = "The variable is an array."
Else
    Msg = "The variable is not an array."
End If
MsgBox Msg, vbOKOnly + vbInformation, "Array Check 1.0"
```

Finding the Bounds of an Array

To find the bounds of an array, use the `LBound` (for the lower bound, the index number of the first item) and `UBound` (for the upper bound, the index number of the last item) functions. They take the following syntax:

```
LBound(array [, dimension])
UBound(array [, dimension])
```

Here, `array` is a required argument specifying the name of the array, and dimension is an optional variant specifying the dimension whose bound you want to return—1 for the first dimension, 2 for the second, and so on. (If you omit the dimension argument, VBA assumes you mean the first dimension.)

For example, to return the upper bound of the second dimension in the array named `MyArray` and display it in a message box, you could use the following statement:

```
MsgBox UBound(MyArray, 2)
```

Displaying Arrays in a List Box or Combo Box

Often, you'll want to display the contents of an array in a list box or combo box of a dialog box to allow the user to pick one of the items in the array. For example, you might want to display a list box showing all the documents in a folder so that the user could choose a particular document. Figure 19.12 shows a dialog box containing such a list box, and Listing 19.3 shows the code used to fill the list box.

FIGURE 19.12

You can display an array in a list box to allow the user to choose one of the items in the array.

Listing 19.3

```
1.  Sub UserForm_Initialize()
2.      Dim FileArray() As String, ffile As String,
    ➥Count As Integer
3.      ffile = Dir("c:\temp\*.doc")
4.      Count = 1
5.      Do While ffile <> ""
6.          If ffile <> "." And ffile <> ".." Then
7.              ReDim Preserve FileArray(Count)
8.              FileArray(Count) = ffile
9.              Count = Count + 1
10.             ffile = Dir()
11.         End If
12.     Loop
13.     FileList.List() = FileArray
14. End Sub
```

Analysis

Listing 19.3 declares and fills an array for a list box in a dialog box, enabling the user to choose a file to work with from the list box.

Line 2 declares the array variable `FileArray`, the variable `ffile` as the String data type, and the `Count` variable as the Integer data type. Line 3 then assigns to `ffile` the result of a directory operation on the designated folder (here, `c:\temp`) for files with a `.doc` extension. Line 4 sets the `Count` counter to 1.

Lines 5 through 12 contain a `Do While...Loop` loop that runs while `ffile` is not an empty string (`" "`):

- Line 6 makes sure that `ffile` is not a folder by comparing it to the single period and double period used to denote folders (directories, if you remember your DOS). If `ffile` is not a folder, line 7 uses a `ReDim Preserve` statement to increase the dimensions of the `FileArray` array to the number in `Count` while retaining the current information in the array, thus building the list of files in the folder.

- Line 9 then adds 1 to `Count`, and line 10 sets `ffile` to the result of the `Dir` function (i.e., the first file name matching the `*.doc` pattern in the designated folder).

- Line 11 ends the `If` condition. Line 12 contains the `Loop` keyword that will continue the loop as long as the `Do While` statement is `True`.

When the loop ends, line 13 sets the `List` property of the `FileList` list box in the dialog box to the contents of `FileArray`, which now contains a list of all the files in the folder.

Customizing the Toolbox

You met the Toolbox way back in Chapter 5, and I hope you've been using it agreeably since then. At that point, I promised to tell you later how you can customize the Toolbox by adding controls to it, removing controls, and even adding new pages of your own. Later has now arrived.

I can see you starting to shake your head doubtfully: the existing controls in the Toolbox seem to be more than enough, you say—after all, we've only just reached the `MultiPage` and `MultiTab` controls in this chapter, and the end of the book is rapidly approaching: why would you want to add more controls to the Toolbox?

One reason is to make available those controls that you use in all your dialog boxes, so that you don't have to create them from scratch each time. For example, in the dialog boxes so far in this book, we've almost always had an OK button that dismissed the dialog box and continued execution of the macro. Each time we've created an OK button, we've had to set its Name property (usually cmdOK), its Caption property (invariably OK), its Accelerator property (O), its Default property (usually True), and even its Height and Width properties (because VBA by default creates huge and clunky command buttons that will dismay a sensitive dialog box). All that effort is wasted after the first time you create an OK button, because you can simply place a copy of the first OK button you create on the Toolbox and reuse it for subsequent forms. (I'll show you how to do this in just a second.)

The other reason to customize the Toolbox is to add really fancy controls that extend the things you can do with dialog boxes and userforms. If you're not interested in this type of control at the moment, I don't blame you. But at least put your most-used controls on the Toolbox to save yourself a little time.

Adding Controls to the Toolbox

Let's start with adding controls to the Toolbox directly from a userform, because this is what you're probably going to want to do first. For example, once you've created OK and Cancel buttons to your liking, you can copy them from the userform to the Toolbox so that you'll be able to reuse them in any userforms you subsequently create.

To copy a control from a displayed userform to the Toolbox, just drag it and drop it, as shown in Figure 19.13.

To add controls to the Toolbox, right-click in the page to which you want to add controls (I'll discuss how to add pages to the Toolbox in a moment), and choose Additional Controls from the context menu to display the Additional Controls dialog box (see Figure 19.14). In the Available Controls list box, select the check boxes for the controls you want to add to the Toolbox, and then click the OK button. (To collapse the list to only the items currently selected, select the Selected Items Only check box in the Show group box.)

You can move a control from one page of the Toolbox to another by dragging it from the page it is on, moving the mouse pointer (still dragging) over the tab of the destination page to display that page, then moving the mouse pointer down (again, still dragging) into the body of that page and dropping the control on it.

FIGURE 19.13

The quickest way to add a control to the Toolbox is to drag it there from a userform.

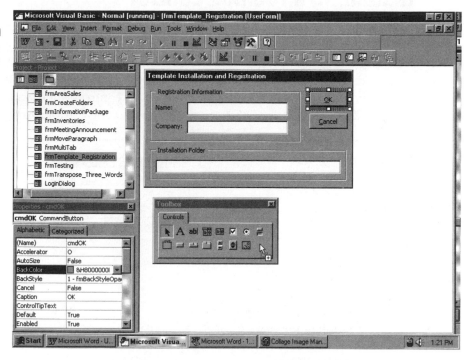

FIGURE 19.14

In the Additional Controls dialog box, select the check boxes for the controls you want to add, and then click the OK button.

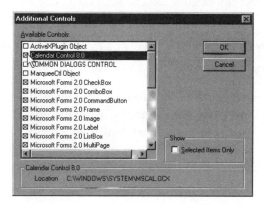

Renaming a Toolbox Control

As you've seen, when you move the mouse pointer over a control in the Toolbox, a screentip appears, showing the name of that control. To rename a control, right-click it in the Toolbox and choose the Customize item from the context menu to display the Customize Control dialog box, shown in Figure 19.15. (The menu item will be identified by the name of the control—for example, if the control is identified as New Label, the menu item will be Customize New Label.)

FIGURE 19.15

In the Customize Control dialog box, enter the name for the control in the Tool Tip Text text box, then use the Edit Picture button or the Load Picture button to assign a button to it.

Enter the name for the control in the Tool Tip Text text box (delete or change the existing name as necessary); this name will appear as a screentip when the user moves the mouse pointer over the control in the Toolbox. Then, if you wish, assign a different picture to the control's Toolbox icon as described in the next section, or click the OK button to close the Customize Control dialog box.

Assigning a Picture to a Control's Toolbox Icon

Each control in the Toolbox is identified by a picture. You can change the picture assigned to the control by using the Edit Picture button or the Load Picture button in the Customize Control dialog box.

Editing or Creating a Picture

To edit the picture assigned to the control, right-click the control, choose the Customize button from the context menu to display the Customize Control dialog box, and click the Edit Picture button to display the Edit Image dialog box (see Figure 19.16). Here, you can adjust the picture in the Picture edit box, pixel by pixel, by choosing the appropriate color or choosing the Erase tool in the Colors group box and clicking in the square you want to change. Use the Move buttons to move the entire image around the edit box (each direction button will be available only if the image does not touch that edge of the edit box); use the Clear button to erase the entire image so that you can start from scratch. Use the Preview group box to see how the picture looks at the resolution at which it will be displayed in the Toolbox.

FIGURE 19.16

In the Edit Image dialog box, you can customize the existing pictures for your Toolbox controls or create new pictures from scratch.

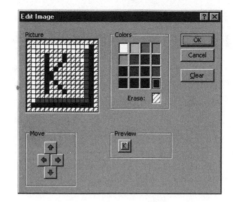

When you've finished adjusting the image, click the OK button to return to the Customize Control dialog box, and click the OK button to close that dialog box.

Loading a Picture

If you have existing pictures for controls (for example, ones that you or your colleagues created on another computer), you can load them for controls to make the controls easy to identify.

To load an existing picture for a control, right-click the control, choose the Customize button from the context menu to display the Customize Control dialog box, and click the Load Picture button in the Customize Control dialog box to display the Load Picture dialog box. Select the picture and click the Open button to load it.

Removing Controls from the Toolbox

To remove a control from the Toolbox, right-click it and choose the Delete item from the context menu. The item will be identified by the name of the control—for example, if you right-click a control named Company Name Combo Box, the menu item will be named Delete Company Name Combo Box. If the item is a custom control, this action gets rid of the control, and you can't restore it (unless you have a copy elsewhere). If the item is a Microsoft-supplied control, you can restore it from the Additional Controls dialog box by selecting the check box for the appropriate object (for example, Microsoft Forms 2.0 CommandButton).

You can also remove controls from the Toolbox by deleting the entire page they are on. I'll discuss how to do this in just a moment.

Adding Pages to the Toolbox

To add a page to the Toolbox, right-click the tab at the top of a page (or the label on the tab) and choose New Page from the context menu. The Visual Basic Editor will add a new page named—surprise—New Page, to which it will add the Select Objects control. This control appears on every page in the Toolbox (so that it's always at hand), and you cannot remove it.

You'll probably want to rename the new page immediately. To do so, follow the procedure in the next section.

Renaming Pages in the Toolbox

To change the name of a page, right-click its tab or label and choose Rename from the context menu to display the Rename dialog box. Enter the caption (i.e., the label) in the Caption text box; enter any control tip text you want to appear in the Control Tip Text text box; and click the OK button to close the dialog box.

Removing Pages from the Toolbox

To remove a page from the Toolbox, right-click its tab or label and choose Delete Page from the context menu. The Visual Basic Editor will remove the page from the Toolbox without any confirmation, whether the page contains controls or not.

Importing and Exporting Toolbox Pages

If you need to share your Toolbox pages, you can save them as separate files and distribute them to your colleagues. Toolbox pages have a `.pag` file extension.

To import a Toolbox page, right-click the tab or label on an existing page in the Toolbox and choose Import Page from the context menu to display the Import Page dialog box, which you'll recognize the Open dialog box in disguise. Select the page you want to import and choose the Open button. The Visual Basic Editor will add the new page after the last page currently in the Toolbox, and will name it New Page rather than any name it may have borne when it was exported. You can then rename the page as described earlier in this section.

Likewise, you can export a Toolbox page that you've created by right-clicking its tab or label and choosing Export Page from the context menu to display the Export Page dialog box, which is a disguised version of the Save As dialog box. Enter a name for the page (change folders if necessary) and choose the Save button to save it. Now anyone can import the page as described above.

Moving Pages in the Toolbox

To move a page in the Toolbox, right-click its tab or label and choose Move from the context menu to display the Page Order dialog box (the same one that you use for rearranging the pages in a multi-page dialog box, and which appeared in Figure 19.7). In the Page Order list box, select the page or pages that you want to move (Shift+click to select multiple contiguous pages, Ctrl+click to select multiple pages individually) and use the Move Up and Move Down buttons to rearrange the pages as desired. Select the OK button to close the Page Order dialog box when you've finished.

Building Forms with ActiveX Controls

As you saw in Chapter 3, you can create forms that use Word's built-in form fields. You can also create forms that use *ActiveX* components; these forms work in a similar way to dialog boxes, but the controls appear in the text of a document rather than in a userform. Such forms are primarily useful for Web pages, but you may want to use them for other purposes as well.

Entering ActiveX Controls in a Document

To enter ActiveX controls in a document, display the Control Toolbox by right-clicking the menu bar or any displayed toolbar and choosing Control Toolbox from the context menu.

Next, enter Design mode. You can do so either manually, by clicking the Design Mode button, or automatically, by clicking one of the other buttons in the Toolbox. Design mode allows you to lay out the form without the ActiveX controls being active; when you exit Design mode, the ActiveX controls in the document will become active, and clicking on them will cause them to perform their regular actions (for example, clicking a check box will select it if it is not currently selected or deselect it if it is currently selected). When you enter Design mode, Word will display the Exit Design Mode toolbar, which contains an Exit Design Mode button; you can also exit Design mode by clicking the Exit Design Mode button in the Control Toolbox (into which the Design Mode button will have metamorphosed).

To place an ActiveX control (such as a check box, a spin button, or a scroll bar), click its button in the Control Toolbox. You can then drag the control to where you want it to appear in the document, and size it to an appropriate size.

Setting the Properties of ActiveX Controls

ActiveX controls that you place in a document have properties similar to the properties that controls in a userform have. To display the properties for a control, enter Design mode if you're not still in it, select the control in the document by clicking it, and then click the Properties button in the Control Toolbox to bring up the Properties window for the item. (Alternatively, right-click the control—again in Design mode—and choose Properties from the context menu.) You can then adjust the properties for the control by working in the Properties window. Figure 19.17 shows the Properties window for a command button.

To view the Properties
window for an ActiveX
control, right-click the
control in Design mode
and choose Properties
from the context menu.

Attaching Code to ActiveX Controls

As with dialog box controls, ActiveX controls in a document or form can have
code attached to them that runs on their `Click` event or `Change` event. For
example, you might attach to an option button code that selects or deselects associated check boxes, or you might attach to a Submit command button on a Web
page code that would transfer the information from the form and then display
another page.

To attach code to a control, you can simply double-click the control. Word will
display the Visual Basic Editor with the code sheet for the current document displayed. The Visual Basic Editor will automatically create a suitably named macro
for you if one does not already exist (for example, if you double-click a command
button named `cmdSubmit`, the Visual Basic Editor will create a macro named
`Private Sub cmdSubmit_Click`). You can also display the Visual Basic
Editor and the code sheet by right-clicking the control and choosing View Code
from the context menu, or by selecting the control and then clicking the View
Code button in the Control Toolbox.

On the code sheet, you create and debug code as usual for the control. To return
to the document, either coolswitch (Alt+Tab) to Word or close the Visual Basic
Editor.

Formatting ActiveX Controls

For straightforward formatting of ActiveX controls, you'll probably find it easiest
to work directly in the Word document. For example, to resize a command button,

you can simply select it and drag its sizing handles. For more complex formatting, or to choose an option such as locking a control's anchor so that it cannot move to another page from the paragraph to which it is anchored, you use the Format Control dialog box.

To display the Format Control dialog box (see Figure 19.18), right-click the appropriate control while in Design mode and choose Format Control from the context menu; alternatively, select the control while in Design mode and choose Format ➤ Control. Choose options on the Size, Position, and Wrapping pages of the Format Control dialog box. Click the OK button to apply your changes and close the Format Control dialog box.

FIGURE 19.18

Choose formatting options for an ActiveX control in the Format Control dialog box.

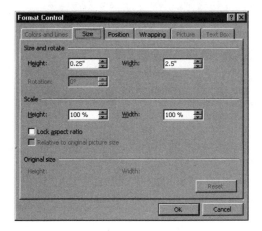

Retrieving Information from a Form

In this final section, I'll discuss briefly how you can retrieve information from a form. First, we'll look at how to retrieve information from ActiveX controls, because we've just been talking about those; then we'll look at how to retrieve information from form fields, which we left way back in Chapter 3.

Retrieving Information from ActiveX Controls

You can retrieve information from ActiveX controls by checking their properties, just as you retrieve information from the controls in a dialog box. For example, to find out whether an option button is selected, you check to see if its `Value` property is `True` (which indicates that it is selected) or `False` (which indicates that it is not). Likewise, to retrieve text from a text box, you check its `Text` property or its `Value` property (either of which returns the same result).

Suppose you have a form which the user can fill in either as an individual or on behalf of their company; in either case, you would want a valid name (either for the individual or for the company), so you could create code such as that shown in Listing 19.4 to check that the text box for the chosen option button was filled in—and that the user had chosen one option button or the other (assuming both option buttons were deselected at first).

Listing 19.4

```
1.  Private Sub cmdSubmit_Click()
2.      Dim Msg As String, MTitle As String
3.      MTitle = "Missing Information"
4.      If optIndividual.Value = True Then
5.          If txtIndividual = "" Then
6.              Msg = "Please enter your name."
7.              MsgBox Msg, vbOKOnly + vbCritical, MTitle
8.              End
9.          End If
10.     ElseIf optCompany.Value = True Then
11.         If txtCompany = "" Then
12.             Msg = "Please enter your company name."
13.             MsgBox Msg, vbOKOnly + vbCritical, MTitle
14.             End
15.         End If
16.     Else
17.         Msg = "Please choose the Individual option button
            ➡or the Company option button."
18.         MsgBox Msg, vbOKOnly + vbCritical, MTitle
19.         End
20.     End If
```

```
21.          'macro continues here
22.      End Sub
23.
24.      Private Sub optCompany_Click()
25.          If optCompany.Value = True Then
             ➥optIndividual.Value = False
26.      End Sub
27.
28.      Private Sub optIndividual_Click()
29.          If optIndividual.Value = True Then
             ➥optCompany.Value = False
30.      End Sub
```

Analysis

This listing shows three macros: cmdSubmit_Click, which runs when the user clicks the Submit button on the form; optCompany_Click, which runs if the user clicks the optCompany option button; and optIndividual_Click, which runs if the user clicks the optIndividual option button.

cmdSubmit_Click checks the condition of the option buttons when the user tries to submit the form. Line 2 declares two strings, Msg (which will hold the text in the message boxes the macro displays when something is wrong) and MTitle (the title bar for the message box). Line 3 then assigns the text Missing Information to MTitle.

Line 4 uses an If statement to check the Value property of the optIndividual option button. If it is True—the option button is selected—the statements in lines 5 to 8 run. Line 5 checks to see if txtIndividual, the text box in which the individual's name should have been entered, contains only a blank string: if so, line 6 assigns appropriate text to the Msg string, line 7 displays a message box consisting of Msg, an OK button and a Wrong icon, and the title stored in MTitle, and line 8 uses an End statement to end execution of the macro and return the user to the form; if not (meaning the user has already entered their name), execution shifts to the End If statement in line 9, and from there to the End If statement in line 20, after which the macro continues.

If the If statement in line 4 is not True, VBA moves to line 10 and evaluates the ElseIf statement, which checks if the optCompany option button is selected. If it is, lines 11 to 15 repeat the actions of lines 5 to 9, but with the txtCompany text box, in which the company name should have been entered. Again, if the text box contains only an empty string, the macro displays a message box requesting the user to enter the company name.

If the `ElseIf` statement in line 10 is not `True`, VBA moves to the `Else` statement in line 16. If execution reaches this statement, the user has selected neither the `optIndividual` option button nor the `optCompany` option button and must be chastised, so line 17 assigns an appropriate message and line 18 displays it in a message box; again, this message box includes an OK button, the Wrong icon, and the `MTitle` string as the title bar.

Line 21 indicates where the macro would continue if the user had passed these labyrinthine checks and the form were ready for submission. Line 22 ends the `cmdSubmit_Click` macro.

Because the option buttons in the form are not contained in a frame, they do not work as an opposing pair—selecting one does not automatically deselect the other. So the form uses the macros `optCompany_Click` and `optIndividual_Click` to deselect the other option button when one option button is selected. `optCompany_Click` simply contains a statement that checks if the `Value` property of the `optCompany` option button is `True`; if it is, it sets the `Value` property of the `optIndividual` option button to `False`. `optIndividual_Click` returns the compliment.

Retrieving Information from Form Fields

At the end of Chapter 3, I left you hanging with an example of transferring information from the form fields in one document to the form fields in another document. In this section, we get to pick up that loose thread and pull it out as far as it goes.

As you'll recall, I suggested creating a macro that accesses the filled-in employment application and inserts relevant pieces of information from it into a letter inviting the applicant to an interview (or turning them down). This letter can be either a form or a document containing bookmarks; a form might be easier.

In your template for the letter to the applicant, you would set up form fields (or bookmarks) for the information you wanted to pull from the application: the various name and address fields, the position sought, and so on. To do so, you simply manipulate the `Result` property of the relevant `FormFields` object in the appropriate document by using strings.

For example, your macro might retrieve part of the information from the open application form like this:

```
With Documents("Application form.doc")
    FirstName$ =.FormFields("FirstName").Result
    MiddleInitial$ =.FormFields("MiddleInitial").Result
    LastName$ =.FormFields("LastName").Result
    JobSought$ =.FormFields("Job").Result
    ReferencesProvided =.FormFields("References").Result
End With
```

Having retrieved that information (and the rest), the macro would then open a new document based on the letter-to-the-applicant template and fill in the relevant fields (FirstName, MiddleInitial, LastName, and so on) in the letter:

```
With Documents("Letter to applicant.doc")
    .FormFields("FirstName").Result = FirstName$
    .FormFields("MiddleInitial").Result = MiddleInitial$
    .FormFields("LastName").Result = LastName$
    .FormFields("JobSought").Result = JobSought$
    If ReferencesProvided = 1 Then          'check box is selected
        .FormFields("ReferencesProvided").Result = "We will
        ➥check your references within the next week."
    Else
        .FormFields("ReferencesProvided").Result = "Please
        ➥provide the names of two references as soon as
        ➥possible."
    EndIf
End With
```

Once you've transferred all the relevant information from the application form to the letter, it'll be ready for a quick scan by the human eye to make sure everything's okay. While that's going on, you could have Word transfer the name and address information to an envelope and print that automatically.

Earlier in the chapter, I mentioned using Word's built-in dialog boxes instead of laboriously crafting complex custom dialog boxes of your own. That's next, whenever you're ready.

CHAPTER

TWENTY

20

Using Word's Built-in Dialog Boxes

In Chapters 7 and 19, you saw how you can create custom dialog boxes to allow the user to supply input to your macros. You learned how to create a dialog box by placing controls on a userform, how to hook the userform into the code of a macro, and how to retrieve from the dialog box the values resulting from the user's choices.

In this chapter, we'll look at how you can use Word's built-in dialog boxes to perform operations that you might otherwise construct a custom dialog box for. First, though, let's look at the reasons for using built-in dialog boxes, as well as the limitations of doing so.

Why Use Built-in Dialog Boxes?

At first, it may seem strange to use a built-in Word dialog box in a macro, but once you accept the idea, the advantages to using a built-in dialog box instead of a custom one are pretty obvious: you don't need to spend any time building the dialog box (just a few minutes inserting the code to summon it and link it to your macro), and you can be sure that it will work. Better yet, users of your macros will probably already be acquainted with the dialog box, especially if it's something as straightforward as an Open dialog box (or one of its many variations, such as the Insert File dialog box) or a formatting dialog box (such as the Font, Paragraph, or Borders and Shading dialog box).

The main disadvantages to using a built-in dialog box are that it may not offer all the actions you want (which might mean that you have to use two built-in dialog boxes, or one built-in dialog box followed by a custom dialog box, message box, or input box, to achieve your goal) and that it may offer the user actions that you do not want them to take. For example, you might require the user to open a file only from a given folder, in which case the Open dialog box would not be suitable, as it lets the user access any folder to which they have file-viewing rights.

As you'll see later in this chapter, you can circumvent some of these problems by retrieving only certain values from a built-in dialog box. This way, you can prevent the user from taking undesired actions. But if the built-in Word dialog box does not provide enough functionality for your needs, you probably shouldn't be using it in the first place.

Displaying a Built-in Dialog Box

To display a built-in dialog box, you need to know two things: first, the name and constant for the dialog box, and second, which method you want to use to display it.

Built-in Word dialog boxes are identified by constants starting with the letters *wdDialog* (as in Word Dialog), followed by the name of the dialog box; the name is derived from the menu commands required to display the dialog box. For example, to refer to the Open dialog box, you use the constant `wdDialogFileOpen`, because you would use the File ➤ Open command to display the dialog box. Likewise, to display the Print dialog box (File ➤ Print), you use the constant `wdDialogFilePrint`, and to display the Options dialog box (Tools ➤ Options), you use the constant `wdDialogToolsOptions`.

You use these constants with the `Dialogs` property, which returns the `Dialogs` collection object. For example, to return the Save As dialog box and display it using the `Show` property (which I'm sure you recall from Chapter 7), you would use the following statement:

```
Dialogs(wdDialogFileSaveAs).Show
```

So far so good. But here's where the plot thickens: VBA provides two methods of displaying built-in dialog boxes on-screen: `Show` and `Display`. The `Show` method not only displays the specified `Dialog` object but also executes the actions the user takes in the dialog box. For example, if you use the `Show` method to display the `wdDialogFileSaveAs` dialog box, and the user enters a name for the file in the File Name box and clicks the Save button, VBA will save the file with the given name in the specified folder (and with any options the user chose). The `Display` method, on the other hand, displays the dialog box on-screen but does *not* execute the actions the user takes in the dialog box; instead, it allows you to return the settings from the dialog box once the user dismisses it and use them for your own purposes. We'll look at how to use the `Show` and `Display` methods in the following sections. First, though, I'll quickly explain how to access the various tabs of tabbed dialog boxes.

Specifying the Tab to Display

If the dialog box you want to display has tabs, you can display the tab of your choice by specifying the `DefaultTab` property. You refer to a tab by the name of the dialog box plus the word *Tab* and the name of the tab, which is quite a mouthful. To illustrate, the constant for the Bullets and Numbering dialog box is `wdDialogFormat-BulletsAndNumbering`, and the constant for its Outline Numbered tab is `wdDialogFormatBulletsAndNumberingTabOutlineNumbered`. Likewise, the Font dialog box is referred to as `wdDialogFormat-Font`, and its Character Spacing tab is referred to as `wdDialogFormatFont-TabCharacterSpacing`; you could display the tab by using the following code, which uses a `With` statement:

```
With Dialogs(wdDialogFormatFont)
    .DefaultTab = wdDialogFormatFontTabCharacterSpacing
    .Show
End With
```

Using the Show Method to Display and Execute a Dialog Box

As I just mentioned, the `Show` method displays the specified dialog box and executes the actions the user takes in it. At the risk of stating the obvious, the `Show` method is useful when you need to have the user perform a conventional interactive action while you're running a macro. As a simple example, in a macro that is supposed to perform certain formatting tasks on the current document , you could check to make sure that a document was open before attempting to perform the formatting; then, if no document was open, you could display the Open dialog box so that the user could open a file. (You might precede the Open dialog box with a message box explaining the problem.) Listing 20.1 shows the code for this part of the macro.

Listing 20.1

```
1.   If Documents.Count = 0 Then
2.       Proceed = MsgBox("There is no document open." + vbCr
     ➥+ vbCr + "Please open a document for the macro
     ➥to work on.", vbOKCancel + vbExclamation, "Format
     ➥Report 1.13")
```

```
3.        If Proceed = vbOK Then
4.            Dialogs(wdDialogFileOpen).Show
5.            If Documents.Count = 0 Then End
6.        Else
7.            End
8.        End If
9.    End If
10.       'rest of macro here
```

Analysis

Line 1 checks the `Count` property of the `Documents` collection to see if no documents are open; if that's the case, the statements in lines 2 through 8 run. Line 2 displays a message box informing the user that no document is open and asking them to open one for the macro to work on. The message box has OK and Cancel buttons, and stores the button chosen in the variable `Proceed`. Line 3 checks to see if the OK button was chosen; if it was, line 4 displays the Open dialog box so that the user can select the file, which VBA will open when they click the Open button in the Open dialog box. (The user can cancel the procedure at this point by clicking the Cancel button in the Open dialog box, so line 5 checks the `Count` property of the `Documents` collection again, and uses an `End` statement to terminate execution of the procedure if there is still no document open.)

If the OK button was not chosen, execution moves from line 3 to the `Else` statement in line 6, and the `End` statement in line 7 ends execution of the macro.

Line 8 contains the `End If` statement for the nested `If` statement, and line 9 contains the `End If` statement for the outer `If` statement. Line 10 contains a comment to indicate that the rest of the macro would run from this point, which is reached only if a document is open.

Using the Display Method to Display a Dialog Box

Unlike the `Show` method, the `Display` method displays a built-in dialog box but does not execute the actions the user takes in the dialog box; instead, you can return the settings that the user made in the dialog box and use whichever of them you want in your macros. The twofold advantage of this method is that the user gets to work with familiar Word dialog boxes, and you get to retrieve only the settings you actually need for the macro.

For example, you'll often need to find out which folder a macro should be working in, such as when you need the location of a number of documents that the user wants to manipulate. To get the folder, you *could* display a straightforward input box (as discussed in Chapter 6) and prompt the user to type in the correct path to the folder. The problem with this is that the user may not know the path or may mistype it, both of which are more likely given Windows 95 and Windows NT's support for long file names containing spaces and punctuation. A possible solution is to display a list box containing the tree of drives, folders, and files, as discussed in Chapter 19; but to do this you need to dimension an array and fill it with the folders and file names, *and* you need to refresh the display every time the user moves up or down the tree—quite a lot of work. You can achieve the same result much more easily by displaying one of Word's built-in dialog boxes—for instance, the Open dialog box, which has the tree built in—and grabbing the settings for your own purposes.

> **NOTE**
>
> In the above example, by using the `Display` method you can grab the name and path of the folder that the user chose in the Open dialog box without having the user actually open a file, whereas if you used the `Show` method to display the Open dialog box, the user would open a file or cancel the dialog box, neither of which you want them to do.

Working with the Settings in a Built-in Dialog Box

In this section, I'll discuss how to work with the settings in Word's built-in dialog boxes. In your macros, you'll need to do the following with these settings:

- Set them appropriately before displaying the dialog box, to provide the user with specific information or to steer the user toward choosing certain settings

- Retrieve them from the dialog box once the user has dismissed it

- Make sure the dialog box contains the current information for the dialog box

Executing the Settings in a Built-in Dialog Box Displayed Using the Display Method

To execute the settings in a built-in dialog box that you've displayed with the `Display` method, you use the `Execute` method. You probably won't want to do this very often, which is why you're reading about it in a separate section rather than in the main text, but there are times when it comes in handy.

Let's say you want to let the user specify the name under which to save a file. To this end, you could use the `Show` method to display the Save As dialog box, which allows the user to choose the folder in which to save the file and to specify the name for the file. When the user then chooses the Save button in the Save As dialog box, the file will be saved in the specified location under the specified name. But if you wanted to make sure that the user saved the file with an 8.3 file name rather than with a long file name, you could use the `Display` method instead of the `Show` method. Then, when the user clicked the Save button to dismiss the Save As dialog box, you could check the file name they had chosen and change it to an 8.3 name if necessary.

Setting Options in a Built-in Dialog Box

You can set the options in a dialog box either with or without displaying the dialog box. Your choice usually depends on the option you're manipulating. For example, when you set the user name on the User Information tab of the Options dialog box, you are writing information to the registry that you can then draw on for other macros; in this case, there's no need to display the dialog box. In other cases, though, you'll need to display the dialog box, because just setting an option without displaying the dialog box has no effect. For example, you might want to display the Save As dialog box showing a suggested name in the File Name text box. To do so, you would set the name in the File Name text box and then display the dialog box, but the name wouldn't be implemented (i.e., the file wouldn't be saved under the name) until the user chose the Save button in the dialog box. (If you simply

635

wanted to save the file under the specified name instead of suggesting a name that the user can change if they want to, you'd do better to use the SaveAs method on the appropriate Document object than mess with the Save As dialog box.)

Before you spend time setting an option in a Word dialog box by specifying the dialog box and the argument for setting one of its options, check whether you can achieve the same effect by using a method without involving a dialog box. In most cases, your cue for using a dialog box will be that you need to involve the user of the macro at some level.

To set an option in a built-in dialog box, use a Set statement to return a dialog object that refers to the object in the Dialogs collection. For example, to set the contents of the File Name text box in the Save As dialog box, you could use the statements shown below. The first statement returns a dialog object called SaveMe that refers to the wdDialogFileSaveAs object in the Dialogs collection. The second statement sets the Name property of SaveMe to **Baroque Castles in Bavaria, Introduction.doc**, and the third statement uses the Show method to display the Save As dialog box.

```
Set SaveMe = Dialogs(wdDialogFileSaveAs)
SaveMe.Name = "Baroque Castles in Bavaria, Introduction.doc"
SaveMe.Show
```

Most of the built-in Word dialog boxes have a number of arguments that you can use for retrieving or setting values in the dialog box. For example, the Open dialog box has arguments for Name (as you just saw), ConfirmConversions, ReadOnly, LinkToSource, AddToMru (adding the document to the Most Recently Used document list at the foot of the File menu), PasswordDoc, and more. Some of these are options that you'll see in the Open dialog box itself; others are associated options that you'll find on the various tabs of the Options dialog box.

You can deduce the names of many of the arguments for a built-in dialog box from the names by which the options are identified in the dialog box itself. For example, in the Font dialog box (wdDialogFormatFont), the Font drop-down list is identified by the Font argument, and the Color drop-down list is identified by the Color argument. Other options, however, have less obvious names: for instance, the Size drop-down list in the Font dialog box is identified by the Points argument, which you might not readily guess. In these cases, the easiest way to access the correct names is to open the VBA Help file (by pressing the F1 key while working in the Visual Basic Editor), click the Help Topics button to display the Help Topics dialog box, select the Index tab, and choose the topic "built-in Word dialog boxes, argument list." This displays a list of all the built-in Word dialog boxes and the names of the arguments they take, as shown in Figure 20.1.

FIGURE 20.1

Use this list to find the arguments you need to manipulate built-in dialog boxes.

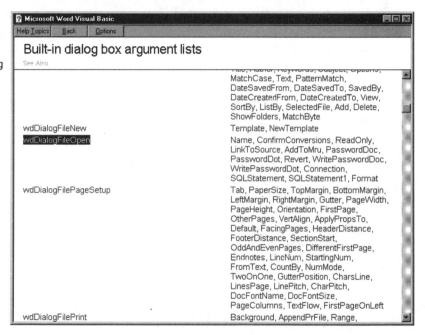

For example, in some macros, you may want to display the Open dialog box showing a particular directory and a particular set of files. If you wanted to display all the .txt files in the \textinput\ folder on the networked drive Mercury\MercuryD\, you would set the Name argument for the dialog box to *.txt. You could use the following statements to set the Name argument and display the Open dialog box showing the appropriate folder and files:

```
ChangeFileOpenDirectory "\\Mercury\MercuryD\textinput"
With Dialogs(wdDialogFileOpen)
    .Name = "*.txt"
    .Show
End With
```

Restoring the Previous Settings in a Built-in Dialog Box

Along with setting options in a dialog box before displaying it to guide the user toward the correct choices, you'll often want to restore the settings in certain dialog boxes at the end of a macro. For instance, if you perform a Find and Replace operation via VBA, the settings will stick at the end of the macro, and the next time the user opens the Find and Replace dialog box, they will see the details of the last operation you performed. This isn't usually too embarrassing, though it can disconcert users who assumed your macro was performing unfathomably complex maneuvers rather than a series of conventional (if subtly planned and beautifully executed) Find and Replace operations; the main problem is that the user will need to clear the settings the macro has left in order to execute a Find and Replace of their own, and if they fail to do so, they may get unexpected results.

You might do well to create a macro that clears the settings in the Find and Replace dialog box. You could then call this macro from the end of any macro that had used Find and Replace. Listing 20.2 shows an example of how this macro might look.

Listing 20.2

```
1.   Sub Clear_Find_and_Replace()
2.       With Selection.Find
3.           .ClearFormatting
4.           .Text = ""
5.           .Replacement.ClearFormatting
6.           .Replacement.Text = ""
7.           .MatchAllWordForms = False
8.           .MatchCase = False
9.           .MatchSoundsLike = False
10.          .MatchWholeWord = False
11.          .MatchWildcards = False
12.          .Wrap = wdFindContinue
13.          .Forward = True
14.      End With
15.  End Sub
```

Analysis

This macro is very straightforward: it simply uses a `With` statement that starts in line 2 and ends in line 14 to set all the relevant properties in the Find and Replace dialog box. Line 3 clears formatting on the `Find` object, and line 4 sets the `Find` object's text to an empty string. Lines 5 and 6 perform the same actions, but for the `Replacement` object. Lines 7 through 11 set the `MatchAllWordForms`, `MatchCase`, `MatchSoundsLike`, `MatchWholeWord`, and `MatchWildcards` properties to `False`, their default state. Line 12 sets the `Wrap` property to `wdFindContinue`, its default value. Line 13 sets the `Forward` property to `True`, its default value. Line 14 ends the `With` statement, and line 15 ends the macro.

> **NOTE**
>
> You could simply include the contents of this macro (lines 2 through 14) at the end of a macro that used Find and Replace, but your code will be much tighter and more efficient if you create this macro as a separate item and then call it from any macro that needs it, as discussed in Chapter 17.

If you use Find and Replace frequently in your macros—and given how useful they are for manipulating text, you're likely to—you may also want to call a macro such as this at the beginning of a macro that uses Find and Replace. By doing so, you can ensure that you're working from a known group of settings and that one of the options will not trip you up with an unexpected setting.

> **TIP**
>
> If you want to be really classy, you can retrieve the details of the last Find and Replace operation and store them in private variables for the duration of the macro, then use them to restore the user's last Find and Replace operation as the macro ends. Under certain circumstances, this might be useful, but in most cases you'll do best to clear the details of the Find and Replace operations you've performed and leave it at that.

Retrieving Values from a Built-in Dialog Box

When you use the `Display` method to display a dialog box, you'll almost always need to return information from the dialog box—otherwise, there's little point in displaying the dialog box (beyond deliberately annoying the user, of course, which displaying a random and useless succession of built-in dialog boxes will do admirably). When you use the `Show` method to display a dialog box and let the user take the usual action the dialog box offers, you may also want to return information from the dialog box.

To return a value from a built-in dialog box, you identify the dialog box, typically by using a `Set` statement to return a dialog object that refers to the appropriate object in the `Dialogs` collection. You then display the dialog box to let the user choose settings; if you want to be able to approve the settings before implementing them, you use the `Display` method instead of the `Show` method so that VBA does not execute the settings when the user dismisses the dialog box. You then check the settings, change any that need changing, and use the `Execute` method to apply the settings or otherwise use them for your own purposes.

For example, say you wanted to display the Drop Cap dialog box to allow the user to specify the size and font of a drop cap, but at the same time you wanted to force the user to position it as a drop cap rather than in the margin (which is one of the positioning options the Drop Cap dialog box provides). You could use the statements shown in Listing 20.3 to return the `Dialog` object for the Drop Cap dialog box, display the dialog box, and make sure the positioning of the drop cap was correct. (This macro involves checking only one of the settings in the dialog box; in more complex dialog boxes, or in procedures in which you want to exert a greater degree of control, you'll often want to check more settings.)

Listing 20.3

```
1.   Set MyDrop = Dialogs(wdDialogFormatDropCap)
2.   With MyDrop
3.       .Position = wdDropNormal
4.       .Font = "Arial"
5.       .DropHeight = 4
6.       .DistFromText = 0.5
7.       BClicked = .Display
8.       If BClicked = 0 Then End
```

```
 9.      If .Position <> wdDropNormal Then
       ➥.Position = wdDropNormal
10.      .Execute
11.  End With
```

Analysis

Line 1 returns the `Dialog` object for the Drop Cap dialog box and stores it in `MyDrop`. Lines 2 to 11 contain a `With` statement for the MyDrop object. Line 3 specifies the `Position` argument for the dialog box, which governs the setting in the Position area of the dialog box. This can be set to None, Dropped, or In Margin; here, `wdDropNormal` specifies the Dropped option. Line 4 sets the `Font` argument to Arial, which sets the Font drop-down list in the dialog box. Line 5 sets the `DropHeight` argument, which sets the Lines to Drop spinner box in the dialog box. Line 6 sets the `DistFromText` argument, which sets the Distance from Text spinner box in the dialog box.

Line 7 displays the dialog box, which appears with the specified settings (see Figure 20.2); the statement sets the result of the dialog box to the variable `Bclicked`, which the macro uses to check which button the user clicked. The user can then make choices in the dialog box, and execution continues when they dismiss the dialog box.

FIGURE 20.2

By setting options in a dialog box before displaying it, you can guide the user of a macro toward the right choice. If they refuse to take the bait, you can check and correct the settings after they dismiss the dialog box.

Line 8 compares the value of `BClicked` to 0, which would indicate that the user had chosen the Cancel button in the dialog box; if it matches, the `End` statement ends the macro without executing the choices the user made in the dialog box. (I'll discuss how to check which button the user chose in a dialog box shortly.)

Line 9 checks the `Position` setting and resets it to `wdDropNormal` if it is set to anything else. Line 10 uses the `Execute` method to execute the settings in the dialog box, implementing the drop cap with the user's choices (and `wdDropNormal`, if the user chose anything else). Line 11 ends the `With` statement.

Getting the Current Values for a Dialog Box

You can use the `Update` method to make sure that you're working with the current values for a dialog box. This is primarily useful when you call a dialog box containing volatile information early in a macro and then need to ensure you have the current values when you use information from that dialog box later in the process.

For example, if, during a macro, you display a modeless dialog box such as Spelling or Find and Replace, the user can make changes to the settings while the macro is executing, so you may need to update the values before using Find and Replace (or Spelling) later in the macro. The first of the following statements declares an object named `MyFind` that references the Replace tab of the Find and Replace dialog box (note that this is referred to as `wdDialogEditReplace` rather than, say, `wdDialogEditFindAndReplaceTabReplace`; this is a legacy of the separate Find dialog box and Replace dialog box from earlier versions of Word). The second line displays the `MyFind` object. The third line indicates where other actions in the macro would take place, and the fourth line uses the `Update` method to update the information in the dialog box.

```
Set MyFind = Dialogs(wdDialogEditReplace)
MyFind.Display
'other actions
MyFind.Update
```

In most cases, however, it makes more sense to delay calling the dialog box until it is needed. By doing so, you will get the current values for the dialog box and will not need to use the `Update` method.

Returning the Button the User Chose in a Dialog Box

The settings in a built-in dialog box are only part of the story. To find out which button the user clicked in a dialog box, you check the return value of the `Show` method or the `Display` method. The return values are as follows:

Return Value	Button Clicked
–2	Close
–1	OK
0	Cancel
1	The first command button
2	The second command button
>2	Subsequent command buttons

You might imagine there's little point in returning the button clicked when using the `Show` method, because `Show` executes the action the user takes in the dialog box before you can check the value the method returns. But in fact, returning the button clicked can tell you if the user chose to close or cancel the dialog box, which can prove invaluable for directing the flow of a macro correctly.

For example, in Listing 20.1 earlier in the chapter, we used an `If Documents .Count = 0 Then End` statement to trap the result of the user's clicking the Cancel button in the Open dialog box (rather than opening a document as expected). In this case, checking the `Count` property worked well because we knew there weren't any documents open, so it was a reasonable way to proceed; but things won't always be this convenient. Instead of checking the `Count` property, we could have trapped the click of the Cancel button by using code such as that shown in Listing 20.4. This technique isn't necessarily better, but you'll find it useful in a far wider variety of circumstances.

Listing 20.4

```
1.   If Documents.Count = 0 Then
2.       Proceed = MsgBox("There is no document open." + vbCr
     ➥+ vbCr + "Please open a document for the macro
     ➥to work on.", vbOKCancel + vbExclamation,
     ➥"Format Report 1.13")
3.       If Proceed = vbOK Then
4.           ButtonChosen = Dialogs(wdDialogFileOpen).Show
5.           If ButtonChosen = 0 Then End
6.       Else
7.           End
8.       End If
9.   End If
10.  'rest of macro here
```

Analysis

Here, the macro proceeds along the same lines as the macro in Listing 20.1 until line 4, which implicitly declares the variable ButtonChosen and assigns to it the result of the Show method for the Open dialog box; so VBA displays the dialog box and stores the button clicked in the ButtonChosen variable. Line 5 then tests the value of ButtonChosen against 0, the value of the Cancel button; if they match, the End statement ends execution of the macro; if they do not match, line 8 ends the nested If statement, line 9 ends the outer If statement, and execution of the macro continues from line 10.

Specifying a Timeout for a Dialog Box

One final thing you can do with built-in dialog boxes is display them only for a specified time rather than having them stay open until the user dismisses them. To do so, you use the TimeOut variant argument with the Show method or the Display method. You specify TimeOut as a number of units, each of which is approximately a thousandth of a second (if the system is busy with many other tasks, the units may be longer). So you could display the User Information tab of the Options dialog box for 15 seconds—long enough for the user to check the Name setting and change it if necessary—by using the following statements:

```
With Dialogs(wdDialogToolsOptions)
    .DefaultTab = wdDialogToolsOptionsTabUserInfo
    .Show (15000)
End With
```

NOTE   `TimeOut` **does not work for custom dialog boxes, only for built-in Word dialog boxes.**

Timing out a dialog box is especially useful for noncritical information like the user name in this example, because it allows the macro to proceed even if the user has left the computer. Likewise, you might want to time out a Save As dialog box in which the macro suggested a viable file name but allowed the user (if present and lucid) to override it. However, for a procedure in which the user's input is essential, you won't want to use the `TimeOut` argument.

By now you should have dialog boxes of various descriptions coming out of your ears, or at least popping up to enhance your macros and allow the user to direct them appropriately. You've also assembled a powerful arsenal of VBA tools that will enable you to automate many procedures in Word. In the next part of the book, I'll discuss how you can put together all that you've learned so far.

PART III

Automating Word
Procedures and Documents

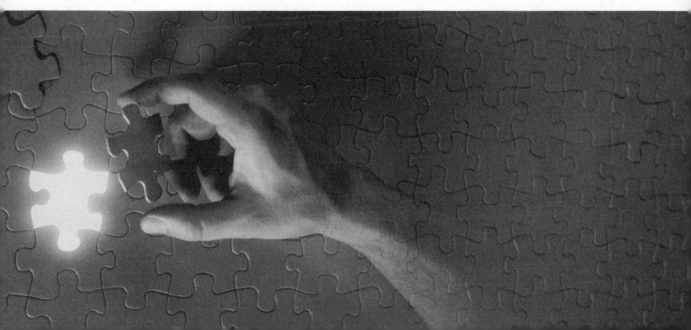

CHAPTER TWENTY-ONE

Word's Automatic Macros, Startup Switches, and the Registry

In Chapter 3, we touched briefly on the five automatic macro names that Word provides for helping you automate your templates. I'll start off this chapter by discussing suitable ways of using these automatic macros. I'll also discuss briefly macro viruses (which are typically based on using automatic macros) and ways of guarding against them.

From automatic macros we'll move on to startup switches, which are instructions that you can run when you load Word to achieve particular results. Startup switches aren't difficult to grasp or to use, but they can come in handy, so reserve some storage in your brain for the middle of the chapter.

Lastly, I'll show you how you can use Word and VBA to access and manipulate the registry—the Windows 95 and Windows NT database that contains configuration information for your computer's hardware and software.

Word's Five Automatic Macros

Word provides the following five names for automatic macros:

- `AutoExec` runs whenever you start Word.

- `AutoExit` runs when you exit Word.

- `AutoNew` runs whenever you create a new file based on a template containing an AutoNew macro.

- `AutoOpen` runs whenever you open a file based on a template containing an AutoOpen macro.

- `AutoClose` runs whenever you close a file based on a template containing an AutoClose macro.

AutoExec

The `AutoExec` macro runs whenever you start Word or whenever you load a global template. The main instance of `AutoExec` lives in the Normal.dot template, in which you can have only one active `AutoExec` macro at a time (if you have more than one, Word will run only the first). You can use an `AutoExec` macro in Normal.dot to set screen preferences, to open the last couple of files you worked on, or to open, say, a log file that you need to update every morning at work. You can use an `AutoExec` macro in a global template to perform other operations as needed.

> **NOTE**
>
> If you start more than one session of Word, the `AutoExec` macro will run in each of those sessions. So it's a mistake to create an `AutoExec` macro that simply starts a fresh copy of Word: each fresh copy would launch another until the afflicted computer ran out of memory. (Before you ask—yes, I have tried this. It was briefly amusing.)

In the next sections, we'll look at a couple of examples of `AutoExec` macros.

Using an AutoExec Macro to Set a Procedure to Run at a Specific Time

One use for an `AutoExec` macro that's not immediately obvious is to automatically set a procedure to run at a specific time. You could use this to do anything from displaying a reminder at a certain time (though Outlook, Office 97's Desktop Information Manager, would usually be easier for such a menial and mechanical task) to running a long information-gathering macro at an antisocial hour every morning.

To run a procedure at a specific time, you use the `OnTime` method with the `Application` object. The `OnTime` method sets a background timer running (you can only run one `OnTime` timer at a time) and takes the following syntax:

```
expression.OnTime(When, Name, Tolerance)
```

Here, `expression` is a required expression that returns an `Application` object. Usually, you'll want to use the `Application` object itself.

`When` is a required variant specifying the time (or date and time) at which to run the procedure. You'll usually want to use a string to specify the time (e.g., `00:01` to run a macro at a minute past midnight, `4/1/97 13:00` to run a macro at 1 p.m. on April Fools' Day 1997), but you can also use a serial time—the numerical format in which applications store dates and times—or a serial date and time if you find that more convenient.

`Name` is a required string specifying the name of the macro you want to run. There are a couple of things to note about this: First, the macro needs to be available both when you run the `OnTime` command (in this case, when Word is started) and at the time specified in `When`. This often means that the macro needs to be in Normal.dot (or another global template you load automatically). Second, if you have multiple macros with the same name, you can make sure that `OnTime` chooses the right one by specifying its complete macro path in the form `projectname.modulename.macroname`. For example, to specify the macro named `Create_Report` in the module named `Sales` in the `Normal` template, you would use the path `Normal.Sales.Create_Report`.

`Tolerance` is an optional variant specifying the number of seconds that VBA should let pass before canceling the running of the macro. `Tolerance` comes into play if something delays the running of the macro at the specified time. For example, if you have a dialog box open at the specified time, or if you're running another macro, the `OnTime` command will not be able to execute until the dialog box is closed or the other macro stops running. If you omit `Tolerance`, or set a tolerance of 0 seconds, VBA runs the macro as soon as it is able to (no matter how long the delay is).

To illustrate, you could use the following `AutoExec` macro to set VBA to run the `Create_Report` macro at one minute past midnight:

```
Sub AutoExec()
    Application.OnTime When:="00:01",
    ↪Name:="Normal.Sales.Create_Report"
End Sub
```

Using an AutoExec Macro to Implement AutoCorrect Settings for Different Users

In Chapter 4, I mentioned some of the pitfalls associated with full use of AutoCorrect—mainly that one person's designated abbreviation for a word or phrase is another person's everyday word in a special context, and that a user who is not accustomed to a full set of AutoCorrect entries will trip up over entries customized to someone else who uses them in every line they type. To remedy this, you could create a simple `AutoExec` macro that checks the name of the user and turns off AutoCorrect's Replace Text as You Type feature for users who don't want it (see Listing 21.1).

Listing 21.1

```
1.  Sub AutoExec()
2.      User = InputBox("Enter your first name:", "Word Logon")
3.      If User = "John" Then
4.          Application.AutoCorrect.ReplaceText = True
5.      Else
6.          Application.AutoCorrect.ReplaceText = False
7.      End If
8.  End Sub
```

Analysis

Line 2 displays an input box that prompts the user to enter their first name. Line 3 uses an If statement to check if the name is John: if it is, line 4 sets the Replace Text property of the AutoCorrect object to True, which enables the Replace Text as You Type feature; if it is not, execution shifts to the Else statement in line 5, and line 6 sets the ReplaceText property of the AutoCorrect object to False, disabling the Replace Text as You Type feature. Line 7 ends the If statement, and line 8 ends the macro.

AutoExit

The AutoExit macro is the logical counterpart to the AutoExec macro, and runs whenever you close down Word or when you unload a global template. Like AutoExec, AutoExit lives in the Normal.dot template (or in a global template), where you can have only one active AutoExit macro at a time.

Typically, it's harder to find convincing uses for an AutoExit macro in Normal.dot than for an AutoExec macro; finding uses for an AutoExit macro in another global template is a little easier. In some special cases, you may want to employ an AutoExit macro in Normal.dot to restore the user environment so that Word is in a suitable condition for the next user. For example, in a classroom or lab environment, you could use an AutoExit macro to reset all keyboard shortcuts, toolbars, and menus to their default settings. Listing 21.2 displays such a macro.

Listing 21.2

```
1.   Sub AutoExit()
2.       On Error GoTo Handle
3.       Documents.Open "c:\Program Files\Microsoft Office\
         ➥Templates\Normal.dot"
4.       KeyBindings.ClearAll
5.       With Application
6.           For Each cb In CommandBars
7.                   .CommandBars(cb.Name).Reset
8.           Next cb
9.           .CommandBars("File").Reset
10.          .CommandBars("Edit").Reset
11.          .CommandBars("View").Reset
12.          .CommandBars("Insert").Reset
13.          .CommandBars("Format").Reset
14.          .CommandBars("Tools").Reset
15.          .CommandBars("Table").Reset
16.          .CommandBars("Window").Reset
17.          .CommandBars("Help").Reset
18.      End With
19.      Documents("Normal.dot").Save
20.      End
21.  Handle:
22.      If Err = -2147467259 Then
23.          Application.CommandBars(cb.Name).Delete
24.          Resume Next
25.      End If
26.  End Sub
```

Analysis

This macro clears all keyboard shortcuts and command-bar customizations, and it deletes any custom toolbars that have been created. Line 2 begins the macro with an On Error statement directing execution to the Handle label in line 21 if an error occurs. You'll see the reason for this in a moment.

Line 3 opens Normal.dot for the changes, and Line 4 uses the ClearAll method on the KeyBindings object to clear all custom key assignments.

Line 5 then begins a `With` statement that ends in line 18. The `For...Next` statement in lines 6 through 8 uses the `Reset` method on the `CommandBar` object identified by the counter in the loop (`cb`) to reset each command bar in turn. The command bars reset this way include all the built-in Word toolbars (Standard, Formatting, AutoText, Web, and so on all the way to seldom-seen toolbars such as the AutoShapes toolbar) and the menu bar, which is a command bar named Menu Bar.

So far, so good; but you cannot reset a custom toolbar, because it has no built-in default values. So when line 7 tries to apply the `Reset` method to a custom toolbar, an error will occur. The error-handling code then shifts execution to the `Handle` label in line 21. Line 22 compares the error to `-2147467259`, the error generated by trying to reset a custom toolbar. If the error matches (as it should), line 23 uses the `Delete` method to delete the custom command bar. Line 24 then uses a `Resume Next` statement to continue execution at the `Next cb` statement in line 8 (the next line after line 7, which generated the error). The `For...Next` loop then continues until all built-in command bars have been reset and all custom command bars have been deleted.

After that, it's the turn of the menus, which (as you'll recall) are considered command bars, but which will not have been reset by the `For...Next` loop. To reset the menus, you need to specify them by name and use the `Reset` method. Line 9 resets the File menu, line 10 the Edit menu, and so on through line 17, which resets the Help menu. (Any custom menus will already have been removed by the `For...Next` loop when it reset the menu bar.)

Line 18 then ends the `With` statement, line 19 saves Normal.dot, and line 20 contains an `End` statement to end execution of the macro before reaching the error handler, which will have been used by this point if it was needed. Line 26 ends the macro.

NOTE   This macro works well, but depending on your circumstances, you might find it easier to simply copy to each computer a "safe" version of Normal.dot from the network or from a location inaccessible to the students. The disadvantage to doing so is that you have to perform the copy operation from outside Word—you cannot mess with Normal.dot like this while it is running.

Another use for an `AutoExit` macro would be to display a message to the user reminding them to perform a particular task, depending on the time of day, before closing Word. For example, an `AutoExit` macro could check to see if the time was between 4 p.m. and 5 p.m. and, if it was, display a reminder for the employee to fill in their timecard for the day or complete some kind of log. You could even check to make sure that a vital file had been created—and prevent them from leaving Word (though not their computer) until it had been.

AutoNew

An `AutoNew` macro runs whenever you open a new file based on the template containing it. You can have only one `AutoNew` macro per template, including Normal.dot. If the the new document you're creating is based on a template that contains an `AutoNew` macro, that macro will run; otherwise, the `AutoNew` macro in Normal.dot will run. If this seems odd, cast your mind back to the discussion of Word's three-layer architecture, and of Normal.dot, in "How Do Templates Work?" in Chapter 3.

Adding an `AutoNew` macro to a template is a great way to create forms: you can automatically pull the latest information from a database into the new document. Likewise, if part of a document can be filled in easily and quickly with a macro, you could display a dialog box to collect that information, then fill it in automatically. Once you'd done that, you could save the document—or prompt the user to save it—in an appropriate location.

> **NOTE**　You can put an `AutoNew` macro in a document, but it won't do you much good, because you can't create a new document based on another document—you can only create a new document based on a template.

Alternatively, you can use an `AutoNew` macro to set up the screen appropriately for the user to work on the document. This might mean making sure that certain toolbars were displayed and that other toolbars weren't, that the application window and document window were maximized, and so on. Listing 21.3 contains such a macro.

Listing 21.3

```
1.   Sub AutoNew()
2.       If Application.WindowState <> wdWindowStateMaximize
     ➥Then
3.           Application.WindowState = wdWindowStateMaximize
4.       End If
5.       If ActiveWindow.WindowState <> wdWindowStateMaximize
     ➥Then
6.           ActiveWindow.WindowState = wdWindowStateMaximize
7.       End If
8.       For Each cmb In Application.CommandBars
9.           With Application.CommandBars(cmb.Name)
10.              If .Name = "Standard" Or .Name = "Formatting"
             ➥Or.Name = "Utilities"
             ➥Or .Name = "Menu Bar" Then
11.                  If .Visible = False Then .Visible = True
12.              Else
13.                  If .Visible = True Then .Visible = False
14.              End If
15.          End With
16.      Next cmb
17.  End Sub
```

Analysis

Line 2 begins by using an If statement to check whether the state of the application window is anything other than maximized (i.e., if it is minimized or "restored"); if so, line 3 maximizes the window. Line 4 ends this If statement.

Line 5 uses a similar If statement to check whether the state of the active window is anything other than maximized; if so, line 6 maximizes the window. Line 7 ends this If statement.

Lines 8 through 16 contain a For Each...Next statement that displays the Standard, Formatting, and Utilities toolbars (Utilities is a toolbar I'm assuming is in the template), and the menu bar, and hides all other displayed toolbars. (As I discussed in Chapter 3, you can't hide the menu bar.)

Here's how this works:

- The `For Each...Next` statement runs for each object (referenced here by the variable `cmb`) in the `CommandBars` collection.

- Line 9 begins a `With` clause that references the `Name` property of the current command bar object specified by `cmb`.

- Line 10 compares the `Name` property of the command bar object specified by `cmb` to the names of the command bars we want to have displayed at the end of the macro: Standard, Formatting, Utilities, and Menu Bar (the menu bar itself). If the name matches, the `If` statement in line 11 runs, checking to see if the `Visible` property is `False` (which means the command bar is hidden) and, if it is, changing it to `True`, thus displaying the command bar.

- If the name does not match those listed in line 10, execution shifts to the `Else` statement in line 12, and line 13 checks the `Visible` property against `True` to see if the command bar is displayed; if it is, the `Then` statement changes the `Visible` property to `False`, hiding the command bar. Line 14 ends the `If` statement, line 15 the `With` statement, line 16 the `For Each...Next` statement, and line 17 the macro.

AutoOpen

An `AutoOpen` macro runs whenever you reopen a file based on the template containing the `AutoOpen` macro. Like `AutoNew`, you can have any number of `AutoOpen` macros, one in Normal.dot and one apiece in any other templates or documents. If the document you're opening contains an `AutoOpen` macro, that macro will run; if, instead, the document you're opening is based on a template that contains an `AutoOpen` macro, that macro will run; otherwise, any `AutoOpen` macro in Normal.dot will run.

Because `AutoOpen` is template-specific, if you want to, say, switch to a particular printer for a given type of document, this would be an easy way to do that. For example, by using an `AutoOpen` macro, you could make sure that the user's default printer was a PostScript printer when they opened a document that required PostScript output (see Listing 21.4).

Listing 21.4

```
1.   Sub AutoOpen()
2.       If ActivePrinter <> "HP LaserJet 4ML PostScript
     ➡on LPT1:" Then
3.           WasPrinter = ActivePrinter
4.           ActivePrinter = "HP LaserJet 4ML PostScript"
5.           Msg = "Word has changed printers from "
         ➡+ WasPrinter + " to " + ActivePrinter + vbCr
6.           Msg = Msg + "because this document requires
         ➡a PostScript printer."
7.           MsgBox Msg, vbOKOnly + vbInformation,
         ➡"Printer Changed"
8.       End If
9.   End Sub
```

Analysis

Line 2 checks to see if the `ActivePrinter` object is `HP LaserJet 4ML PostScript on LPT1`. If it's not, the statements in the `If` condition run:

- Line 3 stores the name of the `ActivePrinter` object in the variable `WasPrinter`.

- Line 4 changes the `ActivePrinter` object to the PostScript printer.

- Lines 5 and 6 build a message in the variable `Msg` informing the user of the change, and line 7 displays a message box containing `Msg`.

Line 8 ends the `If` condition, and line 9 ends the macro.

You'll find many uses for `AutoOpen` macros, so I'll mention just a few here:

- First, you may want to use an `AutoOpen` macro to maximize the application and document windows (or otherwise arrange the windows) and display specified toolbars, much like the `AutoNew` macro shown in Listing 21.3.

- If you're editing a document, you may want to use an `AutoOpen` macro to make sure that Track Changes is switched on (as discussed in Chapter 18).

- If you want to update all fields when you open a document, you could write an `AutoOpen` macro to update the fields (as discussed in Chapter 14):

```
Sub AutoOpen()
    ActiveDocument.Fields.Update
End Sub
```

AutoClose

An `AutoClose` macro runs whenever you close a file based on the template containing the `AutoClose` macro, or when you close a document that contains an `AutoClose` macro. As with `AutoOpen`, any template or document can contain one `AutoClose` macro, as can Normal.dot. If the document is based on a template that contains an `AutoClose` macro, or if the document itself contains an `AutoClose` macro, that macro will run when you close the document; otherwise, any `AutoClose` macro in Normal.dot will run.

You might want to pair `AutoClose` with `AutoOpen` to undo any environmental changes you make—for example, to switch back to the regular printer from the special one, or to switch paper trays on a printer from a letterhead tray to the regular tray.

Disabling Automatic Macros

As you saw in Chapter 3, the automatic macros in Word (and in other word processing applications and spreadsheets) can be used as vectors for macro viruses to attack any computer that opens an infected file. In previous versions of Word, only templates could contain macros, but because you could disguise a template as a document by simply renaming its *.dot* extension to **.doc**, you couldn't be sure that what appeared to be a harmless document was not in fact a macro-bearing template in disguise. So the ability of Word 97 documents to contain macros does not really represent any further threat to security.

Microsoft has built *some* protection against macro viruses into Word (and Excel), but you still need to keep your eyes open and your wits about you. This built-in protection scans each document or template you try to open to see if it contains code (i.e., any macro, function, or userform). If it does, Word displays the Warning dialog box shown in Figure 21.1, offering you four choices:

- Click the Disable Macros button to have Word open the document or template in a read-only mode that prevents any automatic macros from running. This also prevents you from executing any of the code in the document or template yourself. But in read-only mode, you can open the Visual Basic Editor and examine the code in the document or template and establish for yourself whether it is innocent or malevolent. If you give it the thumbs up, you'll need to close the document and open it again. This time, Word will display a message box (shown here) telling you that the document or template was last opened as read-only and asking if you want to open it as read-only again. Choose the No button. Word will respond with the Warning dialog box again. This time, choose the Enable Macros button, and Word will open the document or template normally, so you will be able to run the code it contains.

- Click the Enable Macros button to have Word open the document or template with the macros enabled. Any automatic macros contained in the document or template will execute as usual, and you will be able to run the code yourself either from the Macros dialog box or from the Visual Basic Editor.

- Click the Do Not Open button to cancel the Open operation. This doesn't do much good—it prevents any automatic macros from running, but you don't resolve the question of whether the code in the document or template is good or evil.

- Click the Tell Me More button to display information on macro viruses and how you can visit Microsoft's Web site to buy anti-virus software that will scan your computer's drives for macro viruses and other infections. (This isn't really a choice, because it doesn't take any action on the document; once you've read the information, you still need to choose among the Disable Macros button, the Enable Macros button, and the Do Not Open button.)

FIGURE 21.1

The Warning dialog box alerts you to the presence of code in a document or template.

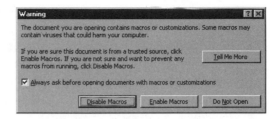

The Always Ask before Opening Documents with Macros or Customizations check box in the Warning dialog box provides a quick way to turn off the virus-scanning feature, which is enabled by default. If you clear this check box, Word will display the Confirm Macro Virus Protection Off dialog box shown in Figure 21.2. Click the Yes button to turn macro virus protection off.

FIGURE 21.2

To turn macro virus protection off, click the Yes button in the Confirm Macro Virus Protection Off dialog box.

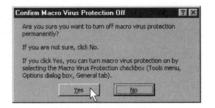

Once you've done this, you can turn macro virus protection back on by selecting the Macro Virus Protection check box on the General tab of the Options dialog box. (As you've probably guessed, you can also clear this check box to turn macro virus protection off before even trying to open a document or template that contains code.)

Word's macro virus protection provides a first line of defense against macro viruses, but if you create numerous documents and templates that contain code and distribute them to your coworkers, you'll quickly find the Warning dialog box a severe irritant, because it will appear whenever any user opens a document containing code or a template containing code. Because the Warning dialog box will thus be appearing frequently, you'll probably want to explore ways of suppressing macro virus protection for documents and templates that you know to be safe, while retaining the protection for documents and templates of dubious origin. The best way to do this is to reduce the threat posed by automatic macros, as described in the following paragraphs.

As I mentioned in Chapter 3, you can temporarily disable automatic macros while opening a document by holding down the Shift key as you issue the Open command (for example, in the Open dialog box, click to select the document, then hold down Shift and click the Open button). This is a good way to approach documents or templates that you suspect of harboring questionable code, which means any code that you haven't created or checked yourself.

To disable automatic macros for the whole of the current session, you need to run a `WordBasic.DisableAutoMacros` statement. You can run this by creating a macro such as the following one and running it from a toolbar button, a menu item, or a keyboard shortcut:

```
Sub DisableAutomaticMacros()
    WordBasic.DisableAutoMacros
End Sub
```

If you wanted to disable automatic macros for every Word session, you could include the `WordBasic.DisableAutoMacros` statement in an `AutoExec` macro. If you do this, you might want to display a message box first to confirm that the user wants to disable automatic macros, as in the following statements:

```
Sub AutoExec()
    If MsgBox("Do you want to disable automatic macros for the
    ➥current session?", vbYesNo + vbQuestion, "Disable
    ➥Automatic Macros") Then WordBasic.DisableAutoMacros
End Sub
```

The problem with disabling automatic macros for a whole session is that it will prevent the user from enjoying the benefits of automatic features such as those we looked at earlier in this chapter; it will also remove many of the benefits from the typical automated form.

Using Startup Switches to Specify Launch Options

As discussed in the previous section, you can use an `AutoExec` macro to affect how Word starts up, an `AutoNew` macro to affect how a new document starts, and an `AutoOpen` macro to affect the behavior of a document that you open. You can also use *startup switches* to affect how Word launches. For example, you can use a switch to prevent Word from creating a new blank document when it launches, or you can have Word create a new document based on a template of your choice rather than on Normal.dot. Table 21.1 lists the available Word startup switches.

TABLE 21.1 Word Startup Switches.

Startup Switch	Effect
/n	Starts Word without creating a new blank document.
/m	Starts Word and prevents any `AutoExec` macro from running.
/m`macroname`	Starts Word and runs the macro specified instead of any `AutoExec` macro.
/l`addinpath`	Starts Word and loads the specified add-in (for example, a global template).
/a	Starts Word; stops add-ins and global templates (including Normal.dot) from loading automatically; prevents Word from reading from or writing to the registry. This is a powerful switch for when you want to prevent the user from accidentally (or deliberately) changing Word settings—for example, in a shared copy of Word for which the settings need to remain constant.
/t`templatename`	Starts Word and creates a new document based on the specified template. Enter the template name in double quotation marks with its path.

To set a startup switch in Windows 95 or Windows NT 4.0, add any switch to the Target line of a Word shortcut. To display the Properties dialog box for a shortcut, right-click the shortcut and choose Properties from the context menu. Click the Shortcut tab to display it, and then add the switch to the Target line (see Figure 21.3). Click the OK button to close the Properties dialog box.

NOTE In Windows NT 3.51, you add the switch to the command line for the Word program icon in Program Manager.

Usually the first shortcut you'll want to change is the one that the Word or Office Setup program creates in the Microsoft Office folder (or whatever the folder is called on your computer), because this is the main shortcut for launching

Word. You can create further shortcuts with different startup switches as necessary. For example, you could create a shortcut on the Desktop with a different startup switch (or switches) from a shortcut you dragged to the Start menu.

FIGURE 21.3

By adding startup switches to the Target line of a Word shortcut, you can launch Word with different options specified.

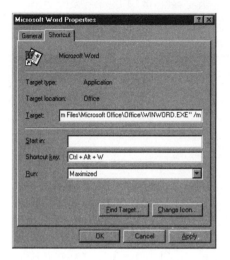

Working with the Registry

In this section, I'll discuss how you can use VBA to work with the Windows 95 or Windows NT registry, the central database of configuration information for the installation of Windows 95 or Windows NT on your computer. You can retrieve information already stored in the registry (for example, the location of the Word program files or templates), and you can write your own information to the registry so that you can retrieve it later.

> **WARNING**
>
> **Before I get into discussing the registry, here's a caveat: if you don't understand what the registry is and does, you probably shouldn't be messing with it. And regardless of whether you're going to tamper with the registry or not, you should keep a backup of your registry so that you will be able to restore it if its configuration goes awry.**

Retrieving Information from the Registry

You can retrieve information from either the Word section of the registry or from any other section of the registry, depending on the property you use. Let's start by looking at how to return information from the Word section of the registry.

Retrieving Information from the Word Section of the Registry

You can retrieve information from the Word section of the registry by using the `ProfileString` property of the `System` object. The `ProfileString` property takes the following syntax:

```
expression.ProfileString(Section, Key)
```

Here, `expression` is an expression that returns a `System` object. Usually, you'll want to use the `System` object itself.

`Section` is a required string that specifies the *key* (the folder, as it were) in the registry. This key has to be located below the main key for Word, which is `HKEY_CURRENT_USER\Software\Microsoft\Office\8.0\Word`.

`Key` is a required string that specifies the value you want to retrieve from the `Section` key.

For example, the `PROGRAMDIR` key, which specifies the folder in which the Word program files are located, is contained in the `Options` key (folder) under the `\Word\` key (folder). You could return the value of `PROGRAMDIR` and display it in a message box by using the following statement:

```
MsgBox System.ProfileString("Options", "PROGRAMDIR")
```

More usefully, you could use the `PROGRAMDIR` key to locate particular files that you needed to access, or you could use the `PICTURE-PATH` key to identify the folder in which Word starts looking for picture files.

Retrieving Information from Other Sections of the Registry

To return information from a section of the registry other than the Word section, you use the `PrivateProfileString` property with the `System` object. The

`PrivateProfileString` property works in a similar way to the `Profile-String` property, but it takes an additional argument, because you can use it not only with the registry but with other settings files as well. The syntax for the `PrivateProfileString` property is as follows:

```
expression.PrivateProfileString(Filename, Section, Key)
```

Again, `expression` is an expression that returns a `System` object, and again, you'll usually want to use the `System` object itself.

`Filename` is a required string specifying the file name of the settings file you want to access. To specify the registry, you use an empty string (""). To specify a settings file, you use its file name and path (you *can* omit the path, in which case VBA assumes the file is in the main Windows folder—usually `\Windows\`—but usually it's a better idea to include it).

TIP

One reason for omitting the path might be that you were sure that the settings file you wanted to access was in the Windows folder, but you weren't sure on which drive the Windows folder would be located or what it would be named. You can retrieve this information by checking the `System-Root` **key in the** `CurrentVersion` **key (folder)—**`HKEY_LOCAL_MACHINE\SOFTWARE\Microsoft\Windows\Current-Version\` **for Windows 95,** `HKEY_LOCAL_MACHINE\SOFTWARE\Microsoft\Windows NT\CurrentVersion\` **for Windows NT.**

`Section` is again a required string that specifies the key in the registry. This time, you need to specify the full path to the key, all the way from `HKEY_CURRENT_USER` down to the key (folder) that contains the key.

`Key` is again a required string that specifies the value you want to retrieve from the `Section` key.

As an example, you could return the path and name of the current AutoCorrect list file by specifying the `Path` key in the `HKEY_CURRENT_USER\Software\Microsoft\Office\8.0\Common\AutoCorrect\` key in the registry by using the following statement:

```
MsgBox System.PrivateProfileString("", "HKEY_CURRENT_USER\
➥Software\Microsoft\Office\8.0\Common\AutoCorrect", "Path")
```

Likewise, you can access the registered owner and registered organization for the copy of Windows 95 or Windows NT on the computer by returning the `RegisteredOwner` and `RegisteredOrganization` keys in the `HKEY_CURRENT_USER\Software\Microsoft\Windows\CurrentVersion\` key (for Windows 95) or `HKEY_CURRENT_USER\Software\Microsoft\ Windows NT\CurrentVersion\` (for Windows NT). You could use this information to suggest registration information for, say, Word templates or macros that you were distributing. We'll look at how you might do so in the next section. First, though, a quick detour to answer that nagging question I sense you're asking: How do you know which key in the registry to use to access information?

Finding the Keys You Need in the Registry

You'll have noticed that in the previous section I was blithely assuming that you knew which keys in the registry you'd need to access for particular information.

Various books are available on the details of the registry in Windows 95 and in Windows NT, but if you just need to know a key or two, you probably won't want to blow a week's worth of lunch and coffee-break money on a specialized book. You can find most of the information you need by diving into the registry headfirst and doing a little guided spelunking.

Diving into the registry means running the RegEdit program, `REGEDIT.EXE`. Microsoft doesn't provide a Start menu entry for RegEdit, undoubtedly to discourage the casual spelunker, but you can easily run RegEdit by choosing Start ➤ Run, typing **regedit** in the Open combo box, and clicking the OK button. The illustration here shows what RegEdit looks like—a mutated version of the Windows/NT Explorer with a lunatic number of folders (keys).

This isn't one of those fifty-dollar tomes on the registry, so I'll keep more or less to the point. As you'll see, the left pane contains six keys: `HKEY_CLASSES_ROOT`, `HKEY_CURRENT_USER`, `HKEY_LOCAL_MACHINE`, `HKEY_USERS`, `HKEY_CURRENT_CONFIG`, and `HKEY_DYN_DATA`. The names are pretty grim; that's because Microsoft had to come up with something even more off-putting than the gaggle of `.ini` files that Windows 3.1x used to store configuration information. (I'd say they succeeded.) `HKEY_CLASSES_ROOT` contains an

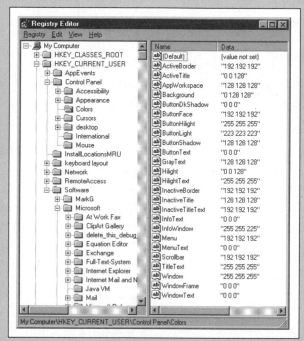

exhaustive list of the file types that Windows recognizes, the applications associated with them, and more. `HKEY_CURRENT_USER` contains information on the current user and their setup. `HKEY_LOCAL_MACHINE` contains information on the hardware and software setup of the computer. `HKEY_USERS` contains information on the users who are set up to use the computer. `HKEY_CURRENT_CONFIG` contains information on the current configuration of the computer. Finally, `HKEY_DYN_DATA` contains dynamic data on what's running on the computer, including performance-monitoring statistics.

You'll find the values you're most likely to need in the keys under `HKEY_CURRENT_USER\Software\`. For example, you'll find information on Office 97 in `HKEY_CURRENT_USER\Software\Microsoft\Office\8.0\` and information on Windows in `HKEY_CURRENT_USER\Software\Microsoft\Windows\` (for Windows 95) or `HKEY_CURRENT_USER\Software\Microsoft\Windows NT\` (for Windows NT).

The alternative to determined spelunking is to use known key names or known values to find information. For example, if you wanted to find where FTP sites were listed, you might search for **FTP Sites**; if you wanted to find out what the entry for the AutoCorrect file was called, you might search for **.acl**, the extension of the AutoCorrect file. You can restrict the search by selecting only the check boxes for the items you're looking at—Keys, Values, or Data—in the Look

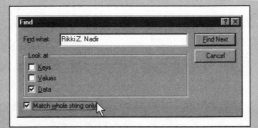

At group box of the Find dialog box (shown here), and you can search for only the entire string (i.e., excluding strings which the string in the Find What text box is part of) by selecting the Match Whole String Only check box.

Because of the volume of information that Windows stashes in the registry, the first match you find may not be the key you need. For example, if you use your company's name as the Find item when looking for the `Registered-Organization` key for Windows, you may find another key (such as the registered organization for Internet Explorer, if it's installed on your computer). Close examination of the key will usually tell you whether you've found the key you were looking for; if not, press the F3 key or choose Edit ➤ Find Next to find the next instance.

Storing Information in the Registry

Retrieving information from the registry is useful for finding out information about the computer's setup and the registered user of the software, but you may also find yourself needing to store information in the registry. Usually, you won't want to change existing values in the registry directly—for example, it makes little sense to change the `PROGRAMDIR` setting for Word that we looked at earlier, because doing so will cause Word to fail—though on occasion you may want to manipulate, say, the folder into which an application automatically downloads data or the `SearchUrl` key for Internet Explorer.

However, you can create your own settings in the registry to store information that you need for your macros. To do so, you use the `PrivateProfileString` property of the `System` object with almost the same syntax as for retrieving a value:

```
expression.PrivateProfileString(Filename, Section, Key) = value
```

Here again, `expression` is an expression that returns a `System` object; you'll usually use `System` itself. `Filename` is the name of the settings file; again, you use an empty string to denote the registry. `Section` is the key (the folder) within the registry that you want to access, and `Key` is the key itself; if `Section` or `Key` does not exist, VBA creates it. `value` is the value that you want to assign to `Key`.

For example, you could set registration information for templates or macros you were distributing by using the macro shown in Listing 21.5.

Listing 21.5

```
1.  Sub Register_Templates()
2.      Load frmTemplate_Registration
3.      frmTemplate_Registration.Show
4.  End Sub
5.
6.  Private Sub cmdOk_Click()
7.      Dim CurFolder As String, DestFolder As String,
        ➥T1 As String, T2 As String, D1 As String,
        ➥D2 As String
8.      frmTemplate_Registration.Hide
9.      Unload frmTemplate_Registration
10.     CurFolder = ActiveDocument.Path
11.     DestFolder = txtInstallationFolder.Text
12.     If Dir(DestFolder, vbDirectory) = "" Then
        ➥MkDir DestFolder
13.     T1 = CurFolder + "\Industry1.dot"
14.     T2 = CurFolder + "\Industry2.dot"
15.     D1 = DestFolder + "\Industry1.dot"
16.     D2 = DestFolder + "\Industry2.dot"
17.     FileCopy T1, D1
18.     FileCopy T2, D2
19.     System.PrivateProfileString("", "HKEY_CURRENT_USER\
        ➥Software\Microsoft\Office\8.0\Common\
        ➥SpecialTemplates", "RegisteredOwner")
        ➥= txtRegisteredOwner.Text
20.     System.PrivateProfileString("", "HKEY_CURRENT_USER\
        ➥Software\Microsoft\Office\8.0\Common\
        ➥SpecialTemplates", "RegisteredOrganization")
        ➥= txtRegisteredCompany.Text
21. End Sub
```

```
22.
23.  Private Sub UserForm_Initialize()
24.      Dim TemplateFolder As String, WRegOwner As String,
         ➥WRegOrg As String
25.      TemplateFolder = System.PrivateProfileString("",
         ➥"HKEY_CURRENT_USER\Software\Microsoft\Office\8.0\
         ➥Common\FileNew\LocalTemplates", "")
         ➥+ "\Special Templates"
26.      WRegOwner = System.PrivateProfileString("",
         ➥"HKEY_LOCAL_MACHINE\Software\Microsoft\Windows\
         ➥CurrentVersion", "RegisteredOwner")
27.      WRegOrg = System.PrivateProfileString("",
         ➥"HKEY_LOCAL_MACHINE\Software\Microsoft\Windows\
         ➥CurrentVersion", "RegisteredOrganization")
28.      txtRegisteredOwner.Text = WRegOwner
29.      txtRegisteredCompany.Text = WRegOrg
30.      txtInstallationFolder.Text = TemplateFolder
31.  End Sub
32.
33.  Private Sub cmdCancel_Click()
34.      End
35.  End Sub
```

Analysis

This listing consists of four separate macros. The first macro, Register_ Templates, simply loads the frmTemplate_Registration userform. This macro appears within a regular module in the document or template that contains it; the other three macros appear on the code sheet for the userform. The second macro, cmdOk_Click, runs when the OK button in the dialog box is chosen, and takes most of the action in this set of macros. The third macro, UserForm_ Initialize, initializes the text boxes in the dialog box and enters the appropriate information in them. The fourth macro, cmdCancel_Click, runs if the user selects the Cancel button (or the close button) in the dialog box.

Here's what happens in the sequence of macros:

1. First, the Register_Templates macro starts running. Line 2 loads the frmTemplate_Registration userform (i.e., dialog box) into memory. This automatically runs the UserForm_Initialize macro, so execution moves to line 23, where this macro starts.

2. Line 24 explicitly declares the variables that this macro needs—three strings:

   - `TemplateFolder`, which will be used to store the name and path of the folder in which local templates on the current computer are stored

   - `WRegOwner`, which will be used to store the name of the registered owner of this copy of Windows

   - `WRegOrg`, which will be used to store the name of the organization to which this copy of Windows is registered

3. Lines 25 through 27 assign information to the three strings:

   - Line 25 assigns to the `TemplateFolder` string the name of the default key (represented in code by an empty string) of the `Local-Templates` key (folder) under `HKEY_CURRENT_USER` in the registry.

   - Line 26 assigns to the `WRegOwner` string the value of the `RegisteredOwner` key under `HKEY_LOCAL_MACHINE`.

   - Line 27 assigns to the `WRegOrg` string the value of the `RegisteredOrganization` key under `HKEY_LOCAL_MACHINE`.

4. Lines 28 through 30 assign the `WRegOwner`, `WRegOrg`, and `Template Folder` strings to the `Text` property of the `txtRegisteredOwner`, `txtRegisteredCompany`, and `txtInstallationFolder` text boxes respectively, thus providing a suggested value for each text box. Line 31 then ends the `UserForm_Initialize` macro, and execution returns to the `Register_Templates` macro at line 3.

5. Line 3 uses the `Show` method to display the userform, the Template Installation and Registration dialog box (see Figure 21.4).

FIGURE 21.4

The Template Installation and Registration dialog box allows the user to correct the user name and company name, and to specify a different folder in which to install the templates.

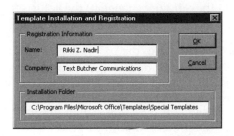

6. When the user dismisses the dialog box, the macro continues:

   - If the user clicks the Cancel button, the `cmdCancel_Click` macro runs, with line 34 ending execution of the macro.

   - If the user clicks the close button on the dialog box, VBA returns execution to line 4, where the `End Sub` statement ends the macro.

   - If the user clicks the OK button (the desired result), the `cmdOk_Click` macro runs, with execution shifting to line 6 (which starts that macro).

7. Line 7 explicitly declares the string variables that the macro needs:

   - `CurFolder`, which will contain the name of the current folder

   - `DestFolder`, which will contain the name of the destination folder for the templates

   - `T1`, which will contain the name and path of the first template to copy

   - `T2`, which will contain the name and path of the second template to copy

   - `D1`, which will contain the name and path of the destination for the first template

   - `D2`, which will contain the name and path of the destination for the second template

8. Line 8 hides the `frmTemplate_Registration` dialog box, and line 9 unloads it from memory.

9. Line 10 assigns to `CurFolder` the `Path` property of the `ActiveDocument` object, and line 11 assigns to `DestFolder` the `Text` property of the `txt InstallationFolder` text box—what the user entered in the text box, or (if they did not change it) the value set during the `UserForm_Initialize` macro.

10. Line 12 uses the `Dir` function to see if the folder specified in `DestFolder` exists. If it does not, VBA uses the `MkDir` function to create `DestFolder`.

11. Line 13 assigns to `T1` the path in `CurFolder` and the name of the first template, `Industry1.dot`. Line 14 repeats the process for `T2` and the second template, `Industry2.dot`.

12. Line 15 assigns to D1 the path in DestFolder and Industry1.dot. Line 16 repeats the process for D2 and Industry2.dot.

13. Line 17 copies the template specified in T1 to the destination specified in D1; line 18 copies T2 to D2.

14. Line 19 uses the PrivateProfileString property of the System object to assign to the key RegisteredOwner in the \Common\SpecialTemplates\ key (folder) the Text property of the txtRegisteredOwner text box. (SpecialTemplates is a custom key that VBA creates at this point. VBA then creates the RegisteredOwner key within the SpecialTemplates key.)

15. Line 20 likewise assigns to the key RegisteredOrganization in the \Common\SpecialTemplates\ key (folder) the Text property of the txtRegisteredCompany text box. (Again, VBA creates the Registered Organization key here.)

16. Line 21 ends the macro. Execution returns to line 4, which ends the first macro and the procedure.

After running this macro, you can access the RegisteredOwner and RegisteredOrganization keys in the SpecialTemplates key at any point by using the PrivateProfileString property of the System object:

```
MsgBox System.PrivateProfileString("", "HKEY_LOCAL_MACHINE\
➥Software\Microsoft\Windows\CurrentVersion","RegisteredOwner")
```

By using automatic macros, you can quickly and effectively optimize the user environment for the task at hand, or reset it to standard parameters after the user has messed it up. And by using the registry, you can access a wide range of useful information to help you manipulate not only Word but also Windows and the other applications on your computer; you can also store information of your own and retrieve it for later use in your macros.

So far, so good—but there's much more automation ahead. In the next chapter, I'll discuss how you can automate everyday procedures in Word.

Automating Regular Word Procedures

In this chapter, I'd like to take a break from grinding through the various VBA statements, methods, properties, etc., and take time to discuss what types of procedures you should be planning to automate and how you should go about automating them.

So far in this book, we've examined a variety of tools that you can use to streamline and improve your work in Word. By now, you know how to do everything from a simple task such as inserting a couple of words in an open document to a complex task such as this: opening a document, finding in it certain pieces of information and extracting them, creating a new document, inserting in the appropriate places the pieces of information from the first document, saving the document under a name and in a folder of your designation, and closing the first document again. You know how to use message boxes to communicate with the users of your macros and to apply the decisions they make to run the macros; how to use input boxes to solicit and apply simple information; and how to use both custom dialog boxes and Word's built-in dialog boxes for gathering more complex information and taking complex actions.

In short, you're pretty much ready to let VBA rip, and you need a victim or two. I'll suggest where you might start looking. This will be a short chapter, so it shouldn't do you any harm to at least skim through it.

Which Procedures Should You Automate with Macros?

The answer to the above question is, pretty much any procedures that you can—within reason, and depending on the amount of time you have at your disposal for working with VBA.

> **NOTE** Before we get into examining what you might want to create a macro for, I'd like to mention once again Word's many automatic features, from styles to templates to AutoCorrect. If you haven't fully explored the possibilities that these features provide, you run the risk of squandering valuable time on writing unnecessary macros. But if you're familiar with these features and have established that you really do need to write a macro to achieve the effects you desire, read on.

You'll find it's instantly obvious that some procedures are not suitable candidates for automating through a macro or macros. For example, you probably shouldn't consider any one-shot editing task as a possible subject for a macro—instead, just grit your teeth and do it. But if, on the other hand, you need to repeat a tedious editing task ad infinitum throughout a 200-page document, you should immediately think of creating a macro to perform the grunt work for you. This might be a simple recorded macro that you could run repeatedly by hand, or you could build in a straightforward loop to repeat the macro for each instance of the item requiring the tedious editing maneuver until the macro reached the end of the document.

The same principles apply to creating a document. If a document is truly a one-time thing, you'll find little within it to automate with a macro. If you create a wide assortment of letters, you can use features such as AutoText and AutoCorrect to fill in boilerplate text such as your address, logo, and salutation as you need them, but you may not be able to improve the process significantly by using macros.

One key indication that you might want to consider creating macros is if you have a template for a particular type of document. Say you create four different types of letters, three types for business (letters requesting products, letters acknowledging receipt of products, and letters evaluating products) and one type for personal use. You'll probably create a template for each type of letter; you might then write a separate macro for each template that quickly inserted a set of related information into the letters (for example, by using boilerplate text stored in the macro).

I hope this discussion hasn't made you think it's tricky to identify procedures that *are* suitable candidates for automating with macros. Once you start creating macros, you'll probably identify so many candidates that you have a hard time stopping. But to get started, try analyzing your working procedures as discussed in the following sections.

Automating Repeated Labor-Intensive Procedures

First, ask yourself this: Does your everyday work include any labor-intensive procedure you find yourself performing repeatedly? This can be anything from a tiny but tedious editing or formatting task (such as transposing three words, or applying complex formatting to an element) to a large-scale procedure involving extracting information from another application and processing it in Word.

> **NOTE**
>
> Chapter 23 discusses how you can use VBA to make Word interact with both the other Office applications and non-Office applications. In that chapter, I'll show you a couple of examples of tedious interapplication procedures that you would do well to streamline with a macro.

One example of a labor-intensive procedure is a complex Find-and-Replace operation that you might want to perform either on documents supplied to you in an unsuitable format or on documents created in an application for which Word does not have a conversion filter. By recording the series of Find-and-Replace operations you perform, you can make it available for instant use with the next document of the offending type.

> **NOTE**
>
> While Word provides conversion filters for a wide range document types from Lotus 1-2-3 to WordPerfect 6.*x*, conversion filters for non-mainstream, old, or niche applications remain a perennial problem. For example, if your company needs to get information from its internal publications created in, say, an old version of Ventura Publisher, you can't simply import the text into Word, because Word doesn't have an import filter for Ventura. However, you can open up the Ventura file as a text document and then use a concerted Find-and-Replace operation to apply Word styles to the paragraphs and elements.

Automating Documents You Create Frequently

Next, evaluate what kinds of Word documents you create frequently: letters, memos, reports, newsletters, articles, and so on. Work out how much overlap there is among the different documents that fall into each of these categories. For example, you might establish that you create three different types of memos, and that within each type, the contents of the memos have strong similarities. Ask yourself if you can create templates to speed up your production of such documents. If so, determine whether you can add macros to the templates to lay out and format the information or simply enter the information into the documents more quickly.

Could you enter basic information in a document more quickly if you were able to use a dialog box to take care of fields strewn throughout the document? Might you be able to speed things up even more if the whole document were a form? (Your decision to use a form will probably depend on whether the document contains areas that will need detailed work rather than just different information you could use a form in the latter situation.)

Automating Tedious Tasks

When evaluating what you could do with a macro, consider even basic tasks that you don't think twice about performing. You don't need to automate the whole of a document; just automating one or two tedious tasks can make a difference.

As an example of a tiny but tedious task, suppose you have an assortment of business-letter templates stored in a `Business Letters` folder within the `\Templates\` folder of your installation of Office. To create a new document based on one of the templates, you'd choose File ➤ New, select the Business Letters tab in the New dialog box (unless this is the last tab you used in the current session of Word, in which case it will already be displayed), choose the template, and click the OK button (or double-click the icon for the template). This is a three-second process involving a mere five clicks of the mouse—but you could reduce it to a one-click process by creating a series of macros, each of which started a new document based on one of the templates, and putting buttons for them on the toolbar; you could also create keyboard shortcuts to run the macros. Alternatively, you could create a macro that would display the Business Letters tab of the New dialog box when you clicked a toolbar button or pressed a keyboard shortcut; this would save less time and effort, but might still be worthwhile.

Another example is clearing the "sticky" settings in the Find and Replace dialog box; if in your previous search in the current Word session you specified formatting, and/or a particular search direction, or a matching option such as Match Case, you'll need to clear those settings for the next search (unless you want to continue using them). So you might create a macro that cleared the settings in the

Find and Replace dialog box before displaying it, using the techniques discussed in Listing 20.2. You could then replace the usual commands for displaying the Find and Replace dialog box (Edit ➤ Find or Ctrl+F, Edit ➤ Replace or Ctrl+H) by reassigning those commands to the macro, so that every time you displayed the dialog box, the settings would be cleared. Alternatively, you could use the macro as a way to display the Find and Replace dialog box when you wanted it to appear with its settings cleared, while keeping the usual commands for displaying the dialog box for those occasions when you wanted to retain the sticky settings.

If you examine your working habits, you'll find any number of other small tasks that you could eliminate or at least reduce by using macros.

NOTE   Chapter 24 discusses how to design and build a special-purpose template to automate tasks involved in creating a particular type of document. These tasks range from the infinitesimal (like the examples above) to the burdensome, but as you'll see, the potential net savings of time makes even the shortest macros worthwhile.

Automating Procedures That Others Can Use

Once you've established that you can create a macro to perform a particular task, ask yourself who will use the macro. If it's just yourself, you'll need to be sure that the macro will actually save you time. On the other hand, if you have a whole department full of colleagues ready to take advantage of your macro, you'll find it much easier to justify the time and effort involved in creating it. (The disadvantage of creating a macro for your colleagues rather than just for yourself is that you'll usually need to spend more time testing it to make sure it works under the widest variety of circumstances that you can imagine. I'll discuss this in a little more detail later in the chapter.)

Automating Complex Tasks

When you need to perform a complex task such as setting configuration information in Word on a number of computers, consider creating a macro to do it for you. For example, if you're responsible for administering templates on a network, you might write a macro that set up the installation of Word automatically (and perhaps performed a few other tasks at the same time) rather than having the users confuse themselves by cavorting around the network drives in the Modify Location dialog box (and other dialog boxes).

When Is It Worth Creating a Macro?

Usually, the key to deciding whether it's worth the effort of creating a macro for a particular task is this: Will you save more time by using the macro than it takes to create it?

For a rough-and-ready macro that you put together for a particular task and discard immediately afterward, the time savings is relatively easy to estimate: the task would take, say, thirty minutes to perform manually; the macro will take five to ten minutes to write and another five to run, so you'll save fifteen minutes. The only fly in the ointment is if you decide to create such a macro and discover that it takes you three times as long as you guessed it would.

But for a macro that will save only a few minutes for each user whenever they need to, say, create a document of a particular type, you may need to think harder to justify spending four or five hours of your time up front. Here the question is not what time savings you can expect in the long haul, because the time will not be your own, but whether creating such a macro will make people's work life easier. If the document in question is one that people create with reasonable frequency, it's probably a good bet to automate; with no more than a little honest self-examination, you should be able to detect whether you're trying to fulfill a real need or you're just taking an opportunity to show off your imagination and your VBA skills.

The main reason for creating a macro that will not necessarily save much time is to automate a process that the user may have difficulty performing, such as choosing a number of setup or configuration options. Such a macro may in fact result in a net savings of time if the user is not competent to perform the task without intensive instruction, but the main thrust behind creating the macro is to get the process done correctly.

A secondary but entirely valid reason for creating a macro that may not necessarily save time is the feel-good factor, both for the people who use the macro and for the person who created it. A couple of clicks here and a few keystrokes there may not save other users of your macros any significant amount of effort, but they're likely to appreciate customization and macros that bring their most-needed commands to their fingertips. And if your own copy of Word is cranked and hotkeyed to the eyeballs, you'll probably not only have a lot more fun using it than if it were soberly configured, but you'll also get more work done. Moreover, if you're constantly on the lookout for ways to improve the user interface, you'll frequently come up with ideas (some sensible, some maniacal) for doing so.

How Should You Approach Automating a Procedure?

Once you've established that you can and should automate a procedure, take a moment to decide how to approach the automation. You could, of course, simply barrel ahead with the macro recorder or start throwing around assorted statements in the Visual Basic Editor, but usually the process of creating a macro will benefit from a little consideration and reflection up front.

The steps to take vary depending on the type and complexity of the procedure involved, but here's a quick list to start with:

- First, define what the macro or set of macros is going to do. In other words, establish the goal of the procedure.

- Second, work out the basic steps of the procedure, either in your head or in writing; one good way of tracking the steps in a macro is to enter them as comment lines in the macro, and then fill in the code between them. (Use the macro recorder if it will make the process easier.)

- Third, if you're creating a set of macros, decide which steps will be performed by which macro. Make your code as modular as possible so that you'll be able to reuse it.

- Fourth, establish roughly what any message boxes, input boxes, or dialog boxes in the procedure will do: at what point you'll call them, which options they will contain, and which actions they will need to take.

Deciding How Sophisticated to Make the Macro

The next thing you'll probably find yourself considering is how sophisticated to make your macro. If you're creating a temporary macro to deal with a particular problem in a particular document (or group of documents), there'll be no need to worry about making the macro as slick as possible—instead, you'll focus solely on making it functional, and you'll probably delete the macro the moment it's done its duty. But as soon as you decide that your colleagues could use a certain macro as well, you need to concern yourself with making it user-friendly or even bombproof. Perhaps your colleagues are sensible enough that you can distribute the macro with basic instructions for its use (e.g., use the macro only with a document open and in Normal view, make a selection before running the macro, etc.) and expect them to deal with the consequences of their not following the instructions; generally speaking, however, this isn't usually the best way to proceed for widely distributed macros. Furthermore, restricting a relatively short macro so that it will run only under the circumstances you intended can take more time than creating the macro itself.

You can mitigate the amount of work involved in rendering a macro bombproof (or harmless) by following the principles of well-behaved macros discussed in Chapter 18. For example, to make sure the macro is running under suitable conditions, you can call separate macros to check the user environment and change its settings if necessary, then restore the original environment at the end of the macro.

Choosing How to Create the Macro

Once you've established what a macro will need to do and roughly how it will do it, take a moment to consider your options for creating it:

- **Create the macro from scratch.** This is the most obvious choice, of course, but before starting to create the macro, you should ask yourself if there's a better way to proceed.

- **Adapt an existing macro.** If you have a similar macro to the one you're trying to create, you may be able to save most of the effort involved in creating a new macro by adapting the code in the existing macro. To adapt an existing macro, you can simply copy its code in the Visual Basic Editor and paste the result under another name. If the macro is in a different template, you can copy the code either by using the Visual Basic Editor or by using the Organizer dialog box. In this case, you don't need to give the new macro a different name from its predecessor, but doing so is usually a good idea and will help you keep your macros straight.

- **Use part of an existing macro.** If you can leverage a number of lines of code from an existing macro (or more than one existing macro), you may be able to save time and effort. Better yet, try the next option.

- **Call existing macros to perform actions in the new macro.** Instead of repurposing code from an existing macro, you may be able to modularize your code (as discussed in Chapter 17) and call separate macros to perform certain functions in the new macro.

TIP As you create new macros, ask yourself if you can repurpose part or all of them to save yourself work in future macros. If you decide you can, build modular code consisting of macros that perform specific tasks applicable to as wide a range of macros as possible; alternatively, segment and comment your code so that you can quickly find blocks of code that can be used in another macro.

Choosing Whether to Write the Macro or Record It

If you choose to create the macro from scratch, you have one more decision to make: whether to write the code yourself or use the macro recorder. In Chapter 5 we began by recording the basic moves for a macro and then opening the macro in the code window of the Visual Basic Editor to adjust the results. This method will give you code that works but that may contain a number of unnecessary statements (because the macro recorder records everything you do, including all the options in the dialog boxes you use when recording the macro). The code is also restricted in that it can only work in the active document rather than using the objects in the `Documents` collection (because you cannot record actions that involve `Document` objects other than the `ActiveDocument` object).

Around Chapters 10 and 11, when we started working in earnest with VBA, you learned the advantages of using the Word object model and creating macros from scratch in the Visual Basic Editor. Since that point, we've concentrated on working in the Visual Basic Editor, perhaps to the detriment of the macro recorder. After all, writing a macro is more difficult (and therefore advanced) than recording a macro, so why does anyone worth their salt record a macro when they could write it instead?

I suggest viewing it this way: however good you are with VBA, you should still always consider the macro recorder as a viable option for creating either rough-and-ready macros or the basis of more complex macros. You'll often find it makes sense to have the macro recorder take as much of the strain of creating a macro as possible. And there's no shame in using the macro recorder to quickly identify the object or property you need to reach in VBA.

Well, that's quite enough of a break from VBA code. It's time to plunge right back into the most entertaining methods and statements we've looked at so far—those that enable you to manipulate applications other than Word.

CHAPTER

TWENTY-THREE

Working with Other Applications

From your day-to-day interactive work with Word, I'm sure you're familiar with the features it offers for exchanging information with other applications, be they the other Office applications (Excel, PowerPoint, Access, or Outlook) or applications outside the Office group (Lotus 1-2-3, CorelDRAW!, etc.). For example, you may have used Access's Publish It with MS Word feature to create Word documents out of an Access report, or you may have performed a mail merge using data from your Outlook address book or an Excel spreadsheet (or both). Likewise, you've probably used OLE/Automation to include in a Word document an object created in another application, such as part of a spreadsheet, a chart, or a slide from a presentation.

In this chapter, I'll discuss how you can use VBA to work automatically with other applications. First, we'll look at integrating Word with the other Microsoft Office applications: Excel, PowerPoint, Outlook, and Access. Because this is what you're mostly likely to be doing at first, this will form the main thrust of the chapter. Then we'll look at how you can use VBA to manipulate non-Office (and non-Microsoft) applications. With such applications, your options are more limited, but you can still transfer information back and forth. Finally, as a wrap-up, I'll mention how you can manipulate the Office Assistant to communicate with or entertain users of your macros.

Your main reason for communicating with other applications is to exchange data with them—either transferring information from the other application to Word, or from Word to the other application. You can also use Word to get the other application to perform certain actions, but unless your ultimate goal is to transfer information, this kind of remote control has little purpose beyond the intellectual stimulation of doing things the hard way.

Tools for Communicating with Other Applications

As mentioned above, Word offers a number of tools for communicating with other applications. I'll concentrate on those tools in the following order, which is roughly the order of preference:

- **Automation,** formerly known as Object Linking and Embedding (OLE), the latest method for transferring information between Windows applications.

- **Dynamic Data Exchange (DDE),** an older method of transferring information between applications that remains a good fallback when Automation is not available.

- **SendKeys,** a (by comparison) prehistoric method of communicating with another application. SendKeys relies on sending keystroke equivalents to the other application rather than manipulating it in the more sophisticated ways that Automation and DDE use. SendKeys is crude but still effective.

Using Automation to Transfer Information

Automation, formerly OLE, provides the snappiest way of communicating with another application and under most circumstances should be your first resort. The only snag is that not every application supports Automation, so you won't always be able to use it. However, with recent Microsoft applications (and especially with the Office 97 applications), it's a pretty safe bet.

To use Automation through VBA, you create an object in VBA that references the application you want to work with. You use the `CreateObject` function to create a new object in another application and the `GetObject` function to retrieve an existing object in another application.

Creating an Object with the CreateObject Function

`CreateObject`, which creates a new object in the specified application, takes the following syntax:

```
CreateObject(class)
```

Here, `class` is a required argument specifying the class of object to create. As you may remember from Chapter 11, the *class* of the object means its formal definition rather than its quality; the `class` argument consists of the name of the application that will provide the object and the type of object to be provided, so it looks like this:

```
applicationname.objecttype
```

For example, to specify the Excel `Application` object as a class, you could use a `class` argument of `Excel.Application`. Here, `Excel` is the name of the application that provides the object, and `Application` is the type of object that Excel provides. Likewise, you could specify `Excel.Sheet` to specify a worksheet object in Excel.

Typically, you'll use a `CreateObject` function with a `Set` statement to assign to an object variable the object that you create. For example, to create a worksheet object in Excel and assign it to the object variable named `NewSheet`, you could use the following statements:

```
Dim NewSheet As Object
Set NewSheet = CreateObject("Excel.Sheet")
```

Returning an Object with the GetObject Function

`GetObject`, which returns an existing object, takes the following syntax:

```
GetObject([pathname] [, class])
```

Here, `pathname` is a variant variable assigned the string data type (Variant/String) specifying the full path and name of the file that contains the object you want to retrieve. `pathname` is optional, but if you don't specify it, you have to specify the `class` argument. `class`, which is optional if you specify `pathname` but required if you don't, is a variant variable assigned the string data type specifying the class of the object you want to return.

As with `CreateObject`, typically you'll use a `GetObject` function with a `Set` statement to assign to an object variable the object that you return with the `GetObject` function. For example, in the second of the following statements, the `GetObject` function returns an object consisting of the workbook `f:\finance\revenue.xls`. The `Set` statement assigns this object to the object variable named `Revenue` declared in the first statement:

```
Dim Revenue As Object
Set Revenue = GetObject("f:\finance\revenue.xls")
```

Here, the workbook is associated with Excel. When this code runs, VBA starts Excel if it isn't already running and activates the workbook. You can then reference the object by referring to its object variable; in this example, you could manipulate the `Revenue` object to affect the workbook `f:\finance\revenue.xls`. I'll show you an example of this in just a moment.

In the next sections, we'll look at two examples of how you can use the `CreateObject` and `GetObject` functions to transfer data.

> **NOTE**
> I don't want to get too deeply into the details of cross-application VBA in this chapter. I'll show you just enough so that you can see that the VBA dialects used by the other VBA applications are closely related to the VBA commands that you've been using to control Word. From there, the initiative's all yours.

Transferring Information from an Excel Spreadsheet to a Word Document

The first example we'll look at here uses the `GetObject` function to retrieve the information from a cell in an Excel spreadsheet and insert it in the current Word document at the current selection. Listing 23.1 contains the code for this macro.

Listing 23.1

```
1.   Sub Getting_Value_from_Excel()
2.       Dim MySpreadsheet As Object, SalesTotal As String
3.       Set MySpreadsheet = GetObject("c:\Corporate\Sales
         ➡Forecast.xls")
4.       With MySpreadsheet
5.           .Application.Visible = True
6.           .Parent.Windows("Sales Forecast.xls")
             ➡.Visible = True
7.           .Application.GoTo Reference:="SalesTotal"
8.           SalesTotal = .Application.ActiveCell.Value
9.           .Application.Workbooks("Sales Forecast.xls")
             ➡.Saved = True
10.          .Application.Quit
11.      End With
12.      Set MySpreadsheet = Nothing
13.      Selection.TypeText SalesTotal
14.  End Sub
```

Analysis

Because this macro retrieves only one piece of information from an Excel spreadsheet, it provides a very simple example of accessing information from another application.

Line 2 declares the object variable `MySpreadsheet` and the string variable `SalesTotal`. Line 3 then uses a `Set` statement and the `GetObject` function to make `MySpreadsheet` reference the spreadsheet `c:\Corporate\Sales Forecast.xls`.

Line 4 then begins a `With` statement that works with the `MySpreadsheet` object; the `With` statement ends in line 11. In between, Word uses VBA to manipulate the properties of the `MySpreadsheet` Excel object. Line 5 sets the `Visible` property of the Excel `Application` object to `True`, displaying Excel. Line 6 sets the `Visible` property of the `Sales Forecast.xls` window object in the `Windows` object collection in the `Parent` object to `True`, displaying the window containing the `Sales Forecast.xls` spreadsheet. Line 7 uses the `GoTo` method of the Excel `Application` object to go to the range referenced by the `SalesTotal` label in the spreadsheet. (Note that this `SalesTotal` is a named range in the Excel spreadsheet, not the Word string named `SalesTotal` we declared in line 2 and which resurfaces in the next line.) Line 8 then assigns to the Word string `SalesTotal` the `Value` property of the `ActiveCell` object (the active cell) in the Excel `Application` object, in essence assigning the information from the active cell to the `SalesTotal` string. Line 9 then changes the `Saved` property of the `Sales Forecast.xls` spreadsheet to `True` so that the macro will be able to close it without Excel prompting to save changes (opening the spreadsheet and manipulating it makes Excel think the spreadsheet has been changed, even though it hasn't), and line 10 uses the `Quit` method on the `Application` object to close Excel and the spreadsheet.

Line 12 assigns to the `MySpreadsheet` object the special value `Nothing` that I discussed way back in Chapter 10. This releases the memory that the object variable has taken up. (Because the macro ends almost immediately afterward, this statement isn't necessary here, but it's good practice to free up the memory assigned to an object when you no longer need to use the object. For example, if this macro continued for a couple hundred more lines of code, releasing the memory at this point could help ensure that the rest of the procedure ran as fast as possible.)

Finally, line 13 uses the `TypeText` method on the `Selection` object in Word to enter the `SalesTotal` string at the current selection. Line 14 ends the macro.

Creating a Binder and Adding a Document and Spreadsheet to It

The second example (shown in Listing 23.2) uses the `CreateObject` function to create a new binder in the Office Binder mini-application, starting Office Binder in the process unless it's already running. The macro then adds two sections to the new binder, names them, activates the first section, and saves and closes the binder.

Listing 23.2

```
 1.    Sub Create_and_Populate_Binder()
 2.        Dim MyBinder As Object
 3.        Set MyBinder = CreateObject("OfficeBinder.Binder")
 4.        With MyBinder
 5.            .Sections.Add Type:="Word.Document"
 6.            .Sections.Add Type:="Word.Document"
 7.            .Sections(1).Name = "Introductory Letter"
 8.            .Sections(2).Name = "Marketing Memo"
 9.            .Sections("Marketing Memo").Activate
10.            'take other actions here
11.            .SaveAs "c:\temp\AutoBinder.obd"
12.            .Close
13.        End With
14.    End Sub
```

Analysis

Like the example in Listing 23.1, this macro is kept simple to clearly illustrate working with the object. The result is a little unrealistic, but functional.

Line 2 declares the object variable `MyBinder`, and line 3 uses a `Set` statement to make `MyBinder` reference the binder object returned by the `CreateObject-("OfficeBinder.Binder")` statement.

Line 4 then begins a `With` statement that runs until line 13 and works with the `MyBinder` object. Line 5 uses the `Add` method to add a section of the type `Word.Document` to the `Sections` collection object in the binder; line 6 then adds another. Line 7 sets the `Name` property of the first object in the `Sections` collection to `Introductory Letter`, and line 8 sets the `Name` property of the second object to `Marketing Memo`. Line 9 activates the section identified as `Marketing Memo`. Line 10 contains a comment line indicating where the macro could take further actions.

Line 11 uses the `SaveAs` method to save the binder, and line 12 uses the `Close` method to close the binder (and the Office Binder application). Line 13 ends the `With` statement, and line 14 ends the macro.

> **NOTE**
>
> Notice that in this procedure, we do not set the `Visible` property of the object to `True`, so the object (and application) are not displayed: the whole procedure takes place in the background.

Starting an Application

As you've already seen, you can start an application by using the `GetObject` or `CreateObject` functions, which will start the appropriate application if it's not already running. This is useful for when you need to create an object or return one from an application.

At other times, you'll want to simply start or run an application without associating it with an object. To do so, you use the `Shell` function. `Shell` can run any executable program, and its syntax is straightforward:

```
Shell(pathname[,windowstyle])
```

`pathname` is the name of the program you want `Shell` to run, together with a path (if needed—anything that's already in the current path should run fine without an explicit path) and any command-line switches or arguments that are needed.

NOTE

Shell **will also run a file whose extension is associated with a known program. For example,** Shell "testfile.txt" **will typically fire up Notepad, because Notepad is usually associated with .txt files. And if** Shell **cannot find the specified application or file, it returns a run-time error.**

windowstyle is an optional argument that you use to specify the type of window in which to run the application. Here are your choices for this argument:

Constant	Value	Window Style
vbHide	0	Minimized and hidden, but with focus
vbNormalFocus	1	Normal ("restored") with focus
vbMinimizedFocus	2	Minimized with focus (the default)
vbMaximizedFocus	3	Maximized with focus
vbNormalNoFocus	4	Normal ("restored") without focus
vbMinimizedNoFocus	6	Minimized without focus

NOTE

If you're feeling curious, you can also use the values 5 (for normal with focus), 7 (for minimized without focus), 8 (for normal without focus), and 9 (for normal with focus) with the Shell **function. These duplicate the values in the above list and have no discernible benefit.**

Returning the Task ID of the Started Application

The Shell function returns a unique task identification number (*task ID*) that identifies the application it has just started. You can use this task ID as a way of quickly accessing the application without having to list all the applications that are running.

To return the task ID of an application, assign it to a variable when you run the Shell statement, as in the following example, which runs Lotus 1-2-3 and assigns the task ID to the MyTaskID variable:

```
MyTaskID = Shell("c:\lotus\123\programs\123w.exe")
```

A Caveat: the Shell Function Runs Asynchronously

The Shell function comes with one big caveat: it runs other programs *asynchronously* rather than *synchronously*. In other words, when Word encounters a Shell statement, it registers the statement as an action to be performed—but the action may not necessarily be finished before the next statement in the macro executes.

On occasion, this may cause some nasty errors. For example, you might need to run an executable file to install its contents during a macro—say, delivering some document files that the macro then worked with, or installing a converter file for a document the macro was about to open. Until the executable file had delivered its contents, the actions in the remainder of the macro couldn't be executed successfully, so you would need to make sure that subsequent actions were not taken until the executable file had finished executing.

If you run into this type of problem, your best approach is usually to allow as much time as possible for the Shell function to execute before taking any action that requires Shell to have finished executing. You might be able to run the Shell function earlier in the process than you otherwise would have done—that is, execute some statements that do not rely on the Shell function having been performed between executing the Shell function and executing statements that depend on it. If the macro is short and you have no latitude with the actions the macro must perform, you can introduce a deliberate time-wasting mechanism to give Word more time to execute the Shell function. For example, you could print a message to the status bar a large number of times to take up a little processor time before proceeding:

```
For i = 1 to 1000
    Application.StatusBar = "Please wait while Word
    ➡processes the information: " + Str$(i) +
    ➡" out of 1000..."
Next i
```

Depending on the speed of your processor, 1,000 iterations of such a loop might take anywhere from a quarter of a second to a second or two—long enough for Word to finish executing the `Shell` function, but probably not long enough for the user to become impatient. If you run into this problem often, you could create a macro named (say) `Delay` that you could run regularly after `Shell` statements.

Activating an Application

So much for starting an application. To work with the application, you'll often need to activate it. To do so, you use the `AppActivate` statement. `AppActivate` activates the other application but does not maximize or restore it, so if the application is minimized, focus will be shifted to its Taskbar icon, but the application will not be displayed. (To maximize, minimize, or restore an application window, you use the `Shell` statement, as discussed earlier in this chapter.)

The syntax for `AppActivate` is as follows:

```
AppActivate title[, wait]
```

Here, `title` is a required string specifying the title contained in the title bar of the application window to be activated. For example, to activate Excel, you would specify **Microsoft Excel** for `title`, because Excel displays "Microsoft Excel" in its title bar:

```
AppActivate "Microsoft Excel"
```

TIP

If you have two or more sessions of Excel running, VBA will arbitrarily pick one. To avoid this random choice, you can specify the full title in the title bar—for example, **Microsoft Excel - Book2.**

`wait` is an optional Boolean value that you can use to specify whether the application that calls the other application needs to have the focus (i.e., be active) before it can call the other application; the default wait setting is False, which specifies that the calling application does not need to have the focus before it can call the other application, but you can set wait to True to have the calling application wait until it has the focus before it can call the other application. You might want to set wait to True to avoid having the calling application interrupt a sensitive process that had the focus.

For example, you could activate PowerPoint by using the following statement:

```
AppActivate "Microsoft PowerPoint"
```

You can also activate an application by using the task ID for the application that you return with the Shell function. Using the task ID eliminates the possibility of confusing multiple sessions of the same application (though you still need to make sure you're using the task ID of the correct session of the application). For example, you could start Lotus 1-2-3 and assign its task ID to a variable, and then use the variable to activate 1-2-3, by using these statements:

```
MyTaskID = Shell("c:\lotus\123\programs\123w.exe")
AppActivate MyTaskID
```

Communicating via DDE

As discussed in the previous section, your first choice for communicating with a recent Windows application should be Automation; but if the other application does not support Automation, DDE (Dynamic Data Exchange) is a viable option. DDE is a protocol that establishes a channel between two applications through which they can automatically exchange data. DDE tends to be a much more ticklish process than Automation, so I'd suggest you not invest time in it unless you find you absolutely need to use it. That said, once you do get DDE going, it can work like a charm.

Beyond giving you a brief overview of the main DDE commands as shown in the following list, I'll leave you to investigate DDE on your own. Given the facility with which you can access information in other applications by using the CreateObject and GetObject functions, you shouldn't need to use DDE frequently—if you need to use it at all.

A typical DDE conversation can contain the following actions:

- Using the DDEInitiate method to start a DDE connection and establish the channel on which the connection operates

- Using the `DDERequest` method to return text from the other application or the `DDEPoke` method to send text to the other application

- Using the `DDEExecute` method to execute a command in the other application

- Using the `DDETerminate` method to close the current DDE channel, or using the `DDETerminateAll` method to close all the DDE channels

Communicating via SendKeys

The simplest level of automatic communication with another application is achieved by using the SendKeys statement. SendKeys is the method to use if neither Automation nor DDE works with the application with which you need to communicate; because SendKeys is relatively limited in what it can do, you'll seldom want to use it unless you absolutely have to. That said, such occasions do arise, so here's the scoop on SendKeys. Compared to DDE, it's dead-simple to use.

SendKeys does pretty much what its name suggests: it sends the specified keystrokes to the destination application. For example, if you want to use SendKeys to send the command to create a new file in, say, Notepad, you would send the keystrokes for **Alt+F** and **N** (to execute the File ➤ New command), and Notepad would react as if you were punching the keys manually.

SendKeys works only with currently running Windows applications; you cannot use SendKeys to start another application (for that you need to use `Shell`, as discussed earlier in this chapter), nor can you use SendKeys to communicate with DOS applications running in virtual DOS machines under Windows.

Syntax

The syntax for the `SendKeys` statement is as follows:

```
SendKeys string[, wait]
```

Here, `string` is a required string expression specifying the keystrokes to be sent to the destination application, and `wait` is an optional Boolean value specifying whether to wait after sending the keystrokes until the application has executed them (`True`) or to immediately return control to the procedure sending the keystrokes (`False`, the default setting).

Typically, `string` will consist of a series of keystrokes—usually there will be little point in sending a single keystroke to an application. All alphanumeric characters that appear on the regular keyboard are represented by the characters themselves: to send the letter *H*, you specify **H** in the string, and to send the word *Hello*, you specify **Hello** in the string. This is all friendly and straightforward. Where `SendKeys` gets a little tricky is with the movement and editing keys (Enter, Backspace, etc.), the meta keys (Alt, Ctrl, Shift), and conventional characters that it uses to denote special keys.

To denote the movement and editing keys, SendKeys uses reasonably intuitive keywords enclosed within braces (`{ }`):

Key	Code
↓	`{DOWN}`
←	`{LEFT}`
→	`{RIGHT}`
↑	`{UP}`
Backspace	`{BACKSPACE}`, `{BS}`, or `{BKSP}`
Break	`{BREAK}`
Caps Lock	`{CAPSLOCK}`
Delete	`{DELETE}` or `{DEL}`
End	`{END}`
Enter	`{ENTER}`
Esc	`{ESC}`
F1, F2, etc.	`{F1}`, `{F2}`, etc. (up to `{F16}`)
Help	`{HELP}`
Home	`{HOME}`
Insert	`{INSERT}` or `{INS}`
Num Lock	`{NUMLOCK}`
Page Down	`{PGDN}`
Page Up	`{PGUP}`

Key	Code
Print Screen	{PRTSC}
Scroll Lock	{SCROLLLOCK}
Tab	{TAB}

The meta keys are denoted with symbols as follows:

Key	Code
Shift	+
Ctrl	^
Alt	%

SendKeys automatically assigns the keystroke after the meta key to the meta key. For example, to send a Ctrl+O keystroke, you specify **^O**, and SendKeys assigns the O to the Ctrl keystroke; the next keystroke after the O is considered to be struck separately. If you need to assign multiple keystrokes to the meta key, enter the keystrokes in parentheses after the meta key. For example, to send Alt+F, Alt+I, Alt+I, you would specify **%(FII)** rather than **%FII**.

As you can see, SendKeys has special meanings for the plus sign (+), caret (^), percent sign (%), and parentheses ( ); the tilde (~) gets special treatment as well. If you need to use these characters to represent themselves, you enter them within braces: {+} sends a straight + sign, {^} a straight caret, {%} a percent sign, {~} a tilde, and {()} parentheses. Likewise, you need to enclose brackets (which have a special meaning in DDE in some applications) within braces; braces themselves also go within braces.

Using SendKeys is much less complex than these details probably make it appear—and with that reassurance, there's one more trick you should know: to repeat a key, enter the key and the number of repetitions in braces. For example, to send five ↑ keystrokes, you would specify **{UP 5}**; to send ten zeroes, you would specify **{0 5}**.

After all that syntax, I expect you're longing for an example. How could I refuse?

Example

As an example of using SendKeys, you could start Notepad and send log-file information to it by using the statements in Listing 23.3.

> **WARNING**
>
> Because SendKeys needs to activate the target application, you can't step into the code in the Visual Basic Editor—the Visual Basic Editor grabs the focus back at the wrong point, directing the keystrokes toward itself rather than the target application. Instead, you need to create the macro (or copy this listing) and then run it from the Macros dialog box in Word.

Listing 23.3

```
1.  Sub Send_to_Notepad()
2.      Dim LogDate As String, SaveLog As String,
        ➥MyNotepad As Variant
3.      LogDate = Month(Now) & "-" & Day(Now) & "-" & Year(Now)
4.      SaveLog = "Log file for " & LogDate & ".txt"
5.      MyNotepad = Shell("notepad.exe", vbNormalFocus)
6.      AppActivate MyNotepad
7.      SendKeys Msg & "%FS" & SaveLog & "{Enter}" & "%{F4}",
        ➥True
8.  End Sub
```

Analysis

This macro starts by declaring in line 2 two string variables it will use to store information, `LogDate` and `SaveLog`, and the variant variable `MyNotepad`. You'll notice that the string variable `Msg` is not declared here; I'm assuming that this is a private variable set by the procedure that calls this macro.

Line 3 assigns to the `LogDate` string a date built of the `Month`, `Day`, and `Year` values for `Now` (which returns the current date and time). For example, if the date is July 11, 1997, `Month(Now)` will return **7**, `Day(Now)` will return **11**, and `Year(Now)` will return **1997**, so the `LogDate` string will contain **7-11-1997**. Line 4 then assigns to the `SaveLog` string (which will be used to supply the file name for the log file) text describing the file, the `LogDate` string, and the `.txt` extension (to continue our example, **Log file for 7-11-1997.txt**).

In line 5, the macro finally gets down to business, using the `Shell` statement to run Notepad in a "normal" (i.e., not maximized or minimized) window with focus, and storing the task ID of the Notepad session in the variable `MyNotepad`. Line 6 then uses an `AppActivate` statement to activate Notepad.

> **WARNING** As I mentioned earlier, the `Shell` function runs asynchronously, which can cause VBA to find itself executing instructions out of order. If you try the code in Listing 23.3 and find it doesn't work, try inserting a delaying mechanism between lines 5 and 6, as discussed in the section "A Caveat: the Shell Function Runs Asynchronously."

Line 7 uses a `SendKeys` statement to send to Notepad the following:

- the information contained in the string `Msg` (which we're assuming to contain the information to be recorded in the log file).
- an Alt+F keystroke (to pull down the File menu), followed by an S keypress to choose the Save item on the menu. This displays the Save As dialog box with the File Name text box selected.
- the `SaveLog` string, which is entered in the File Name text box.
- an Enter keypress to choose the Save button in the Save As dialog box.
- an Alt+F4 keystroke to quit Notepad.

Line 8 ends the macro.

What you'll see when you run this macro (again, you need to run it from Word, not from the Visual Basic Editor) will be this: Notepad will spring to life; the contents of the `Msg` string will appear in the document; the Save As dialog box will display itself, enter the file name in the File Name text box, and dismiss itself; and then Notepad will close.

Even if you don't need to use SendKeys to automate any operations, you may find its ghost-in-the-machine effects useful for unnerving users of your macros.

Controlling the Office Assistant

VBA comes with a full set of commands to let you control the Office Assistant from within Word. I doubt you'll want to make a career out of programming the Office Assistant; however, it not only makes a good party trick but can help break the ice with new interface elements (macros and userforms) that you need your colleagues to use. So I'll spend a few minutes here discussing the Office Assistant, which is implemented in the `Assistant` object in VBA.

Displaying the Office Assistant

Before you do anything else with the Office Assistant, you'll probably want to find out whether the Office Assistant is displayed. To do so, check the `Visible` property of the `Assistant` object; to display the Office Assistant, set the `Visible` property to `True`. For example, to find out if the Office Assistant was displayed and display it if it was not, you could use the following statement:

```
With Assistant
    If .Visible = False Then .Visible = True
End With
```

Setting the Office Assistant Character

To return the file name of the current Office Assistant character, you use the `Filename` property of the `Assistant` object; to set the Office Assistant character, you set the `Filename` property. The names of the files for the nine Office Assistant characters are as follows:

Character	File Name
Clippit	clippit.act
PowerPup	powerpup.act
The Genius	genius.act
Hoverbot	hoverbot.act
Office Logo	logo.act
Scribble	scribble.act
The Dot	dot.act
Mother Nature	mnature.act
Will	will.act

So, for example, you could return the file name of the currently selected Office Assistant character and display it in a message box by using the following statement:

```
MsgBox Assistant.FileName
```

To set the character to The Genius, you could use this statement:

```
Assistant.FileName = "genius.act"
```

You'll find the files for the Office Assistant characters in the \Program Files\Microsoft Office\Office\Actors\ folder.

> **WARNING** Before you attempt to change the Office Assistant character, make sure that the file you intend to use is present on the computer. Depending on the installation options chosen, certain Office Assistant characters may not have been installed.

Playing an Animation

To play an animation, use the Animation property of the Assistant object. For example, to play the Empty Trash animation (PowerPup's best—the animation with the exploding bone), you could use the following statements:

```
With Assistant
    If .FileName <> "powerpup.act" Then
        .FileName = "powerpup.act"
    End If
    If .Visible = False Then
        .Visible = True
    End If
    .Animation = msoAnimationEmptyTrash
End With
```

Displaying a Balloon

Another Office Assistant technique you may find useful is displaying a balloon with text to provide the user with information or allow them to choose a topic. To do so, you use the `NewBalloon` property of the `Assistant` object to return a `Balloon` object. Balloons offer a large number of options, so I'll discuss only the most immediately useful ones here.

First, you get to choose the type of balloon by setting the `BalloonType` property:

Constant	Displays
`msoBalloonTypeButtons`	A balloon with buttons. (This is the default setting.)
`msoBalloonTypeBullets`	A balloon with bullets
`msoBalloonTypeNumbers`	A balloon with a numbered list

You also get a choice of two icons (or none) by setting the `Icon` property: `msoIconAlert` displays a Warning icon, `msoIconTip` displays a Tip icon, and `msoIconNone` displays no icon (the default setting).

Next, choose the buttons you want for the balloon by specifying the `Buttons` property:

Constant	Buttons
`msoButtonSetAbort-RetryIgnore`	Abort, Retry, Ignore
`msoButtonSetBackClose`	Back, Close
`msoButtonSetBackNext-Close`	Back, Next, Close
`msoButtonSetBackNext-Snooze`	Back, Next, Snooze
`msoButtonSetCancel`	Cancel
`msoButtonSetNextClose`	Next, Close
`msoButtonSetNone`	(no button; this setting causes the Office Assistant to disappear and is of no discernible use)

Constant	Buttons
`msoButtonSetOK`	OK
`msoButtonSetOkCancel`	OK, Cancel
`msoButtonSetRetry-Cancel`	Retry, Cancel
`msoButtonSetSearch-Close`	Search, Close
`msoButtonSetTips-OptionsClose`	Tips, Options, Close
`msoButtonSetYesAll-NoCancel`	Yes, Yes to All, No, Cancel
`msoButtonSetYesNo-Cancel`	Yes, No, Cancel
`msoButtonSetYesNo`	Yes, No

To specify a heading, set the `Heading` property by assigning a string to it:

```
With Assistant.NewBalloon
    .Heading = "Designing Your Resume"
End With
```

To specify a single paragraph of text for the balloon, assign a string to its `Text` property:

```
With Assistant.NewBalloon
    .Heading = "Designing Your Resume"
    .Text = "If you spend company time designing your resume,
    ➥you will be fired."
End With
```

To set a number of labels, specify the labels one by one using the `Labels` property:

```
With Assistant.NewBalloon
    .Heading = "Designing Your Resume"
    .Labels(1) = "State your objective."
    .Labels(2) = "Assess your qualifications."
    .Labels(3) = "Subtly exaggerate your positive qualities."
End With
```

Once you've made your choices, you use the Show method to display the balloon. Listing 23.4 produces the simple balloon shown in Figure 23.1.

Listing 23.4

```
 1.  With Assistant.NewBalloon
 2.       .BalloonType = msoBalloonTypeNumbers
 3.       .Icon = msoIconTip
 4.       .Button = msoButtonSetOK
 5.       .Heading = "Creating an Inventory"
 6.       .Text = "The Create_Inventory macro will create the
            ➥appropriate inventory for your current project."
 7.       .Labels(1).Text = "Open the document from which to
            ➥create the inventory."
 8.       .Labels(2).Text = "Run the macro."
 9.       .Labels(3).Text = "Sit back and enjoy the scenery."
10.       .Show
11.  End With
```

Analysis

This listing uses a straightforward With statement to set the properties for the NewBalloon object: line 2 sets the BalloonType property to a numbered list, and line 3 sets the Icon property to the Tip icon. Line 4 sets the Button property to specify an OK button. Line 5 assigns text to the Heading property, and line 6 assigns text to the Text property, which produces the first paragraph at the top of the balloon. Lines 7 through 9 assign text to the `Text` property of three labels in the `Labels` collection. Finally, line 10 uses the `Show` method to display the balloon, and line 11 ends the `With` statement.

NOTE   At this writing, the Office Assistant characters are getting a mixed reception from early adopters of Office 97. Given the rapidity with which the user's initial response of amused interest may turn to disgusted frustration, you'll probably want to give users of your macros a way to avoid the Office Assistant if you decide to employ it.

In the next chapter, I'll discuss how you can put together a special-purpose template to facilitate the production of a particular type of document. I can't promise to use every single VBA command we've used so far in the book, but a good proportion of them will resurface in context. Flip the page.

CHAPTER
TWENTY-FOUR

Building a Special-Purpose Template

Given the extent to which you can customize Word, and the power of the Visual Basic for Applications language, you can even build a special-purpose application that runs itself. For example, if you so wished, you could build a Word application that limited the user to creating a certain type of document: the user would start the application, create the document, and then exit the application, without being able to take any other actions. Generally speaking, though, building a special-purpose application in Word makes little sense because, to help you create any Word document, you will usually want to be able to access other Word documents (for example, for reference, or to cut or copy and paste text); or you might want to perform whatever operation the application was designed to perform while you had other documents open, without closing them and shutting down Word. (With Access, on the other hand, you might want to create an application that opened, let the user choose from and execute a small range of tasks such as updating one component of a database, and then closed.)

In Word, you usually won't want to significantly restrict the functionality available to the user; instead, you'll normally do best to build a special interface with features that guide the user toward the easiest ways of performing the task they're working on. So instead of building a special-purpose application, you'll usually want to construct a special-purpose template that enables the user to perform the task or tasks at hand while retaining the use of Word's regular features.

In this chapter, I'll discuss how you can put together such a template. I'll start by stating the purpose of the template and the goals it's supposed to achieve. Then I'll walk you through a number of different macros designed to help the user create documents in the template. Along the way, I'll touch on a number of the commands we've looked at in the book; I'll also mention a couple of commands you haven't yet encountered.

The Example Template: Magazine Article.dot

The example template I've created for demonstration purposes is named `Magazine Article.dot` and, as its name suggests, it's intended for writing magazine articles. It's distributed by MegaMag Publications Inc., proud purveyors of such magazines as *Icelandic Fashion Review*, *Steamships of the Caucasus*, *Radio Free Liberia Listening Guide*, *The Projection TV Companion*, and more.

The goals of the template are as follows:

- Provide styles for all the permissible elements in the magazine articles.

- Make sure that the writers use the styles to indicate the elements of their articles (headings, pull quotes, notes, sidebars, illustrations, etc.) rather than laying out the elements by using blank paragraphs, tabs, and spaces.

- Make sure that the writers base other documents for MegaMag on the `Magazine Article.dot` template rather than on other templates.

- Make sure that the writers save their articles under names that indicate the writer's name and the title of the article.

- Save the articles in Word 6 format for easy conversion to the desktop-publishing application that MegaMag uses, which can't read files in Word 97 format.

The User Interface

In the section titled "Putting Customization to Use" in Chapter 3, I discussed briefly how to approach customizing the user environment. `Magazine Article.dot` provides an example of how you might customize the user environment for a particular purpose—in this case, providing the user with the appropriate functionality for writing magazine articles. `Magazine Article.dot` features a modified menu bar, two special toolbars, and some reassigned keyboard shortcuts. I'll discuss these in turn in the following sections.

The Menus

The `Magazine Article.dot` template sports stripped-down menus to provide the user with a limited number of options designed to fulfill all their writing needs for MegaMag. Figure 24.1 shows the resulting menu bar.

FIGURE 24.1

The menu bar of the Magazine Article .dot template features a reduced set of menus.

You'll notice that I've removed the Format menu, because all the formatting the user will need is available via the styles built into the template, and any formatting beyond this is superfluous and will cause a processing problem for the desktop-publishing application the template is designed to shield; I've also removed the Table menu, because the writers should not be using tables in their articles. These limitations will apply only to documents based on the Magazine Article.dot template; if the user opens another document, they will still enjoy all the functionality supported by the template on which that document is based.

Styles Menu

So far, so good; but the menu bar also bears two extra menus, Styles and Macros, to make the styles and macros in the template more easily accessible to the user. The Styles menu (shown in Figure 24.2) allows the user to quickly apply a style to the current paragraph or current selection using the keyboard. They can also use the mouse for the Styles menu, but there's little advantage to using the Styles menu with the mouse over using the Style menu on the Formatting toolbar (if the Formatting toolbar is displayed). With the keyboard, however, the user can employ the menu's access key (**S**) to activate the menu and then employ the appropriate access key to trigger the menu item for the desired style.

As I'll show you in a minute, all the styles are also available on the Magazine Article Styles toolbar, which the user can display and hide at will, and on the Styles drop-down list on the Formatting toolbar, which the user can likewise display and hide. This wealth of redundant methods for applying styles should ensure that the user always has the styles on hand no matter which toolbars they currently have displayed.

Most of the menu items (and the corresponding toolbar buttons) are straightforward style items dragged from the Styles category on the Commands tab of the Customize dialog box (choose Tools ➤ Customize, or right-click the menu bar or a displayed toolbar and choose Customize from the context menu to display the Customize dialog box; then select the appropriate template in the Save In

FIGURE 24.2

FIGURE 24.2

The Styles menu provides a quick way to apply styles with the keyboard.

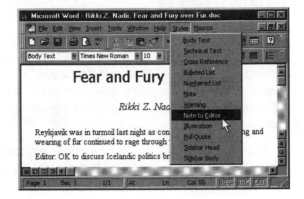

drop-down list on the Commands tab). For example, the Body Text button simply applies the Body Text style, and the Note to Editor button applies the Note to Editor style. The exceptions are the Technical Text and Cross Reference items, which run simple macros to toggle the Technical Text and Cross Reference character styles on and off as appropriate. Listing 24.1 shows the code for both of these macros.

Listing 24.1

```
1.   Sub Technical_Text()
2.       If Selection.Style = "Technical Text" Then
3.           Selection.Style = "Default Paragraph Font"
4.       Else
5.           Selection.Style = "Technical Text"
6.       End If
7.   End Sub
8.
9.   Sub Cross_Reference()
10.      If Selection.Style = "Cross Reference" Then
11.          Selection.Style = "Default Paragraph Font"
12.      Else
13.          Selection.Style = "Cross Reference"
14.      End If
15.  End Sub
```

Analysis

The `Technical_Text` macro (lines 1 through 7) toggles on and off the Technical Text character style. Line 2 compares the `Style` property of the `Selection` object to `Technical Text`; if it matches, line 3 applies the Default Paragraph Font style; if not, the `Else` statement in line 4 runs, and line 5 applies the Technical Text style to the selection. Line 6 ends the `If` statement, and line 7 ends the macro.

The `Cross_Reference` macro in lines 9 through 15 toggles on and off the Cross Reference character style. This macro works in the same way as the `Technical_Text` macro but manipulates the Cross Reference style instead.

Macros Menu

The Macros menu (see Figure 24.3) contains five of the macros included in the `Magazine Article.dot` template:

Macro Name	Macro Menu Item
NewMegaMagDocument	New Magazine Article
Save_in_Word_6_Format	Save in Word 6 Format
Set_Author_Information	Set Author Information
Set_Toolbar_and_View_ Preferences	Set Toolbar and View Preferences
Delete_the_Current File	Delete this Document

FIGURE 24.3

The Macros menu provides quick access to the macros that the user may need to run manually.

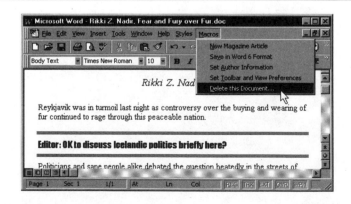

You'll notice that I haven't included the `Technical_Text` and `Cross_ Reference` macros on the Macros menu. Because these simply toggle their namesake styles on and off, they belong on the Styles menu (and Styles toolbar) rather than on the Macros menu and Macros toolbar. (You could put them on both toolbars, but there's little point—it would only serve to clutter the user interface unnecessarily.)

Like the styles, the macros are also available through a toolbar—in this case, the Magazine Article Macros toolbar. Again, this is designed to ensure that the user always has access to them. (As you'll see in a moment, a couple of the macros are also included on the File menu.)

I'll discuss the menu items and their macros in the following sections.

New Magazine Article The New Magazine Article menu item runs the `NewMegaMagDocument` macro, which creates a new template based on the `Magazine Article.dot` template. Listing 24.2 shows the code for the `NewMegaMagDocument` macro.

Listing 24.2

```
1.  Sub NewMegaMagDocument()
2.      Dim TemplateLocation As String
3.      TemplateLocation = System.PrivateProfileString("",
        ➥"HKEY_CURRENT_USER\Software\Microsoft\Office\8.0\
        ➥Common\FileNew\LocalTemplates", "")
4.      Documents.Add Template:=TemplateLocation &
        ➥"\Special Templates\Magazine Article.dot"
5.  End Sub
```

Analysis

Line 2 declares the string `TemplateLocation`, and line 3 assigns to it the value of the `LocalTemplates` key in the `FileNew` key under `HKEY_CURRENT_USER\ Software\Microsoft\Office\8.0\Common\FileNew\` in the registry—the location of the local templates for the current computer. Line 4 then uses the `Add` method on the `Documents` object to create a new object based on the `Magazine Article.dot` template, which is specified as being in `TemplateLocation & \Special Templates\`. Line 5 ends the macro.

NOTE

As you'll remember from Chapter 21, the word *key* has two meanings in the context of the registry: first, it means a folder or container in the registry; and second, it means an individual value inside one of those folder keys.

Save in Word 6 Format   The Save in Word 6 Format menu item runs the `Save_in_Word_6_Format` macro, which saves the current document in Word 6 format (technically, Word 6.0/Word 95 format, but I'll refer to it as Word 6 format here). The macro is very simple:

```
Sub Save_in_Word_6_Format()
    ActiveDocument.SaveAs FileFormat:=
    ➥FileConverters("MSWord6Exp").SaveFormat
End Sub
```

Here, the second line uses the `SaveAs` method and the `SaveFormat` property of the `FileConverters` object (as discussed in Chapter 13) to save the active document in Word 6 format.

As you'll see later in this chapter, the `AutoNew` macro automatically saves each new document based on the `Magazine Article.dot` template in Word 6 format, so the `Save_in_Word_6_Format` macro is for the most part a precautionary step. But it becomes necessary when the user attaches a document based on another template and saved as a Word 97 document (or another type of file) to the `Magazine Article.dot` template. In this case, the next time the user saves the file, the `Save_in_Word_6_Format` macro will suggest saving the file in Word 6 format.

Delete This Document   The Delete This Document menu item runs a more sophisticated version of the `Delete_the_Current_File` macro presented in Listing 13.2 in Chapter 13. As you'll recall, that macro confirmed that the user wants to delete the current document, then closes it and deletes it by using a `Kill` statement. This version of the macro has to be more sophisticated because it is located in the `Magazine Article.dot` template, and when the macro closes the document based on that template, Word stops the rest of the macro from executing, thereby preventing the macro from deleting the document it has just closed. (If two documents based on `Magazine Article.dot` are open, the macro will work fine, but this is unlikely to be the case in most instances.) Listing 24.3 contains the code for the macro.

Listing 24.3

```
1.    Sub Delete_the_Current_File()
2.        Dim Response As Byte, FileToKill As String,
          ➥TestFile As String, TemplateLocation As String,
          ➥CloseMe As String
3.        FileToKill = ActiveDocument.FullName
4.        Response = MsgBox("Do you want to delete "
          ➥+ FileToKill + "?", vbYesNo + vbCritical
          ➥+ vbDefaultButton2, "Delete the Current File")
5.        If Response = vbYes Then
6.            Documents.Add
7.            TemplateLocation = System.PrivateProfileString
              ➥("", "HKEY_CURRENT_USER\Software\Microsoft\
              ➥Office\8.0\Common\FileNew\LocalTemplates", "")
8.            ActiveDocument.AttachedTemplate = TemplateLocation
              ➥& "\Special Templates\Magazine Article.dot"
9.            CloseMe = ActiveDocument.FullName
10.           TestFile = Dir(FileToKill)
11.           Documents(FileToKill).Close SaveChanges:=
              ➥wdDoNotSaveChanges
12.           If Len(TestFile) <> 0 Then
13.               Kill FileToKill
14.           End If
15.           Documents(CloseMe).Close SaveChanges:=
              ➥wdDoNotSaveChanges
16.       End If
17.   End Sub
```

Analysis

The `Delete_the_Current_File` macro begins by declaring in line 2 the various variables it will use: the Byte variable `Response` and four string variables, `FileToKill`, `TestFile`, `TemplateLocation`, and `CloseMe`. Line 3 then assigns to the `FileToKill` variable the `FullName` property of the active document.

Line 4 displays a message box to ensure that the user wants to delete the file, identifying it by name. As in the previous incarnation of this macro, the default button on the message box is No, forcing the user to actively select the Yes button if they want to delete the file. Again as before, line 5 checks `Response` against `vbYes` and proceeds if they match.

Line 6 creates a new document based on Normal.dot. This document will act as a staging horse for closing the document that will be deleted, so it needs to be attached to the `Magazine Article.dot` template. To do so, line 7 returns the `LocalTemplates` key (folder) from the registry and assigns it to the `TemplateLocation` variable, and line 8 sets the `AttachedTemplate` property of the active document (the new document just created) to the location of `Magazine Article.dot`: `TemplateLocation` plus the folder `Special Templates` plus `Magazine Article.dot`. Line 9 then assigns to the variable `CloseMe` the `FullName` property of the active document.

NOTE By creating a document based on Normal.dot and then attaching it to `Magazine Article.dot`, **the macro avoids running the** `AutoNew` **macro in** `Magazine Article.dot`.

Now two documents based on `Magazine Article.dot` are open, so the macro can close the original document and delete it without cutting itself off in the process.

Line 10 uses the `Dir` statement to establish whether the original document exists on disk. Line 11 closes the document without saving changes. Lines 12 through 14 contain a nested `If...Then` condition: if the length of the `TestFile` string is not 0—i.e., if the document exists on disk—the `Kill` statement in line 13 is executed, deleting the document from disk.

All that remains is for line 15 to close the staging-horse document (identified by `CloseMe`) without saving changes, and execution of the macro can end as Word closes the `Magazine Article.dot` template at the same time.

Set Author Information The Set Author Information menu item runs the `Set_Author_Information` macro, which displays the Set Author Information dialog box (see Figure 24.4) for indicating the author's name, ID number, and working folder.

FIGURE 24.4

The Set Author Infor-
mation dialog box.

The `Set_Author_Information` macro contains only the code to display the
dialog box, which is the `frmSet_Author_Information` userform:

```
Sub Set_Author_Information()
    Load frmSet_Author_Information
    frmSet_Author_Information.Show
End Sub
```

Everything else happens on the code sheet for the userform, as shown in
Listing 24.4.

Listing 24.4

```
1.   Private AuthorName As String, AuthorID As Variant,
     ➥SaveFolder As String
2.
3.   Private Sub UserForm_Initialize()
4.       Get_Author_Information
5.       txtAuthorName.Value = AuthorName
6.       txtAuthorID.Value = AuthorID
7.       lblSaveFolder = SaveFolder
8.   End Sub
9.
10.  Private Sub cmdCancel_Click()
11.      End
12.  End Sub
13.
14.  Private Sub cmdChangeFolder_Click()
15.      Dim CurrentName As String, MagSave As Object
16.      CurrentName = lblSaveFolder
17.      ChangeFileOpenDirectory CurrentName
18.      Set MagSave = Dialogs(wdDialogFileSaveAs)
```

```
19.      With MagSave
20.          .Display
21.              lblSaveFolder = CurDir
22.      End With
23.  End Sub
24.
25.  Private Sub cmdOK_Click()
26.      frmSet_Author_Information.Hide
27.      SaveFolder = lblSaveFolder
28.      AuthorName = txtAuthorName.Text
29.      AuthorID = txtAuthorID.Text
30.      Update_Author_Information
31.  End Sub
32.
33.  Sub Update_Author_Information()
34.      Dim RegLoc As String
35.      RegLoc = "HKEY_CURRENT_USER\Software\Microsoft\
         ➥Office\8.0\Common\MagazineArticle"
36.      System.PrivateProfileString("", RegLoc,
         ➥"AuthorName") = AuthorName
37.      System.PrivateProfileString("", RegLoc,
         ➥"AuthorID") = AuthorID
38.      System.PrivateProfileString("", RegLoc,
         ➥"SaveFolder") = SaveFolder
39.  End Sub
40.
41.  Sub Get_Author_Information()
42.      Dim RegLoc As String
43.      RegLoc = "HKEY_CURRENT_USER\Software\Microsoft\
         ➥Office\8.0\Common\MagazineArticle"
44.      AuthorName = System.PrivateProfileString("", RegLoc,
         ➥"AuthorName")
45.      If AuthorName = "" Then AuthorName =
         ➥Application.UserName
46.      AuthorID = System.PrivateProfileString("",
         ➥RegLoc, "AuthorID")
47.      SaveFolder = System.PrivateProfileString("",
         ➥RegLoc, "SaveFolder")
48.      If SaveFolder = "" Then SaveFolder = CurDir
49.  End Sub
```

Analysis

Listing 24.4 contains six macros: `UserForm_Initialize`, `cmdCancel_Click`, `cmdChangeFolder_Click`, `cmdOK_Click`, `Update_Author_Information`, and `Get_Author_Information`.

But first, line 1 declares three private variables: the string variable `AuthorName`, the variant variable `AuthorID`, and the string variable `SaveFolder`. These variables are declared as private rather than local so that they will be available to all the macros in the procedure.

The `UserForm_Initialize` macro (lines 3 through 8) initializes the dialog box. Line 4 runs the `Get_Author_Information` macro, which I'll discuss later in this analysis and which stores values in the `AuthorName`, `AuthorID`, and `SaveFolder` private variables. Line 5 then sets the `Value` property of the `txtAuthorName` text box to the value that `Get_Author_Information` has stored in the `AuthorName` variable; line 6 sets the `Value` property of the `txtAuthorID` text box to the value of `AuthorID`; and line 7 sets the `lblSaveFolder` label to the value of `SaveFolder`. Line 8 then ends the `UserForm_Initialize` macro.

The `cmdCancel_Click` macro (lines 10 through 12) simply cancels the procedure with its `End` statement (line 11) if the user clicks the Cancel button in the dialog box.

The `cmdChangeFolder_Click` macro (lines 14 through 23) runs when the user clicks the `cmdChangeFolder` button (identified in the dialog box as Change Folder for Saving Articles). Line 15 declares the string variable `CurrentName` and the object variable `MagSave`. Line 16 then stores the value of the `lblSaveFolder` label in `CurrentName`, and line 17 changes the File-Open-Directory value to `CurrentName`, so that when the Save As dialog box is displayed, it will be set to the folder in `CurrentName`. Line 18 sets the `MagSave` object variable to reference the Save As dialog box. Lines 19 through 22 contain a `With` statement that works with the `MagSave` object. Line 20 uses the `Display` method to display the dialog box, which suppresses the display of the Set Author Information dialog box and allows the user to choose a folder. When the user clicks the Save button, VBA hides the dialog box and continues execution at line 21, which retrieves the folder the user chose and sets `lblSaveFolder` to reflect it, and then redisplays the Set Author Information dialog box. Line 22 then ends the `With` statement, and line 23 ends this macro.

The `cmdOK_Click` macro (lines 25 through 31) runs when the user clicks the OK button. Line 26 hides the Set Author Information dialog box. Line 27 sets the private variable `SaveFolder` to the value of `lblSaveFolder`. Line 28 sets the private variable `AuthorName` to the `Text` property of the `txtAuthorName` text box. Line 29 sets the private variable `AuthorID` to the `Text` property of the `txtAuthorID` text box. Line 30 then runs the `Update_Author_Information` macro, which is discussed in the next paragraph. Line 31 ends the `cmdOK_Click` macro.

The `Update_Author_Information` macro (lines 33 through 39) updates the author information stored in the registry with the information from the Set Author Information dialog box. Line 34 declares the string variable `RegLoc` (for *registry location*), and line 35 sets the registry location in which this template is storing its information—the `MagazineArticle` key (folder) under `HKEY_CURRENT_USER\ Software\Microsoft\Office\8.0\Common\`, a key unique to this template. Line 36 then sets the `AuthorName` key to the value of the `AuthorName` string. Line 37 sets the `AuthorID` key to the value of the `AuthorID` variant. Line 38 sets the `SaveFolder` key to the value of the `SaveFolder` string. Line 39 then ends this macro.

The `Get_Author_Information` macro (lines 41 through 49) performs the reverse operation from `Update_Author_Information`, retrieving the values for the private variables from the keys stored in the registry, but with a twist: if there is no information in two of the keys, it gets that information from elsewhere. Line 42 again declares the `RegLoc` string variable, and line 43 again assigns to it the appropriate registry location. Line 44 then sets the private variable `Author-Name` to the value of the `AuthorName` key. Line 45 checks to see if the private variable `AuthorName` is an empty string, and if so, assigns to it the `UserName` property of the `Application` object—the registered user's name in Word. Line 46 sets the private variable `AuthorID` to the value of the `AuthorID` key. Line 47 sets the private variable `SaveFolder` to the value of the `SaveFolder` key. Line 48 checks to see if the private variable `SaveFolder` is an empty string, and if so, assigns to it the current folder (`CurDir`). Line 49 then ends the macro.

By this time, the `AuthorName` and `SaveFolder` private variables should have values assigned to them—either values from the registry keys they first target, or (if the keys are blank or do not yet exist) from Word application information.

Set Toolbar and View Preferences The Set Toolbar and View Preferences menu item runs the `Set_Toolbar_and_View_Preferences` macro. This macro simply loads and displays the Toolbar and View Preferences dialog box (see Figure 24.5), which allows the user to specify the toolbars to be displayed and choose view options to be applied for documents based on the `Magazine Article.dot` template.

FIGURE 24.5

The Toolbar and View Preferences dialog box lets the user quickly set toolbar and view preferences to be applied whenever they create or open a document based on the `Magazine Article.dot` template.

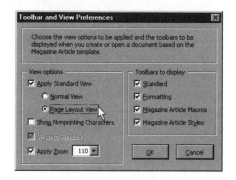

The `Set_Toolbar_and_View_Preferences` macro contains the following code:

```
Sub Set_Toolbar_and_View_Preferences()
    Load frmToolbar_and_View_Preferences
    frmToolbar_and_View_Preferences.Show
End Sub
```

Again, all the action happens on the code sheet for the Toolbar and View Preferences dialog box. Listing 24.5 shows the code for this code sheet. Brace yourself: this is the longest code listing in the book.

Listing 24.5

```
1.   Private Sub UserForm_Initialize()
2.       Dim RegLoc As String, MagStandard, MagFormatting,
         ➥MagMacros, MagStyles, MagZoom, MagZoomPercent,
         ➥MagShowAll, MagWrapToWindow, MagStandardView,
         ➥MagView
3.       cmbZoom.AddItem "50"
4.       cmbZoom.AddItem "75"
5.       cmbZoom.AddItem "100"
```

```
 6.        cmbZoom.AddItem "110"
 7.        cmbZoom.AddItem "120"
 8.        cmbZoom.AddItem "130"
 9.        cmbZoom.AddItem "140"
10.        cmbZoom.AddItem "150"
11.        cmbZoom.AddItem "200"
12.        cmbZoom.AddItem "400"
13.        RegLoc = "HKEY_CURRENT_USER\Software\Microsoft\
           ➥Office\8.0\Common\MagazineArticle"
14.        MagStandardView = System.PrivateProfileString
           ➥("", RegLoc, "StandardView")
15.        MagView = System.PrivateProfileString
           ➥("", RegLoc, "View")
16.        MagShowAll = System.PrivateProfileString
           ➥("", RegLoc, "ShowAll")
17.        MagZoom = System.PrivateProfileString
           ➥("", RegLoc, "Zoom")
18.        MagZoomPercent = System.PrivateProfileString
           ➥("", RegLoc, "ZoomPercentage")
19.        MagStandard = System.PrivateProfileString
           ➥("", RegLoc, "Standard")
20.        MagFormatting = System.PrivateProfileString
           ➥("", RegLoc, "Formatting")
21.        MagMacros = System.PrivateProfileString
           ➥("", RegLoc, "MagMacros")
22.        MagStyles = System.PrivateProfileString
           ➥("", RegLoc, "MagStyles")
23.        MagWrapToWindow = System.PrivateProfileString
           ➥("", RegLoc, "WrapToWindow")
24.        If MagStandard = True Then
25.            chkStandard.Value = True
26.        Else
27.            chkStandard.Value = False
28.        End If
29.        If MagFormatting = True Then
30.            chkFormatting.Value = True
31.        Else
32.            chkFormatting.Value = False
33.        End If
34.        If MagMacros = True Then
35.            chkMagMacros.Value = True
36.        Else
```

```
37.                chkMagMacros.Value = False
38.        End If
39.        If MagStyles = True Then
40.                chkMagStyles.Value = True
41.        Else
42.                chkMagStyles.Value = False
43.        End If
44.        If MagStandardView = True Then
45.                chkStandardView.Value = True
46.                optNormalView.Enabled = True
47.                optPageLayoutView.Enabled = True
48.                If MagView = "Normal" Then
49.                    optNormalView.Value = True
50.                Else
51.                    optPageLayoutView.Value = True
52.                End If
53.        Else
54.                chkStandardView.Value = False
55.        End If
56.        If MagShowAll = True Then
57.                chkShowAll.Value = True
58.        Else
59.                chkShowAll.Value = False
60.        End If
61.        If MagWrapToWindow = True Then
62.                chkWrapToWindow.Value = True
63.                If MagView = "Normal" Then
64.                    chkWrapToWindow.Enabled = True
65.                Else
66.                    chkWrapToWindow.Enabled = False
67.                End If
68.        Else
69.                chkWrapToWindow.Value = False
70.        End If
71.        If MagZoom = True Then
72.                chkZoom.Value = True
73.                cmbZoom.Enabled = True
74.                cmbZoom.Value = MagZoomPercent
75.        Else
76.                chkZoom.Value = False
77.                cmbZoom.Enabled = False
78.                cmbZoom.Value = ""
```

```
79.        End If
80.    End Sub
81.
82.    Private Sub chkStandardView_Click()
83.        If chkStandardView.Value = True Then
84.            optNormalView.Enabled = True
85.            optNormalView.Value = True
86.            optPageLayoutView.Enabled = True
87.        Else
88.            optNormalView.Enabled = False
89.            optNormalView.Value = False
90.            optPageLayoutView.Enabled = False
91.            optPageLayoutView.Value = False
92.        End If
93.    End Sub
94.
95.    Private Sub chkZoom_Click()
96.        If chkZoom.Value = True Then
97.            cmbZoom.Enabled = True
98.            cmbZoom.Value = "100"
99.        Else
100.           cmbZoom.Enabled = False
101.       End If
102.   End Sub
103.
104.   Private Sub cmdOK_Click()
105.       Dim RegLoc As String
106.       RegLoc = "HKEY_CURRENT_USER\Software\Microsoft\
           ➥Office\8.0\Common\MagazineArticle"
107.       frmToolbar_and_View_Preferences.Hide
108.       If chkStandard.Value = True Then
109.           CommandBars("Standard").Visible = True
110.           System.PrivateProfileString("", RegLoc,
           ➥"Standard") = "True"
111.       Else
112.           CommandBars("Standard").Visible = False
113.           System.PrivateProfileString("", RegLoc,
           ➥"Standard") = "False"
114.       End If
115.       If chkFormatting.Value = True Then
116.           CommandBars("Formatting").Visible = True
117.           System.PrivateProfileString("", RegLoc,
           ➥"Formatting") = "True"
```

```
118.      Else
119.          CommandBars("Formatting").Visible = False
120.          System.PrivateProfileString("", RegLoc,
              ➥"Formatting") = "False"
121.      End If
122.      If chkMagMacros.Value = True Then
123.          CommandBars("Magazine Article Macros")
              ➥.Visible = True
124.      System.PrivateProfileString("", RegLoc,
              ➥"MagMacros") = "True"
125.      Else
126.          CommandBars("Magazine Article Macros")
              ➥.Visible = False
127.          System.PrivateProfileString("", RegLoc,
              ➥"MagMacros") = "False"
128.      End If
129.      If chkMagStyles.Value = True Then
130.          CommandBars("Magazine Article Styles")
              ➥.Visible = True
131.          System.PrivateProfileString("", RegLoc,
              ➥"MagStyles") = "True"
132.      Else
133.          CommandBars("Magazine Article Styles")
              ➥.Visible = False
134.          System.PrivateProfileString("", RegLoc,
              ➥"MagStyles") = "False"
135.      End If
136.      With ActiveWindow.View
137.          If chkStandardView.Value = True Then
138.              System.PrivateProfileString("", RegLoc,
                  ➥"StandardView") = "True"
139.              If optNormalView.Value = True Then
140.                  .Type = wdNormalView
141.                  System.PrivateProfileString("", RegLoc,
                      ➥"View") = "Normal"
142.              Else
143.                  .Type = wdPageView
144.                  System.PrivateProfileString("", RegLoc,
                      ➥"View") = "PageLayout"
145.              End If
146.          Else
147.              System.PrivateProfileString("", RegLoc,
                  ➥"StandardView") = "False"
```

```
148.        End If
149.        If chkWrapToWindow.Value = True Then
150.            .WrapToWindow = True
151.            System.PrivateProfileString("", RegLoc,
               ➥"WrapToWindow") = True
152.        Else
153.            .WrapToWindow = False
154.            System.PrivateProfileString("", RegLoc,
               ➥"WrapToWindow") = False
155.        End If
156.        If chkShowAll.Value = True Then
157.            .ShowAll = True
158.            System.PrivateProfileString("", RegLoc,
               ➥"ShowAll") = "True"
159.        Else
160.            .ShowAll = False
161.            System.PrivateProfileString("", RegLoc,
               ➥"ShowAll") = "False"
162.        End If
163.        If chkZoom.Value = True Then
164.            .Zoom = cmbZoom.Value
165.            System.PrivateProfileString("", RegLoc,
               ➥"Zoom") = "True"
166.            System.PrivateProfileString("", RegLoc,
               ➥"ZoomPercentage") = cmbZoom.Value
167.        Else
168.            System.PrivateProfileString("", RegLoc,
               ➥"Zoom") = "False"
169.        End If
170.    End With
171. End Sub
172.
173. Private Sub cmdCancel_Click()
174.    End
175. End Sub
176.
177. Private Sub optPageLayoutView_Click()
178.    If optPageLayoutView.Value = True Then
179.        chkWrapToWindow.Enabled = False
180.    End If
181. End Sub
```

```
182.
183.    Private Sub optNormalView_Click()
184.        If optNormalView.Value = True Then
185.            chkWrapToWindow.Enabled = True
186.        End If
187.    End Sub
```

Analysis

Listing 24.5 contains seven macros:

- `UserForm_Initialize` initializes the userform.

- `chkStandardView_Click` runs when the Apply Standard View check box is clicked (either selected or cleared).

- `chkZoom_Click` runs when the Apply Zoom check box is clicked (again, either selected or cleared).

- `cmdOK_Click` runs when the OK button is chosen.

- `cmdCancel_Click` runs when the Cancel button is chosen.

- `optPageLayoutView_Click` runs when the Page Layout View option button is clicked.

- `optNormalView_Click` runs when the Normal View option button is clicked.

I'll discuss the macros briefly in this section. Because most of them use statements we've been through at length earlier in the book, I won't explain every detail of how they work—instead, I'll point out the main actions the macros are taking.

UserForm_Initialize The `UserForm_Initialize` macro (lines 1 through 80) starts by declaring the `RegLoc` variable to hold the registry location, and ten variables that the macro needs for storing information to be transferred from the registry to the dialog box and vice versa: `MagStandard`, `MagFormatting`, `MagMacros`, `MagStyles`, `MagZoom`, `MagZoomPercent`, `MagShowAll`, `MagWrapToWindow`, `MagStandardView`, and `MagView`.

The macro then adds ten items to the `cmbZoom` combo box, providing zoom percentages from 50 to 400. Note that there's a cluster of zoom percentages just above 100—110, 120, 130, 140, and 150—because these provide suitable zoom percentages for viewing normal text at conventional font sizes (e.g., Times New Roman 12-point) at 800 x 600–pixel resolution (the resolution users are most likely to be using).

Line 13 stores the registry location in `RegLoc`. Lines 14 through 23 then return the individual keys from the `MagazineArticle` key in the registry and store them in the appropriate variables. For example, line 14 stores the `StandardView` key in the `MagStandardView` variable, and line 15 stores the `View` key in the `MagView` variable.

Lines 24 through 43 contain a series of four `If` statements that check the values of the `MagStandard`, `MagFormatting`, `MagMacros`, and `MagStyles` variables and set the check boxes for the corresponding toolbars appropriately. For example, if `MagStandard` contains the value `True`, line 25 sets the `Value` property of the `chkStandard` check box to `True`, selecting the check box; if not, line 27 sets the `Value` of the check box to `False`, deselecting it.

Lines 44 through 55 contain a more complex `If` statement that sets the `Value` property of the `chkStandardView` check box (identified as Apply Standard View in the dialog box) and the two option buttons under it, `optNormalView` and `optPageLayoutView` (identified as Normal View and Page Layout View, respectively). If the `MagStandardView` variable is `True`, the macro selects the `chkStandardView` check box, enables the `optNormalView` and `optPage-LayoutView` option buttons, and uses the value of the `View` variable to determine which of `optNormalView` and `optPageLayoutView` to select. If `MagStandardView` is not `True`, the macro clears the `chkStandardView` check box, and the option buttons (which are disabled in the userform) remain disabled.

Lines 56 through 60 contain an `If` statement that uses the value of the `MagShowAll` variable to determine whether to select or clear the `chkShowAll` check box (identified in the dialog box as Show Nonprinting Characters).

Lines 61 through 70 contain an `If` statement that uses the value of the `Mag-WrapToWindow` variable to determine whether to select or clear the `chkWrap-ToWindow` check box. This is complicated by the Wrap to Window feature not being available in Page Layout view. To reflect this, if `MagWrapToWindow` is `True`, line 63 checks to see if `MagView` is `Normal`; if it is, line 64 enables the `chkWrapToWindow` check box, and if not, line 66 disables the check box.

Lines 71 through 79 contain an `If` statement that uses the value of the `MagZoom` variable to control the `chkZoom` check box and the `cmbZoom` combo box. If `MagZoom` is `True`, line 72 selects the `chkZoom` check box, line 73 enables the `cmbZoom` combo box, and line 74 sets the `Value` of the `cmbZoom` combo box to the value stored in `MagZoomPercent`; if `MagZoom` is not `True`, line 76 clears the `chkZoom` check box, line 77 disables the `cmbZoom` combo box, and line 78 sets the `Value` of the `cmbZoom` combo box to an empty string.

Line 80 ends the `UserForm_Initialize` macro.

chkStandardView_Click The `chkStandardView_Click` macro (lines 82 through 93) adjusts the settings of the `optNormalView` and `optPageLayout-View` option buttons when the user clicks the `chkStandardView` check box (identified in the dialog box as Apply Standard View). The Apply Standard View check box lets the user choose whether to have the template change to a designated view (Normal view or Page Layout view) when they create or open a document based on the `Magazine Article.dot` template. By default, the Apply Standard View check box is cleared, so the `optNormalView` (Normal View) and `optPageLayoutView` (Page Layout view) option buttons are disabled. When the user clicks the `chkStandardView` check box, line 83 checks the `Value` property of `chkStandardView`: if it is `True`, line 84 enables the `optNormalView` option button, line 85 selects it, and line 86 enables the `optPageLayoutView` option button. If the `Value` of `chkStandardView` is not `True`, the `Else` statement in line 87 runs: line 88 disables `optNormalView`, and line 89 deselects it (whether or not it was selected); line 90 disables `optPageLayoutView`, and line 91 deselects it. Line 92 ends the `If` statement, and line 93 ends this macro.

chkZoom_Click The `chkZoom_Click` macro (lines 95 through 102) adjusts the settings of the `cmbZoom` combo box when the user clicks the `chkZoom` check box (identified in the dialog box as Apply Zoom). Line 96 checks the `Value` property of the `chkZoom` check box to see if the user selected the check box or cleared it: if the `Value` is `True` (i.e., the user selected the check box), line 97 enables the `cmbZoom` combo box, and line 98 sets its `Value` to `100`, thus selecting the 100 value in the drop-down list; if the `Value` is `False` (i.e., the user cleared the check box), line 100 disables the `cmbZoom` combo box. (The value 100 remains in the disabled combo box; alternatively, the macro could reset the value of the combo box at this point.) Line 101 ends the `If` statement, and line 102 ends this macro.

cmdOK_Click `cmdOK_Click` (lines 104 through 171) runs when the user selects the OK button in the Toolbar and View Preferences dialog box. The macro sets display options according to the settings chosen and stores details of those choices in the keys in the registry.

First, line 105 declares the string variable RegLoc, and line 106 assigns to it the location of the registry key with which to work. Line 107 then hides the frmToolbar_and_View_Preferences dialog box, removing it from the screen.

Next, the macro uses four If...Then...Else statements (lines 108 through 135) to check the Value property of each of the check boxes governing the display of the toolbars controlled by the dialog box: chkStandard (which controls the Standard toolbar), chkFormatting (the Formatting toolbar), chkMagMacros (the Magazine Article Macros toolbar), and chkMagStyles (the Magazine Article Styles toolbar). If the Value property of the check box item is True, the first of the statements that follow sets the Visible property to True, displaying the toolbar, and the second statement sets the appropriate key in the registry to True; otherwise, the Else statement runs—the first statement after it sets the Visible property of the toolbar to False, hiding the toolbar, and the second statement after it sets the appropriate key in the registry to False.

Line 136 begins a With statement for the View object in the ActiveWindow object; this With statement contains a number of If statements that implement the options in the View Options group box of the dialog box and store their settings in the appropriate keys in the registry:

- Line 137 checks to see if the chkStandardView check box is selected (True). If it is, line 138 sets the StandardView key in the registry to True, and the nested If statement in lines 139 to 145 runs: it checks which of the two option buttons—optNormalView and optPageLayoutView— is selected, and sets the Type property of the View object accordingly to wdNormalView or wdPageView and the View key to Normal or PageLayout. If chkStandardView is not True, line 147 sets the StandardView key to False.

- Lines 149 through 155 use an If...Then...Else statement to check whether the chkWrapToWindow check box is selected. If it is, line 150 sets the WrapToWindow property of the View object to True, activating the Wrap to Window feature, and line 151 sets the WrapToWindow key to True; if not, line 153 sets the WrapToWindow property to False, and line 154 sets the WrapToWindow key to False.

- Lines 156 through 162 use an If statement to check whether the chkShowAll check box (identified as Show Nonprinting Characters in the dialog box) is selected or cleared and to set the ShowAll property of the View object and the ShowAll key accordingly.

- Lines 163 through 169 use an `If` statement to check if the `chkZoom` check box is selected. If it is, line 164 sets the `Zoom` property of the `View` object to the `Value` property of the `cmbZoom` combo box, thus setting the zoom percentage for the active window; line 165 sets the `Zoom` key to `True`, and line 166 sets the `ZoomPercentage` key to the `Value` property of `cmbZoom`. If `chkZoom` is not selected, line 168 sets the `Zoom` key to `False`.

- Line 170 ends the `With` statement, and line 171 ends the macro.

cmdCancel_Click The `cmdCancel_Click` macro (lines 173 through 175) contains nothing but an `End` statement that ends execution of the procedure if the user chooses the Cancel button in the Toolbar and View Preferences dialog box.

optPageLayoutView_Click The `optPageLayoutView_Click` macro (lines 177 through 181) runs when the user clicks the `optPageLayoutView` option button; this macro simply disables the `chkWrapToWindow` check box if the `Value` of `optPageLayoutView` is `True` (again, because the Wrap to Window feature is not available in Page Layout view).

optNormalView_Click Finally, the `optNormalView_Click` macro (lines 183 through 187) runs when the user clicks the `optNormalView` option button. This macro simply enables the `chkWrapToWindow` check box if the `Value` of `optNormalView` is `True`.

File Menu

The File menu for the `Magazine Article.dot` template is modified slightly (see Figure 24.6) to encourage the user to employ the macros discussed in the preceding sections:

- The access key for the New command (**N**) has been reassigned to a new menu item, New Magazine Article, which runs the `NewMegaMagDocument` macro discussed earlier. So when the user presses **Alt+F**, **N**, they will create a new document based on `Magazine Article.dot` instead of displaying the New dialog box, but they can still display the New dialog box by choosing the New item from the menu.

- The Save command has been removed and replaced with the Save in Word 6 Format command, which inherits its access key (**S**). When the user presses **Alt+F**, **S** to save a document, it will automatically be saved in Word 6 format.

- Finally, a Delete this Document item has been added, which runs the `Delete_the_Current_File` macro.

FIGURE 24.6

A modified File menu
replaces the conventional
New and Save items with
custom macros.

The Toolbars

As I mentioned earlier, the `Magazine Article.dot` template includes two
toolbars, Magazine Article Styles and Magazine Article Macros (see Figure 24.7).
These toolbars provide access to the same styles and macros as the Styles and
Macros menus but are easier to use with the mouse than the menus are. As you
just saw, the user can set options in the Toolbars and View Preferences dialog box
to have these toolbars displayed automatically when they create or open a document based on the `Magazine Article.dot` template.

FIGURE 24.7

The template's two tool-
bars, Magazine Article
Styles and Magazine
Article Macros, provide
quick mouse access to
the same features as the
template's special menus.

The Keyboard Shortcuts

Most of the keyboard shortcuts in this template are the regular ones—Ctrl+C for Copy, Ctrl+P for Print, and so on—but there are a couple of changes made to bring the template's macros to the forefront:

- The Ctrl+N keyboard shortcut is assigned to the `NewMegaMagDocument` macro, so pressing Ctrl+N will start a new document based on `Magazine Article.dot` rather than on Normal.dot.

- The Ctrl+S keyboard shortcut is assigned to the `Save_in_Word_6_Format` macro, so pressing Ctrl+S will save the current document in Word 6 format rather than in Word 97 format.

Renaming the Application Window and Document Window

If you want to emphasize to the user that they're working with a special-purpose template (or a custom application, if you decide to develop one in Word), you can rename the application window to one of your choosing by setting the `Caption` property of the `Application` object with a statement such as this:

```
Application.Caption = "Text Butcher Communications"
```

When a document window is maximized, the name of the document window appears after the name of the application in the title bar, separated by a hyphen (for example, "Microsoft Word - Kings of Oblivion.doc"). When no document window is maximized, the application's name appears by itself in the application's title bar.

Renaming an application can have a gratifying effect on the unsophisticated user of your special-purpose template, but think twice before doing it on a whim: once you've renamed an application, its name stays set until you rename it again or until you close the application. So if you rename Word when you create a document in your special-purpose template, Word will stay renamed when the user switches to another window containing a document that has nothing to do with your template. (This is why the `Magazine Article.dot` template does not rename the application.)

When you rename an application, remember that it will appear to Windows and to other applications as the new name you set. For example, if you rename Word and then display the Close Program dialog box, you will see it listed there as the name you gave it rather than as "winword.exe." Likewise, if you reference a renamed application from another application, you'll need to use the name you set rather than the application's "real" name.

As well as renaming the application window you can rename a document window by setting its `Caption` property. For example, to change the name of the active window to "Creating a Magazine Article," you could use the following statement:

```
ActiveWindow.Caption = "Creating a Magazine Article"
```

As with the `Application` object, a window you rename retains its name until you rename it again or close it.

The Automatic Macros

The `Magazine Article.dot` template contains two automatic macros: `AutoNew` and `AutoOpen`. The following sections discuss what these macros do.

The AutoNew Macro

The `AutoNew` macro performs three functions:

- Retrieving and implementing toolbar and view preferences stored in the registry

- Suggesting automatically saving the document with a suitable name, and forcing the Save operation to be in Word 6 format

- Maximizing the document window (but not the application window)

The `AutoNew` macro consists of the following code:

```
Sub AutoNew()
    Toolbar_and_View_Preferences
    frmArticleInformation.Show
    WinMaximize
End Sub
```

As you can see, the `AutoNew` macro first calls the `Toolbar_and_View_Preferences` macro. It then displays the `frmArticleInformation` userform, also known as the Article Information dialog box. Thirdly, it calls the `WinMaximize` macro. We'll look at these in turn.

Toolbar_and_View_Preferences

The `Toolbar_and_View_Preferences` macro retrieves the stored toolbar and view preferences from the registry and implements them. Listing 24.6 contains the code for this macro.

Listing 24.6

```
1.   Sub Toolbar_and_View_Preferences()
2.       Dim RegLoc As String, MagStandard, MagFormatting,
    ➥MagMacros, MagStyles, MagZoom, MagZoomPercent,
    ➥MagShowAll, MagWrapToWindow, MagStandardView,
    ➥MagView
3.       RegLoc = "HKEY_CURRENT_USER\Software\Microsoft\Office\
    ➥8.0\Common\MagazineArticle"
4.       MagWrapToWindow = System.PrivateProfileString("",
    ➥RegLoc, "MagWrapToWindow")
5.       MagStandardView = System.PrivateProfileString("",
    ➥RegLoc, "StandardView")
6.       MagView = System.PrivateProfileString("", RegLoc,
    ➥"View")
7.       MagShowAll = System.PrivateProfileString("",
    ➥RegLoc, "ShowAll")
8.       MagZoom = System.PrivateProfileString("", RegLoc,
    ➥"Zoom")
9.       MagZoomPercent = System.PrivateProfileString("",
    ➥RegLoc, "ZoomPercentage")
10.      MagStandard = System.PrivateProfileString("",
    ➥RegLoc, "Standard")
```

```
11.     MagFormatting = System.PrivateProfileString("",
        ➡RegLoc, "Formatting")
12.     MagMacros = System.PrivateProfileString("",
        ➡RegLoc, "MagMacros")
13.     MagStyles = System.PrivateProfileString("",
        ➡RegLoc, "MagStyles")
14.     If MagStandard = True Then
15.         CommandBars("Standard").Visible = True
16.     Else
17.         CommandBars("Standard").Visible = False
18.     End If
19.     If MagFormatting = True Then
20.         CommandBars("Formatting").Visible = True
21.     Else
22.         CommandBars("Formatting").Visible = False
23.     End If
24.     If MagMacros = True Then
25.         CommandBars("Magazine Article Macros")
            ➡.Visible = True
26.     Else
27.         CommandBars("Magazine Article Macros")
            ➡.Visible = False
28.     End If
29.     If MagStyles = True Then
30.         CommandBars("Magazine Article Styles")
            ➡.Visible = True
31.     Else
32.         CommandBars("Magazine Article Styles")
            ➡.Visible = False
33.     End If
34.     With ActiveWindow.View
35.         If MagStandardView = True Then
36.             If MagView = "Normal" Then
37.                 .Type = wdNormalView
38.             Else
39.                 .Type = wdPageView
40.             End If
41.         End If
42.         If MagWrapToWindow = True Then
43.             .WrapToWindow = True
```

```
44.          Else
45.              .WrapToWindow = False
46.          End If
4/.          If MagShowAll = True Then
48.              .ShowAll = True
49.          Else
50.              .ShowAll = False
51.          End If
52.          If MagZoom = True Then
53.              .Zoom = MagZoomPercent
54.          End If
55.      End With
56.  End Sub
```

Analysis

This macro combines the approaches of the UserForm_Initialize macro and the cmdOK_Click macro attached to the frmToolbar_and_View_ Preferences userform (refer back to Listing 24.5), but it does so without displaying a dialog box; instead it applies the values returned from the registry to set view options directly.

Line 2 declares RegLoc once again for the location of the registry key to work with, plus the ten variables used for storing the information from the registry keys. Line 3 assigns the appropriate location to RegLoc, and lines 4 through 13 assign the information from the registry keys to the variables.

Lines 14 through 33 contain a series of four If statements that use the values stored in MagStandard, MagFormatting, MagMacros, and MagStyles to determine whether to display the Standard, Formatting, Magazine Article Macros, and Magazine Article Styles toolbars. For example, if the MagStandard variable in line 14 is True, line 15 displays the Standard toolbar; if MagStandard is not True, the Else statement in line 16 runs, and line 17 hides the Standard toolbar.

Lines 34 through 55 contain a With statement that uses the values stored in MagStandardView, MagView, MagWrapToWindow, MagShowAll, MagZoom, and MagZoomPercent to set the remaining view options. Line 56 then ends the macro.

The Article Details Dialog Box

Next, the `AutoNew` macro displays `frmArticleInformation`, the Article Details dialog box (see Figure 24.8), to gather information that it will use for naming and identifying the article: the name of the magazine the writer is writing for, the title of the article, and the writer's name.

The `frmArticleInformation` userform has attached to it the code shown in Listing 24.7.

FIGURE 24.8

The Article Details dialog box gathers information about the article.

Listing 24.7

```
1.    Private Sub UserForm_Initialize()
2.        cmbMagazine.AddItem "Icelandic Fashion Review"
3.        cmbMagazine.AddItem "Steamships of the Caucasus"
4.        cmbMagazine.AddItem "Radio Free Liberia Listening Guide"
5.        cmbMagazine.AddItem "The Projection TV Companion"
6.        txtAuthor.Value = System.PrivateProfileString("",
          ➡"HKEY_CURRENT_USER\Software\Microsoft\Office\8.0\
          ➡Common\MagazineArticle", "AuthorName")
7.    End Sub
8.
9.    Private Sub cmdOK_Click()
10.       frmArticleInformation.Hide
11.       Dim MagHeader As String, MagSave As Object,
          ➡MagFolder As String, ButtonClicked
12.       MagHeader = cmbMagazine.Value & ": " & txtTitle.Value
          ➡& " (" + txtAuthor.Value & ")"
13.       ActiveDocument.Sections(1).Headers
          ➡(wdHeaderFooterPrimary).Range.Text = MagHeader
14.       ActiveDocument.Bookmarks("Title").Select
15.       Selection.TypeText txtTitle.Value
16.       ActiveDocument.Bookmarks("Author").Select
17.       Selection.TypeText txtAuthor.Value
```

```
18.        MagFolder = System.PrivateProfileString("",
           ➥"HKEY_CURRENT_USER\Software\Microsoft\Office\8.0\
           ➥Common\MagazineArticle", "SaveFolder")
19.        Set MagSave = Dialogs(wdDialogFileSaveAs)
20.        With MagSave
21.            If MagFolder <> "" Then
               ➥ChangeFileOpenDirectory MagFolder
22.            .Format = FileConverters("MSWord6Exp").SaveFormat
23.            .Name = txtAuthor.Value & ", "
               ➥& txtTitle.Value & ".doc"
24.            ButtonClicked = .Display
25.            If ButtonClicked = 0 Then End
26.            .Format = FileConverters("MSWord6Exp").SaveFormat
27.            .Execute
28.        End With
29.    End Sub
30.
31.    Private Sub cmdCancel_Click()
32.        End
33.    End Sub
```

Analysis

This listing contains three macros: UserForm_Initialize, cmdOK_Click, and cmdCancel_Click.

UserForm_Initialize The UserForm_Initialize macro (lines 1 through 7) initializes the Article Details dialog box. Lines 2 through 5 use the AddItem method to add four magazine names to the cmbMagazine combo box. Line 6 sets the Value property of the txtAuthor text box to the contents of the AuthorName key in the MagazineArticle key in the registry. Line 7 ends the macro.

cmdOK_Click The cmdOK_Click macro (lines 9 through 29), which runs when the user chooses the OK button in the dialog box, enters header, author, and title information in the document and then suggests saving it under a suitable name. Here's what happens:

Line 10 hides the Article Details dialog box.

Lines 11 through 13 arrange the header. Line 11 declares the string variable `MagHeader`, the object variable `MagSave`, the string variable `MagFolder`, and the Variant variable `ButtonClicked`. Line 12 builds a header from the information in the Article Details dialog box and assigns it to `MagHeader`; line 13 then sets the `Text` property of the primary header of the first section of the document to `MagHeader`, thus effectively inserting the `MagHeader` string as the header.

Lines 14 through 17 set the title and author information. Line 14 selects the bookmark `Title` in the document so that line 15 can insert the title contained in the `Value` property of the `txtTitle` text box. Line 16 selects the bookmark `Author` in the document, and line 17 enters the author name stored in the `Value` property of the `txtAuthor` text box.

Lines 18 to 28 prompt the user to save the document under a suitable title. Line 18 sets `MagFolder` to the value of the `SaveFolder` key in the registry— the folder the user chose in the Set Author Information dialog box as the working folder for their articles. Line 19 sets the `MagSave` object variable to reference the Save As dialog box. Lines 20 through 28 then contain a `With` statement that works with the `MagSave` object:

- Line 21 changes the File-Open-Directory setting to `MagFolder` if `MagFolder` is not an empty string (which would mean that the user has not set registry information yet). Line 22 uses the `SaveFormat` property of the `File-Converters` object to specify Word 6 format in the Save As dialog box.

- Line 23 assigns to the `Name` property for the dialog box the value property of the `txtAuthor` text box, a comma, a space, the `Value` property of the `txtTitle` text box, and the `.doc` extension. For example, if the author's name is **Rikki Z. Nadir** and the title of the article is **Cuisine of the Lombardi Mountain Goatherds**, the macro will suggest a document name of `Rikki Z. Nadir, Cuisine of the Lombardi Mountain Goatherds.doc`.

- Line 24 then sets the `ButtonClicked` variable to the return value of the `Display` method, displaying the dialog box with the suggested name, folder, and format; the user can then change the information in the Save As dialog box and click the Save button to proceed.

- When the user dismisses the dialog box, line 25 checks to make sure the button chosen was not the Cancel button; if it was, the `End` statement ends execution of the procedure.

- Line 26 resets the `SaveFormat` property of the `FileConverters` object (in case the user has changed it), thus ensuring that the document is saved in Word 6 format; and line 27 uses the `Execute` method to execute the settings in the dialog box, saving the document.

- Line 28 ends the `With` statement, and line 29 ends the macro.

cmdCancel_Click The `cmdCancel_Click` macro (lines 31 to 33) runs when the user chooses the Cancel button or the close button in the Article Details dialog box. The `End` statement in line 32 ends execution of the procedure.

WinMaximize

The `WinMaximize` macro, which the `AutoNew` macro calls next, does nothing beyond maximize the active document window if it is not maximized:

```
Sub WinMaximize()
    With ActiveWindow
        If .WindowState <> wdWindowStateMaximize Then
            .WindowState = wdWindowStateMaximize
        End If
    End With
End Sub
```

The AutoOpen Macro

Like the `AutoNew` macro, the `AutoOpen` macro has three tasks to perform:

- Retrieve and implement toolbar and view preferences stored in the registry

- Return to the location of the previous edit in the document

- Maximize the document window (but not the application window)

Now that we've been through the macros that the `AutoNew` macro runs, the `AutoOpen` macro is very straightforward:

```
Sub AutoOpen()
    Toolbar_and_View_Preferences
    Application.GoBack
    WinMaximize
End Sub
```

The first statement runs the `Toolbar_and_View_Preferences` macro, retrieving and restoring the toolbar and view preferences stored in the registry. The second statement uses the `GoBack` method to return to the last edit performed on the document—with any luck, the location at which the user was last working and where they will want to resume work. The third statement runs the `WinMaximize` macro, maximizing the document window if it is not currently maximized.

That's about it for this special-purpose template, as well as for the main text of this book.

PART IV

Appendices

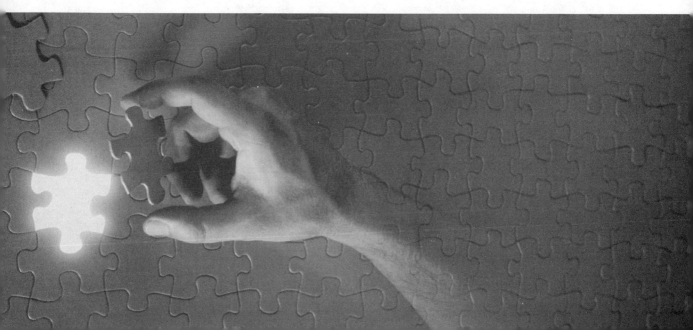

APPENDIX

A

What's on the CD?

The CD in the back of the book contains the following:

- All the numbered code listings from the book, presented in an automated document that lets you quickly access the code you need and transfer it to the Visual Basic Editor, where you can run it or adapt it to your needs.

- Video walk-throughs of key procedures from Chapters 5, 6, and 7, in which you'll explore the Visual Basic Editor, message boxes, input boxes, and dialog boxes.

- The sample template discussed in Chapter 24, `Magazine Article.dot`.

Accessing the Code Listings

The code listings for the book are on the CD in the document named `Word 97 Macro and VBA Handbook Code Listings.doc` in the folder named `Code Listings`.

To access the code listings, open `Word 97 Macro and VBA Handbook Code Listings.doc`. You'll see the document shown in Figure A.1.

FIGURE A.1

To access the code listings for the book, open `Word 97 Macro and VBA Handbook Code Listings.doc`.

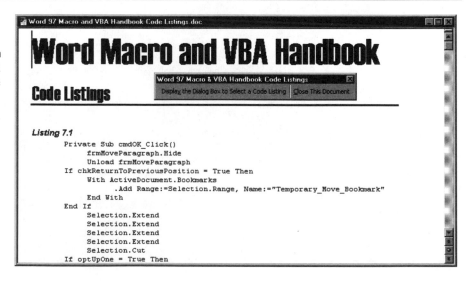

If you have macro virus protection enabled, Word will warn you that the `Word 97 Macro and VBA Handbook Code Listings.doc` document contains macros or customizations. Click the Enable Macros button to open the document with the macros enabled—the document does contain an `AutoOpen` macro that runs automatically when you open the document, but the only action this macro takes is to display a custom toolbar that you need to have available.

Next, click the Display the Dialog Box to Select a Code Listing button on the Word 97 Macro & VBA Handbook Code Listings toolbar to display the Word 97 Macro & VBA Handbook Code Listings dialog box (see Figure A.2).

FIGURE A.2

Click the Display the Dialog Box to Select a Code Listing button on the Word 97 Macro & VBA Handbook Code Listings toolbar to display this dialog box.

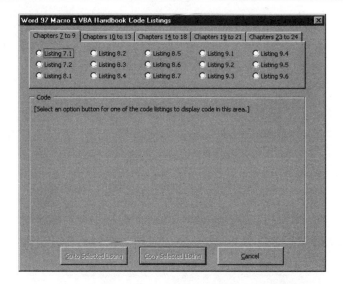

If you've disabled automatic macros (for example, by Shift+clicking to open the file), the Word 97 Macro & VBA Handbook Code Listings toolbar may not be displayed. To display it, right-click the menu bar or any displayed toolbar and choose Word 97 Macro & VBA Handbook Code Listings from the context menu of toolbars.

In the dialog box, select the tab containing the appropriate chapter (Chapters 7 to 9, 10 to 13, 14 to 18, 19 to 21, or 23 to 24), and then select the option button for the code listing you want to work with. The dialog box will display the code (or as much of a long listing as will fit) in the Code group box (see Figure A.3) and will enable the Go to Selected Listing and Copy Selected Listing command buttons.

FIGURE A.3

Select the tab for the appropriate chapter, and then select the code listing you want to work with.

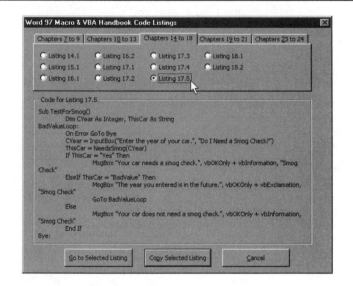

You can now click the Go to Selected Listing command button to move to the beginning of the selected listing, or click the Copy Selected Listing command button to copy the selected listing to the Clipboard so that you can then paste it into the Visual Basic Editor.

TIP

Instead of using the dialog box, you can of course scroll manually through the document to find and copy those lines of code that you need.

Viewing the Walk-Throughs

The `Walk-throughs` folder contains three subfolders—`Chapter 5, Chapter 6,` and `Chapter 7`—which between them contain the following twenty-four walk-throughs of the more important procedures from those chapters:

Chapter 5

Chapter 6

Chapter 7

Creating the Dialog Box, step 6 (page 251)

Creating the Dialog Box, step 7 (page 252)

Creating the Dialog Box, steps 8 and 9 (page 253)

Creating the Dialog Box, step 10 (page 254)

Creating the Dialog Box, step 11 (page 255)

The `Walk-throughs` folder contains each walk-through in two formats: Video for Windows files (`.avi`), and self-executing Microsoft Camcorder files (`.exe`). So for example, you'll find both `Opening the Visual Basic Editor.avi` and `Opening the Visual Basic Editor.exe` in the `Chapter 5` folder. There's no sound on either the AVI files or the Camcorder files.

If you have a Windows video viewer installed and configured (for example, the Windows Media Player), you can run the AVI files by simply double-clicking them in a file-management program (such as Explorer); alternatively, you can run your Windows video viewer first and then open the files from there.

If you don't have a Windows video viewer installed, you can run the self-executing Microsoft Camcorder files instead by double-clicking them in a file-management program.

TIP These walk-throughs are best viewed at a screen resolution of 800 x 600 pixels or greater. I recorded them at 800 x 600 resolution because at 640 x 480 resolution, the windows in the Visual Basic Editor are so small it's hard to work effectively. If you're viewing the walk-throughs at 640 x 480 resolution, they'll run fine, but you won't be able to see the rightmost and bottommost quarters of what was recorded.

Using the Sample Template

The sample template discussed in Chapter 24, `Magazine Article.dot`, is in the folder named `Sample Template` on the CD. To install the sample template on your computer, simply copy it from the `Sample Template` folder to a folder named `Special Templates` under your Office `Templates` folder. You can then start a new document based on the template by choosing File ➤ New and selecting the Magazine Article template on the appropriate tab of the New dialog box.

APPENDIX
B

Converting WordBasic Macros to VBA

In this appendix, I'll discuss how VBA converts WordBasic macros in existing Word 6.0/Word 95 templates to VBA macros in Word 97. VBA handles this conversion transparently as part of the process of converting the templates and their contents (styles, AutoText entries, interface customizations, and so on) to Word 97.

If you have WordBasic macros, you'll probably want to move some or all of them to VBA so that you can continue using them with Word 97. The good news is that Word 97 automatically converts WordBasic macros to VBA. The bad news is that the conversion, while usually effective, results in code that is much less efficient than native VBA code, which means you'll probably want to eventually re-create most of your macros in native VBA to make them run at a decent speed.

Converting Word 6.0/Word 95 Templates to Word 97

To convert a Word 6.0/Word 95 template to Word 97, you simply open it in Word 97 either by using the Open dialog box (File ➤ Open) or by double-clicking the name of the template in a file-management program. (Alternatively, you can place the template in your Office 97/Word 97 `Templates` folder, then start a new document based on it by choosing File ➤ New, selecting the template on the appropriate tab of the New dialog box, and choosing the OK button. Another alternative is to attach an existing document to the template by using the Templates and Add-ins dialog box.)

If you have macro-virus checking enabled (it's controlled by the Macro Virus Protection check box on the General tab of the Options dialog box), Word may warn you that the template you're opening contains code and offer to disable it. If you're sure that the code in the template is benevolent, choose the Enable Macros button. Otherwise, choose the Do Not Open button, examine the code in the template in Word 6 or Word 95 to make sure it's harmless, and then try again.

TIP

It's usually best to open a Word 6.0/Word 95 template from a location outside your Office 97/Word 97 `Templates` folder, then save the converted template in Word 97 format in the appropriate `Templates` folder. This way, you can keep the Word 6.0/Word 95 template available in case anything goes wrong with the conversion or you need to keep the template available for working in Word 6 or Word 95.

As you open the template (or create a new document based on it), Word will automatically convert the macros to VBA. If the template contains a lot of macros, the conversion can take a minute or two; the status bar will display messages tracking the progress of the conversion of each macro in turn.

If there's an `AutoOpen` macro in the template you're opening, Word will try to execute it; likewise if there's an `AutoNew` macro in the template from which you're creating a new document. If Word encounters a problem in running the macro, it will alert you to the problem and display the Visual Basic Editor with the offending code highlighted so that you can try to resolve the problem. Beyond an `AutoOpen` or `AutoNew` macro, however, Word does not check the commands or logical integrity of the converted macros; you'll discover any problem when you go to run them.

Here are the main parameters that the conversion uses:

- VBA converts each of your macros into a module within the template. This can make for a morass of modules that you'll probably want to reorganize more sensibly later—for example, by grouping related macros into descriptively named modules and deleting any unnecessary modules.

- VBA performs most WordBasic actions by calling them through the `WordBasic` property of VBA. The `WordBasic` property is basically an Automation object named `Word.Basic` that provides methods for each WordBasic statement and function in Word 6 and Word 95. We'll look at an example of this in just a couple of minutes.

- VBA explicitly declares all variables at the beginning of the macro that contains them. It gives each variable a single line (rather than declaring multiple variables on a single line), which makes for macros much longer than their originals.

- VBA does not create userforms from any custom dialog boxes in the converted macros (as I mentioned earlier, WordBasic stores each custom dialog box as collections of code within the macro rather than as separate userforms). Instead, it prefaces each statement in the code for the dialog box with a WordBasic call; the statements remain in the VBA code.

When you close a template you've opened, or close the document based on or attached to the template, Word will ask (as usual) if you want to save changes to it; these changes (if you haven't made any others) are the conversions of the macros to VBA and of the templates' other contents to Word 97 format. If you choose to save changes, Word will display the dialog box shown here, which lets you specify whether to overwrite the existing template or create a new template. If you choose the New File button, Word displays the Save As dialog box so that you can name the new file and then save it as usual.

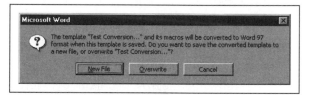

Because the converted macros tend to be much more verbose than the original macros, and because the Word 97 format stores more information about documents and templates (to allow for new features such as Web hyperlinks), templates converted to Word 97 are almost invariably much larger than Word 6.0/Word 95 templates—sometimes three to four times as large. For example, a medium-size template I converted was 169K in its Word 6.0/Word 95 incarnation, and 715K in its Word 97 form; when I converted my whole Normal.dot (which contains an embarrassing number of macros), it ballooned from a stout 393K to a grotesque 1392K—enough to put a serious dent in the performance of a slower computer. Before converting your templates, strip from them any macros that you won't need to convert, and you'll find Word 97 running a little faster than it otherwise would.

Problems Associated with Converting WordBasic Macros to VBA

In general, Word's conversion of WordBasic macros to VBA is quite effective, but with some macros you may run into problems.

I've found that certain expressions cause trouble. For example, WordBasic forced you on occasion to use `End Select` statements differently than VBA does, so if you've used one or more `End Select` statements in your WordBasic macros, you'll often find VBA displaying errors in them, because VBA expects a more logical and more rigid placement of the `End Select` statement.

If Word 97 identifies anything in a macro it knows it can't handle (WordBasic calls to the Windows Application Programming Interface—API—seem to raise a red flag), you'll see this message box:

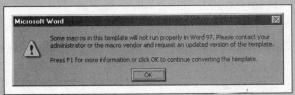

If this message box appears, check the status bar and note the name of the macro that is currently being converted; this macro contains something that VBA doesn't like, and you'll probably need this information in a minute or two.

From this message box, you might be inclined to press the F1 key to display either the Office Assistant (if you haven't disabled it) or VBA Help; however, neither brings up any directly relevant topic. You can search for "WordBasic," but it only produces some (forgive me) basic information on converting macros.

If there's something in a macro that VBA absolutely cannot handle (for example, if a macro has become corrupted), it will convert the rest of the template so that you can use the template's styles, AutoText entries, and customizations. You'll then be able to run those macros in the template that converted properly—but the only way to find out which those are is by trial and error: starting the macros and watching which run and which crash. When a macro crashes, you'll see such cryptic messages as "Compile error in hidden module."

 This is ugly, because there's little you can do about it. But the really bad news is that when you go to open the template's project in the Visual Basic Editor, you'll see the Project Locked dialog box (shown here).

You've just hit the wall: you're now totally locked out of all the macros in the template you've just converted, so you can't even debug the macros that haven't converted properly. Your best recourse is to close the template without saving changes (otherwise you'll end up with a bloated version of the template containing unusable VBA code), open the template in Word 6 or Word 95, remove the macro that caused the "Some macros in this template will not run" message box, and try again. If the conversion founders on a different macro this time, remove that one, too. By doing so, you can usually whittle down a template to the macros that will convert properly, but it's a slow and tedious process.

An Example of a Converted Macro

Listing B.1 shows a short WordBasic macro followed by its VBA conversion. This macro toggles revision marks (Track Changes, in Word 97 parlance) on and off and displays an appropriate message on the status bar informing the reader whether revision marks were turned on or off.

Listing B.1

```
1.   Sub MAIN
2.        Dim TR As ToolsRevisions
3.        GetCurValues TR
4.        If TR.MarkRevisions = 0 Then
5.            ToolsRevisions .MarkRevisions = 1
6.            Print "Revision marks have been turned ON."
7.        Else
8.            ToolsRevisions .MarkRevisions = 0
9.            Print "Revision marks have been turned OFF."
10.       End If
11.  End Sub
12.
13.  Public Sub MATN()
14.       Dim TR As Object: Set TR = WordBasic.DialogRecord.
             ➥ToolsRevisions(False)
15.       WordBasic.CurValues.ToolsRevisions TR
16.       If TR.MarkRevisions = 0 Then
17.           WordBasic.ToolsRevisions MarkRevisions:=1
18.           WordBasic.PrintStatusBar "Revision marks have
             ➥been turned ON. "
19.       Else
20.           WordBasic.ToolsRevisions MarkRevisions:=0
21.           WordBasic.PrintStatusBar "Revision marks have
             ➥been turned OFF."
22.       End If
23.  End Sub
```

Analysis

Lines 1 through 11 contain the original WordBasic macro, which was called
ToggleRevisions; here, it is identified as Sub MAIN, the default name that
WordBasic uses for the main Sub procedure in a macro. Lines 13 through 23 contain the VBA conversion of it. As I mentioned, VBA creates a separate module out
of each macro in a module it converts, so the contents of lines 13 through 23 are
contained in a module named ToggleRevisions; VBA names the macro within
the module MAIN after the WordBasic name.

VBA has translated the Sub MAIN declaration from line 1 of the WordBasic macro into a Public Sub MAIN declaration in line 13. This gives the macro public scope, making it accessible to other macros in the current document, current template, and other active templates (including Normal.dot). This emulates the functionality that the WordBasic macro had in its native template.

Line 2 in the WordBasic macro declares the variable TR and assigns to it the ToolsRevisions object, which represents the Revisions dialog box (under the Tools menu; hence the name). Line 14 shows VBA going one better: it explicitly declares TR as a variable of the Object data type, and then (after a colon, which allows a second statement on the same line) uses a Set statement to assign to TR the ToolsRevisions object (accessed via the DialogRecord object in the WordBasic property).

Line 3 uses a GetCurValues statement to get the current values for the TR object, thus retrieving the current values for the Revisions dialog box. Line 15 performs the same maneuver by calling through the WordBasic property.

Line 4 begins an If...Then...Else statement that checks the value of the MarkRevisions property in the TR object. If TR.MarkRevisions is 0 (indicating revision marking is off), line 5 sets the MarkRevisions property of the ToolsRevisions object to 1, turning revision marking on, and line 6 displays a message on the status bar informing the user of this. If TR.MarkRevisions is 1, execution moves to the Else statement in line 7; line 8 sets the MarkRevisions property of the ToolsRevisions object to 0, and line 9 displays the appropriate message on the status bar. Line 10 ends the If statement, and line 11 ends the macro.

In the VBA macro, the If statement closely parallels the WordBasic one. Line 16 is identical to line 4, because If statements work the same way; likewise lines 19 and 22 are identical to lines 7 and 10. Lines 17 and 20 use the WordBasic property to access the ToolsRevisions object, and lines 18 and 21 use the PrintStatusBar property of the WordBasic property to display the status bar messages.

Using WordBasic through VBA

Since VBA handles existing Word code by running it through the `WordBasic` property, you might ask whether you can't do the same—that is, leverage your knowledge of WordBasic by continuing to use it in your macros in VBA. The answer is that you can, but it's not a great idea: first, you're limiting yourself to the capabilities of WordBasic, which is less powerful than VBA; and second, you'll notice quite a drop in performance if you execute WordBasic code through the `WordBasic` property in VBA.

That said, when you can recall the appropriate WordBasic command for quick macros and do not want to spend time drilling down through the Word object model for the appropriate objects, methods, and properties, using WordBasic through the `WordBasic` property may make sense. (The alternative is to run Help from the Visual Basic Editor, choose the "WordBasic commands, Visual Basic equivalents A-Z" entry on the Index tab of the Help dialog box, and look up the VBA equivalent of the appropriate WordBasic command. This provides a quick way to pull your knowledge of WordBasic into your VBA code.)

INDEX

NOTE: Page numbers in *italics* refer to figures or tables; page numbers in **bold** refer to significant discussions of the topic.

SYMBOLS

A

D

F

G

H

I

N

O

P

S

T

U

V

X

Y

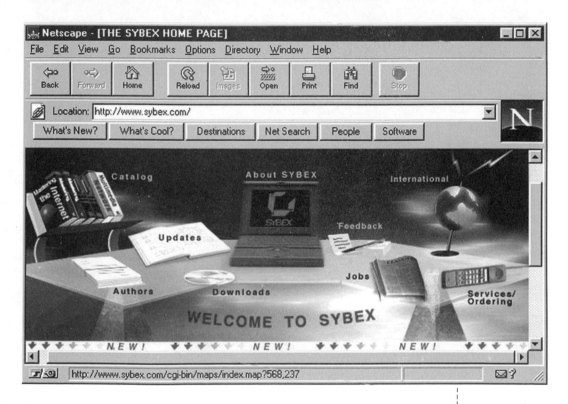

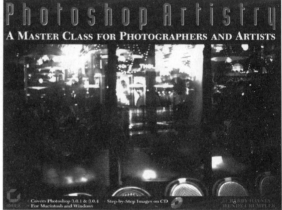

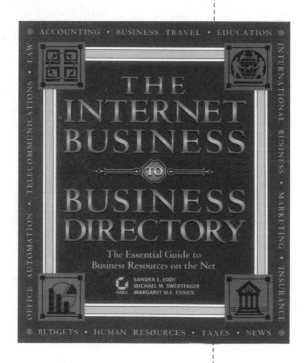

What's on the CD?

The CD included with this book contains the following:

- All the numbered code listings from the book, presented in an automated document that lets you quickly access the code you need and transfer it to the Visual Basic Editor, where you can run it, change it, or otherwise play with it.

- Video walk-throughs of key procedures from Chapters 5, 6, and 7, in which you'll explore the Visual Basic Editor, message boxes, input boxes, and dialog boxes.

- The sample template discussed in Chapter 24, `Magazine Article.dot`.

Appendix A contains instructions on how to use the CD.